DATE DUE

THE
FIRST WORLD WAR

AN EYEWITNESS HISTORY

JOE H. KIRCHBERGER

Facts On File, Inc.

For Joan

The First World War: An Eyewitness History

Copyright © 1992 by Joe H. Kirchberger
All maps courtesy of Neil Hyslop, cartographer.
All rights reserved. No part of this book may be reproduced or utilized in any form or by any means, electronic or mechanical, including photocopying, recording, or by any information storage or retrieval systems, without permission in writing from the publisher. For information contact:

Facts On File, Inc.
132 West 31st Street
New York NY 10001-2006

Library of Congress Cataloging-in-Publication Data
Kirchberger, Joe H.
    The First World War : an eyewitness history / Joe H. Kirchberger
       p. cm.—(The Eyewitness history series)
    Includes bibliographical references and index.
    ISBN 0-8160-2552-5
    1. World War, 1914–1918—General works. 2. World War, 1914–1918—
    Personal narratives. I. Title. II. Series.
    D521.K57 19 92
    940.3—dc20   91-19970

Facts On File books are available at special discounts when purchased in bulk quantities for businesses, associations, institutions or sales promotions. Please call our Special Sales Department in New York at (212) 967-8800 or (800) 322-8755.

You can find Facts On File on the World Wide Web at http://www.factsonfile.com

Jacket design by Keith Lovell

Printed in the United States of America

VB VCS 10 9 8 7

This book is printed on acid-free paper.

Contents

Acknowledgments

My editor at Facts On File, Gary M. Krebs, has been extremely helpful with many valuable and practical suggestions during the whole period of our collaboration on this book. It was a pleasure to work with him.

I also would like to express my appreciation to the German Information Center in New York, the National Archives in Washington, D.C. and various branches of the New York Public Library for providing a large part of the Pictorial material for this book.

The Eyewitness History Series

Historians have long recognized that to truly understand the past we must relive it. We can see past eras and events clearly only when we free our minds from the knowledge of what unfolded between then and now and permit ourselves to experience events with the fresh vision of a contemporary participant or observer.

To stimulate our powers of historical imagination we must begin by immersing ourselves in the documents of the period, so that we can view events as eyewitnesses. The Eyewitness History Series offers readers and students the opportunity to exercise their historical imaginations by providing in a single volume a large collection of excerpts from what historians call "primary sources," the memoirs, diaries, letters, journalism and official documents of the period.

To give these historical raw materials a framework, each chapter begins with a brief summary of the "Historical Context" followed by a detailed "Chronicle of Events." However, the bulk of each chapter consists of a large selection of quotations from eyewitness acounts of the events of the time. These have been selected to give the reader the widest range of views possible. Each has a specific source in the Bibliography to facilitate further study. To further stimulate the reader's historical imagination, a selection of contemporary illustrations is included in each chapter. Modern maps have been included in an appendix for the convenience of readers.

Rather than interrupt the main text with lengthy official documents, we have included them in an appendix. Another appendix includes brief biographies of the major personalities referred to in the text.

Eyewitness Histories are intended to encourage students and readers to discover the powers and the pleasures of historical imagination, while also providing them with comprehensive and self-contained works of reference to significant historical periods.

Preface

IMPACT OF THE WAR

The First World War (1914 to 1918), at the time usually called The Great War, shook Europe at its very foundations and reshaped the rest of the world considerably. It has been said that the 20th century—the first half of which was characterized by two unprecedented international catastrophes, World War I and II—actually began in the last days of July 1914, when the great powers started mobilizing their armies and war became inevitable. What started as a conflict between one major power, Austria-Hungary, and the little Balkan state of Serbia, within a few days involved all the great powers in Europe: Russia, Germany, France and England. Japan and Turkey soon followed, Italy joined the fray in 1915, and finally, when the United States joined the Western Allies in 1917, all major world powers were involved.

While the two main battlefronts of the war developed in France and Russia, large-scale fighting also took place in the Near East; in the Balkans; along the Austro-Italian front; on the Mediterranean; around the German colonies in Africa, New Guinea and some Central Pacific islands; and on the high seas. Australian, New Zealand, Canadian and French troops fought in Europe, Indian soliders fought in the Near East, and about two million U.S. soldiers landed in Europe to participate decisively in the battles during the last months of the war. When, after more than four years of fighting, the Central Powers—Germany, Austria-Hungary, Turkey and Bulgaria—were finally beaten, the face of Europe had changed radically: In 1914, all of the major powers had been monarchies, except for France. None of these Monarchies survived in 1918, except for Great Britain. Russia was torn by civil war and gave rise to a new world power, Soviet communism, and Austria-Hungary was dissolved into a number of states along national lines. The United States had, for the first time in its history, abandoned George Washington's principle of noninvolvement in foreign conflicts. Europe was no longer the center of world events.

REASONS FOR THE OUTBREAK

Was this catastrophe inevitable, and what was the cause of it? The first question has never been answered by any consensus of historians, but it is obvious that there were many reasons, some of them going back to the 17th, 18th and 19th centuries. France and Germany had long been enemies, and tensions had been heightened since the days of Louis XIV and Napoleon I. Although France had been the conqueror in these wars, it had been beaten in their latest conflict, the Franco-German War of 1870–71. This humiliating memory was very much on the minds of most Frenchmen, in particular the loss of Alsace-Lorraine, the population of which for the most part spoke German but considered itself part of France and never accepted the German rule enforced upon it after 1871.

There was also the rivalry between Great Britain—which controlled a vast colonial empire through its superior naval power—and Germany, newly united since 1871, which rapidly developed into the leading power on the European continent with an industrial and naval capacity rivaling and even surpassing Great Britain's. There was also the situation in the Balkans (known as the powder keg of Europe), which was caused by the gradual weakening of the rule of Turkey (known as the "sick man at the Bosporus"). This led to a confrontation between Austria and Russia in southeastern Europe. Both powers were striving to control the Dardanelles Straits, which would have provided Russia with an access to the Mediterranean. There was, last but not least, the personality of the German emperor William II, whose impulsive, undiplomatic speeches and proclamations antagonized both his allies and potential adversaries and created an atmosphere of uncertainty and resentment in European capitals.

It is safe to say that the background for the war was provided by the age of imperialism, which saw the extension of rule by one government or nation over others. Since the end of the age of exploration and discovery, and spirit of imperialism had led to the spreading of peaceful and not so peaceful expansion of the main European powers all over the newly opened world, with Britain and France emerging as the leading world empires.

The German Empire entered into this contest much too late, and its colonies, acquired only in and after the 1880s, never proved themselves profitable, either as markets or as material sources for its growing industry; but its colonial activities did lead to frictions with the older empires. To be sure, there were clashes between the established, ever-expanding empires. The Fashoda crisis (see Document 10) of 1898 almost ended in a British-French war; and in the Dogger Bank episode of 1904 (see CHRONOLOGY, chapter 1), the Russian Fleet, passing through the North Sea on its way to the Far East to fight the Japanese, fired on British trawlers and created an acute crisis between the two nations. Still, when World War I broke out, these nations found themselves fighting on the same side against the Central Powers led by Germany and Austria-Hungary.

Looking at the constantly shifting maze of alliances between the great powers during the 40 years prior to 1914—in particular the ever-vacillating relations between Germany and Russia on the one hand

and Germany and England on the other—one cannot help feeling that the final lineup of 1914 was somewhat accidental. But it also seems clear that the clumsy, unstable German diplomacy since Bismarck's dismissal in 1890, as well as the worldwide unpopularity of the German emperor, contributed to what was regarded by most Germans as a dark conspiracy of the older jealous powers.

WAR GUILT

In retrospect, it appears that the coexistence of so many heavily armed, ambitious powers was bound to lead to an armed confrontation sooner or later, though it is safe to say that in August 1914 none of the main responsible players really wished for a world war or worked toward it. But all of them took certain chances, and the irony of the situation in 1914 was that the two powers least equipped to stand a long war—Austria-Hungary and Russia—took the greatest chances. Among the European powers of the 20th century, Austria was an anachronism: a huge empire, not built on a national basis, but ruled by a small German minority, where only the Hungarians were granted a certain amount of independence in what was called the "Dual Monarchy." The great majority of the population, the Slavs, never enjoyed a satisfactory status within the empire and were looked down upon by their rulers—and by the Hungarians even more than by the Germans. This situation was all the more dangerous as Imperial Russia embraced the idea of Pan-Slavism, making itself the protector of all Slavic peoples under Austrian (and Turkish) rule. In spite of this tense situation, Austria annexed the Balkan provinces of Bosnia and Herzegovina in 1908, which had been under Turkish sovereignty but Austrian administration. It was clear that Russia would object violently to any further extension of Austrian power in the Balkans. Yet this was exactly what Austria attempted in 1914, exploiting the crisis caused by the assassination of Archduke Francis Ferdinand (see chapter 2), successor to the Austrian throne, and in this attempt Austria was given practically a free hand by its ally, the German government. Both Austria and Germany apparently underestimated Russia's readiness to enter a major war that would automatically draw France, Russia's close ally, into the conflict. Britain remained aloof until Belgium's frontier was violated by Germany. After that, Britain felt bound by international treaty to assist Belgium.

THE NEW HORRORS OF THE WAR

Still, it is highly improbable that war would have broken out had any of the responsible players realized what incredible misery and wholesale slaughter lay ahead. There had been no general European war since Napoleon's days, 100 years earlier, and even the heated clashes between some great powers (e.g., the Crimean War of 1854–55, the Prussian-Austrian War of 1866 and the Franco-German War of 1870–71) had been limited affairs in comparison and in 1914 were only remembered by a few survivors. The most recent major war, between Russia and Japan, had been fought at a faraway place.

None of the leaders realized that they were engaging in a four-year struggle that would strain their finances, man power and industrial capacity to the utmost and would leave the whole continent exhausted and impoverished in the end. This war would bear no resemblance to the glorified fighting in the stories of Joan of Arc, Henry V of England, Alexander Nevski of Russia, Frederic II of Prussia and Prince Eugene of Austria. The German emperor, looking at a battlefield with its mass of dead and wounded was most likely sincere when he cried: "I did not want this to happen!" Any of the other men responsible for advancing the conflict might have said the same thing if they had foreseen the slaughter.

SURVIVORS AND NEW LEADERS

Few of the personalities who "led" Europe into the war survived it: Tsar Nicholas II of Russia was forced to abdicate in March 1917 and was shot by the Bolsheviks in July 1918; William II (Kaiser Wilhelm) abdicated and fled to Holland in November 1918; and in Austria, tired, old Emperor Francis Joseph died in November 1916, while his grand-nephew and successor Charles—who tried unsuccessfully to conclude a separate peace with the Allies behind Germany's back—abdicated three days after his "ally" William. Only King Albert I of Belgium, whose resistance in 1914 had helped the Allied cause, and George V of England survived.

Few of the leading statesmen of 1914 outlasted the war. Russian foreign minister Sergei Sazonof, Austrian foreign minister Count Leopold von Berchtold, German chancellor Theobald von Bethmann-Hollweg, English prime minister Herbert Henry Asquith, Turkish leader Enver Pasha and most other leading figures disappeared during the war or at its conclusion. Only in France did the old guard of Poincaré, Clemenceau and Briand stay in power, surviving all crises.

The war also brought many new personalities into the limelight. Among the civil leaders were David Lloyd George of Britain, Woodrow Wilson of the United States and Russian revolutionaries V.I. Lenin and Leon Trotsky. Among the generals—who in many countries, especially Germany, increasingly took control of the governments from the civilians—Paul von Hindenburg, Erich Ludendorff, Erich von Falkenhayn and Max Hoffman of Germany; Austrian Count

Georges Clemenceau. Courtesy of the "Review of Reviews"

Franz Conrad von Hoetzendorf; Joseph-Jacques-Césaire Joffre, Ferdinand Foch and Henri Philippe Pétain of France; Earl Douglas Haig and Viscount Edmund Allenby of Britain; Aleksey A. Brusilov of Russia and John J. Pershing of the United States proved to be excellent strategists.

The navies also had their new heroes: The British had Jellicoe and Beatty, the Germans Scheer and Hipper. And although the war in the air was of minor importance compared to the role it played in World War II, it nevertheless had its own great men and popular heroes: French pilots René Fonck and Georges Guynemer, Englishmen Albert Ball and Edward Mannock, the Canadian W.A. (Billy) Bishop, and Germans Oswald Boelcke, Max Immelmann and Manfred von Richthofen.

NOVELTIES OF THE WAR

The First World War turned out to be an entirely new experience not only for its size and the horrible sacrifices it entailed, but also for the way it was fought. Radically new weapons were introduced: On land there were tanks (first used tentatively in 1917), which played a decisive role in the last stages of the war, and poison gas also was used for the first time. In the air, planes and dirigibles were used for the first time, though only for reconnaissance purposes in the first part of the war. On the high seas, submarines developed into a deadly weapon that came close to deciding the war in favor of the Germans. Naval mines had been known and used occasionally since the 16th century, but only in World War I did they enter into wide use. A more or less stabilized front, 440 miles long between the Swiss border and the North Sea, consisting of a system of fortified trenches and dugouts, barbed wire fences and sandbagged parapets, would have been unthinkable in any earlier war, but it lasted for three years with only minor changes, in spite of desperate attempts on both sides to break through. Rifles, machine guns and artillery had, of course, been known in previous wars, but they had all been refined during the last decades and could be fired at much wider ranges with a far deadlier effect. Most casualties of the war were due to artillery fire, with machine guns coming a close second.

All in all it can be said that in this war (in contrast to World War II) the defense had the upper hand, at least in the congested French-Belgian and Austrian-Italian fronts. In the enormous distances of the Russian Empire and also in the Near East, where the fighting was more fluid, the cavalry still played an important combat role.

THE WAR AT SEA

Of the great rival British and German navies, the former played an important (though not decisive) role in the war, while the German navy was kept away from most of the naval fighting. The British navy protected all merchant ships carrying supplies to Britain and blockaded the North Sea in an attempt to starve Germany. Blockades on a large scale had been known before in world history: Napoleon had tried to cut off all English merchandise from the European continent in 1807, and in the American Civil War the Union navy had successfully blockaded the confederate ports. But a blockade of this size had never before been attempted, and its effect was increased by huge mine belts laid across the North Sea by the British and American Navies. The Germans never broke through the blockade in force during the entire war, although in the one major naval confrontation, the battle of Jutland, the German High Seas Fleet had the edge over the stronger British navy. Yet four years of blockade did not succeed in forcing Germany down to its knees, in spite of great hardships suffered by the civilian population: Perhaps this is because the German economy was efficiently reorganized and adjusted to suit war conditions (see chapter 10).

THE FINAL OUTCOME

The year 1917 saw the low point for the Allied armies. Russia had collapsed, and though the United States had entered the war on the Allies' side, its armies could not be expected to make the decisive difference until the following year. In the meantime, German submarines wreaked havoc with British shipping and brought the country close to disaster, until the convoy system (see chapter 9) reduced the danger.

After millions of German troops had been moved from the eastern to the western front, the Central Powers achieved a numerical superiority at the western front. But the German armies were exhausted and eventually had to face two million fresh troops from the United States. It has been said that the German war mentality is tougher but less resilient than the French, and the last months of the war seem to support this thesis. While the French rallied repeatedly (after the initial crushing defeat at the Marne in 1914 and the setbacks at Verdun in 1916), the German army—after its last great offensive failed in the spring of 1918—was finished for good. The tremendous, almost incomprehensible enthusiasm with which German soldiers had marched into war in 1914 had long disappeared. After years of fighting in mud and cold, the common soldier no longer knew what he was fighting for. The glaring contrast between the war profiteers and "base wallahs" (who stayed away from the front lines) on the one hand and the worn-out soldiers and city dwellers (who had to get by with ever-dwindling food and fuel rations) on the other grew constantly, but was true not only for Germany but also for all warring nations.

What the people all over the world truly wanted was peace. But when peace came, it did not put an end to the hatred within and between nations, in spite of the lofty ideals of world peace and democracy proclaimed by U.S. president Woodrow Wilson. Social unrest and civil wars flared up in Russia, Germany, Austria, Hungary and elsewhere, and the policy of revenge expressed in the Peace Treaties of Paris failed to establish a permanent basis for peaceful coexistence in Europe. On the contrary, it contained most of the elements that, only 20 years later, led to the even greater disaster of World War II.

CONNECTING LINKS BETWEEN THE TWO WORLD WARS

While World War I had a tremendous impact on the generation condemned to live through it, it has been reduced to a pale memory and vague reminiscence as we head toward a new century. There are few survivors with personal memories, and the more recent catastrophe of 1939–1945 has overshadowed the impression it once made. Even the ghastly hell of Verdun has given way, in mankind's memory, to the ghosts of Stalingrad. But it should be remembered that World War II, which formed the political, cultural and economical world such as we know it today—or at least until 1989—would be unthinkable and quite unexplainable without the First World War. The second, of course, had as many complex roots and causes as the first, but in retrospect it seems it was even less inevitable given that it had been a necessity in the mind of only one man. There is no doubt that Adolf Hitler plunged the world into its greatest catastrophe because, consciously or subconsciously, he wanted to reverse the outcome of World War I.

Hitler was a low-ranking soldier, one among millions in the First World War. But quite a number of the future political leaders in World War II did play prominent roles in the World War I. Winston Churchill was first lord of the admiralty at the beginning of the war, then lost his post by the failure of the Dardanelles campaign, but he served again as minister of munitions in 1917 and as secretary of state for war and air in 1918. In the United States, Franklin D. Roosevelt was assistant secretary of the navy during the First World War and Harry S. Truman served as a field artillery captain in France. Henri-Philippe Pétain had been one of the French heroes at Verdun, and Charles de Gaulle had fought with distinction in France until he was captured in 1916. On the German side, Hermann Göring had been something of a hero in the German Air Force during the latter part of the first war.

Many of the future military leaders had also seen action in the earlier war. George Marshall was a a staff officer under General John J. Pershing; George S. Patton Jr. was wounded as a tank brigade commander; both Omar Bradley and Dwight D. Eisenhower saw action in France; and Chester W. Nimitz was chief of staff of the U.S. submarine force. The British generals Archibald Percival Wavell, Bernard L. Montgomery and Harold Rupert Alexander also fought in France during the First World War. On the French side, Maxime Weygand and Maurice-Gustave Gamelin served on Marshal Ferdinand Foch's staff. German generals Erwin Rommel, Karl Rudolf G. von Rundstedt and several others also saw action in World I.

Quite a number of lower ranking U.S. soldiers who landed in France between 1942 and 1945 had been there 25 years earlier, and many of the old war songs by Irving Berlin, George M. Cohan and others once more became as popular as ever. In 1941, the old war tradition was still very much alive in the American nation. The bloodshed and the miseries of 1917 to 1918 were largely forgotten or at least suppressed when the U.S. Army crossed the Atlantic once again, though with less enthusiasm than in 1917–18, because people were less naive this time.

It was the same in Europe: People went to war reluctantly, but they went, and they paid the price. It took the development of the atomic bomb to deter the major participating nations from planning another war—at least for the next 45 years.

1. Europe: 1871 to June 28, 1914

The Historical Context

THE BISMARCK ERA

The European balance of power, established after the Napoleonic wars and maintained by the Holy Alliance, had provided a status quo for the "legitimate" powers—Russia, Austria and Prussia—that amounted to Russian dominance on the Continent during the first half of the century. Two events shook up this situation: the Crimean War (1854–56), which had ended Russian dominance, and Prussia's victorious wars against Austria (1866) and France (1870–71). The first Prussian victory had pushed Austria out of the loose German Confederation and directed it into a close alliance with Hungary and a tendency to extend its power into the Balkans. The second had ended the short European prominence of France under Napoleon III and instead created a strong central power in Europe, the German Empire, under Prussia's leadership.

The first 20 years of the period between 1871 and 1914 were characterized by the personality of Germany's leading statesman, Otto von Bismarck. He considered the German Empire to be saturated and resisted for many years any attempt to extend German influence; he opposed German colonialism. During that time he sought allies to secure Germany's position; he found them in Russia and Austria. A pro-Russian policy had been an old Prussian tradition, and a new alliance with Russia would prevent Germany from being caught in a two-front war. With Austria, Germany shared a common language and culture, and Bismarck had seen to it, by treating defeated Austria generously in 1866, that Austria would not become a permanent and irreconcilable enemy.

The first result of this European policy was the Three Emperors' League, formed in 1873 by Germany, Austria and Russia. The organization's chief aim was to stress monarchical solidarity against subversive elements and to support Germany in the event of a new confrontation with France, where radical monarchists, bent on revenge for 1871, had come into power.

1

But the Three Emperors' League was standing on weak ground: There were constant clashes between Austrian and Russian interests in the Balkans, particularly after the outbreak of insurrections against Turkish rule in Bosnia and Herzegovina in 1875 and in Bulgaria during the following year. In each case, the uprisings had been supported by Russia, and when the Serbs were completely defeated by the Turks and the Bulgarians were subjected to bloody massacres, Russia began to prepare for war against Turkey. Indignation about the Turkish cruelties swept throughout Europe and was especially vehement in England, to the extent that British efforts to support Turkey against the threatening Russian advance in the Balkans were hampered. In spite of British, Austrian and German efforts to mediate, the Russian government yielded to the pressure of Pan-Slavic circles and declared war on Turkey. The Turkish armies were soon overwhelmed, and Russian troops occupied lines just outside of Constantinople. War fever swept through England, and a British fleet was sent to Constantinople in February 1878.

The following month, the Treaty of San Stefano between Russia and Turkey secured the independence of Serbia and Montenegro and provided reforms in Bosnia and Herzegovina and an autonomous state of Bulgaria to be occupied by Russian troops. But the other European powers intervened to check any further Russian advances. In a secret agreement, England promised to defend Turkey against further attacks on her Asian possessions and in return was allowed to occupy Cyprus. A general European conference followed—the Berlin Congress—in which Bismarck offered to play the part of the "honest broker." The treaty that resulted prevented the war which had been looming between Russia on the one side and England and Austria on the other.

But the treaty left Russian Pan-Slavists dissatisfied and also did not meet the hopes of Serbia, Bulgaria and Greece. The Turkish Empire was left with only a few fragments of land in Europe, and these constituted a constant temptation for the neighboring countries. A further result was the cooling off of relations between Germany and Russia— whose representative, Alexander Mikhailovich Gorchakov, felt betrayed by Bismarck—and the beginning of a German rapprochement with Austria. In October 1879 this led to a formal Alliance Treaty between the two countries which was renewed every five years and remained in force until 1918. Its main provision was that if one state were attacked by Russia, the other would support it with all its forces. This treaty was the cornerstone of Bismarck's alliance system, though he could put it through only against the stubborn resistance of his emperor, William I, who viewed Austria as the traditional enemy and rival of Prussia. There was even talk about bringing Britain into this combination; Prime Minister Benjamin Disraeli of Britain, who had been on very friendly terms with Bismarck at the Berlin Conference, was in favor, but in the end nothing came of it. Yet the very idea caused Russia, Britain's old antagonist, to suggest a new Three Emperors' League, which was organized, under strict secrecy, in June 1881. This league obligated the participating powers to maintain friendly neutrality should one of them get into a war with a fourth power (Turkey excluded).

In all of these dealings, France did not play a leading role, except for its establishment of a protectorate over Tunis (on the North African coast). Bismarck had encouraged this in order to get France away from its anti-German revenge policy. But the French initiative created a long period of French-Italian tension which led to a Triple Alliance between Germany, Austria and Italy that was regularly renewed until 1915. In case Italy was attacked by France without provocation, the other two powers would come to its aid; and Italy would help Germany if Germany were attacked by France. This alliance was joined by Serbia and Romania in the following years, and thus a powerful central European bloc was created. However, Italy was not as solidly bound to the other two great powers as they were to one another, and Italy remained a rival of Austria in the Adriatic and the Balkans. Moreover, after the 1866 war there remained problems between Austria and Italy over certain border territories retained by the former, which became known as "unredeemed Italy" (*Italia irredenta*). Most of these territories—Trieste, Trentino, Fiume and Istria—were recovered by Italy as a result of the Treaty of St. Germain in 1919.

In 1883, Bismarck gave in to the growing demand in Germany for developing colonies in Africa. This resulted in an alienation between England and Germany, and, for the first time since 1870, a loose alliance between France and Germany. The latter ended only two years later when French prime minister Jules Ferry, who had collaborated with Bismarck, fell from power.

A period of radical nationalism and agitation followed in France, particularly when the popular General Georges Boulanger became minister of war in January 1886. There was even talk of an intended coup d'état by Boulanger, but he never exploited the situation and he lost his position in May of 1887 when his popularity declined rapidly. Yet some of the French anti-German sentiment had caught fire with Russian nationalists, one more reason for Bismarck to insist on the renewal of the Triple Alliance with Austria and Italy in February of 1887. At the same time, a Mediterranean agreement between Italy and Britain had been concluded, which provided a basis for common action in the event of a hostile action by France or Russia. Bismarck had encouraged this agreement, in the hope of exploiting a French-English conflict over their interests in Egypt. His main achievement, however, was the so-called Reinsurance Treaty with Russia, a secret agreement replacing the old Three Emperors' League that Russia had refused to renew. Russia and Germany now promised each other neutrality if either would get involved in a war with a third power, except for an aggressive war of Germany against France or of Russia against Austria. This treaty enabled Bismarck to prevent Russia from lining up with France. He also promised support to "measures his Majesty [the Tsar] may deem necessary to take to control the key of his empire"—meaning the Dardanelles Straits—which he knew Russia would not be able to secure against the resistance of Britain and Austria.

The extremely complex system of alliances created and maintained by Bismarck could not be perpetuated after his dismissal by the new German emperor, William II (known as the "Kaiser") in March 1890. Under the new chancellor, Count Georg Leo von Caprivi, Germany's foreign policy was largely but unofficially directed by Baron Friedrich von Holstein, known as the "Grey Eminence," who advised not to renew the Reinsurance Treaty with Russia, despite several Russian attempts to reopen the negotiations. Instead, a rapprochement with Britain was attempted, and an exchange was arranged of territories claimed by Germany in East Africa for the island of Heligoland in the North Sea, which Britain had obtained from Denmark in 1815. Germany quickly installed fortifications at Heligoland, and these played a strategic role in both world wars.

This rapprochement, as well as the premature renewal of the Triple Alliance with Austria and Italy—by which Germany wanted to prevent Italy from being drawn over to the French side—initiated the first negotiations between France and Russia in July 1891. A military convention drafted in August 1892 was formally accepted in January 1894. It was to be in force as long as the Triple Alliance existed, and it provided that if France were attacked by Germany—or if Italy were supported by Germany—Russia would muster up all available forces against Germany. In case of a German attack on Russia, France would support the latter with all of its forces. Still, the conclusion of a German-Russian tariff treaty a few months later seemed to indicate Russia's unwillingness to be drawn into hostilities with Germany.

Meanwhile, Britain had followed a policy of "splendid isolation" under Robert Arthur, marquess of Salisbury. His one attempt to develop a common Near Eastern policy with Germany was misunderstood by the German emperor and aggravated relations between the two countries. Matters were further worsened by William's telegram of congratulations to President Paul Kruger of the South African Republic (Transvaal), whose army had defeated some British raiders. This caused a storm of indignation in Britain and began to prepare the ground for Britain to join the Russian-French alliance.

But late in 1897, a conflict arose beteen Britain and Russia over railroad-building rights in Manchuria and Siberia, in which Salisbury suggested a line across all of Asia dividing it into a northern Russia interest sphere and a southern one controlled by Britain. Nothing ever came of it nor of Britain's attempts to involve Japan against Russia (since the Japanese were not yet ready to act). The period of sharp antagonism between Russia and Britain continued when, in May 1898, the latter attempted to enlist German support against Russia's encroachments in the Far East. But the German foreign minister, Bernhard von Buelow, treated the matter evasively, as his sights were set on his country's program to build up its navy.

Another incident that, for the time being, prevented a British-French-Russian alliance was the Fashoda crisis in the fall of 1898. British forces under Lord Horatio Herbert Kitchener were advancing up the Nile and clashed with a French expeditionary force under Major J.B. Marchand at Fashoda in the South Sudan. While the British were seeking to occupy a continuous strip of territory from Cairo to Cape Town, the French desired a land route from the Atlantic to the Red Sea. The English insisted on a French withdrawal, and the two nations came as close to war as they had been since the time of Napoleon. France, which was suffering from internal strife (the famous Dreyfus affair), finally yielded the territory and was given instead some worthless districts in the Sahara Desert. Peace prevailed, but in France some fierce hatred for Britain stayed alive for a long time.

In 1899, the Russian tsar invited 26 nations to an international peace conference at The Hague (seat of government in the West Netherlands), mainly because Russia was suffering under the financial strain of keeping up armaments with the other great powers. Nothing essential was achieved by the tsar; there was neither a limitation of armaments nor the compulsory arbitration for international crises. Only some particularly offensive weapons—such as the infamous dumdum bullets and gas warfare—were forbidden, and a permanent court of arbitration was installed at The Hague. Shortly thereafter, the main promoter of the French-Russian Alliance, French foreign minister Théophile Delcassé, managed to extend this alliance during a visit to St. Petersburg.

At the same time Britain found itself occupied with the South African situation for several years: Since the British raids into Transvaal in 1895, South African president Kruger—who fought for the independence of the Dutch settlers (Boers) in Transvaal—had become convinced that the British intended to acquire the entire rich Transvaal territory, while the British government suspected that Kruger wanted to drive the British out of South Africa altogether.

When war broke out in October 1899, there was much talk of a French-German-Russian intervention on behalf of the Boers of Transvaal, but no power undertook actual steps in this direction. The British, at first greatly outnumbered, finally overwhelmed the Boers, and Johannesburg and Pretoria were taken in May–June of 1900. But the Boers—whose president had fled to Europe, where he tried in vain to interest the other powers to come to his aid—reverted to guerrilla tactics. The strategy so disrupted the country that the British had to resort to ruthless oppression, including large-scale concentration camps in which some 20,000 Boers died. The Boers were finally forced to accept British sovereignty; it was only the 1903 British policy under Joseph Chamberlain that enacted a gradual reconciliation and Anglo-Dutch equality.

In the meantime, the Germans had exploited the British dilemma by establishing some colonies in the Samoan islands and extending their sphere of influence in the Near East by obtaining railway-building concessions from the Turks for a Constantinople-Baghdad railroad line. Their endeavors were furthered by a visit of the German emperor to Constantinople and the Holy Land in 1898, during which time he proclaimed his friendship to the 300 million Muslims in the world. This antagonized the Russians and the French who entertained similar railway schemes. The British were outraged as well, but in the end were pacified by the continuous German support of their complete takeover in Egypt.

Yet a real German-English rapprochement never took place, and the famous "blood is thicker than water" slogan (an English proverb often quoted by William II) never amounted to more than an empty phrase. When the German emperor and his foreign minister, Prince Bernhard von Bülow, visited the English court in November 1898, there were discussions of an Anglo-German agreement. But British public opinion was strongly against it, since the German sympathies with the Boers had not been forgotten, and Bülow shortly thereafter stressed the need for a stronger German navy. A proposed German-British block against Russian expansion in the Far East was disapproved by Bülow, and in May of 1901, Lord Salisbury again pronounced the British policy of "splendid isolation." This ended all German-British alliance negotiations, but did not prevent the British government from aligning with the Japanese in January 1902. England's new king, Edward VII, was known for his pro-French inclinations, and his visit to Paris in May 1903 started the slow but thorough reconciliation between the two powers, which was then furthered by Théophile Delcassé's and French president Emile Loubet's visit to London in July of the same year.

This development was undoubtedly accelerated by the outbreak of the Russian-Japanese war of 1904–5, which was provoked by the Russian expansion into Manchuria. The tsarist government never took the Japanese quite seriously and, consequently, was due for a rude awakening. The war began with the Japanese bottling up the Russian fleet at Port Arthur. The Russians surrendered to the Japanese after a long siege in January 1905. The Russians then suffered another defeat on land at Mukden, in northeastern China. At the end of May the impressive Russian fleet, which had come all the way from Europe, was annihilated by the Japanese navy in the Battle of Tsushima Straits. Japan emerged from this war as a new world power, with Britain as its ally. British-Russian negotiation had broken down after the Russians refused, in November 1903, to agree to partition their influence in the

Persian region. Britain had sided with the eventual winner by signing an alliance with Japan in January 1902 in which it recognized Japan's special interests in Korea. And Britain further strengthened its position when, following the path prepared by Delcassé and later by King Edward, it concluded the Anglo-French Entente Cordiale with France in April 1904, although Russia—France's close ally—was now engaged in a bitter struggle with England's ally Japan!

The Entente Cordiale, concluded after months of negotiations, completely settled all colonial differences between the two powers: Britain guaranteed free navigation on the Suez Canal and was given a free hand in Egypt, in which France had previously invested much capital and had shown considerable political interest. France was given British support in its Moroccan policy and surrendered its traditional rights on the Newfoundland shores. Earlier disputes between Britain and France about Madagascar, the New Hebrides and French Gambia were also settled.

INTERNATIONAL CRISES

This seemed to divide the political world into two clearly distinct groups: the Anglo-French-Russian and the German-Austro-Italian. But during the same year, there was another conflict between Britain and Russia, the so-called Dogger Bank episode in October 1904. The Russian fleet, on the way to the Far East, fired upon British trawlers which were mistaken for Japanese destroyers. The Russian government did not give the British sufficient explanation for the attack, whereupon the British fleet was ordered to stop the Russians at Gibraltar. The crisis was overcome at the last moment by the efforts of the great champion of the Entente Cordiale, Delcassé. Simultaneous German-Russian discussions about a defensive alliance broke down because Russia would not commit itself without consulting its ally France. Germany's countermove was Emperor William's visit to Tangier, which was designed by Chancellor Bülow and Friedrich von Holstein to test the strength of the Anglo-French Entente. This resulted in an outcry in Paris against Delcassé, who had to resign a few months later (in June 1905). His successors were unwilling to get into a conflict with the Germans, and they pleaded for a general conference on Morocco, which took place in Algeciras, Spain in January 1906, where all the powers sided against Germany except Austria. By this time, Chancellor Bülow disagreed with Holstein and forced him to resign.

In the meantime, another attempt to arrange a defensive alliance between Russia and Germany, this time initiated by the two emperors during visits aboard each other's yachts, the so-called Bjoerkoe Treaty of July 1905, was wrecked by the opposition of the Russian foreign office and French objections. And although Britain's new liberal cabinet under Sir Edward Grey was reluctant to promise France outright support in case of a German attack, Anglo-French military and naval conversations now began in earnest.

In February 1906, the British launched their first super-battleship, the *Dreadnought*, which boasted 10 12-inch guns. This started a more intensified race in the buildup of the two navies. A visit of King Edward VII to the German emperor in August of the same year did not change the situation. Neither did the Second Hague Peace Conference, which had been called at President Theodore Roosevelt's suggestion as early as October 1904 but had been postponed by the war in the Far East. When it did convene in the summer of 1906, all British suggestions of armament limitations and compulsory arbitration were rejected by the other powers, with Germany acting as their spokesman. The only successes were in regard to regulations on issues such as voluntary arbitration, the rights of neutrals and collecting debts.

The basic situation had not changed; the final link, the Anglo-Russian Entente, was concluded in August 1907. While the agreement was not as extensive as the one between Russia and France, it did settle all major points of conflict between the two powers: Afghanistan was declared to be within the British sphere of interest, while Persia was divided among three zones, the large and most valuable northern zone being assigned to Russia. China's suzerainty over Tibet was agreed upon, and Britain's dominant position in the Persian Gulf was recognized by Russia.

King Edward, during the following months, was busy consolidating the alliance. He met with Russian foreign minister Alexander Petrovich Izvolski at Marienbad in September 1907, with Tsar Nicholas in June 1908 and with Emperors William and Francis Joseph two months later. The last two meetings had few practical results.

A new crisis developed in October 1908 when Austria announced the annexation of Bosnia and Herzegovina, which had been under Austro-Hungarian administration and occupation since the Congress of Berlin but remained under the sovereignty of the Turkish Sultan. This caused indignation in Serbia and Montenegro and also in Russia, where the public knew nothing of the recent agreement between Izvolski and Austrian foreign minister Count Alois Aehrenthal, who had promised Russia that Austria would not oppose the opening of the Straits (the Dardanelles and the Bosporus) to Russian warships. Izvolski's own prime minister, Peter Arkadevich Stolypin, instructed him to repudiate this agreement. But Germany stuck loyally to its ally Austria. France and Britain, while resenting Izvolski's secret deals, only demanded an international conference. Izvolski's further efforts to secure the Straits through an agreement with Austria were rejected by London, but the question of the two provinces was finally settled between Austria and Turkey when the latter was paid a compensation. This paved the way for the later Austro-German-Turkish alliance during World War I. Yet anti-Austrian animosity was again rising in the annexed provinces, in particular in Sarajevo, the capital of Bosnia.

In July 1909, one of the main actors in the European theater, Prince Bernhard von Bülow, resigned as German chancellor. He had come to disapprove the tremendous naval buildup promoted by his emperor and Admiral Alfred von Tirpitz, but the main reason for his resignation was his role in the *Daily Telegraph* affair in November 1908. The emperor, who was of half-British descent on his mother's side and entertained a strange love-hatred for Great Britain, declared, in an interview with an English nobleman, the English to be fools and himself to be a great friend of England, although German public opinion was hostile to England during the Boer War. He also claimed to have designed a strategy for England to win its struggle in South Africa and added that the German navy was needed only in the Far East but never against England. His declarations, which were never checked by the chancellor nor at the German Foreign Office, caused great indignation in the Reichstag as well as in Britain, where his remarks were regarded as condescending as well as insincere, and made Bülow's position impossible, although he meekly tried to defend the emperor. The incident once again provoked, quite unnecessarily, a crisis between the two powers; representatives at the London Naval Conference, which convened six weeks later, did agree on certain regulations about naval warfare, but this was never ratified. Anglo-German negotiations about the Baghdad Railway in December 1909 also failed, although the Germans were ready to make large concessions; but the British were unwilling to commit themselves without Russian and French approval.

The year 1911 produced another Moroccan Crisis, provoked by France's occupation of Fez in May. Negotiations with German foreign secretary Alfred von Kiderlen-Waechter were handicapped by the formation of a new cabinet in France under Joseph Caillaux and by Germany's next step of sending its gunboat *Panther* to Agadir, Morocco. The British rejected France's request to send in ships, and the Germans finally demanded the entire French Congo as compensation for giving up any claims on Morocco. This aroused David Lloyd George, the British chancellor of the exchequer, who was usually considered to be pacifically minded; on July 21, 1911 he used threatening language against Germany in his "Mansion House Speech." Britain openly prepared for war, but eventually Germany gave France a free hand in Morocco in exchange for the cession of some unimportant sections of land in the French Congo.

In February 1912, a last chance for a cooperation between Britain and Germany arose but was missed. Britain's war secretary, Lord Richard Burdon Haldane, went to Berlin and suggested British support for German colonial plans in Africa if Germany would refrain from increasing its navy. While the new German chancellor, Theobald von Bethmann-Hollweg, and foreign secretary Alfred von Kiderlen-

Waechter were anxious to come to an agreement with England, the emperor and Admiral Tirpitz were determined to continue building up the German navy. On the other hand, the British refused to agree to the formal promise of neutrality demanded by Bethmann.

THE BALKAN SITUATION

So the armament race pressed on: The Germans increased their naval program, France and Russia entered into a naval alliance, and the British began to concentrate their naval strength in the North Sea rather than in the Mediterranean. In March 1912, Bulgaria and Serbia concluded a treaty of alliance under Russian sponsorship, which posed a direct threat to Austria. In spite of warnings by the new Austrian foreign minister, Count Leopold von Berchtold, the two countries declared war against Turkey. This first Balkan War, starting in October 1912, saw Bulgaria, Serbia, Greece and Montenegro fighting against the Turks, and subsequent to several Bulgarian and Serbian victories, the Serbs reached the Adriatic, while Russia warned the Bulgarians against occupying Constantinople.

Austria and then Italy opposed the appearance of the Serbs at the Adriatic, while Russia supported the Salvic Serbs, their "natural friends." In December 1912, both Austria and Russia began to mobilize, but then the Russians abandoned the Serbs. The peace conference, opening in December at London, soon broke down as the Turks refused to give up Adrianople and Crete. When the extreme nationalist Enver Bey gained power in Turkey through a coup d'état, war was resumed. Again the Turks were badly beaten, and in the new Treaty of London, in May 1913, Turkey ceded a great amount of territory which included the island of Crete.

Immediately after, a new Balkan war broke out between the former allies. Serbia and Greece could not agree with Bulgaria on some territories on the Adriatic and in Macedonia. When Romania and Turkey entered the war on the side of Serbia and Greece, Bulgaria was soon defeated. In the Treaty of Bucharest, which followed in August 1913, the Romanians, Serbs and Greeks proved to be the winners. The following month, Turkey regained Adrianople. However, when Serbia invaded Albania during that same month, it was forced by an Austrian ultimatum to withdraw.

Russia had stood by during these crises, but was aroused when German general Liman von Sanders was appointed to reorganize the Turkish army. Russia, supported by the French, protested because it suspected German designs on the Turkish capital; as a result Liman was given a lesser appointment. The Russians had come to the conclusion, as expressed in their crown council of February 1912, that their designs on the Straits could only be attained by a European war. They then began negotiations with the British on an Anglo-Russian naval convention, which was not concluded before the outbreak of the Great War.

Disagreements between the close allies Germany and Austria came out into the open in June 1914, when Austria recommended an alliance with Bulgaria and Turkey (as it actually materialized during the Great War) to prevent a renewal of a Balkan League under French and Russian influence. Germany, instead, suggested a reconciliation of Austria with Serbia, Romania and Greece. One might say that the Balkan wars prepared for the world war in that they satisfied some of Serbia's ambitions and thereby encouraged it to acquire some further parts of Austria-Hungary with a Slavic population; at the same time they caused Austria's resolve to get rid of Serbia as soon as possible. Also, the wars left Bulgaria and Turkey dissatisfied, and therefore inclined to enter any war alliance directed against Russia.

MILITARY PREPARATIONS

While statesmen and diplomats had been busy arranging, dissolving and rearranging alliances, treaties and conventions, the militaries of the great nations had been preparing for the eventualities of war. In Germany, the General Staff had a long and proud tradition, and after Prussia's victories over Austria and France under the generalship of Helmuth von Moltke, an era of pride and conviction of Prussian invincibility prevailed. But Moltke retired in 1888 and when, a year later, Count Alfred von Schlieffen took over, the mood changed. Schlieffen was convinced that Germany would sooner or later have to face a two-front war. He pointed out that the victories of the past had been attained against weaker foes and that entirely different tactics would be required in a coming war. He was convinced that Russia would require much more time to mobilize its armies than France and that Russia could prolong the war by retreating into its vast area as it had done against Napoleon I. Therefore, his solution was to concentrate all available forces for a quick and overwhelming attack on France. This could be done only by enveloping the enemy forces; a frontal attack across the German-French border would be impractical because of the strong fortresses France had built along the border of Alsace-Lorraine. And since the new German Army would be about six times the size of that of 1870, it could develop its full strength only by sweeping through neutral Belgium. Schlieffen discounted Belgian resistance, believing Belgium could be bullied into cooperating. He correctly predicted that France would attack across the Alsace-Lorraine border in order to regain its lost province, and he intended to hold the French in a "sack" while his northern wing would push the French armies deeply into their own territory and then swing around to catch the

Count Alfred von Schlieffen, originator of the German plan of attack in the West. Photo courtesy of the German Information Center, New York City.

southern French wing from behind. It was certainly a reckless, bold scheme, which went against all military tradition; it was even planned to involve the reserve units on the front lines. His paragon was, strangely enough, Hannibal, the Carthaginian general, who had beaten the Romans in 216 B.C. at Cannae by similar enveloping tactics.

But Schlieffen's successor in 1906, Count Helmuth Johannes Ludwig von Moltke, nephew of the Prussian hero, was less bold. He worried about a Russian invasion of East Prussia and the German left wing, which Schlieffen had left in a weak position. The original plan was therefore watered down somewhat, but with the plan of an overwhelming attack through Belgium maintained. Neither Moltke nor Schlieffen seem to have had any qualms about violating Belgium's neutrality and the psychological effect it would have on the neutral countries, in particular the one great unknown factor—Britain.

Across the Rhine, French strategists were aware of the threat of envelopment by the German right wing, but they felt that such an attack would give them a better chance to smash through the German center and left. The French military believed in the offensive, and the molder of their military theory at the time, General Ferdinand Foch, director of the Paris War College, had an almost mystic belief in an all-out attack and a morale based on willpower more than anything else. *Cran* (guts), the military equivalent of Henri Bergson's *élan vital,* became the slogan in the new French army.

But there were also dissenting voices: The vice president of the Supreme War Council, General Augustin Edouard Michel, proposed to meet a German advance through Belgium with a million men along a line at Verdun-Namur-Antwerp; he also suggested the employment of reserve units to increase the strength of the French left wing. But the minister of war, Adolphe Messimy, and such authorities as Joseph Gallieni, the great colonial general, and Marshal Joseph Joffre (the future hero of the Marne) dismissed Michel's ideas as insane. Moreover, the issue of relying on reserve units had become a political one, since the left-wing parties, unpopular with the professional soldiers, believed in a "nation in arms" in the tradition of 1792 to safeguard the Republic against dictatorial designs à la Boulanger. In 1913, therefore, "Plan 17" was adopted, based on Foch's idea of crossing the Rhine at Mayence and heading straight for Berlin. By concentrating on this attack, the greater part of the Belgian frontier was left undefended. This was done with the express approval of Michel's successor Joffre, in spite of the fact that back in 1904 an officer of the German General Staff had betrayed the Schlieffen plan to a French intelligence officer at Brussels, and that as late as 1913 some confidential remarks of Moltke's had gotten into French hands.

In Britain, public opinion was strictly against involvement in a continental war, although there had been some anxiety when Russia was beaten by Japan in 1905 (which would have left France to fight alone should the Germans have decided to attack). This was the beginning of British-French joint military plans, with British officers attending French maneuvers. Yet there was strong resistance to the idea of British army units being employed as mere adjuncts of the French. Instead, the First Sea Lord, Sir John Fisher, suggested, in the event of war, a British landing on the Baltic coast, only 90 miles from Berlin. More serious attempts to define Britain's role in a continental war were developed by the commander of England's Staff College, General Henry Wilson, who established a close relationship with General Foch. Under the impact of the Agadir crisis of July 1911, the Imperial Defense Committee was presided by the new prime minister, Sir Herbert Henry Asquith, and attended by Foreign Secretary Sir Edward Grey, Chancellor of the Exchequer David Lloyd George and Home Secretary Winston Churchill. Fisher's plans of a naval landing were rejected by the Committee and Wilson's ideas for an expeditionary force to be landed in France were adopted. By the spring of 1914, the joint work of the French and British general staffs had been completed in total secrecy. Yet Britain's political leaders kept aloof of any commitment, always emphasizing that under no circumstances should France violate the Belgian neutrality, as such a step would make it impossible for Britain to support France.

The other unknown factor in prewar Europe was the Russian army. Its commitment to the French was unquestionable, but how strong was it and how ready was it to strike? Russia had vast resources; it could muster up one and a half million soldiers in peacetime and over three million upon mobilization, and further reserves in territorials could bring its eventual strength to more than six million troops. But after mobilization, the average Russian soldier would have to be transported no less than 700 miles, four times as far as the German soldier, who could rely on more efficient means of transportation. Could France count on a Russian attack prompt enough to support its own offensive in the West? France's Plan 17 depended on it, and no doubt the Russians were anxious to restore glory to their arms which had been embarrassed by Japan. In 1911 at a staff meeting, French general Auguste Dubail, chief of the war ministry staff, had been assured that Russia would invade East Prussia on "M 16," i.e., on the 16th day after mobilization, with half of their forces of approximately 800,000 men immediately available; the other half would be used to launch an attack across the Austrian border further south.

British observers of the Russian-Japanese war had pointed out serious flaws within the Russian colossus: low intelligence, disregard of secrecy, lack of initiative and poor generalship. There was, furthermore, a strong opposition in the country to the French alliance, particularly among the Baltic barons of German descent and others who felt that an alliance (à la the Three Emperors' League) was much more natural than that of a Western democracy. The Russian minister of war, General Vladimir Sukhomlinov, was intelligent but lazy and pleasure-loving, far more interested in leading an extravagant life than in discussing badly needed innovations in the army system. As a result, Russia had only 60 batteries of heavy artillery (against 380 in the German Army) and only 850 shells per gun (as compared to the 2,000–3,000 in the Western armies).

Sukhomlinov's successor, the Grand Duke Nicholas, was much more capable and popular with the army, but was hated by the reactionaries and the tsarina because the Grand Duke despised her famous protégé, the monk Rasputin. Under Nicholas, a new war plan was worked out, providing that in the event that Germany used its main strength against France, four armies would be used against Austria and two against Germany. Of these, one was to start out from Vilna, the other from Warsaw. The first was to draw all German strength upon itself, while the second (starting out a little later) was to move behind the German forces, cutting off their retreat across the Vistula.

POWDER-KEG EUROPE

In summary, one can say that the military authorities in the four big European powers clearly figured on the possibility, even likelihood, of a general war and tried to prepare for it. The general public, however, was kept in the dark and was completely taken by surprise when the outbreak occurred. The political leaders professed to be peace-loving, but it was obvious that Austria had designs on the Balkans, in particular Serbia, and Russia certainly would not tolerate any further advances in the direction of the Dardanelles. In Germany, the emperor's provocative, if inconsistent, speeches had left an uneasy feeling in the European capitals, particularly in London.

It should also be noted that as early as December 1912, a so-called "war council" took place in Berlin in which William II emphasized that, according to the latest remarks of British war secretary Lord Richard Burdon Haldane, London had refused a proposal of British neutrality in any war Germany might be drawn into, because a victory on the continent would upset the balance of power which British policy had made its guiding principle. The emperor, while regretting that the British blood relatives would consider fighting on the side of the Slavs against their German brethren, stressed that this cleared the situation once and for all. When German chief of staff Moltke openly advocated a preventive war, stating: "the sooner the better," his majesty agreed. Actual measures in this direction were stopped only because Admiral Tirpitz pleaded for a delay of one and a half years to enable the navy to widen the Kiel Canal sufficiently to permit the new German Dreadnought class of warships to pass through so that the German fleet could promptly be committed to either the Baltic or the North Sea.

All of the details about the war council have not been corroborated, neither have the exact utterances and actual significance of the meeting. Chancellor Theobald von Bethmann-Hollweg, who did not participate, apparently was unconvinced that Britain would automatically turn against Germany. But it is safe to say that by the end of 1912, the European nations had come to the brink of war, even before the question of Belgian neutrality had arisen.

It is also obvious, in retrospect, that during the 40 to 50 years preceding the outbreak of the war, a considerable shift in the distribution of power between the five leading European nations—Britain, France, Germany, Austria and Russia—had taken place: While there had been an approximate equality between them at the beginning of the period, Britain's share in the world's manufacturing production fell in these 40 years from one-third to one-seventh by 1913, and the country had fallen from being the world's leading industrial state to third place behind the United States and Germany. France had fallen from being the second industrial nation in the world to number four, and the Dual

Monarchy of Austria-Hungary, once the dominant force in Central Europe, had shrunk into an outwardly glamorous but internally feeble conglomeration of nationalities with a limited industrial capacity. Russia had been humiliated in its battles with Japan and had been left far behind in the technological race of the big nations. While this gradual, almost invisible development may not have been fully understood by all of the European leaders, the new imbalance of power no doubt created the desire to "contain" rising Germany and, on the German side, the fear of encirclement. Increasing mutual distrust and nervousness characterized the last years before 1914, and the only thing missing was a little spark.

CHRONICLE OF EVENTS

1866:
War between Prussia and Austria. Prussian victory at Koeniggraetz (Sadowa). The German Confederation is dissolved and replaced by the North German Confederation dominated by Prussia.

1870–71:
Franco-German War: France, under Emperor Napoleon III, is defeated by the Northern and Southern States, Napoleon taken prisoner. A German empire is founded, with William of Prussia as its first emperor. Alsace-Lorraine is taken from France and becomes a German province.

1871:
August–September: Meetings between emperors William I of Prussia and Francis Joseph of Austria-Hungary.

1872:
September: Meeting of the three emperors in Berlin (Alexander II of Russia had invited himself). No political agreements.

1873:
May 6: Military convention between Russia and Germany, arranged during the visit of Emperor William I, Bismarck and Moltke to St. Petersburg.
June 6: The Three Emperors' League is formed to maintain monarchical solidarity against subversive movements.
September: Italy under King Victor Emmanuel II is loosely associated with the Three Emperors' League.

1875:
Russian Tsar Alexander II and Prime Minister Alexander Mikhailovich Gorchakov visit in Berlin. Friction arises between the latter and Bismarck, who realizes the weakness of the Three Emperors' League.
July: Insurrection takes place in Bosnia and Herzegovina against the Turks, supported by Russia.
November: England's prime minister Benjamin Disraeli purchases Egypt's shares in the Suez Canal from the Khedive (Viceroy).

1876:
May 13: Berlin Memorandum, drawn up by Austrian foreign minister Count Julius Andrassy, Gorchakov and Bismarck, attempts to ease the tension between Russia and England.
May–September: Uprisings in Bulgaria are suppressed brutally by the Turks.
June–July: Serbia and Montenegro declare war on Turkey and are defeated.
September: After their final defeat, the Serbs appeal to the powers for mediation. British indignation over Turkish misrule and horrors hamper Disraeli's policy of supporting the Turks against Russia.
November: Russia prepares for war against Turkey.

1877:
January: Turkey rejects all proposals for the powers for mediation and reforms.
April 24: Russia declares war on Turkey.
December: Turkish defeats, Turkey appeals for mediation.

1878:
January 31: The Russian forces are just outside Constantinople. Armistice. War fever spreads in England (jingoists).
February 15: A British fleet arrives at Constantinople.
March 3: Treaty of San Stefano between Russia and Turkey. Montenegro and Serbia to be independent, reforms in Bosnia and Herzegovina, large territorial concession to Russia.
June 4: Secret British-Turkish agreement in which the British promise defense against fur-

ther attacks. Britain to occupy Cyprus.

June 13–July 13: The Berlin Congress, with Bismarck presiding as the "honest broker." Disraeli, Gorchakov, Andrassy etc. participate. Bulgaria divided in three parts, Austria given a mandate to occupy Bosnia, Romania obtains the Dobrudja, Russia gets Southern Bessarabia. There is very little left of Turkey's European possessioins, but the Pan-Slavists, Greeks and Serbs are dissatisfied.

1879:

September: Dual control of England and France in Egypt.

October 7: Alliance Treaty between Germany and Austria-Hungary, which remains in force until 1918. Complete mutual assistance against Russia and at least neutrality against any other power are assured.

1881:

May: French Protectorate over Tunis established. Beginning of a long period of French-Italian friction.

June 18: Secret Alliance of the Three Emperors, providing neutrality if one of the contracting powers goes to war with a fourth power. It is renewed in 1884.

June 28: Secret treaty between Austria and Serbia in which the latter promises not to tolerate intrigues against Austria. This almost amounts to an Austrian protectorate over Serbia.

1882:

May 20: Triple Alliance between Germany, Austria and Italy, which is renewed every five years until 1915. Germany and Austria to aid Italy should it be attacked by France without provocation, and vice-versa if Germany is attacked by France.

September: British occupation of Egypt, leading to an estrangement between England and France.

1883:

February–April: Beginning of German colonialism in Africa, leading to tension between Germany and England and a loose German-French entente.

October: Alliance between Austria and Romania, following the latter's dissatisfaction with the results of the Berlin Congress. The treaty remains in force until 1916.

November: British setbacks in the Sudan, due to uprisings under the "Mahdi," a fanatic religious leader.

1885:

March: French prime minister Jules Ferry resigns, thereby ending the German-French entente. Reconciliation between Germany and Britain begins.

November: Serbia declares war on Bulgaria and is thoroughly defeated.

1886:

March: Peace between the two countries is restored.

November: Growing tension between Austria and Russia over the Balkan situation. Bismarck tries to mediate by proposing an Austrian (Western) and a Russian (Eastern) sphere of influence.

1886–87:

Revenge for the defeat of 1870–71 agitation in France, headed by the minister of war, General Georges Boulanger.

1887:

February: Agreement between England and Italy on Mediterranean problems.

February 20: The Triple Alliance is renewed for five years.

May: Fall of Boulanger.

June 18: Secret Russian-German Treaty (Reinsurance Treaty), replacing the Three Emperors' League. The two powers promise each other neutrality if either gets involved in war with a third power, except by aggression. German assistance is also promised to Russian efforts to acquire entrance to the Black Sea.

December 12: Second Mediterranean Agreement among Britain, Austria and Italy.

1888:

January 28: Agreement between Germany and Italy, providing the use of Italian forces in case of a German-French war.

February 3: Publication of the German-Austrian Alliance of 1879.

March 9: Death of German emperor William I. His son, Frederick III, ascends the throne as a dying man.

June 15: William II, son of Frederick III and Victoria, daughter of Queen Victoria of England, becomes emperor. Tension between him and Bismarck.

1890:

March 18: Dismissal of Bismarck by William, partly because of a disagreement on Russian policy.

June 18: The German-Russian Reinsurance Treaty is allowed to lapse.

July 1: Anglo-German agreement of exchange of Heligoland which becomes German, against German claims in East Africa.

1891:

February: Anti-German demonstrations in Paris during the visit of Empress Frederick.

May 6: The Triple Alliance between Germany, Austria and Italy is prematurely renewed.

July 4: State visit of Emperor William in London.

July 24: A French navy unit visits Cronstadt in the Gulf of Finland. Demonstrations of Franco-Russian friendship.

1892:

August: French military mission in St. Petersburg. A military convention is drafted.

1893:

December–January 1894: A French-Russian military convention is formally accepted.

1895:

April: Intervention of Russia, Germany and France in the Far East, advising Japan to give up certain territories recently won in a war against China. Beginning of Russian-Japanese friction.

August 5: Interview between William II and the new British prime minister Robert Arthur Talbot Salisbury, who suggests partitioning the Turkish Empire. His ideas are misunderstood and create an era of distrust between the two men.

1896:

January 3: William II sends telegram to President Paul Kruger of Transvaal, South Africa, causing great indignation in England as an anti-British gesture.

March 1: Italian defeat by the Ethiopians at Adua. The British decide to reconquer the Sudan lost in 1883.

1897:

April: War between Greece and Turkey. Greeks suffer defeats, but through an Austrian-Russian agreement the status quo is more or less maintained.

November 14: German forces land at Kiaochow Bay, China and occupy Tsingtao, which is then leased from China for 99 years.

1898:

January 25: Salisbury proposes a division of interests in Asia between England and Russia, in which the more valuable southern sphere is left to England. Instead, the Russians encourage the Chinese to ask for a lease of Port Arthur. New Russian-English estrangement.

March 27: The Chinese give in and lease Port Arthur to the Russians.

March 28: Passage of the first naval law in the German Reichstag. Salisbury tries to get German support against Russian expansion in the Far East.

August 30: Anglo-German Agreement on the future of the Portuguese colonies, since Portugal is bankrupt.

September: Beginning of the Anglo-French Fashoda crisis concerning the area around the Nile at South Sudan. The French at last evacuate Fashoda, as they are unprepared for a war at sea.

October: Visit of Emperor William II to Constantinople and the Holy Land.

1899:

May–July: First Hague Peace Conference called by Tsar Nicholas II. No agreement on disarmament or compulsory arbitration.

November 1: Anglo-German agreement on the respective colonies in the Samoan Islands.

November 25: A railroad concession is given to a German company for the stretch from Constantinople to Ankara.

November: Visit of William and his chancellor Bülow in London. No agreement on closer ties, and a cooling of Anglo-German relations results.

1900:

June 12: Second German naval law passed, providing a fleet of 38 battleships.

June–August: Boxer rising in China which gives Russia the opportunity to occupy Manchuria.

December 14: French-Italian agreement, in which France gets Morocco, Italy Tripoli. Beginning of a French-Italian entente.

1902:

Anglo-Japanese Alliance, marking the end of Britain's "splendid isolation."

1903:

May 1–4: King Edward VII visits Paris. Beginning of the reconciliation between France and Britain

Edward VII, king of England, who helped to establish the French-Russian-British prewar alliance. Photo courtesy of the Author.

July 6–9: Visit of French president Emile-François Loubet and foreign minister Théophile Delcassé to London. Talk about an entente.

August 29: Dismissal of Russian minister of finance Count Sergei Witte, who had opposed Russia's expansion policy in the Far East.

November: Anglo-Russian discussions on Persia and the Far East break down.

1904:

February 4: War between Russia and Japan. The Japanese attack Port Arthur.

April 8: Conclusion of the Anglo-French entente cordiale, hastened by the outbreak of the Russian-Japanese war. Questions regarding Egypt, the Suez Canal, Morocco, Newfoundland, Madagascar, French Gambia and the New Hebrides settled.

April 24–29: Loubet and Delcassé in Rome. King Victor Emmanel III of Italy does not mention the Triple Alliance in his speeches, aggravating Germany and Austria.

May: The Japanese defeat the Russians at the Yalu river and begin the siege of Port Arthur.

October 21: Dogger Bank incident. Russian ships fire on British trawlers. Anglo-Russian crisis. Germany proposes mutual aid in case of attack by another European power, but Russia will not agree without consulting France.

1905:

January 2: Port Arthur surrenders to the Japanese.

February 3: Strong speech of the first lord of the British admiralty against German naval armaments.

February 20–March 9: Russians beaten at Mukden by five Japanese armies.

March 31: First Moroccan crisis. Visit of William II at Tangier, trying to test the Anglo-French Entente.

May 27–29: The Russian fleet is annihilated by the Japanese under Togo at Tsushima Straits.

June 6: Fall of Delcassé, as a result of the first Morocco crisis.

July 24: Bjoerkoe Treaty signed by emperors William II and Nicholas II, but it fails because it is opposed by both governments and by the French.

August 12: Renewal of Anglo-Japanese Alliance for 10 years.

September 5: Treaty of Portsmouth ends Russian-Japanese war, mediated by U.S. president Theodore Roosevelt. Korea left to Japan.

1906:

January: Anglo-French military conversations.

January 16–April 7: Algeciras Conference to settle the Moroccan crisis. All powers except Austria side with France against Germany.

February 10: England launches the *Dreadnought,* the first battleship of her class.

August 15: King Edward VII visits William II at Cronberg. Discussions on the naval situation end without results.

1907:

June–October: Second Hague Peace Conference, as suggested by President Roosevelt. British attempts to come to an agreement on armament limitations are unsuccessful.

July: Renewal of Triple Alliance, although Germany and Austria have doubts about Italy's sincerity.

August 3–5: Emperors William and Nicholas meet at Swinemünde and discuss the Baghdad Railway.

August 31: Anglo-Russian entente. Agreement on Persia and Afghanistan, on Russian interests in the Straits and British interest in the Persian Gulf region.

September: Meeting of Edward VII with Russian foreign minister Alexander Petrovich Izvolski at Marienbad, regarding the new entente.

1908:

January 27: Count Alois Aehrenthal, Austrian foreign minister, antagonizes the Russians and the British with his plans for a railway to Saloniki.

August 11: Edward VII and William II meet at Friedrichshof. The latter refuses any reduction in the German naval program.

August 13: At Ischl, Edward tries to enlist Austrian pressure on Germany regarding naval reductions.

October 6: Austria proclaims the annexation of Bosnia and Herzegovina, of which Izvolski had been advised in advance. Russian prime minister Peter Arkadevich Stolypin overrules him and opposes the move. France and Britain demand a conference.

October 9–14: Izvolski lacks support during a visit in London and his policy collapses.

October 28: William II quoted in interview with the *Daily Telegraph,* creating an uproar in London and Berlin.

1909:

January: Agreement between Austria and Turkey which recognizes Austria's annexation of the two provinces.

March: Intervention of the powers to prevent a war between Austria and Serbia over the provinces.

March 21: Germany asks Russia to recognize the annexation. Izvolski yields, causing British indignation.

July 14: German chancellor Bülow resigns, mainly because of the *Daily Telegraph* affair. His successor, Theobald von Bethmann-Hollweg, is eager for an agreement with England.

1910:

Russian-Austrian reconciliation through an agreement to maintain the status quo in the Balkans.

November 4–5: Tsar Nicholas visits Emperor William at Potsdam. Tentative agreement on the Near East.

1911:

June–November: Second Moroccan crisis. The German Foreign secretary Alfred von Kiderlen-Waechter tries for better relations with France and England, but is frustrated by the French cabinet change (Joseph Caillaux takes over). The arrival of the German gunboat *Panther* antagonizes the French and the British.

July 21: Threatening speech of David Lloyd George, warning Germany about aggression.

November 4: A compromise is found, with France getting a free hand in Morocco.

September 28: War between Italy and Turkey, because of Italian annexation of Tripoli.

November 11: Russians invade Northern Persia, suppressing the reform movement supported by the British.

1912:

February 8: Viscount Richard Burdon Haldane, on mission in Berlin, tries unsuccessfully to stop further increase of the German navy, and

refuses promise of neutrality demanded by Bethmann-Hollweg.

March 13: Treaty of Alliance between Serbia and Bulgaria.

April 18: The Italians bombard the Dardanelles, which are temporarily closed by the Turks.

May 4–16: Italians occupy Rhodes and other Dodecanese islands.

May 29: Alliance between Greece and Bulgaria.

July 16: Naval convention between Russia and France, supplementing the military convention of 1893.

July 22: British admiralty decides to withdraw battleships from the Mediterranean and place them in the North Sea. The French, on the other hand, move their battleships from Brest to the Mediterranean.

August 14: Bulgaria demands autonomy of Macedonia from Turkey.

October 18: War between the Balkan states (Bulgaria, Serbia and Greece) and Turkey.

Peace treaty between Italy and Turkey; Turkey withdraws from Tripoli, while Italy promises withdrawal from the Aegean islands.

October 22–November 3: Bulgarian and Serbian victories against the Turks. The Bulgarians move close to Constantinople.

November 10: The Serbian army reaches the Adriatic.

November 24: Austria opposes Serbian access to the Adriatic and proposes an independent Albania. Russia supports Serbia, Italy and Germany, while England sympathizes with Austria.

Early December: Both Austria and Russia begin to mobilize.

December 5: Last renewal of the Triple Alliance.

December 8: "War council" in Berlin. Moltke's suggestions of a preventive war are finally rejected because Tirpitz declares the navy will not be ready for another year and a half.

1913:

January 6: London Peace Conference on the Balkan situation breaks down.

January 23: Turkish nationalists under Enver

Bey stage a coup d'état. War is resumed with the Balkan states.

May: After further victories against the Turks, the Balkan states have to give up Durazzo and Scutari under Austrian threats.

May 30: Treaty of London ends First Balkan war. Turkey gives up further territory, including Crete.

July: Second Balkan War: After an unauthorized Bulgarian attack, Serbia, Greece, then Romania and Turkey declare war against Bulgaria, which is quickly defeated.

August 10: Treaty of Bucharest, in which Bulgaria loses territory to Romania, Serbia and Greece.

September 29: In the Treaty of Constantinople, the Turks recover Adrianople.

October 18: After an Austrian ultimatum, Serbia evacuates Albania.

November: Tension between Russia and Germany on the appointment of Otto Liman von Sanders to reorganize the Turkish army. Liman is reappointed inspector-general instead.

1914:

February 21: Russian crown council on the Straits.

April 22–24: King George V and Foreign Secretary Edward Grey of Fallodon visit Paris. An Anglo-Russian naval convention is discussed.

June 15: British-German agreement on the Baghdad Railway problem.

June 24: Disagreement between Austria and Germany on the future of Balkan policy, the former advocating an alliance with Bulgaria and Turkey, while Germany urges Vienna to work for a reconciliation with Serbia, Greece and Romania.

EYEWITNESS TESTIMONY

But this war with France, it will come, it will be forced upon us by the emperor of the French . . . I do not believe that he longs for it personally, I even think he would rather avoid it, but his precarious situation will drive him into it. In my calculation the crisis will occur in about two years . . . We shall win, and the result will be the opposite of what Napoleon strives for: the complete unification of Germany without Austria, and probably also Napoleon's fall.

Bismarck to Carl Schurz on January 28/29,
1868, in Schurz's Memoirs.

The details of Prussia's action again show much infamy, and that of France much clumsiness and carelessness. My hope is mainly based on the idea that France can stand the war longer than Prussia . . .

Austrian Emperor Francis Joseph, letter to his
mother, August 3, 1870.

We had conducted victorious wars against two of Europe's major powers; what mattered was to deprive at least one of the two powerful adversaries we had been fighting with of the temptation contained in the prospect of having its revenge by concluding an alliance with other nations. That France could not be this nation was obvious for anyone familiar with history and the French character . . . The choice could only be between Austria and Russia, since the English constitution does not permit alliance of assured permanence . . . I considered the connection with Russia the more promising one.

Bismarck, in his Memoirs, *about the situation*
after the Franco-German War of 1870–71.

France will have but one thought: to reconstitute her forces, gather her energy, nourish her sacred anger, raise her young generation to form an army of the whole people, to work without cease, to study the methods and skills of our enemies, to become again a great France, the France of 1792, the France of an idea with a sword. Then one day she will be irresistible. Then she will take back Alsace-Lorraine.

Victor Hugo, French poet and novelist, after
1871, in Barbara Tuchmann, The Guns of
August *(1962).*

Their Majesties promise each other, even when the interests of their States lead to disputes over special questions, to negotiate so that these disputes may not overshadow the considerations of a higher order which they have at heart.

First clause of the Three Emperors' League,
June 6, 1873.

Turkey possesses a utility almost providential for Austria-Hungary. For Turkey maintains the status quo of the small Balkan states and impedes their (nationalistic) aspirations. If it were not for Turkey, all these aspirations would fall down on our heads . . . if Bosnia-Herzegovina should go to Serbia or Montenegro, or if a new state should be formed there which we cannot prevent, then we should be ruined and should assume ourselves the role of the "Sick Man."

Count Julius Andrassy, Hungarian prime min-
ister and Austro-Hungarian foreign minister, at
a crown council on January 29, 1875.

It cannot correspond to our interests to see the position of Russia seriously and permanently injured by a coalition of the rest of Europe, if fortune is unfavorable to the Russian arms; but it would affect the interests of Germany just as deeply, if the Austrian monarchy was so endangered in its position as European power or in its independence, that one of the factors with which we have to reckon in the European balance of power, threatened to fall out for the future.

Bismarck, on the Balkan conflict of 1876, in
A.J.P. Taylor, The Struggle for Mastery in
Europe *(1954).*

Our misfortune in 1876 and 1877 was that we went with the peoples instead of with the governments. An emperor of Russia ought always to go only with the governments.

Alexander III of Russia, commenting in 1886
on the Balkan conflicts of 1876–77, in A.J.P.
Taylor, The Struggle for Mastery in Europe.

The greatest folly of my political life was the Berlin Congress. I should have let Russia and England fight and devour each other as those two lions in the woods of which only their two tails were left. Then we would have more influence, more quiet and less danger now. But then I conducted politics like a town alderman.

*Bismarck about his role at the Congress of
1878, in W. Richter,* Bismarck.

I want appeasement, I would like to be reconciled. We have no sensible motive for seeking to do you harm; we are rather in the position of owing you reparation.

*Bismarck to French ambassador Courcel in
1882, in A.J.P. Taylor,* The Struggle for
Mastery in Europe.

You authorise me to tell my Minister that you do not have with Italy an alliance as with Austria?— Yes.—May I say that your arrangements with Italy have been made in view of a temporary situation? Yes.—Am I authorised to say that there is nothing written between you?—Goodbye. You will say that what you call the Triple Alliance is the completion of a policy which I follow toward Austria since Sadowa [the main battle in the Prussian-Austrian war of 1866].

*Conversation between French foreign minister
William Henry Waddington and Bismarck,
May 1883, in A.J.P. Taylor,* The Struggle for
Mastery in Europe.

German policy will always be obliged to enter the line of battle if the independence of Austria-Hungary were to be menaced by Russian aggression, or if England or Italy were to be exposed to invasion by French armies.

*Bismarck to British prime minister Lord Robert
Arthur Salisbury, November 22, 1887, in
A.J.P. Taylor,* The Struggle for Mastery in
Europe.

So long as I am minister, I shall not give my consent to a prophylactic attack upon Russia, and I am far from advising Austria to make such an attack, so long as she is not absolutely certain of English cooperation.

*Bismarck on December 15, 1887, in A.J.P.
Taylor,* The Struggle for Mastery in Europe.

Your map of Africa is beautiful, but my map of Africa lies in Europe. Here is Russia and here is France, and we are in the middle. This is my map of Africa.

*Bismarck, 1888, to a colony-enthusiast, in W.
Richter,* Bismarck.

If you cannot have what you like you must like what you have, and today our sole resource is the hope of Russia's support and the anxiety which this simple hope causes Bismarck.

*Paul Cambon, French ambassador, to Spanish
foreign minister Spuller, March 11, 1889, on
the general course of French foreign policy.*

In naval policy, I did not ask how big the navy should be, but how small. There must be a battle and the great war which hangs over Germany's head, must be fought, before we can build as many ships as Germany and especially the Emperor, who is very keen on the development of the navy, want. . . . We have to consider public opinion much more than in Bismarck's time.

*Count Leo von Caprivi, German chancellor
1890–94, in A.J.P. Taylor,* The Struggle for
Mastery in Europe.

In case of war between France and Germany we must immediately hurl ourselves upon the Germans . . . We must correct the mistakes of the past and crush Germany at the first opportunity.

*Tsar Alexander III to foreign minister Nikolai
Karlovich Giers, 1892, in A. J. P. Taylor,* The
Struggle for Mastery in Europe.

You would not be good patriots, you would not be Frenchmen, if you did not hold to the thought that the day will come when you can recover possession of your lost provinces; but there is a great distance between this natural feeling and the idea of provocation to realize it, of revenge in a word; and you have often shown that you want peace above everything and that you know how to wait with dignity.

Tsar Alexander III to French ambassador Montebello. December 16, 1893, in A.J.P. Taylor,
The Struggle for Mastery in Europe.

The object, in the last analysis, is to put England by pacific, but certain means, in the necessity of accepting, if not herself proposing the meeting of a European conference . . . May we not hope that the question of the evacuation of Egypt will follow naturally from that of the Egyptian Sudan?

*Jean Baptiste Marchand, French explorer and
general, on the French expedition to the upper
Nile, 1895, alluding to the British setback in*

the Sudan by the revolt of the Mahdi in 1883,
in A.J.P. Taylor, The Struggle for Mastery
in Europe.

We need the Bosporus and the entrance to the Black Sea. Free passage through the Dardanelles can be got later by diplomacy.
Statement of a Russian crown council, July
1895, in A.J.P. Taylor, The Struggle for
Mastery.

Let me see if Wilhelm can/ Be a little gentleman; Let me see if he is able/ to sit still for once at table!— But Fidgety Will/ He won't sit still.
Punch, *London, February 1896, alluding to the*
story of naughty Philipp in the popular
"Struwwelpeter" children's storybook.

If we can give the English the impression . . . that our Government, pushed on by public opinion, would be capable of occupying Port Said, the demonstration will have a certain effect. But . . . we must know what we want and say it frankly, cordially, but clearly. We have stood too much on our rights and not taken enough account of the facts.
Ambassador Paul Cambon on March 31, 1896,
on the British-French conflict over Egypt.

Chamberlain must not forget that in East Prussia I have one Prussian army-corps against three Russian armies and nine cavalry divisions, from which no Chinese wall divides me and which no English iron-clads hold at arm's length.
William II of Germany to his chancellor Prince
Chlodwig von Hohenlohe, on British prime
minister Joseph Chamberlain's attempts for
closer relations with Germany, April 7, 1898.

Wipe that dirty smile off your face, Barbarossa! Actually, our crusades did not achieve anything either!
Godfrey of Bouillon to Emperor Frederick I, in
Simplicissimus, *a Munich satirical journal,*
with caricature by Th.Th. Heine, referring to
the Crusades of 1099 and 1190 and William II's
journey to the Holy Land 1898.

I do like knowing that it lies entirely with me to decide the ultimate course of the war in South Africa . . . all I need to do is to telegraph orders to all the troops in Turkestan to mobilize and advance to the frontier.
Nicholas II, letter to his sister at the time of the
Boer War, October 21, 1899.

In case the aggressive actions of third powers or new trouble in China, endangering the integrity and free development of this Power, became a threat to their interests, the two Allied Governments would consult on means of safeguarding them.
Franco-Russian declaration of March 20, 1902,
in reaction to the Anglo-Japanese agreement of
the same year.

As I recall, General Kuropatkin reproached Plehve [the reactionary minister of the interior] for having been the only minister who wanted the Russian-Japanese war and who joined the politicians who dragged the peoples into this war. "Kuropatkin," Plehve replied, "you do not known the internal situation in Russia. We do need a little, victorious war in order to dam up the revolutionary tide."
Count Sergei de Witte (Sergei Witte), former
Russian premier, on the events leading us to
conflict with Japan in 1904, in his Memoirs
(1921).

. . . we must avoid two things: firstly that our relations with Russia be injured because of the war . . . on the other hand letting ourselves be pushed forward by Russia against Japan or still more against England.
Bernhard von Bülow, German chancellor, in a
memo to William II in regard to the Russo-
Japanese war, February 14, 1904.

Without the war in the Transvaal, which bled Britain and made her wise, without the war in the Far East which made for reflection on both sides of the Channel and inspired in all the desire to limit the conflict, our agreements would not have been possible.
Paul Cambon, Ambassador to Great Britain, in
a letter to his brother Henri, April 16, 1904,
after the conclusion of the Anglo-French En-
tente Cordiale.

The whole Japanese line was lit up with the glitter of steel flashing from the scabbard . . . Once again the officers quit shelter with ringing shouts of "Banzai", wildly echoed by all the rank and file. Slowly, but not to be denied, they make headway, inspite of the barbed wire, mines and pitfalls and the merciless hail of bullets. Whole units are destroyed—others take their places; the advancing wave pauses for a moment, but sweeps ever onward. Already they are

within a few yards of the trenches. Then, on the Russian side, the long grey line of Siberian Fusiliers forms up in turn, and delivers one last volley before scurrying down the far side of the hill . . .
General François de Négrier, Lessons from the Russo-Japanese War *(1905).*

In the late war, our moral strength was less than that of the Japanese; and it was this inferiority rather than mistakes in generalship, that caused our defeats . . . The lack of martial spirit, of moral exaltation and of heroic impulse affected particularly our stubbornness in battle.
Russian General G. Kuropatkin: The Russian Army and the Japanese War *(1909).*

. . . it should cause European statesmen some anxiety when their people seem to forget that there are millions outside the charmed circle of Western Civilisation who are ready to pluck the sceptre from the nerveless hands so soon as the old spirit is allowed to degenerate . . . Providentially, Japan is our ally . . . England has time, therefore—time to put her military affairs in order.
British Major General Sir Ian Hamilton, analyzing the Japanese victory over Russia, in A Staff Officer's Scrapbook *(1905).*

A quiet and warm day. Alix and I received many people at the farm and our breakfast was delayed by one hour . . . I bathed in the sea. After dinner we went for a walk. From Odessa I received the perplexing news that the crew of the newly arrived "Potemkin" revolted, killed the officers and took possession of the ship. They now threaten to start unrest in the city. One should not think it possible!
Nicholas II, diary of June 15, 1905.

We must be free to go to the help of France as well as free to stand aside . . . If there were no military plans made beforehand we should be unable to come to the assistance of France in time . . . We should in effect not have preserved our freedom to help France, but have cut ourselves off from the possibility of doing so.
Edward Grey of Fallodon, British foreign secretary, on the discussions between the English and French military staffs, January 1906.

If negotiations [with Russia] now in progress lead to a satisfactory result, the effect upon British opinion would be such as very much to facilitate a discussion of the Straits question if it came up later on.
Edward Grey of Fallodon, British foreign secretary, on May 1, 1907, in A.J.P. Taylor, The Struggle for Mastery in Europe.

It was imperative that Russia should act with the greatest prudence towards Germany, and give the latter power no cause for complaint that the improvement of the relations of Russia and England had entailed a corresponding deterioration of the relations of Russia with Germany.
Alexander Petrovich Izvolski, Russian foreign minister, during the British-Russian negotiations, June 12, 1908, in A.J.P. Taylor, The Struggle for Mastery in Europe.

After this easy victory, I should not be surprised if greater demands were made of Russia . . . The Franco-Russian entente has not borne the test; and the Anglo-Russian entente is not sufficiently strong or sufficiently deep-rooted to have any appreciable influence. The hegemony of the Central Powers will be established in Europe, and England will be isolated . . . In past times we have had to fight Holland, Spain and France for this [maritime] supremacy, and personally I am convinced that sooner or later, we shall have to repeat the same struggle with Germany.
Arthur Nicolson, British ambassador in Russia, 1908, on the Bosnia annexation quoted in Winston Churchill, The Unknown War, *1931.*

Aehrenthal's performance comes to look more and more like a subaltern's rag. He told us nothing about it, gave Isvolski and Tittoni such veiled hints that they regard themselves as entirely bamboozled, showed the Sultan who is principally concerned, no consideration at all. He . . . brought the Serbs to boiling-point; irrigated Montenegro to the utmost; has instigated the Cretans to revolt, thrown our Turkish policy, the outcome of twenty years' hard work, on the scrapheap; exasperated the English and promoted them to our place in Stambul; infuriated the Greeks by his friendliness towards the Bulgarians; smashed the Treaty of Berlin into smithereens and has thrown the concert of the powers into the most unholy state of discord; annoyed the Hungarians because Bosnia was to have been incorporated with them . . . That performance, viewed as a whole, is a European record such as no other diplomatist has ever put to his credit. He certainly is not a far-seeing statesman.

William II, commenting on Austria's annexa-
tion of Bosnia, 1908, in Winston Churchill,
The Unknown War.

Since Russia demonstratively joined England at Reval, we could not give up Austria. The European situation was so changed that we must be more reserved to Russian wishes than we used to be.

German Chancellor Bernhard von Bülow, mem-
orandum of October 27, 1908, referring to the
recent meeting of Tsar Nicholas II and King
Edward VII.

[The Bosnian affair] is a question in which the vital interests of Russia are not involved. French public opinion would be unable to comprehend that such a question could lead to a war in which the French and Russian armies would have to take part.

Note of the French Embassy to the Russian
Government, February 26, 1909, after Austria's
annexation of Bosnia and Herzegovina, in
A.J.P. Taylor, The Struggle for Mastery in
Europe.

It may go the way it went between Japan and Russia. One day, the one side will say: It cannot go on this way. Or: If we wait any longer, we will be in a bad position, we will be the weaker party instead of the stronger one. Then catastrophy will set in. Then the great march will start throughout Europe, and 16–18 million men, the flower of the nations, equipped with the best murder weapons, will stand in the field against one another as enemies. But I am convinced that behind the big march stands the big crash—yes, you have laughed about that before, but it will come, it has only be postponed . . . through your doing, because you have carried things to an extreme . . .

August Bebel, German Socialist leader, in the
German Reichstag, in his last speech on foreign
policy, 1911.

The whole policy is of a sort that I cannot cooperate with it. But I ask myself again and again whether the situation will not develop even more dangerously if I go and then probably not alone.

Theobald von Bethmann-Hollweg, German
chancellor, to Secretary of State Alfred von Kid-
erlen-Waechter, January 2, 1912, in A.J.P.
Taylor, The Struggle for Mastery in Europe.

The two governments [British and French], foreseeing the case where one of them would have a grave motive to apprehend either the aggression of a third power, or some event threatening the general peace, agree that they will immediately deliberate on the means for acting together in order to prevent aggression and safeguard peace.

Poincaré's proposal for a British-French agree-
ment, September 1912. The British cabinet al-
tered it to preserve their freedom of action.

The German people must be made to see that we have to attack because of our enemies' provocation. Things must be so built up that war will seem as a deliverance from the great armaments, the financial burdens, the political tensions. We must also prepare for war financially, though without awakening financiers' suspicions . . . If we are attacked, we shall do as our brothers did, a hundred years ago [against Napoleon] . . . Let us remember that many provinces of the old German Empire, such as the County of Burgundy and much of Lorraine, are still in French hands; that thousands of our German brothers groan under the Slav yoke in the Baltic. Germany must regain what formerly she lost.

Helmuth Johannes Ludwig von Moltke, German
chief of staff, in a report to the emperor, March
13, 1913. [This document was known to
the French.]

You can be certain I stand by you and I am ready to draw the sword whenever your action makes it necessary . . . whatever comes from Vienna is for me a command.

William II to Austrian foreign minister Count
Berchtold, as reported by the latter, on October
28, 1913, after the Austrian ultimatum to Ser-
bia regarding Albania.

The least likely hypothesis was a German attack on Epinal-Toul, for it would mean neglecting a possible British intervention, and would tie down large masses of troops in the difficult mountainous country on the upper Moselle . . . Other hypotheses foresaw the debouching of large-scale forces towards the Eifel, destined to fall on the French left via Belgium, and they were amply justified by the enormous sums put up by the Germans for the last ten years to the Metz-Thionville group. In this way, having examined what the role of the Metz-Thionville fortifications was

likely to be, we came to reckon that the German would probably violate Belgian neutrality.
Marshal Joseph Joffre in 1913, quoted in M.
Ferro, The Great War (1973).

Odd as it may seem, reserves became a party-political question. The Right claimed that only the professional army really counted for national defence and objected in principle to the nation in arms, which in their view would mean a mere militia; hence they would use reserves only as a supplement needed to bring the professional army to war strength. They expected the war to be a short one, and therefore lavished attention on the professional army . . . The Left, by contrast could only think in terms of the nation in arms. They objected to long-term service and felt that a few months' training would be enough to fashion the citizen soldier for the coming war.
Marshal Joseph Joffre, 1913, as quoted in M.
Ferro, The Great War.

Battles are beyond everything else struggles of morale. Defeat is inevitable as soon as the hope of conquering ceases to exist. Success comes not to him who has suffered the least but to him whose will is firmest and morale strongest.
From the Field Regulations of the French Army,
October 1913, in Barbara Tuchmann, The
Guns of August.

It is above all the German offensive through Belgium on which we ought to fix our attention. As far as we can foresee the logical consequences of the opening of our campaign, we can say without hesitation that if we take the offensive at the outset we shall be beaten.
Colonel Grouard, French military expert, in his
book La Guerre Eventuelle, 1913, quoted by
Barbara Tuchmann in The Guns of August.

War between Austria and Russia would be very useful to the cause of the revolution in Western Europe. But it is hard to believe that Francis Joseph and Nicholas will give us this pleasure.
Vladimir I. Lenin, in a letter to the Russian
writer Maxim Gorky, 1913, as quoted in E.
Taylor, The Fall of the Dynasties (1963).

The peace of the world will be secure only when the Triple Entente . . . is transformed into a defensive alliance without secret clauses. Then the danger of a German hegemony will be finally ended, and each of us can devote himself to his own affairs: The British can seek a solution of their social problems, the French can get rich, protected from any external threat, and we can consolidate our selves and work on our economic reorganization.
Russian foreign minister Sergei Sazonov to
Ambassador Benckendorff, February 19, 1914.

If there were a really aggressive and menacing attack made by Germany upon France, it was possible that public feeling in Great Britain would justify the Government in helping France. But it was not likely that Germany would make an aggressive and menacing attack upon Russia; and, even if she did, people in Great Britain would be inclined to say that, though Germany might have successes at first, Russia's resources were so great that, in the long run, Germany would be exhausted without our helping Russia.
Edward Grey of Fallodon, British foreign secretary, during a visit with Edward VII in Paris, April 1914. Quoted in A.J.P. Taylor, The Struggle for Mastery in Europe.

You know what interests we have at the Bosporus, how sensitive we are at that point. All southern Russia depends on it, and now you stick a Prussian garrison under our noses!
Sergei Sazonov, Russian foreign minister, to a German journalist after the appointment of Otto Liman von Sanders to reorganize the Turkish army, April 1914.

Whether a European conflagration comes depends solely on the attitude of Germany and England. If we both stand together as guarantors of European peace, which is not prevented by the engagements of either the Triple Alliance or the Entente, provided we pursue this aims on a common plan from the start, war can be avoided.
German chancellor Theobald von Bethmann-Hollweg, to Karl Max von Lichnowsky, German ambassador to London, June 16, 1914.

The open endeavours of Russia to encircle the Monarchy have the ultimate aim of making it impossible for the German Empire to oppose Russia's distant aims of gaining political and economic supremacy.
Count Leopold von Berchtold, Austrian foreign secretary, in a memorandum, June 24, 1914.

2. The Big Crisis and the Outbreak of the War: June 28 to August 4, 1914

THE HISTORICAL CONTEXT

THE ASSASSINATION; AUSTRIA AND SERBIA

The nephew of old Emperor Francis Joseph, Archduke Francis Ferdinand, who had become heir to the throne of Austria-Hungary when the emperor's only son committed suicide in 1889, was an unpopular and arrogant man, but he had some ideas about reorganizing the antiquated empire. He hated the Hungarian aristocracy who made modernization so difficult, and he wanted to accommodate the large percentage of Slavs within the empire by basing the future empire on three, instead of two, "state nations." On the other hand, he thought so little of Serbia that he never would have risked a war on its behalf. He was less than enthusiastic about conducting large military maneuvers in the newly acquired Bosnia, where his presence was taken as a provocation by the separatist radicals and, in fact, a large part of the population. But this was considered a political necessity—one had to show the subjects who was master. Thus he and his wife paid a brief visit at Bosnia's capital, Sarajevo. On June 28, 1914 both were assassinated there by Gavrilo Princip, a young revolutionary.

Princip and other radicals acted as agents of the Serbian society called "The Black Hand," which agitated against Austrian aspirations on Serbia. They all had been trained in Belgrade by men close to the Serbian government. The Viennese government was convinced of this, but wanted to have a clear case and sent a legal expert to Sarajevo to collect evidence. At this point, there was general outrage in the world and sympathy for the Austrian claims for satisfaction. However, Vienna did not yet take any official steps against Serbia but sent an emissary, Count Alexander Hoyos, to Berlin to assure German cooperation in settling, once and for all, the intolerable situation created by

Emperor Francis Joseph of Austria. Photo courtesy of the Austrian Institute, New York City.

the Serbs. Both Count Leopold von Berchtold, the foreign minister, and the chief of the General Staff, Count Francis Conrad von Hoetzendorf, felt that this was the time to do away with Serbia altogether. Emperor Francis Joseph agreed—although it is doubtful he was told the complete story—under the condition that Germany's help was guaranteed.

In Berlin, the emperor and the chancellor promised full support, apparently thinking that the conflict could be localized and convinced that Russia was militarily unprepared to take an extreme stand. William even went further, insisting on a sharply worded ultimatum against Serbia.

The only opposition in Vienna was voiced by the prime minister of Hungary, Count Stephen Tisza, who foresaw a general European conflict. He also asked what, in case of a victory over Serbia, the Austro-Hungarian monarchy would do with so many additional Slav subjects—it had too many already. But after the German pressure was making itself felt, he too gave in. Still, there was no sense of crisis among the European peoples—for the time being. In July, people went into their summer vacations as usual; while in Vienna, the foreign office waited for the end of the French state visit in St. Petersburg.

There, Raymond Poincaré and René Viviani agreed with the Russians to ask England to join with France and Russia in exerting pressure on Austria, although Austria's demands on Serbia were not yet known.

The Austrian ultimatum to Belgrade, dated July 23, demanded suppression of publications hostile to Austria, dissolution of anti-Austrian organizations, cessation of propaganda in the schools, dismissal of certain officials accused of anti-Austrian propaganda, collaboration of Serbian and Austrian officials in the inquiry on the assassination, trials on those accessory to the plot, arrest of two Serbian officials known to be involved, and general explanations and apologies. The Serbian answer, formulated within 48 hours, accepted most of the ultimatum but rejected one major point, the investigation by Austrian officials on Serbian soil, claiming that such an invasion by foreign officials would be incompatible with the Serbian constitution. In retrospect, it is difficult to understand why the Serbian government attached so much importance to this point; a few Austrian officials would have had a difficult time in hostile Belgrade and certainly would not have jeopardized Serbian independence. Belgrade took this chance because it felt confident of Russian support, just as Austria acted tough because of the promised German support.

GERMANY'S AND RUSSIA'S POSITIONS

The two sides were bluffing; both believed they could get away with one more risk without getting into a war. In Austria, the chances did not seem as great as at the time of the annexation of Bosnia and Herzegovina—indeed they may have seemed smaller, because one could point to the inexcusable crime which had started the crisis. The German emperor, a great believer in legitimacy, did not want war with Russia in spite of all his martial speeches, and did not believe that the tsar, whom he addressed in his letters as "Dear Nicky," would send his armies to defend the assassination of a legitimate monarch. Also, his first reaction to the Serbian answer was that it made a conflict unnecessary. But the military in Vienna, Belgrade, St. Petersburg and Berlin thought otherwise, and Count Berchtold's reaction to the Serbian note was to inform the Austrian minister in Belgrade to leave the capital immediately. Serbia had actually started mobilization against Austria even before its reply to Vienna because Serbian officials were sure that they would be supported by Russia. In response, Austria began mobilizing against Serbia. At this point, localization of the conflict was still possible. There was plenty of opposition to the idea of a general European conflict in each of the countries concerned. In Austria, the various Slavic nationalities felt often much closer to Russia than to their German masters, and the hatred between Hungarians and Slavs

Theobold von Bethmann-Holl-
weg, German chancellor who
pursued a moderate policy in
1914. Photo courtesy of the Au-
thor.

was even greater than between Germans and Slavs. In Russia, a good part of the ruling aristocracy was of Baltic-German descent and felt closer to their immediate neighbor in the West than to France, the Latin democracy. Both in France and in Germany, the socialist parties which represented large parts of the population denounced nationalism, proclaimed solidarity of the workers of all nations, advocated arbitration and blamed capitalism for the present crisis; and in Britain, public opinion was overwhelmingly against participation in any conflict on the continent.

But in Vienna, the foreign minister, Count Berchtold, and the chief of staff, Conrad von Hoetzendorf, decided to present a *fait accompli*. When Britain proposed an international conference, Austria answered that it could not submit a question of its national honor to the decision of outsiders. By now, Vienna was receiving confused signals from Berlin. Chancellor Bethmann-Hollweg sent restraining telegrams, while Helmuth von Moltke, chief of the General Staff, advised the mobilization of the whole Austrian army. Berchtold followed his own gambling instincts, declared war on Serbia and bombed Belgrade the following day (July 29). This provoked Russia, which had cautiously accepted the British mediation proposals but now had to live up to its self-proclaimed role of protector of all Slav nations. The tsar, who had been inclined to listen to the German emperor's pleas for Russian-Austrian negotiations, finally yielded to the pressure of his generals and his foreign minister, Sergei Sazonov, who aimed at increasing control in the Balkans. At first, the tsar authorized a limited mobilization only—against Austria. Then, when told that a partial mobilization was technically unfeasible, he ignored German warnings and permitted general mobilization.

ENGLAND AND FRANCE; GERMANY'S ULTIMATUM

The German emperor, meanwhile, still did not believe in Russia's readiness to fight. His military advisers had explained that Russia could not be ready until 1916 or at least would have to confine itself to slow retreat as in 1812 against Napoleon. Now, when Russia assembled huge masses of troops on the Austrian and German borders, William blamed Britain for not having warned Russia in time; this may have been correct, but undoubtedly he could have done the same by warning Austria. His ambassador in London, Prince Karl Max von Lichnowsky, an earnest Anglophile who could think of no greater catastrophe than a conflict between Germany and Britain, had tried his best to support all English efforts to mediate but could not give his emperor a definite assurance that Britain would stay neutral in case of an armed conflict between Germany and Russia and Russia's ally France. France, too, had meanwhile begun to take military steps. So, with the emperor torn between the various moderate and prowar advisers, and with his chancellor—a man of good but rather feeble will who wanted to please everybody—equally undecided, the military in Berlin took over. No serious attempt was made to keep France neutral; on the contrary, Berlin had the temerity to ask Paris if she would stay neutral in a German-Russian conflict and to request, as a guarantee, that France hand over the border fortresses of Toul and Verdun until after the war. The German ambassador in Paris did not dare to pass on this demand to the French government, but the French had intercepted his instructions anyway and simply replied, as could have been expected, that France would act in accordance with its own interests.

At the same time, Berlin demanded from Russia immediate cessation of war preparations, in an ultimatum to be answered within 12 hours. In both cases, Germany had maneuvered into a position in which it had to be the one to declare war and to appear as the aggressor. What was left for Germany to do was to assure Britain's neutrality. But when London requested a declaration that Belgian neutrality would be respected, Berlin's answer was no. Obviously, it would have been impossible to change the Schlieffen-Moltke plan for attack through Belgium, which had worked out to the most minute detail over the preceding years, at the last minute. Still, on August 1, 1914 it seemed for a moment as if Britain's neutrality could be won, although it stood by its guarantee of Belgium's integrity. Lichnowsky reported a British offer that Britain would stay neutral and guarantee France's neutrality if Germany promised not to attack France. The emperor jumped at this offer. Now he could throw his whole army, which was about to invade Luxembourg and Belgium, against Russia. He summoned Moltke at once and told him to change all plans accordingly. Moltke declared immediately that this was impossible. A plan involving millions of troops could not be reversed at a moment's notice. The emperor replied: "Your uncle would have given me a different answer!"

As it turned out, Lichnowsky had misunderstood the British foreign minister who, in a very roundabout way, had promised to keep France neutral if Germany would not attack France *or Russia;* his eagerness to find a compromise had gotten the better of him. So the machines began to roll as planned. Germany declared war on Russia, since its ultimatum had remained unanswered. Apparently, the German thought was that the Russian mobilization amounted practically to a declaration of war, so that the German declaration was only a formality. This may have been correct for a country whose whole strategy was built on quick, overwhelming attack, in which every hour of every day counted, but it did not necessarily apply to Russia, whose leaders interpreted the German war declaration as a clear act of aggression. In fact, the German chancellor had explained to the Reichstag: "Should we further wait until the powerful nations we are wedged between choose the moment of attack? To expose Germany to this danger would have been criminal." This amounted, in the eyes of the world, to an admission of blatant aggression; this was worsened when, two days later, war on France was explained by flimsy excuses of alleged border violations—which proved to be entirely untrue.

ENGLAND JOINS IN

Britain had tried but failed to preserve the peace. It seemed clear that it was in Britain's interest not to let Germany win and dominate the continent. And again, Germany supplied Britain with a sufficient reason to interfere: the invasion of Belgium, or rather, the resistance of Belgium and its heart-rending appeals for help. This was enough to reverse the opinion of the British public, which had been uninformed of its country's military involvements and was averse to the idea of putting up a large army. Britain, of all the great powers, had no conscription and would never be expected to fight side by side with the traditional enemy, Russia. There still was plenty of opposition among the Irish, the Laborites, the socialist groups, pacifists such as Lord Bertrand Russell and some unconvinced Liberals. But their voices were hardly heard, as it had become easy for the government to denounce Germany as the power-hungry, inhuman aggressor with no respect for innocent civilians and international law. As late as August 1, 12 of 18 cabinet members had still been opposed to promising aid to threatened France. Now, on August 3, after Foreign Secretary Edward Grey's great speech in Parliament, there could be no more question that Britain made Belgium the issue, and the Lower House reacted with overwhelming applause. And while Prime Minister Herbert Henry Asquith let another 24 hours go by before putting the decisive question to the German government, the outcome could no longer be in doubt.

PEACE EFFORTS

Inside the other powers, opposition disappeared even faster, swept away by an unprecedented, unexpected wave of nationalism and fighting enthusiasm. In Germany, the huge Social Democratic Party, which controlled more than one-third of the seats in the Reichstag elected in 1912, had condemned the Austrian ultimatum and had sent an emissary, Hermann Mueller, to Paris in an attempt to draft a common strategy to preserve the peace. But the French socialists declared that France was threatened by Germany and that they had to come to the aid of their country. When Mueller replied the threat was not coming from Berlin but from tsarist despotism, no one listened. The question of approving the credits demanded by the German government for conducting the war was debated passionately among the socialist delegates of the Reichstag. In the end, only a small minority of 14 members was opposed to the approval and they at last gave in to the majority. Everyone, from the bourgeois intellectual to the lowest worker, was ready to march for the fatherland, which everyone believed had been encircled by jealous neighbors, forcing it to fight for its life and its proper place among the nations.

In Russia—which had been near a revolution ever since the ruthlessly suppressed uprising of 1905—no opposition could speak up. In Austria, the semi-senile emperor, Francis Joseph, 84 years old, had lost control of the government and went along with what his ambitious, reckless advisers told him. In France, the last hope for pacifist opposition died when Jean Jaurès, the eloquent, brilliant pacifist leader of the socialists, was assassinated by a radical nationalist on July 31.

WARTIME PSYCHOLOGY

The decisions which led to an international catastrophe had been made by only a few men, the ruling monarchs and leaders of government. The parliaments in Germany, Austria and Russia had not been consulted, nor had the internationally experienced businessmen and sociologists, but these leaders had managed to convince the masses on each side that their country was the innocent victim of dark intrigue. Many people felt with great relief that the depressing time of party bickering and class conflicts was over and that finally a great, liberating storm was uniting their country, giving even the least significant citizen the chance to become a hero.

A "short war" had been promised. The emperor told the departing troops that they would "be home before the leaves have fallen from the trees," and a German officer leaving for the western front said he expected to have breakfast at the Café de la Paix in Paris on Sedan Day, September 2! In Russia, officers planned to be in Berlin by that time, and Russians who expected the war to last six months were looked upon as defeatists. The Russian minister of justice declared that "Vasilii Fedorovitch" (William, son of Frederick—the German emperor) had made a mistake; he would be unable to hold out for long. He based his opinion on the fact that Germany had a stockpile of nitrates, needed for the production of gunpowder, that would only last six months. Only the timely discovery by Fritz Haber of a process by which to fix nitrogen out of the air saved Germany from this dilemma. The French were so convinced of a quick victory that they did not waste any troops on the defense of the extremely valuable Lorraine iron basin; the result was that they lost most of their iron ore for the duration.

There were exceptions to the general optimism. Both Moltke and Joffre foresaw a wearisome struggle of several years, and Lord Horatio Herbert Kitchener, recalled to become Britain's minister of war on August 4, predicted a war of at least three years. But these were rare cases, and they kept their opinions to themselves. One has the impression that all of Europe had entered a dream-world during the first days of August and that only in Britain did people remain sober and realistic enough to understand that a deadly serious, desperate time lay ahead of them, for their own country and for the entire continent.

In Germany, a special note was added to the general enthusiasm and optimism—the hatred of "treacherous" England. Not the hereditary enemy, France, nor the "barbarous" Russians who were soon to devastate German soil, but the "blood relative" who had suddenly shown his real face when Germany was engaged in a life and death struggle with its neighbors became the object of furious hatred. This started with the emperor, who had been naive enough to believe that neither his friend Nicky nor his relative George would ever attack him. He believed in some kind of solidarity between legitimate monarchs, above all clashes between their nations. When Nicky disappointed him, he resented it greatly, but after all, Russia had been known to be the close ally of France. With England—which he secretly admired— the case was different, the disappointment much deeper. When the last diplomatic effort of Germany to assure British neutrality had failed, the emperor, impulsive as ever, blamed it all on the sly machinations of his uncle, the late Edward VII, who had trapped Germany in order to destroy her.

WHO WAS RESPONSIBLE?

In retrospect, it seems clear that while nobody aimed at a general war, no one was entirely innocent in 1914. They all took chances and gambled with their nations' fortunes, often for no more than prestige or "national honor" or to help dubious allies. What happened to Belgrade was of no vital importance to St. Petersburg, Berlin or Paris, and was not worth risking the existence of any great nation. But the situation had been explosive for years, and with the particular constellation of 1914, it would have taken extremely wise and energetic men to prevent the great conflagration. As Lloyd George put it shortly after the war: "It was something into which they glided or rather staggered and stumbled, perhaps through folly, and a discussion, I have no doubt, would have averted it."

CHRONICLE OF EVENTS

1914:

June 28: Archduke Francis Ferdinand of Austria and his wife are assassinated at Sarajevo by Gavrilo Princip, a Bosnian revolutionary belonging to a terrorist organization.

July 5–6: Consultation of Count Alexander Hoyos, confidant of Austrian foreign minister Count Leopold von Berchtold, and the Austrian ambassador with the German emperor and chancellor. Austria is promised full support for drastic action against Serbia, of whose complicity in the assassination the Austrian government is convinced. Austria sends a legal expert to Sarajevo to collect evidence.

July 7: Austrian crown council. Most members are in favor of war against Serbia, but Count Stephen Tisza, premier of Hungary, insists on diplomacy to avoid larger complications.

July 13: While Germany urges steps while world opinion is supporting Austria, the Austrian emissary reports that he is unable to find conclusive evidence of Serbian complicity.

July 14: In a new crown council, Tisza agrees to military action, if no Serbian territory is annexed.

July 20–23: Visit of French President Raymond Poincaré and Premier René Viviani to St. Petersburg. Agreement to ask Britain to join with France and Russia to exert pressure on Vienna.

July 23: Austrian ultimatum to Serbia, limited to 48 hours.

July 24: Russian policy is formulated: Serbia must not be attacked and devoured by Austria.

July 25: Austria assures Russia that no territory of Serbia will be annexed.

Russian crown council decides on first military measures against Austria and also on war, should Serbia be attacked.

France assures Russia of support.

Serbia's reply to Austria's ultimatum is in general favorable, but rejects a crucial point.

Austrian minister leaves Belgrade.

Serbia orders mobilization against Austria.

Partial mobilization of Austria-Hungary against Serbia.

July 26: Preparatory war measures in Russia, British foreign secretary Edward Grey proposes conference. France accepts, Austria and Germany decline. Russia accepts in principle, but prefers direct talks with Vienna.

July 27: First French preparatory war measures. British fleet ordered not to disband after maneuvers.

Grey promises Russia diplomatic support.

July 28: William II considers Serbian reply as satisfactory.

July 28: Austria declares war on Serbia. Austrian-Russian discussions interrupted.

Germany urges Austria to occupy Belgrade.

July 29: Belgrade bombarded by Austrians. The German chancellor urges Austria to resume discussions with Russia. He also promises not to take French territory in Europe, nor Belgian territory if England promises neutrality. His plan is rejected.

The tsar agrees to general mobilization demanded by the military and foreign minister Sergei Sazonov. After receiving a telegram from the German emperor he recalls this order and decides on mobilization against Austria alone.

July 30: Conversations between St. Petersburg and Vienna resume, but Russia decides on general mobilization. Frontier guard put up by France.

July 31: "State of threatening danger of war" declared in Germany. Germany, in a 12-hour ultimatum to Russia, demands cessation of war preparations on the German border. Berlin inquires about France's stand in a German-Russian conflict.

July 31: A British request that Belgian neutrality be respected is rejected by Germany. At 5:00 P.M., Austria decrees general mobilization.

August 1: France replies to the German note of July 31 that she "would be guided by her own interests."

3:55 P.M.: French mobilization.

4:00 P.M.: German mobilization.

Germany offers to Britain a promise not to attack France if French neutrality would be guaranteed by Britain.

7:00 P.M.: As no reply has been received to the German ultimatum, Germany declares war on Russia.

August 2: After much discussion, the British cabinet votes to assure France to protect the coast against German attacks.

Germans begin to invade Luxembourg.

Germany demands Belgian permission to cross Belgian territory, promising to uphold Belgian integrity. The demand is rejected.

August 3: Germany declares war on France, claiming border violations. Germany begins the invasion of Belgium.

DECLARATIONS OF WAR, 1914–1918

1914:

July 28:	Austria on Serbia.
August 1:	Germany on Russia.
August 3:	Germany on France.
August 4:	Germany on Belgium.
	Britain on Germany.
August 5:	Montenegro on Austria.
August 6:	Austria on Russia.
	Serbia on Germany.
August 8:	Montenegro on Germany.
August 12:	France on Austria.
	Britain on Austria.
August 23:	Japan on Germany.
August 25:	Japan on Austria.
August 28:	Austria on Belgium.
November 2:	Russia on Turkey.
	Serbia on Turkey.
November 5:	Britain on Turkey.
	France on Turkey.

1915:

May 23:	Italy on Austria.
June 3:	San Marino on Austria.
August 21:	Italy on Turkey.
October 14:	Bulgaria on Serbia.
October 15:	Britain on Bulgaria.
	Montenegro on Bulgaria.
October 16:	France on Bulgaria.
October 19:	Russia on Bulgaria.
	Italy on Bulgaria.

1916:

March 9:	Germany on Portugal.
March 15:	Austria on Portugal.
August 27:	Romania on Austria.
August 28:	Italy on Germany.
	Germany on Romania.
August 30:	Turkey on Romania.

1917:

April 6:	United States on Germany.
April 7:	Panama on Germany.
	Cuba on Germany.
April 23:	Turkey severs relations with United States.
June 27:	Greece on Austria, Bulgaria, Germany and Turkey.
July 22:	Siam (Thailand) on Germany and Austria.
August 4:	Liberia on Germany.
August 14:	China on Germany and Austria.
October 6:	Peru severs relations with Germany.
October 7:	Uruguay severs relations with Germany.
October 26:	Brazil on Germany.
December 7:	United States on Austria.
December 8:	Ecuador severs relations with Germany.
December 10:	Panama on Austria.
December 16:	Cuba on Austria.

1918:

April 23:	Guatemala on Germany.
May 8:	Nicaragua on Germany and Austria.
May 23:	Costa Rica on Germany.
July 12:	Haiti on Germany.
July 19:	Honduras on Germany.

Eyewitness Testimony

I am a bird of ill omen. When I was stationed in Turkey they had a revolution. When I was in China, it was the boxers . . . But now I am resting. Nothing ever happens in Brussels.

Von Below-Saleske, German minister in Brussels, to a visitor, early 1914, in Barbara Tuchman, The Guns of August.

I am a South Slav nationalist. My aim is the union of all Yugoslavs, under whatever political regime, and their liberation from Austria—by terrorism.

Gavrilo Princip at his trial, as quoted by E. Taylor, The Fall of the Dynasties, *1963.*

Try to put yourself in our position! We were revolutionaries . . . and would not have been any, had we not made use of the opportunity to kill a future monarch. . . . It was organized too poorly.

Ivo Kranjtschewitsch, coconspirator at Sarajevo on June 28, 1914, at an interview with the Northwest German Rundfunk, *1950.*

Horrible. The Almighty does not allow himself to be challenged with impunity. A higher power has restored the order which I unfortunately was unable to uphold.

Emperor Francis Joseph to his aide-de-camp, Count Edouard Paar, at the news of his nephew's assassination at Sarajevo. He was referring to Francis Ferdinand's morganatic marriage to Countess Sophie Chotek. The emperor had never forgiven him for this misalliance.

Tisza was against war with Serbia; he was anxious, fearing that Russia might strike at us and Germany leave us in the lurch. Stürgkh, the Prime Minister, on the other hand, expressed the opinion that an inquiry would provide us grounds for going forward. I put forward the view that nothing but a powerful attack could prevent the danger threatened from Serbia. The murder committed under the patronage of Serbia was the reason for war.

Austrian general Count Franz Conrad von Hoetzendorf, about a meeting on July 1, 1914, in Winston Churchill, The Unknown War *(1931).*

Action against Serbia should not be delayed . . . Even if it should come to a war between Austria and Russia, we could be convinced that Germany would stand by our side with her accustomed faithfulness as an ally.

Austrian ambassador Szoegyeny, report to Foreign Secretary Count von Berchtold after his talk with Emperor William II, July 5, 1914.

Austria must judge what is to be done to clear up her relations with Serbia; but whatever Austria's decision, she could count with certainty upon it that Germany will stand behind her as an ally . . . If war must break out, better now than in one or two years' time when the Entente will be stronger.

Szoegyeny's report to Berchtold, July 6, 1914, relating his talk with German chancellor Theobald von Bethmann-Hollweg.

Such an attack upon Serbia would, in human possibility, provoke the world war, in which case I—despite all optimism in Berlin—should be obliged to regard Roumania's neutrality as at least very questionable. Public opinion there would passionately demand war against us . . . a war provoked by us would probably have to be fought under very unfavorable conditions . . .

Count Tisza, memorandum to Emperor Francis Joseph, July 7, 1914, in Winston Churchill, The Unknown War.

Almost twenty-five years have passed since our two countries have united their diplomatic efforts, clearly recognizing their destinies. The happy results of this permanent bond can be observed every day on the balance of the world. Your majesty may be assured that, tomorrow as well as yesterday, France will continue to promote peace and civilisation in close cooperation with her ally, a goal that both governments have never ceased to work on.

Raymond Poincaré, president of the French Republic, during his visit in St. Petersburg, as reported by the French newspaper Le Matin, *July 20, 1914.*

He [the tsar] thanked me for my visit and told me the Tsarina and he would be happy to reciprocate during the summer of 1915. As far as he personally was concerned, he promised this without reservation. Concerning the Tsarina he added that he hoped her health which had improved recently would allow her to undertake the journey. The vision of a war did not appear before his eyes for one moment.

Raymond Poincaré, Memoirs *(1930).*

Our relations [with Germany] are very much better than they were a few years ago . . . The two great Empires begin to realize they can co-operate for common ends, and that the points of co-operation are greater and more numerous and more important than the points of possible controversy.

David Lloyd George, chancellor of the exchequer, in a speech in the House of Commons, July 23, 1914.

The wishes of the (Austrian) Monarchy are in the main fulfilled. A capitulation of the most humiliating character is enshrined there, and every ground for war disappeared. But the piece of paper is only of value when it is translated into fact. The Serbs are Orientals, false and procrastinating. In order that these fair promises materialize, a *douce violence* must be applied. Austria could hold Belgrade as a guarantee. The Austrian Army must have a visible *satisfaction d'honneur*. That is the condition of my mediation.

William II to Foreign Minister Gottlieb E. von Jagow, in reaction to the Serbian reply of July 25, 1914.

Maybe for the first time in 30 years I feel myself as an Austrian, and would like to have a try once more with this empire that offers little hope. The spirit all around is excellent.

Sigmund Freud, letter to Karl Abraham, July 26, 1914.

For the diplomats the situation was clear. It was otherwise for the Chief of the General Staff, who on the one hand must keep before him the rapid and decisive war against Serbia, but on the other must be prepared suddenly to divert everything towards a war with Russia. This was a dilemma involving in itself the gravest responsibility and a most unfavourable situation from the point of view of operations . . .

Austrian general Conrad von Hoetzendorf on July 26, 1914, in Winston Churchill, The Unknown War.

In this most serious moment I appeal to you to help me. An ignoble war has been declared to a weak country. The indignation in Russia shared fully by me is enormous. I foresee that very soon I shall be overwhelmed by the pressure brought upon me and be forced to take extreme measures which will lead to war. To try and avoid such a calamity as a European war, I beg you in the name of our old friendship to do what you can to stop your allies from going too far. Nicky.

Tsar Nicholas to Emperor William, telegram of July 28, 1914.

. . . with regard to the hearty and tender friendship which binds us both from long ago with firm ties, I am exerting my utmost influence to induce the Austrians to deal straightly to arrive at a satisfactory understanding with you. I confidently hope you will help me in my efforts to smooth over difficulties that may still arise. Your very sincere and devoted friend and cousin, Willy.

Emperor William II, telegram [in English] to Tsar Nicholas, July 29, 1914.

Thank you heartily for your quick answer . . . The military measures which have now come into force were decided five days ago for reasons of defence on account of Austria's preparations. I hope from all my heart that these measures won't in any way interfere with your part as mediator which I greatly value. We need your strong pressure on Austria to come to an understanding with us.

Nicholas II, telegram to William II, July 30, 1914.

The preliminary mobilization of my entire army and of my navy which I have ordered today will be followed in the shortest possible time by definite mobilization . . . In this momentous struggle it is of the greatest importance that Austria should direct her main forces against Russia and should not divide her forces by an offensive against Serbia. This is the more important as a large part of my army will be tied by France. In this battle of giants . . . Serbia plays quite a subsidiary part, which calls only for such defensive measures as are absolutely necessary. . . . I beg of you further to do all you can by meeting her wishes to induce Italy to take part. All else must be subordinated to the entry of a united Triple Alliance into the war.

Emperor William II of Germany, telegram to Emperor Francis Joseph of Austria, July 31, 1914.

We are warning Russia not to create a situation by mobilizing which will conjure up the bloodiest genocide, but could also cause the end to tsarism! . . . We implore France to use all her influence on Russia

William (Wilhelm) II, emperor of Germany. Photo courtesy of the German Information Center, New York City.

. . . But we also warn most urgently, once again, the German government not to go too far! The people . . . want peace . . .

Vorwaerts, German Socialist newspaper, on July 31, 1914.

. . . we could, and must hold fast to the idea of the offensive against Serbia, the more so since we had to bear in mind that Russia might merely intend to restrain us from action against Serbia by a threat, without proceeding to war against us . . . It was not until July 31 that there came suddenly the decided declaration of Germany that she herself was now willing to carry through the Great War against France and Russia. This produced an entirely new situation . . . It was immediately reckoned here that we must put in the preponderating mass of our forces in the North, and I beg your Excellency to accept the assurance that, in spite of the great complications caused by our transport of troops to the South which has already been completed, this will be carried through.

Conrad von Hoetzendorf to Moltke, on August 1, 1914, in Winston Churchill, The Unknown War.

We sat down to dine . . . when Le Mee grasped my arm. "Listen!" A loud murmur rose from the street through the open window. At the same moment, something magnetic, not to be put into words, yet very definite passed through each of us . . . "It's come." . . . We ran to the window. Down below in the street, moving toward the barracks, we saw a rolling wave of heads. Every face wore the same expression of blank stupor and distraction; in all eyes was the same strange phosphorescent gleam. Then came a hoarse strangled sound of women's voices. "Here's to us." And picking up our swords we ran back to barracks.

Paul Lintier, Journal of a French Gunner, August 1, 1914 in France, in Guy Chapman (ed.), Vain Glory (1937).

So this is the height of culture we have reached: Hundreds of thousands, the healthiest, most valuable and precious elements are trembling that something vague, a hint of the rulers of Europe, some malice or sadistic whim, some Caesarian madness or a business speculation, some hollow word or a vague idea of honor will drive them from their homes tomorrow, away from wife and child, from all that was built up laboriously, into death. Any insane accident may call today, tomorrow, any minute, and all, all will come.

Franz Pfemfert, editor of Die Aktion, in an article entitled "The Possessed," August 1, 1914.

Recklessness and weakness will plunge the world into the most horrible war aimed to destroy Germany. For there can be no longer any doubts: England, France and Russia have conspired . . . to wage a war of annihilation against us . . . This is in nuce [in a nutshell] the whole, naked situation, contrived slowly but surely by Edward VII, and now put into action. The stupidity and clumsiness of our ally was used to trap us. Finally, the famous encirclement of Germany has become an undeniable fact . . . Sneering England has her most brilliant success of her consistent, purely anti-German world policy . . .

a magnificent achievement, to be admired even by him who is perishing through it! Edward is stronger in death than I am in life . . .

William II, memo after the Russian mobilization was announced in Emil Ludwig, Wilhelm der Zweite *(1926).*

Your Majesty, it cannot be done. The deployment of millions cannot be improvised. If your Majesty insists on leading the whole army to the East, it will not be an army ready for battle but a disorganized mob of armed men with no arrangements for supply. Those arrangements took a whole year of intricate labor to complete.

Helmuth von Moltke to William II on August 1, 1914, when the emperor suddenly demanded to shift the entire army against Russia, in Barbara Tuchman, The Guns of August *(1962).*

Even if all else be so veiled and dark that we cannot see into the future, one thing I am certain of: *Germany cannot perish.* I do not, like the braggarts, base this assertion of any conviction of the perfection of our attainments, but on the knowledge that we have not yet fully realized ourselves . . . We may have said all we have to say in music, but . . . above all, in the moulding of life, we have not yet fulfilled our destiny . . . I want to fight for the preservation of the German spirit and for its fulfilment. Who and what could hold me back from this?

Otto Braun, war volunteer, letter, August 2, 1914, to Julie Vogelstein.

I ask the House from the point of view of British interests to consider what may be at stake. If France is beaten to her knees . . . if Belgium fell under the same influence and then Holland and then Denmark . . . if, in a crisis like this, we run away from these obligations of honor and interest as regards the Belgian Treaty . . . I do not believe for a moment that, at the end of this war, even if we stood aside, we should be able to undo what had happened, in the course of the war, to prevent the whole of the West of Europe opposite us from falling under the domination of a single power . . . and we should, I believe, sacrifice our respect and good name and reputation before the world and should not escape the most serious and grave economic consequences.

British foreign secretary Sir Edward Grey, in his speech to the Parliament, August 3, 1914.

. . . if the German fleet came down the Channel and bombarded and battered the undefended coasts of France, we could not stand aside and see this going on practically within sight of our eyes, with our arms folded, looking on dispassionately, doing nothing!

Sir Edward Grey, in his speech to the Parliament.

An hour later Sir Edward Grey returned to the Foreign Office. Nicolson went upstairs to see him. The Secretary of State was leaning gloomily by the window. Nicolson congratulated him on the success of his speech. Sir Edward did not answer. He moved to the center of the room and raised his hands with clenched fists above his head. He brought his fists with a crash upon the table. "I hate war," he groaned, "I hate war."

Harold Nicolson, English historian and diplomat, in Peacemaking *(1919), in Guy Chapman (ed.),* Vain Glory *(1937).*

Our Allies are dropping away even before the war has started, like rotten apples! A total collapse of the German and Austrian foreign diplomacy. That could and should have been avoided.

William II, marginal note on a report advising that Romania would not join the Central Powers, August 4, 1914, in Emil Ludwig, Wilhelm der Zweite.

The lamps are going out all over Europe; we shall not see them lit again in our lifetime.

Sir Edward Grey, August 4, 1914.

Our hearts beat with enthusiasm. A kind of intoxication takes possession of us. My muscles and arteries tingle with happy strength. The spirit is contagious. Along the line track walkers wave to us. Women hold up their children. We are carried away by the greeting of the land, the mystery that the future holds, the thought of glorious adventure, and the pride of being chosen to share it.

André Fribourg, soldier in the French 106th Regiment, on moving to the front, August 4, 1914, in The Flaming Crucible *(1918).*

For now they are singing. All of them are singing, except one poor man in a remote corner who weeps thinking of those he left behind. The others sing gravely, religiously, passionately. And with them I sing the hymn that stirs the profoundest depths of the soul [the Marseillaise]. It is the chant of the hour. Every line thrills. A month before we sang it lightly. Now it stirs every fibre of our beings.

André Fribourg, on moving to the front, August 4, 1914, in The Flaming Crucible.

The next day the German Embassy was turned over to me. I went to see the German Ambassador at three o'clock in the afternoon. He came down in his pyjamas, a crazy man. I feared he might literally go mad. He was of the anti-war party and he had done his best and utterly failed. This interview was one of the most pathetic of my life. The poor man had not slept for several nights. Then came the crowds of frightened Germans, afraid that they would be arrested. They besieged the German Embassy and our Embassy . . . All London has been awake for a week. Every day Germans are arrested on suspicion; and several of them have committed suicide. . . . I shall never forget Sir Edward Grey's telling me of the ultimatum—while he wept . . . nor the King as he declaimed at me for half an hour and threw up his hands and said. "My God, Mr. Page, what else could we do?"

Walter H. Page, U.S. ambassador in London in Life and Letters: August 4, 1914, *in Guy Chapman (ed.),* Vain Glory.

Our troops have occupied Luxembourg and perhaps are already in Belgium . . . We knew that France was standing ready to invade Belgium . . . Our invasion of Belgium is contrary to international law, but the wrong—I speak openly—we are committing we will make good as soon as our military goal has been achieved.

Chancellor Theobald von Bethmann-Hollweg, in the German Reichstag, August 4, 1914.

In the morning to Berlin in one of the few trains still running . . Now is the time when all elemental emotions are brought into the foreground, pain, brotherliness, readyness to help, manliness. Every one is thinking of his rightful duties and tasks. All are united in one mighty aim, all trivial things vanish . . . Then we went to Reichstag. One of the greatest days one could live through, for, however it may end, this 4th of August is immortal.—The Chancellor's face was almost tragic.

Otto Braun, Diary, *August 4, 1914.*

We are up against the mightiest War-machine of all times, wonderful in organisation, joining the savagery of the barbarian to the deadliest resources of modern science. The revelation of the black soul of Germany is the greatest and most hideous surprise of this month of months . . . the torture and massacre of old men, women and children, the shooting of hostages, the sack and burning of towns and destruction of ancient seats of learning.

Punch, *London, August 1914.*

Medical Officer: "Sorry I must reject you on account of your teeth." Would-be Recruit: "Man, ye're making a gran' mistake. I'm no wanting to bite the Germans, I'm wanting to shoot 'em."

Cartoon in Punch, *London, August 1914.*

I did find a number of *"Gott strafe England"* medals. Conversation with the Germans revealed that they all regarded the invasion of Belgium as unfortunate, but a national necessity. Conscientious German Christians seemed sincere as they endeavored to justify the invasion. The weak argument was invariably advanced that if Germany had not invaded Belgium, France would have done so. They went on to explain that it was not a war of aggression on the part of Germany, but one of protection against the so-termed encircling policy, *"Einkreisung-Politik,"* of British diplomacy.

Conrad Hoffman, In the Prison Camps of Germany *(1915).*

One very soon recognized that for Germany war was a business. All was in most efficient readiness for war, so that when it came the regular routine of life continued to go with comparatively little interruption or alteration. True, in Wilhelmstrasse, the home of the War Ministry and Foreign Offices, officialdom became more active and the offices there developed into veritable beehives of activity; but even there it was a year or more before expansion of the War Ministry became necessary in view of the unanticipated long duration and extent of the War.

Conrad Hoffmann, In the Prison Camps of Germany.

French and Russian they matter not, / A blow for a blow and a shot for a shot; / We love them not, we hate them not, / We hold the Vistula and the Vosges-gate, / We have but one and only hate, / We love as one, we hate as one, / We "hate" one for and one alone—ENGLAND! . . .

Ernst Lissauer, German writer, in "Hassgesang"
("Song of Hate"), 1914.

Had there been a Bismarck in Germany, a Palmerston or a Disraeli in Britain, a Roosevelt in America, or a Clemenceau in authority in Paris, the catastrophe might, and I believe would have been averted.

David Lloyd George, War Memoirs, vol. 1
(1933).

3. The War in the West: August 4 to the End of 1914

The Historical Context

GERMANY'S INVASION OF BELGIUM

When Chancellor Bethmann-Hollweg declared at the Reichstag on August 4, 1914 that German troops had occupied Luxembourg and "perhaps" were already in Belgium, German army units had been in Belgium for eight hours. Seven German armies, in all about 1,500,000 men, had been posted along the French and Belgian borders. In accordance with the Schlieffen plan, the northern wing—consisting of the First, Second and Third Armies—was the strongest with 34 divisions in each army. The central Fourth and Fifth Armies consisted of 20 divisions each, while the southern Sixth and Seventh Armies were made up of 16 divisions each. A cavalry corps of three divisions was attached to the right wing, as well.

Still, the northern wing—intended to move through Belgium—was not quite as strong as Schlieffen had planned it, simply because Schlieffen had not figured on a two-front war. Moltke was forced to leave a minimum force to defend East Prussia against the Russians. Moreover, there were, at the outbreak of war, several unknown factors: Would Britain join France, and if so, how fast and how many British units could cross the Channel to aid France? Would Belgium put up just a token resistance, or would it try to make a real stand against the overwhelming German forces?

Britain entered the war but had delayed the decision for two days and sent only four, instead of six, divisions. Belgium, to the amazement of the greater part of the world, decided to fight. The moral force behind the effort was King Albert, who also showed more common sense and military insight than most of his generals. Belgium had built the huge forts of Liège and Namur 30 years earlier and relied on them entirely for its defense. They were manned by garrisons of reserve units, and the king concentrated all of Belgium's six divisions on the Meuse River, where the great fortresses could be reinforced. But these efforts were frustrated by his General Staff, which had the divisions stationed all around the country to face any potential aggressor and now refused to change its established strategy. The staff expected Liège to hold out for months against any attempt to capture it, as Port Arthur had done 10 years earlier against the Japanese. But it ignored the huge siege guns developed recently by Skoda, the Austrian munitions firm, and by Krupp in Essen. The Belgian army, on the other hand, had hardly any of the heavy field artillery it needed for the defense of the terrain between the forts of Liège and Namur.

Still, the German advance force met with unexpected, stubborn resistance at Liège. Infantry assaults, still executed in the old fashion of advancing almost shoulder to shoulder, were mowed down by Belgian machine guns. But on the evening of August 5, a comparatively unknown German general, Erich Ludendorff, took over the command of a brigade whose general had been killed; he managed to break through between the forts and reached the heights of the right bank of the Meuse River which overlooked the city and the citadel. He then sent an emissary to the Belgian commander of Liège, General Gérard Mathieu Leman, and threatened to destroy the city by zeppelin raids if the German army were not allowed to march through. After Leman's refusal, one zeppelin appeared and dropped 13 bombs, killing nine civilians—the first air raid victims of the century. Since no French or English help arrived, the king as well as Leman realized that the city could not be held and withdrew the defending army—not, as Joffre had wanted, to form a northern extension of the French armies, but in the direction of Antwerp, where Leman's armies could make a last stand but could not aid French efforts to stop the German northern wing. Still, none of the Liège forts had yet been taken, and it took many days of disassembling and reassembling, loading and unloading of the Krupp and Skoda mammoth guns to transport them into a position to attack the forts. Once that was accomplished, the forts had no chance. Eleven forts had fallen by August 16, and on the following day Leman was knocked unconscious in the last fort, Loncin.

With Liège out of the way, the German advance could no longer be detained. On August 20, the Belgian army took refuge in the fortress of Antwerp, while the Second German Army appeared before the only remaining fortress of Namur which barred the route up the Meuse River into France. This time the Germans used their heavy guns immediately and took the city after two days.

THE FRENCH ARMY

The French army had not been able to help, as it had launched the great offensive in the south, according to the Plan 17, which was kept so secret that even the French government had never been consulted about it. Alsace-Lorraine was invaded by 17 French divisions, which took Sarrebourg and Mulhouse without meeting any resistance. They were greeted with tremendous enthusiasm by the greater part of the population. But Mulhouse soon had to be abandoned when the Germans counterattacked with troops brought in from Strasbourg. In the fiercely fought battle of Morhanges-Sarrebourg (Saarburg), the French were driven back with huge losses to their own line of fortifications—a rather humiliating defeat after they had presented themselves as the great liberators and vanguards of "revanche." However, the French public did not learn much about these reverses. Joffre kept all decisions and information to himself; cabinet ministers complained that they learned more of the movements of the German armies than of the French, and President Poincaré protested that he was never told about reverses. False rumors began to spread. The veteran General Joseph-Simon Gallieni, whom the jealous Joffre kept idle in Paris until the last minute, overheard in a Paris café that General Gallieni had just entered Colmar with 30,000 men.

These setbacks, however, had put the French southernmost armies in a better position to utilize their interior railway system and thus shift to the north, where the first gigantic battle of the war was in the making.

The northernmost First German Army under General Alexander von Kluck had begun its great push through Belgium right after Liège had fallen. The Second Army, to his left, under General Karl von Buelow, and the Third, under General Max Klemens von Hausen, followed in their sweep through Belgium. Joffre was ill-prepared to meet this overwhelming attack. There had been enough warnings, in particular from General Charles Lanrezac, the commander of his northernmost army, the Fifth, and also from Gallieni, who by then had been transferred to the Paris War Ministry. All that Joffre could provide was a makeshift defense force consisting of territorial troops who were shifted to the section between the Channel and the first fortress on French soil, Maubeuge. The fortress was poorly prepared to withstand a siege, and the British Expeditionary Force which was supposed to link up with the French had not yet made any difference in the overall situation.

THE BRITISH EXPEDITIONARY FORCE

There had been a great debate among the top British military as to where to commit the four British divisions, about 80,000 men who had crossed the Channel between August 12 and 17, protected by the British navy. They had landed at the seaports of Le Havre and Boulogne and further up the Seine River at Rouen. Lord Kitchener, Secretary of War, who anticipated a long, drawn-out war, was unwilling to expose his small force of highly trained soldiers to annihilation by the huge

German armies. He suggested that they concentrate around Amiens, on the Somme, and urged the government to build up a large army at home in the meantime. Other top leaders wanted to move to Antwerp to help the Belgian army. The opinion of the commander of the British Expeditionary Force (BEF), Sir John French, prevailed, and, in accordance with plans developed long before the war, an attempt was made to link up with the French Fifth Army under General Lanrezac, which was in danger of being overrun by the Germans. Once again the numerical superiority as well as the extension of the arc formed by the German armies was underestimated by Joffre. Lanrezac was forced to retreat and was fired by Joffre, while the British had to bear the brunt of the German attack at Mons in southern Belgium. In their first contact with the Germans, the British put up a valiant but futile resistance and had to withdraw in order to avoid being enveloped by Kluck's rapidly advancing troops.

The British public was never given the full picture of the situation, which became more desperate every day. They only heard of successes and were never treated to an explanation for why the front was moving deeper and deeper into France. The battle of Mons was supposed to have saved France, while actually the British had been in touch with no more than three German corps out of a total of 30. The cooperation between the French and British was poor, and in spite of further delaying action fought by the British at Le Cateau, the spectacular German advance continued. By August 25, the German armies seemed to be on the point of victory. British headquarters had withdrawn to Compiègne, 40 miles north of Paris, and on August 31 Lord Kitchener received a report from Sir John French in which he declared his intention to retire behind the Seine, and thus, for all practical purposes, to abandon his ally, the French. While Kitchener rushed to France, desperately trying to organize a coordinated resistance, Kluck's army had taken Compiègne and stood 30 miles from Paris, engaged in action on September 1 against the rear guards of the French Sixth Army and the BEF. This hastily assembled new army, under General Michel-Joseph Maunoury, was also forced to retreat toward Paris; on September 3, against the advice of President Poincaré, the French government moved to Bordeaux.

DILEMMA OF THE GERMAN ARMIES, AND RETREAT

But the German military command had troubles of its own. Moltke, sitting in his headquarters at Luxembourg, did not keep in close enough contact with his army commanders and was not the man to inspire them or their soldiers. Contrary to sound military judgment, the Russians did not wait until their mobilization could be completed but—on the urgent request of their French allies—attacked Austria and

Count Helmuth von Moltke (the Younger), loser of the battle of the Marne, 1914. Photo courtesy of the New York Public Library.

invaded East Prussia, probably prematurely. However, Moltke felt obliged to dispatch two army corps and a cavalry division to the east, where they arrived too late to partake in the decisive battle. He also found that he could no longer follow the original Schlieffen plan, which had been watered down anyway by the strengthening of the southern German armies against the French attack in Alsace-Lorraine.

Now Moltke found he lacked the strength to move west of Paris. He realized that the French had been pushed back with great losses, but their lines had not been broken nor had the wide encirclement foreseen by the Schlieffen plan been achieved. Further, the Belgian army was now entrenched at Antwerp—reinforced by British marines—in the back of the German forces. And finally, it became evident that the three German armies of the northern wing—with soldiers exhausted from endless marches—were not cooperating well with one another. General Karl von Bülow had to worry about Kluck on his right, who went ahead too fast, and Hausen on his left, who advanced too cautiously.

But on August 30, when Bülow asked Kluck to assist him in pursuing the Fifth French Army he had beaten at St. Quentin, Kluck agreed. Instead of heading straight for Paris, Kluck decided to move southeast to get behind the retreating Fifth Army. When this move was discovered by British air reconnaissance, the new military commander in Paris, Gallieni, saw that Kluck's right flank was now exposed to him; though the new French Sixth Army, of whose existence the Germans were unaware, was formed strictly for the defense of Paris, Gallieni pleaded immediately with Joffre and the French Sixth Army to join him in an all-out counterattack, which would involve not just the Sixth Army but every French unit along the Paris-Verdun line. He convinced Joffre—who in turn persuaded Sir John French—to cooperate.

Kluck, meanwhile, continued to move south of the Marne River, although his troops had by now outrun their supply lines and suffered from hunger as well as utter fatigue. Only the thought of their great victory and of heading for Paris kept them going; they did not realize that they were no longer marching toward the French capital. In Berlin, too, people expected the fall of Paris by September 4. By September 5, the German First Army had reached its farthest point south of the Marne, since Kluck had disregarded Moltke's orders of September 4 to stand fast. When he realized the threat on his right flank, Kluck was forced to turn west to face the enemy, and in doing so, a dangerous gap developed between his troops and in Bǔlow's Second Army. The French-British counterattack was now in full swing.

On the same day, Moltke's chief of intelligence, Colonel Richard Hentsch, had arrived at Kluck's headquarters after a 175-mile drive from Luxembourg. He informed Kluck that the southern German armies under the Crown Prince and Grand Duke Rupprecht of Bavaria were deadlocked in battles before the great French fortresses and that there was imminent danger of an attack from the west. This time, Kluck gave in. When he had been close to defeating Maunoury's Sixth Army, the latter had been reinforced, on Gallieni's initiative, from Paris by means of some 600 taxi cabs which rushed about 6,000 troops to the front, about 45 miles to the east. The effect of this move was mainly psychological, but it permitted Maunoury to stand fast. Joffre spent an anxious day because he felt Gallieni had ordered the attack prematurely before the necessary numerical superiority over the Germans had been achieved. But Joffre was helped by the stubborn resistance of the French armies at the right wing who withstood all attacks in the Verdun and Nancy areas and the fact that the British, though slowly, moved into the gap between the First and Second German Armies. On a second visit on September 8, Colonel Hentsch advised Bǔlow to retreat, after which Kluck's withdrawal automatically followed. By September 13, the German armies had withdrawn to the north of the Aisne River; all efforts of the Allies to dislodge them there ended in failure.

Thus ended the first battle of the Marne, probably the most dramatic conflict of the whole war, and one of the most decisive ones, even though the war was to last another four years. Germany had almost

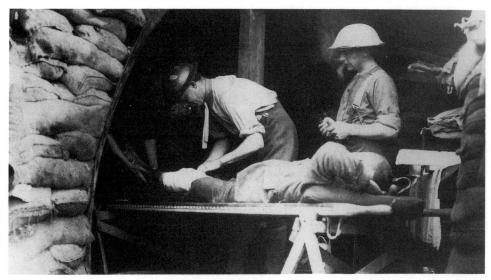

Scottish soldiers at a dressing station in Belgium, 1914. Photo courtesy of the National Archives, Washington, D.C.

but not quite reached its great goal—to overrun France—and had squandered its great initial advantage, since it had at its disposal the best prepared and equipped army in Europe. Experts have claimed that had the original Schlieffen plan been followed rigidly, France might have fallen. However, Schlieffen could not foresee Russia's early participation nor Belgium's brave resistance. As far as strategy is concerned, it is easy to see in retrospect that both sides committed grave errors. The French had neglected to provide proper defenses where it mattered most: along the Belgian-French frontier. Instead, they had put their main effort into the attack into Alsace-Lorraine, which proved quite futile and extremely costly to them. On the positive side, they produced in Joffre and Gallieni leaders who never lost their confidence and saw the opportunity to strike back at crucial moments. The small British force did not play a decisive role, and its leader, Sir John French, seemed most of the time more concerned about preserving his independence than helping the Allied cause.

On the German side, most observers agree that Kluck's headlong offensive across the Marne had given his enemies the golden opportunity, but that the main fault was with the supreme commander Moltke, whose indecisiveness may have made the difference between victory and defeat during the critical days of September 1–5. Moltke, though not a personally timid man (he even dared to speak up to the emperor), was self-critical and melancholy by nature, as he always felt himself to be in the shadow of his celebrated uncle. Apparently, he lost his nerve when Joffre did not, and that may have been what made the difference.

Alexander von Kluck, commander of the First German Army, in Belgium. Photo courtesy of the National Archives, Washington, D.C.

THE WAR TURNS STATIC

After the great battle, the Germans had lost their numerical superiority in the west and were forced to dig in to fight a war of attrition. They had also missed the chance to occupy the Channel ports of Dunkirk, Boulogne and Calais, which they could have taken easily during the initial push. Yet the territory the German armies now occupied left one-tenth of France—including about three-quarters of its heavy industry—and practically all of Belgium in enemy hands, except for the region around Antwerp which could have served as a basis for an Allied attack of the Belgian coast. But when the Germans began their bombardment of the outer forts by the end of September, little help was forthcoming from the Allies to support the outgunned and outnumbered troops inside the fortress. By October 7, the city itself was being bombarded. Two days later, when Antwerp capitulated, the Belgian army withdrew, and thenceforth it defended a small strip of Belgian land not occupied by the enemy until the end of the war. The Belgian government was established at LeHavre.

For the huge armies which had fought at the Marne and were now facing each other alongside the Aisne River, there was room to maneuver only in the north. Each side attempted to outflank the other. During the next few days after the fall of Antwerp, the Germans, now under the supreme command of General Erich von Falkenhayn (who had replaced Moltke), took Ghent, Bruges and Ostend and, further south, the city of Lille. In the meantime, the whole British Expeditionary Force, now consisting of six infantry and two cavalry divisions, had been secretly transferred from the Aisne section to Flanders. It arrived in time to be engaged in Falkenhayn's next major drive, a massive attack through Flanders in the direction of the seaports which mainly concentrated around the Ypres area. The numerically superior German units made deep inroads into the Allied lines but never succeeded in breaking through. Their final defeat in the middle of November, was principally a British victory. The English infantrymen, all professional soldiers, had mastered rapid rifle shooting to such an extent that the Germans suspected great numbers of British machine guns where there were hardly any. Many of the British marksmen could discharge 30 rounds per minute. The allies were also helped by the determined stand of Belgian King Albert, who did not hesitate to have the lock gates of the canalized Yser River opened at Nieuport to throw back the advancing Germans. Meanwhile, the British commander, Sir John French, vacillated between complacency, wild optimism and premature despair which, at one point, caused him to suggest an evacuation camp for the BEF at Boulogne. It took the

King Albert I of Belgium, who organized stiff resistance to the German invasion, 1914. Photo courtesy of the New York Public Library.

persuasiveness of Joffre's deputy in the north, General Ferdinand Foch, to make him take a firm stand at Ypres.

In the First Battle of Ypres, the Germans had employed 402 battalions against 267 Allied, and disposed of twice as much cavalry. The losses on both sides were staggering. The British lost more than half of the original BEF. One of their divisions, the Seventh, lost 350 of its 400 officers and 20% of its enlisted men. But the "race to the sea" was won by the Allies and access to the all important Channel seaports was denied to the Germans.

Winter set in, and as the last major piece of mobile warfare had come to an end in the west, both sides dug in and strengthened their defenses. It was clear by now that this would be a long war, and all previous estimates of ammunition requirements had proven hopelessly short. Trench warfare required different weapons such as grenades, mortars, high-explosive shells and illuminating flares. Both sides needed time to catch up with the production of these and with filling the ranks of their armies, for the casualties of the first few months of fighting in the west had been appalling: 850,000 French were killed, wounded or captured; and about 675,000 for the Germans.

A firm line now ran from the Swiss border in the south to the English Channel in the north which, in the course of the next three years, would hardly vary by more than 10 miles. In the south, Verdun, Rheims, and Soissons remained in Allied hands; further north, Noyon, Peronne and Bapaume were in German hands; Montdidier, Albert and Aras were in French hands. Further up, Lens and La Bassée were German; Armentières, Ypres and Nieuport were British; and Passchendaele, Dixmude and Ostend were German.

CHRONICLE OF EVENTS

1914:

August 4: German armies cross the frontier of Luxembourg and Belgium.

August 5–6: German units, under General Otto von Emmich, get past the forts of Liège.

August 6–17: The forts of Liège are reduced by heavy German artillery. Belgians fall back on Brussels, then on Antwerp.

August 7–17: A British Expeditionary Force, under Sir John French, lands at Le Havre.

August 14–25: Battle of the Frontiers, in Lorraine. The French invasion is checked by German forces and French armies are driven out of Lorraine with heavy losses.

August 18–19: Battle of Tirlement. The German First Army under General Alexander von Kluck drives back Belgian forces.

August 20: Kluck's army enters Brussels.

August 21–24: French armies under General Charles Lanrezac are defeated at Charleroi and driven back from Luxembourg.

August 23: Battle of Mons. First contact between German and British troops. The latter, and the French Fifth Army, are forced to fall back.

August 25: The Belgian fortress Namur is taken by the Germans.

August 26: The British, under General Horace Lockwood Smith-Dorrien, fight a delaying action at Le Cateau.

August 27: French fortress Longwy is taken by the Germans.

August 30: German armies take Montmédy. Kluck gives up his advance to the west of Paris to keep contact with the German Second Army (Bülow).

September 1: German armies take Soissons.

September 2: German armies take Laon.

September 3: German armies take Rheims. The French government moves from Paris to Bordeaux.

September 4: The German Commander in Chief, Helmuth von Moltke, orders the German First and Second armies to turn southwest to meet the newly formed French Sixth Army under under General Michel-Joseph Maunoury.

German infantry attacking, August 1914. Photo courtesy of the National Archives, Washington D.C.

September 5–12: Battle of the Marne. Joffre orders a general counteroffensive.

September 7: Maubeuge is taken by the Germans.

September 9: The German First and Second armies (Kluck and Bülow) begin to fall back, following instructions from Moltke in Luxembourg passed on by Colonel Richard Hentsch.

September 13: The German armies retreat to north of the Aisne River.

September 15–18: Battle of the Aisne. Allies fail to dislodge German positions.

September 22–25: German attacks in the Verdun region. St. Mihiel is taken. Fighting in the Picardy and in the Channel region.

September 27: Fighting in the Artois region, between the Picardy and Flanders.

October 1–9: German troops, under General Hans von Beseler, attack the last remaining Belgian fortress, Antwerp, with heavy guns. The Belgian army and the supporting British troops are forced to evacuate.

October 10: The race for the seaports begins.

October 11: German troops occupy Ghent.

October 12: In the south, German troops occupy Lille.

October 14: German troops take Bruges.

October 15: Germans occupy Ostend.

October 18: Battle of the Yser begins.

October 30–November 24: First Battle of Ypres.

December 14–24: Allied armies attack along the whole front, from Nieuport on the seacoast to Verdun in the south, without making any substantial gains.

December 20: First battle of Champagne, in northeast France, begins.

German infantry entrenched in Belgium, 1914. Photo courtesy of the National Archives, Washington, D.C.

EYEWITNESS TESTIMONY

. . . But I am envying you for being allowed to be an officer in this army, to be victorious in France, especially in France which one has to castigate because one loves her. It is strange, but I would muster up more vigour against those I after all esteem the highest than anyone else, for their arrogance was the beginning of all the misery.

Stefan Zweig, well-known Austrian writer, letter to his publisher Anton Kippenberg, end of 1914.

For all we have and are,/ For all our children's fate,/ Stand up and take the war./ The Hun is at the gate! . . . There is but one task for all,/ One life for each to give./ What stands if Freedom fall?/ Who dies if England live?

Rudyard Kipling, "For All We Have and Are," 1914.

God heard the embattled nations sing and shout: "Gott strafe England"—"God save the King"—"God this"—"God that"—and "God the other thing." "My God," said God, "I've got my work cut out."

J.C. Squire, English poet, as quoted by A.J.P. Taylor, Illustrated History of the First World War, 1964.

We went outside to see the scene of the "battle," as it was called in the despatches; a field in the first flush of the war, where the headless lances of Belgian and German cavalrymen were still scattered about. The peasants had broken off the lance-heads for the steel, which was something to pay for the grain smouldering in the barn which had been shelled and burned . . . A superficial survey was enough to show that it had been only a reconnaissance by the Germans . . .

Frederick Palmer, near Louvain, Belgium, August 1914, My Year of the Great War (1915).

A peasant woman came out of the house beside the battlefield . . . "Les Anglais" she cried at the sight of us. Seeing that we had some lances in the car, she rushed into her house and brought out half a dozen more. If the English wanted lances they should have them . . . Her eyes were burning with appeal to us and flashing with hate as she shook her fist toward the Germans. When were the English coming? All her trust was in the English, the invincible English, to save her country.

Frederick Palmer, near Louvain, Belgium, August 1914, My Year of the Great War.

The bitterest incident of all was when we passed through a little [Belgian] village, we trod underfoot a strip of cloth which had hung in greeting across the street, and which bore the words: "Welcome to our saviours, the British!"

British Captain C.A.L. Brownlow, in "The Breaking of the Storm: August 25, 1914," quoted in Vain Glory (1937).

And silence, only silence, in Paris, the silence of the old men and the women, and of children who had ceased to play and could not understand. . . . No one might see what was going on unless he carried a rifle. No one might even see the wounded. Paris was spared this, isolated in the midst of war.

Frederick Palmer, in Paris, end of August 1914, My Year of the Great War.

Until now I have not been afraid, and in the bottom of my heart, I have been a little vain of the fact. But the suddenness, the mystery of this night attack surprises me. To fight in the daylight, even against an unseen enemy, is bearable; but a rare control of the nerves is needed to await coolly, in pitch darkness, a foe whose position and strength are unknown . . . A flood of anguish surges over us while the bullets whistle about our ears, and suddenly, while my brain remains very clear, and I count on the almost certain repulse of the attack, my overstrung nerves shake my conquered body, my teeth chatter, my legs, arms, hands and fingers tremble; my will loses control over my rebellious frame and while loading the cartridges into the stock of my rifle, I jam the weapon.

André Fribourg, on fighting in France, September 1914, The Flaming Crucible (1918).

"Hide!" At the brief command we squat in the hedge lining the road at the end of the village of Mouilly. Yonder, to the east, above the green crest plumed with tall columns of smoke, a German balloon has appeared. The "sausage" held captive by her wire, seems motionless; but curious, she rises little by little. If an observer were to catch sight of us and signal our whereabouts, we should be quickly showered. We wait. The danger passes. An hour later we are in the woods . . . We arrive at the front. The relief takes place within 200 yards of the foe . . . We tumble into the trench, a furrow eighty centimetres dug into the stony soil.

André Fribourg, at the front, September 1914, The Flaming Crucible.

As we are to begin the battle upon which depends the fate of our country, it is necessary to remind all that the time for retreat has ended. Every effort must be made to drive back the enemy. A soldier who can no longer advance must guard the territory already held, no matter what the cost. He must be killed in his tracks rather than draw back.

Marchal Joseph Joffre, order to the French forces on September 5, 1914.

We fired like madmen, blackened with powder, the rifles scorching our fingers, and between rounds

Marshal Joseph-Jacques-Césaire Joffre of France, victor in the first battle of the Marne. Photo courtesy of the New York Public Library.

thrusting our hands into the earth to fling up a miserable shelter. On all sides, cries, screams and groans . . . Péguy remained standing in spite of our shouts of "Lie down." He drew himself up as if in challenge to the storm of bullets, as it were to summon the death he had glorified in his verse. At that moment a bullet pierced his noble forehead. He fell on the hillside without a cry. . . . When, some yards farther on, frantically leaping forward, I glanced behind me, I saw stretched on the hot, dusty earth, among the broad green leaves, a black and scarlet stain in the midst of so many others, the body of our beloved brave lieutenant.

Victor Boudon, French soldier, about the death of the French poet and writer Charles Péguy at the Marne, September 5, 1914, in Guy Chapman (ed.), Vain Glory *(1937).*

Things go badly. We shall lose the battles East of Paris. One of our armies will have to retreat, and the others must follow. The war, so hopefully begun, will turn right around. I have to bear what happens, and will stand or fall with my country. We must suffocate in this fight against East and West. The campaign is not yet lost, no more than it is for the French, but the French élan that was about to fade away will again burst into flames and I fear our people in their flush of victory will hardly be able to bear such a disaster.

Helmut von Moltke, letter to his wife from Luxembourg, September 9, 1914.

The flames of a village destroyed by shellfire, a livid moonlight and a terrific storm, such were the precursors of our entrance this morning into a pretty village in the Vosges, where a dozen houses were gutted, burned or totally demolished by shells. Chickens were pecking at the door-sills of the deserted houses. That is war! Our men might have been put in bad humour by this. But no! . . . They are laughing and chatting now while the German bombs are falling not far from us . . .

Letter from a French soldier in the Alsace, September 14, 1914, in Albert Geouffre de Lapradelle, War Letters from France *(1915).*

The battle of the Marne was not only a giant conflict of great armies, but also a significant struggle between two methods of command. The military method practiced on the French side had been inspired by the teachings of Napoleon. This doctrine calls for the commander-in-chief to direct the battle from beginning to end. . . . In the German camp, a quite different doctrine was being followed. It had been bequeathed to the armies of the empire by old Marshal von Moltke. The victor of the battles of Sadowa and Sedan taught that the actual direction of a battle falls principally upon the subordinate command.

The commander-in-chief, after having drawn the general plan of battle, makes way for the initiative of his army commanders.

Marshal Joseph Joffre, "Narrative of the Battle of the Marne" (1927).

We have been living in a sheltered valley for generations. We have been too comfortable and too indulgent . . . and the stern hand of fate has scourged us to an elevation where we can see the great everlasting things that matter for a nation—the great peaks we had forgotten, of Honour, Duty, Patriotism, and, clad in glittering white, the great pinnacle of Sacrifice pointing like a rugged finger to Heaven.

David Lloyd George, Queen's Hall speech, September 19, 1914.

The French are led excellently, which is not the case with us, unfortunately. Moltke has collapsed physically. Don't say a word about that! But our situation has become extremely dangerous since Austria has been such a failure. Of 800,000 men in Galicia there are supposed to be only 500,000 left. In the West, things also have become very difficult for us. I would not write this to you, but I talked to a gentleman from Berlin yesterday who knew it all and told me, all this was known in Berlin.

Alfred von Tirpitz, secretary of the German Marine, in a private letter, September 21, 1914.

When the cannon is still at night, I hear the groans and the death rattle of the wounded who have not been picked up in front of the trenches facing the enemy . . . Quite often the Prussians dispatch our wounded soldiers with a lance thrust or a blow with a butt of a musket. I know what I am talking about for I have seen it.

Letter of a French soldier between Aisne and Marne, September 26, 1914, in A.G. de Lapradelle, War Letters from France (1915).

We have been putting in our time here at very hard drilling and are supposed to have learned in six weeks what the ordinary recruit in times of peace takes all his two years at. We rise at 5 and work stops in the afternoon at 5. A twelve hours day at one sou a day.

Alan Seeger, American poet who joined the French Foreign Legion, in a letter to his mother from Toulouse, September 28, 1914.

Four weeks ago this country could be called rich. Plenty of cattle and pigs. Now it is empty. There is no wine cellar in any of the towns that was not confiscated by the Germans. No grocery-, egg-, butter-, flourshop that does not have to supply to the Germans only. No horse that was not taken away, no automobile, gasoline, railroad car, no house, no coal, oil, electricity that does not work for us, is not utilized by us. I buy some useful and comfortable things for myself and my men, give him a slip of paper with my name on it and the merchant stands in his shop, bowing. From the cellar of Chevalier van der B. I take fifteen bottles of the best Bordeaux and some bottles of old port . . . and do not even thank the cellarman with a two-franc coin. I take . . . pigs, chickens, potatoes, apples of the natives who fled or were expelled. They do not even get a receipt . . . Whom would I give it to?

Rudolf G. Binding, German poet, on Belgium in 1914, in War Poems and Diaries (1940).

. . . on the 13th of September Joffre, always unboastful and laconic, announced the rolling back of the invaders, on the 15th the battle of the Aisne began. What an Iliad of agony, endurance and heroism lies behind these dates, the ordeal and deliverance of Paris, the steadfastness of the "Contemptibles," the martyrdom of Belgium! Day by day Germany unmasks herself in her true colours from the highest to lowest.

Punch, London, September 1914.

Over there are men separated from me by everything; whom I hate, not only because they kill us and we kill them; but because between them and me there is a wide moral abyss and the weight of the past. Their inborn brutality, their coarseness, their insolence of soul fill me with horror . . . How I should like to kill them in the intoxication of battle! But at this minute, in the calm of the autumn night, I feel that I hate them less than I did during the August rush. I remember that they love as I love; that they undergo the same sufferings; that they are brave; that death is watching them as it watches each one of us, and that to many a one the words of Christ apply: "Father, forgive them, for they know not what they do." The same kind of a life from day to day ends by creating invisible ties.

André Fribourg, fighting in Lorraine, October 1, 1914, The Flaming Crucible.

For nearly a month I have not undressed, or taken off my shoes. I have washed twice, once in a pool, and once in a ditch near a dead horse. I have never been near a mattress. Two or three times I slept in a barn, on straw. All my other nights I passed on the earth or in the earth . . . Here, often we pilfer fifteen minutes of rest as, in the city, a hungry man steals a loaf of bread.

André Fribourg, on life in the trenches of Lorraine, October 1914, The Flaming Crucible.

Preceding me, his belt on a level with my eyes, is Giesecke . . . one of the few young men of the company who left Chalons the last Friday of July and are still alive . . . A shell has carried off his "kepi," and his fatigue cap, worn sideways, gives him a savage appearance . . . occasionally he talks softly and sadly, like one who knows he is soon to die. I have seen no one so deeply convinced that he is marked for death, yet who faces danger so calmly, and who survives so long.

André Fribourg, on fighting in Lorraine, October 1914, The Flaming Crucible.

Mailly was about the furthest point reached by the Germans before the French success in the battle of the Marne forced them to retreat . . . Some of the buildings in the village are damaged by shells . . . Last night two Germans were found in the woods near here by a patrol. One was dead from hunger and exposure and the other nearly so. He said the reason they had not surrendered was that their officers had told them that they would be shot.

Alan Seeger, diary, at Mailly, France, October 4, 1914.

It has rained for forty hours. All night, without stopping, the downpour has kept up, steadily and monotonously. A dirty gray day is rising over the trees . . . We are chilled; the rain has penetrated cap and garments; overcoat, vest, and shirt are like a sponge. The water rolls down my back and over my skin. There are twelve inches of it in the trench. We are hungry; yesterday they gave each man a piece of meat that I have kept by precaution on my bag.

André Fribourg, on life in the trenches of Lorraine, October 10, 1914, The Flaming Crucible.

I am very calm; in full control of myself; and it is at this exact moment that my being feels a terrible revolt. "Oh, stupid and brutal force; miserable force, mad force, I hate you; I despise you! You are nothing! You cannot harm me! You are going to kill me, but what will that prove? You shall not overwhelm me! Others already have my heart and my soul; and if you crush me, my spirit will break you! You are nothing! Kindness and charity alone count in this world. I will be good. I have suffered too much. I have seen too much suffering. I have made too many suffer. I will be good. I swear it. Henceforth all my life will be good." Then, in the awful tumult, the earth opens; I am swept by a frightful blast; I feel a shock in my forehead, a shock in my loins; a flame passes before my eyes. I fall; and know no more.

André Fribourg, on being wounded in a bombardment in Lorraine, October 10, 1914, The Flaming Crucible.

The men in the firing trenches we pass look at us enviously. After these fearful days and more fearful nights, after having endured every bodily agony and mental strain, these men, whose courage, coolness, and spirit of sacrifice can never be enough praised, shiver in their dark holes at the passing of our sad procession . . . One man whom I know by sight . . . says to me in a compassionate tone: "Don't worry old man! You are lucky. You are wounded. Some are dead. There is Rigollet, there is . . . there is . . ." and he adds my own name. I should like to protest, but I am so weary, and he is so sure that I am dead.

André Fribourg recalls being carried back from the front on a stretcher, October 1914, The Flaming Crucible.

About trenches—said Dunn [the Company Commander] Well, we don't know as much about trenches as the French do, and not near as much as Fritz does. We can't expect Fritz to help, but the French might do something. They are too greedy to let us have the benefit of their inventions. What wouldn't we give for their parachute-lights and aerial torpedoes! But there is never any connexion between the two armies, unless a battle is on, and then we generally let each other down.

Robert Graves, with a Welsh regiment in France, fall of 1914, Good-by to All That (1929).

Only 126 out of 256 are left in our company and not a single captain in the regiment . . . for exactly twenty-one days we have been living like moles, underground solidly entrenched on three hills, only 800 or 900 meters from the enemy . . .

Letter of a French soldier in Belgium, October 1914, in A.G. de Lapradelle, War Letters from France (1915).

The prophets are no longer so optimistic in predicting when the war will end. One of Mr. Punch's young men suggests Christmas, 1918. But 500 German prisoners have arrived at Templeton, co. Tipperary. It's a long long way, but they've got there at last.

Punch, London, October 1914.

A German flare shot up, broke into bright flame, dropped slowly and went hissing into the grass just behind our trench . . . Instinctively I moved. "It's bad to do that, sir" the sentry said, as a rifle bullet cracked between us. "Keep still, Sir, and they can't spot you. Not but what a flare is a bad thing to fall on you. I've seen them burn a hole in a man."

Robert Graves, with a Welsh regiment in France, fall of 1914, Good-Bye to All That.

Our men slept in Verzy in their harness, that is, wearing the cartridge belt, with sack and gun at our head. At four we got up and marched here . . . There were three graves by the roadside at a place where we stopped, a post above each and a placard reading: Espion, traître à son pays [Spy, traitor of his country].

Alan Seeger, diary, Verzenay, France, October 23, 1914.

We have made a march of about 75 kilometers in four days and are now on the front, ready to be called on at any moment. . . . How beautiful the view is here, over the sunny vineyards! And what a curious anomaly. On this slope the grape pickers are singing merrily at their work, on the other the batteries are roaring. Boom! Boom! This will spoil one for any other kind of life . . .

Alan Seeger, letter to his mother, near Reims, October 23, 1914.

Unfortunately I am compelled to use the severest measures of military law against the town of Orchies. There, doctors, sanitary personnel and about twenty German soldiers have been attacked and murdered. The worst atrocities have been committed in an incredible manner (ears cut off, eyes torn out and similar bestialities). Therefore I ordered the town to be completely destroyed. Orchies, formerly a town of 5000 inhabitants, exists no longer: Houses, townhall, church have disappeared, there are no more inhabitants.

Major von Mehring, German Commandant of Valenciennes, Proclamation of November 8, 1914, E. Engel, Tagebuch (1915).

Fifth day of our second period in the trenches. Five days and nights of pure misery . . . The increasing cold will make this kind of existence insupportable, with its accompaniments of vermin and dysentery. Could we only attack or be attacked! I would hear the order with delight. The real courage of the soldier is not facing the balls, but the fatigue and discomfort and misery.

Alan Seeger, diary, near Cuiry, France, November 10, 1914.

We had been in a fight, had seen loaded ambulances going to the rear, had crossed roads filed with corpses and passed ravaged farms . . . No wonder we were astonished to read in our official communication: "Situation unchanged and in the Vosges."

Letter of a French soldier in Lorraine, November 14, 1914, in A.G. de Lapradelle, War Letters from France (1915).

You know how for the last three weeks the Germans have been spreading the news that Verdun is besieged, taken, destroyed. It is one of our favorite jokes here. Whenever anyone of us is going to Verdun we tell him it is useless to start, seeing that Verdun is destroyed.

Letter of a French soldier near Verdun, November 1914, in A.G. de Lapradelle, War Letters from France.

. . . there seemed no limit to the cheerfulness of Belgians. At a hospital in Calais I met a Belgian professor with his head a white ball of bandages, showing a hole for one eye and a slit for the mouth. He had been one of the cyclists which took account of many German cavalry scouts in the first two weeks of the war. A staff automobile had run over him on the road. "I think the driver of the car was careless" he said mildly . . .

Frederick Palmer, at Calais, November 1914,
My Year of the Great War (1915).

In clear weather aeroplanes buzz overhead all day long. Both sides bombard them with shrapnel, which makes a queer little whir when it explodes high in the air . . . Never have I seen the lines bring an airman down, for the puffs of yellow smoke break too low, and high up in the clouds the machine goes humming on, contemptuously dropping its signal fuses . . . Standing facing them (the enemy's trenches) from his ramparts the sentinel has ample time for reflection. Alone under the stars, war in its cosmic rather than its moral aspect reveals itself to him. Regarded from this more abstract plane the question of right or wrong disappears . . . He is on the side he is fighting for, not in the last analysis from ethical motives at all, but because destiny has set him in such a constellation . . . Playing a part in the life of the nations he is taking part in the largest movement his planet allows him.

Alan Seeger, letter to the New York Sun,
from a trench in France, December 8, 1914.

The typical trench dugout resembles catacombs more than anything else. A long gallery is cut in the ground with pick and shovel. Its dimensions are about those of the cages which Louis XI devised for those of his prisoners he wished especially to torture, that is, the height is not great enough to permit a man to stand up and the breadth does not allow him to stretch out . . . The roof of the dugout is built by laying long logs across the top of the excavation; felling trees for these coverings occupies a large part of our rest intervals. On the completeness with which these beams are covered with earth depends the comfort and safety of the trench. Wicker screens are often made and laid across the logs, sods are fitted over the screens so as to make a tight covering and then loose earth is thrown back on top. This is an effective protection against all but the heaviest shells.

Alan Seeger, letter to the New York Sun *from*
the woods of France, December 14, 1914.

In the early days of war prison history in Germany one of our secretaries asked the British Tommies for a list of the things which they wanted most. These men had just come from the front, had not yet had time to receive food parcels from home, and up to date had had no letters from home. The list received was the following: Hair-cutting scissors, razors, razor strops, shaving soap, shaving brushes, hair brushes, combs, clothing brushes, toilet soap, laundry soap, boot brushes—all articles for the maintenance of personal cleanliness. These were the things that these British Tommies wanted most at a time when one would have thought desire for food would be uppermost.

Conrad Hoffmann, recalling events of late 1914,
In the Prison Camps of Germany (1920).

4. The Eastern Front: August 1914 to March 1915

THE HISTORICAL CONTEXT

RUSSIA'S INVASIONS OF EAST PRUSSIA, AND INITIAL SUCCESS

Fortunately for the French, it was not war minister Vladimir Sukhomlinov who was appointed commander in chief of the Russian forces when the war broke out. Instead it was his arch rival, Grand Duke Nicholas (Nikolai Nikolayevich), the grandson of Tsar Nicholas I. The grand duke represented the reforming tendency within the army and disliked Germany and he was the most admired figure in the Russian army. Sukhomlinov, on the other hand, was (according to foreign minister Sazonov) lazy and untrustworthy. Clearly he was German-oriented and dead set against any reform or modernization of the army. He boasted that he had not read a military manual in 25 years. Somehow he remained as war minister for another year anyway, after which he was dismissed and convicted of corruption, abuse of power and inactivity.

Grand Duke Nicholas was not particularly popular at the St. Petersburg court. He was hated by Tsarina Alexandra, a German princess who never concealed her sympathies for the German cause. Since 1911 she had been under the spell of Grigori Yefimovich Rasputin, a semiliterate peasant and self-appointed "holy man" who apparently exercised a great amount of personal magnetism and political power under the protection of the tsarina. Since the grand duke despised Rasputin, he was hated by the tsarina, who wrote to her husband in June 1915: "I have absolutely no faith in Nikolasha [the grand duke]. I know him to be far from clever and having gone against a man of God, his work cannot be blessed or his advice good."

Nicholas knew that immediate action against Germany was needed to help France, and he listened to the urgent appeals of French ambassador Maurice Paléologue. He disregarded shortages of motor transport, telephone and telegraph equipment. In order to meet the date for attack promised to the French (16 days after mobilization), improvisations had to be introduced at the last moment; but on August 12, an advance cavalry and infantry unit led by General Pavel K. Rennenkampf's First Army invaded East Prussia. On August 17, Nicholas opened his full-scale offensive on a 35-mile-wide front, heading for the Insterburg Gap, an area of open land between the Masurian Lakes to the south and the fortified Koenigsberg area to the north. Russia's Second Army started two days later and had a longer approach to the German border. It was supposed to go around the Masurian Lakes from the south and join up with the First Army near the town of Allenstein, thus catching the German army engaged with the First Army from the south and behind. The Russian Second Army's leader, General Alexsander Samsonov, was not familiar with the region nor with his troops and staff. The Russians were encouraged by the news that Japan had declared support for the Allies on August 15, which automatically freed large contingents of Russian troops for service on the European front. This was a deep disappointment in Berlin where, in the very first days of the war, crowds had cheered the Japanese embassy upon rumors that Japan had declared war on her old enemy—Russia!

The German Eighth Army was just about strong enough to cope with one Russian army but not with two. Its commander, General Friedrich Wilhelm von Prittwitz and Gaffron, was good at entertaining the emperor with anecdotes, but he was not much of a military leader and his chief of staff, Count von Waldersee, was ill at the time. Fortunately for him, Prittwitz had two excellent officers by his side, General Hermann von François, commander of the first corps, an energetic, though somewhat impetuous, leader, and Colonel Max Hoffmann, deputy chief of operations, a specialist in Russian affairs.

Cautiously, Prittwitz sent only half of his troops to meet Rennenkamp's army. François disregarded his orders, established himself at Gumbinnen, only 25 miles from the Russian border, advanced even farther and engaged the Russians five miles inside the border. His first encounter with the Russians was successful, but when on the following day, August 19, the Russians attacked in full force, bringing in their heavy guns, the two corps sent up to help François were routed and had to withdraw. The Battle of Gumbinnen was essentially a Russian victory, and Prittwitz felt that he could no longer hope to hold up the two advancing Russian armies. He proposed to retire the entire army behind the Vistula River, thus leaving all of East Prussia to the Russians. François and Hoffmann protested, the latter pointing out that retreat was impossible, as the Second Russian Army was by now nearer to the Vistula than the Germans. Prittwitz cut him short, contacted Moltke at Coblenz and announced his retreat, adding that the waters of the Vistula were extremely low in summer and that he was not sure he could even hold the river line without reinforcements.

Pavel K. Rennenkampf, commander of the First Russian Army invading East Prussia, loser at Tannenberg. Photo courtesy of the New York Public Library.

GERMANY'S COUNTEROFFENSIVE: TANNENBERG

The idea of abandoning East Prussia to the Russians was unacceptable to the emperor and to Moltke. It would have meant a terrible blow to the morale of the population. If the Russians could cross the Vistula, they would become a direct threat to Berlin and to the Austrian flank. Also, this was the worst time to ask Moltke for reinforcements, as the battle of the west was in full swing and every battalion was needed. The reaction of the German headquarters, at that time still at Coblenz, was decisive. Prittwitz and his deputy Waldersee were dismissed and a new Chief of Staff, Erich Ludendorff, was appointed for the German Eighth Army. Ludendorff had been successful at Liège and was now with Bülow's Second Army at the outskirts of Namur. Ludendorff left within 15 minutes after he received the news on August 22. During his drive through Belgium he was informed that the Oberste Heeresleitung (OHL) had also selected a new commander, Paul von Beneckendorff und Hindenburg, a 68-year-old retired general who had fought against Austria in 1866 and against France at Sedan in 1870. He was a native of what was then West Prussia and was therefore completely familiar with the East Prussian terrain. Hindenburg joined Ludendorff's train at Hannover and thus began a team that worked together for practically the duration of the war and in the end became more powerful than the emperor and the civilian government.

Paul von Hindenburg, German field marshal, victor at Tannenberg, 1914. Photo courtesy of the German Information Center, New York City.

In the meantime, a heated debate had been going on at the East Prussian headquarters in Marienburg, where Max Hoffmann and his immediate superior, General Gruenert, tried to convince Prittwitz that the situation could be saved by moving François' advanced corps and other units to the south to help the weak German forces against Samsonov's left wing, which was closest to the Vistula. This was possible only if Rennenkampf in the north did not pursue immediately. Hoffmann was sure that he would not, and he turned out to be correct. The Russians had communication problems and sent many messages in the clear, so that the German High Command was informed that Rennenkampf moved toward Koenigsberg—away from the German forces—and that Samsonov, urged by his superiors, was hurrying forward in the belief that he had beaten the weak German units opposing him. This decided the issue. Ludendorff and Hindenburg approved of Hoffmann's dispositions and quickly concentrated all available troops around Samsonov's Second Army, forming a half-moon facing southeast around Samsonov's center. Though François, much to Ludendorff's chagrin, did not attack as soon as he had been ordered, practically the full force of the entire German Eastern Army was launched on August 27 against Samsonov's exhausted and half-starved troops. Both his flanks were turned, and the superior Russian cavalry was employed too wide and did not play a decisive role in the battle. Even at this point, Samsonov refused to retreat and ordered his center to push northward. The result was the complete disintegration of his army on August 29 and 30. Samsonov himself, stumbling through the woods on foot, committed suicide on August 29. Nothing remained of his

Second Army. The Germans took 92,000 unwounded prisoners, and 60 trains were required to take them to the rear. Of the 600 guns, about 500 were captured. The German losses amounted to 10,000–15,000 men.

Why Rennenkampf failed to pursue the retreating Germans and help Samsonov when there was time, has never been satisfactorily explained. Some Russian leaders, because of Rennenkampf's German descent, declared him a traitor, but there has never been any proof of that, nor that he failed to help Samsonov because of a private quarrel he had with him during the Russo-Japanese War. Most likely Rennenkampf simply had lost contact with the German forces and hesitated to push forward too fast to give the Second Army a better chance to come around and cut the Germans off from the Vistula. At any rate, when he finally turned south, it was too late, and contact between the two armies was never again established. Rennenkampf now had to face the whole German Eighth Army, reinforced by the two corps from the west that had arrived too late to participate in Samsonov's disaster that became known as the Battle of Tannenberg, a small town in the Western Masurian section where 500 years before Polish and Lithuanian forces had defeated the Teutonic knights.

BATTLE OF THE MASURIAN LAKES

The second great battle in East Prussia began only a week later. The German army, now under General August von Mackensen—whose corps had been badly beaten by the Russians at Gumbinnen—attacked on September 5 while another corps under François tried to cut off Russian supply and communication lines by attacking the difficult Lake region. Rennenkampf retreated but delayed the German movements by counterattacking vigorously at the center and thereby managing to keep open his escape to the east. Even so, the demoralized Russian forces suffered great losses. Thousands were driven into the lakes and swamps of the region. In all, Rennenkampf's army suffered about 100,000 casualties and 45,000 prisoners, and the Germans advanced across the border to the Niemen River. East Prussia was free of Russian troops, but not for long; in October most of the German units had to be withdrawn to help their Austrian allies further south.

RUSSIAN ATTACKS AND AUSTRIAN-GERMAN COUNTERATTACKS IN GALICIA

The Russian commander in chief, Grand Duke Nicholas, had amassed the greater part of his forces—no less than four armies—along the Austrian border. Nevertheless, Conrad von Hoetzendorf, chief of staff

August von Mackensen, German field marshal, victor at the Masurian Lakes. Photo courtesy of the New York Public Library.

under Archduke Frederick, aggressively minded and a long-time advocate of a preventive war, planned to attack the Russians at the outset of the war, although he was also engaged in hostilities against Serbia. He argued that the Russians, who in his estimate had about 30 divisions on the Austrian border, would soon have 52 and thereby heavily outnumber his own 39 divisions. Also, since Italy's attitude at the time was doubtful, he did not want his country to get into the situation Germany found itself in: a two-front war. He therefore started a drive from Lemberg and Przemysl straight north into Russian Poland toward the heavily fortified city of Warsaw, hoping that a German drive south from East Prussia would support him and cut off all Russian forces in the great Polish salient. The aim of the Russian strategists, on the other hand, was an advance into East Prussia and into Galicia in the south, establishing a straight line between Danzig (Gdansk) and Cracow.

Neither side knew the intentions of the enemy. The commander of the southern Russian armies expected an Austrian push eastward while Hoetzendorf expected little resistance on his way via Cholm and Lublin, where he could have cut off the rail lines into Warsaw. In their first clashes with the Russians at Krasnik and Komarov at the end of August, the Austrians were successful. But Hoetzendorf had seriously underestimated Russian strength, and when, on August 30, General Alexei Brusilov, commander of the Eighth Army and Russia's most successful general, counterattacked in strength, the Austrian right collapsed and retreated in panic. On September 3, Hoetzendorf had to evacuate Lemberg, Austria's great gateway to Eastern Galicia and railroad center. Nevertheless, he persisted with the attack, ordering General Moritz von Auffenberg Komarov to engage the advancing Russians from the north—with disastrous results. Russian generalship proved quite superior to that of the Austrians. Hoetzendorf had to order general retreats, Przemysl, the great Austrian fortress west of Lemberg, was invested by the Russians in the third week of September, and all of Eastern Galicia was abandoned. The whole campaign had cost the Austrians a total of 130,000 killed, wounded and captured. Most of the latter were Slavs who had never shown much enthusiasm for the Austrian cause and felt closer to the Russians than to their German masters. The Russians advanced all the way to the Carpathians, occupied Czernowitz and by the end of September started an attack on the Carpathian passes leading into northern Hungary.

In this situation the Austrians asked their German ally for help. Hindenburg, who, since Tannenberg, had enjoyed a tremendous (probably not quite deserved) prestige, was made chief commander of all eastern German armies, and a great combined attack on the Russian armies in Poland was designed. As a result, the German armies in East Prussia had to limit themselves to a defense line along the Masurian Lakes, so that some border districts of East Prussia were again invaded by the Russians. But on October 4, the Austrian attack in Galicia was launched, and von Mackensen advanced on the Austrian left flank. By October 12 he was close to Warsaw, but he had to withdraw when the Austrians, counterattacked further east, retreated to Cracow. Przemysl, which had been relieved with the first onslaught, was besieged again, and northern Hungary was invaded a second time. A large-scale offensive was suggested by Ludendorff and Hindenburg; this would have required reinforcements from the west and was therefore rejected by the new German chief of the general staff, Falkenhayn, who was still engaged in a drive for the Channel ports (see chapter three). But the few divisions sent from the west enabled the Germans to take Lodz, southwest of Warsaw; at the same time, the Austrian offensive in the south was successful at Limonova, though the Russian positions before Cracow could not be broken.

Thus the fighting on the Russian front during the winter months was inconclusive. But in February, a second, prolonged battle was fought at the Masurian Lakes in which the Tenth Russian Army was decisively beaten by the Germans, who then also occupied Memel, an important seaport at the northernmost tip of Germany. During the following month, the Russians succeeded in retaking the city, but only for a few days, after which the Russians were driven out of Germany permanently. Simultaneously, however, they finally succeeded in occupying the great fortress of Przemysl in Galicia. With a lack of heavy siege guns on the Russian side, no assault had been possible, but the besieged Galician fortress had finally run out of supplies.

SUMMARY

The fighting in the East had shown the weaknesses of the various armies. The Austrian army had suffered from rather poor generalship and the fact that it consisted of 11 different nationalities. Most of the troops were Slavs and could not understand their German-speaking officers. The morale of the troops was severely shaken in the first months of fighting, in which the Serbian front had been deprived of troops in order to beat the Russians; but the latter had occupied Galicia and even infiltrated the great natural defense line, the Carpathian Mountains. What still held the empire together was a sentimental loyalty of all its peoples to the old emperor Francis Joseph—and German help.

The Russian position, after the end of the winter campaign, looked fairly good on paper. Their armies held more Austrian territory than the Germans did Russian. But a dismal lack of supplies became more and more apparent. About 30 times as many shells had been fired as could be produced in Russia during this period, and many other types of war supplies were critically scarce. It also became apparent that with the stabilization of the eastern front, more German units would be transferred to the east, a strategy vigorously advocated by Hindenburg and Ludendorff. The former had at one time even threatened to resign. The emperor finally gave in, and a new Tenth Army was formed, but Falkenhayn saw to it that it would not go to the northeastern front but to Galicia, partly to relieve the Austrians and partly because he hoped to cut into the southern Russian front and thereby force a Russian withdrawal from Poland.

CHRONICLE OF EVENTS

1914:

July 29: Austrians bombard Belgrade.

August 3: Grand Duke Nicholai Nicolayevich is made commander in chief of the Russian troops.

August 12: A detachment of General Rennenkampf's First Russian Army invades East Prussia.

August 13: Austrians begin the first invasion of Serbia, crossing the Drina River.

August 17–21: At the battle of the Tser and the Jadar, Serbian forces defeat the Austrians, forcing them to withdraw from Serbian territory.

August 17: Rennenkampf's First Russian Army advances in full force into Germany.

August 19–20: Battle of Gumbinnen. Rennenkampf's army defeats the German Eighth Army under General Friedrich Wilhelm von Prittwitz.

August 22: Prittwitz, who has suggested withdrawal to the Vistula River, is dismissed by Moltke and replaced by General Erich Ludendorff, who is to serve as chief of staff to General Paul von Beneckendorff und Hindenburg, who comes out of retirement.

August 23: Hindenburg and Ludendorff arrive at Marienburg, East Prussia and decide to turn against the Second Russian Army under General Alexander V. Samsonov, who has invaded East Prussia from the southeast.

August 26–30: Battle of Tannenberg. The German army surrounds and defeats Samsonov's army decisively.

August 26–September 2: In Galicia, an Austrian army under General Moritz von Auffenberg-Komarow, defeat the Russians at Zamosc, but larger Russian forces under General Alexei Brusilov drive back the Austrian right wing.

September 3: Russian armies occupy Lemberg (Lvov) in the western Ukraine.

September 6–15: In East Prussia, battle of the Masurian Lakes. German forces under General August von Mackensen attack and defeat Rennenkampf's First Army. German troops then advance to the lower Niemen River, across the border.

September 8: Austrian troops again cross the Drina River into Serbia, while the Serbs invade Austria and take Zemlin on September 10.

September 8–17: Battle of the Drina. The Serbs are ultimately forced to retreat.

September 18: Hindenburg is made commander in chief of the German armies in the east.

September 21: The Russians take Czernowitz in the Bukovina, and Jaroslav, and besiege the key fortress of Przemysl in the Carpathian foothills.

Erich Ludendorff, Hindenburg's chief of staff. After 1916 he was Germany's main strategist. Photo courtesy of the New York Public Library.

September 24: Russian armies launch an attack on the passes of the Carpathians which lead into northern Hungary.

October 4: Combined German-Austrian counterattack. The Austrians launch an offensive in Galicia, while the Germans push toward the Vistula.

October 12: German troops under Mackensen advance to Warsaw but retreat when the Russians counterattack the Austrians further east.

Early November: The Austrians retreat to Cracow.

November 10: Przemysl is again besieged by the Russians.

November 11: The German Ninth Army, under Mackensen, begins a drive southeast from Thorn (Torun).

November 15: Russian armies renew the invasion of northern Hungary.

November 16–December 2: Battle of Cracow.

November 16–25: Battles of Lodz and Lowicz.

December 2: Austrians take Belgrade.

December 5–17: Successful attack of the Austrian armies in the battle of Limanova, but Russian positions before Cracow are not broken.

December 6: Before Lodz, the Germans have received reinforcements from the west and finally take the city.

December 6: Serbian forces attack the Austrians and defeat them at Kolubara.

December 15: Belgrade is retaken by the Serbs. The Austrian troops recross the frontier, ending the second invasion of Serbia.

1915:

February 4–22: Winter battle in Masuria (East Prussia). German advance.

February 17: German troops occupy Memel (Klaypeda) in Lithuania.

February 22–27: Russian victory in the battle of Przasnysz, near Kovno (Kaunas), Lithuania.

March 18: Russians retake Memel.

March 21: Russians are again driven out of Memel.

March 22: Russians take the fortress of Przemysl, north of the Carpathians, and advance through the mountain passes into northern Hungary.

EYEWITNESS TESTIMONY

We must tackle France in the open field; we cannot involve ourselves in a prolonged war of position before her barricaded Eastern frontier . . . I am sorry that blood should flow, but Belgium has rudely rebuffed all our most far-reaching assurances . . . This war, which sets almost the whole of Europe alight, will probably cost us our fleet, but the decision will be reached on land. The spirit of our people is excellent . . . There is an angry bitterness against faithless Russia; our mobilization is developing like clockwork . . . Assemble your whole force against Russia. Even Italy cannot be such a dirty dog as to fall upon your rear. Let the Bulgarians loose against Serbia and leave the pack of them to tear each other to pieces. There must now be only one objective—Russia. Thrust the knout-carriers into the marshes of the Pripyat and drown them there.

Helmut von Moltke to Conrad von Hoetzendorf, August 5, 1914.

Count Franz Conrad von Hoetzendorf, head of the Austro-Hungarian armies. Photo courtesy of the New York Public Library.

We have taken today the first Russian battery from a cavalry brigade. The Russians attack most stupidly and are shot down everywhere . . . We already have over five hundred prisoners, who are glad to get something to eat. The Belgians are quite negligible, incapable of attack.

Moltke to Hoetzendorf, August 9, 1914.

I believe this war has come to our time and to every individual as a fiery test to make men of us all, men prepared for the terrific events in the years to come.

Otto Braun, Diary, August 18, 1914.

In Serbia, the offensive a failure . . . in East Prussia, the German army in retreat; the stroke towards Syedlets not to be counted on; Roumania has fallen away, and her intervention on the Eastern wing did not come about; Russian troops on that wing thus set free; Bulgaria and Turkey in passive expectancy; Italy tending to turn hostile; in Vienna, forces behind the scenes at work, agitating against A.O.K. [the Austrian Army Chief Command], and before us the Russian superiority of force gathering to strike an annihilating blow. Nevertheless I held fast to taking the initiative in the North, for the enemy there must be grappled, so that he should not disturb the vic-

torious advance of the German armies against France, so that the German Eastern army should not be given over to face a blow in isolation, and finally so that Russia should not gain time to gather together her full numerical superiority.

Conrad von Hoetzendorf on the situation of August 20, 1914, Memoirs.

There is not much to say about our successes compared with those of the Germans, mainly because the German victories have been gained at our expense; for of the hundred divisions which Germany is forming she has given only nine regular and three landwehr divisions to the Eastern theater. Thus the enormous weight of the Russian Army is thrown upon us. The enclosed copy of a report by Potiorek gives an authentic picture of the failure in Serbia. That a complete infantry division should simply scatter, and abandon its guns and material, was the less to be expected as our troops otherwise are everywhere fighting just as gallantly as the Germans, who are engaged not against Russians, but *only against Frenchmen.*

Conrad von Hoetzendorf, letter of August 27, 1914, in Winston Churchill, The Unknown War (1931).

In restaurants and bars, even beer is not being served any longer. Yet you always meet a lot of drunks in the streets . . . Not far from here there is a tearoom "Petrograd," the favorite hide-out for the officials and soldiers of our camp. I have been there several times and never met a single man who was not drunk. Yet, they sell no alcohol there. The solution of the puzzle is simple. Next to the tearoom there is a pharmacy where people line up to buy Eau de Cologne # 3 which was put on the market by the Ferrein Pharmacy as a war product after the sale of alcohol was forbidden. It contains fifty percent of alcohol, plus certain ingredients tasting of lemon . . . I must confess that I also tried this Eau de Cologne after I had received my pay of six rubles. I spent three rubles, half of my monthly pay . . .

J. Oskine, Russian soldier, describing the situation in Moscow, end of August 1914, Le carnet d'un soldat ("A Soldier's Notebook") (1931).

I am gradually learning what a marvelous educational institution the Prussian Army is! You cannot have any idea how intolerable it is to one's self-respect to listen to the disgusting swearing of the N.C.O.s, but combined with stable duty it is truly an incomparable schooling. You just learn to bear everything, and to pull yourself together, because you have to, I'm sure there will be times when I shall be even wearier than to-day, but does it matter?

Otto Braun, letter from Grudziadz (Graudenz), Poland, to his parents, September 21, 1914.

Even after Samsonoff's defeat Rennenkampf continued to advance, either from a misunderstanding or, deliberately, to prevent Hindenburg from striking for Warsaw . . . Rennenkampf was quick in retreat, as in advance, and the German soldiers were exhausted after their forced marches.

R.R. McCormick, referring to the fighting in East Prussia, 1914, in With the Russian Army (1915).

At yesterday's reception for foreign journalists the Oberpraesident [chief administrator of a province] submitted a survey of the war damage East Prussia has suffered: 400,000 persons have left the province, but the largest part has returned in the meantime. The Russians killed, as far as is known, 1,620 civilians, wounded 433, carried off to Russia 5,419 men, 2,587 women and 2,719 children. Many of the men

are old and helpless. Unfortunately it has to be assumed that many of these carried off persons have been killed. The number of rapes and molestations cannot be established since many of the people involved are reluctant to supply information. People of all age groups have been affected, from children to old women. Twenty-four towns, 572 villages and 236 estates have been destroyed by enemy arson.

Chronicle of the Frankfurter Zeitung: "The Great War 1914–1918."

On Christmas Day, with the roar of the cannon, in a big barn with horses shuffling and champing; sitting on a small box writing by the light of a guttering candle; opposite me a man searching his dog for lice and telling me that he found only three today—have I ever written you a letter in such romantic circumstances?

Otto Braun, letter to his parents from the eastern front, December 25, 1914.

When we marched from Kielce to the front, it seemed to me as if the world stopped where the railroad ended and the war lay in front of me, in great emptiness. Always the same picture. Simple wooden crosses along the roads, and shot up houses, still smoldering. The same tragic note repeating itself: Nothing but the lonely chimney with the stove looming up, like a sad, forsaken fellow waiting for the return of his loved ones. And a second thing is repeated every evening: the retreating Russians set fire to villages and especially bridges . . .

Peter Frenzel, German student, letter from the Russian front, 1915. Quoted in War Letters of Fallen Students (1929).

One of the marvelous things abut war is that the elementary, primitive and simple reigns not only over our minds and spirit, but permeates all things down to the very smallest. It is only now that we find out what home and hearth and all those objects of daily use . . . mean, what they actually consist of, stripped of all ephemeral ornamentation, it is only now, when we have to make them ourselves, that we discover it. . . . War, which was for our ancestors the fulfilment of their romantic passions, yea, the ideal of romanticism, is for us a sublime fate, an inevitable necessity . . .

Otto Braun, letter to his parents from the eastern front, January 17, 1915.

This war, however far-reaching its consequences, does not seem to me to be one single event. It is part of our present age, so that one will have to say: This age began with the war which stamped the whole character of the period. A surging age is being born. . . . A new world is coming to life! Thus, in the wars of Alexander was Hellenism born . . . the bourgeois world in the Napoleonic wars, and our age . . . will bring forth with tremendous convulsions the unprecedented and unforeseen.

Otto Braun, letter to his parents from the eastern front, February 1, 1915.

When we arrived at the Nida river, after marching some days, there were some cases of cholera in our regiment. The villages we had been passing through had been occupied by Austrian troops one month ago, and the inhabitants claimed that the cholera had appeared already when the Austrians were there. . . . Samfarov warned us not to eat fresh pork or fowl, and advised to drink only boiled water with a few drops of lemon juice mixed in. We should keep meticulously clean and wash our hands before eating . . . How could such measures help when, for instance, my detachment of forty men had only a ramshackled house to stay in, where we slept on the ground, pressed together like herrings? . . . The doctors displayed an exemplary devotion, particularly Blum who had been made the chief medic. When he noticed me he gave me some advice: Eat as much as possible, first of all, not just the soldier's ratio, eat boiled pork or roast and drink plenty of tea, and never leave the stomach empty. When I objected that all this was contrary to the official orders posted near us, he laughed and said that this stupid order of Samfarov's had been put up over his protest.

J. Oskine, Galicia, 1915, Le carnet d'un soldat.

Our situation was worsened because at least one third of our men had no rifles . . . At this moment, not only rifles, but also ammunition was missing. A short while ago, when we marched through Galicia and constantly expected to meet the enemy, every soldier was supposed to have not just the regular amount of 120 cartridges, but much more. Sometimes, everyone of us had up to 300 cartridges. They weigh almost one pud [16.4 kg]. On those long marches, these heavy loads bothered the men. To remedy the situation they threw the cartridges into the ditches where no one picked them up. . . . When the soldiers rested for the night somewhere, they took the rifles apart and used the butts to build a fire. I have done this myself several times, to warm us up and to boil water for tea . . . So now, during the retreat from Galicia, many of the soldiers go into a fight without weapons. They wait for the dead and the wounded to acquire a rifle.

J. Oskine, on fighting in Galicia, 1915, Le carnet d'un soldat.

I cannot tell you . . . how wonderful I feel in the trenches. The feeling of danger and the first baptism of fire has a tremendous fascination. In spite of all the horror that accompanies it, the gruesome unburied dead, the destruction and desolation everywhere, this combat does make life so much more intense. Believe me, never have I more ardently wished to go on living, never have I felt the beauty of life more deeply than now, when for the first time . . . I look into the face of death. Life is incomplete without death . . .

Otto Braun, letter to his parents from the eastern front, March 25, 1915.

As the battalion that we are to replace is back . . . , we "need" not go there any more; instead of that, we shall get the honorable task of repairing the road! I tell you honestly that I sometimes think of joining the infantry if this goes on: drover, mender, but never soldier.

Otto Braun, letter to his parents from Poland, March 25, 1915.

We marched into the mountains . . . But the inhabitants, and the houses! All wooden log-cabins where people and cattle live together with lice and fleas. Only the jews stand out a little by their somewhat greater humanity though they are still running around in their habits and with their long beards. Yet they take all the money from our soldiers as long as they have any, though they have come to protect them from the Russians. . . . Of course, we are not here for the fun of it, but to throw the Russians out of Galicia; that will not be easy, because of the mountains and rivers. But all our boys are full of enthusiasm. We all have the intention to make them run and then make an end to it. Today we move into position. Then the order will come to attack . . .

Ernst Guenther Schallert, German student, letter from Plarona, Galicia, April 1915, in War Letters of Fallen Students *(1929).*

Hindenburg has undertaken two offensives against Russia, to cripple her long enough to get time to finish France. The first time he was glad to get across the frontier with his army, the second time he met a far more bloody repulse than Cold Harbor [General Ulysses S. Grant's defeat in June 1864].

R.R. McCormick, referring to the German-Russian battles in 1914 and early 1915, in With the Russian Army *(1915).*

5. The Mediterranean Area: July 1914 to the End of 1916

The Historical Context

Even before the great armies at the western and eastern fronts had begun their action, some dramatic and, in the long run, extremely important events had taken place in the Mediterranean.

TURKEY'S NEUTRALITY

Both Britain and France depended on control of the Mediterranean for communication with their African colonies, and Russia would, in case of war, need the Dardanelles Straits more than ever to have an all-year open outlet to the sea. But the Dardanelles were in Turkish hands, and in July 1914 it was not known on which side Turkey would stand in case of an open conflict. England had been the traditional protector of the weak old Ottoman Empire, but of late had tired of depending on "scandalous, crumbling, decrepit, penniless Turkey," as Winston Churchill, First Lord of the Admiralty, had put it. William Gladstone, the leader of the Liberal opposition had appealed to the world to condemn Turkish atrocities, and the Liberal British government, in power since 1906, pursued a decidedly anti-Turkish policy. Germany, on the other hand, had cultivated friendly relations with Turkey for some time and in July 1914 became quite anxious to secure an ally who could cut off Russia from English and French supplies. On August 1, a secret offensive and defensive alliance between the two powers was concluded, under the auspices of the strong man in the Turkish cabinet, war minister Enver Pasha. But Turkey hesitated to fight against England and France, both of which had powerful naval units in the Mediterranean, while Germany was far away. Two events decided the Turkish decision with far-reaching consequences: The first was that

Sir Winston Churchill, first lord of the British admiralty in 1915. Photo courtesy of the New York Public Library.

England seized two Turkish battleships in the British yards where they were built. Apparently, the British feared that these ships could turn out on the wrong side when war broke out. The second was the role that two German warships played during the first week of August.

The French had the largest fleet in the Mediterranean and needed it to transport their colonial troops from the African ports of Bone, Philippeville and Algiers to Toulon and Marseilles. The bulk of the British fleet had recently been stationed at Scapa Flow in the Orkney Islands, but the British Mediterranean fleet, stationed at Malta and headed by three battle cruisers, was also considerable. The Germans had only two warships, the battle cruiser *Goeben*—as large as a Dreadnought— and the light cruiser *Breslau;* both were modern, well-equipped ships, under the command of Admiral Wilhelm Souchon. The Austrian fleet included two Dreadnought ships which were stationed at Pola, at the northern end of the Adriatic, and would remain inactive.

GERMAN WARSHIPS DECIDE THE ISSUE

The Western Allies expected Souchon to interfere with French troop movements and then to turn west, and the First Lord of the Admiralty, Winston Churchill, was anxious to have the two German ships followed and attacked as soon as possible. But Britain was not yet officially in the war and also had to reckon with interference from the Austrian fleet. Souchon had his own troubles as the *Goeben* was due for boiler repair, and Italian ports refused to coal his ships—the first indication that Germany could not rely on Italy as an ally. Still, Souchon managed to get some supplies from a German merchant boat and was proceeding west to the French ports when he received orders from Admiral Tirpitz to head for Constantinople. The idea was to exert pressure on the Turks to join actively on the German side. Souchon did not immediately obey, but proceeded to shell Philippeville and Bone after running up a Russian flag—a clear violation of international laws. He was repeatedly sighted by British ships, but the British admiral, Sir Berkeley Milne, was slow in pursuing him, even after England had officially entered into the war and assumed wrongly that Souchon was heading west or moving up the Adriatic toward Pola, the Austrian strong point.

Only a small British squadron under Admiral Ernest Charles Troubridge followed the Germans, and they did not dare to attack until, on August 7, near the Greek coast, the British light cruiser *Gloucester* attacked both ships; after some shots were exchanged, the *Gloucester* dropped back and was then ordered by Admiral Milne not to pursue any further. The two German ships could again refuel in the Greek Isles, and although Tirpitz had withdrawn his instructions, Souchon decided on his own to proceed to Costantinople. Close to the Dardanelles, which were guarded by mine fields, he asked the Turkish government for permission to enter. After some hesitation, Enver granted the permission, also assuring the German military representative that any British warships following the Germans would be fired upon. On August 10, a Turkish destroyer led the two boats through the Dardanelles.

At first, the Turks, still maintaining a semblance of neutrality, insisted that the German ships be disarmed but then agreed to buy the two boats as a substitute for the two battleships confiscated in England.

Churchill, furious at the failure of the vastly superior British fleet to deal with the Germans, suggested sending a torpedo flotilla through the Dardanelles to sink the two boats—as had already been proposed by French general Joseph Gallieni—but was vetoed by Lord Kitchener, who was afraid to alienate the Muslim world by such an act of violence.

For three months, the Allies tried to come to terms with Turkey; Russia was even prepared to renounce Constantinople—which they had called "Tzargrad" for some time—while the German military influence in Constantinople increased from day to day. By the end of October, Berlin felt Turkey's active participation had become imperative, and on October 28 the two warships, provided with Turkish names but under Souchon's command, entered the Black Sea and shelled three Russian ports. Now there was no way back, and Russia, Britain and France declared war on Turkey.

The result was that for imports Russia was left dependent on the ports of Arkangelsk (which was icebound for half the year) and Vladivostok (which was 8,000 miles away). Russian exports and imports almost immediately dropped by about 95%. Without the daring cruise of the *Goeben* and the *Breslau*, Turkey may never have sided with the Central Powers, and the extremely costly and unsuccessful Gallipoli campaign and the difficult, long-lasting Allied campaigns in Mesopotamia, Suez and what was then known as Palestine would probably have been unnecessary.

THE BRITISH DARDANELLES EXPEDITION

But Churchill had not given up on subduing Turkey by direct attack. When, in January 1915, Grand Duke Nicholas appealed for help from the British to provide relief from Turkish pressure the war council in London decided on naval action against the Dardanelles, in the hope that a joint action of the British and French fleets would be sufficient to destroy the Turkish forts on the Gallipoli peninsula, west of the straits, so they could eventually occupy Constantinople. Such a campaign, if successful, would have knocked out the Turkish Empire, swayed the Balkan states, killed all attempts of the Turks to seize the Suez Canal and provided Russia with much needed supplies. However, the Russians, though repeatedly urged by Churchill, declined to cooperate by launching a local offensive, since they were fully occupied at the eastern front, and while Greek prime minister Eleutherios Venizelos offered help, he was opposed by King Constantine of Greece and forced to resign. Probably the Russians would have been opposed to Greek participation anyway because they suspected the Greeks to be interested in Constantinople themselves.

Naval action began on February 19, when the Dardanelles were bombed, and the Greek island of Lemnos was occupied. The outer forts of the peninsula were old and outranged by the warships, and the Turkish howitzers were rather ineffective. Yet a month later, when British Admiral John de Robeck tried to force the Narrows with 18 warships, it turned out that the minesweeping actions preceding the attack had been woefully insufficient. Several warships were struck and sunk, and de Robeck decided that ships alone could not force the passage. The Turks, outgunned and almost down to their last shells, were amazed to see the Allied fleets withdraw. The element of surprise was lost, and while Kitchener had a force of about 70,000 men—mainly Australians and New Zealanders—the Turks had increased their troops from two to six divisions (about 100,000 men). German

General Otto Liman von Sanders was placed in overall command of the Turkish forces, and he immediately updated and strengthened the Turkish defenses.

The Allied invasion forces landed on several points of the peninsula and on the Asiatic side of the straits, but the commander, British general Ian Hamilton, soon lost control and never established sufficient coordination. The Turks put up heroic resistance and managed to keep the various units from reaching the heights. It was here that Mustafa Kemal, a young colonel who later became president of the Turkish Republic, rose to prominence. By strengthening the critically important ridges of Chunk and Sari Bair, he succeeded in holding off the initial onslaught of Anzac (Australian and New Zealand Army Corps) troops at the last moment. Operations at Cape Helles, the southern end of the peninsula, were equally uncoordinated. Instead of overrunning the Turkish positions, the troops began to dig in, and the next few months produced a stalemate. By then, the Allies were outnumbered by 15 Turkish divisions, and Hamilton attempted to cut the Turks off by landing at Suvla Bay with the help of five additional, newly arrived British divisions. Again, the strategically sound plan was poorly executed, the general in charge (Sir Frederick Stopford) being unfamiliar with the situation. In the meantime, several British warships had been sunk by hostile submarines, and the one raid Allied submarines staged on Constantinople did not change the situation.

By late autumn, the British government realized that there was no hope of success. Hamilton was recalled and his successor, Sir Charles Munro, called for an immediate evacuation. This operation, which was expected to be very costly, was the only operation executed efficiently during the whole campaign. All troops were withdrawn without a single loss of life. But the entire unfortunate operation had cost the Allies about 250,000 casualties out of a total number of 480,000 troops committed. Turkish losses were probably even higher—but the Straits remained closed.

ITALY JOINS THE ALLIES

While the Gallipoli campaign was under way, the decision on the other unknown element in the Mediterranean—Italy—had also fallen. From the outset, Italy had claimed that Austria was the aggressor against Serbia and that joining the Central Powers would therefore be incompatible with the terms of the Triple Alliance. But at the same time, Italy claimed under the terms of the same treaty the right to receive compensation to counterbalance Austrian expansion in the Balkans. In Berlin, the government was willing to make concessions to keep Italy at least neutral, and in December 1914, former chancellor Bernhard von Bülow, on a special mission to Rome, recognized the

Italian right to the Trentino. But Austrian foreign minister Count Berchtold rejected all concessions. When Berchtold was replaced by the less adamant Count Stephen Burian, Italy extended its demands to South Tyrol and other territories and, at the same time, started negotiating with the Allies about joining their side. When, in May of 1915, the Germans had finally persuaded their Austrian ally to accept the Italian conditions, it was too late, as a secret treaty between Italy, England, France and Russia had already been concluded. Italian prime minister Antonio Salandra, a convinced interventionist, who had recently been supported by Benito Mussolini (then editor of the Socialist newspaper *Avanti*), had won out over former prime minister Giovanni Giolitti, who advocated neutrality. The Allies, stalled at the western front, were ready to offer a great deal, in spite of Russian opposition to the assignment of the Dalmatian coast to Italy because of Serbia's designs on that region. In the final agreement, South Tyrol, Trentino, Gorizia, Trieste, Istria, most Dalmatian Islands and some other territories were promised to Italy—as well as full sovereignty in the Dodecanese Islands already occupied by Italy and a share in the German colonies. Italy was also given a loan and the promise of a part of the war indemnities expected after victory, and finally diplomatic support was promised in case the pope should intervene in favor of a compromise peace. In May 1915, Italy first denounced the Triple Alliance and then declared war on Austria-Hungary.

THE ISONZO FRONT

Yet the country was poorly prepared to enter the world conflict. When Supreme Commander Luigi Cadorna took over in July 1914, he discovered that plans had been worked out only for defense. Because of the utter secrecy of the negotiations on both sides, the military staff was only informed of the change of alliance in May 1915. Also, the Italian belief that Austria had been almost knocked out by Russia was quite erroneous. After the Russian defeat at Gorlice, more Austrian troops were transferred to the Italian front. Still Italy, with only one front to fight on, had a numerical superiority of about four to three at this front but suffered from ammunition shortage early on.

The Italian-Austrian front ran through the Alps, and both sides attempted to push to the open plains on either side. Neither succeeded until 1917. The main battles were fought along the Isonzo River, a front only about 60 miles long. During 1915, four battles were fought there, the first two in July, the last two in winter. But Cadorna never managed to advance more than 10–12 miles. The Austrian troops, under Archduke Eugene, were more willing to fight the Italians than the Russians; Italy was the national enemy to the Slavs in the Austrian Empire because of its designs on Dalmatia, whose population was

Erich von Falkenhayn, commander of the German forces in France, 1915–1916. Photo courtesy of the German Information Center, New York City.

mostly Slav. During the year, the Italians never managed to take either of the two important bridgeheads held by the Austrians, Gorizia and Tolmino.

After the fifth Isonzo battle, which lasted over a month, and in which the Italians again failed to gain anything substantial, Austrian Supreme Commander Conrad von Hoetzendorf tried to induce the German high command to organize an attack in the Trentino on the Italian rear and flank. But Germany was not yet at war with Italy, and Falkenhayn needed all available troops for his offensive at Verdun. Therefore, the Austrians attempted an offensive in the Trentino by themselves and advanced to Asiago and Arsiero by the end of May 1916. But they lacked sufficient troops, and in a counteroffensive during the following month, the Italians recovered most of the lost territory, though under severe losses. In the sixth battle of the Isonzo, they finally managed to take the one bridgehead at Gorizia and immediately thereafter declared war on Germany, apparently concerned that Italy would be left out in the forthcoming partition of the Turkish Empire. Three more battles were fought on the Isonzo River in 1916, without tangible results; but by engaging the Germans, Italy had invited disaster in the year to come.

CHRONICLE OF EVENTS

1914:

August 3: The German cruisers *Goeben* and *Breslau* under Admiral Wilhelm Souchon bombard the ports of Bone and Philippeville in French Africa.

August 6: Goeben and *Breslau* evade a British squadron north of Messina by using the southern end of the Straits.

August 11: Both ships arrive at the Dardanelles and are permitted to enter.

October 29: Turkish warships, including the renamed *Goeben* and *Breslau*, bombard Odessa, Sevastopol and other Russian Black Sea ports.

November 2: Russia declares war on Turkey.

November 5: Britain and France declare war on Turkey. Britain announces the annexation of

Wilhelm Souchon, German admiral, who led two German warships to Constantinople in August 1914. Photo courtesy of the German Information Center, New York City.

the island of Cyprus which it had occupied since 1878.

November 14: The Sultan, as Khalif, proclaims a Holy War (*Jihad*) against all nations waging war against Turkey or its allies.

December 18: The British proclaim a protectorate over Egypt, occupied since 1882.

1915:

Early January: Russia appeals to England for action in the Mediterranean to relieve Turkish pressure.

February 19: Beginning of the British naval action against the Dardanelles.

February 23: British forces occupy the island of Lemnos as a base for the Dardanelles operations.

March 4: Russian foreign minister Sergei Sazonov, in a note to the British and French representatives, claims Constantinople for Russia in the event of a successful campaign in the Dardanelles.

March 18: The British Navy, under Admiral John de Robeck, attempts to force the Dardanelles Narrows with 18 warships, but gives up after four ships strike mines.

April 25: Landing of British, New Zealand and Australian troops at several places on the Dardanelles peninsula with devastating losses.

April 26: Secret treaty between England, France, Russia and Italy regarding Italian intervention on the side of the Entente.

May 3: Italy denounces the Triple Alliance.

May 10: Naval convention between England, France and Italy.

May 12: Hostile submarines sink three British warships in the Dardanelles Straits.

May 23: Italy declares war on Austria-Hungary.

May 24: Germany severs relations with Italy.

June 29–July 7: First battle of the Isonzo River.

July 18–August 10: Second battle of the Isonzo.

August 6: British forces land at Suvla, in order to cut behind Turkish position at the Narrows.

August 6–10: Battle of Sari Bair. The Turks hold their positions against British attacks.

October 16: Sir Ian Hamilton, British commander at the Dardanelles, is replaced by Sir Charles Munro, who prepares for evacuation.

October 18–November 3: Third battle of the Isonzo.

November 10–December 10: Fourth battle of the Isonzo.

December 19–January 9, 1916: British and Anzac forces are withdrawn from the Gallipoli peninsula without losses.

1916:

February 15–March 17: Fifth battle of the Isonzo, leading to no substantial change.

May 15–June 3: Austrian offensive in the Trentino sector.

May 31: Austrian troops take Asiago and Arsiero.

June 17–July 7: Italian counteroffensive, recovering most of the lost territory.

August 6–17: Sixth battle of the Isonzo. The Italians take the bridgehead at Gorizia.

August 28: Italy declares war on Germany.

September 14–18: Seventh battle of the Isonzo.

October 9–12: Eighth battle of the Isonzo.

October 31–November 4: Ninth battle of the Isonzo, still without tangible results.

EYEWITNESS TESTIMONY

Assume command of squadron off Dardanelles. Your sole duty is to sink *Goeben* and *Breslau* if they come out no matter what flag they fly. We are not at war with Turkey but Admiral Souchon is now Commander-in-Charge Turkish Navy and Germans are largely controlling it.

Winston Churchill, telegram to Vice-Admiral S.H. Carden, mid-September 1914.

The Grand Duke Nicholas . . . has asked if it would be possible for Lord Kitchener to arrange for a demonstration of some kind against the Turks elsewhere, either naval or military, and to so spread reports as to cause the Turks, who he says are very liable to go off at a tangent, to withdraw some of the forces now acting against the Russians in the Caucasus, and thus ease the position of the Russians.

Sir George Buchanan, British ambassador in Petrograd, in a letter to Lord Kitchener, end of December 1914, in Alan Moorehead, Gallipoli *(1956).*

The only place that a demonstration might have some effect in stopping Turkish reinforcements going east would be the Dardanelles. Particularly if, as the Grand Duke says, reports could be spread at the same time that Constantinople was being threatened.

Lord Kitchener, letter to Churchill, January 2, 1915, discussing actions to help the Russians, in Alan Moorehead, Gallipoli *(1956).*

Lord Kitchener thought the plan worth trying. We could leave off the bombardment if it did not prove effective . . . The Admiralty should prepare for a naval expedition in February to bombard and attack the Gallipoli Peninsula with Constantinople as its objective.

Minutes of the London War Council of January 13, 1915.

We were fired at from all directions. One saw stabs of light in the hills and in the direction of the 6-inch battery covering the minefields on both sides of the straits, followed by the whine of little shells, the bursting of shrapnel, and the scream of heavy projectiles which threw up fountains of water. It was a pretty sight. The fire was very wild, and the *Canopus* was not hit, but for all the good we did towards dousing the searchlights we might just as well have been firing at the moon.

Roger Keyes, Admiral Carden's chief of staff, about the naval attack on March 10, in Alan Moorehead, Gallipoli *(1956).*

I do not understand why minesweepers should be interfered with by firing which causes no casualties. Two or three hundred casualties would be a moderate price to pay for sweeping up as far as the Narrows. I highly approve your proposal to obtain volunteers from the Fleet for minesweeping. This work has to be done whatever the loss of life and small craft . . . Secondly, we have information that the Turkish forts are short of ammunition, that the German officers have made despondent reports and have appealed to Germany for more . . . it is being seriously considered to send a German or an Austrian submarine, but apparently they have not started yet. Above is absolutely secret. All this makes it clear that the operation should now be pressed forward methodically and resolutely at night and day . . . The enemy is harassed and anxious now. The time is precious . . .

Winston Churchill, telegram to Admiral Carden, March 14, 1915.

I do not intend to commence in bad weather leaving result undecided as from experience on first day I am convinced given favorable weather conditions that the reduction of the forts at the entrance can be completed in one day.

Admiral Carden, message to the Admiralty before the attack on March 18.

I had a most indelible impression that we were in the presence of a beaten foe. I thought he was beaten at 2 P.M., I knew he was beaten at 4 P.M., and at midnight I knew with still greater certainty that he was absolutely beaten; and it only remained for us to organize a proper sweeping force and devise some means of dealing with the drifting mines to reap the fruits of our efforts. I felt the guns of the forts and batteries and the concealed howitzers and mobile field guns were no longer a menace.

Roger Keyes, de Robeck's chief of staff, on the naval attack on March 18, 1915 in Alan Moorehead, Gallipoli *(1956).*

Let them dare to destroy the embassy. I'll get even with them. If they fire a single shot at it we'll blow up the French and the British Embassies. Go tell the British Admiral that, won't you? Tell him also that we have the dynamite ready to do it.

Baron von Wangenheim, German ambassador at Constantinople, to Henry Morganthau, the American ambassador, after the British attack on March 18, 1915.

So I said good-bye to old K. (Lord Kitchener) as casually as if we were to meet together at dinner . . . He did not even wish me luck and I did not expect him to, but he did say, rather unexpectedly, *after* I had said good-bye and just as I was taking up my cap from the table, "If the Fleet gets through, Constantinople will fall of itself and you will have won, not a battle, but the war."

General Sir Ian Hamilton, appointed commander in chief for the Gallipoli expedition, in his diary, March 1915.

I am most reluctantly driven to the conclusion that the straits are not likely to be forced by battleships, as at one time seemed probable, and that, if my troops are to take part, it will not take the subsidiary form anticipated. The Army's part will be more than mere landing parties to destroy forts; it must be a deliberate and prepared military operation, carried out at full strength, so as to open a passage for the Navy.

General Hamilton to Lord Kitchener, March 19, 1915, in Alan Moorehead, Gallipoli.

During the battle I had cabled that the chances of the Navy pushing through on their own were hardly fair fighting chances, but since then de Robeck, the man who should know, had twice said that he *did* think there was a fair fighting chance. Had he stuck to the opinion . . . then I was ready, as a soldier, to make light of military croaks about troop-ships . . . But once the Admiral said his battleships could not fight through without help, there was no foothold left for the views of a landsman.

General Hamilton, diary, after the battle of March 18.

We have not got through the Narrows, and some sceptical critics are asking what we should do if we got through to Constantinople, without a land force. It is a great scheme, if it comes off; and the only begetter of it, if report is true, is Mr. Winston Chur-

chill, the strategist of the Antwerp expedition, who now aspires to be the Dardanelson of our age.

Punch, London, March 1915.

I regarded it as only the first of several days' fighting, though the loss in ships sunk or disabled was unpleasant. It never occurred to me for a moment that we should not go on . . . till we had reached a decision one way or another. I found Lord Fisher and Sir Arthur Wilson in the same mood . . . For the first time since the war began, high words were used around the octagonal table . . .

Churchill in his report to the Dardanelles Commission, 1916.

There was a fever of excitement about the 'Constantinople Expedition' among the young men in England. It's too wonderful for belief. I had not imagined Fate could be so kind . . . Will Hero's Tower crumble under the 15-inch guns? Shall I loot mosaics from St. Sophia, and Turkish Delight and carpets? Should we be a Turning Point in History? . . . I suddenly realize that the ambition of my life has been—since I was two—to go on a military expedition against Constantinople.

Rupert Brooke, English poet, setting out on the Dardanelles expedition in 1915, in Alan Moorehead, Gallipoli.

Even more than in the Fleet I find in the Air Force the profound conviction that, if they only could get into direct touch with Winston Churchill, all would be well. Their faith in the First Lord is, in every sense, touching. But they can't get the contact and they are thoroughly imbued with the idea that the Sea Lords are at best half-hearted; at the worst, actively antagonistic to us and the whole of our enterprise.

General Hamilton in his diary, 1915.

Once in a generation a mysterious wish for war passes through the people. Their instinct tells them that *there is no other way* of progress and of escape from habits that no longer fit them. Whole generations of statesmen will fumble over reform for a lifetime which are put into full-blooded execution within a week of a declaration of war . . . Only by intense sufferings can the nations grow . . .

General Hamilton in his diary, 1915.

Captain, you must either send up reinforcements and drive the enemy into the sea or let us evacuate this place because it is absolutely certain that they will land more troops tonight. Send the doctors to carry off my wounded. Alas alas, Captain, for God's sake send me reinforcements because hundreds of soldiers are landing. Hurry! What on earth will happen, Captain?

Turkish message captured on April 26, 1915 at Cape Helles at the southern tip of the Gallipoli peninsula, in Alan Moorehead, Gallipoli.

Both my divisional generals and brigadiers have represented to me that they fear their men are thoroughly disorganized by shrapnel fire to which they have been subjected all day after exhaustion and gallant work in the morning. Numbers have dribbled back from the firing line and cannot be collected in this difficult country. Even the New Zealand Brigade which has only recently been engaged, lost heavily and is, to some extent, demoralized. If troops are subjected to shell fire again tomorrow morning there is likely to be a fiasco, as I have no fresh troops to replace those in the firing line. I know my representation is most serious, but if we are to reembark it must be at once.

General Sir William Birdwood to his commander in chief Hamilton, after the fighting on April 26, 1915, in Alan Moorehead, Gallipoli.

Your news is indeed serious. But there is nothing for it but to dig yourselves right in and stick it out. It would take at least two days to reembark as Admiral Thursby will explain to you . . . Make a personal appeal to your men and General Godley's to make a supreme effort to hold their ground. P.S. You have got through the difficult business, now you have only to dig, dig, dig, until you are safe.

General Ian Hamilton to Birdwood, April 27, 1915, in Alan Moorehead, Gallipoli.

One fresh man on Gallipoli today was worth five afloat on the Mediterranean or fifty loafing around London in the Central forces. At home they are carefully totting up figures—I know them—and explaining to the P.M. [Prime Minister] . . . with some complacency that the 60,000 effective bayonets left me are enough—seeing they are British—to overthrow the Turkish Empire. So they would if I had that number, or anything like it, for my line of battle. But what are the facts? Exactly one half of my "bayonets" spend the whole night carrying water, ammunition and supplies between the beach and the firing line. The other half . . . , those left in the firing line, are up the whole night armed mostly with spades digging desperately into the earth. Now and then there is a hell of a fight, but that is incidental and a relief.

General Ian Hamilton in his diary, end of April 1915.

If you could only spare me two fresh divisions organized as a corps, I could push on with great hopes of success both from Cape Helles [in the South] and Gaba Tepe [in the north of the peninsula]; otherwise I am afraid we shall degenerate into trench warfare with its resultant slowness.

Hamilton, message to Kitchener, around May 8, 1915.

A combative grimness had taken place of his Lord Fisher's usual genial greeting; the lower lip of his set mouth thrust forward, and the droop at the corner was more marked than usual . . . "I have resigned" was his greeting, and on my inquiring the reason he replied "I can stand it no longer." He then informed that he was on his way to see the Prime Minister, having made up his mind to take no further part in the Dardanelles 'foolishness,' and was off to Scotland that night.

David Lloyd George, on Lord Fisher's resignation, May 16, 1915, in Alan Moorehead, Gallipoli.

The question whether we can long support two fields of operation draining on our resources requires grave consideration. I know that I can rely on you to do your utmost to bring the present unfortunate state of affairs in the Dardanelles to as early a conclusion as possible, so that any consideration of a withdrawal, with all its dangers in the East, may be prevented from entering the field of possible solutions.

Kitchener to Hamilton, May 19, 1915.

K. [Kitchener] tells me Egypt is mine and the fatness thereof; yet no sooner do I make the most modest suggestion concerning anything or anyone Egyptian than K. is got at and I find he is the Barmecide and I Schac'abac.

General Hamilton, in his diary, around May 20, 1915, referring to a story in the Arabian Nights in which empty dishes are served to a hungry man.

Then the fearful smell of death began as we came upon scattered bodies. We mounted over a plateau and down through gullies filled with thyme, where there lay about 4,000 Turkish dead. It was indescribable. One was grateful for the rain and the grey sky. A turkish Red Crescent man came and gave me some antiseptic wool with scent on it . . .

Captain Aubrey Herbert, on Gaba Tepe beach in the north of the peninsula, during a truce, May 24, 1915, quoted in Alan Moorehead, Gallipoli.

I am much surprised at the change in Winston Churchill. He looks years older, he seems very depressed and to feel keenly his retirement from the Admiralty . . . he suddenly burst forth into a tremendous discourse on the Expedition and what might have been, addressed directly across the table in the form of a lecture to his mother, who listened most attentively. Winston seemed unconscious of the limited number of his audience, and continued quite heedless of those around him. He insisted over and over again that the battle of March 18th had never been fought to a finish, and, had it been, the Fleet must have got through the Narrows. This is the great obsession of his mind, and will ever remain so . . .

Ellis Ashmead-Bartlett, British war correspondent, in his diary, end of May 1915.

Mingling among them all is the wily Greek, avaricious and plausible, making much money out of both of the others [the French and the British], having every sort of commodity from onions to Turkish Delight and Beecham's Pills.

Admiral Wemyss, governor of the island of Imbros, describing conditions at Mudros, Imbros' harbor, during the Gallipoli campaign, June 1915, in Alan Moorehead, Gallipoli.

I missed the gate and hit the net. I was brought up from eighty feet to forty-five feet in three seconds, but luckily only thrown fifteen degrees off my course. There was a tremendous noise, scraping, banging, tearing and rumbling, and it sounded as if there were two distinct obstructions, as the noise nearly ceased and then came on again, and we were appreciably checked twice. It took about twenty seconds to get through.

British submarine commander Boyle, describing breaking the steel net drawn across the straits by the Germans, July 1915.

A purely passive defence is not possible for us, it implies losing ground by degrees—and we have not a yard to lose . . . But to expect us to attack without giving us fair share—on Western standards—of high explosive and howitzers shows lack of military imagination . . . If only [Kitchener] would come and see for himself! Failing that—if only it were possible for me to run home and put my own case.

General Hamilton, diary, July 1915.

In two months' fighting in Gallipoli our casualties have largely exceeded those sustained by us during the whole of the Boer War. And financial purists may be pardoned for their protest against extravagant expenditures in view of the announcement that the war is now costing us well over three millions daily.

Punch, London, July 1915.

The one next to me was Sir Frederick Stopford, a man of great kindliness and personal charm, whose conversation at lunch left me at the end of the meal completely without hope of victory at Suvla. The reason . . . was his inability to quash the new General opposite who . . . was holding forth almost truculently about the folly of the plan of operations drawn up by the General Staff . . . I longed for Sir Frederick to rebuke his disagreeable and discouraging junior; but he was deprecating, courteous, fatherly, anything except the commander of an army corps which had been entrusted with a major operation that might change the whole course of the war . . . in twenty-four hours.

Compton Mackenzie in his memoirs on General Stopford, commander of the Suvla campaign, August 1915.

How long the Fifth Army can hold the enemy is more than I can prophesy. If no ammunition comes through from Germany, it can only be a question of a short time . . . it is a matter of life and death. The opinion of the Turkish General Headquarters appears to me to incline to a hazardous optimism.

Admiral von Usedom, German commander of the defenses of the Dardanelles, letter to Emperor William II on July 30, 1915.

I had seen Enver in many moods, but the unbridled rage which Sir Edward's [Grey's] admonition now caused was something entirely new. As I read the telegram his face became livid, and he absolutely lost control of himself. The European polish which Enver had sedulously acquired dropped like a mask; I now saw him for what he really was—a savage, bloodthirsty Turk. "They shall never come back," he shouted, "I shall let them stay until they rot. I would like to see those English touch me." And he added, "Don't ever threaten me." In the end, however, he calmed down and agreed that the hostages could come back to Constantinople.

Henry Morgenthau's report on his talk to Enver Bey, who had sent British captives to Gallipoli, which was constantly bombed by the British. Grey stated that Enver and his ministers would be held personally responsible for any injury to these hostages. In Alan Moorehead, Gallipoli.

Just been ashore where I found all quiet. No rifle fire, no artillery fire, and apparently no Turks. IX Corps resting. Feel confident that golden opportunities are being lost and look upon situation as serious.

British Colonel Aspinall, message to General Hamilton after a visit on Suvla, August 8, 1915.

. . . then off we dashed, all hand in hand, a most perfect advance . . . At the top we met the Turks; Le Marchand was down, a bayonet through his heart. I got one through the leg, and then for what appeared to be ten minutes, we fought hand to hand, we bit and fisted, and used rifles and pistols as clubs; and then the Turks turned and fled, and I felt a very proud man; the key of the whole peninsula was ours, and our losses had not been so great for such a result. Below I saw the straits . . . As I looked round I saw that we were not being supported, and I thought I could help best by going after those who had retreated in front of us. We dashed down towards Maidos, but had only got about 100 feet down when suddenly our own Navy put twelve-inch monitor shells into us, and all was terrible confusion. It was a deplorable disaster; we were obviously mistaken for Turks, and we had to get back . . .

British Major Allanson, on the attack on Anzac Ridge, August 8, 1915, in Alan Moorehead, Gallipoli.

Message: An attack has been ordered on Chunuk-Bair. To whom should I give this order? I am looking for the battalion commanders, but I cannot find them. Everything is in a muddle.

Message: I have received no information about what is going on. All the officers are killed and wounded.

I do not even know the name of the place where I am. I request in the name of the safety of the nation that an officer be appointed who knows the area well.

Messages received by Turkish commander Lieutenant-Colonel Potrih at Chunuk Bair, on top of the Northern Ridge, August 9, 1915, in Alan Moorehead, Gallipoli.

We found Stopford about four or five hundred yards to the east of Ghazi Baba, busy with a part of a Field Company of engineers supervising the building of some splinterproof headquarters huts for himself and his staff. He was absorbed in the work, and he said it would be well to make a thorough good job of the dug-outs as we should probably be here for a very long time . . . As to this morning's hold-up, Stopford took it very philosophically.

General Hamilton in his diary, after the British attack on Tekke Tepe Ridge had failed disastrously on August 9, 1915.

If you deem it necessary to replace Stopford, Mahon and Hammersley, have you any competent generals to take their place? From your report I think Stopford ought to come home.
I hope Stopford has been relieved by you already.

Kitchener, cable to Hamilton, August 14, 1915.

The fact is, you are just a bit above our trenches. If you could only get your fire rather lower you will be right into them, and here exactly is the dugout of our captain, Risa Kiazim Bey, a poor, good man. You miss him all the time. If you take a line on that pine tree you will get him.

Captain Aubrey Herbert reporting on a Turkish prisoner who volunteered advice to the British in the trenches on how to take better aim against his former Turkish comrades. August 1915, during the lull after the Anzac attacks had failed, quoted in Alan Moorehead, Gallipoli.

One quarter would probably get off quite easily, then the trouble would begin. We might be very lucky and lose considerably less than I have estimated [the loss of half the men]. On the other hand, with all these raw troops at Suvla and all these Senegalese at Cape Helles, we might have a veritable catastrophe.

Hamilton to Kitchener, who had asked about potential losses in a withdrawal from Gallipoli, October 12, 1915.

Sedition is talked around every tin of bully beef on the peninsula . . . I shall always remember the stricken face of a young English lieutenant when I told him he must make up his mind for a winter campaign . . . I do not like to dictate this sentence . . . but the fact is that after the first day at Suvla an order had to be issued to officers to shoot without mercy any soldier who lagged behind or loitered in an advance.

Keith Murdoch, Australian journalist, on the situation in October 1915. His claims are probably overstated, in Alan Moorehead, Gallipoli.

If you western-front generals don't like the idea of attacking, at least be ready to take advantage of our naval attack when we deliver it.

Admiral Roger Keyes to the British generals, advocating another naval attack at the straits on November 17, 1915.

Thus the Admiral [de Robeck] and the general [Kitchener] who were really entirely responsible for the lamentable policy of evacuation left the execution of this unpleasant task to an Admiral [Keyes] and a General [Birdwood] who were strongly opposed to it.

Keyes, after the withdrawal was decided upon on November 24, 1915, in Alan Moorehead, Gallipoli.

I wish to draw in no impressionist colours, but it must in all probability arise. The evacuation and the final scenes will be enacted at night. Our guns will continue firing until the last moment . . . but the trenches will have been taken one by one, and a moment must come when the final *sauve qui peut* takes place, and when a disorganized crowd will press in despairing tumult on to the shores and into the boats. Shells will be falling and bullets ploughing their way into the mass of retreating humanity . . . Conceive crowding into the boats of thousands of half-crazy men, the swamping of craft, the nocturnal panic, the agony of the wounded, the hecatombs of slain. It requires no imagination to create a scene that, when it is told, will be burned into the hearts and consciences of the British people for generations to come.

Lord Curzon, as member of the War Committee, in a letter to the cabinet on the forthcoming evacuation at Gallipoli, November 1915.

Lord Kitchener's personal qualities and position played at this time a very great part in the decision of events. His prestige and authority were immense. He was the sole mouthpiece of War Office opinion in the War Council. Everyone had the greatest admiration for this character, and everyone felt fortified, amid the terrible and incalculable events of the opening months of the war, by his commanding presence. When he gave a decision it was invariably accepted as final. He was never, to my belief, overruled by the War Council or the war cabinet in any military matter, great or small. No single unit was ever sent or withheld, not merely to his agreement, but to his advice. Scarcely anyone ever ventured to argue with him in Council . . . All powerful, imperturbable, reserved, he dominated absolutely our counsels at this time.

Winston Churchill, report to the Dardanelles Commission in 1916.

Lucinico (a village near Goritzia on the Isonzo front) is nothing more than a heap of grey stones; except for a bit of the church wall and the gable end of a house one cannot even speak of its ruins. But in one place among the rubble I saw the splintered top and a leg of a grand piano. Podgora hill, which was no doubt once neatly terraced and cultivated, is like a scrap of landscape from some airless, treeless planet.

Herbert George (H.G.) Wells, on the Isonzo front, January 1916, Italy, France and Britain at War (1917):

As I descended the upper track two bandaged men were coming down on led mules. It was mid August, and they were suffering from frost bite . . . For everywhere upon the icy pinnacles are observation posts directing the fire of the big guns on the slopes below . . . Snow and frost may cut them off absolutely for weeks from the rest of mankind. The sick and wounded must begin their journey down . . . in a giddy basket that swings down to the head of the mule track below.

Herbert George (H.G.) Wells, about the Isonzo-Dolomites front, January 1916, Italy, France and Britain at War.

Among these mountains avalanches are frequent; and they come down regardless of human strategy. In many cases the trenches cross avalanche tracks; they and the men in them are periodically swept away and periodically replaced. They are positions

that must be held; if the Italians will not face such sacrifices, the Austrians will.
George (H.G.) Wells, about the Isonzo front January 1916, Italy, France and Britain at War.

The Dardanelles failure was due not so much to Mr. Churchill's precipitancy as to Lord Kitchener's and Mr. Asquith's procrastination . . . [Churchill's] removal from the admiralty was a cruel and unjust degradation.
David Lloyd George, War Memoirs *(1933).*

A naval attack executed with rapidity and vigour at the outbreak of the war might have been successful . . . if the Entente Fleets had appeared before Constantinople the eight divisions retained there would have been impotent to defend it.
Report of the Turkish staff after the war, in Alan Moorehead, Gallipoli.

It is impossible to read all the evidence, or to study the voluminous papers which have been submitted to us, without being struck by the atmosphere of vagueness and want of precision which seems to have characterized the proceedings of the War Council . . . How can a fleet 'take' a peninsula?
Report of the Dardanelles Commissioners, 1917, on the British naval expedition against the Dardanelles.

Of the great mistakes made by Germany perhaps the greatest was in reckoning on the detachment of the Dominions. The Canadians have made an answer on a hundred stricken fields before and after Vimy Ridge. Australia gave her goodliest at Gallipoli . . . The immortal dead, British, Australians, New Zealanders, who fell in the great adventure of the narrow straits [of Gallipoli] are not forgotten in the hour of triumph.
Punch, *London, November 1918.*

6. The Western Front: January to December 1915

THE HISTORICAL CONTEXT

STALEMATE AND FUTILE ATTACKS

The events of 1914 had created a unique situation in military history: Here was a front of over 350 miles, by now heavily fortified, manned by millions of men who lived in trenches and dugouts, and protected by barbed wire and thousands of machine guns, which made a frontal assault unlikely to succeed and in any case extremely costly. Yet flanking movements enabling the attacker to engage the enemy from the side or the rear were no longer possible. Also, the element of surprise which had played such a vital role in all previous wars hardly existed, since the barbed-wire defenses called for long artillery barrages before an attack was launched. Still, most of the military leaders on both sides, convinced that a decision would have to be won on the western front, gathered all available men and equipment into this area. The result was a terrible war of attrition which cost hundreds of thousands of lives with very little to show for it. What had developed, in fact, was the very opposite of what Schlieffen had envisioned: a stalemate in the west and an offensive war against Russia in the east.

The Allies were wrong in their calculation that in the new war of attrition German and Allied losses would be about even. It turned out that in the many, almost suicidal massive attacks by the Allies during the next two years, their losses would be almost twice as high as those of their enemy. The chance of the German army eventually running out of manpower, therefore, was quite slim.

For a whole month, the Germans attacked in the Soissons and La Bassée Canal region in the Champagne, making only slight gains. From the middle of February 1915 onward, the French counterattacked German positions in the eastern Champagne but had little to show for the extremely heavy bombardment preceding the attacks and the heavy infantry losses they incurred. Then in March came Britain's turn. They attacked in the Artois region and actually broke through the German lines in the vicinity of Neuve Chapelle, but they were somehow unable to exploit their success.

Next came heavy French attacks in the Verdun section, where the German salient south of the fortress always threatened to cut off Verdun. But the attacks at St. Mihiel did not essentially change the situation in this region either.

In all of these battles, first-line trenches had been frequently overrun by the attacking troops. Usually the advance against the second line of defense was frustrated by surviving machine crews, and supports could not be brought up fast enough for a second drive. Often counterattacks overwhelmed the attacker before a proper defense could be organized.

GAS WARFARE

In April, the Germans came up with a new and peculiarly horrible weapon: poison gas. The possibility of using gas in warfare had been known since the 19th century, and it seems that the French even had

The largest French gun, firing at night. Photo courtesy of the National Archives, Washington, D.C.

some advance notice about Germany's intentions. Yet the surprise was complete, and though the means of spreading chlorine was still primitive, the attack probably could have succeeded if it had been conducted on a larger scale. The gas was compressed in cylinders, released from the parapets (breastworks) and carried by the wind, which meant that when the wind changed, it would play havoc with the attackers. At first, there was no defense available against the poison which caused lung damage, blisters, sometimes death, except a wet rag pressed to the face, but soon enough regular gas masks were distributed on both sides. A gas shell was developed by the French and proved to be much more effective than the wind-blown gas. Aside from chlorine, other gases, such as Lewisite and Mustard Gas, were introduced and for the rest of the war, poison gas was frequently used by both sides, although it did not play a decisive role in the outcome of the war.

The first use of chlorine took place at Ypres where the Allies were preparing a major May offensive. The German gas attack created a panic, and some units fled, leaving Ypres exposed. Yet the breach was small; the reserves brought up were insufficient and hesitated to advance through the gassed area. British units moved in and closed the gap; the chief effect of this attack was that it ruined full participation of the British in Joffre's great offensive in the Artois region. Having begun on May 9, the encounter lasted almost six weeks and resulted in over 300,000 Allied casualties—with a gain of hardly eight square miles.

BATTLES IN THE ARTOIS AND CHAMPAGNE REGIONS

Thereafter, the Western front remained fairly quiet while Joffre prepared for his fall offensive. The main battle took place in the Champagne, between Rheims and the Argonne, after an unprecedented artillery barrage. But although huge masses of infantry were thrown into the battle, the German troops held the heights between Ste. Menehould and Rheims, and after almost six weeks of intense fighting, the French had gained little ground.

Further north, in the Artois region, the British tried to support the French efforts by starting a large-scale attack just a few days later. They had fewer guns at their disposal than the French and therefore, with less of a preceding bombardment, achieved an element of surprise. They assaulted under cover of gas clouds, and as they greatly outnumbered the opposing German units, succeeded in driving them back, particularly in the mining area of Loos where the battle raged for two weeks. They came near a breakthrough but had no reserves in the vicinity except for cavalry units, which were of little use in this densely built-up area. Thus the gap in the German line was closed again, and subsequent fighting did not alter the situation.

Joffre had hoped that this double offensive in northern France would work like a pair of pincers, thereby forcing a general German withdrawal. But after weeks of fighting, only some bulges had been produced, and the Allies had suffered a quarter of a million casualties. The great stalemate continued.

CHRONICLE OF EVENTS

1915:

January 8–February 5: In the Champagne, heavy fighting in the Soissons and La Bassée Canal sections. Minor German gains.

February 16–March 30: In the Eastern Champagne, heavy French attacks after intense bombardment, with minor gains only.

March 10–13: British attack in the Artois region, resulting in a breakthrough near Neuve Chapelle, but no permanent gains.

March 30–April 15: In the southern sector, heavy French attacks on the German salient at St. Mihiel, without tangible results.

April 22–May 25: Second battle of Ypres. A major offensive planned by the British is frustrated by the German use of poison gas (chlorine). Initial German gains are not exploited.

May 9–June 18: Second battle of Artois. French units under General Henri-Philippe Pétain break through German lines north of Arras, but advance only three miles, suffering huge losses.

September 22–November 6: Second battle of Champagne. Joffre attacks between Rheims and the Argonne, after an immense artillery preparation. Insignificant French gains.

September 25–October 15: Third battle of Artois. The British attack, using gas for the first time. Germans are driven back near Loos, but British fail to exploit their advantage.

Ruins of St. Martin's Church, Ypres, Belgium, 1914. Photo courtesy of the National Archives, Washington, D.C.

EYEWITNESS TESTIMONY

. . . I was standing guard under the wall of a chateaux-park with a comrade when a patrol sneaked up on the other side and threw a hand grenade over, which sputtered a moment at our feet and went out without exploding. I . . . called out the corporal of the guard. We walked back . . . when another bomb came over which exploded among us with a tremendous detonation. In the confusion that followed the attacking party burst in the door . . . and poured a volley into our midst, killing our corporal instantly and getting away before we had time to fire a shot.

Alan Seeger, letter to his father, near Cuiry,
France, January 11, 1915.

The Kaiser has had his first War birthday and, as the Prussian government has ordered that there shall be no public celebrations, this confirms the rumours that he now wishes he had never been born.

Punch, *London, January 1915.*

Poor ruined villages of Northern France! There they lie like so many silent graveyards, each little house the tomb of some scattered family's happiness. Where are the simple, peace-loving country folk that dwelt here when these windows were squares of yellow lamplight, not, as now, blank as holes in a skull? The men away at the war or already in their graves, the women and children refugees in the South, dependent upon charity. The pity of it all is that the French guns have done and have had to do the material damage . . . It is frightful to think that only at such a price can the French regain their conquered territory. If the enemy are to be driven across the frontier does it not mean that every town and village between must be laid in ruins?

Alan Seeger, letter to the New York Sun,
from a trench in France, February 5, 1915.

The interior of the church was filled with rubble and bodies and parts of bodies, one corpse naked, burned by a flame-thrower . . . In the trench there were several corpses. The heels of one of ours were sticking out, the heads of others . . . The most dreadful sight was an arm in field grey with a white hand which protruded from the white wall of the right saphead. Everywhere we dug, we dug into corpses. More of ours than of the French. Whenever

a mine exploded, pieces of flesh fell into our position. Shreds of a dead Frenchman hung from the branches of a tree . . .

Richard Courant, diary, at Vauquois, France,
in February 1915, in Constance Reid, Courant
(1976).

I am dulled and stupefied, look neither ahead nor behind, do nothing except take a few photographs . . . What seemed interesting and important and unusual to me only a few months ago is of absolutely no consequence now. The word "culture" sounds almost like a sneer.

Richard Courant, diary, at Vauquois, France,
in February 1915, in Constance Reid, Courant.

In the diocese of Namur 26 priests have been killed. 25 were shot, one hanged. In the diocese of Luettich [Liège] 6 priests were shot, in the diocese of Mecheln 13, in the diocese of Tournai 2 priests were shot. The episcopal offices claim that all killed were innocent. Information on the reasons for the shootings could only come from the troops involved.

Statement of the German governor general in
Belgium, dated February 28, 1915.

Two German prisoners, being escorted by as many cavalrymen, failed to salute a French colonel. He . . . made them stand at attention and then stormed at them in a manner that made me fear he was about to order a summary execution. After he left I looked at the Germans' faces. They betrayed anger, not fear.

R.R. McCormick, recalling events at Arras,
France, March 1915, With the Russian Army
(1915).

You might be walking across the fields and minded to go through a hedge, and bump into a block of steel with a gun's crew grinning behind it. They would grin because you had given proof how well their gun was concealed. But they wouldn't grin as much as they would if they saw the enemy plunking shells into another hedge two hundred yards distant, where the German aeroplane observer thought he had seen a battery and had not.

Frederick Palmer, in Flanders, March 1915,
My Year in the Great War *(1915).*

The wonder was that any ditch could be cut in soil which the rains had turned into syrup. Mud oozed from the sandbags, through the wire netting, and between the wood supports which held the walls in place. It was jast as bad over in the German trenches. General Mud laid siege to both armies . . . The tug of war was strife against landslides, rheumatism, pneumonia and frozen feet.

Frederick Palmer, at the British front in France,
March 1915, My Year in the Great War.

I like to ask that question, "Were you at Mons?" and get the answer, "Yes, sir, I was; I was through it all!" without boasting—a Mons veteran need not boast—but in the spirit of pride. To have been at Mons, where the hard-bought retreat of one against five began, will ever be enough glory for English, Scotch, Irish or Welsh. It is like saying "I was in Pickett's charge."

Frederick Palmer, in Flanders, in March 1915,
My Year in the Great War.

The Germans were as busy as beavers dam building. They had a lot of work to do before they got their new defences right. We heard them driving stakes and spading; we heard their voices . . . and occasionally the energetic, shouted, guttural commands of their officers. All through that night I never heard a British officer speak above a conversational tone. The orders were definitive enough, but given with a certain companionable kindliness.

Frederick Palmer, in the trenches of Flanders,
March 1915, My Year in the Great War.

A man who can be the same in a trench in Flanders as in a drawing room has my admiration. They never lose their manners, these English officers. They carry it into the charge and back in the ambulance with them to England where they wish nothing so much as that their friends will "cut out the hero stuff," as our own officers say.

Frederick Palmer, in Flanders, March 1915,
My Year in the Great War.

These veterans could "grouse," as the British call it. Grousing is one of Tommy's privileges. When they got to grousing worst on the retreat from Mons, their officers knew that what they really wanted was to make another stand. They were tired of falling back; they meant to take a rest and fight a while.

Frederick Palmer, in Flanders, March 1915,
My Year in the Great War.

Mr. Thomas Atkins [the name for the typical British foot soldier], none other, is the hero of that retreat from Mons. The first statue raised in London after the war ought to be of him. If there had been five hundred thousand of him in Belgium at the end of the second week in August, Brussels would now be under the Belgian flag.

Frederick Palmer, My Year in the Great War.

The French pilot has really dropped five bombs, and unfortunately, only Germans were killed. Now the people of Charleville are glad about their hero who played this trick on us, and we are good-hearted enough to repair the damage for those fellows. The Emperor is furious; now, Buckingham Palace will be no longer off limits. He really believed in a silent agreement between the ruling houses to spare each other—a strange way of thinking.

Alfred von Tirpitz, letter from the Imperial
Headquarters at Charleville, April 15, 1915, in
H.H. Welchert, Weltgewitter *(n.d.)*

A few of our own men had reached us, and night fell. We could not remain where we were. To the right there was still nobody. I could see the trench for some thirty yards . . . Should I go and see what was happening there? By an effort of will, I made my decision. The trench was full of French corpses. There was blood everywhere. At first I went with great circumspection, with little assurance. I was alone with all these dead! . . . Then little by little I grew bolder. I dared to look at the bodies, and it seemed to me as if they returned my stare . . .

French lieutenant Jacques Pericard, "Face à
Face," on the fighting at Bois d'Ailly, France,
April 1915, in Guy Chapman (ed.), Vain
Glory *(1937).*

British soldiers died in vain on Aubers Ridge on Sunday because more shells were needed. The Government, who have so seriously failed to organize adequately our national resources, must beat their share of grave responsibility.

London Times, *after the British offensive in*
Aubers Ridge, France, April 1915.

Soon . . . a peculiar smell was noticed, accompanied by smarting of the eyes and tingling of the nose and throat. It was some little time, however, before I realized that the yellow clouds were due to the gas about which warnings had been received, and almost

British guns on the battlefield. Photo courtesy of the National Archives, Washington, D.C.

simultaneously French coloured troops, without officers, began drifting down the roads through the back areas of the V Corps . . . It was impossible to understand what the Africans said, but from the way they coughed and pointed to their throats, it was evident that, if not suffering from the effects of gas, they were thoroughly scared. Teams and wagons of the French field artillery next appeared retiring, and the throng of fugitives soon became thicker and more disordered.

British brigadier general J.E. Edmonds, describing the first German gas attack at Ypres, April 22, 1915, in Guy Chapman (ed.), Vain Glory.

At sundown . . . we march out to the posts. Some of these are in a cemetery that got in the way of the flood tide of the Battle of the Aisne. The retreating Germans must have made a stand behind the mounds and grave stones, for the place has been frightfully bombarded. The shells that do not respect even the dead have shattered the monuments and burst open the sepulchres. Quantities of chloride of lime, liberally sprinkled about, are a remedy that is not much better than the evil, and the rats as big as rabbits that scurry under the banks and hedges and discourage one from lying down between watches make this the

least desirable of all posts. . . . Further up the slope the voices of the enemy are plainly audible.

Alan Seeger, letter to the New York Sun, *from the Aisne, April 28, 1915.*

Is the sport of war dead? Not for Archibald [name of the British anti-aircraft gunner]! Here you see a target—which is rare these days when British infantrymen have stormed and taken trenches without ever seeing a German—and the target is a bird, a man-bird. Puffs of smoke with bursting hearts of death are clustered around the Taube [German plane]. One follows another in quick succession, for more than one Archibald is firing . . .

Frederick Palmer on the British antiaircraft units in Flanders, spring 1915, My Year in the Great War.

. . . the next puff may get him. Who knows this better than the aviator? He is, likely, an old hand at the game; or, if he is not, he has all the experience of other veterans to go by. His ruse is the same as that of the escaped prisoner who runs from the fire of the guard in zigzag course, and more than that. If a puff comes near on the right, he turns to the left . . . if one comes under, he rises; over, he dips. This means that the next shell fired at the same point will be wide of the target.

Frederick Palmer, with British antiaircraft units in Flanders, spring 1915, My Year in the Great War.

There is no flustering the French population. That very day I heard an old peasant, who asked a British soldier if he could not get permission for the old man to wear some kind of an armband which both sides would respect, so that he could cut his field between the trenches. Why not? Wasn't it his wheat? Didn't he need the crop?

Frederick Palmer, with a British artillery unit in Flanders, spring 1915, My Year in the Great War.

Last night a lot of German stuff was flying about, including shrapnel, I heard one shell wish-wishing towards me and dropped flat. It burst just over the trench where "Petticoat Lane" runs into "Lowndes Square." My ears sang as though there were gnats in them, and a bright scarlet light shone over everything. My shoulder got twisted in falling, and I thought I had been hit, but I hadn't been. The vibration made my chest sing, too, in a curious way, and I lost sense of equilibrium. I was ashamed when the sergeant-major came along the trench and found me on all fours, still unable to stand up straight.

Robert Graves, in the trenches in France, May 28, 1915, Good-bye to All That *(1929).*

The lines here are so near that the two sides can talk to each other easily. We told them a few nights ago that Italy had declared war and they yelled back: "Yes, but against you!" Won't they be furious when they learn the truth!

Alan Seeger, diary, at Puisieulx, in the Champagne, May 29, 1915.

They have pushed in very close . . . at one point less than 100 meters . . . Once in a while a German cries out—"Hey, Français—kaput, kaput." Then piquant dialogues begin, either in French or German . . . we can hear them playing their harmonicas and accordions, a kind of music the German soldiers seem very fond of.

Alan Seeger, diary, in the Champagne, June 10, 1915.

Only half an hour before one of the officers had been shot through the head by a sniper. He was a popular officer. The others had messed with him and marched with him . . . No one dwelt on the incident. What was there to say? The trembling lip, trembling in spite of itself, was the only outward sign of the depth of feeling . . . at tea in the dugout. The subject was changed to something about the living. One must carry on cheerfully . . .

Frederick Palmer, Flanders, June 1915, My Year in the Great War.

Looking over the parapet of the communication trench you saw fields, lifeless except for the singing birds in the wheat, who had also the spirit of battle. The more shells, the more they warble . . . Between the screams you heard their full-pitched chorus . . . Mostly, the birds seemed to take cover like mankind; but I saw one sweep up . . . toward the men-brothers with their wings of cloth.

Frederick Palmer, in Flanders, June 1915, My Year in the Great War.

That morning a soldier had been shot through the heart and arm sideways back of the trench. He had lain down unnoticed for a nap in the sun, it was supposed. When he awoke, presumably he sat up and yawned and Herr Schmidt, from some platform in a tree, had a bloody reward for his patience.

Frederick Palmer, in Flanders, June 1915, My Year in the Great War.

The next morning I saw the British take their revenge. Some German who thought he could not be seen in the mist of dawn was walking along the German parapet. What hopes! Four or five men took careful aim and fired. That dim figure collapsed in a way that was convincing.

Frederick Palmer, in Flanders, June 1915, My Year in the Great War.

. . . following some instinct of survival, I tried after a few minutes to crawl to the rear. I could not do it by myself, and two men from the neighboring battalion came to my aid. One of them was shortly hit in the leg, and immediately afterwards I was hit by a second rifle shot which took great pieces of flesh from my left lower arm. I was beginning to lose consciousness . . . although my other companion tightened a tourniquet about my arm in a shell crater.

The man who had been hit had his leg dressed while the other man rolled me into a coat, put me on my back and dragged me along the ground with a piece of cord from a breadsack. In my dazed state I tried to help by making rowing movements . . . We advanced only by inches. The noise, bullets and shrapnel, was infernal. The English advance was imminent. I remember that during the hours of being pulled I was constantly concerned with whether we were actually going in the right direction, since no definite line of demarcation separated us from the English. I was overjoyed when I finally saw the familiar pile of straw in front of our barricade and . . . placed on a stretcher . . .

Richard Courant, German mathematician, about his experience in fighting the British at Douai, France, August 1915. Reported in Constance Reid, Courant *(1976).*

"Inspections! They are second nature to us!" said a new army man. "We were inspected and inspected at home and we are inspected and inspected out here. If there is anything wrong with us it is the general's own fault if it isn't found out. When a general is not inspecting, some man from the medical corps is disinfecting."

Frederick Palmer, with the British army in France, summer 1915, in My Year in the Great War.

. . . there is also a prince with the British army in France. No lieutenant looks younger for his years than this one in the Grenadier Guards, and he seems of the same type as the others when you see him marching with his regiment or off for a walk smoking a briar-wood pipe. There are some officers who would rather not accompany him on his walks, for he can go fast and far. He makes regular reports of his observations, and he has opportunities for learning which other subalterns lack, for he may have both the staff and the army as personal instructors. Otherwise, his life is that of any subaltern; for there is an instrument called the British Constitution which regulates many things. A little shy, very desirous to learn, is Albert Edward, Prince of Wales, heir to the throne of Great Britain and Ireland and the Empire of India. He might be called the willing prince.

Frederick Palmer, about the future King Edward VIII, summer 1915, in France, My Year in the Great War.

The Germans had special regimental snipers, trained in camouflaging themselves. I saw one killed at Cuinchy who had been firing all day from a shell-hole between the lines. He wore a sort of cape made of imitation grass, his face was painted green and brown, and his rifle was also green-fringed. A number of empty cartridges lay beside him, and his cap bore the special oak-leaf badge . . . The Germans had the advantage of having many times more telescopic sights than we did, and bullet-proof steel loop-holes. Also a system by which snipers were kept for months in the same sector until they knew all the loop-holes and shallow places in our trenches . . . It puzzled us that when a sniper had been spotted and killed, another sniper would often begin operations next day from the same position. The Germans probably underrated us, and regarded their loss as an accident.

Robert Graves, in France, summer 1915, Good-bye to All That.

We had pulled socks, with the toes cut off, over our bare knees, to prevent them showing up in the dark and to make crawling easier. We went ten yards at a time, slowly, not on all fours, but wriggling flat along the ground. After each movement we lay and watched for about ten minutes. We crawled through our own wire entanglements and along a dry ditch; ripping our clothes on more barbed wire, glaring into the darkness until it began turning round and round. Once I snatched my fingers in horror from where I had planted them on the slimy body of an old corpse . . . We got home after making a journey of perhaps two hundred yards in rather more than two hours . . . After this I went on patrol fairly often, finding that the only thing respected in young officers was personal courage. Besides, I had cannily worked it out like this. My best way of lasting through the end of the war would be to get wounded. The best time to get wounded would be at night and in the open, with rifle-fire more or less unaimed and my whole body exposed. Best, also, to get wounded, when there was no rush in the dressing room services . . .

Robert Graves, in France, summer 1915, Good-bye to All That.

One day, walking along a trench at Cambrin, I suddenly dropped flat on my face; two seconds later a whizz-bang struck the back of the trench exactly where my head had been. The sergeant who was with me, walking a few steps ahead, turned round:

"Are you killed, Sir?" The shell was fired from a battery near Les Briques Farm, only a thousand yards away, so that I must have reacted almost simultaneously with the explosion of the gun. How did I know that the shell would be coming my way?
Robert Graves, in France, summer 1915,
Good-bye to All That.

From the morning of September 24th to the night of October 3rd, I had in all eight hours of sleep. I kept myself alive and awake by drinking about a bottle of whiskey a day. I had never drunk it before, and have seldom drunk it since; it certainly helped me then. We had no blankets, greatcoats, or waterproof sheets, nor any time or material to build shelters. The rain continued.
Robert Graves, on fighting in France, fall of 1915, Good-bye to All That.

I find it very difficult to like the French here, except occasional members of the official class. Even when billeted in villages where no troops have been before, I have not met a single case of hospitality that one meets among the peasants of other countries. It is worse than inhospitality here, for after all we are fighting for their dirty little lives. They are sucking enormous quantities of money out of us, too.
Robert Graves, letter from the French front, fall of 1915, Good-bye to All That.

. . . we crossed the open space between the lines, over the barbed wire, where not so many of our men were lying as I had feared (thanks to the efficacy of the bombardment) and over the German trench, knocked to pieces and filled with their dead. In some places they still resisted in isolated groups. Opposite us all was over and the herds of prisoners were being led down as we went up. We cheered, more in triumph than in hate, but the poor devils, terror-stricken, held up their hands, begged for their lives, cried "Kamerad," "Bon Français," even "Vive la France."
Alan Seeger, letter to his mother after the battle in Champagne, October 25, 1915.

Meanwhile the Hamburg *Fremdenblatt* asserts that "we Germans would gladly follow the Kaiser's lead through the very gates of hell, were it necessary." The qualification is surely superfluous, in the light of the murder of the heroic English hospital matron, Edith Cavell . . . Her life was one long act of mercy.

She died with unshaken fortitude after the mockery of a trial . . . her great offence was that she was English . . . Many years will pass before the echoes of that volley fired at dawn in a Brussels prison yard will die away.
Punch, London, October 1915. Edith Cavell was a British nurse in Brussels, who was shot as a spy by the Germans.

It is still a law that when a company of infantry marches through London it must be escorted by a policeman. This means a good deal: that civil power is superior to military power. It is a symbol of what Englishmen have fought for with spades and pitchforks . . . England is fighting for it in this struggle; and starting unready against a foe who was ready, as the free peoples always have, she was fighting for time and experience before she could strike her sturdiest blows.
Frederick Palmer, My Year in the Great War.

At the start of the war the Germans had the advantage of many mobile howitzers and immense stores of high explosive shells, while the French were dependent on their soixante-quinze (seventy-five) and shrapnel; and at this disadvantage the brilliancy of their work with this wonderful field gun on the Marne and in Lorraine was the most important contributory in saving France next to the vital one of French courage and organization.
Frederick Palmer, My Second Year of the War *(1917).*

General Joffre, grounded in the France of the people and the soil, was a thrifty general. Indeed, from the lips of Frenchmen in high places the Germans might have learned that the French Army was running short of men. Joffre seemed never to have any more divisions to spare; yet never came a crisis that he did not find another division in the toe of his stocking, which he gave up grumblingly as the peasant parts with a gold piece.
Frederick Palmer, My Second Year of the War.

No less than General Joffre, Sir Douglas [Haig] lived by the rule. He, too, insisted on sleeping well at night and rising fresh for his day's work. During the period of preparation for an offensive his routine began with a stroll in the garden before breakfast . . . At luncheon very likely he might not talk of war . . . Every day at half-past two he went for a ride and with him an escort of his own regiment of Lancers.

Frederick Palmer, My Second Year of the War.

England had Lord Kitchener, who could hold the imagination and the confidence of the nation through the long months of preparation, when there was little to show . . . It required a man with a big conception and patience and authority to carry it through, and recruits with an unflinching sense of duty. The immensity of the task of transforming a non-military people into a great fighting force grew on one in all its humdrum and vital details . . . "Are you learning to think in big numbers?" was Lord Kitchener's question to his generals.

Frederick Palmer, in Britain, end of 1914, My Year in the Great War.

Take Lord Kitchener's maximum (four machine guns per battalion); square it, multiply that result by two—and when you are in sight of that, double it again for good luck.

David Lloyd George, as minister of munitions, 1915, thus suggesting 64 machine guns per battalion. Toward the end of the war, every British battalion had about 43 machine guns, and was asking for more. Quoted in A.J.P. Taylor, Illustrated History of the First World War, *1964.*

At the Prussian ministry for war, several donations for the army were received in November. We are mentioning among those for special military accomplishments: 500.- Mark for the first young German warrior who plants the first German flag on English or Scottish soil. / 500.- Mark for the first German airman who drops a bomb on London.

Proclamation, in E. Engel, Ein Tagebuch *(1915).*

If there was a strike, the British press made the most of it for it was big news. Pessimism is the Englishman's natural way of arousing himself to fresh energy. It is also against habit to be demonstrative in his effort . . . Then, pessimism brought recruits; it made the Englishman say, "I've got to put my back into it!"

Frederick Palmer, on conditions in Britain in 1915, My Year in the Great War.

If I should die, think only this of me:/ That there's some corner of a foreign field/ That is forever England . . . This heart, all evil shed away,/ a pulse in the eternal mind, no less/ Gives somewhere back the thoughts by England given.

Rupert Brooke, English poet, 1887–1915: "The Soldier" *(1915).*

7. The Eastern Front: May 1915 to March 1917

THE HISTORICAL CONTEXT

GERMAN-AUSTRIAN ATTACKS IN THE CARPATHIANS AND POLAND

By April/May 1915, the Russians had more than six million men "under arms," but only in the widest sense considering how poorly they were equipped. The morale of the troops was still high, and when spring came, a Russian attack through the Carpathian Mountains could have developed into a fatal blow for the Dual Monarchy. But the Central Powers were the first to attack: From early April on, Austrian forces, supported by the German South Army, drove the Russians from the mountains, and an Eleventh German Army, under General August von Mackensen, also cooperating with Austrian forces, prepared for a drive from southeast of Cracow in the direction of Przemysl, now in Russian hands.

The main offensive began on May 1 and started with a heavy bombardment of Gorlice just inside the Russian lines. Russian defenses were weak, their trenches were poorly dug and their dugouts were not deep enough. After a day of fighting, the Germans broke right through, and within two weeks they had advanced almost two hundred miles, reaching the San River and crossing it within another week. Przemysl, on the upper San, could no longer be held by the Russians and fell after five weeks; Lemberg followed less than three weeks later. After a continued advance of eight weeks, the southern Russian front collapsed entirely, Galicia and the Bukovina were "liberated," and Warsaw was threatened from the south. Within this incredibly short time, the Russian situation had turned so desperate that recruits were sent to the firing line after only one month's training and, sometimes armed only with clubs, were advised to pick up rifles from their fallen comrades.

The Central Powers made use of this favorable situation by offering immediate peace to Tsar Nicholas, under which the prewar frontiers should be reestablished. Knowing that his material inferiority could never be rectified, the temptation must have been great for the tsar, but as an honorable man he stuck to his promises to his allies and refused. Possibly, by doing that, he provoked the outbreak of the Great Revolution in his country, thereby sealing his own fate.

Three months after the offensive began, Warsaw fell to the German and Austrian troops, in a second great offensive sweep in which the Austrians, under Archduke Joseph Ferdinand, took Lublin and Cholm in the south, then stormed Ivangorod. In the Narev, a new Twelfth German Army under General Max von Gallwitz attacked in northern Poland and Courland and occupied Windau and Mitau (Yelgava) in what is now Latvia. By September, the Austrians had taken Lutsk and Dubno, while the Germans had advanced to Kovno and Vilna (Vilnius) in Lithuania. Even the great fortress of Novo-Georgiesk near Warsaw, and, further east, Brest-Litovsk on the Bug River, were taken by the Germans. Again, the extensive but obsolete fortifications of the Russian fortresses were no match for Germany's big siege guns.

By September, however, Russian resistance stiffened. They held Tarno against the Austrians; and in the north, Dvinsk on the Dvina River against the Germans. Riga, the Latvian capital on the Dvina River and an important Baltic port, also held out, only to fall to the Germans two years later. Still, when the German advance came to a halt in September, all of Poland, Lithuania and Courland had been lost as well as more than half a million men. The line ran now almost straight from near Czernowitz to Dvinsk and then westward along the Dvina River with Riga, Dvinsk, Pinsk, Dubno and Tarnopol remaining on the Russian side; Baranovitchi, Vilna and Mitau on the German-Austrian side. At the instigation of the tsarina and Rasputin, Grand Duke Nicholas was relieved of his supreme command and sent to the Caucasus, where he achieved successes against the Turks in the following year. The tsar himself took over the supreme command of the Russian armies. This necessitated his absence from the capital, and led to an increase in the influence Rasputin and the tsarina exerted in political and military affairs.

RUSSIAN COUNTERATTACKS IN 1916: BRUSILOV

Again, by the end of 1915 it looked as if Russia was beaten, but during the following year it rose once again. And for the second time, Russia attacked to support allies in the west. First, it launched an offensive near Lake Naroch to relieve the pressure of the Germans at Verdun. After six weeks of fighting, very little had been achieved, but the main blow was yet to come. General Alexei Brusilov, one of the more successful army commanders in the past, was now put in command of four armies, the eighth, eleventh, seventh and ninth.

In preparing his great offensive, several factors worked in his favor. Russian industry had been reorganized during the winter, and the country was now producing 100,000 rifles a month; also, huge supplies had come in from her allies. Both Germany and Austria had been forced to withdraw troops from the Russian front, Falkenhayn for his big onslaught on Verdun, Austria to bolster its offensive in Italy. Brusilov had planned his attack for July, but due to urgent appeals from France and a personal telegram from the king of Italy to the tsar, he started somewhat prematurely.

The great attack started all along the Galician front in the beginning of June and was immediately successful, although Brusilov had no more than a parity of strength against the Austrians. By letting all four armies attack at the same time, after a minimum of artillery preparation, he achieved a complete surprise. Conrad von Hoetzendorf had been confident that his elaborate defenses of five lines of deep trenches would be more than enough to frustrate any onslaught, but he was mistaken. Masses of Czech troops in the Austrian army went over to the enemy without firing a shot, and the lines were broken on an almost 200-mile front.

On the first day alone, 13,000 prisoners were taken, and in three weeks the Austrian army had lost 200,000 men, mostly by desertion. The Russians advanced from 16 to 78 miles in the region south of Pinsk and took Lutsk and Czernowitz in June. But due to their poor railway systems, they were unable to bring up enough reserves from the north. Still, the Austro-Hungarian Empire seemed in danger of collapse, particularly because, in late August, Romania decided to declare war on Austria. This country had wavered for two years, but now, when Brusilov's offensive seemed irresistible, it saw its opportunity to acquire Transylvania to the north, which Romanians considered to be part of their country, but which had become an integral part of Hungary in 1867. Romanian troops invaded the greater part of this province, instead of attacking across Austria's almost undefended frontier, which possibly could have caused the downfall of the Dual Monarchy. By her shortsighted action, Romania gave Germany the chance to prop up the Austrian front against Russia and to organize a two-pronged attack on Romania, which was soon completely beaten and was occupied by the Central Powers before the year was over. The conquest of Romanian oil fields and wheat lands proved to be of considerable help to the Central Powers, but the conquest had required great numbers of troops needed elsewhere; additionally, another 250 miles had been added to the overlong eastern front.

NEW STALEMATE

Brusilov, successful as he had been in the beginning, had probably overreached himself by attacking simultaneously in the north—in the region of the Pripet Marshes—where he was faced by German units and made no progress whatsoever. In fact, after some reinforcements had arrived, the Germans started to counterattack at Brusilov's northern flank.

By July, German units were employed all along the eastern front, and Conrad von Hoetzendorf was relieved of his command. Brusilov probably would have broken off his offensive at this point, but he was urged on by his superiors in St. Petersburg. He continued his attacks until September and managed some further advances, but replenishment of men and material had become extremely difficult or impossible. His great offensive had brought Russia 350,000 prisoners and also the conquest of the Bukovina and large parts of Galicia, but Russian casualties had amounted to a million men; the country was exhausted and the Russian soldiers' will to fight had been sapped. The country was ready for a revolution. On the other hand, one could argue that Brusilov's main adversary, Austria, had also been dealt a death blow. Austria's eastern front could only be maintained by the constant pouring in of German units, and German generals took over on the eastern front and in Romania. When Emperor Franz Joseph, who had ruled since 1848, finally died in November 1916, the last connecting link between the peoples and nations constituting the Austrian Empire had disappeared. His successor and grand-nephew Karl, married to Zita of Bourbon-Parma—who had great influence over him and entertained sympathies to the Allies—realized from the beginning that his empire could be saved only by the conclusion of a quick peace. But this again would have to be negotiated behind the back of his great ally and mainstay, Germany.

CHRONICLE OF EVENTS

1915:

April 1–25: Austrian forces, supported by the German South Army under General Alexander von Linsingen, drive the Russians from the Carpathians.

April 26: German offensive in Courland.

May 2: Great Austrian-German offensive in Galicia begins. Battle of Gorlice-Tarnow.

May 3–5: Austrian-German forces cross the Dunajec River.

May 14: Jaroslav taken.

May 15–23: German-Austrian troops force a crossing of the San River.

June 3: The fortress of Przemysl is retaken by German-Austrian forces.

June 5: Zuravno taken.

June 8: Stanislav taken.

June 22: Lemberg retaken.

June 23–27: German-Austrian troops cross the Dniester River. Galicia and the Bukovina are again under Austrian-German control.

July 1: The second great offensive of the Central Powers begins.

July 18: The Germans take Windau in Courland.

July 31: The Austrians, under Archduke Joseph Ferdinand, take Lublin and Cholm.

August 1: The Germans take Mitau in Courland.

August 4: The Austrians take Invangorod.

August 4–7: The German Twelfth Army, under Max von Gallwitz, advances in northern Poland to the Narev River and takes Warsaw.

August 18: Kovno, on the Niemen River, is taken by the Germans.

August 20: The fortress of Novo-Georgievsk is stormed by the Germans.

August 25: Brest-Litovsk is taken by the Germans.

August 31: The Austrians take Lutsk in the south.

September 2: The fortress of Grodno falls to the Germans.

September 5: Grand Duke Nicholas is relieved of the supreme command.

September 6: The battle of Tarnopol begins, with Russians offering stiff resistance.

September 8: The Austrians take Dubno.

September 9: Beginning of the battle of Dvinsk, Germans meet stiff resistance by the Russians.

September 19: Germans take Vilna (Vilnius) on the Neris River. The great offensive comes to a halt.

1916:

March 19–April 30: Russian offensive at Lake Naroch, with insignificant results.

April 4: General Alexei Brusilov is appointed commander of the Russian southern front.

June 4: Beginning of Brusilov's great offensive. The Austrians fall back.

June 8: Russian troops take the fortress of Lutsk.

June 11–30: Battle of the Strypa.

June 18: Czernowitz taken by Russian troops.

July 2–9: Battle of Baranovici.

July 28–August 17: Battle of Kovel. Great Russian advances, but they fail to take the important railway center of Kovel and Lemberg.

August 27: Romania declares war on Austria-Hungary.

August 28: Romanian troops invade Transylvania and occupy Kronstadt (Brasov) and Hermanstadt (Sibiu).

September 27–29: Counterattack of German-Austrian forces, under General Erich von Falkenhayn, in Transylvania. Romanians surrounded at Hermanstadt (Sibiu).

September 26–November 23: German-Bulgarian forces, under General August von Mackensen, attack Romanian forces in the Dobrudja.

October 7–9: Battle of Kronstadt (Brasov). The city is retaken by German-Austrian troops.

October 22: Constanza in the Dobrudja is taken by German-Bulgarian forces.

October 25: Cernavoda in the Dobrudja is taken.

November 21: Death of Emperor Francis Joseph of Austria.

November 23: Mackensen's forces cross the Danube and advance toward Bucharest.

December 1–5: Romanians counterattack at Argesul, but are defeated.

December 6: Bucharest is occupied by the Central Powers. The Romanian government moves to Jassy.

1917

January 5: German-Austrian forces advance to Braila.

January 15: Most of Romania is in the hands of the Central Powers. Romanian forces have retreated to the Sereth River.

EYEWITNESS TESTIMONY

I consider him [the Grand Duke Nicholas] the greatest soldier that the war produced. Certainly he is the unknown quantity that threw out the forty years of methodical calculations of the German General Staff. In the first months of the war he struck down the Austrians with one hand and with the other dragged back the Prussians from the gates of Paris.

R.R. McCormick, observations from St. Petersburg, April 1915, With the Russian Army *(1915).*

The Russian physique is far ahead of any other in Europe . . . Perhaps he has shot less well than his enemy, but has certainly been his physical superior. I have been through the English, French and Russian armies and have seen thousands of Austrian and German prisoners. The Russian soldier averages half a head taller than other soldiers, weighs 24 pounds heavier . . . He is trained in marksmanship and shoots the long range as well as any trained soldier, but to fire at a man ten feet away would not occur to him . . . The equipment of the Russian soldier is . . . an extraordinary combination of usefulness and economy, and certainly shows up the equipment of Western armies for what it is—the product of theorists and amateurs . . . Before going to Russia I had always imagined that the Russian soldier's boot was a clumsy affair and a hindrance to marching and activity. Nothing could be further from the truth. The leather is as flexible as kid . . .

R.R. McCormick, With the Russian Army.

After my return from Russia I was astounded to hear from a European military officer that the Kazacks [Cossacks] were an irregular body of guerrillas, useful to harry a defeated enemy, but unable to contend with regular troops. The truth about this is that they are to regular troops what regular troops are to the militia . . . The Kazacks are frontiersmen. We know the superiority of frontiersmen over all other troops of equal training . . . they are an hereditary military organisation like the Samurai of Japan . . . they are trained from childhood . . . There is no considerable body of troops in the world that can, mounted, offer any serious resistance to the Kazacks.

R.R. McCormick, With the Russian Army.

I expected to find Warsaw desolate. The sight that met me was of a city living as in time of peace. Certainly the war had made less impression here than upon the civil population in France.

R.R. McCormick, With the Russian Army.

As regards the Poles, my opinions are divided. A nation that, for the sake of an insignificant number of really cultured aristocrats, turns all the rest of its people into half-brutes, which has concentrated all its culture in a few spots, which has preserved its little castles and allowed the other "human beings" to live immediately beyond their walls in filth knee-deep, stinking, blunted and stupefied—such a nation has pronounced its own verdict.

Otto Braun, letter to his parents from Lodz, April 21, 1915.

We came upon long trains of Austrian prisoners, most of them happy and well, but some footsore and ill. There was about one guard for every 100 prisoners . . . Evidently there was no attempt . . . to escape. Many of them are of the Slav race and feel as much or more at home among the Russians as among the Austrians . . . Such a paucity of escorts could never have kept Siberians, or men from the Caucasus, or Kazacks, or cowboys.

R.R. McCormick in Galicia, May 1915, With the Russian Army.

I am dreaming such strange things lately. The other day I met C. S. for coffee, as we had often done in peacetime . . . I could not get rid of a weird feeling but did not know what it was. Finally I could not help asking: "How is this, haven't you been killed long ago?" "Yes," he said, "and so have you. All the people you see here have fallen . . ." What do you think of such crazy dreams? Premonitions?

Walter Lange, German student serving in Poland, letter of June 18, 1915. He was killed two months later. Quoted in War Letters of Fallen Students *(1929).*

In the middle of the day our regimental commander, Colonel Samfarov, showed up. The men can't stand him . . . He made the rounds through the companies, checking weapons and equipment. Suddenly he shouted with a piercing voice at Lieutenant Chancev: Why are the boots of the men red? Why haven't they been polished?" "Colonel, sir," Chancev answered, "it has been several months that our company has been in the fight without being relieved—not only have they no polish, but, as you can see, they are marching in completely torn boots. It is impossible to clean such footwear—" "Lieutenant, please do not argue with me," Samfarov replied. "When I command that the boots have to be black, then they have to be black."

J. Oskine, on fighting in Galicia, June 1915, in
Le carnet d'un soldat *(1931).*

As I found it in France so I found it in Galicia. The citizens who had been in the immediate theatre of war were ruined, but those nearby were getting rich selling supplies to the soldiers.

R.R. McCormick, near Sambar, Galicia, summer 1915, With the Russian Army.

The Austrian trenches were clearly visible through the glasses. They were of covered type, built with loop-holes and exceedingly strong against shrapnel and rifle fire. Another half mile beyond lay the supporting trenches, and around these, lounging in full view, were groups of Austrian soldiers clearly visible in their blue gray uniforms so badly adapted to modern warfare.

R.R. McCormick, in Galicia, summer 1915,
With the Russian Army.

I was ordered to ride over to a company that had moved up the line, and bring them back . . . I took R. with me, and we galloped along in complete darkness, jumping the Russian trenches, and rode straight through the village. The road bent sharply to the right and shrubs blocked the view. Suddenly I heard men moving and some Russian words. R. was riding a little behind me and said: "Oh, the Russians!," turned his horse sharply and tried to escape. We tore along when suddenly R. disappeared. It would have ben madness to stop. I tried to get to the 3rd Company . . . and make them occupy Rudnik. They did not take any notice of my request . . . I have never felt so awful, because I was sure that R. was dead or taken prisoner. On my return I heard that R. had only lost his horse, but saved himself by crawling through barns . . . Never have I been so happy. The next morning they said a lot of nice things about me, quite without cause, because it was pure luck to have found the Division

so soon. But the important thing is, my comrade is alive!

Otto Braun, diary at the eastern front, August 14, 1915.

"Station is Stradom, delousing!" At daybreak, one emerged from the train half asleep . . . Our train returned to the lousy front, we shall get a new, disinfected train after delousing. . . . There are about five to seven "Lausoleums" at the border, each has cost almost a million marks, but apparently they are necessary, because, according to the calculation of a professor, a Russian prisoner is feeding about 9000 lice . . .

Walter Schmidt, German student, letter from the Russian front, September 27, 1915. Quoted in War Letters of Fallen Students *(1929).*

The task of those at home seems to me to be that of preserving the continuity of civilisation . . . Even though we do not know when peace will come, come one day it will, and the future will belong not to the victorious or defeated nation, but to the one which will know how to turn the new era into one of peace, and which will win out in the conflicts of peace-time.

Otto Braun, letter to his parents from the Russian front, December 13, 1915.

I chanced to hear a soldier whom I had, well, not exactly cursed, but spoken to rather sharply . . . say to another: "As long as Lieut. Braun is in command I shall go everywhere with him." I do not suppose you know how glad a remark like this makes one . . . When all is said and done, it cannot be denied that leadership is *the* profession. I can't tell you how much I am learning here.

Otto Braun, letter to his parents from the Russian front, February 3, 1916.

Very interesting patrol duty at night. Under a clear starry sky crawled slowly forward on soft new-fallen snow . . . to within about 80 yards of the Russians. Finally, we got to a perfectly smooth surface of ice that might have broken any moment; there was no cover . . . It was a risky affair, for the Russians shot each time the ice cracked. At such times I am always pleased at my composure.

Otto Braun, diary, at the Russian front, February 28, 1916.

Our lake is getting more beautiful from day to day . . . The change of the landscape has not been lost on the Russians who are much greater lovers of nature than we are. For some time now, no shot has been fired on either side . . . We are watching each other, but think it stupid to alarm each other by shooting. When the Russian guard takes over, he feels that his vis-à-vis should know about it. He shouts "Morning, Aujuscht" across the lake, and takes his leave in the same manner. I don't know why the Ruski prefers to call the German "August," but he means better than the Frenchman for whom we are only the "boches." At the beginning, "Aujuscht" did not cooperate, kept his reserve in the face of all advances, and once in a while sent a bullet across. Then we heard "damned Germanski, no shoot." Most of the troops are Poles and Lithuanians and know a little German. It is good that there is a large lake between us, otherwise some of them would have deserted.

Oskar Greulich, German student, letter from the Russian front, April 24, 1916 in War Letters of Fallen Students.

One sometimes comes across people who are quite done for. Just now there passed a Pfc who obviously has St. Vitus' Dance, while the night before last, an Austrian platoon commander came running like mad and shouting: "The Russians, the Russians are coming." Then he was gone. You have to be one of those naif and arrogant "base wallahs" who have never been at the front to condemn these people.

Otto Braun, diary, at the Russian front, July 6, 1916.

The worst of the first day was that we had to stand the whole concentrated Russian fire without being able to retaliate in any way. Suddenly, like the prince in a fairy tale, just during the worst rain of shells, two young field artillery officers came along and said that they had just arrived with their battery and wanted to shoot, but they had no idea what was going on. We quickly told them, and in ten minutes the first purring shells whistled over our heads, like joy bells for us . . .

Otto Braun, letter to his parents from the Russian front, July 6, 1916.

Some of the men are quite exhausted, on the point of breaking up altogether, and some are already down and out, e.g. the crew of one machine gun that got three direct hits one after another. Nobody was wounded, but the men are finished, staggering about, screaming, and so on . . . There is one picture I shall never forget: In a wood where every stump was shot away lay a Russian, a German and another Russian; all three of them with expressions of most terrible fury on their faces, particularly the German with his bayonet fiercely clutched in his hand, his left clenched above his head, and beneath his heart the deep wound of a three-edged Russian bayonet.

Otto Braun, diary at the Russian front, July 10, 1916.

It was marvellous to see the Medics tearing about, under heavy fire, here, there and everywhere, with never a word of failing courage, joking occasionally and proud of being able to help the men. There was hardly a word of complaint from the wounded, just calmness and understanding. There are some things out here in the filth and the beastliness that are finer and more wonderful than many works of peace.

Otto Braun, letter to his parents from the Russian front, July 16, 1916.

The war theater is still divided into two great parties: Not Russians and Germans, but officers and men. "The superiors" somebody said the other day "are the cancer sore of the army." Very true. But that is good—for if the terror from behind is greater than that from the front then a violent urge will inspire the whole army . . . to rush to the front. Amen.

Kurt Tucholsky, political writer, letter to Hans E. Blaich, July 21, 1916.

Great cheers here that Hindenburg, now at Brest-Litowsk, has taken over the supreme command . . . Hindenburg's leadership gives us all a great feeling of calm, for under him, nothing has ever gone wrong. The men were so cheerful with the news that I was quite amazed about my Hanseatic and Mecklenburg men. Of course, a furlough is out of the question now. I would not leave my company to anyone else. I do feel much better as company commander than as an adjutant . . .

Hans Stegemann, German student, letter from the Russian front, August 4, 1916, in War Letters of Fallen Students.

Some of my best people have been killed in the last few days. And if you imagine the often heart-breaking letters of their relatives, whose only bread-winner, father of a family, or son, has been killed, you may realise the awful pictures. But what are we to do? Unshakable faith . . . keeps us going.

Otto Braun, letter from the Russian front to Atha N., September 26, 1916.

Now I must tell you how I was wounded . . . I was just beginning to write you a letter when the Russians attacked us repeatedly with machine-gun fire. We were right in the line of fire and I got hit on my left forearm as if with an iron rod; it knocked me down. In falling I must have received the shot in the face. It went in just above the jaw and out just under the eye, without touching my mouth, a piece of exceptional good luck. First I was lying there quite confused and discovered that I had been hit—without believing it. I went to the dug-out and got bandaged,—bleeding like a wounded wild pig; my coat and trousers were covered with blood, and my arm hurt very much, but I did not lose consciousness. Then they gave me morphia which didn't help much . . . the men were quite speechless. N. almost cried as I was driven away next day . . . and I nearly did too. One does not realise how attached one is to the company.

Otto Braun, letter to his father, from the Military Hospital at Lemberg, November 14, 1916.

Like many of us, I impatiently awaited medical help. We had thought the doctors would examine our wounds, and make bandages for us. That hope was in vain. Only on the third day, two young ambulance men showed up, accompanied by a young and elegant captain of the medical corps. They walked through our freight car, looked nonchalantly in our faces and left. I noticed some doctors and ambulance men who strolled about in front of the train. This criminal negligence of the medical service incensed the wounded. We expressed loudly our indignation, but in vain, since none was in the car but the wounded.

J. Oskine, at the caucasus front, 1916, in Le carnet d'un soldat.

He [the Grand Duke Paul] said a family council had convened and authorized him to respectfully beg his Majesty to agree to a constitution, as long as there is time for it. It would prove that the ruler anticipated the wishes of his people. He said: "There is an excellent opportunity. In three days we are celebrating the Saint-Nicholas festival. Announce on this day that the constitution has been granted, that Stuermer [the prime minister] and Protopopov have been removed, and you will see the enthusiasm and love of your faithful people cheering you." The ruler became contemplative. Then, with a tired gesture, he knocked off the ashes from his cigarette and, while the Czarina shook her head disapprovingly, said: "What you ask me to do is impossible. On the day of my coronation I have sworn an oath on the absolute rule. I must conserve this oath unimpaired for my son."

Princesse Paley, wife of Grand Duke Paul, relating the conversation of her husband with the tsar, December 3, 1916, Souvenirs de Russie *(1923).*

The real drama is that the Czarina is being accused of showing a lot of sympathy for the German interests. Everybody believes she wants peace and does not want to fight against Germany. She even organizes political parties in Russia that undoubtedly help William in his fight against us. I personally do not believe this, but all the world is sure that she who knows so much, is helping the enemy.

Alexander Dubenskij, historian at the Imperial court, in his diary, 1916.

You told me more than once that you do not trust anyone and that you are being deceived. If that is so, don't you think that your wife is being deceived too, who loves you dearly, but is being confused and flattered by the people around her. You trust Alexandra Feodorovna. That is only natural. But what she says is not the truth; she only repeats what is skillfully suggested to her by those around her.

Grand Duke Nicholas, letter to the tsar, end of 1916.

The political situation in Poland, created by the proclamation of November 5 has raised the impression among large parts of the population . . . that the German administration has nothing more to say and that Poland is now a completely independent country, relieved of any burden of war as is borne by every country in Europe. This opinion is erroneous. Since Polish authorities are just being instituted, there exists not yet any Polish administration, but it would have to impose the same requisitions and burdens as the German authorities who for the time being take their place.

Proclamation of the German General Governor, published in the Warschauer Zeitung *(German-language newspaper in Warsaw) December 31, 1916.*

Frosts have caught us by surprise in our summer outfits. The shoes we received in Tula were worn down by the long marches and open on all sides. Now we miss the woollen belts, the bashliks, the warm underwear which we left in Ustilug . . . Being immovable on the frozen ground during the cold spell caused many sicknesses, of course. Sometimes, ten men had to step out of the ranks. In my section, some left for the hospital with frozen feet or hands, day after day.

J. Oskine, recalling the winter of 1916/17, in Le carnet d'un soldat.

His opinion of foreign policy and international was intelligent. Too many journalists suspected him for no good reason, of wanting to come to terms with the Germans; but, if I would mention in these notes all the days when I heard him say "One has to admit that these boches are, nevertheless, pigs," it would sound monotonous . . . Undoubtedly he was poorly informed on some subjects, particularly about events of the day and what was being thought in his empire. That was inevitable. He read no newspapers but only excerpts. No original documents were submitted to him, but only condensed notes and reports.

General Janin, head of the French military commission at the Russian Headquarters, referring to the tsar, late 1916, in Le Monde Slave *(1926).*

Nicholas II had many faults as a ruler, but even more as a man. His greatest weakness turned this truly kind, sensitive and well educated man into a monster: alcoholism. Nicholas drank much, was often drunk, and during those moments he was horrible.

Aron Simonovice, secretary of Rasputin, Raspoutine (1930).

First . . . I have to pass on to you the following request of our friend Rasputin which came to him in a vision during the night. He asks you to order the offensive near Riga. He says it is necessary, as otherwise the Germans will dig in there for the whole winter . . . He says this is the main thing and asks you sincerely to order the attack.

Tsarina Alexandra Feodorovna, letter to the tsar, 1916.

January 10: Anastasia Sapovalenkove, wife of a doctor, has presented Rasputin with a carpet.
January 16: During the visit of . . . Rasputin held the prostitute on his knees, fondled her, and whispered inaudible words to her.
January 18: Maria Gill, wife of the commander of the 145. regiment, slept with Rasputin.
January 23: An unknown clergyman has brought some fish to Rasputin.
January 26: Last night Rasputin gave a party in honor of an individual just released from prison. They carried on very indecently and sang and drank into the morning hours.
January 28: Bokvone brought a case of wine to Rasputin today.
February 21: Simonovice, Rasputin's secretary, arrived with a case containing six bottles of wine, caviar and cheese.
April 3: Rasputin returned around one o'clock in the morning, accompanied by an unknown female who spent the night with him.

Police reports on Rasputin, 1916, reported by R. Fueloep-Miller, in Raspoutine et les femmes, *1952.*

I do not believe that Rasputin is an agent paid by the Germans, but he certainly was a fearful instrument in the hands of the German General Headquarters, which was intensely interested to preserve the life of such a valuable ally and therefore had surrounded him with spies who served, at the same time, as his bodyguard. The Germans had found an extremely effective way to compromise the court, and they exploited it.

Pierre Gilliard, the tutor of Alexei, the tsarevich, The Tragic Destiny of Nicholas and His Family *(1921).*

With the ladies and young girls of high society [Rasputin] behaved quite insolently, and the presence of their husbands or mothers did not bother him in the least. Even an oaf would have been insulted by his conduct. Yet hardly anybody ever took offense. One was afraid of him, and therefore he was surrounded by flatteries and courtesies, no matter what he did. The women kissed his dirty hands which were covered with the leftovers of his meals, and disregarded his repulsive, black fingernails.

Aron Simonovice, Raspoutine *(1930).*

Through years of observation I have tried to explain Rasputin's influence over their majesties. I came to the definite conclusion that his presence in the palace was closely connected with the illness of Aleksej [the young successor to the throne] . . . When Rasputin was presented to [the tsarina] she was convinced that, should she turn to him during Aleksej's illness, he would "personally" pray to God, and that God would hear his prayers. She was convinced Rasputin was the mediator between her and God, since her own prayers had no success. Both majesties saw in Rasputin a half-saint. I noticed it since I had lived with them for four years, they loved me. Yet, in front of me they never mentioned Rasputin with a single word. I clearly felt their fear that I, a Calvinist, would not understand their ideas about Rasputin . . .

Pierre Gilliard, The Tragic Destiny of Nicholas and His Family.

First I thought that there must have been an error, and that a third-class passenger got by mistake into the first-class compartment. The man was dressed like an ordinary peasant. His attire seemed to fit the person who wore it: coarse, poorly educated, hair like brushwood, a long beard showing remnants of his last meal. Both his hands and face were in need of thorough scrubbing . . . I noticed that people on the platform paid much respect to him and, passing him, made the sign of the cross. I asked one of the porters: "Who is this man?" He answered: "Grigori Rasputin."

Jones Stinton, English journalist, in Russia in Revolution *(1917).*

[Rasputin's] mouth was very large, and instead of teeth one only saw blackish stumps. Often, during meals, leftovers got stuck in his beard. He never ate meat, no sweets and no cake. His favorite food was potatoes and fruit sent to him by his many female admirers. He was anything from being an abstinent man. But he was not interested in Cognac, nor in

brandy or schnapps. He preferred Madeira and portwine to all other sorts of wine. He had gotten used to the wines of the South when he lived in monasteries, and could stand incredible amounts of them.

Aron Simonovice, Raspoutine *(1930).*

A tall man, dressed in a black caftan as worn by the Muziks on holidays, approaches the countess in large steps and kisses her noisily. That is the Starec Rasputin . . . I had time to observe him. Brown hair, long and dishevelled, a black, dense beard, high forehead, a broad and protruding nose, a muscular mouth. But the whole expression of the face is concentrated in the eyes—flax-blue eyes with a strange lustre, a strange inscrutability and magnetism. His glance is piercing and at the same time flattering, both naïve and shrewd, direct and remote. When he talks vivaciously one feels that his pupils take on a coat of phosphorus and magnetism. This "man of God," this mystic lecher at least makes no bones about his baseness, for his whole physical and moral personality surrounds itself with a rotten odor, a lusty smell, acid- and animal-like, the stench of a he-goat.

Maurice Paléologue, Alexandra Feodorovna, Imperatrice de Russie *(1932).*

Everybody is talking about Rasputin's assassination. In officers' circles the news has unleashed tremendous and noisy delight: a battle won with 100,000 prisoners could not have excited them more. Colonel Bazarov, usually quite restrained, was beaming all over his face and explained to me that even William's death would not have given him so much joy. . . . How many people have said: Now is the time to get the Czarina into a nunnery.

General Janin, recalling December 17, 1916, in Le Monde Slave.

The appointments that recently took place prove that you decided once and for all to pursue an interior policy which is the exact opposite of the wishes of your faithful subjects. This policy only plays into the hands of the left elements whose principle is "the worse, the better," and the more the discontent grows, the more the monarchic principle itself will begin to shake. Those who defend the idea that Russia cannot exist without a tsar will have no leg to stand on since the disorder and despotism will be known to all.

Grand Duke Alexander to the tsar, January 1, 1917.

He [the Tsar] appeared, simply dressed, in a grey cossak cerkesska, with a bloated face, tired but gracious . . . He asked trivial questions without showing much interest in the answers. The court seemed worried . . . The lackeys, splendidly dressed, talked to one another uninhibitedly. What striking contrast to the straight posture, the excellent behavior, the "fine taste" they still displayed last week! Something is wrong in the machinery, and that affects the engine, all the way to the servants of the palace . . . Before leaving the golden hall in which he had played his symbolic role, Nicholas II turned on the threshold to the guests, with a gloomy look and clenched fist. Alas! This provoking pose was more that of an automat winding itself up than that of an autocratic ruler prepared to break any resistance . . . Only power keeps him going, but for how long? They say that six regiments of the Guards are revolting . . .

Charles de Chambrun, secretary of the French ambassador, on the tsar's New Year's reception, January 1, 1917.

In our company soldiers have begun to desert. Almost every morning a few men are missing at roll call. Guards have been placed, upon order of the commandant, not only on every door but even every spot where the fences . . . can be climbed. . . . However, it does not help. It happened a few times that the guards themselves have thrown away their rifles and fled.

J. Oskine, recalling the mood early in 1917, Le carnet d'un soldat.

I cannot understand why books on Russia still like to describe the peasant as a slave tyrannized by a cruel despot. . . . I have lived in a Russian village for a long time and have seen time and time again how the peasants prevented their children from going to school . . . , saying it would be ridiculous to teach them stupidities, and that it was much better to leave the children with their families who would teach them to till the soil, which is much more useful than writing and calculating . . . In fact the peasants lived without missing anything, and if they did not know cleanliness, it was their own doing, because they did not feel the need for it. Unfortunately, there was vodka everywhere, a very strong drink on which all peasants got tight.

Alexander Eddalin, La Révolution Russe (1920).

8. The Balkans and the Orient: 1914–1918

THE HISTORICAL CONTEXT

Turkish Attacks on Russia and Against Suez

The fighting in the Balkans and in the Near East throughout the war did not directly affect the decisions on the main fronts, but it did divert considerable troop contingents on both sides, and it played a decisive role in the reorganization of Eastern Europe as well as the Eastern Mediterranean countries after the end of the war.

In the Balkans, Serbia and little Montenegro were in on the Allied side from the beginning. Bulgaria joined the Central Powers in October 1915, and Romania the Allies in August 1916. Finally, Greece came in with the Allies in June 1917.

All these moves were reactions to Turkey's decision in October 1914 to side with Germany against its arch enemy, the Russians. In November, the sultan of Turkey, as khalif the religious ruler over all Muslims, proclaimed a *jihad*, a holy war against all nations fighting Turkey or its allies—a move that did not influence events to a large extent. Britain, concerned that its presence in Egypt was jeopardized by Turkey's entry into the war, established a protectorate over Egypt, which Britain had occupied since 1882. The defense of Egypt was hastily organized, and the first troops from Australia and New Zealand arrived there in December 1914.

The idea conceived by the German general Otto Liman von Sanders, military attaché in Constantinople, to attempt an invasion of the Ukraine (which would have brought Romania in on the side of the Central Powers), was rejected by Turkey's new strong man, Enver Pasha. Instead, an offensive against Kars in Armenia—which had been Russian-occupied since 1878—was undertaken. At first, the Russians were pushed back, and Tabriz in Azerbaijan was taken by the Turks, but a Russian counterattack at the end of January 1915 succeeded, and the Turkish offensive came to an end. A few months later, the deportation and massacre of hundreds of thousands of Armenians began

123

when the Turks accused them of aiding the invading Russians. Thereupon the Armenians revolted and resisted in the mountain fortress of Van until they were released by a Russian force in May. Sporadic fighting in the Caucasus contained until August, when Van was reoccupied by the Turks.

In February 1915 the Turks also attacked the Suez Canal, but they were easily beaten by British and Anzac units. Still, a constant threat to vital English interests in the Near East continued to exist, and several British statesmen, notably Winston Churchill, Lloyd George and Lord Kitchener, proposed to leave the western front entirely in French hands and attack in the Near East, thus bringing the Balkan states in on the Allied side. These ideas were vigorously opposed by Joffre and Sir John French, and all plans of sending forces to the Gulf of Alexandretta or to Salonica had to be shelved until the Russians' appeal to the British for help in the Dardanelles was resolved (see Chapter 5). Bulgaria, Greece and Romania were still quite exhausted from the Balkan wars of 1912–13 and at first proclaimed neutrality in the world conflict. From the beginning, however, Russia tried hard to get Romania on its side, which would have been a great help in the forthcoming Galician campaign. As long as King Carol, who had been ready to join Austria and Germany, lived, this was impossible. After his death in October 1914, Ion Bratianu, prime minister under Carol's successor, Ferdinand, demanded from the Russians Transylvania, part of the Bukovina and the so-called Banat region in Southern Hungary as a reward. When the Russians seemed ready to concede all of this, the Romanians demanded further that the Allies should keep 500,000 men in the Balkans, and Russia another 200,000 in the Bessarabia. Thus, the year 1915 was spent in futile negotiations.

THE FIGHT FOR THE BALKAN STATES

Bulgaria was equally beleaguered by the Allies to join, and was offered part of Macedonia and Thrace; but again, the Bulgarians asked for more territory, including the Dobrudja region lost to Romania in the second Balkan war. After the failure of the Dardanelles campaign, the Allies renewed their offer to Bulgaria; in fact, they promised Bulgaria regions which would have to be taken from their ally Serbia and from Greece, whose support they also courted. But by June 1915, Bulgaria leaned to the Central Powers. In August, the German government persuaded the Turks to cede some territory along the Maritza River, and the Central Powers provided a loan of 400 million francs to Bulgaria, which thereupon began to mobilize. In October 1915, Serbia and Bulgaria declared war on each other.

This again brought Greece into the foreground. The Serbs, already at war with Austria, felt threatened by Bulgaria and appealed to

Greece for aid. Eleutherios Venizelos, the Greek prime minister, had recently returned to power and was ready to cooperate, allowing one British and one French division to land in Salonika in northern Greece. But again King Constantine refused to join the Allies, and Venizelos was forced to resign. The Allies now fostered a rival Greek government in Salonika under Venizelos which declared war on Austria and Germany.

Serbia, of course, had borne the brunt of the attack by the Central Powers. Belgrade had been bombed on July 29, 1914, and the Austrians started their first invasion of the country two weeks later. But they were unable to concentrate as much power as originally intended because of Russian pressure, and the Serbian army repulsed them in battles of the Tser and the Jadar, forcing the Austrians to withdraw from their territory. They even managed to invade Austria, but after a second Austrian invasion and prolonged fighting along the Drina River, they had to retreat, and Belgrade was taken on December 2, 1914 for a few days. The Serbs counterattacked, defeated the Austrians in the battle of Kolubara and retook the city on December 15, thus ending the second invasion of their country.

The end came for Serbia when in October 1915 an Austro-German campaign under General August von Mackensen was launched. Belgrade fell within a few days and the Bulgarians joined in; the Allied forces at Salonika were of no help to the Serbs. By December, the British were ready to discontinue the Salonica adventure. But the French, under General Maurice Sarrail, insisted on staying and demanded reinforcements, which tied up more troops but did not help the Serbs; they were forced out of their own country by the Bulgarians and the Austrians. Most troops fled into Albania and Montenegro (which was also overrun), though mountain warfare between Austrians and Italians continued in Albania for the duration of the war.

New friction between Greece and the Allies arose when the French, in January 1916, occupied the island of Corfu (Kerkira), off the northwestern Greek coast, to create a refuge for the beaten Serbian troops. Greek protests were ignored. A provisional Albanian government at Durres (Durazzo) had to leave for Naples under Italian protection, after Scutari (Shkoder) and Berat had been taken by the Austrians. By the spring of 1916, the position of the Central Powers seemed quite favorable, particularly after a German-Bulgarian force had occupied a fortress in Greek Macedonia, which seemed to indicate that King Constantine of Greece had finally decided in favor of the Central Powers. Within a month, this provoked an ultimatum from the Allies demanding from Greece demobilization and the formation of a new government. The Greeks gave in but were lukewarm in their support of a new Allied drive, consisting of Serbian troops from Corfu and some Russian and Italian contingents which advanced against Bulgaria but were pushed back by German and Bulgarian counterattacks. A voluntary Greek corps fighting with the Allies surrendered. This infuriated the Allies, who thereupon demanded the surrender of the Greek fleet. When further Allied demands were rejected, British and French units landed at Piraeus on December 1, 1916, but they withdrew after some weeks. Clashes between the Greek government supporters and the pro-Allied Venizelists occurred, and the British decided to recognize Venizelos. By this time, the Salonica troops under Sarrail had started their great offensive in Macedonia and had taken Monastir (Bitola), but they did not manage to advance on the Bulgarian frontier.

New fighting broke out in Macedonia in the spring of 1917. After two inconclusive battles, again at Monastir and Lake Presba, and another engagement in May, the Allies realized that without the cooperation of a reliable Greek government, they could not succeed. Therefore, another Allied ultimatum was handed to the Greek government demanding King Constantine's abdication. Simultaneously, French troops occupied the Isthmus of Corinth, and Allied forces also invaded Thessaly. On June 12, Constantine abdicated, his son Alexander made Venizelos premier, and within one day Greece severed its relations with the Central Powers. Since Romania had fallen in January of 1917, there was no Balkan power left on the side of the Central Powers, except Bulgaria.

THE NEAR EAST

The war in the Near East began on a rather small scale when, in November 1914, a British force from India occupied Basra in southern Mesopotamia (Iraq) to protect the oil pipeline from Persia (Iran). The British, under General Sir John Nixon, then extended their territory and defeated Turkish attacks on Basra in April 1915. Another British force, under General Charles Vere Townshend, advanced to the Tigris and Euphrates rivers and began a push toward Baghdad, defeating the Turks at Kut-el-Amara. However, after another engagement at Ctesiphon on the Tigris in November of the same year, Townshend was forced to fall back and was then besieged at Kut-el-Amara. Three times the British attempted to relieve the garrison, but their troops were held up by floods. They then tried to buy off the Turks but to no avail. In April 1916 all of their 10,000 men had to surrender.

Some months earlier, the Russians had invaded western Iran and then started an offensive in Armenia. After a successful drive south, they turned west to flank the Turks in Iraq and by May 1916 joined hands with the British at the Tigris River. Large parts of Armenia—including the towns of Erzerum and Trebizond—also fell to the Russians, but in June, the Turkish counterdrive began, which lasted until the middle of August; thereafter, it was checked by the Russians.

In 1915 and 1916, the British in Egypt were threatened from two sides, by the Senussi Tribes from the west and by the Turks from the northeast. The Senussi uprising was suppressed in March 1916 when the British reoccupied the town of Sollum; but their campaign against the Sultan of Darfur occupied them for the rest of the year. In April, a Turkish unit under German command surprised the British and seized several outposts controlling the approach to the Suez Canal. But they were driven out again, and a larger Turkish attempt against the canal, undertaken in August, came to an end when the Turks were almost surrounded at Rumani and forced to retreat.

In April 1916, Britain, France and Russia agreed on the future partition of the vast Turkish possessions in Asia. Constantinople had already been promised to the Russians in early 1915. It was decided that Britain should control Mesopotamia (Iraq) and Syria; France, the Syrian coast, Cilicia and southern Kurdistan; and Russia, Armenia and parts of Kurdistan and northern Anatolia. A year later, Italy was granted some concessions in the Smyrna region. In all of these arrangements, the British made commitments which were at odds with promises they had made to some Arab leaders.

Naturally, the British and French did their best to assure Arab assistance against the Turkish rule. From July 1915 to early 1916, there were negotiations between London and Arab leaders, in particular, Hussein ibn Ali, the Grand Sherif of Mecca. An agreement was reached in January 1916; in June, the great Arab revolt started with an attack on the Turkish garrison at Medina, which was forced to surrender, whereupon Hussein proclaimed himself king of the Arab countries. The British recognized him as king of the Hejaz and, under the leadership of General Archibald Murray, began a drive from Egypt into Palestine and the Sinai peninsula. This offensive was at first successful, but then the Turks managed to get in reinforcements and were aided by German troops under Falkenhayn. In the second battle of Gaza, the British were forced to withdraw and suffered heavy losses. Murray was then replaced by Sir Edmund Allenby, a cavalry officer who had last commanded the Fifth British Army in France.

Allenby, although operating far from his home base and confronting the Turkish Empire in a region it had controlled for centuries, had two factors going in his favor. The first was that from spring 1917 on, the Turks were convinced that the Russian Empire had collapsed for good and gambled on an early German victory. Therefore, their main interest was now directed toward territorial pickings in the Caucasus region, and they considered the Palestine front against the British operating from Egypt as secondary.

Secondly, Allenby not only had the help of King Hussein, whose diplomatic skill did much to control the disparate Arab tribes, but also that of a new, spectacular war hero, Colonel Thomas Edward Lawrence, who joined the army of Hussein's son Faisal as an adviser in

Viscount Edmund Henry Allenby, conqueror of Palestine and Jerusalem. Photo courtesy of the New York Public Library.

1916 and soon assumed a leading role in the Arab uprisings. Lawrence was an English scholar who had traveled widely in the Near and Middle East and had worked in Egypt for British Army Intelligence. He was thoroughly at home in the Arab world and had mastered colloquial Arabic. He was almost given a free hand by Allenby and was provided with weapons and money. His idea was to organize small, mobile striking forces who often worked far behind the Turkish lines and to strike at the few vital railways on which the Turks depended for supplies. With only a few thousand men at his disposal, he managed to tie down large parts of the Turkish army. Lawrence fought passionately for Arab independence, and it was the tragedy of his life that the hopes he had raised among the Arabs were not fulfilled at the Paris Peace Conferences.

TURKEY'S COLLAPSE

Allenby's attack on the Palestine front began in October 1917. After a month of heavy fighting, the British managed to roll up the Turkish lines, taking the towns of Beersheba, Gaza and Jagga in November, and finally Jerusalem in December. Then his advance came to a stop, as he had to give up large contingents of his army to meet the crisis in France. His final attack—which led to the collapse of Turkey—only began in September 1918. The three Turkish armies, led by the German general Otto Liman von Sanders with headquarters in Nazareth, ran from Arsuf on the Mediterranean to the Jordan Valley. Only one railway line came down from Damascus in the North; it branched out to Megiddo and Haifa on the Mediterranean in the west, and was constantly harassed by Arab tribes. Allenby made the Turks believe that his main thrust would take place in the Jordan Valley. Instead, he attacked along the sea coast, and his superior cavalry pushed far enough along the coast to swing around to the east, behind the lines of two of the Turkish armies, occupying their communication centers. The German corps managed to escape into Transjordan, but the greater part of Turkish military might was destroyed within a few days. The British advance could not be stopped: Damascus, Homs and Aleppo were taken in October, and French navy units captured Beirut in the same month. Within five weeks, the British had advanced 300 miles and had taken 75,000 prisoners, losing less than 5,000 men themselves. The Turks appealed for an armistice.

In Mesopotamia, the British started their new attack on Turkish forces in December 1916 and—after prolonged fighting at Kut-el-Amara during January and February 1917—occupied Baghdad in March. Meanwhile, the Russians had advanced in Western Persia (Iran) until July 1917, whereafter they retreated, as a result of the Russian Revolution. The British, further advancing to the north, captured Ramadi on the Euphrates and Tikrit on the Tigris in September 1917.

CHRONICLE OF EVENTS

1914:

October 10: King Carol of Romania, a supporter of the Central Powers, dies. His successor Ferdinand and his prime minister Ion Bratianu start negotiations with the Entente Cordiale.

November 22: British forces from India occupy Basra, the only port of Mesopotamia (Iraq), then spread into the surrounding territories.

December 17: The Turks begin their drive toward Kars in Armenia.

December 29–January 2: Battle of Sarikamish. The Turks advance and occupy Tabriz in northwest Iran.

1915:

January 30: Tabriz is retaken by the Russians.

February 3–4: Turkish attacks on the Suez Canal are repulsed by the British.

March 6: Greek prime minister Eleutherios Venizelos resigns because his king, Constantine, refuses to support the Allies at the Dardanelles.

April: Turks begin deportation and massacre of the Armenians, accused of aiding the Russian invaders.

April 11–13: British forces, under Sir John Nixon, repulse Turkish attacks on Basra.

April 20: Armenian uprising at Van, eastern Turkey.

May 19: Van is relieved by a Russian force.

June 3: British General Charles Vere Townshend occupies Amara on the Tigris River.

July 25: Townshend takes the town of Nasiriya on the Euphrates and begins his advance toward Baghdad.

August 5: Van is reoccupied by the Turks.

September 21: Bulgarians begin to mobilize.

September 28: In the battle of Kut-el-Amara, Townshend's army defeats the Turks.

October 3–5: One British and one French division land at Salonika (Thessaloniki) in Macedonia.

October 5: Greek prime minister Venizelos resigns again since King Constantine refuses to join in the war.

October 6: German-Austrian campaign in Serbia, led by General August von Mackensen.

October 9: Belgrade is taken by the Central Powers.

October 11: Bulgarian troops cross into Serbia.

October 14: Bulgaria and Serbia declare war on each other.

October 15: England and France declare war on Bulgaria.

October 22: Bulgarian troops under General Nicolas Jekov occupy Skopje (Uskub) in Serbian Macedonia.

November 5: Nish is taken by the Bulgarians.

November 16: Prilep is taken by the Bulgarians.

November 22–24: Battle of Ctesiphon, southeast of Baghdad. Indecisive outcome, both Turkish and British troops retreat, the British all the way to Kut-el-Amara.

December 2: Bulgarians occupy Monastir (Bitolje).

December 6: Austrian troops occupy Plevje abd Ipek in Serbia.

December 6–10: Allied forces, operating from Salonika, are repulsed on the Vardar River.

December 7–April 29, 1916: The Turks besiege Kut-el-Amara.

1916:

January 11: French occupy Corfu.

January 13: Cettinje, Serbia, is taken by the Austrians. King Nicholas of Montenegro retires to Italy.

January 15: Serbian refugee troops land in Corfu, over Greek protests.

January 18: Russian offensive in Armenia. Koprikoi is taken.

January 18–21: Vain attempt is made by the British to relieve the garrison at Kut-el-Amara.

February 13–16: Battle at Erzerum, which falls to the Russians.

February 18: Russians take Mush in Armenia.

February 26: In their advance into western Persia (Iran), the Russians take Kirmanshah.

February 27: Austrians take Durazzo (Durres), Albania. The Albanian government has left for Naples.

March 2: Bitlis, Armenia, falls to the Russians.

March 8: Another British attempt to relieve the troops at Kut-el-Amara fails.

March 12: Russians occupy Karind, in Iran.

April 1–9: Last British effort to relieve the garrison at Kut-el-Amara.

April 17: Russians occupy the Black Sea port of Trebizond (Trabzom).

April 26: Anglo-French-Russian agreement regarding the future partition of the Turkish Empire in Asia.

April 29: British forces at Kut-el-Amara capitulate to the Turks.

May 15: The Russians take Khanikin and Rowanduz in Armenia.

May 26: A Bulgarian-German force occupies Fort Rupel in Greek Macedonia.

June 5: Arab revolt against the Turks begins. Attack on the Turkish garrison at Medina.

Turkish counteroffensive in western Iran begins. Khanikin is retaken.

July 1: Kirmanshah is retaken by the Turks.

August 2–21: Battle of Doiran. Allied troops advance against the Bulgarians on the Salonika front.

August 4: Turkish forces attacking the Suez Canal are almost surrounded near Rumani, and retreat.

August 17–19: Battle of Florina. Bulgarian and German troops push back the Allied Salonika forces.

September 29: Venizelos and Admiral Paul Condouriotis establish a provisional, pro-Allied government in Crete.

October 5–December 11: Allied Salonika forces under French general Maurice Sarrail attack in Macedonia.

October 29: Hussein, Grand Sherif of Mecca, is proclaimed king of the Arabs.

November 19: Monastir (Bitolje) in Macedonia is taken by Sarrail's troops.

November 20: British offensive in Sinai and Palestine under Sir Archibald Murray.

December 15: British recognize Hussein as king of the Hejaz.

December 21: British take El Arish.

December 23: British take the fortified post of Maghdaba.

1917:

January 9: British take Rafah.

March 11–19: Second battle of Monastir is inconclusive. Battle at Vardar is also undecided.

March 11: British occupy Baghdad.

March 26–27: Battle of Gaza. British fail to take the town.

April 17–19: Second battle of Gaza. The Turks, reinforced by German units, force back the British with heavy losses.

June 12: King Constantine of Greece abdicates in favor of his son, Alexander.

June 27: Venizelos again is premier in Greece. Relations with the Central Powers are severed.

June 28: In Palestine Sir Archibald Murray is replaced by Sir Edmund Allenby.

July 6: British Colonel T.E. Lawrence begins coordinating the Arab movement and operating behind Turkish lines in Palestine.

July 8: Russians begin to retreat from western Iran.

September 29: British take Ramadi on the Euphrates.

October: Beginning of the British offensive, under General Allenby, on the Palestine front.

October 31: British take Beersheba.

November 7: British force the evacuation of Gaza.

November 16: Jaffa is evacuated by the Turks.

December 8: Allenby enters Jerusalem.

1918:

September 18, 1918: British offensive in Palestine. In the battle of Megiddo, the Turkish lines are broken.

October 1–2: British and Arabs take Damascus.

October 7: French naval forces take Beirut.

October 15: Homs falls to the Allies.

October 26: Aleppo is taken by the Allies. The

Young Turk ministers are dismissed by Sultan Mohammed VI.

October 30: Armistice between Turkey and the Allies is concluded at Mudros.

November 12: The Allied fleet passes the Dardanelles and arrives at Constantinople.

EYEWITNESS TESTIMONY

It had been nine years since I had been in Marseille. Then it had impressed me as being a rather sleepy city, partaking of the repose of the South. Now we found it bustling with life, the gayest city, I think, I have ever seen.

R.W. Imbrie, recalling impressions on the way to the Orient, October 1916, Behind the Wheel *(1918).*

The atmosphere was oppressive, deadly. There seemed no life in it. It was not burning hot, but held a moisture and sense of great age and exhaustion such as seemed to belong to no other place: not a passion of smells like Smyrna, Naples or Marseilles, but a feeling of long use, of exhalations of many people, of continued bath-heat and sweat. One would say that for years Jidda had not been swept through by a firm breeze: that its streets kept their air from year's end to year's end, from the day they were built for so long as the houses would endure. There was nothing in the Bazaars to buy.

T.E. Lawrence, on arriving at Jidda, port of Mecca, on the Red Sea, October 1916, Revolt in the Desert *(1926).*

Ali would not let me start till after sunset, lest any of his followers see me leave the camp. He kept my journey a secret even from his slaves, and gave me an Arab cloak and headcloth to wrap around myself and my uniform, that I might present a proper silhouette in the dark upon my camel. I had no food with me; so he instructed Tafas [Lawrence's guide] to get something to eat at Bir el Sheiks, the first settlement, some sixty miles out, and charged him most stringently to keep me from questioning and curiosity on the way, and to avoid all camps and encounters.

T.E. Lawrence, on the way from Rabegh, on the Red Sea, to meet Faisal, October 1916, Revolt in the Desert.

[Faisal] looked very tall and pillar-like, very slender, in his long white silk robes and his brown headcloth . . . His eyelids were dropped; and his black beard and colourless face were like a mask . . . I greeted him . . . "And do you like our place here in Wadi Safra?" "Well; but it is far from Damascus."

The word had fallen like a sword into their midst. There was a quiver. Then everybody present stiffened and held his breath for a silent minute. Some, perhaps, were dreaming of far off success; others may have thought it a reflection on their late defeat. Feisal at length lifted his eyes, smiling at me and said, "Praise be to God, there are Turks nearer to us than that." We all smiled with him; and I rose and excused myself for the moment.

T.E. Lawrence, on his meeting with Faisal, October 1916, Revolt in the Desert.

Sections of Beni Ali tribesmen approached the Turkish command with an offer to surrender, if their villages be spared. Fakhri [the Turkish Pash] played with them, and in the ensuing lull of hostilities surrounded the Awali suburb with his troops; whom he suddenly ordered to carry it by assault and to massacre every living thing within its walls. Hundreds

Thomas Edward Lawrence ("Lawrence of Arabia"). Photo courtesy of the New York Public Library.

of the inhabitants were raped and butchered, the houses fired, and living and dead alike thrown back into the flames. Fakhri and his men had served together and had learned arts of both the slow and the fast kill upon the Armenians in the North. This bitter taste of the Turkish mode of war sent a shock across Arabia; for the first rule of Arab war was that women were inviolable; the second that the lives of children too young to fight with the men were to be spared: the third, that property impossible to carry off should be left undamaged.

T.E. Lawrence with Faisal, November 1916. In Revolt in the Desert.

At this moment two German prisoners . . . pass by within six feet of us. The colonel's lips draw back like the unsheathing of a bayonet, his eyes stab and his unbandaged hand opens and closes as though gripping a throat. "Sales cochons ("dirty pigs")," he mutters. "Nom de Dieu, how I hate them." The prisoners pass placidly by and you feel it is well that our friend cannot have his way with them.

R.W. Imbrie, in Macedonia, November 1916, Behind the Wheel.

It's wonderful what a cheering effect the arrival of the post had on us. Throughout the winter it was about our only comfort. In France it had been welcome, but in the Orient we seemed to be so cut off from the world that letters were a luxury . . . When they came it didn't so much matter that a man was cold or hungry and caked with mud, that the quarters leaked and that the snow drifted in on his blankets.

R.W. Imbrie, in Florina, Northern Macedonia, early December 1916, Behind the Wheel.

. . . more shells came in, scattered about the city . . . Crossing the stream we saw the body of a man hanging half over the wall, and nearby the shattered paving where the shell had struck. In such an atmosphere we lived. Each day brought its message of death. On December 19th, I saw a spy taken out to be shot. On the 20th, a house next to quarters was hit. Two days later, when evacuating under shrapnel fire, I saw two men killed . . .

R.W. Imbrie, in Monastir (now Bitola), Macedonia, December 1916, Behind the Wheel.

Monastir (Bitola) is a city without cellars, a city for the most part of flimsy mud walls . . . About all one can hope for in a bombardment is that by sticking close to a house the smaller éclat (fragments) may be stopped. To be strafed on Christmas Day . . . before the only real meal in months, was surely the refinement of cruelty, worthy of the Huns . . . Somehow the dinner was not a great success. I guess we were all just a bit homesick. Not even the plum pudding aroused our spirits. There was only one toast: "To the folks back there!"

R.W. Imbrie, in Monastir (Bitola), Macedonia, Christmas 1916, Behind the Wheel.

The following day we had five cars demolished, my own among the number. Its sides were blown in and the entire vehicle was plastered with blood, and strips of human flesh, the shell which did the damage having torn a little girl who was standing by it at the time. In all the war I have seen no more horrible sight than that of the child's family gathering the still warm particles of flesh . . .

R.W. Imbrie, in Monastir (Bitola), Macedonia, December 29, 1916, Behind the Wheel.

As we drove along, we left consternation in our wake. Mountain ponies, forsaking the habit of years, climbed imaginary trees and kicked their loads loose with a carefree abandon of a great desire to be elsewhere. Terror-stricken peasants gave us one look and took to the fields . . . An elephant pulling a baby-carriage up Fifth Avenue would excite no greater wonder than did our car rolling through the streets of Coritza.

R.W. Imbrie, in Albania, January 1917, Behind the Wheel.

"It isn't the fire we fear,/ It isn't the bullets that whine,/ It isn't the business career/ Of a shell or the bust of a mine;/ It isn't the snipers who seek/ To nip our young hopes in the bud;/ No, it isn't the guns/ And it ain't the Huns -/ It's the Mud, Mud, Mud!"

Army song, quoted by R.W. Imbrie, January 1917, in Behind the Wheel.

We saw much of the Italians. Long lines of their troops were constantly marching forward, little men with ill-formed packs. As soldiers they did not impress us, but they had a splendid motor transport, big powerful cars, well adapted to the Balkan mud, and handled by the most reckless and skillful drivers in the Allied armies. The men were a vivacious lot and often sang as they marched.

R.W. Imbrie, in Brode, Serbia, January 1917, Behind the Wheel.

In marked contrast [to the Italians] were the Serbs, the "poor relation of the Allies." For the most part they were middle-aged men, clad in non-descript uniforms and with varied equipment. They slogged by silently—almost mournfully. I never saw one laugh and they smiled but rarely. They went unobtrusive, almost unnoticed, yet when a car was mired, they were always the first to help, and withal they were invested with a quiet dignity which seemed to set them apart. I never talked with a soldier of any army who had seen them in action, but who praised their prowess.

R.W. Imbrie, in Brode, Serbia, January 1917
Behind the Wheel.

If Verdun had seemed the City of the Dead, Monastir (Bitola) was the place of Souls Condemned to Wander in the Twilight of Purgatory. The fate of the population was a pitiful one. In a world of war, they had no status. Food, save the farina issued by the military, was unobtainable, and fuel equally wanting. Scores were killed. As for the wounded, their situation was terrible. Drugs were too precious, bandages too valuable and surgeons' time too well occupied for their treatment.

R.W. Imbrie, in Monastir (Bitola), Macedonia,
February 13, 1917, Behind the Wheel.

The sole disquieting feature was the very real success of the Turks in frightening the Arabs by artillery. The sound of a fired cannon sent every man within earshot behind cover. They thought weapons destructive in proportion to their noise. They were not afraid of bullets, nor indeed overmuch of dying: just the manner of death by shellfire was unendurable. It seemed to me that their moral confidence was to be restored only by having guns, useful or useless, but noisy, on their side. From the magnificent Faisal down to the most naked stripling in the army the theme was artillery, artillery . . .

T.E. Lawrence, with Faisal, winter of 1916/17,
Revolt in the Desert.

We must not take Medina. The Turk was harmless there. In prison in Egypt he would cost us food and guards . . . Our ideal was to keep his railway just working, but only just, with a maximum of loss and discomfort . . . His stupidity would be our ally, for he would like to hold, or to think he held, as much of his old provinces as possible. This pride in his

imperial heritage would keep him in his present absurd position—all flanks and no front.

T.E. Lawrence, recalling how he explained his
strategy to the Arabs, spring 1917, Revolt in
the Desert.

As soon as I entered the Chief handed me a gas mask and warned me to keep it slung. The night before the enemy had, for the first time, shelled with gas. As a result, 344 *civils* had been killed, and some few soldiers. Dead horses, dogs and the few remaining fowls lay about the streets, suffocated by the deadly chlorine . . . Several of the men had been nearly overcome before they were awakened and their masks fixed.

R.W. Imbrie, in Monastir (Bitola), Macedonia,
March 1917, Behind the Wheel.

It is not possible to convey an idea of the horror of Monastir during the period. The panic-stricken population fleeing the city, the burning houses—for the enemy had added incendiary shells to his repertoire of frightfulness—the rotting carcasses . . . , the field dressing-stations with their blackened, bloody occupants . . . the air itself, bearing the breath of death . . . Another horror was added . . . when the enemy's planes flew over the city dropping a salvo of bombs. The fire of our antiaircraft did not seem to have the slightest effect . . .

R.W. Imbrie, in Monastir (Bitola), Macedonia,
March 1917, Behind the Wheel.

Having not a mouthful of water we of course ate nothing. Yet the certainty of drink on the morrow let us sleep easily, lying on our bellies to prevent the inflation of foodlessness. Arab habit was to fill to vomiting point at each well, and either to go dry to the next; or, if they carried water, to use it lavishly at the first halt, drinking and bread-making.

T.E. Lawrence, riding through the desert, May
1917, in Revolt in the Desert.

A strange thing was the snakes' habit, at night, of lying beside us, probably for warmth, under or on the blanket. When we learned this our rising was with infinite care, and the first up would search around his fellows with a stick till he could prove them unencumbered. Our party of fifty men killed perhaps twenty snakes daily; at last they got so on our nerves that the boldest of us feared to touch ground . . .

T.E. Lawrence, in the Arab desert, May 1917,
Revolt in the Desert.

It was never easy for us to keep our movements secret, as we lived by preaching to the local people, and the unconvinced would tell the Turks. Our long march into Wadi Sirhan was known to the enemy, and the most civilian owl could not fail to see that the only fit objective was Akaba.

T.E. Lawrence, crossing the desert, June 1917, Revolt in the Desert.

. . . we rode steadily through the flowing mirage till afternoon, when we descended on the [railway] line; and, having delivered a long stretch of it from guards and patrols, began on the many bridges of the captured section. The little garrison of Ghadir el Haj sallied out with the valour of ignorance against us, but the heat-haze blinded them, and we drove them off with loss.

T.E. Lawrence, on sabotage work 60 miles northeast of Akaba, summer 1917, Revolt in the Desert.

Fortunately the poor handling of the enemy gave us an unearned advantage. [The Turks] slept on in the valley, while we crowned the hills in wide circle about them unobserved. We began to snipe them steadily in their positions under the slopes and rock-faces by the water, hoping to provoke them out and up the hill in charge against us . . . It was terribly hot - hotter than ever before I had felt in Arabia - and the anxiety and constant movement made it hard for us. Some even of the tough tribesmen broke down under the cruelty of the sun, and crawled or had to be thrown under rocks to recover in their shade. We ran up and down to supply our lack of numbers by mobility . . . The hill-sides were steep and exhausted our breath . . . Our rifles grew so hot with sun and shooting that they seared our hands, and we had to be grudging our rounds, considering every shot. The rocks on which we flung ourselves for aim were burning . . . We consoled ourselves with knowledge that the enemy's enclosed valley would be hotter than our open hills: Also that they were Turks, men of white meat, little apt for warm weather.

T.E. Lawrence, fighting the way to the sea, near Akaba, summer 1917, Revolt in the Desert.

Now [the captured Turkish commander] sidled up by me and, his swollen eyelids and long nose betraying the moroseness of the man, began to complain that an Arab had insulted him with a gross

Turkish word. I apologized, pointing out that it must have been learned from the mouth of one of his Turkish fellow-governors. The Arab was repaying Caesar.

T.E. Lawrence, on the way to the sea, July 1917. In Revolt in the Desert.

In the last four weeks I had ridden fourteen hundred miles by camel, not sparing myself anything to advance the war; but I refused to spend a single superfluous night with the familiar vermin. I wanted a bath, and something with ice in it to drink: to change clothes, all sticking to my saddle sores in filthiness . . . to eat something more tractable than green date and camel sinew. I got through again to the Inland Water Transport and talked like Chrysostom. It had no effect, so I became vivid. Then, once more, they cut me off. I was growing very vivid, when friendly northern accents from the military exchange floated down the line: "It's no bluidy good, sir, talking to them . . . water boogers."

T.E. Lawrence, in Akaba, summer 1917, Revolt in the Desert.

The notes we had issued at Bair . . . were pencilled promises, on army telegraph forms, to pay so much to bearer in Akaba. It was a great system, but no one had dared issue notes before in Arabia, because the Bedouins had neither pockets in their shirts nor strong-rooms in their tents, and notes could not be buried for safety. So there was an unconquerable prejudice against them . . .

T.E. Lawrence, in Cairo, summer 1917, Revolt in the Desert.

Before I was clothed, the Commander-in-Chief sent for me, curiously . . . It was a comic interview, for Allenby was physically large and confident, and morally so great that the comprehension of our littleness came slow to him . . . He was full of Western ideas of gun power and weight - the worst training for our war - , but, as a cavalry-man, was already half persuaded to throw up the new school, in this different world of Asia . . . He did not ask many questions, nor talk much, but studied the map and listened to my unfolding of Eastern Syria and its inhabitants. At the end he put up his chin and said quite directly: "Well, I will do for you what I can," and that ended it. I was not sure how far I had caught him; but we learned gradually that he meant exactly what he said;

and that what General Allenby could do was enough for his very greediest servant.

T.E. Lawrence, Cairo, summer 1917, Revolt in the Desert.

The King Hussein came down from Mecca and talked discursively . . . the proposed transfer of Faisal to Allenby was accepted at once, King Hussein taking the opportunity to stress his complete loyalty to our alliance. Then, changing his subject, as usual without obvious coherence, he began to expose his religious position, neither strong Shia nor strong Sunni . . . In foreign politics he betrayed a mind as narrow as it had been broad in unwordly things; with much of that destructive tendency of little men to deny the honesty of opponents. I grasped something of the fixed jealousy which made the modern Faisal suspect in his father's court; and realized how easily mischief-makers could corrode the King.

T.E. Lawrence, on Hussein's meeting with the British at Jidda, summer 1917, Revolt in the Desert.

No one group would ride or speak with another, and I passed back and forth all day like a shuttle, talking first to one lowering sheikh, and then to another, striving to draw them together, so that before a cry to action came there might be solidarity . . . For my private part [Sheikh Zaal] was the only one to be trusted farther than eyesight. Of the others, it seemed to me that neither their words nor their counsels, perhaps not their rifles, were sure.

T.E. Lawrence, on the beginning of Allenby's campaign, September 1917, Revolt in the Desert.

. . . in the late afternoon we came to the well. It was an open pool, a few yards square, in a hollow valley . . . The stagnant water looked uninviting. Over its face lay a thick mantle of green slime, from which swelled curious bladder-islands of floating fatty pink. The Arabs explained that the Turks had thrown dead camels into the pool to make the water foul; but that time had passed and the effect was grown faint . . . Yet it was all the drink we could get up here . . . so we set to and filled our waterskins.

T.E. Lawrence, on Allenby's campaign, September 1917, Revolt in the Desert.

I could hear the racket coming, as I sat on my hillock by the bridge to give the signal to Salem [Faisal's slave] who danced round the exploder on his knees, crying with excitement and calling urgently on God to make him fruitful . . . I wondered with how many men we were going to have affair, and if the mine would be advantage enough for our eighty fellows to equal them . . . when the front "driver" of the second engine was on the bridge, I raised my hand to Salem. There followed a terrific roar, and the line vanished from sight behind a spouting column of black dust and smoke . . . Out of the darkness came shattering crashes and long, loud metallic clangings of ripped steel . . . while one entire wheel of a locomotive whirled up suddenly black out of the cloud against the sky . . . I saw the train stationary and dismembered along the track, with its wagon sides jumping under the bullets . . . while Turks were falling out from the far doors to gain the shelter of the railway embankment. As I watched, our machine guns chattered out over my head, and long rows of Turks on the carriage roofs rolled over and were swept off the top like bales of cotton . . .

T.E. Lawrence, on blowing up the Hejaz railway behind the Turkish lines, fall of 1917, Revolt in the Desert.

The valley was a weird sight. The Arabs, going raving mad, were rushing about at top speed, bareheaded and half naked, screaming, shooting in the air, clawing one another nail and fist while they burst open trucks and staggered back and forward with immense bales which they ripped by the railside, and tossed through, smashing what they did not want . . . the Arabs, having lost their wits, were as ready to assault friend as foe. Three times I had to defend myself when they pretended not to know me and snatched at my things.

T.E. Lawrence, on looting of the blown-up Turkish train, fall 1917, Revolt in the Desert.

We on the Arab front were very intimate with the enemy. Our Arab officers had been Turkish officers, and knew every leader on the other side personally. . . . In consequence our intelligence service was the widest, fullest and most certain imaginable . . . We hoped Allenby would be given a month's fine weather; and, in that case, expected him to take not merely Jerusalem, but Haifa, too . . . I weighed the English army in my mind, and could not honestly assure myself of them. The men were often gallant fighters, but their generals as often gave away in stupidity what they had gained in ignorance. Allenby was quite untried, and his troops had broken down in and been broken by the General Archibald Murray period . . .

T.E. Lawrence, on Allenby's offensive, October 1917, Revolt in the Desert.

[Emir] Abd el Kader was gone up to the enemy, with information of our plans and strength. The Turks, if they took the most reasonable precautions, would trap us at the bridge [over the river Yarmuk]. We . . . decided to push on none the less, trusting to the usual incompetence of our enemy. It was not a confident decision . . . we rode a few yards further, to the top of a stone knoll and there found ourselves looking down upon a retreating party of Circassian horsemen, sent out by the Turks to report if the waters were occupied. They had missed us, to our mutual benefit, by five minutes. At dawn we marched leisurely until the desert ended in a three-foot depression at the edge of a clean plain which extended flatly to the metals of the railway some miles off. We halted for dusk to make its crossing possible. Our plan was to slip over secretly . . .

T.E. Lawrence, on trying to cut off the retreating Turks from their base at Damascus, November 1917, Revolt in the Desert.

Round the bend, whistling its loudest, came the train, a splendid two-engined thing of twelve passenger coaches . . . I touched off under the first driving wheel of the first locomotive, and the explosion was terrific. The ground spouted blackly into my face and I was sent spinning helplessly. Recovering myself, I hobbled towards the upper valley, whence the Arabs were now shooting fast into the crowded coaches. When the enemy began to return the fire, I found myself much between the two. . . . One of the coaches was a saloon, decorated with flags. In it had been Mehmed Jemal Pasha, commanding the Eighth Army Corps, hurrying down to defend Jerusalem against Allenby . . . There had been some four hundred men on board, and the survivors, now recovering from the shock, were now under shelter and shooting hard at us.

T.E. Lawrence, on blowing up a bridge on the Damascus railway line, November 1917, Revolt in the Desert.

. . . flew me to Suez. Thence I went up to Allenby's headquarters beyond Gaza. He was so full of victories that my short statement that we had failed to carry at Yarmuk bridge was sufficient, and the miserable details of failure could remain concealed. While I was still with him, word came that Jerusalem had fallen; and Allenby made ready to enter in the official manner which the catholic imagination of Mark Sykes of the British Foreign Office had devised. He was good enough, although I had done nothing for the success, to let Clayton take me along as his staff officer for the day. The personal Staff tricked me out in their spare clothes till I looked like a major in the British Army . . . so that I had the gauds of my appointment in the ceremony of the Jaffa Gate, which for me was the supreme moment of the war.

T.E. Lawrence, December 1917, Revolt in the Desert.

On our return to Akaba domestic affairs engaged the remaining free days. My part mostly concerned the body guard which I formed for private protection, as rumour gradually magnified my importance . . . the Turks . . . began to offer a reward of one hundred pounds for a British officer dead or alive. As time went on they not only increased the general figure, but made a special bid for me . . . after we blew up Jemal Pasha they put Ali and me at the head of their list, worth twenty thousand pounds alive or ten thousand dead.

T.E. Lawrence, January 1918, Revolt in the Desert.

. . . I rode for Akaba . . . alone now with six silent, unquestioning guards, who followed after me like shadows, harmonious and submerged in their natural sand and bush and hill; and a home-sickness came over me, stressing vividly my outcast life among these Arabs, while I exploited their highest ideals and made their love of freedom one more tool to help England win.

T.E. Lawrence, July 1918, Revolt in the Desert.

[Major] Young and I cut the telegraph, here an important network of trunk and local lines, indeed the Palestine army's main link with their homeland. It was pleasant to imagine Liman von Sanders' fresh curse, in Nazareth [German headquarters], as each severed wire tanged back from the clippers . . . The Turks' hopeless lack of initiative made their army a "directed" one, so that by destroying the telegraphs we went far towards turning them into a leaderless mob.

T.E. Lawrence on cutting the main Turkish communication lines at Mezerib, south of Damascus, fall of 1918, Revolt in the Desert.

An English aeroplane flew round and round, wondering if we were the Arab force. Major Young spread out ground signals, and to him they dropped a message that Bulgaria had surrendered to the Allies. We had not known there was an offensive in the Balkans, so the news came orphaned, and as it were insignificant to us. Undoubtedly the end, not only of the great war, but of our war, was near.

T.E. Lawrence, south of Damascus, September 1918, Revolt in the Desert.

The mass rising we had so long prepared was now in flood, rising higher as each success armed more rebels. In two days' time we might have sixty thousand armed men in movement . . . A man cantered in, to inform [Sheik] Tallal that the Germans had set fire to aeroplanes and store-houses, and stood ready to evacuate the town of Deraa, south of Damascus.

T.E. Lawrence, near Deraa, south of Damascus, September 1918, Revolt in the Desert.

The third party, the smallest, was mostly made up of German and Austrian machine gunners grouped around three motor-cars and a handful of mounted officers or troopers. They fought magnificently and repulsed us time and again despite our hardiness. The Arabs were fighting like devils, the sweat blurring their eyes, dust parching their throats; while the flame of cruelty and revenge which was burning on their bodies so twisted them that their hands could hardly shoot. By my order we took no prisoners, for the only time in our war.

T.E. Lawrence, on the last rear guard fighting near Deraa, September 1918, Revolt in the Desert.

I grew proud of the enemy [the Germans] who had killed my brothers. They were two thousand miles from home, without hope and without guides, in conditions mad enough to break the bravest nerves. Yet their sections held together in firm rank, sheering through the wrack of Turk and Arab like armored ships, high-faced and silent. When attacked they halted, took position, fired to order. There was no haste, no crying, no hesitation. They were glorious.

T.E. Lawrence, on the last fights before the Turkish surrender, September 1918, Revolt in the Desert.

9. The War at Sea: 1914–1918

The Historical Context

THE BRITISH AND GERMAN NAVIES

When war broke out, Britain was without question the domineering sea power in the world. The Grand Fleet consisted of 24 Dreadnoughts, all big-gun battleships which had first been developed in 1906. But Britain's closest sea rival, Germany, was not far behind: The Germans had started building the same type of ships soon after and had about sixteen of them ready in August 1914. In the lower classes of warships, the British navy was also superior to the German navy. The Russian fleet, in land-locked seas, was a negligible factor, and the Austrian navy, pent up in the Adriatic, was no match for the French and British units in the Mediterranean. Yet Winston Churchill, first lord of the admiralty, had good reason to be worried when war was declared.

While Germany did not need its fleet to attack its continental neighbors, Britain's very life depended on its own naval supremacy: Two-thirds of Britain's food was imported, and its merchant fleet carried

German battleship squadron in the North Sea, 1914. Photo courtesy of the National Archives, Washington, D.C.

141

more than half of the world's overseas trade. The Grand Fleet faced an enormous task: It had to escort the British Expeditionary Force (BEF) across the Channel; bring in troops from India to add to the small regular army; prevent an invasion of the British Isles; and, most of all, organize a blockade of all German ports to protect the seaborne commerce on all oceans.

The danger of an invasion by the German army was soon discounted as impracticable by the British Imperial Defense Committee, but an attack on the British fleet seemed logical since Britain could not afford to take any chances with its most vital weapon, while Germany could take the risk. Germany had not only its High Seas Fleet stationed at Kiel in the Baltic Sea and at Wilhelmshaven in the North Sea (the two by then connected by a canal wide enough to carry the largest warships). Germany also had at least 40 fast steamers that could be converted into commerce destroyers. Moreover, the British Grand Fleet, under Admiral Sir John Jellicoe—now assembled at Scapa Flow in the Orkneys off Northern Scotland—was by no means safe from enemy attack: Its base was not yet equipped with land-based guns, fixed mine fields, antisubmarine nets or dry docks for the large battleships. It was known that the Germans were sowing mines with disregard for the limits set by international agreements, and when a British light cruiser rammed and sank a German submarine on August 9, Jellicoe was more concerned than pleased by the news.

Yet a major attack on the British coastline or warships was never undertaken, although the spiritual father of the German fleet, Admiral Alfred von Tirpitz—who had held the post of Secretary of the Navy longer than any German minister since Bismarck—urgently advocated an aggressive policy. For many years, he was not even shown the war plans supposedly laid out by the Naval Staff, headed by his chief, Admiral Hugo von Pohl. When war broke out, Tirpitz discovered that there was no plan to include his navy in the war effort. No attempt was made to interfere with the BEF landings in France. One reason was apparently the ignorance and ineptitude of the German Naval Staff; Tirpitz claimed that he had more in his little finger than Pohl in his whole anatomy. Then there was the ambivalent attitude of the emperor. On the one hand, William pronounced time and again that Germany's future was on the water and that a strong navy was the weapon to cut through a threatening encirclement by the European powers, particularly after he had been impressed by a book by American naval officer and historian Alfred Thayer Mahan called *The Influence of Sea Power on History* (1890). On the other hand, William, with his love-hatred for England, could not really convince himself that he was able to beat a nation that could hark back to Sir Francis Drake and Horatio Nelson. His advisers were equally divided. Some warned that Churchill had declared the German navy to be the Alsace-Lorraine in Anglo-German relations, and claimed that a "navy-less" Germany might actually be stronger than one with a money-and-men-consuming navy. The result was a splendid navy—in gunnery even superior to the British—but without concentrated action when the opportunity presented itself.

GERMAN SHIPS AT LARGE; BATTLE OF THE FALKLANDS

There were, of course, powerful German warships at large when the war started. (The decisive role of the *Goeben* and *Breslau* has been discussed in Chapter 5). A squadron under Admiral Maximilian Count von Spee in the Pacific bombarded Papeete in Polynesia and destroyed the British cable station at Fanning Island in the Central Pacific. Spee

Earl John Rushworth Jellicoe, commander in chief of the British Grand Fleet. Photo courtesy of the New York Public Library.

received reinforcements at Easter Island in October, and in an engagement on November 1 with a small British squadron under Admiral Christopher Cradock, sank two of his three ships. Cradock and 1,600 men perished in this action.

The Admiralty was stunned but reacted rapidly. All available warships were assembled off the southeast coast of South America, and a strong naval unit, led by the *Invincible* and *Inflexible*, under Admiral Frederick Charles Sturdee, hunted down the German unit and caught up with it at the Falkland Islands, a British crown colony 300 miles east of the Magellan Straits. Berlin had issued orders instructing Spee to return home at once, but he apparently missed getting this information at Valparaiso. Instead, he lost some time trying to refuel for the long trip home and also decided to destroy British installations at the Falklands. But the British were waiting for him; and in the ensuing battle, in the most southerly naval engagement ever fought, Spee's squadron was outgunned and destroyed. Four of his ships were sunk, and 1,800 men, including Spee and his two sons, went down. Only the *Dresden* escaped, but it was hunted down by the British at the Juan Fernandez Islands, off the Chilean coast, in March 1915. The *Dresden*, short of ammunition, coal and food, was scuttled by her crew.

Several German raiders were also threatening the Allied merchant ships, the most successful being the *Emden*. Under Captain Karl von Mueller the *Emden* had been roaming through the Indian Ocean. It bombarded Madras on the Bay of Bengal in southeast India and sank a great number of merchant ships before it in turn was sunk by the Australian cruiser *Sydney* off the Cocos Islands in the Indian Ocean. The last of these light cruisers to be hunted down was the *Koenigsberg*, led by Captain Max Looff. Though not quite as successful as the *Emden*, it had threatened shipping lanes from Australia, sunk the old British cruiser *Pegasus* and the steamer *City of Winchester*, and visited Zanzibar, the Mozambique Channel, Madagascar and other places in the Indian Ocean, after which it vanished. Looff thereby succeeded in tying down a considerable British fleet searching for him. His ship was finally discovered in the Rufiji River in Tanganyika, East Africa, and after a nine-month blockade was overwhelmed by the British in July 1915. Looff scuttled his ship, and his crew made it on land to the German colony of East Africa where they joined the German colonial forces under General Paul von Lettow-Vorbeck and held out against the British all through the war. Between them, the *Emden* and the *Koenigsberg* had destroyed 41 Allied merchant boats.

The converted armed merchant vessels, used by both sides, played a minor role in the first months of the war and were uninvolved later on. More than half of the German merchant marine, about 670 boats, were holed up in neutral ports. Only five of the 40 German raiders expected by the British materialized and only one battle developed between the British ex-Cunard liner *Carmania* under Captain James C.

Barr and the German *Cap Trafalgar* under Captain Hans Langerhansz. They met off the Venezuelan coast in early September 1914 and engaged in what was called the longest single naval engagement. Although the *Carmania* was slower and outgunned by the *Cap Trafalgar*, she outmaneuvered the German ship and sank her after having received 79 hits, and she made it to Pernambuco, Brazil, severely damaged. Another German raider, the *Kronprinz Wilhelm*, which had operated in the vicinity, failed to help the *Cap Trafalgar* and did not pursue the *Carmania* but managed to raid the South Atlantic for several months before she was interned.

MINES AND SUBMARINES; DOGGERBANK AND HELIGOLAND

German mines also took their toll soon after war broke out. On October 27, 1914 the British super-Dreadnought *Audacious* struck a mine off the north coast of Ireland and sank. This loss was never made public by the British until after the armistice. Even more serious was, right from the beginning, the naval weapon which came closest to defeating the British: the submarine. This became apparent when, on September 22, the German U-Boat *U-9*, under Captain Otto Weddigen, managed to sneak up on three old British cruisers, the *Aboukir*, the *Hogue* and the *Cressy* off the Dutch coast. When the *Aboukir* was struck by a torpedo, her captain, John E. Drummond, thought he had hit a mine and signaled the other cruisers to come closer, which facilitated Weddigen's task. The *Hogue* was struck, by two torpedoes, and both ships were sinking fast. The British now believed to be surrounded by several submarines, and both the sinking *Hogue* and the remaining *Cressy* engaged in wild firing, to no effect since the submarine emerged only to deliver the final blow. When the *Cressy* was hit by two torpedoes and sank quickly, the nearly 1,000 men who had survived the torpedoes were floating through the oily, littered surface. Help from two small Dutch steamers and a British trawler arrived only an hour later, and a British destroyer flotilla, arriving two hours thereafter, could only carry 837 survivors back to Harwich, England. More than 1,400 British sailors had perished. The submarine, which had not been taken quite seriously by either admiralty, had proven itself a formidable weapon. Weddigen, who had become a hero in Germany overnight, did not survive his fame for long. As commander of the *U-29*, he sank six merchant ships during one patrol, but in March 1915, when he faced the Grand Fleet near the naval base of Moray Firth off the Scottish coast, his submarine was rammed by a Dreadnought and sank with all aboard. Yet the British were reluctant to learn that their majestic warships required a destroyer screen against U-boats, and on New

Year's night, the battleship *Formidable* was struck by a German torpedo in the North Sea and sank. Only 200 of the 800 crew men were saved.

As early as November and December 1914 the Germans had engaged in naval actions against British coastal installations at Yarmouth, Scarborough and Hartepool. Now, three weeks after the sinking of the *Formidable*, German admiral Franz von Hipper directed a battle-cruiser squadron attack off the Dogger Bank—a shoaling area between Britain and Denmark—and was soon battling a superior British fleet. He did considerable damage to the British flagship but lost his battle cruiser *Bluecher*.

The attacks the British launched from their home bases were not particularly successful. Their battle cruiser attack on the German naval base at Heligoland Bight (Bay) at the end of August brought the German cruisers out, and Admiral Sir David Beatty had to retire at first, yet managed to bring up reinforcements and sink three German ships. But the *Inflexible*, fresh back from the Falklands, and the battleships *Majestic* and *Triumph* were incapacitated at the Dardanelles, and the French fared no better in the Mediterranean, losing their cruiser *Provence* with 930 men.

THE GERMAN COLONIES

On the other hand, the Allies were entirely successful in occupying the far-flung German colonies which received no help from their navy. In Africa, Togoland capitulated to a British-French force at the end of August 1914. The Cameroons and German Southwest Africa were invaded by English forces in September. In the latter, the invaders were supported by troops of the Union of South Africa under General Louis Botha, and the Germans capitulated in July 1915. In the Cameroons, the French joined British forces and pushed the Germans back and forced them to cross into Spanish territory in early 1916.

Only in their East African colony did the Germans hold their own. The British bombed their coast town as early as August 8, 1914, and then brought in Indian forces. But the extremely able German commander, General Paul von Lettow-Vorbeck, defeated a superior landing force at Tanga in November. Skirmishing continued for a whole year. Then the British established a naval force at Lake Tanganyika and in the summer of 1916 took Tanga and Bagamoyo. Units of Africans and Portuguese under South African general Jan Christiaan Smuts joined the British, and when, in September 1916, Dar-es-Salaam, Lindi and Tabora were taken, Lettow-Vorbeck had to retreat to the southeast corner of the colony. But the Germans hit back at Mahiwa and invaded Portuguese East Africa in October of 1917, advancing almost to the mouth of the Zambezi River. When the armistice went into effect on November 14, 1918, Lettow-Vorbeck had just begun the invasion of Rhodesia.

The small German possessions outside of Africa fell quickly: Samoa to a New Zealand expeditionary force in August 1914 and the New Guinea and Bismarck Archipelago colonies to the Australians in September. In October Japan attacked Tsingtao in the Shantung province, East China, and the fortress capitulated in November. German possessions in the Marshall Islands, Carolines and Mariannas were occupied simultaneously by Japanese naval units.

THE BRITISH BLOCKADE

Britain's main naval weapon against Germany was the blockade of the North Sea which began in early September 1914. The German navy—after the losses it had taken in the Heligoland action and with the Kaiser's reluctance to risk his "darlings"—did nothing to interfere. Eventually, Germany developed a counter-weapon in a greatly enlarged submarine fleet.

But for the time being, Britain's main difficulty was the antagonism its blockade aroused in a neutral country: the United States. It was the old clash of interests that had caused the war of 1812, the conflict between the neutral's right of commerce and the belligerent's right to restrain commerce. In a London conference—an outgrowth of the second Hague Conference—the major seafaring nations had followed the British lead and favored the neutral's right to trade, over the protests of the United States delegate Admiral Alfred Thayer Mahan. According to the London Declaration of 1909, only absolute contraband (i.e., articles for military use) could be seized by a belligerent after it had declared a blockade; a second class, so-called conditional contraband, consisting of merchandise usable for military *or* civilian use, could only be seized if the enemy destination were proved. All other articles, including food, were to be free. However, when the British government began to have second thoughts about these rules, the declaration was stopped by the House of Lords, and it was never ratified. One problem was that blockades were no longer instituted close to the enemy port, since submarines, floating mines and the wide-ranging cannons necessitated a policy of distant blockade in which the destination of the neutral party could not be easily established. And when the war broke out, Britain was determined not to let food shipments reach Holland that were meant to feed the German armies invading Belgium. When the United States requested all belligerents to confirm their adherence to the London Declaration, Germany and Austria readily agreed, while the British paid only lip service to the declaration and issued new and more vigorous interpretations of the term contraband. In November they declared the North Sea a military zone, whereupon the Germans declared a submarine blockade of Britain to begin in February 1915. In response, the British declared that all goods destined to go to the enemy were contraband, applying the old doctrine of continuous voyage which had been invented in the 18th century and extensively applied by the Union government during the American Civil War: Conditional contraband would be subject to capture if consigned to the enemy or an agent of the enemy. This policy, which ultimately led to Germany's unrestricted submarine warfare, was vigorously opposed in the United States and in particular by President Woodrow Wilson, who wanted to be the champion of the rights of the neutrals by standing up for the freedom of the seas. However, once the British blockade of the North Sea was firmly established, and it turned out that American trade with the Allies increased much more than it lost in trade with the Central Powers, the United States gradually acquiesced in the situation created by Britain. Their trade with Germany and Austria declined from $169 million in 1914 to $1 million in 1916, but during the same period their trade with the Allies increased from $824 million to $3 billion. Most of these goods had to be purchased on credits granted by the United States, which had become the banker and weapons supplier for the Allies and thus had a direct interest in an Allied victory.

AMERICAN-GERMAN CLASHES AT SEA

The German-American relations further deteriorated when American lives were lost as a result of the new German policy. The first victim was an American on board the British steamer *Falaba*, sunk in March 1915. Then an American tanker, the *Gulflight*, was torpedoed without warning, with the loss of three American lives. But the main clash occurred on May 7, 1915, when the 32,000-ton Cunard liner *Lusitania* was torpedoed by the German submarine *U-20* in sight of the Irish coast; 1,198 lives, including 139 American, were lost. The incident brought the United States and Germany to the verge of war. Public indignation over the murder of innocent women and children rose high in the United States, while the sinking was hailed as a great success in Germany. The question of guilt was not as clear-cut as either side was trying to make out. The American embassy had warned against sailing on the *Lusitania*, which did carry a partial cargo of ammunitions and small arms. Also, her captain had failed to zigzag his course as he had been instructed to do and thus got in the submarine's range. But President Wilson sent a strongly worded note of protest to Berlin, demanding reparations and refraining from such practices in the future. His pacifistic secretary of state, William Jennings Bryan, who had been a three-time presidential candidate in the past, resigned and was re-

William Jennings Bryan, Wilson's secretary of state, who resigned because of the Lusitania *incident.*

placed by Robert Lansing, a strong, though not outspoken, advocate of U.S. participation in the war.

Another crisis occurred when the liner *Arabic* was sunk two months later with the loss of two American lives. This time, the German ambassador to Washington, D.C., Count Johann Heinrich von Bernstorff, finally convinced his government of the acute danger of getting into war with the United States, and the German government promised that in the future no liners would be sunk without warning and safety would be provided for noncombatants. These assurances were observed for the next few months and the United States remained neutral for a while longer.

In February of 1916, however, the Germans stepped up their submarine warfare. They announced that thenceforth armed merchantmen would be treated as warships. Subsequently, the British cross-channel steamer *Sussex* was torpedoed with loss of Americans; this time, Washington was not reconciled until the Germans discontinued their "extended" warfare. Around the same time, Tirpitz resigned as marine minister, as he disagreed with the kaiser's unwillingness to make full use of German sea power. Also, Admiral Reinhard Scheer, a much more dynamic and brilliant tactician, succeeded Admiral Pohl in the command of the High Seas Fleet. He staged some bombardments of

Yarmouth and Lowecraft by a German squadron which did not do much damage, but caused an uproar among the English populace; who asked what their Grand Fleet was doing.

THE BATTLE OF JUTLAND

The one and only major sea battle between the two rivaling navies was the battle of Jutland (named after the peninsula occupied by Denmark and Schleswig). It occurred at the end of May. British admirals David Beatty and John Jellicoe as well as Scheer had worked out schemes to lure the enemy fleet into battle. German Admiral Franz von Hipper was sent out with a battle-cruiser squadron and came into contact with British cruisers under Beatty which ran ahead of the Grand Fleet. Hipper, though outnumbered, sank two of Beatty's ships through superior marksmanship. Then the main fleets under Jellicoe and Scheer joined in the battle. Jellicoe tried to cut off the German retreat, but Scheer, executing several sharp turns, launched a torpedo attack, forcing Jellicoe to retreat. Before he could continue his pursuit, Hipper and his battle cruisers attacked, enabling the High Seas Fleet to escape to the south when night fell. It reached its home base around 3:30 in the morning. By using excellent tactics and superior marksmanship, the Germans had achieved a major success in spite of the superiority of the British Force.

In this battle of Jutland—called the battle of Skagerrak by the Germans—the British fleet had lost a total of 14 warships, grossing about 114,000 tons, almost twice as much tonnage as their enemy had lost. The Grand Fleet lost the new battleships, the *Queen Mary* and *Invinci-*

First Earl David Beatty, British admiral, who played a major part in the battle of Jutland. Photo courtesy of the New York Public Library.

ble, as well as the *Indefatigable, Defence, Warrior* and five destroyers. The Germans lost the battleships *Luetzow* and *Pommern,* four cruisers and five destroyers. British losses amounted to 6,000 men, while the Germans only suffered about half of that. The German success was undeniable, due in part to Jellicoe's overcautiousness. But clearly the ultimate result was that the Grand Fleet could not be decisively defeated and the blockade could not be broken by the German fleet. The German High Seas Fleet made no further attempt to challenge the British. But the Germans staged some raids on the English coast in August and again in October 1916, while at the same time, several German raiders slipped through the blockade lines and wreaked havoc with Allied merchant shipping. Among the raiders were the *Moewe,* an armed merchantman under Count Nikolaus zu Dohna-Schlodien; the *Seeadler* under Count Felix von Luckner; and the *Wolf* under Captain Karl Nerger. Their leaders became heroes in German eyes, and the submarine *Deutschland* under Captain Hans Rose created a sensation when it landed in Baltimore in June of 1916—the first submarine to cross the Atlantic—and returned safely after sinking more merchants on her way back.

GERMAN SUBMARINE WARFARE

While these exploits did not change the course of the war, the stepped-up submarine warfare certainly did. By the end of 1916, German U-boats were destroying about 300,000 tons of Allied shipping per month. In early 1917, Germany had 120 submarines operating, and the United States was notified that unrestricted submarine war would begin on February 1, 1917. The German High Command entertained the hopes of winning the war by the destruction of the English food supply. In April 1917, the German successes reached the high point; submarines sank 875,000 tons of Allied shipping, half of them British. While the United States had entered the war on April 6, its presence had not yet been felt, and Jellicoe had to admit that Britain was on its way to losing the war within a few months. To fight this peril, the Allies developed depth charges, so-called Q-ships—armed vessels disguised as merchantmen—and the convoy system, introduced on the insistence of British prime minister David Lloyd George. The first escorted merchant convoy was tried out in May 1917 and turned out to be a success. At the same time, the British increased their number of submarine chasers and destroyers and introduced a system of scouting with hydroplanes. They also pushed their shipbuilding to the very limit.

This turned the tide. By October 1917, the Allies had lost eight million tons of shipping to submarines, but the Germans had lost fifty submarines, and the raids of the remainder fleet had become less and

Alfred Thayer Mahan, American naval officer and historian.

less effective. At the end of the year, Allied shipyards were building more ships than the Germans could sink. By 1918, U.S. shipyards were producing ships at a very rapid rate, thus building up a merchant marine fleet that would rank first among the fleets of the world after the war. By the fall of 1917, the U.S. Navy had delivered almost 150,000 American soldiers to France, suffering few, if any, losses in the process. During the first months of 1918, however, serious losses were incurred: On February 5 the newly launched 14,400-ton *Tuscania* was sunk by a torpedo near the north coast of Scotland, with a loss of 116 lives.

AMERICAN NAVAL LOSSES

As late as July 19, 1918, the U.S. armed cruiser *San Diego* hit a mine about 10 miles southeast of Fire Island and sank rapidly. Yet, through the excellent evacuation procedure organized by Captain H.H. Christy, only six men of the crew of 1,100 were lost. Still, the *San Diego* was the largest American warship lost in the war.

SABOTAGE

But the worst blow to the United States' shipping was the mysterious disappearance of the huge collier *Cyclops*, with 309 soldiers aboard. Her captain, George Worley (originally Georg Wichmann) of German descent, was a heavy drinker, had expressed sympathies for Germany during the early stages of the war, and was a sick man on his last voyage. His ship was last seen at Barbados in early March, on her way from Rio to Baltimore, and then disappeared without a trace. The Germans asserted that the German navy did not sink or capture the *Cyclops*. German sabotage may have been responsible, but it has never been proven.

Undoubtedly, the Central Powers resorted frequently to sabotage. In the summer of 1916, the munition stores at Black Tom Island, New Jersey, exploded with millions of dollars' worth of ammunition. This was the work of German saboteurs, who also destroyed the Kingsley, New Jersey, munition plant in January 1917. Austrian saboteurs blew up the Italian battleship *Leonardo da Vinci* at the Taranto pier and another warship, the *Benedetto Brin*, burned down for no apparent reason. At the end of 1915, the armed British cruiser *Natal* sank at Scapa Flow with heavy loss of life, and suspicion persists that the disaster was also due to sabotage.

In spite of these setbacks and other losses through German mines, it was clear by the summer of 1918 that the Allies had won the battle of the seas. The British blockade had never been broken and a mine belt laid by the American and British navies further sealed the Atlantic. The bulk of the German navy had been kept at its bases since 1916, with the result that mutiny broke out among the crews, who had been idle for years. Rumors of a last-minute, desperate attempt to break out and challenge the Allied navies circulated at Kiel and Wilhelmshaven. Actually, the German navy was so short of lubricating oil that it could not even achieve normal speed, let alone fight a battle. After the armistice had been concluded, the entire German High Seas Fleet surrendered to the British at Scapa Flow. In June 1919, instead of turning over the ships to their former enemies, the Germans scuttled their fleet of 70 ships before the British could intervene, an unprecedented naval suicide that destroyed more ships than had been sunk during the battle of Jutland.

CHRONICLE OF EVENTS

1914:

August 8: British bombard the coast towns of Bagamoyo and Dar-es-Salaam in German East Africa.

August 26: German defense force at Togoland, West Africa, capitulates to a Anglo-French force.

August 28: British cruisers and battle cruisers raid Heligoland Bay. They are first driven off, then return, reinforced, and sink three German ships.

August 30: A New Zealand force occupies the German colony at Samoa.

September: British start blockade of the North Sea.

Early September: The armed ex-Cunard liner *Carmania* and the German *Cap Trafalgar* meet off the Venezuela coast. After a prolonged battle, the *Cap Trafalgar* is sunk.

September 7: British troops from Nigeria invade the German colony of Cameroons, West Africa.

September 11: Australian troops land on the German-held Bismarck Archipelago.

September 22: German submarine *U-9*, under Captain Otto Wediggen, sinks three British cruisers off the Dutch coast.

September 22: A German flotilla under Admiral Maximilian von Spee, coming from the China coast, bombards Papeete and destroys the British cable station at Fanning Island in the central Pacific.

October 12–18: Two additional German cruisers join Spee at Easter Island.

October 15: The British warship *Hawke* is sunk by a German submarine.

October 18: German submarine raid on the British naval base at Scapa Flow.

October 31: A Japanese assault on the German fortress of Tsingtao on the China coast fails.

November 1: Spee's flotilla defeats a British squadron under Admiral Christopher Cradock off Coronel, sinking two of his ships.

The inside of a German submarine. Photo courtesy of the National Archives, Washington, D.C.

German battle cruiser Scharnhorst, *sunk off the Falkland Islands.*

November 2–5: German commander Paul von Lettow-Vorbeck defeats a superior force at Tanga, German East Africa.

November 3: German cruisers, under Admiral Franz von Hipper, raid the English coast at Yarmouth.

November 7: German forces at Tsingtao capitulate to the Japanese.

November 9: The German cruiser *Emden,* successful raider in the Indian Ocean, is sunk by the Australian cruiser *Sydney* off the Cocos Islands.

November: Japanese occupy German island colonies in the Marshall Islands, Mariannas, Palau and the Carolines.

December 8: Sea battle of the Falkland Islands. Admiral Spee's flotilla is caught by a British squadron under Admiral Frederick Charles Sturdee and destroyed. Some 1,800 men, including Spee and his two sons, perish.

December 16: German battle cruisers bombard the British coast at Scarborough and Hartlepool.

1915:

January 14: General Louis Botha of the Union of South Africa crosses the Orange River and occupies Swakopmund in German Southwest Africa.

January 24: Naval encounter between British and German battle-cruiser squadrons off the Dogger Bank. The outnumbered German unit under Hipper does much damage to the Brit-ish, but has to retreat and loses the cruiser *Bluecher.*

February 4: The German government announces that its submarine blockade of Great Britain will begin on February 18.

March 14: The German cruiser *Dresden,* which escaped from the Falklands, is cornered at Juan Fernandez and is blown up by her crew.

March: German submarine captain Otto Weddigen is killed when his *U-29,* after sinking six merchant ships, is rammed by a British dreadnought off the Scottish coast.

March 28: British steamer *Falaba,* a passenger boat, is sunk by a German submarine.

May 1: The American tanker *Gulflight* is torpedoed without warning.

May 7: The huge Cunard liner *Lusitania* is torpedoed off the Irish coast; 1,198 lives, including 139 Americans, are lost.

Reinhard Scheer, German admiral during the battle of Jutland. Photo courtesy of the German Information Center, New York City.

May 9: American President Woodrow Wilson protests the sinking of the *Lusitania.*

June 8: William Jennings Bryan, American secretary of state, resigns and is succeeded by Robert Lansing. A much stronger note is dispatched to Berlin.

August 19: The liner *Arabic* is sunk, two American lives are lost. New tension between Washington and Berlin.

September 1: The German government gives assurances to neutrals on future sea warfare.

November: British secure naval control on Lake Tanganyika in German East Africa.

1916:

February 21: The German government advises the United States that armed merchantmen would be treated as cruisers, as of March 1.

March: Admiral Alfred von Tirpitz, German minister of the marine, resigns. Admiral Reinhard Scheer takes over the command of the German High Seas Fleet.

March 24: The British cross-channel steamer *Sussex* is torpedoed in the Channel, with the loss of American lives. Washington insists on German restriction of its "extended" submarine campaign.

Ruins of the Cathedral of St. Quentin, on the Somme River. Photo courtesy of the National Archives, Washington, D.C.

April 24–25: British positions at Yarmouth and Lowestoft are bombarded by a German squadron.

May 10: Germany gives reassurances regarding its unrestricted submarine warfare.

May 31–June 1: Battle of Jutland (Skagerrak), the only major naval engagement between the two fleets. British losses are almost twice as high as the German losses, but the Germans retreat in the end.

June: The German submarine *Deutschland*, under Captain Hans Rose, crosses the Atlantic, lands in Baltimore and returns safely.

August 19: New German raids on the English coast.

October 26–27: Further German raids on the English coast.

December 12: German units attack British convoys in the North Sea.

1917:

January: The munitions plant at Kingley, N.J. is destroyed by German sabotage.

January 14: German units raid the English coast.

January 31: Germany notifies the United States that unrestricted submarine warfare will begin on February 1.

February 5: The troopship *Tuscania* is torpedoed off the Scottish coast, with the loss of 116 lives.

February 15: Further raids of the English coast.

March: The American collier *Cyclops*, with 300 soldiers aboard, disappears mysteriously in the Atlantic.

April: High point of the submarine warfare. Some 875,000 tons of shipping are sunk in one month.

May 10: First transatlantic convoy is launched by the Allies.

October 17: Germans attack British convoys in the North Sea.

October 18: German victory at Mahiwa, East Africa.

November 17: A British light cruiser attack off Heligoland is beaten back.

1918:

April 23: A large-scale attack on the moles at Zeebrugge and Ostend, aimed at blocking German submarine bases, is only partly successful.

July 19: The U.S. armed cruiser *San Diego* hits a mine off Fire island. Only six of the 1,100-man crew are lost.

October 17–20: The advancing British land forces take Zeebrugge, Ostend and the other Channel ports.

November 2: Lettow-Vorbeck, still fighting in East Africa, invades Rhodesia.

EYEWITNESS TESTIMONY

That first broadside from the enemy raked the *Carmania* fore and aft in the upper works . . . for most of us it was our first baptism of fire and some indiscriminate ducking took place. I myself remember thinking how horribly mean it was to be so rough. I . . . heard the German ship calling for assistance. I knew a little German and loosed off on our transmitter wishing to confuse the enemy operator and any enemy warships listening in. The *Cap Trafalgar's* operator interrupted his call and sent "was?" ["what?"]. I was a bit rattled at this moment as the W/T cabin was severely shaken by several shell explosions—I replied "Wie geht's?" The enemy operator gave this a miss and began calling up his pals again.

St. John, wireless chief on the Carmania, *reporting on the battle between his ship and the German* Cap Trafalgar, *September 14, 1914, in A.A. Hoehling,* The Great War at Sea, *Crowell, N.Y. (1965).*

I jammed the communication as hard as I could for a few minutes and then there happened the grandfather of all explosions—the cabin rocked and was filled with smoke and the apparatus ceased to function. A couple of 4-inch shells had hit the base after funnel and exploded simultaneously, tearing away our aerial connections . . . We had a good view of the conflict just as it was at its hottest . . . One of our starboard guns was hit and the crew knocked out, the gun layer being killed. The gun was quickly remanned and in action again. The two ships were maneuvering around each other at full speed, our captain endeavouring to steer the *Carmania* so that the enemy ship could be ranged on our quarter, thus enabling five of our guns to bear. Our gunners concentrated their aim upon the *Cap Trafalgar's* bow wave and waterline. This eventually had its effect . . . The noise was terrific . . . A striking feature of the working of the after guns was the decorative language of the Royal Marine gunners . . . It wasn't vulgar. It sounded poetic and inspiring.

St. John on the Carmania, *on the battle with the* Cap Trafalgar, *in A.A. Hoehling,* The Great War at Sea.

We decided that our fire superiority was, at best, doubtful. Captain Wirth decided to bring the *Cap Trafalgar* into range of our machine guns, in order to make all the trouble possible for our enemy . . . Enemy shells and shrapnel tore to bits the flowers in our elegant Wintergarten. Marble was torn from the walls . . . Our fire-fighting parties worked bravely to extinguish the many fires about the ship, sustaining casualties as they did so . . . Water gushed over the deck, steam billowed in clouds from the broken pipes. Nevertheless we kept our guns firing effectively, until a shot coming in on the starboard made it difficult to aim . . . We were now but 1,800 meters distant from the enemy. We put to good use our machine guns . . . until all ammunition was expended. Soon we were firing with only two cannons, as was the enemy. He turned away, burning, leading us to believe we were the victor. However, we kept listing more and more to starboard. A lucky shot, piercing below the waterline, had knocked out a main bulkhead and flooded the engine and boiler rooms so badly that pumps could not control the inrush of water.

Otto W. Steffan, radio officer on the Cap Trafalgar, *reporting on the battle with the* Carmania, *September 14, 1914, in A.A. Hoehling,* The Great War at Sea.

Cap Trafalgar sank with flags flying. The sea was thick with debris. In such a situation, we couldn't count for sure on our rescue. However, I clung to a plank until the *Eleonore Woermann*, which had not forgotten us, picked me up. During Captain Collmorgen's search he rescued most of the survivors, including wounded.

Otto W. Steffan, on the end of the Cap Trafalgar, *September 14, 1914, in A.A. Hoehling,* The Great War at Sea.

. . . I submerged completely and laid my course so as to bring up the center of the trio which held a sort of triangular formation. I could see their gray-black sides riding high over the water . . . A fountain of water, a burst of smoke, a flash of fire, and a part of the cruiser rose in the air . . . I heard a roar and felt reverberations sent through the water by the detonation. She had been broken apart and sank in a few minutes.

German submarine Captain Otto Weddigen on the torpedoeing of the British Aboukir, *September 22, 1914, A.A. Hoehling,* The Great War at Sea.

. . . within suitable range I sent away my third attack. This time I sent a second torpedo after the first to make the strike doubly certain. My crew were aiming like sharpshooters and both torpedoes went to their bull's-eye.

Captain Otto Weddigen on the sinking of the Cressy, *September 22, 1914, A.A. Hoehling,* The Great War at Sea.

As the vessel went over I was washed off by a big wave. Before this I had stripped. I saw the *Cressy*, keel upwards; there were perhaps fifty men clinging to her, and when she finally went down I was surprised to find only a little bit of suction. Luckily I am a good swimmer, and after I had gone 100 yards I came across a long plank to which half a dozen men were clinging. They were men I knew and they asked me to share it with them, which I did, with the object of giving them some directions. I told them to hold on with one hand and move their legs about. After . . . a quarter of an hour, some of the men were giving out and began to sit on the wood, forcing it under the water. Leaving the plank, I struck out on my own and swam on for some time till I came across a man who beckoned to me. I . . . found he had a table under one arm and a piece of wood under the other. He gave up the table to me . . . I looked round for something to swim to and caught sight of a fishing smack . . . After a long swim I found I was getting nearer and nearer, and began to shout to it . . . The only human forms I came across were two or three dead bodies—men who were bent over the wood or wreckage to which they had clung. As I got nearer to the smack I shouted for all I was worth. I would shout, swim a hundred yards, and shout again. At last the crew spotted me and sent their small boat which picked me up.

Dr. Gerald Noel Martin, temporary surgeon aboard the Cressy, *about his rescue when his ship was sunk, September 22, 1914, A.A. Hoehling, in* The Great War at Sea.

It was a very difficult undertaking, as the survivors were exhausted and we were rolling heavily. All were practically naked and some were so exhausted that they had to be hauled aboard with tackle.

Captain Voorham of the Flora, *a small Dutch steamer that came to the rescue of the* Aboukir, Hogue *and* Cressy *survivors, September 22, 1914, in A.A. Hoehling,* The Great War at Sea.

. . . natural promptings of humanity have in this case led to heavy losses which would have been avoided by strict adhesion to military consideration . . . it has become necessary to point out that the conditions which prevail when one vessel of a squadron is injured in the mine field, or is exposed to submarine attack, are analogous to those which occur in action, and that the rule of leaving ships to their own resources is applicable, so far, at any rate, as large vessels are concerned.

Ruling of the British Admiralty after the disaster of September 22, 1914 when three cruisers were sunk, in A.A. Hoehling, The Great War at Sea.

I have the honor to request in the name of humanity that you now surrender your ship to me. To show you how much I appreciate your gallantry, I will recapitulate the position. You are ashore, three funnels and most guns disabled. You cannot leave this island, and my ship is intact. In the event of your surrendering, in which I venture to remind you is no disgrace but rather your misfortune, I will endeavour all I can for your sick and wounded . . .

Captain J. Glossop to German Captain K. von Mueller, commander of the Emden, *November 9, 1914.*

It is almost in our heart to regret that the *Emden* has been destroyed. Von Mueller has been enterprising, daring in making war on our shipping, and has revealed a nice sense of humour. He has, moreover, shown every possible consideration to the crews of his prizes. There is not a survivor who does not speak well of this young German . . . The war at sea will lose something of its piquancy, its humour and its interest now that the *Emden* has gone.

Daily Telegraph, *a few days after the destruction of the* Emden, *November 1914.*

Orders re-echoed in the block house and reached us below. The transmitter shrieked, speaking tubes blew and were shouted through. The floor of the central station shook and vibrated to every salvo that rolled from the ship. The finest music, the music of battle. It soothed the nerves after the anxious wait of the long morning . . .

Hans Pochhammer, first officer of the German cruiser Gneisenau, *on the beginning of the battle of the Falkland Islands, December 8, 1914, quoted by A.A. Hoehling,* The Great War at Sea.

It was hard to understand how the *Nuernberg* could survive so long. At times she was completely obscured by smoke and we thought she must have sunk, but as soon as the smoke cleared away, there she was, looking much the same as ever and still firing her guns . . . After crossing her bow, we turned to port till we were nearly on parallel courses again . . . This was a great joy to the crews of our port broadside guns, as up to now they had not had a chance to fire . . . At last, at 6:36, the *Nuernberg* ceased firing, and we ceased firing, too. There was the *Nuernberg* about 5000 yards away, stopped and burning gloriously . . . We had to sink her, there could be no doubt about that, so at 6:45 we opened fire again. After five minutes . . . she hauled down her colours. We immediately ceased firing. We could see now she was sinking. Orders were given to gets the boats ready for lowering . . .

John D. Allen, Captain of the Kent, *on the battle of the Falkland Islands, December 8, 1914, A.A. Hoehling,* The Great War at Sea.

Here at least we can salute the vanquished. Admiral von Spee, who went down with his doomed squadron, was a gallant and chivalrous antagonist, like Captain Mueller, of the *Emden*. Germany's retort, eight days later, by bombarding Scarborough and Whitby, reveals the normal Hun.

Punch, *London, December 1914.*

Had [Vice-Admiral Sir David Beatty's] portrait not appeared in the press, one would have been inclined to say that a first lieutenant had put on a vice-admiral's coat by mistake. He was about the age of a first lieutenant of our own battleships . . . The British navy did not wait for the war again to teach the lesson of "youth for action!" It saved time by putting youth in charge at once.

Frederick Palmer, the British base at Scapa Flow, North Scotland, early 1915, in My Year in the Great War (1915).

That night ride convinced me that however many Germans might be moving about in England under the guise of cockney or of Lancashire dialects in quest of information, none has any chance in Scotland. He could never get the burr, I am sure, unless born in Scotland; and if he were, once he had it the triumph ought to make him a Scotchman at heart.

Frederick Palmer, at Scapa Flow, early 1915, in My Year in the Great War.

All the waters surrounding Great Britain and Ireland, including the whole of the English Channel, are hereby declared a war zone . . . every merchant ship found within this zone will be destroyed without it being always possible to avoid danger to the crews and passengers . . . It is impossible to avoid attacks being made on neutral vessels in mistake for those of the enemy.

German Proclamation, in spring 1915, in A.A. Hoehling, The Great War at Sea.

Notice! Travellers intending to embark on the Atlantic voyage are reminded that a state of war exists between Germany and her allies and Great Britain and her allies; that the zone of war includes the waters adjacent to the British Isles; that in accordance with formal notice given by the Imperial German Government, vessels flying the flag of Great Britain, or of any of her allies are liable to destruction in those waters and that travellers sailing in the war zone on ships of Great Britain or her allies do so at their own risk.

Imperial German Embassy, Washington, D.C., April 22, 1915, before the departure of the Lusitania.

Official comment is of course reticent. The freely expressed unofficial feeling is that the United States must declare war or forfeit European respect. If the U.S. do come in, the moral and physical effect will be to bring peace quickly and to give the U.S. a great influence in ending the war and in so reorganizing the world as to prevent its recurrence.

Ambassador Walter Hines Page, U.S. ambassador in London: Cable to President Wilson after the sinking of the Lusitania, *May 8, 1915.*

We have all been very excited about the news of the *Lusitania*. . . . Why in the name of all dignity does not the American government act or shut up . . . ? I cannot understand the American state of mind, nor why Americans have the temerity to venture into a declared war-zone, much less let their wives and children go there, when anyone with a grain of sense might have foreseen what has happened. They might just as well come over and go Maying in front of our barbed wire.

Alan Seeger, letter to his mother, May 10, 1915.

We often think that we must have got to the end of German "frightfulness," only to have our illusions promptly shattered by some fresh and amazing explosion of calculated ferocity. Last month it was poison gas; now it is the sinking of the *Lusitania*. . . . Many unofficial voices have been raised in horror, indignation and even in loud calls for intervention. The leaven works, but President Wilson, though not unmoved, gives little sign of abandoning his philosophic neutrality.

Punch, *London, May 1915.*

. . . the responsibility for the death of so many Americans which is deeply regretted by everyone in Germany, in a large measure falls upon the American government. It could not admit that Americans were being used as shields for English contraband. In this regard America has permitted herself to be misused in a disgraceful manner by England. And now, instead of calling England to account, she sends a note to the German government.

Vossische Zeitung, Berlin, on May 18, 1915, after the sinking of the Lusitania.

If only these crazy Pan-Germans and Navy bosses will not get us into a mess! The result will be first, that half of our merchant marine—a quarter in American, a quarter in Italian ports—will be confiscated and used against us, so that the number of British ships will be increased—what these asses do not take into consideration—second that we shall have 500,000 American volunteer sportsmen, excellently equipped, come up against our tired troops—what these asses do not believe—third 40 million marks in cash for our enemies—fourth another three years of war, meaning certain disaster, fifth Romania, Greece etc. against us, and all so that Mr. Tirpitz "can show what he is capable of doing." Nothing more stupid has ever been thought up.

Max Weber, prominent German sociologist, about the forthcoming unlimited submarine warfare, in a letter of February 23, 1916, published in Wolfgang J. Mommsen, Max Weber, *(1959).*

The High Seas Fleet was denied its formal radius of action—to steam into the battleground of the North Atlantic, where, alone, a decision was possible. Only in the North Sea, our fleet presented no great danger to the Grand Fleet. The Royal Navy there had but to put into operation the war plans envisioned before 1914. The blame, thus, for the defeat lay not with the soldiers, the sailors and the officers of the High Seas Fleet, but in the continental-mindedness of our government, of our army leadership, and with the entire German people . . . for the first time 1914 was a sea contest and the greatest sea might was on the side of our opponent, whom we could fight with hope of success only in the Atlantic. And this we did not understand.

German U-Boat Lieutenant Karl Doenitz, in a letter to A.A. Hoehling, quoted in his Great War at Sea.

Most remarkable of all has been Mr. Churchill's intervention in the debate on the Naval Estimates, his gloomy review of the situation—Mr. Churchill is always a pessimist when out of office—and the marvellous magnanimity of his suggestion that Lord Fisher should be reinstated at the Admiralty, on the ground that his former antagonist was the only possible First Sea Lord.

Punch, *London, March 1916.*

. . . the most startling personal event of the month has been the dismissal of Grand Admiral Tirpitz. According to one account, he resigned because he could not take the German Fleet out. According to another, it was because he could no longer take the German people in.

Punch, *London, March 1916.*

From 4:15 to 4:43 p.m. the conflict between the opposing battle cruisers was of a very fierce and resolute character . . . Our fire began to tell, the accuracy and rapidity of that of the enemy depreciating considerably. At 4:18, the third enemy ship was seen to be on fire. The visibility . . . had become considerably reduced, and the outline of the ships very indistinct, This, no doubt, was largely due to the constant use of smoke balls or charges by the enemy, under cover of which they were continually altering course or zigzagging.

Admiral John Jellicoe reporting on the battle of Jutland, May 31, 1916, in A.A. Hoehling, The Great War at Sea.

Two or three shots falling together hit *Indefatigable*, about outer edge of upper deck in line with after turret. A small explosion followed and she swung out of line, sinking by the stern. Hit again almost instantly near 'A' turret by another salvo, she listed heavily to port, turned over and disappeared.

Rear Admiral W.C. Pakenham on the sinking of the battleship during the battle of Jutland, May 31, 1916. None of the crew of 1,017 survived. In A.A. Hoehling, The Great War at Sea.

. . . something—I don't pretend to understand what it was—seemed to be urging me to get away, so I clambered up over the slimy bilge keel and fell off into the water, followed, I think, by five other men. I struck away from the ship as hard as I could and must have covered nearly fifty yards when there was a final smash . . . the air seemed full of fragments and flying pieces. A large piece seemed to be right above my head, and acting on impulse I dipped under to avoid being struck . . . I stayed under as long as I could and then came on top again . . . coming behind me I heard a rush of water, which looked very much like surf on a beach, and I realized it was the suction or backwash from the ship which had just gone.

Gunner's Mate E. Francis, on the sinking of the Queen Mary *in the battle of Jutland, May 31, 1916. Of her 1266 officers and men only 18 were saved. In A.A. Hoehling,* The Great War at Sea.

A dense veil of smoke drifts toward from ahead. A destroyer attack! It looks innocent enough but may easily cost us our lives. Through my excellent marine glasses I can just make out four destroyers in the smoke, and upon these our quick-firing guns open rapid fire . . . How long can the enemy destroyers hold out under such fire? As they are steaming 30 knots, they cover a mile in two minutes. The success of the attack depends as much on the endurance of the destroyers as on the accuracy of our gunnery. We are firing at random, however, for there is no time for range firing and the smoke prevents observation of the splashes . . . Now our heavy guns join in the bombardment of the destroyers, chiefly for the sake of the morale effect. This seems to be successful, for the destroyers turn about . . . The important thing is to keep a sharp look-out through the glasses for the enemy torpedoes which have assuredly been fired . . . Then I discover through my glasses, in the distance, a slight ruffling of the surface . . . It is coming toward us . . . In such moments the brain works with immeasurable speed . . . The torpedo is coming ahead of our beam, so I do not hesitate, but

shout at once: "Hard to starboard!" I at once feel a certain relief, although Clinton-Baker [the captain] has still to repeat my words, and the man at the wheel to put down the helm, after which a short time must elapse before the ship, with her speed of 20 knots, responds . . . The ship swings sharply to starboard. I lose sight of both the torpedoes astern and see only the third, now approaching us at an acute angle and very close. A short moment later it has passed . . .

Finnish Commodore G. von Schoultz, observer for the tsar, on board the British battleship Hercules *during the battle of Jutland, May 31, 1916, in A.A. Hoehling,* The Great War at Sea.

Meanwhile the commander in chief had realized the danger to which our fleet was exposed. The van of our fleet was shut in by the semicircle of the enemy. We were in a regular death trap. There was only one way to escape . . . to turn the line about and withdraw on the opposite course . . . But this maneuver had to be carried out unnoticed and unhindered . . . The signal man on our bridge read the message aloud . . . Without moving an eyelid the captain gave the order: "Full speed ahead. Course southeast." Followed by the *Seydlitz, Moltke* and *Von der Tann,* we altered course at 9:15 P.M. and headed straight for the enemy's van. The *Derfflinger,* as leading ship, came under a particularly deadly fire. Several ships were engaging us at the same time. I could feel that our fire soothed the nerves of the ship's company. If we had ceased fire at this time the whole ship's company would have been overwhelmed by despair.

Commander Georg von Hase, gunnery officer on the Derfflinger. *The battle of Jutland, May 31, 1916, in A.A. Hoehling,* The Great War at Sea.

Salvo after salvo fell around us, hit after hit struck our ship. They were stirring minutes. A 38-cm. [15-in.] shell pierced the armor of the *Caesar* turret and exploded inside . . . The shell set on fire two shell cases in the turret . . . The burning cartridge-cases emitted great tongues of flame which shot up out of the turrets as high as a house; but they only blazed; they did not explode as had been the case with the enemy. This saved the ship, but the result of the fire was catastrophic. The huge tapering killed everyone within their reach. Of the seventy-eight men inside the turret only five managed to save themselves through the hole provided for throwing out empty shell-cases . . . The other seventy-three men died together like heroes in the fierce fever of battle, loyally obeying the orders of their turret officer.

Georg von Hase on the Derfflinger, *at the battle of Jutland, on the evening of May 31, 1916, in A.A. Hoehling,* The Great War at Sea, *Crowell, N.Y. 1965.*

Suddenly, we seemed to hear the crack of doom. A terrific roar, a tremendous explosion and then darkness, in which we felt a colossal blow. The whole conning tower seemed to be hurled into the air . . . The shell exploded . . . Poisonous greenish-yellow gases poured through the aperture into our control. I called out: "Down gas-masks!," and immediately every man pulled down his gas-mask over his face. I went on controlling the fire with my gas mask on, which made it difficult to make myself understood . . . The terrific blow had burst open the heavy armoured door of the tower which now stood wide open. Two men strove in vain to force it back . . . Then came unexpected assistance. Once more we heard a colossal roar and and crash . . . a 38-cm. shell exploded under the bridge. Amongst other things, the chart house, with all the charts . . . vanished from the scene forever. And one extraordinary thing happened: The terrific concussion . . . shut the armoured door of the fore-control. A polite race, the English! They had opened the door for us and it was they who shut it again. I wonder if they meant to?

Georg von Hase on the Derfflinger, *on the evening of the battle of Jutland, May 31, 1916, in A.A. Hoehling,* The Great War at Sea.

. . . a shell crashed into the ship and destroyed utterly the after dressing station; other shells followed and finally a fire broke out resulting in many casualties . . . The wounded were carried along the decks from the scene of disaster to the forward station . . . then, to add to the terrible character of the situation, the electric lights went out . . . These various circumstances rendered the dressing station a kind of inferno. But courage and devotion discounted even such great troubles . . . Mess tables were rapidly cleared away and the wounded brought to a place of comfort with all speed . . . A bathroom forward of the sick bay was selected as an operating theater. As soon as it was ready the surgeons set to

work . . . All through the long hours they toiled, knowing little or nothing of what passed upon the seas about them . . . Several bodies were rent in pieces; many limbs were torn from bodies; some men were stripped naked. Among the operations performed by the light of the guttering candles, upon a sinking ship in a gale of wind, were amputations, ligaturing of bleeding vessels and removal of shell splinters.

Contemporary British newspaper account after the battle of Jutland, in A.A. Hoehling, The Great War at Sea.

England's invincibility on the seas is broken. The German fleet has torn the venerable Trafalgar legend into shreds.

Leipziger Neueste Nachrichten, *German newspaper, after the battle of Jutland, in A.A. Hoehling,* The Great War at Sea.

The German Fleet, badly battered, retires to port; and despite the paeans of exultation [from] their Admirals, Kaiser and Imperial Chancellor, remains there throughout the month. Will it ever come out again? Meanwhile, Wilhelmshaven is closed indefinitely, and nobody is allowed to see sheep in Wolff's clothing—the "victorious fleet." The true verdict, so far as we can judge, may be expressed in the homely phrase: The British Navy has taken a knock but given a harder one. We can stand it and they can't.

Punch, *London, June 1916, after the Battle of Jutland.*

In a sense [Lord Kitchener's] loss is irreparable, yet his great work was accomplished before he died. Sometimes accused of expecting others to achieve the impossible, he had achieved it himself in the crowning miracle of his life, the improvisation of the New Armies.

Punch, *London, June 1916.*

Mr. Lloyd George, the new War Secretary, without wasting breath on the pessimistic comments of his colleague Mr. Churchill, has given an encouraging survey of the general situation . . . Better still is the solemn assurance of the Premier that the Government are taking steps to discover the identity of those who are in any way responsible for the judicial mur-

der of Captain Fryatt—the worst instance of calculated atrocity since the murder of Nurse Cavell.
Punch, London, August 1916. Captain Charles A. Fryatt, master of the British merchant vessel Brussels, was accused of attempting to ram a German submarine, and was executed as a franc-tireur by the Germans.

Norwegian (to Swede): "What—you here, too. I thought you were a friend of Germany?" Swede: "I was."
Cartoon in Punch, London, November 1916, showing two torpedoed sailors clinging to a mast in the open ocean, with a German submarine in the background.

. . . Lucien J. Jerome, of the British diplomatic service . . . interjected: "Considering the zone and the class of this ship, I should put it down at two hundred and fifty to one that we don't meet a sub." At this moment the ship gave a sudden lurch sideways and forward. There was a muffled noise like the slamming of some door at a good distance away. The slightness of the shock and the meekness of the report compared with my imagination were disappointing. Every man in the room was on his feet in an instant . . . Then came the five blasts on the whistle . . . We were running, but there was no panic . . . I saw the chief steward opening an electric switch box . . . instantly the boat decks were illuminated. That illumination saved lives. The torpedo had hit us well astern on the starboard side and had missed the engines and dynamos . . . Already the boat was loading up . . .
Floyd Gibbons, reporter for the Chicago Tribune, on the sinking of the Cunard liner Laconia, February 25, 1917, in A.A. Hoehling, The Great War at Sea.

My beloved mother and sister . . . have been foully murdered on the high seas . . . I call upon my government to preserve its citizens' self-respect and save others of my countrymen from such deep grief as I now feel. I am of military age, able to fight. If my country can use me against these brutal assassins, I am at its call. If it stultifies my manhood and my nation's by remaining passive under outrage, I shall seek a man's chance under another flag.
Austin Y. Hoy, American businessman in London whose mother and sister had died from exposure in a lifeboat after the Laconia was sunk, in a cable to President Wilson, in A.A. Hoehling, The Great War at Sea.

The introduction of the convoy system in 1917 robbed [the submarine service] of its opportunity to become a decisive factor. The oceans at once became bare and empty . . . then suddenly up would loom a huge concourse of ships, thirty or fifty or more of them surrounded by a strong escort of warships of all types.
Karl Doenitz, German submarine officer (later chief naval commander under Hitler), in A.A. Hoehling, The Great War at Sea.

The proposal by the United States that we lay a mine barrier across the North Sea was not received with enthusiasm by the British. The reason for this is complex: first, and most potent, was their reluctance to interpose anything to the northward that might hamper the movements of the British fleet, either, I presume, in chase or retreat . . . It has been said that Jellicoe's great caution at one phase of the battle of Jutland was due to an edict from the authorities at London that the fleet *must* survive. In carrying out an injunction of that kind, it necessarily admits that the enemy's fleet may survive also, and that is not what fleets are built for. There was some possibility that the proposed barrage would hamper the British fleet, but the risk was remote . . . Behind the reason given above, there also lay the reluctance of the British to accept a scheme which did not originate with them . . .
Admiral Joseph Strauss, former head of the U.S. Navy's Bureau of Ordnance, in his unpublished memoirs, in A.A. Hoehling, The Great War at Sea.

I called by appointment on Admiral Sir David Beatty on the *Queen Elizabeth* at Scapa Flow . . . discussing the mine situation. Beatty was at the time a man of forth-seven. His rise in his profession had been phenomenal . . . His advancement was due entirely to merit, and not, as I learned, to any family influence . . . He was wholly lacking in geniality, and that contributed a little, I suppose, to his undoubted unpopularity in the British Navy . . . This advancement might have been well received had Beatty been of a prominent family . . .
Admiral Joseph Strauss, in his unpublished memoirs, in A.A. Hoehling, The Great War at Sea.

It will be readily understood that the way had to be made smooth for the mine planters. As long as it was so, all would go well; but a single well-placed torpedo or mine, or a few enemy shells, would certainly finish one vessel, and probably destroy all ten of them. Each mine planter carried from 21 tons to 120 tons of high explosive, a total of nearly 800 tons in the squadron, many times more than the amount that devastated Halifax. With this on board, the squadron was hardly a welcome visitor anywhere.

U.S. Captain Reginald R. Belknap, commander of a mine-laying squadron that planted more than 60,000 mines across the northern exit of the North Sea in early fall of 1917, in A.A. Hoehling, The Great War at Sea.

. . . the great depth of the water in this part of the North Sea made it possible for U-boats to avoid the barrier by travelling at a sufficient depth below the surface. So far as we could ascertain, we suffered no losses in U-boats from these mines.

German Admiral Reinhard Scheer on the mine-laying operation in fall of 1917, in A.A. Hoehling, The Great War at Sea.

The only thing that I look forth to now is the few months leave that I expect to get after leaving the hospital to recuperate . . . I have no news regarding the war to write, only hope that the German people will soon see their error and hang the Kaiser and his whole followers and then have peace.

George Worley, commander of the Cyclops, *in one of his last letters before he and his ship disappeared, January 1918, in A.A. Hoehling,* The Great War at Sea.

This, then, is the end for which the Kaiser has lavished his millions on his 'incomparable' navy! A navy powerful enough to conquer all the navies of the world combined—bar the British . . . Strangely enough, the German surrender lacked the thrill of victory . . . The prevalent emotion, so far as I could ascertain, was pity. It carried even to our great commander in chief who I believe was the least thrilled and most disappointed person present. In speaking to us after the surrender he remarked: "It was a most disappointing day. It was a pitiful day, to see those great ships coming in like sheep being herded by dogs to their fold, without an effort on anybody's part." And no one of his audience dissented . . . They were the husks of their former fighting selves

U.S. battleship New Jersey, *in camouflage coat, 1918. Photo courtesy of the National Archives, Washington, D.C.*

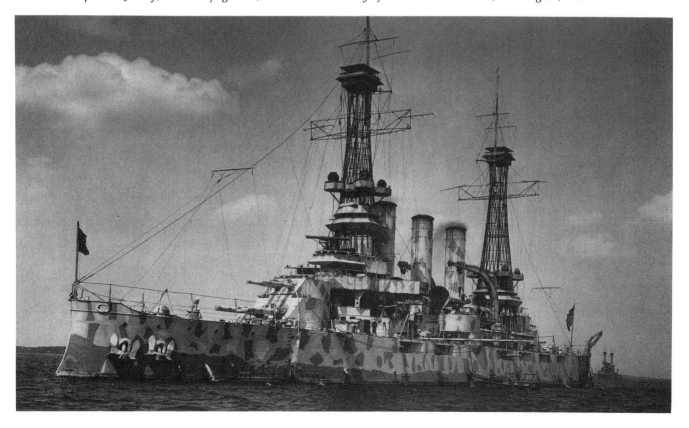

in a miserable state as to equipment, upkeep, and repair.

Francis T. Hunter, lieutenant aboard the New York, *flagship of the American battle fleet, on the surrender of the German navy November 21, 1918, in A.A. Hoehling,* The Great War at Sea.

Your comrades in the Grand Fleet regret your departure. We trust it is only temporary and that the exchange of squadrons from the two great fleets of the Anglo-Saxon race may be repeated. We wish you good-bye, good luck, a good time; and come back soon!

The British commander in chief to the departing United States Navy, November 1918, in A.A. Hoehling, The Great War at Sea.

It was very thorough. We put explosive charges smuggled on the mail boat under the big seawater contenders, which, when destroyed, would allow a torrent of water into the bilges. We set the sea-cocks on a hair-turning and lubricated them heavily. We placed large hammers beside any valve which, when knocked off, would allow the water to rush in. We did our job efficiently on every ship—and very secretly.

Friedrich Ruge, captain of a torpedo boat, about the preparations for scuttling the German fleet, mid-May 1919, in A.A. Hoehling, The Great War at Sea.

Before I send you ashore as a prisoner of war, I would like to express my indignation at the deed which you have perpetrated and which was that of a traitor violating the action of the arrangement entered into by the Allies. The German fleet was in a sense more interned than actually imprisoned. The vessels were resting here as a sort of goodwill from the German government until peace had been signed. It is not the first occasion on which the Germans have violated all the decent laws and rules of the seas.

British admiral Sidney Fremantle to German admiral Ludwig von Reuter after the scuttling, June 21, 1919, in A.A. Hoehling, The Great War at Sea.

10. The Home Fronts During the War: 1914–1917

THE HISTORICAL CONTEXT

WAR PSYCHOSIS

Before the war broke out the tension between the great powers was hardly felt by their populations. It is doubtful that they would have wanted war had they foreseen it. The great industrialists certainly did not want war. German industry, in particular, felt that their country would soon be the leading economic power in Europe with or without war. Many people in France and England were more apprehensive of Russia, their ally, than of Germany. The last election in France, in April 1914, had witnessed a pacifically-oriented majority of Socialists and radicals; in Germany, the pacifist Social Democrats were by far the strongest party in the Reichstag, and in England both public opinion and the liberal Asquith government were strongly against any military involvement on the continent; least of all did they want to be drawn into what they called a "Balkan quarrel."

All of this changed rapidly and radically as soon as war was declared and the men were called to arms. An incredible, almost incomprehensible wave of enthusiasm and patriotism swept over each country. None of the populations, not even the British, was fully informed of the machinations and secret arrangements its government had performed, and they all felt that their homeland was in danger and had to be defended. While the governments in Vienna and St. Petersburg had certainly schemed to enlarge their empires, the peoples of these countries marched only for Holy Russia and the Grand Danube Monarchy. Germany did not want any additional territory; their masses joined to defend the fatherland that, they were told, was surrounded and viciously attacked by her jealous neighbors. France wanted Alsace-Lorraine back but marched for "La Patrie." The British felt secure behind their Channel and their Grand Fleet, but they went to war for a cause—the neutrality of Belgium. They were the first to talk in general idealistic terms of the "war to end war" and the "war to make the

*Herbert Henry Asquith, first earl
of Oxford, British prime minister
1908–1916. Photo courtesy of the
New York Public Library.*

world safe for democracy"—slogans which were later picked up in the
United States.

The political opposition to war disappeared overnight. In France, Socialists became ministers for the first time in the name of the "union
sacrée"; in Germany, a tiny minority of opposing Social Democrats
yielded to party discipline; and in England, only a few members of
Parliament abstained from supporting the government, while no one
voted against it. In Vienna, the Parliament was not consulted, but in
Hungary the parliament unanimously voted for war. In St. Petersburg,
the few Bolshevik votes against the war were ignored by the strictly
conservative fourth Duma.

The war fever seized everybody, rich and poor, sophisticated and
simple. Only a few of the intellectuals tried to swim against the tide:
In England, there was Bertrand Russell, philosopher and mathematician, who became an active pacifist when war broke out and was imprisoned for six months by the government in 1918. In France, Romain
Rolland, novelist and Nobel Prize winner, went into self-imposed exile
in Switzerland. In Germany, Hermann Hesse fled to Switzerland when
war broke out, while writers such as Gerhart Hauptmann and Thomas
Mann—whose works had hardly revealed any strong nationalism in
the past—now turned into fanatic patriots along with the large major-

ity of artists, scientists and even philosophers in all belligerent countries.

ECONOMIC AND SOCIAL PROBLEMS

Civilian life changed quickly within the first few months. No one had foreseen a long war, and no one had realized that such a war required a strictly organized economy. New industries had to be created, workers had to be persuaded or compelled to change their jobs and relax their standards of living. Employers had to work under government orders. The French had some tradition in this respect, as they had already resorted to some planned economy under Napoleon I. The Germans had little experience in this regard, but once they got organized, they achieved an excellent economic control. This was mostly the work of one man, the industrialist Walther Rathenau, who, as the head of the Raw Material Department, put a strict control on production and consumption of metals, textiles, chemicals and all other essential materials which had become largely unattainable through the effect of the British blockade.

New social problems also arose, such as welfare for soldiers and munition workers, for maintaining families of the absent soldiers, and for keeping the war profiteers under control—an almost insoluble problem which was to contribute greatly to the general discontent of the poorer classes.

The problem of financing the war was not tackled responsibly by any of the belligerents. No one tried to cover the huge costs by increased taxation; some countries, including Germany, actually lowered some taxes to make up for other hardships of war. Each country expected to win and make the enemy pay for all expenses. In Germany, government-inspired propaganda preceded each new war loan ("Kriegsanleihe"); the masses responded enthusiastically, though it was clear that they could never be paid back unless the war was won. Government propaganda was particularly intense in Britain, where traditionally the government had interfered with personal freedom and enterprise as little as possible. But Britain had no compulsory military service and now needed millions of soldiers in a hurry to help her hardpressed ally, France, across the Channel. Posters showing the well-known face of Lord Kitchener, regarded as the greatest British soldier and now secretary of war, called on all his countrymen to volunteer for the army. The success was overwhelming: Five hundred thousand volunteers reported during the first month—more than the small regular army could handle—and, altogether, Great Britain raised more than three million volunteers. During the first winter of the war, thousands of men lived under canvas and drilled in civilian clothes, using walking sticks for rifles. Great orators such as David Lloyd George—who at first had not been an enthusiastic advocate of the war—and Horatio Bottomley, the "People's Tribune," aroused the general enthusiasm higher and higher. In London, young women went through the streets offering white feathers as symbols of cowardice to any young man still in civilian clothes.

PROPAGANDA AND RUMORS

While the masses supported their governments wholeheartedly, the governments did not reciprocate with frankness toward the people: News on setbacks at the front were usually withheld, and with the lack of appropriate information, wild rumors flourished in all countries. In England, people were convinced that a hundred thousand or even a million Russian soldiers had landed at Aberdeen, Scotland and were on the way to the western front. People even claimed they had seen the snow on their boots. Wild stories about German atrocities in Belgium were believed by almost everyone. There is no doubt that the German military were extremely severe, even cruel and certainly unnecessarily reckless in their retaliations against actual or imagined francs-tireurs (snipers). But the gruesome stories of babies' hands and nuns' breasts being cut off were either the outgrowth of the fertile imagination of some war journalists or deliberate propaganda. In showing the Germans as "huns," Allied propaganda was much more successful than the Germans in their efforts to paint the Allies as barbarians, illiterate Russians, degenerate democratic Frenchmen or perfidious, jealous British merchants.

Whenever news of setbacks leaked through, they were attributed by the population to enemy spies who, apparently, were everywhere. In August, 1914 rumors circulated in Berlin that the Russians were only 11 miles from Berlin, and that they had poisoned all wells and water reservoirs. In England, rich people who had tennis courts installed in the suburbs were suspected of preparing gun-emplacements from which the invading Germans could bombard the capital. In France, every railway compartment displayed a warning notice that "the enemy was listening in." In most countries—Austria being a notable exception—mass internments of enemy aliens took place, and in many major Allied cities, German shops or even shops only bearing a foreign-sounding name were looted. In Berlin, elegant hotels with English names, such as "Bristol," renamed themselves patriotically in German. Many foreign words in the German language were also replaced by German ones. In 1917 the royal house in England, changed its name from Saxe-Coburg-Gotha to Windsor, and in the same year Admiral von Battenberg—who had married a granddaughter of Queen Victoria—anglicized his name to Mountbatten.

As the war progressed and the initial enthusiasm ebbed away, new problems arose. There were thousands of refugees fleeing before the advancing armies who had to be settled elsewhere. The Belgians had no place to go, as practically their whole country was occupied by German troops. Over one hundred thousand went to England, where people were disappointed to discover that the Belgians were not the heroes described by the London papers, but ordinary workers who did not fit too well in English factories. Finally, a whole munitions town was given to Belgian workers in Northumberland.

GROWING OPPOSITION TO THE WAR. CHANGES OF GOVERNMENTS

Old controversies within the countries subsided, others flared up. In England, the suffragettes ended their violent campaigns, and the Irish—who had bitterly opposed the English in the question of Home Rule—eagerly volunteered in the beginning to help Belgium, in Ulster as well as in southern Ireland. Even Irish writer George Bernard Shaw, the severe critic of English society, who had shocked the public by declaring that the defense of Belgium was only a pretext for British participation in the war, supported the war effort and became an honored guest at headquarters.

On the other hand, the tighter the economies were controlled, the more maximum prices, food restrictions and distribution systems had to be instituted, the less social justice could prevail. The beneficiaries of inflation and government controls were the big industrialists, who had all the orders and all the profits they could wish for; the farmers, who always had enough to eat and could always make fine profits on the black market; the middlemen, whose businesses flourished; and the heavy industrial workers, who received bigger rations because they had to be kept physically strong. The losers were the employees with fixed salaries, the pensioners, the war widows and the old bourgeoisie. The result was hatred of the little people against the war profiteers and estrangement and hostility between farmers and the masses in the big cities who were hardest hit. And since the government and the civil administrations could not alleviate these injustices, their reputations sank; people expected more from the new heroes, the real war leaders, the field marshals and generals.

The civil government leaders could not remain unaffected by the tremendous upheavals the war brought about in all countries. In England, the Asquith ministry was reorganized in May 1915. Because of the British failure at the Dardanelles, Winston Churchill resigned as first lord of the Admiralty and was replaced by Arthur Balfour. A war committee, a Dardanelles committee and finally a ministry of munitions were established during the same summer, and a ministry of blockade in early 1916. By this time, it had become necessary to introduce compulsory military recruiting; the one million British already stationed in France were no longer sufficient.

Shortly thereafter, England had to face the only national rebellion during the war. Many Irish now felt that the time of England's troubles was the great opportunity to strike out for Irish freedom. Sir Roger Davis Casement, an Ulster Protestant, became an ardent Irish nationalist and went to the United States, then Germany to secure support for an Irish uprising. His attempts to persuade the Germans to provide arms and land men in Ireland were unsuccessful. When he returned to Ireland in a German submarine, he was arrested within a few hours. Other leaders of the movement tried to call off the uprising; but on Easter Sunday 1916 it took place anyway. About 2,000 men failed to occupy Dublin Castle, the center of British administration, though it had a garrison of only 20 men. The fighting went on for five days, after which the Irish surrendered. The rebels had not been particularly popular in their own country, since so many families had members or friends in the British army; but the extremely harsh treatment the captured rebel leaders received turned them into heroes. All leaders who had signed the Proclamation of the Irish Republic were shot, as were all the Volunteer commandants. Casement was hanged.

Five weeks later, Field Marshal Lord Kitchener, on a secret mission to Russia, was killed when his cruiser, the *Hampshire*, struck a mine off the Orkney Islands. Lloyd George, who succeeded him in the war office, found that the restrictions he himself had put on this office now worked against him. He therefore strove for a reorganization of the whole structure of government. In December 1916 he managed to oust Prime Minister Asquith and form his own coalition cabinet. He created a small war cabinet, sometimes enlarged by representatives of the dominions, and established for the first time a cabinet secretariat. For the rest of the war, Lloyd George was the most powerful man in England. While often at odds with his generals, he was largely responsible for the unification of the military command under Marshal Ferdinand Foch. His bold and aggressive policies, in particular the organization of convoys to meet the danger of the German submarines, greatly helped bring about the ultimate military success. Sir Edward Grey resigned as foreign secretary and was succeeded by Arthur James, the Earl of Balfour.

In France, foreign minister Théophile Delcassé, the creator of the Entente Cordiale, had resigned in October 1915, and his office was taken over by prime minister René Viviani, but only for a few weeks; then a new coalition under Aristide Briand, a great orator, took over. His great rival was Marshal Joseph Joffre, who claimed for himself the role of a war dictator, but this was vehemently opposed by the Chamber of Deputies. Briand, in turn, had to resign in March 1917, and his successor, Alexandre Ribot, did not last much longer, as he was blamed for the failure of the Nivelle offensive in 1917 (see chapter 13). His successor, foreign minister Paul Painlevé, could not stem the general war-weariness in the fall of 1917. Things took a turn for the better in November, when Georges Clemenceau became prime minister and energetically began to organize his country for victory.

Social unrest spread in Austria as well. Prime Minister Count Carl Stürgkh, who had been violently opposed by liberals and Social Democrats, was assassinated by a young socialist. A month later, Emperor Francis Joseph died; he had ruled since 1848 and represented the last link that held his various peoples together. He was succeeded by his grandnephew Charles, who knew from the beginning that his country could no longer afford the war. Count Czernin became Austrian foreign minister and supported his emperor's private peace-making attempts behind the back of his ally, Germany.

DEBATES WITHIN GERMANY

In Germany, a permanent debate was going on about the war aims. The Social Democrats were the only party who consistently rejected any conquests. At the other end of the scale, the super-patriots, called Pan-Germans (Alldeutsche), demanded security against any future aggressions: Belgium was to be kept; the French coastline all the way to the Somme estuary was to remain occupied; and even the Normandy peninsula was to become German because of its valuable ore deposits. The belt of fortresses from Belfort to Verdun should be taken over, as well as the Baltic provinces and parts of Polish Russia. Even moderate politicians such as Gustav Stresemann and Mathias Erzberger propagated war aims of a similar nature. Nobody dared tell the people that the bloody fighting of three or four years should have been for nothing—if only the status quo were to be restored. Between these debating parties stood the official government—the kaiser and his chancellor, Theobald von Bethmann-Hollweg. William, described by the Allied propaganda as the bloodthirsty king of the "Huns," no longer stood in the limelight. He had become a subdued and depressed man since the war lasted beyond his control. He backed his moderate counselor, the chancellor who, trying to please all sides, antagonized both the right and the left in the end. Since he was reluctant to make clear decisions, a solution of the burning issues of the day was time and time again postponed.

Aside from the debate on war aims, a heated discussion on the question of the proposed unlimited submarine warfare took place. The admiralty, the super-patriots, the Pan-Germans and every other political hothead urged it to get started, and the man in the street was inclined to go along. The masses were half-starved, thanks to Britain's blockade—why not retaliate in a similar fashion? Vicious rumors were circulated: The Kaiser was against it because he himself was half-English, Bethmann had his money at the Bank of England, etc. Bethmann was sure that unlimited submarine warfare would draw the United States into the war. His opponents claimed that Britain would be finished before American help could make any difference, and that the troops' movements across the ocean could be stopped by submarines. Bethmann guessed they were wrong on both counts, and he was correct. He also knew that there was a moral question involved: Unlimited submarine warfare would show Germany as the lawless "Hun" its enemies claimed it to be.

Finally, there was the question of the German and the Prussian constitution. Even conservatives such as Admiral Alfred von Tirpitz recognized that one could not expect the masses—who had carried the war under incredible hardships—to be governed by authority any longer; democracy was on the march, even in Germany. Social Democrats were fighting at the fronts and working at the war factories; without them the war effort could not have been kept up for a single day. But they did not have a voice in the decisions to be made, since the chancellor was not responsible to the parliament but only to the emperor. While Bethmann, as usual, hesitated and urged the warring parties to postpone any decision while the war lasted, the kaiser, in his Easter message of 1917, announced the end of the thoroughly antiquated three-class voting system in Prussia. Three months later he introduced equal, direct and secret suffrage. By this time, Bethmann had lost all support of the military and in the Reichstag and resigned; but his successors Georg Michaelis and Count Georg von Hertling wielded even less authority. More and more, Erich Ludendorff turned into the only real power in Germany. Still, the Reichstag, under the leadership of Mathias Erzberger and his Catholic Center Party, passed a resolution advocating a peace of understanding, without annexations, in July 1917. But Chancellor Michaelis did nothing to support the resolution, and he himself could not last since he did not have the confidence of the Social Democrats and, most important, that of Ludendorff.

On paper, Germany looked like the winner in the summer of 1917. Russia was down and out, the United States had not yet landed troops in France, and German submarines threatened to throttle England's very lifelines. Yet the weak and confused civilian leadership in Germany failed to diplomatically exploit the situation, and more and more of Germany's political and economic leaders began to understand what some of its military leaders had feared since the failure of the battle of the Marne: Germany could not win the war.

CHRONICLE OF EVENTS

1915:

May 25: The Asquith government in London is reorganized as a coalition.

May 27: Winston Churchill resigns as first lord of the admiralty and is succeeded by Arthur Balfour.

June 3: Allied conference in Paris to coordinate action in economic matters.

June 7: The British War Committee, later called the Dardanelles Committee, takes over the conduct of war operations.

June 26: General Vladimir Sukhomlinov, Russian war minister, is removed from his post, later tried for misconduct.

July 2: In London, a ministry of munitions is set up.

October 13: French foreign minister Théophile Delcassé resigns and is succeeded by the prime minister, René Viviani.

October 29: The Viviani cabinet resigns, and a new cabinet is formed by Aristide Briand, who also takes over the foreign ministry.

November 25: Arrangements for inter-allied munitions control, and restrictions of trade with Germany, are arranged at the Paris conference.

December 23: Introduction of a black list of materials not to be shipped to Germany.

1916:

January 6: Compulsory military service is introduced in Britain.

January 27: Establishment of an inter-allied Shipping Control Commission.

February 1: Ivan L. Goremykin, the Russian minister-president, resigns and is succeeded by Boris V. Stuermer.

February 23: Organization of a ministry of blockade in London.

April 20: Sir Roger Casement, Irish rebellion leader, is brought to the Irish coast by a German submarine.

April 24: The great Easter Rebellion starts in Dublin and other parts of Ireland.

May 1: After heavy fighting and much bloodshed, the Irish rebellion is repressed.

June 5: Field Marshal Lord Kitchener dies on a secret mission to Russia when his boat hits a mine off the Orkney Islands.

June 11: In Rome, the Salandra Cabinet resigns and is succeeded by a cabinet formed by Paolo Boselli.

July 7: David Lloyd George becomes secretary of state for war, succeeding Lord Kitchener.

July 22: Russian foreign minister Sergei D. Sazonov resigns. His ministry is taken over by minister-president Stuermer.

October 21: Count Carl Stürgkh, Austrian prime minister, is assassinated by a young socialist, and is succeeded by Ernst von Koerber.

November 20: Gottlieb von Jagow, German foreign minister, resigns and replaced by Dr. Arthur Zimmermann.

December 14: The Koerber cabinet in Vienna resigns and is succeeded by a cabinet under Count Richard Clam-Martinitz, with Count Ottokar Czernin succeeding Count Burian as foreign minister.

1917:

March 17: In Paris, the Briand cabinet resigns and is succeeded by Alexandre Ribot as prime minister and Paul Painlevé as foreign minister.

April 7: Emperor William's Easter message, announcing the end of the outmoded voting system in Prussia.

May 23: The Hungarian ministry under Count Stephen Tisza resigns.

June 15: New ministry under Count Maurice Esterhazy in Hungary.

June 18: The Austrian cabinet under Clam-Martinitz resigns and is replaced by a cabinet under Dr. Ernst von Seidler.

July 14: German Chancellor Theobold von Bethmann-Hollweg resigns. His successor is Dr. Georg Michaelis.

November 21: Emperor Francis Joseph of Austria-Hungary dies and is succeeded by his grandnephew Charles.

November 24: Russian prime minister Stuermer resigns and is replaced by Alexander Trepov.

December 4: In London, the Asquith cabinet resigns. Lloyd George forms a war cabinet, in which Arthur James Balfour replaces Sir Edward Grey at the foreign office.

December 12: The Briand cabinet is reorganized in Paris, and a war cabinet of five ministers is formed.

July 19: The German Reichstag passes a resolution, sponsored by Mathias Erzberger, favoring a peace of understanding, without annexations.

August 1: Pope Benedict XV proposes outlines to serve as a basis for peace.

August 5: Richard von Kuehlmann replaces Dr. Arthur Zimmermann as minister for foreign affairs.

August 21: New ministry under Count Alexander Wekerle in Hungary.

September 12: New French cabinet under Paul Painlevé with Ribot as foreign minister.

October 23: Jean-Louis Barthou succeeds Alexandre Ribot as foreign minister in Paris.

October 25: The Boselli cabinet in Italy resigns due to the disaster at Caporetto.

October 29: New Italian cabinet under Vittorio Emanuele Orlando.

October 30: In Germany, Count Georg von Hertling succeeds Michaelis as chancellor.

November 16: The Painlevé cabinet resigns in Paris. New cabinet under Georges Clemenceau, who is also minister of war. Stephen J.M. Pichon becomes foreign minister.

EYEWITNESS TESTIMONY

. . . in August 1914, men were equal. No one wished to count for more than anyone else. On the streets and avenues men looked each other in the eye and rejoiced in their togetherness. The doctor, the judge . . . the worker, the manufacturer . . . carried the same obligation . . . No one grumbled. The most distasteful men were willing and amicable. There were no longer any superfluous men. It was like a rebirth.

Rudolf Binding, German officer and writer, in his memoirs, Erlebtes Leben *("The Life I Lived") (1928).*

. . . But you are not satisfied to lay your hands on live Belgium. You make war against the dead and their century-old glory! You are bombing Mecheln, you set fire to Rubens! Loewen [Louvain] with its artistic and scientific treasures, sacred Loewen is but a heap of ashes! But you, Hauptmann, who are you and how do you wish to be called from here on since you reject the title of "barbarian?" Are you a descendant of Goethe's or Attila's? Are you waging war against armies or the human spirit?

Romain Rolland, French writer, letter to Gerhart Hauptmann, German playwright, August 29, 1914.

My landlord says: You watch it, at the end it will turn out that we were the worst scoundrels . . . When men go to war, everyone laughs and cheers, and there is no end to the hullabaloo . . . But when the horses are requisitioned, they all lament and cry, and they stroke and kiss the animals, again and again . . .

Georg Hermann, German novelist, in his diary, end of August, 1914.

. . . a great many of us believe that at least a quarter of a million Russians have passed through England on their way to France. The number of people who have seen them is large: that of those who have seen people who have seen them is enormous.

Punch, London, September 1914.

Recently, I am following regularly the official reports quoting foreign papers and find that in particular the rendition of official French bulletins is being falsified here. I could mention many instances. The falsification consists always in the omission of essential remarks as for instance: "The Prussian Guards regiment was completely repulsed," so that a reprint of the official French report shows an entirely different picture than the original. Does one think we have such weak nerves . . . ?

Eberhard von Bodenhausen, director of Krupp, to Karl Helfferich, member of the German Reichstag, October 4, 1914.

First I have organized the total economy of the metals, then that of military woollen cloth of jute, chemicals, and now I am about to have large factories built for the production of niter, the shortage of which, as I can tell you in confidence, could have had serious consequences by next Spring. Everything is under control now. Further we have to take care of rubber, cotton, flax, leather and a number of other materials of lesser importance. It will still take months of very intense work to get everything under control . . .

Walther Rathenau, letter to Captain G. von Diezelsky, October 10, 1914. In Rathenau's Letters, *vol. 1 (1926).*

The wonderful, truthful German people have no distinct sense of liberty. They love authority, want to be governed, they surrender and want to obey. This half-virtue, however, is a crime, seen in the light of history. We are ruled by a class, competent, self-assured, but without initiative . . . The people do not take over their responsibility, as they must. Now they must wash clean with their blood the mistakes

Walter Rathenau, organizer of the German war economy. Photo courtesy of the German Information Center, New York City.

of their masters, and they believe trustingly that God wanted it this way.

Walther Rathenau, letter to Fanny Kuenstler,
November 1, 1914. In Rathenau's Letters, *vol.*
1 (1926).

I do not doubt that mankind will get over this war, too, but I am certain that I and my contemporaries will never see again a happy world . . . I know that science only appears to be dead, but humanity really seems to be dead.

Sigmund Freud, letter to Lou Andreas-Salome,
November 25, 1914.

Gentlemen, the horror of the war is being felt more and more in all countries . . . My party, as representative of international socialism has always been the party of peace and knows that this is true as well for the socialists of other countries. We wish for a lasting peace, one that does not include new entanglements and does not contain germs for new conflicts. This will be achieved when no nation violates another, when the peoples, instead, see their responsibilities in a peaceful exchange of cultural values.

Hugo Haase, socialist member of the Reichstag,
speech on March 10, 1915.

He who in wartime insists on speaking up for peace among men knows that he is jeopardizing his peace of mind, his reputation and even his friendships for his conviction . . . The passions will vanish, reason . . . and love will remain. We shall always try to find how these two are blossoming again in the midst of blossoming ruins.

Romain Rolland, French writer, in Journal de
Genève, *March 1915.*

The main enemy of the German people is to be found in Germany: German imperialism, the German war party, German secret diplomacy. It is the job of the German people to fight against this enemy in our own country.

Karl Liebknecht, illegal leaflet, distributed in
May of 1915.

We cannot say how all this slaughter will end. I do not feel comfortable either when individual victories are being broadcast ever so arrogantly. Fate does not like it if one tries to anticipate one's triumph. But in my soul I do feel we shall prevail. The external

values this war is destroying it will replace by internal values.

Peter Rosegger, Austrian writer, in an essay in
Daheim, *June 1915.*

We had seen all the schools of war and the Conscientious Objectors' battalion—those extreme pacifists who refuse to kill their fellow men. Their opinions being respected by English freedom and individualism, they were set to repairing roads and like tasks.

Frederick Palmer, reporting on London in 1915,
in My Second Year of the War *(1917).*

One heard much about the campaign against the use of foreign words in the German language. This was particularly intense in the early days of the War, but the more reasonable elements soon cautioned the people to moderation in this connection. Thus it happened that none of the streets in Berlin having foreign names, such as Paris Place, French Street, and the like, were changed. Furthermore, the French high school in Berlin was continued throughout the War.

Conrad Hoffmann, In the Prison Camps of
Germany *(1915).*

The French soldiers feel, more or less distinctly, but firmly and strongly that they are the soldiers of Christ and Mary, the defenders of the faith, and that to die the French way means to die the Christian way. Cheers to Christ who loves the French.

Archbishop of Cambrai, pastoral letter, 1915.

. . . the universal eruption of posters imploring us to subscribe to the War Loan indicates the emergence of a new art—that of government by advertisement. To the obvious appeal to duty, patriotism, conscience, appeals to shame, appeals romantic and even facetious are now added. It may be necessary, but the method is not dignified. All that can be said is that "Govertisement," or government by advertisement, is better than government by the press, a new terror with which we are daily threatened.

Punch, *London, August 1915.*

Lord Milner has gone so far in the House of Lords as to say that "such war news as is published has from first to last been seriously misleading." The Balkan intelligence that is allowed to reach us does not exactly deserve this censure. To call it misleading would be too high a praise; it seldom rises beyond a level of blameless irrelevance.

Punch, *London, November 1915.*

The mood of the poorer population in the German cities has turned sullen, particularly because of the food situation . . . The days are over when the German people were satisfied to eat their potatoes with salt; they now demand butter, margerine or at least lard.

Albert Ballin, prominent German shipowner, letter to General von Stilzmann, December 15, 1915.

The National Thrift Campaign is carried on with great earnestness in Parliament. Luxury, waste, unnecessary banquets, high legal salaries have all come under the lash of the economy hunters. Of the maxim that "Charity begins at home," they have, however, so far shown no appreciation beyond abstaining from voting any addition to their salary of £400 a year. Mr. Asquith's announcement that he takes his salary, and is going to continue taking it, has naturally lifted a great weight from the minds of these vicarious champions of economy.

Punch, *London, December 1915.*

Lloyd George was up in the air on one of his "glory of the Welsh Hills" speeches. The power of his rhetoric amazed me. The substance of the speech might be commonplace, idle and false, but I had to fight hard against abandoning myself with the rest of his audience. He sucked power from his listeners and spurted it back at them. Afterwards, my father introduced me to Lloyd George, and when I looked closely at his eyes they seemed like those of a sleep-walker.

Robert Graves, recalling a Welsh literary club dinner in London in April 1916, in Good-bye to All That *(1929).*

Who sees the Kaiser in Berlin,/ Dejected, haggard, old as sin,/ And shaking in his hoary skin?/ The Neutral./ Who says he's quite a Sunny Jim,/ That buoyant health and youthful vim/ Are sticking out all over him?/ The Neutral./ Who tells us tales of Krupp's new guns,/ Much larger than the other ones,/ And endless trains chock-full of Huns?/ The Neutral./ And then, when our last hope has fled,/ Declares the Huns are either dead/ Or hopelessly dispirited??/ The Neutral.

Punch, *London, April 1916.*

The downing of the Zepp at Cuffley by Lieutenant Robinson gave North London the most thrilling aerial spectacle ever witnessed. There has been much diversity of opinion as to the safest place to be during a Zeppelin raid—under cover or in the open, on the top floor or in the basement; but recent experiences suggest that by far the most dangerous place on those occasions is in a Zeppelin.

Punch, *London, September 1916.*

The Emperor sent me a letter of the Crown Prince, addressed to his Majesty, with the urgent request to dismiss the chancellor whose only support were jews and . . . social democrats: Throw the guy out.

Admiral Georg A. von Mueller, War Diaries: October 14, 1916.

Francis Joseph of Austria has died on the tottering throne which has been his for nearly seventy years. In early days he had been hated, but he had shown valour. Later he shown wisdom, and had been pitied for his misfortunes. It was a crowning irony of fate which condemned him in old age to become the dupe and tool of an Assassin. He should have died before the War—certainly before the tragedy of Sarajevo.

Punch, *London, November 1916.*

The middle classes can expect no war profits, neither the grants of millions nor through wages increased by 400–500 percent. On the one hand, war profits provide the possibility to pay the most phantastic prices, on the other hand wages go up correspondingly, and the income of a civil servant cannot keep pace with them. The middle classes sit in between. They bear the main burden of this war of starvation.

Der Tuermer, German monthly, February 1917.

Mr. Bernard Shaw, returned from his "joy-ride" at the Front, has declared that "there is no monument more enduring than brass;" the general feeling is, however, that there is a kind of brass that is beyond enduring. Armageddon is justified since it has given him a perfectly glorious time . . . He entered and emerged from the battle zone without any vulgar emotion; remaining immune from pity, sorrow, or tears. In short:

He went through the fiery furnace, but never a

hair was missed/ From the heels of our most colossal Arch-Super-Egotist.

Punch, London, March 1917.

The people are paying the penalty for their leaders. That is, I believe, the meaning of the war. And this atonement is just, for they have accepted their leadership the way they came along.

Walther Rathenau to the economist Gustav von Schmoller, May 12, 1917.

Bethmann-Hollweg, immortalized by one fatal phrase [the "scrap of paper"], has been at last hunted from office by the extremists whom he sought to restrain, and Dr. Michaelis, a second-rate administrator, of negligible antecedents, succeeds to his uneasy chair, while the Kaiser maintains his pose as the friend of the people.

Punch, London, July 1917.

At this moment, all European churches leave the impression of being state institutions whose tasks it is to promote political-military goals by religious means.

Leopold von Wiese, sociologist, in his book Der Liberalismus *(1917).*

Therefore: Belgium must become German! The country will be divided in two parts which correspond to the division of the population into Walloons and Flemings . . . Both borderlands will be administered dictatorially and will have a status resembling that of the "provinces" in the Roman Empire . . . the former Belgians must not have any political rights in the Empire, for the time being . . .

Program of the Pan-German Federation, 1917, published in Harry Pross, Die Zerstoerung der deutschen Politik *(1959).*

On both sides there exists a minority that seriously believes in a decisive victory. But one thing that no one believes any longer who still possesses some ability to think rationally, is that those ideals of humanity can be attained of which so much is being said in the speeches of all the politicians. The bigger, the bloodier and more destructive the final battles of the world war will turn out to be, the less will be achieved for the future . . .

Herman Hesse, German writer living in Switzerland, in the "Neue Zuercher Zeitung," December 1917.

The strike movement in Greater Berlin is expanding, although it developed without the cooperation of the labor unions and without preparatory organisation by the working classes. Last night, the number of strikers was estimated to be 150,000, by official count 120,000.

Frankfurter Zeitung, January 29, 1918.

Compulsory rationing is now an established fact . . . another lyrist has addressed this touching hymn to margarine: Whether the years prove fat or lean/ This vow I here rehearse: / I take you, dearest Margarine/ For butter or for worse.

Punch, London, March 1918.

Ireland throughout the month has dominated the proceedings, aloof and irreconcilable, brooding over past wrongs, blind to the issues of the War, and turning her back on its realities. Mr. Lloyd George's plan of making Home Rule contingent on compulsory service has been described by Mr. O'Brien as a declaration of war on Ireland.

Punch, London, April 1918.

What should one cry about? Politics? The people? One month of war expenses would have eliminated all misery in the world. Another month would have given security to all intellectuals. A third would have turned the cities into paradises. A fourth would have freed all research, a fifth the arts from all material restrictions . . .

Walter Rathenau, letter to Leopold Ziegler, German philosopher, July 22, 1918.

In all the larger cities the Government requisitioned all brass door-knobs, window-locks, and other brass trimmings from private houses, heavy penalty being inflicted where people failed to report the quantity of such material in their homes. The copper roofing and window-sill plating of all buildings, both public and private, in Berlin were being removed and replaced by galvanized iron. We have all heard of how the church bells were requisitioned in order to supplement the rapidly decreasing supply of copper and provide adequate quantities for the needs of the munition factories.

Conrad Hoffmann, In the Prison Camps of Germany (1918).

When we get together, we face each other silently. Our urge for an open exchange of views is greater than ever, but we cannot be frank any longer. No one still believes we can win the war. All know we have lost it but no one will open his mouth. We are irritated, even when someone says what we secretly believe ourselves; as if we were superstitious that such things should not be spoken out loud.

Josef Hofmiller, Bavarian writer, diary of August 19, 1918.

On the other hand, the handbills dropped by the Allied aeroplanes over German lines, in which information concerning the true situation was given, apparently had their effect in dangerously undermining the German morale, and heavy penalties were inflicted for the sending of such handbills to the homeland by the troops at the front. Personally, however, I saw any number of these handbills in the homes of German families whose husbands or sons were at the front, showing that in spite of the threatened penalty men were unafraid and did send the dangerous leaven to the home folks.

Conrad Hoffmann, In the Prison Camps of Germany *(1918).*

. . . some of the excellent supplies were being sent to our American doughboys . . . proposed to purchase them from the individual prisoners. Needless to say this was a big temptation, on the basis of the prices which prevailed for such commodities as chocolate, sugar, butter, tobacco, and the like. Sergeant Halyburton emphatically refused, replying to the German noncommissioned officers, "You have shown us German discipline, we will show you that we, too, have discipline," and at once he issued a bulletin warning the doughboys of the camp that anyone caught selling American goods to the Germans would be punished most severely. As a result very little if any of the supplies our doughboys at Rastatt received were sold to the Germans, who were most anxious to buy.

Conrad Hoffman, In the Prison Camps of Germany.

11. Life of the Soldiers: 1914–1918

The Historical Context

TRENCH WARFARE

Defense had a great advantage in the static war after the first rush for four main reasons: the increased rapidity, accuracy and range of rifle fire; the appearance of the modern machine gun, the increased use of the spade, and the invention of the barbed-wire fence. The British were the only ones who had at least gathered some experience of these innovations, in the Boer War; but there the wide open spaces of South Africa and the limited amount of war material at the Boers' disposal had left them vulnerable to attack.

In the bogged-down trench war in France, an infantry attack by bayonet after shrapnel fire cannot succeed where no outflanking was possible for lack of open spaces. The offensive is therefore preceded by

German prisoners in a French camp. Photo courtesy of the National Archives, Washington, D.C.

artillery fire that seeks to destroy the enemy wire defenses. But the opposite artillery has the exact range of its own trenches: should the first line of trenches be captured, it can concentrate on it and wipe it out. The answer is deeper trenches and dugouts and a whole system of trenches, connected by narrow, zig-zagging communication trenches which enable the potential attacker to survive artillery barrages. The second and third lines are far enough behind the front and therefore invisible to the enemy. This is where the airplane comes in. Provided one side can gain sufficient superiority in the air, its planes can provide headquarters with the exact positions of secondary trenches, gun emplacements and machine-gun positions. Now, in theory, a properly executed attack can succeed. The defenders' batteries are overpowered by a severe preliminary bombardment, the secondary fortifications and dugouts are eliminated, and barrage fire will shut off any support for the front line trenches—whose men are held down by concentrated artillery fire until the attacking infantry can take over and establish itself in the captured trenches.

Such an attack requires not only a great superiority in men but also in accurate artillery and unobstructed air observation. But in the meantime, antiaircraft guns have been introduced. Even if they cannot shoot down the enemy, they can force a plane to stay high enough in the air to make accurate observation and photos impossible. Also, camouflage of installations on the ground and dummy installations can mislead the enemy by making the interpretation of photos taken from the air extremely difficult. Other means of attack were also tried. Poison gas, after the first shock effect, proved to be a failure not only because gas masks will render most gases ineffective, but also because a changing wind may blow the gas back into the lines of the attacker. Moreover, since gas cannot be propelled into great distances, the attacker will soon find himself in terrain which he himself has turned into deadly ground.

The tank, developed by the British and promoted energetically by Churchill, was first put in use at the Somme in September 1916. At first, the tank was used tentatively and incorrectly, but in November 1917, 300 British tanks attacked the German lines at Cambrai and shattered them on a six-mile front. By this time, the Allies had added trench-bridging to their tank equipment and learned to avoid the one great danger the tanks faced: By moving up too far, without sufficient infantry support, they were in danger of becoming isolated. Instead, the tanks now attacked en masse, usually behind a smokescreen and followed by the infantry. They could wipe out machine-gun nests, mow down barbed-wire defenses and, being more mobile, could outmaneuver fire. In the decisive breakthrough at Amiens in August 1918, British tanks played the main role. The United States entered the war too late to play any part in tank warfare: When the war ended,

23,000 tanks were on order from U.S. factories but only 26 were completed.

CHARACTERISTICS OF THE VARIOUS ARMIES

In this kind of warfare, the traditional formation of the fighting infantry man was bound to change radically. At first this was not realized by the leaders on either side. The Germans still attacked in a close disciplined order, almost shoulder to shoulder in the first battle of the Marne. The British did the same as late as in the great Somme offensive of 1916, in which they suffered 60,000 casualties on the first day. The new infantryman had to be individualized again, geared for "scrapping" with knife, bayonet, club or revolver. In trying to get through the enemy's barbed-wire defenses and fighting it out in the enemy's trench, it was every man for himself. The training methods of the professional armies, relying on "drilling" the men and on their unthinking, blind obedience, ended in unnecessary losses. Many nonprofessionals, such as businessmen, engineers and teachers, turned out to be successful commanders because they were more flexible than their colleagues of the old army class and because they were able to keep close contact with their subordinates—whom they wanted to be as versatile and self-reliant as possible, men who could operate a light machine gun, cut wire fences, throw a hand grenade and dig a trench. The French were particularly efficient in adapting to this new kind of warfare. Before an attack, every man would be given a large-scale map of the ground he was to cover, and his particular job was explained to him. The new Allied infantryman became well-versed in the various specialties required in field combat which consisted of terms such as "rushing," "scrapping" and "digging in."

The German army was the first to put large-scale "digging in" into practice when, after their setback in the first battle of the Marne, they settled behind the Aisne River. From the beginning, the German army was not only the largest but also the best disciplined, trained and equipped force on the continent. Their heavy artillery was especially superior, and they had the best organized transportation system, enabling them to ship large contingents of troops from one front to the other with little loss of time. The British, who proudly called themselves "old contemptibles" (since the kaiser had once spoken of England's "contemptible little army"), had at first only a small but well-trained professional force. The new volunteer army, "Kitchener's Boys," produced fine infantry, guns and airplanes, but the coordination between their various branches tended to be amateurish, and many initial advances were spoiled by inefficient follow-ups. Many of the higher grade British officers were brave, and conscientious and im-

maculate in their upbringing and bearing, but were not always up to
the intellectual tasks expected of them in modern warfare. As a result,
British advances were usually slower and involved higher casualties
than French advances, particularly during the first part of the war.

The French army had, of course, to bear the brunt of the German
onslaught all through the war, even after millions of British and American
soldiers had come to its support. At the beginning of the war,
France mustered 62 divisions, some 1,600,000 men, but increased its
army to about 3.5 million soldiers later. The French army was the
strongest in Europe next to the German, had élan and great recuperative
powers, and its light, 75-mm gun with its unique recoil system
was the best of its type. But it had little medium and heavy field artillery—only
about 300 guns compared to the German 3,500. Its officer
corps was often involved in politics and inclined to adhere to the doctrine
of constant attack which, during the first months, was certainly
the wrong theory to apply.

Except for Russia, France was the first country in which widespread
mutinies occurred, after the failure of the great offensive of April 1917.
But the French soldier was resilient enough to come back under the
leadership of Foch and Clemenceau and win the war.

The Austro-Hungarian army reached a maximum of about 2,700,000
men. Its heavy artillery and most of its junior officers were excellent.
But its supply system was insufficient, its staff work poor, and there
was no homogeneity since only 25% of the soldiers understood German
(the rest being Slavic and Hungarian speakers), while 75% of the
officers were of Germanic origin.

The Russian soldier was physically strong, hardy and brave, and the
cavalry was probably the best in Europe. But there were great deficiencies
in artillery and ammunition. Many of its commanders were selected
because of their social standing only and proved to be incompetent.
The Russian army reached a peak strength of almost six million
men and was frequently victorious against the Austrians, particularly
after Austria had to open a second front against Italy. In their battles
with the Germans, the Russian armies were usually beaten, and only
the vast spaces of retreat prevented their annihilation.

AIR WAR

Air warfare was in its infancy when the war began, the airplane having
been invented only seven years before 1914. But during the last
months of the war, ground battles were preceded or accompanied by
regular air battles, in which sometimes hundreds of planes participated.
Strafing of troops and bombing of cities had become part of the
airplane's role. The Germans raided London through 1918, Paris as
late as September 1918; and the British Royal Flying Corps (now called

German aviator dropping a bomb on the western front. Photo courtesy of the National Archives, Washington, D.C.

the Royal Air Force), as well as the American Independent Air Force, dropped hundreds of tons of bombs on German industrial targets. The French air force was the largest, comprising about 3,800 planes. Each country developed its own type of bomber and fighter plane: the British, the De Havilland and Handley-Page; the French, the Spad and Nieuport; and the Germans, the Fokkers and Gothas. Thus the era of air heroes and single dog-fights in the air began. Only a few of these international celebrities were animated by hatred of the enemy. Mick Mannock of the Royal Flying Corps, who brought down 73 Germans before he was shot down, hated Germany as did René Dormé, the French ace whose village had been destroyed by the Germans. Likewise, Manfred von Richthofen, greatest of the German aces, was a killer by instinct, and his diary shows that he thoroughly enjoyed shooting down 80 Allied planes until he was finally shot down in

Edward Vernon ("Eddie") Rickenbacker, American flying ace. Photo courtesy of the National Archives, Washington, D.C.

April 1918. One member of his squadron who survived the war made a career for himself in the next war: Hermann Goering.

But these hater-pilots were the exceptions. Georges Guynemer, the French ace, was frail, sickly and did not hold a grudge against anyone. When he was shot down, after killing 53 Germans, his body could not be found, and in France the legend persisted that he had flown so high that he just couldn't come down. Oswald Boelcke, German ace in the early stages of the war, was a gentle man who used to visit the graves of his victims and prayed for them. There were many others who did not enjoy killing, and were mostly pleasant, convivial souls who fought machines rather than men: The British had Albert Ball; the French had René Fonck and Charles Nungesser; the Americans had Eddie Rickenbacker and Elliott Springs; the Germans had Ernst Udet, Max Immelmann and Werner Voss; and the Canadians had Billy Bishop. These men faced death every time they took off. They flew without parachutes and in frail tinderboxes that would ignite easily. On the ground they were pampered and treated like no other soldiers, yet most infantrymen looked at them not with envy but with a shudder, seeing the flimsy contraptions take off to fight enemy planes and antiaircraft shells.

While the role of airplanes increased steadily, the other air weapon, the rigid airship inflated with hydrogen, named after the German inventor Count Ferdinand von Zeppelin, had only a limited and temporary success. The Germans used zeppelins for high-seas patrolling and scouting and, after January 1915, for air raids on England. Nine zeppelins attempted to raid Liverpool in January 1916. Since they had to stay at great heights, their bombing could never be accurate, and by the end of 1916, the German Command realized that zeppelin raids were simply too costly. In October of that year, eleven zeppelins attacked England. They met with some foul weather, drifted over France, and four were destroyed. All in all, they had undertaken 51 raids, had dropped 196 tons of bombs and killed 557 persons. But 77 of the aircraft had been lost in the process, and on top of it, the British successfully bombed the German zeppelin bases at Tondern in North Schleswig in July 1918.

Tethered observation balloons were used by both sides throughout the war. The observers, perched in tiny baskets, were sitting ducks for any air or ground attack and often had to escape in parachutes, since the huge balloons above them were easy targets for the enemy.

SUFFERINGS OF THE SOLDIERS

The war in the air, while highly visible and dramatic since it was new, constituted only a tiny percentage of the whole war, as far as men involved were concerned. Even the combats at sea, while expensive in materiel, were relatively cheap in human life. Britain suffered about 40,000 naval casualties, plus 14,600 killed in the merchant marine; Germany, about 25,000 killed, 30,000 wounded and 12,200 prisoners. Tragic as these figures appear to be, they are minuscule compared to the total of about nine million men killed during the war. By far, the greatest burden of the war was carried by the men in or near the trenches. For weeks, sometimes months, they were confined to cold, water-logged, rat- and vermin-infested holes in the ground, constantly exposed to rifle, machine-gun, shrapnel and artillery fire without being able to fight back. They were sent to run into the enemy's machine-gun fire and barbed-wire fences, sometimes after long, exhausting marches through the cold and the mud. The casualty rate in this type of warfare was horrible. While in World War II, an infantry unit was normally considered used up when it had suffered 10–15% casualties, infantry companies in the First World War were sometimes expected to hold out and fight back when they had left no more than 25% of their original strength. In retrospect, it seems a miracle that men could live under such incredible strain and that more mutinies did not occur. Practically all of the men had gone to war because they knew their country was in the right, and in the hope of a better world after the fighting had ended. They fought the enemy to defend their country, not because they hated the men in the opposite trench. Occasional fraternizations across the trenches between Germans and Russians, Germans and Frenchmen, Germans and British soldiers showed that. As the war continued—much longer than anyone had thought possible—the ideals disappeared. The frontline soldier began to hate—not the enemy, but the "base wallahs" behind the lines, the war profiteers, the politicians who would not put an end to the senseless slaughter. But the soldiers fought on, as they were ordered, to the bitter end.

PRISONERS OF WAR

A total of 8,400,000 prisoners were taken during the war. International rules for their treatment had been provided by the Hague Conference of 1899, and were then widened by the Hague Convention of 1907. But these regulations proved insufficient, so that after the war a more complete code was proposed by the International Red Cross, resulting in the 1929 Geneva Convention. The existing rules were by and large respected by the belligerents, but the actual treatment of enemy prisoners depended to a large extent on the economic situation of the captor's country.

Consequently, captives of the Turks suffered the most, but the Russians also only provided minimum needs of food and clothing. Health care was so poor that many prisoners contracted contagious diseases. The Russians also sought to indoctrinate their prisoners, first with Slavic-nationalist propaganda, then with Bolshevik ideas of world revolution. The Germans, on the other hand, violated international rules by deporting Belgian prisoners to the Ruhr district for forced labor. The French, for their part, often treated German prisoners—in particular officers—very roughly, since they despised the invaders of their country. But all in all, it is probably safe to say that the average prisoner of war was better off than his comrade who had to fight at the front for two, three or four years.

EYEWITNESS TESTIMONY

. . . It is understood that bullets whistle, just as horses neigh . . . But how poor the word is ! How pale and niggardly in expressing the extraordinary richness of the music ! . . . the differences of distance, of speed, of calibre, of direction, of the grouping of the guns . . . of dampness, heat, cold wind; the differences of the setting of the battle, whether in plain, valley, forest, glade or on a hill; the differences of intensity of fire are such that there is a veritable scale of sounds of an infinite variety of combinations . . . Very soon you learn to distinguish the sound of the Mannlicher from the sound of a Lebel. The S bullet leaves the rifle dryly, with a sharp note. The cry of the D is deeper, making many echoes . . .

André Fribourg, on fighting in Lorraine, October 2, 1914, The Flaming Crucible *(1918).*

. . . now we are ignorant of what is outside of the square of our company . . . the prehistoric man had his earth, his wife and his children. The soldier of today has lost all ties. In the end he learns to accept this empty existence, but at the beginning and from time to time he undergoes profound anguish.

André Fribourg, in the trenches of Lorraine, October 3, 1914, The Flaming Crucible.

We have just buried Thévenier in a grave dug a little back of the trench . . . It was only yesterday that Th. and I were chatting in the silent trench. He was a kindly and upright man; a scrupulous *employé* who adored his wife and child. He had just been reading me a letter from the unhappy woman who loved him passionately and who in her written words poured out her fears and her tears. "I have no one but you. Guard yourself ! Keep yourself for those who wait for you . . ." Reading, Th., sitting on his knapsack, turned to me with streaming eyes. "Old friend, it breaks me all up to think that they will suffer because I am not there. Poor little fellow; never again will I toss him on my knees, and as for her, she will soon be signing herself the Widow Thévenier." . . . Is it necessary for me to be stranded in the muddy ditches to understand the immortal truth and beauty of the "Iliad"? . . . The letter of the poor loving wife is simply an unconscious translation of the farewell of Andromache to Hector . . .

André Fribourg, on fighting in Lorraine, October 1914, The Flaming Crucible.

The first time I ever encountered a German plane in the air both the pilot, Harvey-Kelley, and myself were completely unarmed . . . We were taking photographs . . . of the trench system to the north of Neuve Chapelle when I suddenly espied a German two-seater about 100 yards away and just below us. The German observer did not appear to be shooting at us. There was nothing to be done. We waved a hand to the enemy and proceeded with our task. The enemy did likewise. At the time this did not appear to me in any way ridiculous—there is a bond of sympathy between all who fly, even between enemies. But afterwards just for safety's sake I always carried a carbine with me in the air. In the ensuing two or three months I had an occasional shot at a German engine. But these encounters can hardly be dignified by the name of "fights." We scarcely expected to shoot the enemy down . . .

R.A.F. Commander Sir Sholto Douglas, about his first flying experience in 1914, in Quentin Reynolds, They Fought for the Sky *(1957).*

On these horrible minutes! One is afraid to die, and during such hours one could long for death out of fear to die in this fashion. I have been in two assaults. May there not be another one! . . . Where did all the courage go? We had enough of waging war. One does not have to be a coward, but humane sentiment revolts against this barbarity, this gruesome slaughter. Finish this war, finish it as quickly as possible!

Kurt Peterson, German student, letter to his parents, October 1914, in War Letters of Fallen Students *(1929).*

Six days is the regular period for service in the trenches under normal conditions. Often enough it seems close to the limit of physical and moral strain which a man can bear. The last night the company packs up its belongings and either in the twilight of the evening or dawn assembles and waits for the shadowy arrival of the relieving sections to whom the position is surrendered without regret.

Alan Seeger, letter to the New York Sun, *from a trench in France, December 8, 1914.*

Cramped quarters breed ill temper and disputes. The impossibility of the simplest kind of personal cleanliness make vermin a universal ill against which there is no remedy . . . the soldier's life comes to mean to him simply the test of the most misery that the human organism can support. He longs for an attack . . .

Alan Seeger, letter to the New York Sun, *December 8, 1914.*

This style of [trench] warfare is extremely modern and for the artillerymen is doubtless very interesting, but for the poor common soldier it is anything but romantic. His role is simply to dig himself a hole in the ground and to keep hidden in it as tightly as possible. Continually under the fire of the opposing batteries, he is yet never allowed to get a glimpse of the enemy. Exposed to all the dangers of war, but none of its enthusiasms or splendid élan, he is condemned to sit like an animal in its burrow and hear the shells whistle over his head and take their little daily toll from his comrades . . . His feet are numb, his canteen frozen, but he is not allowed to make a fire . . . he is not even permitted to light a candle, but must fold himself in his blanket and lie down cramped in the dirty straw to sleep as best he may. How different from the popular notion of the evening campfire, the songs and good cheer.

Alan Seeger, letter to the New York Sun, *from a trench in France, December 8, 1914.*

A squad has stayed behind in the woods to bring us the day's provisions. Before daylight it arrives and the distribution takes place. Great loaves of bread are handed down the lines; each man takes his ration of half a loaf. There is one box of sardines for each two men. A cup of coffee, a small piece of cheese, a bar of chocolate must last us all day, until darkness permits another squad to leave the trench to go down after evening soup. After food comes mail. Too much praise cannot be given the Government for handling the soldier's mail so well.

Alan Seeger, letter to the New York Sun *from the woods of France, December 14, 1914.*

I was at noon today in a place on the Belgian seacoast, a witness of the safe return of a naval airman First Lieutenant von Prondzynsk . . . He had reached Dover and there thrown several bombs, one of which might have hit the harbour railway station . . . The bold airman was heartily congratulated for this first excursion of a German seaplane to the English coast.

Dr. George Wagener in Koelnische Zeitung, *December 1914, in Quentin Reynolds, They Fought for the Sky.*

New Year's Eve was quite strange. An English officer appeared with a white flag and asked for a truce between 11 and 3 o'clock for burying the dead (shortly before Christmas there had been violent enemy attacks in which the English had lost many dead and wounded). It was granted. It is good not to see the corpses lying around any more. The truce was then extended. The English came out of their trenches, and midways cigarettes, canned meat, also photographs were exchanged. They said they did not want to shoot any more. So there was an absolute quiet that struck you as strange . . . It could not go on this way, so we sent word they should return to their trenches, as we would shoot. Then the officer said, he was sorry, but his men did not obey him. They said they could not lie any longer in those wet trenches, and that France was gone. Actually, they are much dirtier than we, have more water in their trenches and many sick. They are mercenaries, so they just go on strike. Of course, we did not shoot. Does the whole English army strike, spoiling the game of those gentlemen in London?

Karl Aldag, German student, letter of January 3, 1915, in War Letters of Fallen Students *(1929).*

One hundred and fifty yards away across a dead field was another wall of sandbags. The distance is important. It is always in all descriptions. One hundred and fifty yards is not much. Only when you get within forty or fifty yards you have something to brag about. Yet three hundred yards may be more dangerous, if an artillery "hate" is on.—Look for an hour and all you see is the wall of sandbags. Not even a rabbit runs across that dead space.

Frederick Palmer, in the French trenches, January 1915, My Year in the Great War *(1915).*

If you prefer the realistic to the romantic school and wish to appreciate the nature of trench warfare in winter, find a piece of wet, flat country, dig a ditch seven or eight feet deep and stand in icy water looking across at another ditch, and sleep in a cellar that you have dug in the wall, and you are near understanding what Mr. Atkins [Tommy Atkins, the name given to the typical British soldier] has been doing for his country . . . Of course, the moist walls will be continually falling in and require mending in a drenching, freezing rain of the kind the Lord visits on all who wage war underground in Flanders. Incidentally, you must look after the pumps, lest the water rise to your neck . . . To carry realism to the limit of the Grand Guignol school, then, arrange some bags of bullets with dynamite charges on the wire . . . plant some dynamite in the parapet . . . and sink heavier charges under your feet, which will do for mines—and set them off, while you engage someone to toss grenades and bombs at you.

Frederick Palmer, on trench warfare in Flanders, January 1915, on My Year in the Great War.

"Guard" means standing here with every nerve strained on the dark world outside . . . When moon or star light makes it possible to see some distance into the orchard, field or grove outside this job is not so bad. But when the sky is covered and complete darkness draws the lurking menace down to within a few meters of this post then the sentinel creates for himself a thousand imaginary dangers.

Alan Seeger, letter to the New York Sun, *from a trench in France, February 5, 1915.*

The Germans are marvellous. You hear their rifles only a few hundred yards off, you feel them about you all the time, and yet you can never see them. Only last night when the moon set behind the crest, it silhouetted the heads of two sentinels in their big trench on top . . . It is four months now that we have been on the firing line,—four months with the noise of the cannon continually in our ears.

Alan Seeger, letter to his father, from a French trench, February 26, 1915.

Then one of the German searchlights that had been swinging its stream of light across the paths of the flares lay its fierce, comet eye on us, glistening on the froth-streaked mud and showing each mud-splashed figure in heavy coat in weird silhouette. "Stand Still," that is the order whenever searchlights come spying in your direction . . . The searchlight swept on. Perhaps Hans at the machine gun was nodding or perhaps he did not think us worth while.

Frederick Palmer, in the trenches of Flanders, March 1915, My Year in the Great War.

They are not emotional, the British, perhaps, but they are given to cheeriness, if not laughter, and they have a way of smiling at times when smiles are much needed. The smile is more often found at the front than back at Headquarters; or perhaps it is more noticeable there.

Frederick Palmer, in the trenches of Flanders, March 1915, My Year in the Great War.

A sort of "after-you-gentlemen-if-you-fire-we-shall" understanding sometimes exists between the foes up to a certain point. Each side understands instinctively the limitation of that point. Too much noise in working; a number of men going out to bury dead or making enough noise to be heard, and the ball begins.

Frederick Palmer, Flanders, March 1915, My Year in the Great War.

Started with Guerder after a Boche reported at Couvres and caught up with him over Pierrefonds. Shot one belt, machine gun jammed, the unjammed. The Boche fled and landed in the direction of Laon. At Coucy we turned back and saw an Aviatik going toward Soissons . . . We followed him, and as soon as he was within our lines we dived and placed ourselves about fifty meters under and behind him at the left. At our first salvo, the Aviatik lurched, and we saw a part of the machine crack. He replied with a rifle shot, one ball hitting a wing, another grazing Guerder's hand and head. At our last shot the pilot sank down on the body-frame, the observer raised his arms, and the Aviatik fell straight downward in flames, between the trenches . . .

Georges Guynemer, a French flying ace, March 1915, in Quentin Reynolds, They Fought for the Sky.

No bad odour assails our nostrils wherever you may go in the British lines. Its cleanliness, if nothing else, would make British army comradeship enjoyable. My wonder never ceases how Tommy keeps himself so neat; how he manages to shave every day and get a part, at least, of the mud off his uniform.

Frederick Palmer, in the trenches of Flanders, March 1915, My Year in the Great War.

Seven weeks ago two Polish deserters came into the lines and gave us valuable information. That night the patrol that went out left the prisoners' menu card for that day stuck on the barbed wire in front of a German post. A few days ago another patrol passing the same spot found a basket in which the Germans had placed two bottles of Munich beer, a box of cigarettes, some chocolate, sandwiches and other samples of their diet, which, it must be said in justice to them, was not bad. On top were three letters addressed to us, "Dear Comrades," and couched in excellent French. The tone of these was most polite. They said that they had been here all winter in front of us and felt we were quite old friends now, though they had never seen any of us . . . They said that they had seen in our press reports to the effect that they were suffering from hunger and so enclosed this specimen of their daily fare to show what they were really enjoying . . . if we wanted peace all we had to do was to come out and sign; that England was the real enemy . . .

Alan Seeger, letter to the New York Sun *from the Aisne, April 28, 1915.*

I have always thought that in a sense his night patrol work was the most exciting on the nerves of all soldiers' duties. In great actions where comrades fight elbow to elbow there are all sorts of external stimulants and supports . . . Besides one sees clearly, knows from which direction the danger will come and pretty much what to expect . . . To the member of the little company creeping out over a battlefield in cold blood in the dead of night, all this is lacking. From every side, the menace points, behind every turn the ambush may be hidden. He has nothing to rely on but his own sang-froid. Advancing over the ground strewn with bodies he faces in every shadow the possibility of a sudden volley at point blank that will lay him cold among them.

Alan Seeger, letter to the New York Sun, from the Aisne, April 28, 1915.

The soldier does not object to danger, which is his business to face, but he does decidedly object to the hard labor incident to trench warfare, which he feels is really not his affair at all, but that of the engineer corps, whose number, however, is quite inadequate to the immensity of the task.

Alan Seeger, letter to the New York Sun, *from the Aisne, April 28, 1915.*

In the field all neurotic symptoms seem to disappear as if by magic; and one's whole system is charged with energy and vitality. Perhaps this is due to the open air life with its simplified standards, freed from all the complex exigencies of society's laws and unhampered by conventionalities.

Fritz Kreisler, violin virtuoso who served in the Austrian army, Four Weeks in the Trenches *(1915).*

This is the most distressing thing about the kind of warfare we are up against here. Never a sight of the enemy, and then some fine day when a man is almost tempted to forget that he is on the front . . . bang! and he is carried off or mangled by a cannon fired five kilometers away. It is not glorious. The gunner has not the satisfaction of knowing that he has hit, nor the wounded at least of hitting back.

Alan Seeger, letter to the New York Sun, *from the French front, May 22, 1915.*

Actually, fear is nothing but the anticipation of approaching calamity which you can hardly escape by caution. I see my healthy limbs, hear the crashing of the shrapnels, the whirring of the shell fragments and involuntarily get the idea that such a thing can tear me to pieces. I have seen the wounds such missiles can inflict. Iron against human flesh! Along with the fear runs the sweet-gruesome foreboding of death in which one does not want to believe but that you cannot escape. The best way to overcome these feelings is to write about them, as I am doing now . . .

Adolf Witte, German student, letter from Galica, June 1915, from War Letters of Fallen Students.

"A Boche gas shell!" we were told as we passed an informal excavation in the communication trench on our way back. "Asphyxiating effect. No time to put on respirators when one explodes. Laid out half a dozen men like fish, gasping for air,—but they will recover."

Frederick Palmer, in Flanders, summer 1915, My Year in the First War.

There was a new terror of trench holding and dwelling. Now a man who lay down in a dugout for the night was not only in danger of being blown heavenward by a mine, or buried by the explosion of a heavy shell, or compelled to spring up in answer to the ring of a gong which announced a gas attack, but he might be awakened by the outcry of sentries who had been overpowered by the stealthy rush of

the shadowy figures of the night, and while he got to his feet be killed by the burst of a bomb thrown by men whom he supposed were also fast asleep in their own quarters two or three hundred yards away.
Frederick Palmer, with the Canadians in France, 1915, My Second Year of the War.

Credit for the trench raid, which was developed through the winter of 1915, belongs to the Canadian . . . The Canadian proposed to enter the German trenches by surprise, remain long enough to make the most of the resulting confusion, and then to return to his own trenches without trying to hold and organize the enemy's position and thus draw upon his head while busy with the spade a murderous volume of shell fire.
Frederick Palmer, with the Canadians in France, 1915, My Second Year of the War.

That one still has that idea: If only we would be home again! It has disappointed us a thousand times. We hoped for the end of October, then for Christmas, then for Easter, then Pentecost, then the 1st of August, then for Christmas 1915, and now we have to accept the thought that the end will come at Eastertime 1916, at the earliest. These two years of war are an interruption of one's life, and yet are such an important part of it; but what the war wants to teach us as human beings, we have not learned and we won't. We hoped for a conciliation of social contrasts by getting to know each other better, a simplification of the conduct of life . . . and only very little of that has happened and is already on the decline. This living-for-one-another is quite inadequate, egotism rules supreme at the front and at home.
Walter Schmidt, German student, letter from the Russian front, July 18, 1915, in War Letters of Fallen Students.

. . . Well, as Mr. Atkins had remarked in his own terse way, a battle was a lot of noise all around you, and suddenly a big bang in your ear; and then somebody said, ''Please open your mouth and take this!'' and you found yourself in a white, silent place full of cots.
Frederick Palmer, Flanders, summer 1915, My Year in the Great War.

A bullet makes the merciful wound; and a bullet through the head is a simple way of going. The bad wounds come mostly from shells; but there is some-

thing about seeing any one hit by a sniper which is more horrible. It is a cold-blooded kind of killing, more suggestive of murder, this single shot from a sharpshooter waiting as patiently as a cat for a mouse . . .
Frederick Palmer, in the British trenches in Flanders, summer 1915, My Year in the Great War.

The Russian prisoners of war most frequently fell victims to this system. Unfortunately they were receiving little help from their own Government, and the great distances and the ignorance of the majority of the Russian people resulted in few parcels being sent by their relatives to the Russian prisoners. The latter were accordingly more or less dependent upon German food or such other food as they could secure by begging or by purchase from their more fortunate British and French fellow-prisoners. French hard-tack biscuits, such as were sent by the French Government to French prisoners of war, were often sold to these hungry Russians at as high as five and six marks apiece.
Conrad Hoffman, In the Prison Camps of Germany *(1915).*

This plane had no reason to fear me. I was going straight for it, my nose aimed at it, and they couldn't possibly have any reason to fear bullets fired through my propeller. While approaching, I thought what a deadly accurate stream of lead I could send into the plane. It would be just like shooting a sitting rabbit because the pilot could not shoot back . . . Suddenly, I decided that the whole job could go to hell. It was too much like 'cold meat' to suit me. I had no stomach for the whole business, not any wish to kill Frenchmen for Germans. Let them do their own killing . . . After a brief argument, it was agreed that a regular German pilot would take up the plane. Lieutenant Oswald Boelcke, later to be the first German ace, was assigned to the job.
Anthony Herman Gerard Fokker, Dutch, about the first tryout of his new fighter plane, 1915, in Quentin Reynolds, They Fought for the Sky.

When half a mile from sheds, put machine into dive and came down to 700 feet. Observed men lined up to right of shed, number estimated 300 to 500. Dropped one bomb in enclosure to put gunners off aim and when in correct position put two into shed.

The fourth bomb failed to release. Made several unsuccessful attempts to get it away, turned, went down to just above surface of lake and made off.

British Flight Lieutenant Sippe, logbook describing raid on zeppelin sheds at Friedrichshaven on Lake Constance, 1915, in Quentin Reynolds, They fought for the Sky.

I decided to dive at her . . . firing a burst straight into her as I came. I let her have another burst as I passed under her and then banked my machine over, sat under her tail and flying along underneath her pumped lead into her for all I was worth . . . As I was firing, I noticed her to begin to go red inside like an enormous Chinese lantern. She shot up about two hundred feet, paused, and came roaring down straight on to me before I had time to get out of the way. I nose-dived for all I was worth, with the zeppelin tearing after me . . . I put my machine into a spin and just managed to corkscrew out of the way as she shot past me, roaring like a furnace . . . then proceeded to fire off dozens of green Very lights in the exuberance of my feelings.

British Lieutenant W.J. Tempest, on shooting down a zeppelin at Potters Bar, October 1915, in Quentin Reynolds, They Fought for the Sky.

It is amazing how much all the men now get into politics. All agree that the privileges of the officers class must come to an end after the war . . . Among the men there are some who talk quite freely and uninhibitedly about what must be done. Their main argument is: What can "they" do if we all do not want it any longer? They cannot put all of us in prison. There are many passionate discussions on the question if Germany should keep any of the occupied territories. The most radical socialist opinions are uttered. Nobody asks if an officer is close by.

Richard Stumpf, on board the Helgoland, *August 23, 1915,* War Diary *(1927).*

The way we are being used is careless and criminal. Please inform Hugo Haase [socialist member of the Reichstag] if necessary. The whole battalion has only one doctor, and what kind of! . . . For our company of 500 men there are two medical orderlies,—and what kind of! . . . The food leaves much to be desired, only potatoes are in the fields plentifully, and very good ones. No tobacco—that hurts espe-

German plane brought down in the Argonne by American machine gunners. Photo courtesy of the National Archives, Washington, D.C.

cially, because it is the only stimulant. In the rear area there are all sorts of things, for instance two cigars and two cigarettes per day. Aside from this the greatest hardship is the lack of lighting. After half past six it is dark. No candles, nothing. You hang around, cannot read or write and crawl into one's "bed," that is one's straw and wrap oneself in the unheated stable or barn into one's coat or a thin blanket, often dripping wet, freezing all night . . .

Karl Liebknecht, socialist leader, letter to his wife from the eastern front, September 20, 1915.

. . . this time only the wounded appeared coming back, no prisoners. I went out and gave water to one of these . . . It was a young soldier, wounded in the hand. His face and voice bespoke the emotion he had been through in a way I will never forget. "Ah, les salauds (bastards)!" he cried, "They let us come right up to the barbed wire without firing. Then a hail of grenades and balls. My comrade fell, shot through the leg, got up, and the next moment had his head taken off by a grenade before my eyes." "And the barbed wire, wasn't it cut down by the bombardment?" "Not at all in front of us."

Alan Seeger, letter to his mother, recalling combat in the Champagne, October 25, 1915.

. . . letters from the front still show the same genius of making light of hardship and deadly peril, the same happy gift of extracting amusement from trivial incidents. So those who spend their days and

nights under heavy shell fire and heavy rain write to tell you that "tea is the dominating factor of war," or that "the mushrooming and ratting in their latest quarters" are satisfactory.
Punch, *London, October 1915.*

I have here principally to tell you a very disagreeable occurrence. As I left my orderly room this morning, I came upon a group of soldiers; I will not particularize their company. One of these soldiers was in conversation with a lance-corporal. You may not believe me, but it is a fact that he addressed the corporal by his Christian name: he called him Jack! To think that the First Battalion has sunk to a level where such familiarity is possible . . . Naturally, I put the corporal under arrest . . . I reduced him to the ranks, and awarded the man Field Punishment for using insubordinate language to an N.C.O. But I warn you, if any further cases of this sort come to my notice . . .
Colonel Ford, known as "Scatter" because he spent his allowance so lavishly, addressing the officers of his battalion at Montagne, France, December 1915, in Robert Graves, Good-bye to All That.

As for atrocities against soldiers—where should one draw the line? The British soldier, at first, regarded the use of bowie-knives by German patrols as atrocious. After a time, he learned to use them himself; they were cleaner killing weapons than revolvers or bombs. The German regarded as equally atrocious the British Mark VII rifle-bullet, which was more apt on striking than the German bullet.
Robert Graves, Good-bye to All That.

The troops with the worst reputation for acts of violence against prisoners were the Canadians (and later the Australians). The Canadians' motive was said to be revenge for a Canadian found crucified with bayonets through his hands and feet in a German trench. This atrocity had never been substantiated; nor did we believe the story, freely circulated, that the Canadians crucified a German officer in revenge shortly afterwards . . . At all events, most overseas men, and some British troops, made atrocities against prisoners a boast, not a confession.
Robert Graves, Good-bye to All That.

Patriotism, in the trenches, was too remote a sentiment, and at once rejected as fit only for civilians,

or prisoners. A new arrival who talked patriotism would soon be told to cut it out . . . The trench-soldier . . . thought of Germany as a nation in arms, a unified nation inspired with the sort of patriotism that he himself despised.
Robert Graves, Good-bye to All That.

Hardly one soldier in a hundred was inspired by religious feeling of even the crudest kind. It would have been difficult to remain religious in the trenches even if one had survived the irreligion of the training battalion at home. A regular sergeant at Montagne . . . had recently told me that he did not hold with religion in time of war. He said that the "niggers" (meaning the Indians) were right in officially relaxing their religious rules while fighting. "And all this damned nonsense, Sir—excuse me, Sir—that we read in the papers, Sir, about how miraculous it is that the wayside crucifixes are always getting shot at, but that the figure of our Lord Jesus somehow don't get hurt, it fairly makes me sick, Sir."
Robert Graves, Good-bye to All That.

In the early days of German prison organization it was the policy of the German authorities to house Russian, French, and British prisoners all within the same barracks, rather than to segregate them by nationalities. It was urged that as long as these nationalities were allies they had better become well acquainted with one another. However, this promiscuous mixing of the different nationalities provoked such continued friction and dissatisfaction that the Germans gradually substituted the national principle in the distribution of prisoners.
Conrad Hoffmann, In the Prison Camps of Germany.

I was shown a pound of walnuts among which one had been found which had been opened, a note enclosed, and then carefully resealed. Obviously no more walnuts were permitted by the Germans to reach the prisoners of war after this discovery. Letters and newspapers baked into loaves of bread were not uncommon; in one camp I was shown a bottle of whiskey baked within a loaf of bread. False bottoms in canned goods and letters in tins of butter or lard, had been discovered at various times. Needless to say, the Germans instigated a most rigorous censorship thereafter of all supplies sent in to prisoners of war. All canned goods were opened before issuance, very much to the discomfort of the prisoners.

Conrad Hoffmann, In the Prison Camps of Germany.

It was fortunate that the need of man power in Germany became so urgent, for it resulted in the sending out of most of the prisoners of war into the agricultural communities to work on the farms, and food conditions there were far superior to those which prevailed in the prison camps. Personally, I regard this feature of employment of the prisoners as providential in the case of the Russians, Serbians, and Roumanians, for had it not taken place and had all these men been compelled to remain in the camps and to subsist on the food which the German authorities were able to provide, death by starvation would have been appalling in the number of victims it would have claimed. The British prisoners of war, as well as the French and many of the Italians were much better off, for their respective governments sent in food in large quantities to care for them.

Conrad Hoffmann, In the Prison Camps of Germany.

At the Burg Officers' Camp I was present on the arrival of a soldier who had recently been captured at the Somme and had been sent to this officers' camp to serve as orderly to one of the officers. It was most amusing to see the generals and other high officers long imprisoned asking the orderly for his opinion with reference to the future and the outcome of the War, because he had the most recent information on the situation. In this same camp fourteen attempts to escape by tunneling had been made. One tunnel was fifty-eight meters, or 174 feet, long before it was discovered by the German authorities and the attempted escape frustrated.

Conrad Hoffmann, In the Prison Camps of Germany.

In this same camp a group of the older men took upon themselves the responsibility of looking after the younger element, a group of some twenty-odd boys ranging in age from sixteen to twenty years. Similarly efforts were made to look after the colored men in the camp who were housed in a separate barrack of their own and numbered over 100. A Canadian student organized a Bible class among these

men which met regularly and had a wholesome effect on the men.

Conrad Hoffmann, In the Prison Camps of Germany.

Time and again I saw groups of Germans just drafted into service and still in their civilian dress march down the streets, escorted by armed German guards as though they were prisoners, to some garrison where they were equipped with uniform and gun. They were a sorry sight and reminded me of "sheep being marched to slaughter." Often the wives accompanied the men, tearfully bidding farewell as they left on the troop trains. On the sides of these trains one found many jests of all characters written in chalk. Among the many vulgar, ridiculous, and ribald jests the following serious sentence attracted my attention: *"Unsere Kinder sollen es gut haben."* (Our posterity will benefit.)

Conrad Hoffmann, In the Prison Camps of Germany.

The only man who still enjoys the sympathy and trust of the common soldier is that loud-mouth Liebknecht. "Scheidemann and Legien [moderate social democrats] should join the agrarians; as social democrats they will never see the Reichstag again." That is the mood among the men in field-gray, not what the journalists drivel. Still, I do not believe in the familiar slogan: "There will be no peace until we turn the rifles around." But there will be a terrible reckoning . . .

Johannes Haas, German student, letter of January 29, 1916, published in War Letters of Fallen Students.

In the waiting rooms, and on the platforms, the badly wounded are lying on the stretchers; those on the road to recovery are grouped under the awning; sick men arriving from the hospital are somehow helped along. Everywhere wan, unshaven faces, bandages, the stretched-out bodies of Zouaves or Algerians, sleepy or restless, but always quiet, gazing without seeing . . . I see Daré . . . he sees me, tries to smile at me and says in a low voice: "You see how ugly, stupid and sad a sick man is in the war. How many of those stretched out there will die from their imprudent flight! They will drag along, getting thinner and thinner from their suffering. Pity them, for they will not have been struck down in the drunk-

enness of battle; they will have more pain and less glory; the injustice of man will add to the injustice of fate. The happy ones, you see, are those who die at one blow . . ."
André Fribourg, at the railway station of Bierne, Flanders, March 1916, The Flaming Crucible.

Scattered with British wounded taking cover in new and old shell-craters was No Man's Land as the living passed. A Briton and his prisoner would take cover together. An explosion and the prisoner might be blown to bits, or if the captor were, another Briton took charge of the prisoner.
Frederick Palmer, on the Battle of the Somme, July 1916, My Second Year of the War.

The professional soldier expressing his admiration of the way the German charges, handles his artillery, or the desperate courage of his machine gun crews may speak of him as "Brother Boche," or the "old Boche" in a sort of amiable recognition of the fact of how worthy he is of an enemy's steel if only he would refrain from certain unsportsmanlike habits.
Frederick Palmer, at the Somme, July 1916, My Second Year of the War.

Oh, these light German cigars! Sometimes I believe they were the real mainstay of the German army organization. Cigars gone, spirit gone! I have seen an utterly weary German prisoner as he delivered his papers to his captor bring out his last cigar and thrust it in to his mouth to forestall its being taken as a tribute, with his captor saying with characteristic British cheerfulness, "Keep it, Bochy! It smells too much like a disinfectant to me, but let's have your steel helmet."
Frederick Palmer, at the Somme, July 1916, My Second Year of the War.

Unlike the English, these victors were articulate; they rejoiced in their experiences and were glad to tell about them. If one had fought it out at close quarters with a German and got his man, he made the incident into a dramatic episode for your edification.
Frederick Palmer, with the French at the Somme, July 1916, My Second Year of the War.

German prisoners used to say on the Somme that their aviators were "funks," though the Allied aviators knew that it was not their opponents lack of courage which was the principal fault, even if they had lost morale from being the underdog and lacked British and French initiative, but numbers and material. It was resource against resource again.
Frederick Palmer, at the Somme, Summer 1916, My Second Year of the War.

Make no mistake about that nine-inch howitzer, which appears to be only a monstrous tube of steel firing a monstrous shell, not being a delicately adjusted piece of mechanism. The gunner, his clothes oil-soaked, who has her breech apart, pays no attention to the field of guns around him or the burst of a shell a hundred yards away . . . Is he a soldier? Yes, by his uniform, but primarily a mechanic, this man from Birmingham, who is polishing that heavy piece of steel . . .
Frederick Palmer, at the Somme, August 1916, My Second Year of the War.

The education of those on the Home Front is also proceeding. There are some maids who announce the approach of zeppelins as if they were ordinary visitors. There are others who politely decline to exchange a seat at an attic window for the security of the basement.
Punch, London, August 1916.

Returning from my morning fly/ I met a Fokker in the sky,/ And, judging from its swift descent, / It had a nasty accident./ On thinking further of the same/ I rather fear I was to blame.
Poem of a British pilot, in Punch, London, *August 1916.*

The first time I saw a tank, the way that the monster was blocking a road gorged with transport had something of the ludicrousness of, say, a pliocene monster weighing fifty tons which had nonchalantly lain down at Piccadilly Circus when the traffic was densest. Only the motor-truck drivers and battalions which were halted some distance away minded the delay. Those nearby were sufficiently entertained by the spectacle which stopped them. They gathered around the tank and gaped and grinned.

Did the Germans know that the tanks were building? I think they had some inkling some weeks before the tanks' appearance that something of the sort was under construction . . . Some German prisoners said that their first intimation of this new affliction was when the tanks appeared out of the morning mist, bearing down on the trenches; others said that German sausage balloons had seen something resembling giant turtles moving across the fields . . . and had given warning to the infantry.

Frederick Palmer, at the Somme, September 1916, My Second Year of the War.

No wonder that the German prisoners who had escaped alive from a trench filled with dead, when they saw a tank on the road as they passed to the rear threw up their hands with a guttural: "Mein Gott ! There is another ! There is no fighting that ! This is not war; it is butchery !" . . . Germans surrendered to a tank in bodies after they saw the hopelessness of turning their own machine gun and rifle fire upon that steel hide . . . There seemed a strange loss of dignity when a Prussian colonel delivered himself to a tank . . .

Frederick Palmer, at the Somme, September 1916, My Second Year of the War.

The average layman conceives of a charge as a rush. So it is on the drill-ground, but not where its movement is timed to arrival on the second before a hissing storm of death, and the attackers must not be winded when there is hot work awaiting them in close encounters . . . No one was sprinting ahead of his companions; no one crying, "Come on, boys!," no one swinging his steel helmet aloft, for he needed it for protection . . . All were advancing at a rapid pace, keeping line and intervals except where they had to pass shell-craters.

Frederick Palmer, on the British attack at Thiepval during the Somme offensive, fall 1916, My Second Year of the War.

Some leaped directly into the trench, others ran along the parapet a few steps looking for a vantage point or throwing a bomb as they went before they descended. It was a quick, urgent, hit-and-run sort of business and in an instant all were out of sight and the fighting was man to man, with the guns of both sides keeping their hands off this conflict under ground.

Frederick Palmer, on the British attack at the Somme, Fall 1916, My Second Year of the War.

Soon after the taking of Fort Douaumont when I was at Verdun, Beauchamp, blond, blue-eyed and gentle of manner, who had thrilled all France by bombing Essen, said, "Now they will expect me to go further and do something greater," and I was not surprised to learn a month later that he had been killed. Something in the way he spoke convinced me that he foresaw death and accepted it as a matter of course.

Frederick Palmer, with the French aviators near Verdun, Fall 1916, My Second Year of the War.

What stories the stretcher-bearers brought in of wounded blown off litters by shells, of the necessity of choosing the man most likely to survive when only one of two could be carried, of whispered messages from the dying, and themselves keeping to their work with cheery British phlegm; and the water men told of new gun positions . . .

Frederick Palmer, at the Somme, Fall 1916, My Second Year of the War.

The men were three-quarters of the distance, now. As they were nearer to the barrage another apprehension numbed your thought. You feared to see a "short"—one of the shells from their own guns which did not carry far enough bursting among the men— and this, as one English soldier who had been knocked over by a short said, with dry humor, was "very discouraging though I suppose it is well meant." A terrible thing that, to the public, killing your own men with your own shells. It is better to lose a few of them this way than many from German machine guns by lifting the barrage too soon, but fear of public indignation had its influence in the early days of British gunnery. The better the gunnery the closer the infantry can go . . . And there were no shorts that day. Every shell that I burst was "on."

Frederick Palmer, on the British attack at the Somme, fall of 1916, My Second Year of the War.

Personal! Only to be processed by officers! One of the most regrettable consequences of the destructive effects of the heavy battles at our Western front is our unproportionly high loss of un-wounded prisoners. I recognize readily that there can be situations where further resistance is useless . . . But we must maintain the principle that in general it is a disgrace for troops to be taken prisoner while armed.

Circular of the crown prince of Germany, October 27, 1916.

The types [of planes] changed so fast that the best plane on the line one day might very well be called obsolete the next day. The resources of almost the entire world were engaged in producing the best possible aircraft, and the results achieved certainly justified the efforts expended.

Major Henry H. Arnold, later chief of the U.S. Air Forces in World War II, on the development of the warplane in 1916, in Quentin Reynolds, They Fought for the Sky.

Both men were shooting. It was probable that the Englishman would fall at any moment. Suddenly I noticed an unnatural movement of the two German flying machines. Immediately I thought: Collision. I had not yet seen a collision in the air. I imagined that it would look quite different. In reality, what happened was not a collision. The two machines merely touched on another. However, if two machines go at the tremendous pace of flying machines, the slightest contact has the effect of a violent concussion. Boelcke drew away from his victim and descended in large curves. He did not seem to be falling, but when I saw him descending below me I noticed that part of his plane had broken off. Now his machine was no longer steerable. It fell accompanied all the time by Boelcke's faithful friend. When we reached home we found the report "Boelcke is dead" had already arrived . . . The greatest pain was, of course, felt by the man who had the misfortune to be involved in the accident.

Manfred von Richthofen in his diary, October 28, 1916, in Quentin Reynolds, They Fought for the Sky.

The Englishman tried to catch me up in the rear while I tried to get behind him . . . The circles we made round one another were so narrow that the diameter was probably no more than 250 or 300 feet. I had time to take a good look at my opponent. I looked down into his carriage and could see every movement of his head. My Englishman was a good sportsman, but by and by the thing became a little too hot for him. He had to decide whether he would land on German ground or whether he would fly back to the English lines. Of course he tried the

latter, after endeavouring in vain to escape me by loopings and such tricks. At that time his first bullets were flying around me, for so far neither of us had been able to do any shooting. When he had come down to about 300 feet he tried to escape by flying in a zigzag course . . . That was my most favourable moment. I followed him at an altitude of from 250 to 150 feet, firing all the time. The Englishman could not help falling. But the jamming of my gun nearly robbed me of my success.

Manfred von Richthofen, November 23, 1916, on downing the English ace, Major Lanoe G. Hawker, in Quentin Reynolds, They Fought for the Sky.

One returns from a flight and finds a three-inch antiaircraft gunshell has gone through the body of his plane. "So that was it ! Hardly felt it !" he said. If the shell had exploded? . . . the pilot would be in the German lines unrecognizable among the debris of his machine after a "crasher." Where in the old

Manfred Baron von Richthofen, German flying ace. Photo courtesy of the National Archives, Washington, D.C.

West gunmen used to put a notch on their revolver handle for every man killed, now in each aviator's record is the number of enemy planes which he has brought down.

Frederick Palmer, with the British aviators in France, 1916, My Second Year of the War.

Once the longing for this peace within reach broke into the open: A Swiss military band played right between the two hostile fronts, and there applause surged up, first on our side, then over there, and both fronts were united in one sentiment, and for half an hour even the dullest turned strangely soft, and suddenly talked of home, of the future, of peace.

Gustav Radbruch, German jurist, later minister of justice, letter from the front near the Swiss border, Christmas 1916.

Modern combat is played out almost entirely invisibly; the new day of fighting demands of the soldier that he . . . withdraw from the sight of the opponent. He can not fight upright on the earth but must crawl into and under it; at sea he fights most securely when he is concealed under the surface of the water, and in the air when he flies so high that he no longer offers a target.

Robert Michaels, Briefe eines Hauptmanns, (1916).

Between this war and the last, we did not die: We ended. Neatly, in the shelter of a room, in the warmth of a bed. Now, we die. It is the wet death, the muddy death, death dripping with blood, death by drowning, death by sucking under, death in the slaughter house. The bodies lie frozen in the earth which gradually sucks them in. The luckiest depart, wrapped in canvas from a tent, to sleep in the nearest cemetery.

Louis Mairet, French officer, in Le Carnet d'un soldat on March 10, 1917, quoted in Guy Chapman (ed.), Vain Glory (1937). Mairet was killed in action in April 1917.

. . . won't it be nice when all this beastly killing is over, and we can just enjoy ourselves and not hurt anyone ? I hate this game, but it is the only thing one must do just now.

Am indeed looked after by God, but Oh! I do get tired of always living to kill, and I am really beginning to feel like a murderer.

British Captain Albert Ball, in letters to his fiancee and his father, May 5, 1917, in Quen-

tin Reynolds, They Fought for the Sky. Two days later, Ball disappeared on a flight without leaving a trace.

The first two salvos always make you jump. The balls of smoke appear miraculously in the sky, then you hear the woof! woof! woof! The shorter the period between seeing and hearing, the nearer the shell is to you. When they coincide you've no more interest in things! When the shells burst below or behind you get the woof! first, and that can be nerve-jerking too. But worst is to get them say fifty yards in front of you, first the flash red flame, then the burst of smoke, the the woof!, then chunks of shrapnel tearing gashes in your wings, and maybe in you too. A second later you are frying through the smoke, which has a sharp, acrid smell, and you realise it isn't black but very dark brown.

A.G. Lee, at the Battle of Messines, June 9, 1917, in No Parachute (1968).

Today's query from home—why do I carry a Colt in the cockpit? For the reason we all do. Not to stage a one-man battle against a platoon of Boche soldiery when forced down the other side—I'd be butchered instantly. No, it's the fear of being set alight. It's something nobody talks about, but it's at the back of everybody's mind, and each of us knows he couldn't take it. To be burned alive, however soon it's over, is the one thing we can't face. Better use the gun and end it in a split second.

A.G. Lee, at the Battle of Messines, June 1917, in No Parachute.

We had a good laugh at an article in one of today's newspapers about the way the Huns paint their machines all the colours of the rainbow. They do it, wrote some expert, in order to give each other confidence. What drivel! They don't need war-paint to give themselves confidence, they've got too much already, with their Albatross D-IIIs outclassing us on almost every count. The fact that nearly all the Huns are coloured, while we're chocolate brown, is very useful in dog-fights, when your shooting is in split-second bursts, because you instantly know who is who. And their colourings sometimes help us to know who we're scrapping with. For example, every Albatross in the Richthofen-Circus has some red paint on it, and the Baron himself has an all-red machine. That's what the chaps say. . . .

A.G. Lee, at the Vimy front, June 1917, in No Parachute.

This is the hell of dog-fights, with every pilot shooting at every Hun, and the whole thing over in a couple of minutes. Just to see one drop out of the fight doesn't count for much. You may use all your ammo, your machine may be riddled, you may have escaped death by inches in a fierce little battle, yet you've nothing positive to report, and it's all written off the records as—an indecisive with E.A. [enemy aircraft].

A.G. Lee, at the Vimy front, June 29, 1917, in
No Parachute.

Plenty of scrapping in the air now every day. Three of us went up and run right into nine Hun machines yesterday . . . They gave us a hell of a time, although we held our own. I made the old bus do some horrible things on that occasion. I believe the whole front from Lens to Arras was looking at us. They hopped it in the end, and I hadn't a bullet hole anywhere on the machine . . . I sent a parcel off to you yesterday. Pilots' boot which belonged to a dead pilot. Goggles belonging to another . . . The piece of fabric with a number on it is from another Hun-two-seater . . . The other little brown packet is field dressing carried by a Hun observer for dressing wounds when in the air . . . I have several other things which I cannot send home, they will do later . . .

Edward Mannock, British ace, in a letter to his friend Jim Eyles, August 1, 1917, in Quentin Reynolds, They Fought for the Sky.

And the captured gun! It is a prize no less dear to the infantry's heart today than it was a hundred years ago. Our battalion took a battery! There is a thrill for every officer and man and all the friends at home. Muzzle cracked by a direct hit, recoil cylinder broken . . . there you have a trophy which is proof of accuracy to all gunners . . .

Frederick Palmer, My Second Year of the War.

I am making this statement as an act of wilful defiance of military authority, because I believe that the war is being deliberately prolonged by those who have the power to end it. I am a soldier, convinced that I am acting on behalf of soldiers. I believe that this war, upon which I entered as a war of defence and liberation, has now become a war of aggression and conquest . . . I am not protesting against the conduct of the war, but against the political errors and insincerities for which the fighting men are being sacrificed.

Statement of Siegfried Sassoon, English poet and novelist who enlisted on August 3, 1914 and had served with distinction in France, but turned conscientious objector, July 1917, in Robert Graves, Good-bye to All That.

. . . why should God grant me any special favour? The Hun I'm fighting may be calling on him too. It isn't as though I had any great faith in religion, but even if I had, would it divert a bullet? Anyway, how can anybody who had to fight believe in God with all the mass killings and with British, French and German priests all shouting that God is on their side? How can I call on God to help me shoot down a man in flames?

A.G. Lee, at the Arras front, September 21, 1917, in No Parachute.

McDonald died of wounds, but Bird and Williams are prisoners. We get this information through Huns flying over our side periodically with a streamered message bag containing the list of . . . casualties. We do the same for them, and even more. For instance, when Boelcke, then their top scorer, was killed last October the R.F.C. not only dropped a message but also a wreath because the chaps thought him a brave and chivalrous opponent. This mutual consideration is one of the few decent things in this mutual-killing business. In the trenches anything like it would be looked upon officially as fraternisation, which shows that us flyers on both sides have our own code in this nasty war . . . our scrapping is impersonal. We don't hate each other. In fact, we probably hate strikers at home, stabbing us in the back, far more than the Huns, who are risking their skins for their country just as we are . . .

A.G. Lee, at the Arras front, September 23, 1917, in No Parachute.

This trench-strafing is becoming rather a strain. In air fighting, what counts, apart from having an efficient plane, are things like experience, skill, tactics, good flying, good shooting. Plus luck, of course, though chance is only one of the factors. But trench-strafing is *all* chance, no matter how skilled you are. To make sure of your target you have to expose yourself to the concentration of dozens of machine guns and hundreds of rifles. Compared with this,

archie [antiaircraft guns] is practically a joke . . . I've got to admit it gives me the shakes . . .
A.G. Lee, at the Battle of Cambrai, November 29, 1917, in No Parachute.

Last year, at this time, I lay awake in a windy tent in the middle of a vast dreadful encampment . . . chiefly I thought of a very strange look on all faces in that camp. An incomprehensible look which a man will never see in England; nor can it be seen in any battle. But only in Étaples. It was not despair, or terror, it was more terrible than terror, for it was a blindfold look, and without expression, like a dead rabbit's. It will never be painted, and no actor will ever seize it.
Wilfred Owen, English poet, diary, December 1917, in Guy Chapman (ed.), Vain Glory.

I had to come up quite close. That observer, whoever he was, was a first-class fighting man. He was a devil for courage and energy. I flew within five yards of him, until he had enough, and that in spite of the fact that I believe I had hit him before. Even to the very last moment, he kept shooting at me. The slightest mistake, and I should have rammed him in the air . . .
Manfred von Richthofen, on bringing down his seventy-fifty enemy plane, quoted by Quentin Reynolds, They Fought for the Sky.

No weary legs hamper him; he does not have to crawl over the dead or stand up to his knees in the mire. He is the pampered aristocrat of the war, the golden youth of adventure. He leaves a comfortable bed, with bath, a good breakfast, the comradeship of a pleasant mess, the care of servants . . . When he returns he only has to slip out of his seat. Mechanics look after his plane . . .
German writer, after visiting headquarters of Richthofen's squadron, known as his "Flying Circus," early 1918, in Quentin Reynolds, They Fought for the Sky.

Ever since the war began the air services have been cursed by the feudings and intrigues that arose from the competition between the War Office and the Admiralty over the provision of aircraft for the R.F.C. and the R.N.A.S. These preposterous rivalries, which led to tragic inadequacies of equipment in the R.F.C. in the field, worked almost to stalemate in an area of divided responsibilities such as Home Defence.

A.G. Lee, on the rivalry between the British Royal Flying Corps and the Navy, in No Parachute.

Trenches rise up, gray clay, three or four feet above the ground. Save for one or two men—snipers at the sap-head—the country was deserted. No sign of humanity—a dead land. And yet thousands of men were there, like rabbits concealed.
In Laurence Housman, Letters of Fallen Englishmen *(1930).*

I have noticed that the normal healthy man arriving from England showed definite signs of physical fear when first coming under fire. This fear very shortly wore off and was replaced by a type of callousness which sometimes increased until a man took very little trouble to protect himself. I noticed in several cases that when this condition was well advanced a man became liable to break down mentally . . .
J.F.C. Fuller, testifying before the British War Office, 1922, in Eric J. Leed, No Man's Land *(1979).*

It seems to me as if we stand before the enemy released from everything that has formerly bound us; we stand entirely free there, death can no longer sever our ties too painfully. Our entire thoughts and feelings are completely rearranged; if I were not afraid of being misunderstood I would almost say that we are somehow "estranged" from the men and things of our former life.
In War Letters of Fallen Students *(1936).*

They [his French comrades] have the air of supplicants who offer the napes of their necks to the executioner . . . The peals of thunder in all those moments have revealed the terrible disproportion between the engines of death and the tiny soldier, in whom the nervous system was not up to the magnitude of these shocks.
Jean Galtier-Boissier, French soldier, in Jean N. Cru, Témoins *(1928).*

The petty, aimless, lazy peacetime life is over. Life has suddenly been reduced to its simplest terms. Every moment is meticulously precise, every touch determined, every action directly aimed toward its goal. All things move straight ahead, and all have their clear, unmistakable meaning.
Franz Schauwecker, German soldier and writer, The Fiery Way *(1921).*

We are soldiers and the weapon is the tool with which we proceed to shape ourselves. Our work is killing, and it is our duty to do this work well and completely . . . For every age expresses itself not only in practical life, in love, in science and art, but also in the frightful. And it is the meaning of the soldier to be frightful.

Ernst Juenger, German officer and writer, Fire and Blood *(1935).*

When moving about in the trenches you turn a corner every few yards, which makes it seem like walking in a maze. It is impossible to keep your sense of direction and infinitely tiring to proceed at all. When the trenches have been fought over the confusion becomes all the greater. Instead of neat, parallel trench lines, you make the best use of existing trenches which might run in any direction other than the one you would prefer, until an old battlefield, like that of the Somme, became a labyrinth of trenches without any plan.

Charles Edmunds, British soldier, Subaltern's War *(1929).*

A little further on the real trenches lay—one long burrow . . . To go down into that never-ending pit is to plunge into the sudden twilight smelling thickly of earth; to feel cut off from the world and close to the terrible heart of things. Round bend after bend you go, scraping twin walls, a prisoner held lengthwise . . .

Henri Barbusse, French soldier and writer, I Saw It Myself *(1928).*

I know . . . what trench warfare is all about, but that is child's play compared to a fight in the coal pit. There, one has the feeling of being in his tunneled-out grave or already roasting in hell. The weight of enormous masses of earth around you gives you the feeling of complete isolation and makes you think that if you die here no one would ever find you again.

Ernst Juenger, German soldier and writer, Sturm *(1963).*

I quote at this time from a report of one of our secretaries to show just what prison life and imprisonment meant to the men. He writes as follows:

"A month ago, a Russian general whom I have often visited presented me with a book by a Russian author, Dosdojewski, which he had translated into French. It was entitled *'Souvenir de la Maison des Morts'* and contained recollections of Dosdojewski's imprisonment in Siberia. The general told me that what is said in the first part of the book regarding the spiritual condition of the prisoners is very typical of his own prison captivity. I have read the book, which explains what is already expressed in the title and is so similar to the condition of the prisoners in the camps I am now visiting. In a true sense of the word they are 'dead men.' "

Conrad Hoffman, In the Prison Camps of Germany.

One evening, after securing permission from the German authorities, we had the band strike up "My Country, 'Tis of Thee," and asked the men to sing. When the first strain of the music was heard it did one's heart good to see the way hats and caps were removed and the men all straightened up to an erect standing or sitting position. And how they did sing! It was not long before we had learned the words of all four verses and on every occasion all four were sung. One night by a happy inspiration I pulled out my silk American flag which I had always carried with me, waving it to the tune of the last verse as it was being played. The effect on the men of seeing Old Glory thus displayed there in the prison camp can be imagined. There was a spontaneous outburst of wild cheers and ringing applause, and then all joined in with even greater intensity than ever in the singing of the last verse.

Conrad Hoffman, In the Prison Camps of Germany.

They are all here now, friends and simple comrades. This one is Gérard, my captain at Les Eparges, whose nerves were so shaken that, coming out of the hospital after his wound was cured, he shot himself through the head. A strange story! This man, who had dared death, who had dealt death, who had threatened us with death, who had played with death, escaped death only to meet her again. How did she rejoin him? By what subtle detour did she find her prey?

André Fribourg, reminiscing after his return from the war, The Flaming Crucible.

12. Governments and Diplomacy During the War: 1914–1918

THE HISTORICAL CONTEXT

In 1914, all sides were convinced that the war would be brief. The French were sure their great attack would take them to Berlin within a few weeks; the Germans had no doubt they would take Paris in September; and the Russians knew their "steamroller" was irresistible. When these hopes came to naught, the idea of settling this incredibly bloody, insane mass slaughter in one way or another certainly entered the minds of many reasonable people. But for a long time to come, peace talks did not stand a chance whatsoever.

The European nations were strong and rich when the war started. Tremendous industrial progress had been made during the last 60 or 70 years, and a great deal of accumulated energy broke loose and exploded in the great national efforts. Every country thought it was personally attacked, but all had their moments of aggression: the French in Alsace-Lorraine, the Germans through Belgium, the Russians in East Prussia. None of these grandiose, carefully worked-out plans succeeded, and by the end of 1914, it was clear that an endless struggle of attrition lay ahead. All subsequent major offensives failed to reach their objectives and ended in senseless massacres of hundreds of thousands of soldiers. When the great British scheme, the attack at the Dardanelles, fell apart in 1915, no sweeping success for either side was forseeable. But nobody talked of peace. Instead, a struggle for new allies began. The Central Powers had secured the support of Turkey; the Allies won Italy; the Central Powers, Bulgaria. In 1916, Romania joined the Allies and a year later, so did Greece. Thus, the war extended into new areas, but no decision was in sight.

THE PROPAGANDA MACHINES

One of the main reasons why efforts for a settlement were not undertaken was the feverish propaganda launched by both sides. Allied propaganda was superior to that of the Central Powers. It painted the Germans as the main—in fact, the only—important enemy, though the war had really started with Austria. The Germans were ruthless, bloodthirsty militarists and referred to as "Huns" or "Boches" (a French word for "swine") out to conquer the world. The words of philosopher Friedrich Nietzsche, the kaiser and Pan-German fanatics supported this claim. Only the German armies occupied enemy territory, making it easy to blame them alone for cruelties and willful destruction as long as the Allied armies had not been given the same chance. To break Prussian militarism once and for all had to be the aim of all peace-loving democracies. Russia, of course, did not fit into this picture, as it obviously represented the most autocratic, least democratic state of all. But propaganda in wartime does not address subtle analysts, rather it tries to incite emotions through simple, drastic images and phrases.

German submarine warfare and incidents such as the sinking of the *Lusitania* seemed to bear out the Allied thesis of German ruthlessness, but the English blockade—designed to starve millions of civilians, including women and children—was not in accordance with international law either and in its effect was at least cruel and inhuman. Still, Allied propaganda was effective, but the more it spread and the more intense it became, the more difficult it would be for any Allied government to enter into peace negotiations.

German propaganda was less streamlined. It was not clear from the beginning who was the main enemy. France was the traditional foe since the days of Louis XIV and Napoleon, but only the German veterans of the 1870–71 war would look at the present conflict in this way. Russia was the main enemy for the political left, since the Social Democrats tried to see the great conflict as a struggle between despotic Russia and a progressive, democratic—or near-democratic—Germany. But soon most Germans concentrated their hatred on England, since, from the kaiser down, they had regarded England as a friendly, blood-related nation. Britain's entry into the war was seen as a stab in the back, an act of cowardice and petty jealousy. Also, through Britain's involvement the war was no longer a continental conflict as earlier European wars had been. The war on land had become a world war, and Britain safeguarded all overseas supplies it and its Allies required, while Germany was cut off and isolated. Last but not least: Britain constituted the bridge to the one great power that was not yet involved in the war: the United States of America.

THE UNITED STATES AS MEDIATOR

From the outbreak of the war, President Woodrow Wilson apparently felt the opportunity would arise for him to step into the conflict as a mediator and peacemaker. In 1914, the great majority of the American people supported neutrality, which was in accordance with George Washington's famous warning against involvement in European affairs that had been adhered to by almost all American presidents up to this point. It is, however, safe to say that there was more sympathy for the Allies than for Germany. The Americans considered the Germans to be arrogant, and the kaiser and the Prussian Junker class were often ridiculed and not taken seriously. Germany's violation of Belgian neutrality, America's natural sympathy for France as the underdog, and the fact that the controlling American newspapers and communication media were located in the U.S. Northeast, where English and French sympathizers had the upper hand, slowly altered public opinion. British propaganda, again, did the better job in the United States, too. The story of Germany's execution of British nurse Edith Cavell—convicted of aiding Allied soldiers to escape—went around the world, though the French had executed nine women as spies during the war, including the famous Mata Hari. Clumsy attempts of German propaganda in the United States backfired, and espionage cases involving German diplomats such as Franz von Papen (later chancellor in the Weimar Republic) and Carl von Boy-Ed, both of whom had to be recalled, turned public opinion more and more against Germany.

Wilson's first attempt to mediate took place in January and February 1916 when he sent his close personal adviser, Colonel Edward M. House, to Europe to consult with leading statesmen of the countries at war. The resulting memorandum, which reflected mainly his discussions with British foreign secretary Sir Edward Grey, announced that the president was ready to propose a peace conference whenever Britain and France were ready. It also hinted that, should the proposal be rejected by Germany but accepted by the Allies, the United States would probably join the war on the Allied side. American mediation terms would include restoration of Serbia and Belgium, the cession of Alsace-Lorraine to France, the transfer of Italian-speaking border regions from Austria to Italy, and the acquisition of Constantinople by Russia. Germany would retain some colonies, while Poland would be independent. The proposal favored the Allied side who in 1916 were still counting on a decisive victory through big offensives. While his efforts did not lead to any progress during the year, Wilson ran for reelection under the slogan "he kept us out of war" and won, by a narrow margin, over the Republican candidate, Charles Evans Hughes.

In December 1916, the German government asked the United States to inform the Allies of German and Austrian willingness to negotiate peace. Specific terms were not mentioned, and since the military situation was favorable to the Germans at the time, the move may have been just an attempt to prevent any unfavorable effects of the planned declaration of unrestricted submarine warfare and to keep the United States neutral. The English and French governments, led by David Lloyd George and Aristide Briand, rejected the proposal; only a few days later, Wilson announced his own proposals, suggesting that the belligerents should state their terms for peace and guarantees to prevent any further conflicts. The Central Powers replied favorably but again without stating any terms, while the Allied answer included terms so favorable to the Allied cause that Wilson did not go along. In his speech of January 22, 1917, he proclaimed the idea of "peace without victory" and then urged the German government to state its own aims. Berlin obliged, but the terms were so one-sided that again no progress was made, though Wilson and the moderate and skillful German ambassador in Washington, Count Johann Heinrich Bernstorff, continued to negotiate. In January 1917, events seemed to force the Allies to ask for American aid, and thus to accept the idea of peace without victory. But two German actions once again tipped the balance in favor of the Allies.

THE ZIMMERMANN NOTE. THE UNITED STATES ENTERS THE WAR

On January 19, a secret message of German foreign secretary Arthur Zimmermann to his ambassador in Washington was intercepted and deciphered by the British. In it Zimmermann proposed that in case war would break out between Germany and the United States, Mexico should be induced to declare war on the United States. As a reward, Germany promised to see to it that, after the war, the lost territories of Texas, Arizona and New Mexico would be restored to Mexico. The British lost no time in informing Washington of this note, and the indignation against Germany rose to new heights in the United States. Yet the greatest factor in getting the United States into the Allied camp was the declaration of unrestricted submarine warfare on January 31, which led to the immediate severing of relations between the United States and Germany. A number of South American states, including Brazil, followed suit. However, Wilson waited until the Germans had committed an overt act of hostility by sinking American ships. This happened soon enough, and war was declared in April.

While some "preparedness measures" had been taken in the States in 1916, the country and its leaders had little experience in modern warfare and needed a whole year to marshal its full military strength. Except for the short Spanish-American War in 1898, there had been no occasion for Americans to fight since 1865. As late as January 1918, the chairman of the Senate Committee on Military Affairs stated that "the military establishment of America had broken down." But before that year was out, the country had shown its economic and military potential.

A War Industry Board was set up, headed by Bernard M. Baruch. It established priorities, allocated raw materials and regulated all production needed for the war effort. A U.S. Shipping Board was also formed to provide vessels needed for overseas deliveries, and since railroads provided practically the only land transportation at the time, a Railroad Administration was established to coordinate all traffic and expedite freight deliveries—a measure that was not even considered necessary during the much greater war effort of 1941–45. Furthermore, a Fuel Organization organized the conservation of coal, gas and petroleum, closed down nonessential industrial production for a short period and introduced fuel-less Mondays. A Food Administration, set up under Herbert Hoover with the slogan "Food will win the war," endeavored to increase production and curtail domestic consumption by introducing meatless and wheatless days. The labor shortage resulting from men being put into military service was met by encouraging women to work in munition plants and other war industries. Taxes were increased, but the "Liberty Loan" and the final "Victory Loan" drives provided even larger financial resources. The total cost of the American war effort amounted to approximately 25 billion dollars, and the public debt rose from one billion in 1914 to about 26 billion six years later.

Public support for all these measures was very strong from the beginning. All voluntary restrictions were accepted, and government loan drives and Red Cross campaigns were subscribed to. A Committee on Public Information did all it could to make all citizens pitch in. No less than 75,000 people, called the Four-Minute-Men, volunteered to speak publicly in support of the draft and in behalf of the Loan Drives, and millions of pamphlets and leaflets, printed in various languages, were distributed to inspire public morale.

Sometimes, these activities led to intolerance against perfectly loyal German-Americans, or against anyone criticizing any aspect of the war efforts. In some states, teaching of the German language was banned and orchestras were forbidden to play German music. There were even attempts to rename sauerkraut "liberty cabbage" and German measles "liberty measles"! An Espionage Act was passed in June 1917, later also a Sedition Act, hundreds of people were arrested on suspicion of spying or sabotage, and Eugene Debs, the Socialist leader, received a ten-year sentence for having spoken out against the war. People who disagreed with the majority opinion were in constant danger of denunciation and even conviction for subversive activities. Yet President Wilson's fears that the Constitution might not survive a general war hysteria proved to be unfounded, and in the long run, democratic freedom in the country survived the crisis.

A Selective Service Act was passed in May 1917 and within a few months nine million men had registered. Ultimately, the total number of men between 18 and 45 who registered amounted to over 24 million, of whom almost three million men and women were inducted into the service. At the end of the war, the United States had 4.8 million men and women under arms in the Army, Navy and National Guard. The American Expeditionary Force (AEF) which went overseas in ever increasing numbers—without suffering any substantial losses in the process—was eager to go into combat but hardly prepared for the dismal experience of actual warfare. Yet the overwhelming majority of the men acquitted themselves well at the front. Few of the men were interested in adventure and glory. Rather, they wanted the job done as quickly as possible, so that they could go home. Homesickness pervaded all ranks, but the high spirit of the AEF was never quite subdued and expressed itself in many First World War songs, some of which lived on and were revived in the Second World War.

PEACE FEELERS OF EMPEROR CHARLES AND THE POPE

Before the American presence on the European war front could make itself felt, two further attempts were made to prepare for a negotiated peace. Emperor Charles of Austria, successor to Francis Joseph, seems to have been determined, from the time of his accession, to make peace for his country, if necessary without Germany. He induced his brother-in-law, Prince Sixtus of Bourbon, to contact Allied leaders and to inform them that he would support French claims for Alsace-Lorraine and the restoration of Belgium and Serbia. French leaders Raymond Poincaré and Aristide Briand, as well as British prime minister David Lloyd George, warmly received these offers, but they asked for gains to Italy. Since the Austrians were unwilling to cede Trieste, the secret negotiations—though continued for several months—ended in failure. They became known to the public only after the war and caused great indignation as Germany felt betrayed by an ally it had helped out many times during the war.

The other peace proposal was launched by Pope Benedict XV in August 1917. He recommended disarmament, freedom of the seas, renunciation of indemnities, and a friendly examination of conflicting territorial claims over Alsace-Lorraine, the Balkans and Poland, as well as evacuation and restoration of occupied territory. Germany accepted in principle but evaded territorial commitment. The Allies took the attitude that the present German leaders could not be trusted, and definite commitments as to Belgium and Alsace-Lorraine would be the

Raymond Poincaré, president of France 1913–1920. Photo courtesy of the New York Public Library.

first condition. The pope's efforts to obtain such commitments were successful in regard to Belgium but not to Alsace-Lorraine. Again, the two sides could not get together. Pacifist sentiments ran high in many countries at this point, furthered by the international strong Socialist parties. At the great international Socialist Congress at Stockholm—which favored peace conditions similar to the pope's—Russian, German, Austrian and Scandinavian delegates gave enthusiastic support to the peace movement. But this was frustrated because the British, American and French delegates could not participate, as their government had refused them passports.

LLOYD GEORGE'S AND WILSON'S PEACE PROPOSALS

By the beginning of 1918, Russia was out of the war and the situation for the Allies was far from favorable. Yet the Allies were inclined to take a firmer stand since it had become clear by Germany's policy in Russia and Romania that Germany had not given up its expansionist policies. On January 8, when Lloyd George formulated the British war aims, he did not sound conciliatory. He proposed restoration of Belgium, Serbia, Montenegro and the occupied sections of France, Italy and Romania; self-government of the nationalities in the Austro-Hungarian Monarchy; the establishment of an independent Poland; the acceptance of Italian and Romanian territorial claims; and reconsideration of the "great wrong done to France in 1870–71"—in other words, the

Woodrow Wilson, president of the United States. 1913–21.

restoration of Alsace-Lorraine. Finally, he proposed the recognition of the separate national conditions in Arabia, Mesopotamia, Syria and Palestine, which amounted to the dissolution of the Turkish Empire. Since Germany, under Ludendorff's leadership, had just then planned the great offensive in France, there was no chance that the Central Powers would respond. But three days later, President Wilson, in an address to Congress, brought forth his own peace program in his famous Fourteen Points speech. It included freedom of navigation, open covenants, removal of all economic barriers, disarmament to the lowest possible level, impartial adjustment of all colonial claims with the proviso that the interests of the populations must be considered, evacuation of Russia and Belgium, evacuation of French territory, restoration of Alsace-Lorraine to France, autonomous development for the peoples of Austro-Hungary, evacuation of Romania and Serbia, autonomous development in Turkey, opening of the Dardanelles under international guaranties, an independent Poland, and finally an association of nations formed to guarantee political independence and territorial integrity for both great and small states.

There was no immediate reaction to Wilson's program, and American military efforts to support the Allied armies continued. It was only in October of the same year that the German government under Prince Max von Baden, in an appeal to Wilson, accepted the Fourteen Points. By this time, the huge German offensive in France had failed, and Germany was decisively beaten. Still, the idealism expressed in Wilson's program raised great—though false—hopes in Europe, particularly in Germany, and when Wilson arrived in Paris to join the peace talks, he was received in Europe with warm ovations and wild enthusiasm as the savior of the future. The one point in which he succeeded was the plan for a League of Nations. But the United States did not become a member due to the opposition Wilson encountered in his own country. In the final peace treaties with the Central Powers, very little was left of Wilson's idealistic vision of fair and peaceful international relations and of self-determination of the peoples.

CHRONICLE OF EVENTS

1916:

January–February: Edward M. House, President Wilson's adviser, visits the leading European statesmen and discusses possibilities for peace.

February 22: In the so-called House Memorandum, it is stated that President Wilson is ready to propose a peace conference.

November 7: Woodrow Wilson is reelected president, largely on a peace platform.

December 12: The German government advises the United States to inform the Allied governments of the willingness of the Central Powers to negotiate peace.

December 18: Wilson announces his own proposals, asking the warring powers to state their terms for peace.

December 26: The Central Powers reply and call for a meeting, without stating their terms.

December 30: The German move of December 12 is rejected by the French and British cabinets.

1917:

January 8: At Pless, the highest military and civilian German authorities conclude that the unrestricted use of the submarine will be the only way to win the war.

January 10: The Allies reply to Wilson's proposal of December 18, naming their specific terms.

January 19: In a note to the German ambassador in Mexico, German foreign minister Zimmermann suggests an alliance with Mexico and Japan against the United States, proposing that in case of victory Texas, Arizona and New Mexico should be restored to Mexico.

January 22: Wilson's "peace without victory" speech to the U.S. Senate.

January 29: Germany's terms for a peace conference are confidentially communicated to President Wilson.

January 31: Germany notifies the United States

Charles (Karl) of Habsburg, last emperor of Austria. Photo courtesy of the Austrian Press and Information Service, New York City.

that unrestricted warfare will begin on February 1.

February–June: Secret negotiations between Austrian emperor Charles and the British and French governments.

February 3: The United States government severs relations with the German government. The Latin American states and China do likewise during the following weeks.

March 24: Prince Sixtus of Bourbon transmits a letter of Emperor Charles of Austria in Paris in which the latter supports the "just French claims relative to Alsace-Lorraine."

April 6: The United States declares war on Germany.

April 19–21: At the St. Jean de Maurienne Conference, the Italians demand the return of the Trentino and Trieste to Italy. The Austrians refuse Trieste.

May 6–8: Second visit of Prince Sixtus to Vienna. After this, negotiations collapse.

May 10: International Socialist Congress meets at Stockholm, attended by German, Austrian, Russian and Scandinavian delegates. It is frustrated by the absence of American, British and French delegates, who had not been permitted to go by their governments.

August 1: Pope Benedict XV proposes outlines for a basis of peace, including disarmament, freedom of the seas, no indemnities and evacuation of occupied territories.

1918:

January 5: In an address to the Trades Unions Congress, Lloyd George announces the British war aims, which include the restoration of Belgium, Serbia, Montenegro and of the occupied parts of France, Italy and Romania.

January 8: In a speech before Congress, President Wilson formulates a peace program consisting of Fourteen Points, which include open covenants, freedom of navigation, removal of economic barriers, reduction of armaments, evacuation of Russia and Belgium, impartial adjustment of colonial claims, an independent Poland and an association of nations to maintain peace.

David Lloyd George, British prime minister. Photo courtesy of the New York Public Library.

EYEWITNESS TESTIMONY

A deputation of Belgians has arrived in this country to invoke our assistance in the time of their deadly need. What action our government can or will take I know not. It has been announced that no action can be taken that will interfere with our entire neutrality . . . Of course it would be folly to jump into the gulf ourselves for no good purpose; and in every probability nothing that we could have done would have helped Belgium.

Theodore Roosevelt in The Outlook, *September 23, 1914, in Allan Nevins,* American Press Opinion *(1969).*

The French were almost popular. The Kaiser had spoken of them as "brave foes." What quarrel could France and Germany have? France had been the dupe of England . . . If hate helps you to win, why not hate as hard as you can? Don't you go to war to win? There is no use talking of sporting rules and saying this and that is "not done" in humane circles—win!

Frederick Palmer, on public opinion in Germany, December 1914. In My Year in the Great War *(1915).*

At our mess we get the Berlin dailies promptly. Soon after the Germans are reading the war correspondence from their own front we are reading it, and laughing at jokes in their comic papers and cartoons which exhibit John Bull as a stricken old ogre and Britannia who Rules the Waves with corners of her mouth drawn down to the bottom of her chin, as she sees that havoc that von Tirpitz is making with submarines—which do not stop us from receiving our German jokes regularly across the channel.

Frederick Palmer, with British war correspondents in France, January 1915. In My Year in the Great War.

Mr. Asquith reminds me very much of the Lincoln of war times, . . . the patient, comprehending politician who bore on the force of his personality the strains, jealousies, hatred and the distrusts which threatened to wreck the machinery of his government. If the war turns out well for his country, Mr. Asquith's name will become immortal. If it turns out ill, there will be no more democratic government in Europe for several centuries.

Robert Rutherford McCormick, on events of February 15, 1915, With the Russian Army *(1915).*

Next to the Grand Duke Nicholas he [Churchill] is the most aggressive person I ever met, and I think that if he had had a military instead of an academic education, he would have made a great general or admiral.

R.R. McCormick, visiting England in February 1915, With the Russian Army.

There is such a thing as a man being too proud to fight.

Woodrow Wilson, in an address to foreign-born citizens, May 10, 1915.

On the whole, America and her representatives were judiciously and courteously handled. Accusation of violation of neutrality was universal, but rarely was there an answer when attention was called to the fact that it was Germany who objected to the proposal made at the Hague Conference that a neutral country should not be permitted to ship ammunition to any country at war. The common people were surprised and astonished when they were told of this, evidently not having heard of it previously.

Conrad Hoffmann, In the Prison Camps of Germany *(1915).*

Mr. Henry Ford's voyage to Europe on the *Oscar II* with a strangely assorted group of pacifists does more credit to his heart than his head, and the conflicting elements in his party have earned for his ship the name of "The Tug of Peace." Anyhow, England is taking no risks on the strength of these irregular "overtures." A vote has been passed for a further increase of our "contemptible little Army" to four millions—

Punch, London, December 1915, *referring to Ford's peace expedition, which failed dismally.*

The miraculous forbearance of President Wilson, in face of the activities of Count Bernstorff [the German ambassador at Washington], is even more trying to a good many of his countrymen than it is to the belligerent Briton. Mr. [Theodore] Roosevelt, for instance, derives no satisfaction from being the fellow-countryman of a man who can "knock spots" off Job for patience. The *New York Life* has long criticised the President with a freedom far eclipsing anything in the British Press. It has now crowned its "interventionist" campaign by a "John Bull number," the most generous and graceful tribute ever paid to England by the American Press.

Punch, *London, February 1916.*

It may be possible for us to inflict appreciable damage on the enemy, but there can be no doubt that even the most favorable issue of a battle on the high seas will not compel England to make peace in this war. The disadvantage of our geographical position, compared with that of the Island Empire, and her great material superiority, cannot be compensated for by our fleet.

Admiral Reinhard Scheer, report to the kaiser after the battle of Jutland, quoted in A.A. Hoehling, The Great War at Sea *(1965).*

Many thousands of Democrats among the professional and business men of the country withdrew their allegiance [to Wilson] because of the infirmities of his foreign policy. Many thousands of the Irish and German-Americans became his bitter and unscrupulous enemies because of his benevolent neutrality toward the Allies. One can only guess how much the default has amounted to, but taking all the people with grievances together it could hardly have been less than 500 000 votes.

The *New Republic, November 11, 1916, after Woodrow Wilson's reelection, in Allan Nevins,* American Press Opinion.

In the current issue of the "Metropolitan Magazine" Mr. Roosevelt breaks loose in a violent onslaught upon the idea and the advocates of a League to Enforce Peace . . . The truth is, of course, precisely the opposite of what Mr. Roosevelt now proclaims it to be. What takes the curse out of American naval and military preparedness is the official support of the peace league. It is because we have begun to prepare that the peace league should become part of American foreign policy.

The *New Republic, January 13, 1917, in Allan Nevins,* American Press Opinion.

Mr. Wilson has launched a new phrase in the world—"Peace without Victory"; but War is not going to be ended by phrases, and the man who is doing more than anyone else to end it—the British infantryman—has no use for them.

Punch, *London, January 1917.*

This war marked the collapse of the system of entangling alliances intriguing for the balance of power. Civilization, in its own interest, is now compelled to take a step forward. Is American democracy to hold aloof? Have we no obligation whatever to the rest of mankind which would impel us to throw our influence into the balance to prevent a repetition of this war? Because George Washington in 1796 wisely decided that a policy of isolation was then for the best interest of the United States, must we refuse to admit that there has been any change in the world since 1796 and that our interests and obligations are now precisely what they were then? . . . Before many months have elapsed the American people must decide whether the United States in relation to other nations is living in the year 1796 or the year 1917. Are they ready to cooperate with the other great countries in the common interest, or are they by the policy of isolation to invite the other great countries to cooperate against them?

New York World, *January 30, 1917, as quoted in Allan Nevins,* American Press Opinion.

I think you will agree with me that this government has no alternative consistent with the dignity and honor of the United States . . . I have therefore directed the Secretary of State to announce to his Excellency the German Ambassador that all diplomatic relations between the United States and the German Empire are severed and to hand to his Excellency his passports.

President Woodrow Wilson, addressing the joint session of Congress on February 3, 1917.

The decision of President Wilson has amazed and disappointed us. Since the Entente had rejected our peace offer no other step was left for us to defend our existence but the unlimited submarine warfare. The United States have refused to support us in our struggle against the violations of international law by the Entente. We have made no unconditional promises to forego unlimited U-Boat warfare, and have broken no promises.

Arthur Zimmermann, German foreign secretary, to American journalists in Berlin, February 5, 1917.

. . . if this attempt is not successful, we propose an alliance on the following basis with Mexico: that

President Wilson before Congress, February 3, 1917. Photo courtesy of the National Archives, Washington, D.C.

we shall make war together and together make peace. We shall give general financial support, and it is understood that Mexico is to reconquer the lost territory in New Mexico, Texas and Arizona . . .

Arthur Zimmermann, German foreign minister, in a cable to his legation in Mexico, February 1917.

For fifteen years a body of German reservists disguised as citizens have been marching and countermarching. They grew at length bold enough to rally to the support of a Pan-German scheme of conquest and a pro-German propaganda of "kultur," basing its effrontery on the German-American vote which began its agitation by threatening us with civil war if we dared to go to war with Germany. Then followed the assassin sea-monsters and the airship campaign of murder. All the while we looked on with either simpering idiocy or dazed apathy. It was no affair of ours. Belgium? Why should we worry? . . . Even the *Lusitania* did not awaken us to a sense of danger . . . First of all on bended knees we should pray God to forgive us. Then erect as men, Christian men, soldierly men, to the flag and the fray . . . through France to Flanders—across the Low Countries to Koeln, Bonn and Koblenz—tumbling the for-

tress of Ehrenbreitstein into the Rhine as we pass and damming the mouth of the Moselle with the ruin we make of it—then, on to Berlin . . . the cry being "Hail the French Republic—hail the Republic of Russia—welcome the Commonwealth of the Vaterland— no peace with the Kaiser—no parley with Autocracy, Absolutism, and the divine right of kings—to hell with the Hapsburg and the Hohenzollern!"

Louisville Courier-Journal, April 7, 1917, one day after war was declared, as quoted in Allan Nevins, American Press Opinion.

A recent resolution of the Reichstag has been welcomed by Mr. Ramsay MacDonald [the Labor leader] as a solemn pronouncement of a sovereign people, only requiring the endorsement of the British Government to produce an immediate and equitable peace. But not much was left of this pleasant theory after Mr. Asquith had dealt it a few sledge-hammer blows. "So far as we know," he said, "the influence of the Reichstag, not only upon the composition but upon the policy of the German Government, remains what it always has been—a practically negligible quantity.

Punch, London, August 1917.

What will be achieved in the East [Brest-Litovsk], nobody knows, nor how long Kuehlmann [foreign secretary] and Hertling [chancellor] even can hold their own against the men of the heavy industry and the Pan-Germans who still make contact with the Supreme Military Headquarters. For Ludendorff, as far as non-military matters are concerned, is utterly blind.

*Max Weber, German sociologist, on January
13, 1918, in Wolfgang Mommsen, Max Weber
und die deutsche Politik (1959).*

The Zeppelins and airplanes are continually bombarding undefended English and French cities and have killed women and children by the hundreds. The submarines have waged war with callous mercilessness. Their crews have continually practiced torture on the prisoners they have taken. They leave women and children to drown. They shoot into lifeboats. At this moment Americans are dying from poison gas which the Germans, in contemptuous defiance of the Hague rules, have made an ordinary weapon of war. I have just been talking with an American soldier absolutely trustworthy who himself saw the body of a Canadian whom the Germans had just crucified.

*Theodore Roosevelt in the Kansas City Star,
May 2, 1918, as per Allan Nevins, American
Press Opinion.*

Wilson's demands, paradoxically, are an obstacle to peace . . . Any liberation of German people will necessitate corresponding liberation of allied people. Complications in this "making world safe for democracy."

*H.V. O'Brien, May 13, 1918 in Wine,
Women and War (Diary), 1926.*

Movie star Douglas Fairbanks, speaking for Liberty Loans in New York, April 1918. Photo courtesy of the National Archives, Washington, D.C.

. . . many Americans are now undoubtedly finding compensation for the neutral indifference and pacific irresponsibility of their former attitude toward the war by a disposition to be more European than the Europeans, more warlike than the Gauls and about as intolerant of dissenting opinion as were the British Tories in 1800. This is particularly true of the Middle West . . .

*The New Republic, August 3, 1918, in Allan
Nevins, American Press Opinion.*

13. The Western Front: January 1916 to March 1918

THE HISTORICAL CONTEXT

The war of attrition continued on a larger, fiercer and more intensified scale. Industrial mobilization had become the key word, for it was now clear that this war was on the side of the big factories as well as the big battalions. As for the latter, Britain took the next step, unprecedented in its history: General conscription, committing itself to a mass army. General Douglas Haig (who was known for both stubbornness and ruthlessness) had succeeded the rather inadequate Sir John

U.S. troops embarking for France, 1917. Photo courtesy of the National Archives, Washington, D.C.

French and planned an offensive in Flanders; but Marshal Joseph Joffre insisted on attacking in the Somme area. There even had been a meeting of French, British, Russian, Italian and Japanese military delegates who agreed on simultaneous offensives in the east and west and on the Italian front. But the Germans beat the Allies to the punch.

THE BATTLE OF VERDUN

Erich von Falkenhayn, ever the advocate of concentrating all available German power in the west, was able to transfer almost half a million men to France to attack the great French salient around the fortress of Verdun. His main reliance was on heavy artillery, which had performed so well against the Belgian fortresses. Verdun had been a maze of concrete and steel forts, arranged in concentric circles around the town. But after 1914 it had become a quiet sector, and Joffre had in fact stripped the formidable forts and reduced their troop strength. Moreover, the Verdun area, being a salient into German-occupied territory, had vulnerable communication lines.

The German preparations were so massive that they could not be kept secret. Joffre had plans of his own and only increased the northeast sector on February 21, the day when the German bombardment began with 1,400 guns on an eight-mile front. Even so, the French were outnumbered at least three to one in this, the greatest bombardment of the war. Their first great strongpoint, Fort Douaumont—a major link in the chain of forts—was taken unoccupied four days later but only after French *mitrailleuses* (machine guns) had received heavy pounding from the attacking German elite troops.

On the eastern flank, the French now retired to the heights of the Meuse River, leaving the city of Verdun half surrounded by German forces. Then word came from the Briand government: Any commander who gives orders to retreat will be brought before court-martial! A few days later, when the first great assault had run its course, a new general—Philippe Pétain—took over at Verdun, bringing in reinforcements and a renewed will to resist. A series of counterattacks and new assaults followed that surpassed anything this war had previously seen. Falkenhayn had, it seems, not aimed for a breakthrough, but planned to bleed the French army dry in the belief that his losses would be lower than that of the French—a theory which was probably incorrect. Pétain made excellent use of the superior French light artillery and employed a better observation service by means of balloons and planes and of the automobile (a vehicle the use of which in combat was underestimated by the Germans, although it had played an important part in the battle of the Marne). Now Pétain organized huge columns of trucks that kept on supplying Verdun on the *Voie sacrée* (the "sacred road"), the only link open for the defenders. An army of over 400,000 men and 136,000 horses and mules was thus kept alive. At peak capacity, one truck came through every 14 seconds, day and night.

In early March, a new wave of German assaults began, this time from the west bank of the Meuse. Endless attacks and counterattacks took place until "Dead Man Hill" and "Hill 304" were at last taken by the Germans. The latter had been renamed "Hill 297" because, due to constant shelling, its height had been reduced from 304 to 297 meters! Fort Douaumont, on the east bank, had become the base for the German attacks but was kept under constant shelling until, on May 8, a terrific explosion occurred inside the fort, killing hundreds of Germans. Two weeks later, the French almost managed to retake the fort, but another fierce German assault brought the other strong fortification, Fort Vaux, into German hands. During this battle, hundreds of Germans had climbed on top of the fort, but for hours could not penetrate it. When the French finally surrendered, they claimed it was only because the water well inside the fort had given out.

The furthest advance the German assault units achieved was in June when, after prolonged fighting, forts Thiaumont and Fleury were taken and some troops got within two miles of the city. A new, vicious poison gas was introduced in these attacks that proved successful against the primitive French masks. But French stubbornness and bravery prevailed, and when the last great attacks against Fort Souville failed, German troops had to be withdrawn, particularly since the British had in the meantime started their great offensive along the Somme River. Falkenhayn and the German crown prince, who had been nominally in charge of the offensive, were forced to withdraw. In the middle of August, Falkenhayn was replaced as chief commander by the Hindenburg-Ludendorff team. Ludendorff, though now persuaded that the fighting had to be forced in the west—not at the Russian front—was less "prestige-conscious"—and more practical—than his predecessor. He had Fort Vaux evacuated. By September, German morale in this section had sunk very low, and whole units, including their officers, began to surrender. Before the end of the year, most of the terrain overrun by the Germans had been retaken, and this part of the front became relatively quiet until 1918, when American units attacked the St. Mihiel sector, south of Verdun.

The horror of this futile battle has been described often: the mountains of dead that could not be buried; the thousands of wounded left behind; the soldiers stuck in their shellholes full of water; the rats; the foul smell of the dead everywhere. Also the shelling of artillery into their own lines, the horrible effects of the gas attacks, soldiers going insane, the deep gap between front lines and communication zones, the vainglorious generals, the unsung heroes and the apathy at the end, sometimes mixed with open revolts and desertions on both sides.

The battle of Verdun, the most horrible mass slaughter—maybe with

Philippe Pétain, French hero of Verdun. Photo courtesy of the New York Public Library.

the exception of Stalingrad in World War II—has taken on legendary proportions, and some exaggerations have crept into the accounts of this battle. The number of casualties was not near a million but "only" some 760,000; 460,000 included the best French troops. The famous *tranche des baïonnettes* (trench of the bayonets) shown to thousands of visitors ever since the war, which displays a row of bayonets sticking out of the ground—supposedly of French soldiers buried in a German artillery barrage when about to attack—is a fake. It was debunked as early as 1930 but was still shown to visitors during the Second World War. On the other hand, the woods around Verdun do not include a single old tree but only growths since the war, clear testimony of the incredible devastation the region must have been subjected to.

THE BRITISH SOMME OFFENSIVE

It is possible that Verdun was saved by the British, who did not participate in its defense but started their great offensive of the Somme on July 1, 1916. Supported by French forces in the southern sector and after a long and intense bombardment, the British attacked with 12 divisions, with 7 more in reserve, along a front of 15 miles. At this point, Allied planes had the upper hand, since the German Fokker had been surpassed by the French Nieuport and the British De Havilland. However, the Somme sector had been heavily fortified by the Germans for two years. There were fortified villages, deep dugouts, interlocking barriers of iron stakes and barbed wire, deep cellars and underground shelters. Haig had warned that this part of the front was practically impregnable, but Joffre had prevailed. The result was wholesale slaughter: The Germans survived the artillery assault in their safe shelters, and when the British went "over the top" in waves, their lines were mowed down by machine guns. They lost 60,000 men on the first day of attack, the worst day ever for the British army. The French had fared somewhat better, but there was no break-through.

In the following weeks, Haig continued the attack regardless of losses, and since the Germans were greatly outnumbered, the Allies eventually drove salients and bulges into the German lines astride the Somme, mainly in the area of Peronne and Beaumont. But in weeks of bitter fighting, they gained no more than five to seven miles of ground. While at first the British announced the offensive as a great victory, it turned out to be a disaster in view of the frightful losses suffered for the gain of little terrain. The appearance of the British sur-prise weapon, the tank, in the middle of September, did not change the picture. Only 18, then 36, tanks were employed in the first as-saults, and the coordination between them and the infantry was poor. Torrential rains in October brought this battle to an end. Again, both sides had bled each other white. The British had lost over 400,000 men; the French, close to 200,000; the Germans, between 400,000 and 500,000.

The battle of the Somme ended Joffre's career; he was retired by Briand and promoted to marshal of France. He was replaced by Mar-shal Robert-Georges Nivelle, a young, promising officer who had gained prominence as chief assistant to Pétain at Verdun. Falkenhayn, the apostle of attrition tactics, was also recalled and sent to the Ro-

Robert-Georges Nivelle, who succeeded Joffre as French com-mander in chief. Photo courtesy of the New York Public Library.

manian front, where he, together with Mackensen, succeeded in subduing this new enemy in one quick campaign.

GERMAN RETREAT AND NIVELLE'S OFFENSIVE

In the beginning of 1917, the German armies in the west were greatly outnumbered by the Allied forces, about four million to 2.5 million. Ludendorff, wanting to concentrate his efforts on aid to Austria against Italy and on submarine warfare, therefore decided on a defensive move. Between February and April, he carried out a withdrawal from the so-called Noyon bulge, which at its most advanced point was still hardly less than 60 miles from Paris, to a much shorter, well-prepared and fortified line called the Hindenburg or Siegfried line. No less than 31 miles of French territory were given up, much more than the total number Allied attacks won from the Germans in 1915–16. But the shortened line could be defended with 13 fewer divisions, and the abandoned land had been turned into wasteland by the German "scorched earth" policy. Wreckages were booby-trapped, wells were poisoned and villages, railroads and roads were destroyed.

This move should have frustrated Nivelle, who had planned a gigantic blow against the very salient that no longer existed. Many of his objectives—Bapaume, Peronne, Noyon and Chauny—had been abandoned by the Germans anyway, but in spite of warnings from his own generals, war minister Paul Painlevé and others, Nivelle persisted, threatening to resign unless he could have his offensive. He even talked openly about the forthcoming battle at London dinner parties. So the Germans were well-prepared.

The French offensive was preceded by that of the British, whose Third Army, under General Sir Edmund Allenby, attacked the northwestern flank of the Hindenburg line at Arras on Easter Sunday, April 9. Supreme Commander Haig believed he could overcome previous failures by using more artillery this time. The preliminary bombardment lasted a week, and in the attack gas projectors were employed to support the infantry. The Canadians took Vimy Ridge, which dominated the area, and the British advanced two to five miles. But there was no breakthrough, and while they took 18,000 prisoners and caused 57,000 German casualties, Allied forces lost 84,000 men.

Before the battle was over, Nivelle launched his own offensive, attacking on April 16 on a 50-mile front from Soissons to Rheims with no less than 54 divisions. He began this so-called Second Battle of the Aisne with 11 million rounds of shell bombardment, but the Germans were well-supported by a terrain full of ravines which they had turned into strong fortifications. Nivelle's great "breakthrough" to end the war was stopped on the first day. Though he kept on attacking, his only success was the capture of the elevated plateau of Chemin des

Dames on May 21. When the battle died out a few days later, the French had lost 220,000 men; and, as a result of this senseless slaughter, large parts of his army mutinied in what amounted to the most widespread revolt of the war. There were many contributing factors: the endless battles, insufficient leaves for the troops, the wide gulf between officers and men, agitation on the home front, the doctrines of revolution seeping in from Russia, German propaganda, and antiwar strikes at home. Whole divisions refused to obey and battalions ordered to the front dispersed into the woods. Soldiers on leave sang the "Internationale" in the trains. Two Russian brigades fighting in France who had suffered heavily became so rebellious that artillery had to be turned against them.

BRITISH ATTACKS AT YPRES AND CAMBRAI

In this dismal situation, Nivelle was dismissed and the hero of Verdun, Pétain, was put in his place. He had a feel for the common soldier, the *"poilu,"* visited the divisions, listened to their complaints, and eliminated some of the hardships. He got things under control again but decided to stay on the defensive until the reinforcements expected from the United States would make themselves felt. At the same time, he proceeded with great rigor against pacifist agitators, and more than 50 ringleaders were executed. He also urged the British to take the initiative to give the French armies a chance to recuperate. Haig was ready to do just that, although the situation was becoming more difficult from week to week. Huge masses of German troops, no longer needed against Russia, were reinforcing the Hindenburg line. Haig had also planned an attack in Flanders for a long time—as an effort to take the Belgian ports serving as German submarine bases—and to roll up the German right flank. The French would have preferred an offensive further south, but after Nivelle's disaster, Haig enjoyed greater freedom to act. On June 7 he started with an attack at Messines, south of Ypres, by detonating some 500 tons of explosives placed under the German positions through long, deep tunnels. The surprise was complete, and the Second British Army, under General Herbert Charles Plumer, took the Messines Ridge the same day, inflicting higher casualties on the German defenders than he himself suffered. This straightened out the Ypres salient. Haig's main objective, the advance into the Flanders plain, was opposed by Lloyd George and some of Haig's subordinates, and by the time Haig launched his main push, at the end of July, the Germans had strengthened their lines and brought in reserves.

So the third battle of Ypres (or Passchendaele) became one of the bloodiest of the whole war. No less than eight heavy attacks were launched, carried through driving rain and fought on waterlogged and muddy terrain. The Germans used a new chemical called mustard gas, actually a colorless liquid causing burning sensations which could lead to blindness and even death. Canals and drainage ditches broke down from the constant shelling, turning the farmlands to fields of mud. When winter set in, Canadian troops took Passchendaele Ridge; the German frontlines were never broken through, however, and the Ypres salient had deepened but not widened and remained as inconvenient as ever. In all, the British and Canadian armies gained about five miles of territory and lost close to 400,000 men, almost twice as many as the Germans.

The French had made some rather weak attempts to support the British efforts. They attacked in the Verdun area in August and retook several key positions, including the east bank of the Meuse. Also, in October, they attacked at Malmaison on the Aisne, along the Chemin des Dames and, cut off a German salient near Soissons, forcing the German units to fall back to the Oise-Aisne Canal. These well-prepared though limited successes did much to restore the self-confidence in the French ranks. On the other hand, the devastating battles of Ypres caused a great amount of demoralization in the British army. It seems that the extent of French and British demoralization during this year was kept so secret that the German High Command never heard about it until it was too late to exploit.

In November 1917, when Georges Clemenceau ("The Tiger") became premier of France, French morale was sufficiently restored, and the British attempted another major attack, with new tactics. At Cambrai they started a surprise assault, without artillery preparation, with 380 tanks under cover of smoke for camouflage. The tank had come of age. Without great difficulties, the British broke through three German lines, but then the exhausted troops found themselves unable to take advantage of the situation. About 180 tanks were put out of action, but only 65 of those due to German fire; the others had broken down. The British had advanced five miles on a six-mile front, but a few days later a heavy German surprise counterattack forced them to give up much of the conquered ground. While the lack of tank and infantry reserves deprived the British of a great opportunity, the tank had proved its worth. British troops had gained as much ground in one day as they had won at Ypres in three months, and it was clear that in the next great offensive in the west the tank would become even more decisive.

None of the massive attempts to break through the enemy lines in France and Belgium had succeeded in 1916 and 1917: Neither the German attack on Verdun nor the Allied offensives at the Somme, Arras, the Aisne, Ypres, Malmaison and Cambrai had reached their objectives. Only on one major European front was a breakthrough achieved, within one day in fact: in the Austro-Italian battle zone.

THE ISONZO FRONT

On the Isonzo front, the year 1917 ended in a catastrophe for the Allies. During the first part of the year, the Italian army under General Luigi Cadorna had kept up its attack on the Isonzo front, but after the 11th battle of the Isonzo—which lasted from August through September—it had gained a total of 10 miles after two years of fighting and had advanced only halfway to Trieste. It suffered from insufficient supplies of ammunition and inadequate artillery, but all of Cadorna's appeals for help from France and England—though supported by Lloyd George and Foch—had been rejected by Haig, who was preparing his great Flanders offensive. This gave Ludendorff a chance. He planned a decisive blow against Italy similar to the ones he had dealt to Romania and Serbia. Six German divisions were sent to the Isonzo region to reinforce the nine Austrian divisions. Although their presence was detected by the Italians, orders to prepare defensive positions were not properly followed, and on October 24 the Austrian-German forces, under cover of fog, attacked in full force. Although the Italians had numerical superiority, the troops were broken at once. The Germans under General Otto von Below used infiltration, heavy, short bombardments, the by-passing of resistance centers and advanced rapidly through the Italian lines; the hard-won gains in 11 battles were lost in only one day.

CAPORETTO

The battle of Caporetto turned into complete disaster. The demoralized Italians surrendered by the thousands and were almost prevented from crossing the Tagliamento in retreat. Finally, they fell back to the Piave River, 70 miles below the Isonzo front. French and British troops were brought in quickly to help establish a new frontline, and the Austro-German forces, who had outrun their supply system, were forced to slow down. The Italian army had lost 300,000 troops, including 265,000 prisoners, and Cadorna was replaced by General Armando Diaz. But the Piave front held, Diaz managed to restore the morale of the troops, and all further efforts to eliminate the Italian army failed. In October 1918, a combined Allied counterattack routed the Austrians, who by that time were near collapse.

CHRONICLE OF EVENTS

1915:

December 19: Sir Douglas Haig succeeds Sir John French as commander in chief of the British forces in the west.

1916:

February 21: Beginning of the Battle of Verdun. The Germans under Crown Prince William attack on the right bank of the Meuse after a terrific bombardment.

February 25: Fort Douaumont is taken by the Germans.

End of February: French reinforcements arrive.

March 6: Beginning of new attacks, on both sides of the salient formed by the French lines.

April 10: Temporary halt of the attacks.

May: General Robert-Georges Nivelle replaces General Henri-Philippe Pétain as French commander of the Verdun sector. French counter-attacks.

June 2: Germans take Fort Vaux.

June 23: Germans take Thiaumont.

July 1: Beginning of the Battle of the Somme. British advance toward Bapaume, the French toward Peronne.

July 11: End of the heavy German attacks at Verdun.

July–August: Slow and extremely costly advance of the Allied forces in the Somme battle.

August 29: Hindenburg succeeds Falkenhayn in the west.

September 15: For the first time, British use tanks in the battle.

October 24–middle of December: French counter-attacks at Verdun.

November 2: Forts Vaux and Douaumont retaken by the French.

Hindenburg, William II, and Ludendorff in General Headquarters, January 1917. Photo courtesy of the National Archives, Washington, D.C.

November 18: End of the Battle of the Somme. Maximum Allied advance seven miles.

December 12: General Robert-Georges Nivelle replaces General Joseph Joffre as commander in chief of the French armies.

1917:

February 23: Ludendorff orders a preliminary withdrawal of the German lines to make them more defensible, between Arras and Soissons.

March 4–April 5: Withdrawal of the German forces to the so-called Hindenburg line, abandoning Bapaume, Peronne, Roye, Noyon and Chauny.

April 9–May 4: Battle of Arras. General Sir Edmund Allenby's Third British Army advances after heavy bombardments and gas attacks. Canadian troops take Vimy Ridge.

April 16: Second Battle of the Aisne begins, as well as the Third Battle of Champagne. The great French offensive meets with little success.

May 15: Nivelle is dismissed and replaced by General Henri-Philippe Pétain.

May 21: French units take the Chemin des Dames, after heavy losses.

May–June 8: Tenth, inconclusive battle of the Isonzo, on the Italian front.

May–June: Widespread mutinies in the French army, affecting 17 corps.

June 7: British General Herbert Charles Plumer launches a surprise attack on Messines Ridge and succeeds in straightening out the Ypres salient.

July 31: Beginning of the Third Battle of Ypres, consisting of eight heavy attacks, resulting in little gain and very heavy British losses. Fighting in this area stops only in November.

August 17–September 12: On the Italian front, the 11th and last battle of the Isonzo is inconclusive.

August 20: Beginning of the Second Battle of Verdun, intended to relieve the British at the Ypres front. French take some key positions on the east bank of the Meuse. Fighting continues in this area until middle of December.

October 23–November 1: Battle of Malmaison. French attack at Chemin des Dames and force the Germans back to the Oise-Aisne Canal.

October 24–December 26: On the Isonzo front, the Caporetto campaign. German-Austrian forces, under General Otto von Below, break through the Italian lines. Italians fall back to the Piave.

November 3–4: French and British troops are rushed to hold the collapsed front.

November 7: General Luigi Cadorna is replaced by General Armando Diaz.

November 20–December 3: Battle of Cambrai. British launch a surprise attack with 380 tanks and penetrate the German lines, but cannot follow through.

November 30: A German counterattack forces the British to abandon much of the conquered territory.

EYEWITNESS TESTIMONY

They are fighting on the sands. When we march, our feet sink into the soft dunes. When we lie down, the wind blows the sand over us. It is white sand where it has not been stained with blood . . . It flutters, whirls, gets in our eyes and ears and the mechanism of our rifles, grits in our teeth . . . The sea is on our left . . . and above, the tumult of the cannon, the roaring of the waves, and the crying of the wind, there rises another sound: The sharpshooters of the Morocco are charging. Their bayonets gleam as they dash forward towards the Great Dune. Faces are aflame with the love of battle. There are tawny Semitic heads with huge noses, and mongrel negro features with flat noses . . . The rusty scabbards of their bayonets clank against their velvet-trimmed trousers as they hurl themselves savagely towards the foe.

André Fribourg, fighting in Flanders, January 29, 1916, The Flaming Crucible *(1918).*

I've had about two hours sleep in the last forty, during which I have driven close to 300 kilometers, been three times under fire, and had but two hot meals . . .

Robert Whitney Imbrie, near Compiègne, France, February 1916, Behind the Wheel of a War Ambulance *(1918).*

Perhaps I was not frightened by those first shells; curiosity may have here supplanted other sensations, but as time went on and I saw the awful, destructive power of shell fire, when I had seen buildings leveled and men torn to bloody shreds, the realization of their terribleness became mine, and with it came a terror of that horrible soul melting shriek. And now after a year and a half of war, . . . I am no more reconciled to shellfire than at first. If anything, the sensation is worse, and personally I do not believe there is such a thing as getting "used" to it.

Robert Whitney Imbrie, at the Aisne River, France, early 1916, Behind the Wheel of a War Ambulance.

Nearly every house had its cellar, and these cellars were deepened, roofed with timbers and piled high with sand-bags. A cave so constructed was reasonably bomb-proof from small shells . . . The resident population of the town was limited to a group of *brancardiers* [litter-bearers], some grave-diggers, the crews of several goulash batteries and some doctors and surgeons. I must not forget to mention the sole remaining representative of the civil population. He was an old, old man, so old it seemed the very shells respected his age . . . at any hour of the day or night he could be seen making his uncertain way among what were the ruins of what had been once a prosperous town—his town. With him, also tottering, was also a wizened old dog . . . And daily, as their town crumbled, they crumbled, until at last one morning we found the old chap dead, his dog by his side.

Robert Whitney Imbrie at Cappy, France, March 1916, Behind the Wheel of a War Ambulance.

. . . At kilometer eight my engine began to miss . . . The opiate given the blessé had begun to wear off, and his groans sounded above the whistling of the wind . . . With the aid of light, I was able to make some repairs, though my hands were so benumbed I could scarcely hold the tools. The car now marched better and I started ahead. Several times a "qui vive" came out of the darkness, to which I ejaculated a startled "France" . . . But the "load" had come through safely.

Robert Whitney Imbrie, near the Somme, early March 1916, Behind the Wheel of a War Ambulance.

I was . . . instructed not to go down this road too far as I would drive into enemy lines. How was I to determine what was "too far" until it was "too late"? . . . I was going on my third hill . . . I beheld a soldier wildly semaphoring . . . Reaching the bottom, I drew up by the soldier who informed me that the crest of the hill was in full view of the enemy and under fire from the machine guns. I felt the information was timely.

Robert Whitney Imbrie, at the Somme, March 1916, Behind the Wheel of a War Ambulance.

Five soldiers rose and bade me welcome. They were a group of grave-diggers, and here they dwelt amid their (wooden) crosses. Their profession did not seem to have affected their spirits, and they were as jolly a lot as I have ever seen, constantly chaffing each other, and when the chap at the piano—who,

by-the-way, before the war had been a musician at the Carlton in London and who spoke excellent English struck a chord, they all automatically broke into song . . . The piano they had rescued from a wrecked chateau at the other end of town . . .
Robert Whitney Imbrie, at Cappy, France, March 1916, Behind the Wheel of a War Ambulance.

The officers were a genial lot, like most Frenchmen delightfully courteous . . . Their chief occupation was the making of paper knives from copper shrapnel bands, and they never lacked for material . . . One of these chaps, through constant opportunity and long practice could give a startling imitation of the shriek of a shell, an accomplishment which got him into trouble, for happening one day to perform this specialty while a non-appreciative and startled Colonel was passing, he was presented with eight days' arrest.
Robert Whitney Imbrie, at Cappy, France, March 1916, Behind the Wheel of a War Ambulance.

As I drove my mud-sputtered ambulance down [Amiens's] main street, I felt singularly out of place. An hour and a half before I had been within rifle range of the German trenches where men were battling to the death and big guns barked their hate, and now, as though transported by a magic carpet, I found myself in the midst of a peace where dainty women tripped by, children laughed at play and life, untrammeled by war, ran its course . . . the transition was at first stupefying.
Robert Whitney Imbrie, at Amiens, end of March 1916, Behind the Wheel of a War Ambulance.

The messroom presented a ghastly sight this morning, a hand grenade having been accidentally exploded, blowing two men to bits which bits are still hanging to the walls.
Robert Whitney Imbrie, at Cappy, France, April 8, 1916, Behind the Wheel of a War Ambulance.

It is a simple statement—"our division moved." But think of 20,000 men plodding along, 20,000 brown guns bobbing and 20,000 bayonets flopping against as many hips. Think of 20,000 blue steel helmets covering as many sweaty, dusty heads . . . the horses straining in their traces, the creaking wagons, the rumbling of artillery, the clanging soup wagons, the whizzing staff cars . . .
Robert Whitney Imbrie, at Mericourt, France, May 1916, Behind the Wheel of a War Ambulance.

The Senegalese were an amusing lot. I have been in Senegal . . . so I know a few words of their language. When I hailed them in this they would immediately freeze into ebony statues, then their white teeth would flash in a dazzling smile as they hailed me as a white chief who knew their home. They were armed with deadly bush knives, and for a dash over the top made splendid soldiers. In the trenches, however, they were nearly useless, as artillery fire would put fears into their souls. It was said they never took or were taken prisoners, and many gruesome tales were current regarding this. Most certainly they must have been useful in night manoeuvres . . .
Robert Whitney Imbrie, near Cappy, France, June 1916, Behind the Wheel of a War Ambulance.

The Epic of the Dardanelles is closed; that of Verdun has begun, and all eyes are focused on the tremendous struggle for the famous fortress. The Crown Prince has still his laurels to win, and it is clear that no sacrifice of German "cannon fodder" will be too great to deter him from pushing the stroke home. . . . The War-lords of Germany are sorely in need of a spectacular success even though they purchase it at a great price . . .
Punch, *London, February 1916.*

. . . Yet in spite of the terrible execution of the French shrapnel, the Germans remained motionless. There was not a shout, not the slightest movement of disorder; everybody bore witness to the calm resignation over the enemy's line. The battery ceased fire, and a silence even more disturbing fell . . . What was going to happen? These men whom we saw clearly, steadily under a hail of fire and steel the guns were raining on them, what had they in store for us? Two, three minutes passed . . . not a move. The French guns opened again, dropped still more shells, and silence persisted . . . When at last day appeared, we were able to perceive that our guns had been bombarding an enormous heap of German corpses.

E. Diatz-Retg, French officer in "The Assault against Verdun," about the fighting in 1916, in Guy Chapman (ed.), Vain Glory (1937).

Verdun still holds out: that is the best news of the month. The French with inexorable logic continue to exact the highest price for the smallest gain of ground. If the Germans are ready to give 100,000 men for a hill or part of a hill they may have it. If they will give a million men they may perhaps have Verdun itself. But so far their Pyrrhic victories have stopped short of this limit, and Verdun . . . remains a symbol of Allied tenacity and the will to resist.
Punch, London, May 1916.

So we came to June 4th, a day still more terrible. About 8.30 a.m., the Boches carried out two attacks in combination; one against the barricade of the observation post, the other on the barricade of the left arches. Through the loopholes, they poured flame and gas, which gave off an intolerable smell and gripped our throats. Shouts of "gas masks" came from both ends of the fort. In the left arches, the garrison, driven back by flame and smoke, fell back towards the central gallery. Here was posted brave Lieut. Girard. He dashed forward into the smoke to the machine guns which his men had been forced to abandon. He had the luck to get there before the Boches, and at once opened fire . . . Inspired by his example, his men came back, stood to their gun and fired for an hour without stopping . . .
French Commandant Raynal, journal, recalling the fighting at Fort Vaux near Verdun, June 4, 1916, in Guy Chapman (ed.), Vain Glory.

I took a turn in the corridors. What I saw was frightening. Men were overcome with vomiting due to the urine in the stomach, for so wretched were they that they had reached the point of drinking their own urine. Some lost consciousness. In the main gallery, a man was licking a little wet streak on the wall . . . 7th June! Day broke, and we scarcely noticed it . . . I sent off my last message, the last salute for the fort and its defenders to their country. Then I turned to my men: "It is all over, my friends. You have done your duty, the whole of your duty. Thank you." They understood, and together in one shout we repeated the last message which my instrument had sent off: "Vive la France!" In the minutes which followed a silence as of death fell upon the fort.

French Commandant Raynal, journal, recalling the fall of Fort Vaux, June 7, 1916, in Guy Chapman (ed.), Vain Glory.

Since St. Mihiel was in [the Germans'] hands, the first [rail]road was eliminated, and though the second was not in enemy's hands, it was commanded by their batteries. This left the position at Verdun without supporting railroads, heretofore considered necessary for maintaining an army. But the Hun had reckoned without two things, the wonderful organisation of the French motor transport, and the *Voie sacrée*. Never had a road been called upon to bear the burdens which were thrown upon this way. An armada of 10,000 motor *camions* [trucks] was launched, and day and night in two unbroken lines this fleet held its course and served the defending armies at Verdun.
Robert Whitney Imbrie, at Verdun, end of June 1916, Behind the Wheel of a War Ambulance.

I descended from my car in an endeavour to find a way through (the shell holes), and the enemy chose this opportune time to shell the hill. It was then I performed a feat which for years I had essayed . . . without success—the feat of falling on the face without extending the arms to break the fall. Whether it was the concussion of the shell which blew me over or whether I really accomplished the stunt unaided, I am unable to say . . . I found myself flat on the ground, my head swimming from the explosion and a cloud of dust above me. My first impression—that this was a particularly unhealthy spot—here found confirmation. I managed to get my car turned and made my way back to where I had noticed a crumbling wall. A head appeared from beneath the stones and a *brancardier* [litter bearer] crawled out of a subterranean passage. It was Fort Fillat.
Robert Whitney Imbrie, at Verdun, July 1916, Behind the Wheel of a War Ambulance.

. . . we worked without thought of schedule, with little sleep and without regard to time. Now and then we ate, more from habit than because we were hungry, but when we were not rolling we did not rest; we could not, the agitation of unrest so permeated the very air.
Robert Whitney Imbrie, at Verdun, July 1916, Behind the Wheel of a War Ambulance.

"The Real Strategists"—hunger, winter and time—cartoon, circa 1915. Courtesy of the New York Public Library.

. . . And then, suddenly, the silence fell, silence save for the whirring screech of a shell. It seemed hours in coming. Something told us it would strike very close, perhaps within. . . . we had dropped on our faces. Then it bust—just beyond the wall. Eclat [fragments] tore gaps in the door draping and whirred spitefully across the room, raining against the wall. "Le luminaire, le luminaire" shouted a voice, and the light was dashed out. There we lay, a mixed mass of arms and legs, lay and waited for another shell. But no more came . . .

Robert Whitney Imbrie, July 1916, Behind the Wheel of a War Ambulance.

It was a strange experience, my wandering in this deserted, stricken city. It gave one something of the sensation Pompeii does. Though the sun shone brightly enough, the chill of ruin and desolation prevailed . . . in scores, hundreds of places there remained but a pile of stones and a yawning hole where once had stood a house.

Robert Whitney Imbrie, at Verdun, July 1916. Behind the Wheel of a War Ambulance.

In the pitchy streets of Verdun, with the debris piled high on either side it was impossible to see a bayonet thrust ahead. Eyes were of no avail; one steered by *feel.* Several times cars met head on. Again, on several occasions, it occurred that a driver, overcome by weariness, fell asleep at wheel to be awakened by his car's crashing into a wall or ditch . . .

There were the usual miraculous escapes. Giles was blown off his feet by the concussion of a shell.
Robert Whitney Imbrie, at Verdun, September 1916, Behind the Wheel of a War Ambulance.

Over in his office in the municipal building where we went after dinner the general [Nivelle] took something wrapped in tissue paper out of a drawer and from his manner, had he been a collector, I should have known that it was some rare treasure. When he undid the paper I saw a photograph of General Joffre autographed with a sentiment for the occasion. "He gave it to me for Douaumont!" said General Nivelle, a touch of pride in his voice—the only sign of pride that I noticed.
Frederick Palmer, near Verdun, fall 1916, My Second Year of the War *(1917).*

Verdun was German valor at its best, and German gunnery at its mightiest . . . and the high-water mark of German persistence was where you stood on the edge of the area of mounds that shells had heaped and craters that shells had scooped by the concentration of fire on Fort Souville. A few Germans in charge reached here, but none returned. The survivors entered Verdun, the French will tell you with a shrug, as prisoners . . . On that hill [of Douaumont] German prestige and system reached their zenith; and the answer, eight months later was French élan which, in two hours . . . swept the Germans off the summit.
Frederick Palmer, Verdun, fall 1916, My Second Year of the War.

. . . Then we started off in the heat of the day on what was without exception the hardest march I have ever made. There were 20 kilometers to do through the blazing sun and in a cloud of dust. Something around 30 kilos on the back. About 50 percent dropped by the way. By making a supreme effort I managed to get in at the finish with the fifteen men that were all that was left of the section . . . The battlefield has no terrors after trials like these that demand just as much grit and often more suffering.
Alan Seeger, letter to a friend from the Somme, June 24, 1916.

We go up to the attack tomorrow. This will probably be the biggest thing yet. We are to have the honor of marching in the first wave . . . I am glad to be going in the first wave. If you are in this thing at all it is best to be in to the limit. And this is the supreme experience.

Alan Seeger, letter to a friend (his last letter), from the Somme, June 28, 1916.

. . . he had not mentioned that there was to be any offensive and I had not. We had kept the faith of military secrecy. Besides, I really did not know, unless I opened a pigeonhole in my brain. It also was my business not to know—the only business I had with the "big push" except to look on . . . To keep such immense preparations wholly a secret among any English-speaking people would be out of the question. Only the Japanese are mentally equipped for security of information.

Frederick Palmer, before the Somme offensive, 1916, My Second Year of the War.

At seven-thirty something seemed to crack in our brains. There was no visible sign that a wave of men twenty-five miles long, reaching from Gommecourt to Soyecourt, wherever the trenches ran across the fields through villages and along slopes to the banks of the Somme and beyond, had left their parapets.

Frederick Palmer, on the beginning of the great Somme offensive, July 1, 1916, My Second Year of the War.

It seemed that all the guns in the world must be firing as you listened from a distance, although when you came into the area where the guns were in tiers behind the cover of a favorable slope you found that many were silent. The men of one battery might be asleep while its neighbor was sending shells with a one-two-three deliberation. Any sleep or rest that the men got must be there in the midst of this crashing babel from steel throats.

Frederick Palmer, the beginning of the Somme offensive, 1916, My Second Year of the War.

There is no race, it seems to me, who know quite so well how to enjoy victory as the French. They make it glow with a rare quality which absorbs you into their own exhilaration. I had the feeling that the pulse of every citizen in France had quickened a few beats. All the peasant women as they walked along the road stood a little straighter, and the old men and old women were renewing their youth in quiet triumph.

Frederick Palmer, on the initial successes at the Somme, July 1916, My Second Year of the War.

The results of the battle of the Somme are shown in a variety of ways: by the reticence and admissions of the German press, by its efforts to divert attention to the exploits of the commercial submarine cruiser *Deutschland*; above all, by the Kaiser's fresh explosions of piety. "The Devil was sick, the Devil a monk would be."

Punch, London, *July 1916.*

In general, calmness and indifference . . . But they shoot "regardless" . . . Their faults: They look on war as a sport. Too much calmness which leads to a "go-to-hell" attitude . . . No consistency in their work. They attack in and out of season, break down when they ought to go through; and with a certain spiritual strength, say: "Oh, well, failed to-day; it'll be all right tomorrow." Nevertheless, there are still so many shells wasted and so many men lost. To sum it up, they still lack savoir-faire.

Louis Mairet, French officer, on the British fighting at the Somme, 1916, in Le carnet d'un soldat.

That evening, the [Royal Army Medical Corps] orderlies dared not lift me from the stretcher into a hospital train bunk, for fear of starting a haemorrhage in the lung. So they laid the stretcher above it, with the handles resting on the head-rail and foot-rail. I had now been on the same stretcher for five days. I remember the journey as a nightmare. My back was sagging, and I could not raise my knees to relieve the cramp, the bunk above me being only a few inches away. A German flying-officer, on the other side of the carriage, with a compound fracture of the leg from an aeroplane crash, groaned and wept without pause . . . Though the other wounded men cursed him, telling him to stow it and to be a man, he continued pitiably, keeping everyone awake. He was not delirious—just frightened and in great pain.

Robert Graves, at the Somme, July 1916, Good-bye to All That *(1929).*

When [the Anzacs] went to Gallipoli it was said that they had no discipline; and certainly at first discipline did irritate them as a snaffle bit irritates a high spirited horse. "Little Kitch" [after Lord Kitchener], as the stalwart Anzacs called the New Army

Englishman, thought they broke all the military commandments of the drill grounds in a way that would be their undoing . . . But after the Australians had fought the Turk a while it was evident that they knew how to fight, and that their general, Sir Charles Birdwood, supplied the discipline which is necessary if fighting power is not to be wasted in misplaced emotion.

Frederick Palmer, on the Anzacs at the Somme, July 1916, My Second Year of the War.

Being now off duty, I fell asleep in the trench without waiting for the bombardment to stop. It would be no worse getting killed asleep than awake. There were no dug-outs, of course. I found it easy now to sleep through bombardments; though vaguely conscious of the noise, I let it go by. Yet if anybody came to wake me for my watch, or shouted "Stand-to!", I was always alert in a second. I could fall asleep sitting down, standing, marching, lying on a stone floor, or in any other position, at a moment's notice at any time of day or night.

Robert Graves, at the Somme, July 1916, Good-bye to All That.

Gunners rubbed their eyes at the vision as they saw the horsemen pass and infantry stood amazed to see them crossing trenches, Briton and Indian on their way up to the Ridge. How they passed the crest without being decimated by a curtain of fire would be a mystery if there were any mysteries in this war, where everything seems to be worked out like geometry or chemical formulae . . . There had been some Germans in hiding in the grass who were taken unawares by this rush of gallopers with lances. Every participant agreed to the complete astonishment of the enemy.

Frederick Palmer, on a rare cavalry charge at the Somme, July 1916, My Second Year of the War.

. . . we decided to move back fifty yards at a rush. As we did so, an eight-inch shell burst three paces behind me. I heard the explosion and I felt as though I had been punched rather hard between the shoulder blades, but without any pain. I took the punch merely for the shock of the explosion; then blood trickled into my eye, and, turning faint, I called to M.: "I've been hit." Then I fell.

Robert Graves, on fighting at the Somme, July 1916, Good-bye to All That.

How the British ever took Mametz Wood I do not understand; or how they took Trônes Wood later, for that matter. A visit to the woods only heightened perplexity . . . they went in by the west where the machine guns were not waiting and the heavy guns were not registered, as I understand it. A piece of strategy of that kind might have won a decisive battle in an old-time war, but I confess it did not occur to me to ask who planned it . . . Strategists became so common on the Somme . . .

Frederick Palmer, at the Somme, near Mametz, July 1916, My Second Year of the War.

Scattered among the Colonial Corps, whether on the march or in the billets, were the black men. There is no prejudice against the "chocolates," as they are called . . . No Frenchman could approach the pride of the blacks over those captured guns, which brought grins that left only half of their ebony countenances as a background for the whites of their eyes and teeth.

Frederick Palmer, at the Somme, July 1916, My Second Year of the War.

Joffre, Catelnau and Foch were the three great names in the French army which the public knew after the Marne, and of the three Foch has, perhaps, more of the dash which the world associated with the French military type. He simplified victory . . . "It went well! It goes well!" he said with dramatic brevity . . . There was no mistaking his happiness. It was not that of a general, but the common happiness of all France.

Frederick Palmer, at the Somme, July 1916, My Second Year of the War.

And the litter over the whole field! . . . Shell-fragments were mixed with the earth; piles of cartridge cases lay beside pools of blood. Trench mortars poked their half-filled muzzles out of the toppled trench walls. Bundles of rocket flares, empty ammunition boxes, steel helmets crushed in by shell-fragments, gas bags, eye-protectors against lachrymatory shells, spades, water bottles, unused rifle grenades, egg bombs, long stick-handled German bombs, map cases, bits of German "K.K." bread, rifles . . . were scattered about the field . . .

Frederick Palmer, on the battlefields of the Somme, July 1916, My Second Year of the War.

In order to make them fight better they had been told that the British gave no quarter . . . They were wholly lacking in military dignity as they filed by; but it returned as by magic touch when a non-commissioned officer was bidden to take charge of a batch and march them to an inclosure. Then, in answer to the command, shoulders squared, heels rapped together, and the instinct of long training put a ramrod to their backbones . . .

Frederick Palmer, on German prisoners at the Somme, July 1916; My Second Year of the War.

In the first rush a lot of Tyneside Scots were marooned from joining in the retreat. They fortified themselves in German dugouts and waited in siege . . . When the British returned eighty of the Scots were still full of fight if short of food and "verra well" otherwise, thank you. At times they had been under blasts from both sides, and again they had been in an oasis of peace, with neither British nor German gunners certain whether they would kill friend or foe.

Frederick Palmer, at the Somme, in the Mametz Woods, July 1916, My Second Year of the War.

Where the young officer had said that it had not gone well this time and a private had said, "We must try again, sir!" the general had said that repulse was an incident of a prolonged operation in the initial stage, which sounded more professional but was no more illuminating. All spoke of lessons for the future. Thus they had stood the supreme test which repulse alone can give.

Frederick Palmer, the Battle of the Somme, July 1916, My Second Year of the War.

Covered with chalk dust from crawling, their bandages blood-soaked, bespattered with the blood of comrades as they lay on litters or hobbled down a communication trench, they looked blank when they mentioned the scenes they had witnessed; but they gave no impression of despair. It did not occur to them that they had been beaten; they had been roughly handled in one round of a many-round fight.

Frederick Palmer, the Battle of the Somme, July 1916, My Second Year of the War.

Why all the trees were not cut down by the continual bombardments of both sides was past under-standing. There was one lone tree on the skyline near Longueval which I had watched for weeks. It still had a limb, yes, the luxury of a limb . . . pointing with a kind of defiance in its immunity. Of course it had been struck many times. Bits of steel were imbedded in its trunk; but only a direct hit on the trunk will bring down a tree.

Frederick Palmer, at the battle of the Somme, August 1916, My Second Year of the War.

I saw a (German) officer marching at the head of the survivors of his battalion along the road from Montauban one day with his head up, a cigar stuck in the corner of his mouth at an aggressive angle, his unshaven chin and dusty clothes heightening his attitude of "You go to —, you English!" The hatred of the British was a strengthening factor in the defense. Should they, the Prussians, be beaten by New Army men? No! Die first! said the Prussian officers.

Frederick Palmer, at the Somme, August 1916, My Second Year of the War.

A fall of rain came as a blessing to Briton and German alike. German prisoners worn with exhaustion had complexions the tint of their uniform. If the British seemed weary sometimes, one only had to see the prisoners to realize that the defensive was suffering more than the offensive. The fatigue of some of the men was of the kind that one week's sleep or a month's rest will not cure; something fixed in their beings.

Frederick Palmer, at the Somme, August 1916, My Second Year of the War.

"A live prisoner would be of more use to his fatherland one day than a dead one, even though he has no more chance to fight again than a rabbit held up by his ears," as one of the German prisoners said. "More use to yourself, too," remarked his captor.

Frederick Palmer, at the Somme, fall 1916, My Second Year of the War.

Von Falkenhayn was gone from power; the Crown Prince who thirsted for war had had his fill and said that war was an "idiocy." It was the sentiment of the German trenches which put von Falkenhayn out; the silent ballots of all public opinion . . . which no officer can control by mere orders.

Frederick Palmer, at the end of August 1916, My Second Year of the War.

No country wanted war less than Canada, but when war came its flame made Canada molten with Canadian patriotism. As George III brought the Carolinas and Massachusetts together, so the Kaiser brought the Canadian provinces together.

Frederick Palmer, at Ypres, fall of 1916, My Second Year of the War.

When a Canadian officer was asked if he had organized some trenches that his battalion had taken his reply, "How can you organize pea soup?" filled a long-felt want in expression to characterize the nature of trench-making in that terrain.

Frederick Palmer, at Ypres, fall 1916, My Second Year of the War.

The names of the new German lines—Wotan and Siegfried and Hunding—are not without significance. We accept the omen: It will not be long before we hear of fresh German activities in the *Goetterdaemmerung* line.

Punch, *London, April 1917.*

Little Willie (of Prussia): "As one Crown Prince to another, isn't your Hindenburg line getting a bit shaky?"

Rupprecht (of Bavaria): "Well, as one Crown Prince to another, what about your Hohenzollern line?"

Cartoon in Punch, *London, April 1917.*

Last night, lying awake in the still small hours, I kept thinking about the Hun observer I hit, and wondering if I killed him. If I did, he's the first man I've ever killed. Being so close when I fired, and seeing him collapse, made him another human being,

Emperor William's pyramid of skulls (British caricature, 1915). Courtesy of the New York Public Library.

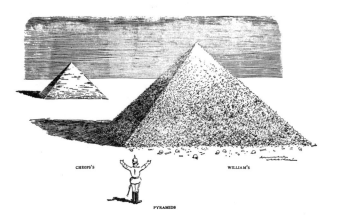

not just a target in an aeroplane. But I can't say it worries me terribly—after all, he started it.

A.G. Lee, at the Ypres front, May 1917, No Parachute *(1968).*

The month has witnessed the amendment of the President's [Wilson's] much discussed phrase: "Too proud to fight" has now become "Proud to fight too."

Punch, *London, May 1917.*

Then I started to come down to have a closer look at things, but the maze of zigzagging trenches was too confusing to disentangle, they seemed so interlocking that but for the shadowy lines of barbed wire, I couldn't have picked out no-man's land, nor which was our frontline, and which the German. Lower still, I saw the brown earth was pockmarked by millions of shell holes, many gleaming with water.

A.G. Lee, lieutenant in the Royal Flying Corps (later air vice-marshal, R.A.F.) flying over the Ypres front, May 23, 1917, No Parachute.

Then at 3.10 exactly, with no preliminary shelling at all, there came a most God-almighty roar, the deep blast of a long and terrible explosion. The sky lit up with a vivid red glare, The ground shook as if we were in an earthquake, in fact the hut seemed to jump off the ground. I've never heard such a stupendous noise before, like the thunderclap of doom. It seemed so close it could have come from just across the canal, instead of a dozen miles away, as we were soon to discover. Then as the roar ended, a hurricane bombardment began, a continuous rapid throbbing of guns, thousands of them. The hut vibrated without pause, the ground shuddered. All hell had been let loose up north.

A.G. Lee, on the opening of the Battle of Messines by an underground explosion of 19 mines under the German positions, June 7, 1917, No Parachute.

Apropos of resentment, England has lost first place in Germany, for America is said to be the most hated country now. The 'morning hate' of the German family with ragtime obbligato must be a terrible thing! General von Blume, it is true, says that America's intervention is no more than "a straw." But which straw? The last?

Punch, *London, July 1917.*

Dear friend, the experiences we have acquired in the eleventh battle of the Isonzo has led me to believe that we should fare far worse in a Twelfth. My commanders and brave troops have decided that such an unfortunate situation might be anticipated by an offensive. We have not the necessary means as regards troops in the theater of war and will have to get them from the eastern front. Please arrange to replace Austrian troops there by German. We need artillery, heavy in particular, not infantry.

Emperor Charles of Austria, letter to William II, August 20, 1917.

But the most reassuring news comes from the enemy Press. "It is simply a miracle" says the *Cologne Gazette*, "that the Germans have so loyally stood by their leaders," and for once we are wholly in agreement with our German contemporary.

Punch, *London, January 1918.*

The General Staff is now trying to run the Air Service with just as much knowledge of it as a hog knows about skating. It is terrible to have a fight with an organization of this kind, instead of devoting all our attention to the powerful enemy on our front. I have had many talks with General Pershing . . . some of them very heated, with pounding on the table on both sides. One time he told me that if I kept insisting that the organization of the Air Service be changed he would send me home. I answered that if he did he would soon come after me. That made him laugh and our talk ended admirably.

General Billy Mitchell in his diary, early 1918, in Quentin Reynolds, They Fought for the Sky.

14. The Eastern Front, from the Russian Revolution to the End of the War: March 1917 to November 1918

THE HISTORICAL CONTEXT

Fierce battles were being fought all through 1917, particularly on the western front. But, aside from America's entry into the war (see chapter 12), the event of the year that had the greatest impact on the war was the collapse of Russia.

RUSSIA BEFORE THE REVOLUTION

After the defeat by Japan and the abortive revolution of 1905, Russia had never come to a complete political rest. Tsar Nicholas was an autocrat by conviction, had sabotaged the reforms of prime minister Peter Arkadevich Stolypin as much as possible, and had done his best to whittle away the few prerogatives of his legislative body, the Duma. The mass of the population had no voice in the Duma, was as much as ever under the control of the nobility, and maintained a sullen hostility toward the regime. The agitation and activities of reactionary organizations such as the "Black Hundreds"—who fought for an unreconstructed autocracy by stirring up waves of anti-Jewish and other riots—poisoned the atmosphere even further, especially after Stolypin had been assassinated by a revolutionary, apparently with the connivance of some reactionaries in the government. During the international crisis of 1914, the Russian government was faced with a great dilemma. It was bound by international treaties to support France and England, and was solemnly committed to protect slavic Serbia when

243

threatened by Austria. On the other hand, the alliance with Russia's traditional antagonist, Britain, was anything but popular, and all but the most ardent Russian imperialists realized that a fight with Germany's powerful war machine could end in defeat and revolution. Some experts feel that a refusal to come to Serbia's help would have provoked a general uprising even sooner. In any case, in spite of the tsar's personal ties to the German emperor, the Russian government did nothing to work out a compromise through mediation, but by its sudden mobilization became instrumental to the outbreak of hostilities.

By the end of 1916, after General Alexei Brusilov's great offensive had finally ended in failure, the crisis caused by the war came to a head. Terrible casualty lists, food shortages (particularly in the great cities), Nicholas' refusal to permit liberal reforms suggested by the progressive bloc in the Duma, the unfortunate role played by the unpopular Empress Alexandra and, even more, by her favorite, the notorious adventurer Grigori Rasputin: All of these factors had resulted in the complete erosion of the patriotism manifest in the first months of the war. It did not help that in November 1916 Boris Stuermer, the archconservative and allegedly pro-German chief of the cabinet, was replaced by Alexander Trepov—who embarked on a policy of ruthless suppression of all opposition—and that Rasputin was assassinated by some aristocrats at the end of December. In the first months of 1917,

Rasputin, the "holy man," at the St. Petersburg Court. Photo courtesy of the New York Public Library.

there were increasing demonstrations, strikes and riots, which in the beginning of March culminated in a wild demonstration of women waiting in line at food stores in Petrograd. After two days, when the garrison was called upon to defend the government, the soldiers simply melted away. The Duma disobeyed the tsar's order to dissolve, fires were lit in the streets, one guard regiment murdered its officers, and the prisons were opened. By March 12, the tsar's orders were ignored in Petrograd, and within a few days he had ceased to command authority anywhere in his former empire.

THE TSAR ABDICATES TO A PROVISIONAL GOVERNMENT

On March 15, at the headquarters of the northern armies, the tsar abdicated in the presence of emissaries of the Duma, which now claimed supreme power. His brother Michael refused the crown in favor of a provisional government headed by Prince Georgi Yevgenyevich Lvov. A few days later, the tsar was arrested, and the rule of the house of Romanov had ended. An autocratic regime, unable to provide the country with the authority and strength required in times of crisis, had not been overthrown by revolution but had simply collapsed.

In the struggle for power that followed, the liberals of the new government tried to carry out their program. They proclaimed civic liberties and legal equality of all citizens and accepted the independence of Poland and Finland and the autonomy of Estonia. But before all these measures could be approved by a constituent assembly, the new regime found itself in conflict with the Petrograd Soviet, the Council of Workers' and Soldiers' Deputies, organized by the Socialists. While the government insisted on continuing the war and on increasing the efficiency of the army by some cautious measures of democratization, the Soviets wanted a speedy conclusion of the war, a general democratic peace, and a radical revision of all war aims. Since the generals were suspected to be counterrevolutionaries, the Soviets deprived the officers of all authority except for strategic operations, placing the administration of the army in the hands of committees elected by officers and men. The counterorders of the government were practically ignored.

The resistance of the Soviets was strengthened when, in the middle of April, a group of Bolshevik leaders arrived at Petrograd. It included Lenin (Vladimir Ilyich Ulyanov), Grigori Zinoviev, Karl Radek, Anatoly Lunacharski and other exiles who had been transported from Switzerland through Germany in a sealed train. The German High Command had correctly assumed that these radicals would undermine the provisional government's efforts to keep on fighting for the Allies. Lenin, the most energetic personality of the group, proclaimed a pro-

V. I. Lenin (Vladimir Ilyich Ulyanov), Russian revolutionary. Photo courtesy of the New York Public Library.

gram in which the power of the "bourgeois" government would be transferred to the Soviets (councils of workers and soldiers), the war would be ended immediately (even if it required accepting a separate peace with the Central Powers) and, in addition, land would be seized by the farmers and control of the industry would be taken over by committees of workers. He was soon joined by Leon Trotsky (Lev Bronstein), who had just returned from exile in New York and had developed a particularly radical program of "permanent revolution." Thus the liberals who believed in democratic elections as practiced by the western democracies faced a dangerous opposition at the moment when they had reason to believe their hour had finally come. For the time being, they were saved by the fact that their Socialist enemies were split into several factions. There were the Social Revolutionaries, the party of the peasants, and the Social Democrats, the followers of Karl Marx—who again were divided into the more moderate Mensheviks and the hard-liners, the Bolsheviks. The borderline between these two factions was sometimes blurred, and some of the leaders, like Trotsky, had vacillated between them in the past. The Mensheviks believed that the proletariat in Russia was not yet ready to take over and that a period of cooperation with the liberal-democratic bourgeoisie was needed, while the Bolsheviks—meaning "the Majority" (although they were actually in the minority until 1917)—wanted an immediate takeover by the Soviets, by violence, if necessary. The Social Revolutionaries proposed a program to rebuild Russia from the peasant base upward, which in former days made good sense, as the overwhelming majority of the Russian people were peasants. But it was difficult to see how such a state could compete with other countries in the new imperialistic-industrial age.

The link between these diverging parties was, for the time being, Alexander Kerensky, the only socialist in Lvov's cabinet. First he was minister of justice, then, from May 1917 on, he became minister of war with General Brusilov as his commander in chief. An idealist and great orator, he managed to bring forth some kind of consensus for a moderate democratic regime. But the gap between his policies and the aims of the Petrograd Soviets was too great. Kerensky's foreign minister, Paul Miliukov, intended to continue the old tsarist line with its alliances and secret treaties and foresaw Russia fighting on to victory. This led to demonstrations in Petrograd in which soldiers and workers poured into the streets demanding peace at once and denounced the policy of conquest of the ruling classes. Miliukov and Kerensky's minister of war, Alexander Guchkov, resigned, and six members of the Soviet executive committee entered the government. But the rift was unbridgeable: On the one hand was the provisional government, more or less representing privileged, educated Russia; on the other was the new "Soviet Russia," the peasant masses on the farms, the peasants in uniforms and the peasants in factories, now known as proletarians.

The next clash occurred when Kerensky began a great offensive on the Galician front in the beginning of July. Brusilov used the best and least affected units at his disposal, mostly Siberian and Finnish troops, and his drive in the direction of Lemberg made some progress, in particular in the south, where General Lavr Kornilov operated against Austrian, Turkish and some German troops. But the triumph was short-lived. The Central Powers transferred a few divisions from the west and launched a counterattack on July 19, and the Russian front quickly dissolved. Tarnopol, Czernowitz and other cities were retaken, and Brusilov was dismissed and replaced by Kornilov. But with an army decimated by wholesale desertions, Kornilov was no more successful than his predecessor. In the beginning of September, the Germans crossed the Dvina River and surrounded and took Riga. Their tactics were, once again, those worked out by their commander, General Oskar von Huitier: a short, heavy artillery preparation, night marches, surprise attacks and infiltrations.

By this time, the Bolsheviks in Petrograd had attempted a coup d'état, which proved to be premature. The Lvov government suppressed the movement and arrested many of the leaders, including Trotsky, while Lenin went into hiding in Finland. This incident—and the deep disagreements within the government on the question of land reform and the handling of national minorities—led to Prince Lvov's resignation on July 20. Kerensky took his place, but with the weak, divided government on one side and the revolutionary Soviets on the other (who were represented by unwieldy bodies, such as the Petrograd assembly, which numbered about 3,000 members), it became clearer from day to day that the heir to tsarist autocracy would have to be a dictatorship. For a moment, it looked as if the right had a good chance. Kornilov, a former peasant and certainly not a reactionary, was convinced that only a military dictatorship could save Russia from disintegration and began to move his most reliable troops in the direction of Petrograd. He avowed that his aim was to liberate the government from Socialist domination; but he was prepared to take over if the opportunity presented itself. Kerensky dismissed him, but Kornilov disobeyed and approached the capital. Kerensky now appealed to the Socialists for support against the "counterrevolution." Trotsky and other Bolshevik leaders were released from prison, and Soviet agitators were sent out to meet the troops. Under their persuasion, Kornilov's troops simply disintegrated, and his move had the opposite effect. The masses now suspected not only the army commanders but also the provisional government.

Kerensky found himself under the domination of his Bolshevik allies. Their propaganda made rapid headway among the soldiers of the capital's garrison and the factory workers. Kornilov's attempt had resulted in the opposite of what he had intended: the revival of the revolutionary impetus. By fall, the Bolsheviks had gained control of many urban soviets, and they were the only party that clearly identified itself with all aims of the stirred-up masses: immediate peace, land for the peasants, bread for the hungry, self-determination of the minority groups and social justice. Yet the Bolshevik leaders never let themselves be carried away by the masses but stuck to their program—the dictatorship of the proletariat. They would never turn against the masses, but they acted as manipulators of the popular will, not as mere agents of the people.

By the end of October, the Mensheviks had lost much of their influence, and Lenin's party could claim majorities in almost all major cities. Only in Siberia were the old Social Revolutionaries still powerful. Lenin, though an orthodox Marxist, realized that the proletariat (in which he included the "poorest peasantry") would form too weak a basis for his ideal—an advanced social system—and that he would be unable to keep control for any length of time without using terroristic methods, which were not part of the orthodox Marxist program. But he and Trotsky counted on international support since they expected a revolution of the masses throughout the capitalistic world. The war, as they interpreted it, was paving the way for socialist states all over Europe.

THE BOLSHEVIK COUP D'ETAT

Lenin, still in hiding, felt the time had come for the seizure of power. The execution of the coup on November 6 was less Lenin's work than that of Trotsky, a brilliant organizer and orator. The Bolsheviks, led by the revolutionary committee, the soldiers from the Petrograd garrison and sailors from Kronstadt, captured most of the government offices, stormed the Winter Palace and arrested the members of the provisional government. Kerensky escaped, tried in vain to organize some resistance and finally went into exile. On the following day, the All-Russian Congress of Soviets approved the action and handed the power to the Bolsheviks. The new government, called Council of the People's Commissars, was headed by Lenin and included Trotsky as commissar for foreign affairs and Josef Stalin as commissar for national minorities. Within a few days, Lenin had declared the end of the provisional government, the end of the war and the handing over of the land to the peasants.

Yet the majority of the people were not behind the Bolsheviks. On November 25, the elections of the Constituent Assembly were disappointing for Lenin. While the privileged groups and even the Mensheviks fared poorly, four-fifths of the vote went to the Social Revolutionaries plus the Bolsheviks, but the Bolsheviks themselves received less than a quarter of the total. Luckily for them, the left Social Revolutionaries cooperated with the Bolsheviks, so the anti-Bolshevik majority could not be tabulated. The Assembly was permitted to gather in January 1918, but it was surrounded by Red Guards. When the anti-Bolsheviks took over, the Bolsheviks walked out. The remaining members supported the decrees on land distribution and declared Russia a democratic, progressive republic. In the early morning hours of January 19, the speaker was informed that the guards were tired and wanted to go home. The assembly adjourned, and when the delegates returned, the doors were barred. The Central Executive Committee had declared that the Constituent Assembly be dissolved. Thus ended the abortive attempt of parliamentarism, for which Lenin never had any use anyway. Whatever attempts had been undertaken for a revolution from below had come to an end.

While it would take the Bolsheviks several years to get full control of the country, they made it clear from the beginning that they would fight against dissolution or reduction of the Russian Empire, although their country had lost the war and the enemy's armies had penetrated deep into Russian territory. From November 1917 on, all expressions of spontaneity encouraged by the revolutionary spirit were beginning to be repressed again and, as it turned out, by methods much harsher than those used by the tsarist regime. To fight any counterrevolutionary activities, the dreaded political police, the Cheka, was created to send emissaries into pro-tsarist Don Cossack territory to prevent any anti-Bolshevik uprising. The bourgeoisie was slowly and methodically annihilated; the aristocrats who had not fled the country were even more ruthlessly exterminated.

THE BOLSHEVIK REGIME AND THE GERMANS

But dealing with the victorious Germans was another matter. As early as November 1916, Germany had announced the formation of an independent Polish state, though their hope to enlist the Poles on Germany's side failed. The provisional government had recognized Polish independence in March 1917, and the British adhered to the principle of an independent Poland. A constitution was granted to Poland and a regency council was appointed by the Central Powers. After the Bolshevik takeover, the Ukrainians and the Estonians declared themselves independent, with Finland, Moldavia and Latvia following suit. The Central Powers recognized the independence of these states, and Russia's western allies did not try to interfere. A separate peace treaty between the Ukraine and the Central Powers was concluded in February, but the main negotiations between the Bolshevik regime and the Central Powers at Brest-Litovsk in Eastern Poland, which had started in December 1917, brought no results. The Russians were represented by Trotsky, the Central Powers by German foreign secretary Richard von Kuehlmann and the Austrian foreign minister, Count Ottokar von Czernin.

The Russians, actually powerless, tried to play a double game. They negotiated with the capitalist powers because they had to and, at the same time, assumed the role of leaders in the coming world revolution that would shortly overthrow their present adversaries. Lenin had the secret treaties of the Allies published to show the workings of imperialism; his agitators delivered inflammatory speeches everywhere; and his agents tried fraternization at the front and indoctrination in the prisoner-of-war camps, fomenting revolution against capitalist and colonial exploiters. They also repudiated all foreign debts of the old regime. They had some success with German troops with all of this propaganda, and some of the German units at the eastern front proved quite worthless in the final days at the western front because they had been indoctrinated by the Communist visions of a world free from exploitation, hunger, injustice, and—above all—war.

But propaganda did not work at Brest-Litovsk. Here Trotsky employed stalling tactics and engaged in endless discussions with Kuehlmann, always hoping for the great international revolution to break out. He refused to recognize the new Baltic states without a plebiscite (in favor of independence), and then, in February 1918, declared that the war was over, although Germany's extremely harsh conditions had not been met. Now the Central Powers resumed hostilities, occupied the Baltic States and moved within 100 miles of Petrograd, causing Lenin to move his capital to Moscow. They also moved into the Ukraine and even to the Crimea and the Caucasus. In parts of the country, a regular civil war broke out, with the Germans supporting the anti-Bolshevik "Whites." Now Lenin insisted on the renewal of the negotiations, and within a few days the treaty was signed. The German conditions were incredibly harsh. Russia was losing its Baltic provinces, all of Poland, the Ukraine and valuable territories in the Caucasus, which were to be taken over by Turkey. The territorial gains of two centuries of expansion—Russia's most modern industrial center, its coal and iron resources, its granary, much of its oil and almost one-third of its population—were lost in one blow. When the terms became known in the United States, people refused to believe that any Russian delegates could have accepted them and thought that Trotsky and his assistants had been bribed by the Germans. The ironic truth was that Germany had indeed subsidized the Bolsheviks for a long time—as long as they had thereby undermined the tsarist and Kerensky regimes. Germany discontinued the subsidies, apparently around the time the peace treaty was concluded.

The Bolshevik party was deeply divided over the peace conditions. Its most extreme elements advocated a revolutionary war by fighting the Germans with any means available and asking the masses to make a last stand, however hopeless, and many of the old Social Revolutionaries supported this policy. Lenin's argument was that a disastrous peace was still preferable to open chaos and civil war, particularly since the position of the Communist regime was still weak and might not stand the ultimate test. Lenin won out, but hostilities continued for some time. German troops were in Odessa and Sevastopol and in April landed in Finland, taking Helsingfors (Helsinki) and Viborg (Viipuri). Here a regular civil war was raging between the Whites—supported by the German units—and the Reds, until the latter were defeated in a five-day battle. On other fronts, such as the Caucasus, Siberia and the Ukraine, anti-Bolshevik groups continued to fight. The largest of these armies was the Czechoslovak Legion, about 40,000 men formed of deserters or prisoners from the Austro-Hungarian armies, who had fought in the final Kerensky offensive. They rejected the Brest-Litovsk treaty and attempted to join the Allies by marching through central Russia toward Vladivostok. They seized sections of the Trans-Siberian railroad and encouraged White uprisings in Siberia. When they reached Ekaterinburg in the Ural Mountains—where the tsar and his family had been imprisoned since April—local Bolshevik authorities, afraid that the city would be captured and the tsar liberated, had the whole imperial family shot in the cellar they occupied. Recent research has revealed that Lenin's government was indeed consulted and approved the action. Trotsky declared later that the execution had been necessary, not only to deprive the Whites of any hope for restoration, but also to show the revolutionary masses that there was no way back for them.

UPRISINGS AND ALLIED INTERVENTIONS

After the Treaty of Brest-Litovsk, the Western Allies considered the Bolshevik regime as a mere puppet of the Germans and developed various plans to reestablish an eastern front, with the aim of preventing a large-scale transfer of German troops to France. In June 1918, a British force under General Frederick Poole, joined by some American contingents, landed at Murmansk on the Barents Sea, north of Petrograd. After a pro-Allied revolution at Arkhangelsk, the British took over this port. The Czech army in Siberia seized Samara and Kazan on the Volga and took Omsk, Irkutsk and other cities on the Trans-Siberian railway. In July, they were joined by some Japanese forces. Japanese troops also joined a British contingent that had landed at Vladivostok. At Omsk, Admiral Alexander Kolchak overthrew the Social Revolutionary government in November 1918 and assumed dictatorship over Siberia. He was recognized by the Allies and at first was successful in fighting Bolshevik armies; but during the following year he was defeated by the Communists, who had him shot.

Due to these military interventions and the frequent uprisings of the Social Revolutionaries, the Bolshevik regime had come close to collapse in August 1918. The Petrograd chief of the Cheka was assassinated, and Lenin himself was severely wounded by an assassin. But the Bolsheviks fought back, and the new Red Army, trained under Trotsky, began to show great fighting qualities. By September, the Social Revolutionaries had been beaten. The armistice in the west in November 1918 annulled the treaty of Brest-Litovsk and reopened the Ukraine and the Baltic states to Soviet forces. The German troops were withdrawn, but British ships entered the Baltic Sea and the Caspian Sea and French forces occupied some of the Black Sea ports. It took the Soviet regime another year to achieve the withdrawal of Allied intervention, and another two years to end the civil war in the devastated, impoverished and starving country.

Compared to their efforts on the western front, Allied interventions in Russia were insignificant in size, but they had far-reaching effects nevertheless. Allied troops and the supply of food and war materials helped Kolchak and his successor, General Anton Denikin, to advance his troops close to Moscow. Allied intervention also caused Trotsky to abandon his military aid to Bela Kun, the Communist dictator in Hungary, causing his downfall and the rise of Hungary's "white terror" regime. French and British help strengthened the Polish state sufficiently to repulse Soviet advances on Warsaw at the last moment. Above all, neither Finland nor the Baltic would have been able to maintain their declared independence without Allied support. In view of all this, the Soviets considered themselves surrounded and constantly threatened by all capitalist countries, and during the following years, Soviet exaggerated descriptions of Allied intervention played a vital part in their international propaganda campaigns.

CHRONICLE OF EVENTS

1916:

November 18: In a stormy meeting of the Duma, the government is warned of impending disaster unless its policy is changed immediately.

December 30: Grigori Yefimovich Rasputin is assassinated by Prince Felix Yussupov and other aristocrats.

1917:

March 8: Strikes and riots in St. Petersburg (renamed Petrograd).

Rasputin, the Tsar and the Tsarina, caricature, 1917. Courtesy of the New York Public Library.

March 10: Mutiny of the troops in the capital.

March 11: The Duma refuses to obey an imperial order to dissolve.

March 12: The Petrograd Soviet, Council of Workers' and Soldiers' Deputies, is organized by the Socialists.

The Duma establishes a Provisional Government, headed by Prince George Lvov and including Paul Miliukov, Alexander Guchkov and Alexander Kerensky.

March 14: The Soviet issues Order No. 1, depriving officers of all authority except in strategic operations.

March 15: Tsar Nicholas II abdicates in favor of his son, and his son in favor of Nicholas' brother Michael.

March 16: Michael abdicates in favor of the provisional government.

March 18: The Provisional Government pledges to continue the war.

March 21: Finland is recognized as independent within the Russian Federation.

March 30: Poland's independence is recognized. Far-reaching land reforms are announced.

April 12: Estonia is granted autonomy.

April 16: Lenin (Vladimir Ilyich Ulyanov), Grigori Zinoviev, Karl Radek, Anatoly Lunacharski and other Bolshevik leaders arrive at Petrograd from Switzerland.

Early May: Leon Trotsky (Lev Bronstein) returns from exile in the United States and England.

May 14–16: Guchkov and Miliukov resign from the Provisional Government. Kerensky is made minister of war.

June 30: General Alexei Kaledin is made *hetman* ("commander in chief") of the Cossacks.

July 1: Beginning of Brusilov's great offensive in Galicia. The Russians advance in the battles of Brzezany, Koniuchy and Zloczow.

July 16–18: Attempt of the Bolsheviks to seize power in Petrograd fails. Trotsky arrested, Lenin escapes to Finland.

July 20: Finnish declaration of complete independence.

Prince Lvov resigns and is replaced by Alexander Kerensky.

July 20–28: German counterattack in East Galicia. Russians are driven back.

July 24–26: German troops retake Halicz, Tarnopol and Stanislav.

August 1: General Brusilov is replaced by General Lavr Georgievich Kornilov.

August 3: Germans retake Czernowitz.

September 3–5: Battle of Riga. The city is surrounded by the Germans and taken.

September 8–14: Kornilov marches on Petrograd as leader of a counterrevolution, but fails.

October 11–20: German troops overrun Latvia and conquer the Baltic islands Oesel, Moon Island and Dago.

October: The Bolsheviks secure a majority in the Soviet.

November 6–7: (old calendar, *October 24–25*): Bolsheviks coup d'état. Kerensky escapes.

November 7: The Second All-Russian Congress of Soviets approves the coup.

The new government is organized under the name of Council of the People's Commissars, headed by Lenin and including Trotsky and Josef Stalin.

The government publishes a decree of peace, appealing to all states to start peace parleys.

November 21: General Nicholas Dukhonin, Russian Commander, is dismissed and replaced by the Bolshevik Nicolai Krylenko.

November 22: Trotsky again proposes an armistice.

November 25: Election of the Constituent Assembly. Four hundred twenty Social Revolutionaries and only 225 Bolsheviks are elected.

November 28: The Bolshevik government offers armistice and peace to the German government.

December 5: The Bolshevik government makes public the secret treaties between Russia and her allies. Armistice is declared between Russia and the Central Powers. Negotiations open at Brest-Litovsk.

December 9: Revolt of the Don Cossacks, led by General Kornilov and General Alexei Kaledin.

December 11: Lithuania establishes an independent government.

December 15: Moldavia declares itself independent. Armistice on the entire eastern front.

December 20: An Extraordinary Committee to Combat Counter-Revolution (Cheka, later called G.P.U.) is organized.

December 28: Negotiations at Brest-Litovsk break down.

December 30: Japanese land at Vladivostok.

1918:

January 10: An Independent Republic of the Don is declared.

January 18: The Constituent Assembly convenes but is dispersed by Red Troops.

January 28: The Ukraine declares itself independent.

February 9: The Ukraine concludes a separate peace.

February 10: The Bolsheviks try to end the war by proclamation.

February 18: German troops resume the offensive.

Bolsheviks take Kiev.

March 2: German troops push Bolsheviks out of Kiev.

March 3: Treaty of Brest-Litovsk. Russia loses the Ukraine, Poland and all borderlands occupied by non-Russians.

March 9: The Soviet government moves to Moscow.

March 13: Germans occupy Odessa.

April: The tsar and his family are moved from Tobolsk to Ekaterinburg.

April 13: General Kornilov is killed in battle with the Bolsheviks. General Anton Denikin and General Peter N. Krasnov take over the anti-Bolshevik forces in the south.

April 22: The Caucasian states declare their independence.

June: Czech troops seize control of the Trans-Siberian Railway.

June 23: British troops land at Murmansk.

July 6: The German ambassador in Moscow,

Count Wilhelm von Mirbach, is assassinated by a Social Revolutionary.

July 10: The new Soviet constitution is promulgated.

July 16: Tsar Nicholas II and his entire family are killed by local Bolsheviks.

August 30: Unsuccessful attempt is made by a Social Revolutionary to assassinate Lenin.

August: British and French troops occupy Arkhangelsk and set up a puppet government of northern Russia.

November 18: Anti-Bolshevik coup at Omsk. Admiral Alexander Kolchak is proclaimed Supreme Ruler of Russia.

December 24: Kolchak occupies Perm.

1919:

January: Bolshevik counteroffensive, resulting in Kolchak's capture and execution.

Eyewitness Testimony

Imagine the hopeless spectacle before our eyes. One could cry. The soldiers do not report for duty, they are ambling about, hands in pockets, besiege the streetcars, walk around, arm in arm with noisy women, do not even salute their officers and mock them,—if they do not kill them.

Charles de Chambrun, secretary of the French ambassador in Petrograd, letter to Princess Lucien Murat, early 1917.

Things are getting more serious. . . An officer cadet invaded a factory where the workers had ordered an "Iatian strike" (with folded arms in front of the machines), and ordered to fire. His soldiers refused to obey him. Thereupon the officer fired three pistol shots which claimed three victims, two women and one worker. The crowd wanted to lynch him, but he managed to escape . . . A similar case at the tobacco factory Laferme. There was only one dead, but the workers laid the body out at the court of the factory and asked the crowd to walk past him. There is increased irritation: Shops have been sacked and devastated.

Marylie Markovich, French journalist, on events of February 15, 1917, La Révolution Russe *(1918).*

The mob ganged up in front of the half empty bakeries. But I remember well that there were, among the rioters, people who, in this not really desperate situation conducted themselves so violently as if it was their plan to exploit the situation. Shops were pillaged, and suddenly hordes of people waving red flags were in the streets. They maneuvered everywhere in the same way, using the same tactics by cheering the companies of Cossacks sent out to confront them. They were proud and eager to clear their name and to get rid of their reputation as butchers of the people . . . and responded smiling: "No, we will not shoot at our brothers." A week later, they showed they had been sincere in changing their attitude when they threw themselves upon policemen and constables.

Ludovic Naudeau, French journalist, on the Petrograd riots, in Le Temps, *February 18, 1917.*

Almost all the shops are open. The promenading crowd runs from the sidewalks to the roadway. No shouting: Firm determination combined with complete cold-bloodedness. How different from the eccentric and entranced masses of 1905 who lived in a legend, in an atmosphere of mystery and religious pomp. The people of 1917 are realistic. Two years of war have matured them more than a century of peace and quiet did.

Marylie Markovitch, on Petrograd on February 24, 1917, La Révolution Russe.

A man, probably of the working class, broke the show window of a shop and shouted to the crowd to do the same with other shops. He was arrested by some soldiers on order of their officers. They pulled him away quite brutally, but when he pulled out a card and showed it to the officer he was released immediately; it was his identification as a police agent. In the general excitement the crowd did not notice this and thought the police had freed the man out of the kindness of their hearts.

Jones Stinton, English journalist. Report of February 25, 1917, Russia in Revolution *(1917).*

I was witness to the first murder . . . an orator who incites the huge crowd to fight the government. Nearby was a detachment of mounted Cossacks who, however, do not interfere. But then a group of policemen, led by an officer, appears, and he commands them to shoot at the crowd. Trumpets sound, announcing that rifle fire will start immediately. The crowd gets agitated, but the orator continues his speech. After the third trumpet call I see clearly that one of the Cossacks takes aim and shoots. The police officer falls and is dead. That is the signal. The policemen are being disarmed by the crowd and flee . . . I still see the picture of a young girl, a Red Cross nurse, wounded in the leg by a police bullet . . . also recall the Cossacks who wave their rifles, ride through the crowd and shout that they will not shoot, that they are with the people . . . They are loudly cheered by the crowd . . . In some places they sing the "Marseillaise". . .

Vladimir Zenzinov, Russian revolutionary, recalling the Petrograd riots February 25, 1917, Memoirs *(1919).*

At nine o'clock in the evening I receive a telegram from his Majesty: "I order that by tomorrow the riots in the capital which are unlawful during the war with Germany and Austria are to be stopped. Nicholas." This telegram, I have to admit quite frankly, was a terrible blow to me. How could I end the riots by tomorrow? . . . Now that they had written on their flags "down with the autocratic regime" one could not pacify them with bread any longer. So what to do? The Tsar had commanded, so we had to resort to arms.

General Chabalov, governor of Petrograd, at a hearing before the Provisional Government, about February 25, 1917.

It would have been sufficient if two or three regiments had sided with the government and resisted the uprising; it would have saved the imperial regime. During the night from Sunday to Monday and in the morning hours of Monday the desertion of the army became final. That is the only thing I am really sure of.

Ludovic Naudeau, recalling Monday, February 27, 1917 in Petrograd, Les dessous du Chaos Russe *(1921).*

It happened that a particularly hated police officer in the district of the poor was seized in the street. The mob, consisting of the lowest elements of the region, got into such a frenzy that it simply tore the unfortunate man to pieces. . . I came to the scene a few minutes later and the awful sight of his . . . remnants was sufficient evidence of this terrible event.

Jones Stinton, recalling events in Petrograd, February 1917, Russia in Revolution.

And now the people take their revenge. There are fires everywhere in Petrograd, in all prisons, all police headquarters. If they set fire to the Palace of Justice it is because in the eyes of the people it was a fortress for the police, in the same way as the Bastille was the symbol of tyranny for the people of Paris.

Marylie Markovich, on events in Petrograd in February 1917, La Révolution Russe.

While his admirers triumphantly put him down on the stage, Paléologue turns to me and mumbles: "This is Marat's triumph." Standing upright on the stage, as if he had guessed this thought which perhaps had come to him too, Kerenski shouted in a flood of words: "I shall not be the Marat of the Russian Revolution!" He was a born orator . . . I

think he does not know exactly what he will say when he takes the floor. His words spurt forward, his mind becomes dull. Does he know the way while he is talking? His words guide him as a cane guides a blind man . . . When he has finished his speech and thunderous applause surrounds him, the moderate tribune does not seem to remember what he had said. He stops, exhausted, with a dry throat, silenced by his eloquence . . .

Charles de Chambrun, Secretary of the French ambassador in Petrograd, in a letter to Princess Lucien Murat, end of February 1917.

It was clear from the beginning that the little confidence this cabinet was enjoying was only due to the fact that a very popular man, the Social Revolutionary Kerenskij was one of its members. But the initial program approved by the cabinet showed clearly the pressure exerted by the so-called soviets, the council of workers and soldiers which was to gain additional foothold all the time. The famous order #1 was announced and telegraphed to all units at the front. It ordered the election of officers and the formation of soldiers' committees in every regiment. This measure which ruined all discipline did not originate, as people here have believed naïvely, with the cabinet, but with the Soviets. Its execution immediately had a fatal effect at the front. Until then the fighting troops had only vague ideas of the changes in Petrograd . . .

Ludovic Naudeau in Le Temps, *Paris, February 28, 1917.*

I think it was the evening of March 1—I had been at a meeting of the military commission—when X. ran up to me, pale and trembling, and said: "They are bringing Sukhomlinov [the former minister of war] into the Duma. The soldiers are furious. They look as if they want to tear him to pieces . . ." I rushed to the hallway. The tumultuous crowd pushed forward . . . Immediately I covered Sukhomlinov with my body. Only I was between him and his attackers. I shouted at them I would not permit them to kill him and to stain the name of the revolution. I declared they could get to him only over my dead body. This was indeed a terrible moment . . . For a moment, they were undecided, and then I had the upper hand. The crowd began to retreat and we managed to push Sukhomlinov through the door which closed behind him while the guards crossed

their bayonets. Sukhomlinovs' appearance incensed the prisoners. No one wanted to sit next to him . . .
Alexander Kerensky, La Révolution Russe
(1917).

From Paris is reported that political and financial circles as well as the business world in France have no fear regarding the stability of the new political regime in Russia. At the Paris stock exchange, the ruble and Russian securities have climbed up.
Journal de Petrograd, *March 7, 1917.*

Some of the soldiers filling the streets are wearing white armbands. There are the patriotic revolutionaries who only want a constitution and an improvement of the situation of the people. They took over the responsibility of the police. Where do the innumerable policemen hide? . . . It is true, the populace of Petrograd murdered a great number of them on the first day. The others are probably in hiding. The soldiers who wear red cockades in public are regular street robbers. They pillage, set fire to houses and have opened up some prisons.
Louise Patin, recalling events of March 1917,
"Journal d'une française," *1917–19.*

Leisurely, the soldiers walk around in groups, with a red cockade on their kepis or on their chests. Their "freedom" consists of not saluting the officers, not even the old generals, to sit down in the first class railway compartments without paying and . . . to smoke and spit there . . . In the schools, too, the fever of independence is raging: The pupils want to elect their teachers and to control their ratings . . .
Louise Patin, recalling events of March 1917,
"Journal d'une française," *1917–19.*

Internal disturbances threaten to affect fatally the further development of this persistent war. The destiny of Russia, the honor of our heroic army, the welfare of the people and the whole future of our dear fatherland demand that the war be continued at all costs until its victorious conclusion. Our cruel enemy is making his last efforts and the moment is near when our brave army, together with our glorious Allies, will fling him down once and for all. In these days, decisive for the existence of Russia, We believe, following Our conscience, it to be Our duty to pave the way for a close unity of our people and for the organization of all its powers in order to achieve a quick victory. We therefore consider it

proper, in agreement with the Duma, to renounce the crown of the Empire and to give up the throne.
From Tsar Nicholas' abdication proclamation,
March 15, 1917.

Recently there has been much talk about the great number of deserters. In the past, this problem was not discussed, not for lack of interest, but because it was forbidden to mention it. It is true, there are still deserters, particularly because of the rumours circulating about the redistribution of the soil, but in general, the earliest deserters are returning to their ranks.
Journal de Petrograd, *March 23, 1917, publishing an announcement by Kerensky.*

I awaited this meeting with the ex-Tsar with a certain amount of uneasiness. I feared I would lose my coolheadedness when facing for the first time the man I had always hated. Only one day ago I had told a member of the Provisional Government regarding the abolishment of the death penalty: "I believe the only death sentence I could sign would be one against Nicholas II" . . . I felt his insecurity and that of the whole family toward the terrible revolutionary. Resolutely I walked toward him and called out my name, as I always did: "Kerensky." He pressed my hand vigorously and, visibly relieved, led me to his family. His son and daughers seemed full of curiosity and stared at me. Aleksandra Fedorovna, stiff, proud and arrogant, gave me her hand unwillingly, and our palms hardly touched. The difference in character and temperament between husband and wife manifested itself in typical fashion. I felt immediately that Aleksandra, though completely broken down and excited, was an intelligent woman with great will power. In a few seconds, I understood the psychological drama that had taken place within the walls of the palace for years.
Alexander Kerensky, recalling a Visit at Nicholas' summer palace at Tsarskoe Selo, late March 1917, In The Truth about the Massacre of the Romanovs *(1936).*

With the end of Tsardom in Russia, the fall of Baghdad and the strategic retreat of Hindenburg on the Western front, all crowded into one month, March fully maintains its reputation for making history at the expense of Caesars and Kaisers.
Punch, *London, March 1917.*

While the old order dissolved, new creative powers emerged which began to affect the life of the nation. But this developed very slowly since around us everything was in flames. We had no time to watch, to listen and to be patient. We expected from the people a degree of maturity, discipline, unselfishness, spirit of sacrifice and political prudence which it could not have reached. For it was just slowly recovered from a despotic regime spoiled by Rasputin, and had seen the blood sacrifices of the war . . . We had no time to philosophize . . .

Alexander Kerensky, recalling events of April 1917, Memoirs *(n.d.).*

The London cabinet sent to the ambassador accredited with the Provisional Government instruction which amounted to the following: The invitation to the Tsar and his family to come to England must be withdrawn, but appearances must be preserved, as if the initiative for the rejection had originated with the representatives of the Russian government . . . so that the British and liberals would not cause any trouble to the cabinet "at this critical moment of the war."

Alexander Kerensky, recalling the spring of 1917, The Truth about the Massacre of the Romanovs *(1936).*

At all these gatherings one heard the "Marseillaise," but not the beautiful "Marseillaise" sung in France that led the French people to victory. It was a gruesome, monotonous and sorrowful song, sad as Russian folk songs . . . There was not one meeting—and there were enough of them, for this first revolution was mainly foolish drivel—without this russified "Marseillaise."

Princesse Paley, recalling the mood at Tsarskoe Selo, April 1917, Souvenirs de Russie *(1923).*

For almost one hour Zinoviev [Grigori Zinoviev, friend and close collaborator of Lenin] talks violently against the capitalism, militarism and imperialism of—the Allies. Always the same wrong conclusions we have heard a hundred times, cleverly mixed with some basic truths, so that they seem acceptable. Only the Germans emerge pure as white as snow from these terrible accusations.

Marylie Markovich, recalling May 1917 in Petrograd, La Révolution Russe.

You simpletons, braggards, idiots, you think history is made in the salons, where little democratic parvenus make friends with noble liberals, where little backward people, shysters from the provinces learn quickly to kiss the tender hands of the highborn excellencies. Simpletons, braggards, idiots! History is made in the trenches where every soldier, intoxicated by nightmares and the war, thrusts his bayonet into the body of an officer, then flees on the bumpers of a train into his native village to start fires there on the roof of the estate owner!

Lenin in a speech to the farmers, reported in Trotsky's Histoire de la Révolution *(1934).*

Mr. Pereverzev, Minister of Justice, hands me some authentic texts of some telegrams exchanged between Lenin, Zinoviev, Ganeckij and other Bolshevik leaders. They show clearly that they received enormous amounts of money from abroad via Stockholm. This was undeniable proof of high treason. I ask . . . why the Provisional Government has not yet started any court proceedings against the guilty ones, and learn the sad fact: Mr. Kerenski and several other ministers have objected.

Gregoire Alexinsky, a Social Democrat, during the Bolshevik riots, July 1917, Memoirs *(n.d.).*

Since then we Bolsheviks were tormented and accused to be spies in the pay of imperialistic Germany. Government authorities demanded of Lenin and Zinoviev to show up . . . but I, knowing the spirit of the reaction, know that the two responsible Bolsheviks would risk to be murdered by these young fanatic officers without any court procedure . . . There was no choice but to help Lenin to go underground. I played the barber, cut off his beard and moustache to make him unrecognizable. Then I accompanied him through the dark streets to the Finland Station.

Josef Stalin, after the Bolshevik uprising of July 1917 had been suppressed, My Life *(1956).*

Starvation will exterminate Petrograd, the German armies will suppress liberty, pogroms will devastate Russia unless we all, workers, soldiers and responsible citizens work together . . . Do not trust the promises of the Bolsheviks! Their promise of an immediate peace is a lie! Their promise to provide bread is fraud! Their promise to distribute the land is a fairy tale for children!

Alexander Kerensky, Proclamation on August 21, 1917 after Riga was taken by the German armies, Memoirs (n.d.).

I soon realized that Kerenski was only a sick man who had borrowed much of Dostojevskij's characters, an actor who sincerely believed in the messianic significance of his destiny while plunging headlong into the abyss . . . By the crest of the first revolutionary wave he was carried up like a flimsy wood shaving. Russia played with this innocent man . . .
V. Vysotski, Alexandre Kerenski (1917).

Something extraordinary: All liberals in Petrograd, no matter of which persuasion, have now put their trust in him, some because he is a wonderful leader of men, the others because they believe in his prudence and moderation. He knows how to come to terms with the call of the hour by clever compromise, without giving up his principles. He is both: A great socialist and a convinced patriot.
Marylie Markovich, about Kerensky, La Révolution Russe.

I had to be everywhere at the same time. They called me, they picked me up from all directions. Day and night I ran through the Duma in fear, sometimes pushing myself through heavy walls of human bodies to get through, sometimes ambling about in the desolation of empty hallways. Sometimes I swooned, losing consciousness for 15 to 20 minutes, until they got me around by having me drink a glass of cognac or black coffee.
Alexander Kerensky, La Révolution Russe.

Russians, our great fatherland is dying. The day of its end is near. I, General Kornilov, declare that the Provisional Government under Bolshevik pressure is acting in complete accordance with members of the German General Staff . . . I swear I shall beat the enemy and give to the people a constituent assembly by which it may decide its own destiny and choose the organization of its new political life. I cannot deliver Russia to her hereditary enemy and let the Russian people become Germany's slaves . . .
General Kornilov, Proclamation on August 27, 1917.

The shops are open, people buy, eat and drink . . . Some signs remind you that there is a war going on. Military personnel mixes in with the crowds, no doubt men on furlough . . . Still, I am worried. The number of soldiers increases from day to day, and one thing which did not bother me in the beginning now makes me wonder more and more. The bandages for wounds and amputations of fingers, hands, legs are without exception, on the left side. That means that all these wounded men have mutilated themselves voluntarily, shooting with their right hands. There can be no doubt. The collapse of the army is continuing.
Richard Kohn, member of the French Sanitary Commission in Kiev, recalling conditions in August 1917, in his unpublished memoirs.

In Russia the Provisional Government has been dissolved and a Republic declared. If eloquence can save the situation, Mr. Kerensky is the man to do it; but so far the men of few words have gone farthest in the war. A "History of the Russian Revolution" has already been published. The pen may not be mightier than the sword today, but is manages to keep ahead of it.
Punch, London, September 1917.

Kerenski realized the seriousness of the situation so little that, three or four days before the armed Bolsheviks took to the streets, he declared to be sure he would triumph and prepared to undertake a propaganda trip to the provincial governments to, as he put it, "rouse enthusiasm" . . . I had occasion . . . to ask the prime minister if he had taken measures to fight the uprisings and if he believed he could rely on capable and loyal troops. Mr. Kerenski answered that several divisions were on the march toward Petrograd, but I saw from his words and vague gestures that nothing had been organized. No doubt he figured on some lucky accident as had come to his help during the first Bolshevik attempt in July.
Joseph Noulens, French ambassador, recalling October 22, 1917, in his Mémoires (1933).

The Provisional Government is completely powerless. Actually the bourgeoisie is ruling, but under the disguise of a fake coalition with the radical parties. The peasants are tired to wait for the land they were promised, and revolt, and there is the same discontent among all working classes throughout the country. The bourgeoisie can stay in power only by means of a civil war. Kornilov's method is the only way for it to secure its power . . . Our first action will be an immediate armistice on all fronts . . .

Leon Trotsky speech in Petrograd, October 1917.

I don't think it is funny when I see how the Allies put all their bets, ludicrously, on . . . Kerenski, Savinkov, Kaledin etc., who are unpopular and have no real strength. It seems to me a lack of political feeling and common sense to support these men without noticing that they no longer represent anything any more except for a few widows, bourgeois and functionaries . . .

Jacques Sadoul, French captain, recalling October 24, 1917, In Notes on the Bolshevik Revolution *(1919).*

The main operation started at two o'clock in the morning. Small groups of soldiers, usually with a core of armed workers or sailors, led by a commissar, occupied simultaneously or one after the other the railroad stations, the main electricity plant, the arsenals and silos, the water works, the palace bridge, the national bank, the large printing offices, and took control of the telegraph office and the post office.

Leon Trotsky recalling conditions on October 25, 1917, Historie de la Révolution *(1934).*

One could eat in the restaurants, but preferably in the back rooms . . . Walls and fences were covered with placards warning the population not to demonstrate. But already new leaflets came out announcing the victory of the revolution. There had been no time to post them and they were being distributed from automobiles. These papers had just come from the printing office and still smelled of fresh ink . . . Cautiously and still lacking self-confidence the armed worker establishes order in the capital he has conquered for himself.

Leon Trotsky recalling conditions on October 25, 1917, Historie de la Révolution.

First, measures must be taken for the realization of peace . . . We shall offer to all peoples of the warring nations peace on the basis of Soviet conditions: No annexations, no reparations, self-determination of the peoples. At the time we shall make public all secret pacts and declare them invalid . . . The government asks all governments and peoples of the belligerent countries to conclude an armistice immediately . . .

From Lenin's speech from the second Congress of the Soviets in Moscow, October 25, 1917.

Every revolution is risky, but our chances of success are excellent. It has been prepared in all details . . . Almost the whole army has been won over. The masses of the peasants will be on our side because of the surrender of the large estates . . . One sweep of the broom was sufficient to chase from power those mediocre and lifeless people. They have lost the trust of the democracy forever. It is regrettable of course, that the Mensheviks abstained from voting. But they had asked for too much . . . It is very annoying that Kerenski was not arrested the day before yesterday when it was easy. This half-crazy man will make trouble which will be easy to overcome but which will prolong the crisis.

Leon Trotsky to Jacques Sadoul, October 25, 1917, in Moscow, in Sadoul's Birth of the U.S.S.R. *(1946).*

Leon Trotsky (Lev Davidovich Bronstein), Russian revolutionary. Photo courtesy of the New York Public Library.

What happened then probably took place during the following morning which was hardly separated from the last day by a sleepness night. [Lenin] looked tired. He smiled and said: "The transition from living in hiding and the fear of Pereverzev [the former minister of justice] to power is too sudden—I am dizzy." He added, in German, "I don't know why" . . . After this one personal remark that I heard from him in connection with our assumption of power we simply reverted to our daily business.

Leon Trotsky recalling events of October 26, 1917, Lénine (1925).

I remember that one morning, a day or two days after the coup, I entered a room of the Smol'nyj [a monastery turned into a girls' school] where I met Vladimir Il'ic [Lenin], Lev Davidovic [Trotsky] and, I believe Dzerzhinsky, Joffe and many others. They all had a grey-greenish complexion, the color of people who have not slept, deep-set eyes and dirty collars. The room was contaminated with tobacco smoke . . . Someone sat at a table, next to him a group of people waiting for orders. Lenin and Trotsky were surrounded. It seemed to me instructions were passed on as in a dream. There was something somnambulant, something moonstruck in the motions, in the words. For a minute I thought I myself was asleep when I saw all that, and that the revolution would fail unless "they" got a good night of sleep and put on clean collars . . .

Mrs. Trotsky's recollection, in Leon Trotsky's Histoire de la Révolution.

No congratulations came in from anywhere. As much as the Berlin Government was ready to flirt with the Bolsheviks, it sent a hostile radio message from Nauen . . . But if Berlin and Vienna vacillated between their hatred of the revolution and their hope for an advantageous peace, all other countries, not only the belligerents, but also the neutrals, expressed in their various languages the feelings and thoughts of the ruling classes in old Russia that had just been toppled by us. In this chorus, the Eiffel tower was particularly prominent in its furious outbursts. It even started to speak Russian, apparently hoping to reach the conscience of the Russian people in this manner. When I read the radio messages from Paris, I sometimes had the illusion Clemenceau was sitting in person on top of the tower. I knew him well

enough as a journalist to recognize if not his style, but his spirit . . .

Leon Trotsky early November 1917, Histoire de la Révolution.

The following people are to be shot, according to our lists: All cadets, all policemen, the representatives of the old regime and—regardless who they are—princes and counts in all the prison camps of Moscow, all gaols and enclosures.

F.E. Dzerzhinsky, head of the Cheka (secret police), shortly after its establishment on December 7, 1917.

I am no prophet. But one thing is sure, the state of capitalism and free trade, represented, for instance until recently by England, this state is dying. The future state will monopolise everything, buy everything, sell everything. Inevitably, the development of the world will lead to socialism through various transitional stages, various phases of a trend which is striving for one goal . . . In Germany or France where the old structures are much more durable, it will be much harder to start a revolution. But if a socialist regime would be established in France or Germany, it would have an easier time to stay in power . . . One great truth cannot be overlooked: the old world cannot exist much longer . . . All one can say against the state as an entrepreneur has not prevented, not held up a development following its own rules.

Lenin to Ludovic Naudeau, correspondent of Le Temps, around December 1917, in Les Densons de Chaos Russe (1921).

I shall never forget the first dinner with the Russians. I was sitting between Joffe and Sokol'nikov, now the commissary for finances. Across from me the working man who obviously had trouble with the various parts of the tableware. He tried this and that . . . but used the fork only to clean his teeth . . . Next to Prince Hohenlohe a peasant, a typically Russian sight with long gray curls and a primeval forest-type beard. He caused the servants to smile just once when he was offered red or white wine and he inquired which of the two was the stronger one, as that one would be his preference.

General Max Hoffmann, German negotiator at Brest-Litovsk, Der Krieg (1923).

The trenches were almost empty. Nobody dared to mention even the possibility of continuing the war. Peace, peace at any cost! . . . Thus, there was not the slightest shadow of a difference of opinion between Vladimir Il'ic [Lenin] and myself about the impossibility of a revolutionary war.

Leon Trotsky on negotiations with the Germans at Brest-Litovsk, Lénine.

[Trotsky's] face showed clearly that he would have much rather put a quick and thorough end to these very disagreeable negotiations by throwing a few hand grenades across the green table if this would have been in accordance with his total political concept . . . A Munich friend had already told me that next to Lenin, Trotsky had the best head among the Bolshevik leaders. Since I knew that Trotsky was especially proud of his dialectics I was all the more resolved to avoid anything that could have provided him with material for agitation among the German socialists.

Richard von Kuehlmann, German foreign secretary, at Brest-Litovsk, Memoirs (1948).

Kuehlmann had a better head than Czernin [leader of the Austrian delegation], and, I believe than the other diplomats I had occasion to meet. One noticed he has character . . . and a good portion of sarcasm, not only toward us—where he met with resistance—but also toward his allies. When the problem of occupied territories was discussed, Kuehlmann gave himself some airs and said, raising his voice: "Thank God, we in Germany have no occupied territory!" Whereupon Czernin shrank and turned green in the face, for it was probably he whom Kuehlmann had in mind.

Leon Trotsky, Ma Vie (My Life) (1930).

General Hoffmann, on the other hand, lent a refreshing character to the conference. He showed no sympathy for deceitful diplomacy and on several occasions put his soldier's boot right on the negotiating table. As far as we were concerned, we never doubted for a second that the only reality to be taken seriously amidst all this talk was Hoffmann's boot.

Leon Trotsky negotiating at Brest-Litovsk, Ma Vie.

When I, replying to Hoffmann's usual attacks, without second thoughts mentioned the German government General Hoffmann interrupted me furiously, in a hoarse voice: "I do not represent here the German government, but the High Command of the German army!" I answered that I was not authorized to judge the relations between the government of the German Empire and its High Command, but only to negotiate with the government. Kuehlmann, gritting his teeth, took note of my declaration and agreed.

Leon Trotsky at Brest-Litovsk, Ma Vie.

We, the sailors of the Black Sea Fleet, are worried about the welfare of the families of those comrades who fell in the heroic fight for the freedom of our people on January 27, 28 and 29. We are dedicating to them a commemoration to provide support for them. We hope that the population will show up in great numbers on our cruisers. In order that they may deposit their gifts without reservation we implore the association of thieves not to go into action in the course of this night.

Notice in the Odessa newspapers, early January 1918, referring to the riots of January 1917.

The association of thieves is ready to participate in this splendid action of relief and human solidarity organized by our glorious sailors, and promises explicitly that no searching will take place during the night of January 31.

Answering notice in the Odessa newspapers, January 1918.

These posters showing the number of the ballot box in large letters are obviously meant for the uneducated people. The posters of the Bolsheviks are red: "Vote for Number four; then you will have bread! land! peace!" The pale blue posters of the cadets are more moderate. The Cossacks have white placards with the number one. And at every corner, at the squares, in the parks there are gatherings of Bolshevik soldiers, talking bombastically, shouting, and raging with furious voices.

Louise Patin, about the election campaign for the Constituent Assembly that convened in January 1918, Journal d'une française.

This telegram from Commissar Karelin to the palace officer Colonel Kobylinskij advised that the people had no longer the means to maintain the Imperial family. The Soviets could only supply soldiers' rations, housing, heating and lighting. This telegram that arrived at Tobol'sk on February 23 said further that from now on the Imperial family would have to pay for its upkeep and could not spend more than 600 roubles per person monthly.

Nicolas Sokoloff, account of February 1918 at Tobol'sk where the Imperial family had been moved. In his Enquête judiciaire sur l'assassinat *(1929).*

Though [Lenin] is an atheist he has no qualms to maintain certain religious ceremonies—which was a surprise in the beginning. One does not exterminate religion by preventing millions of peasants who have just been proletarised from making the sign of the cross in front of an icon, and from greeting the pope, but one has to discontinue the religious instruction of children and explain to them the stupidity of idolatry.

Henri Guilbeaux, recalling events of February 1918, Authentic Portrait of Lenin *(1924).*

In spite of all the insults and the damage I and my people have suffered form our former friends I cannot deny my purely human sympathy to the family of the Tsar, and if it were in my power, I would do all possible to see to it that the Russian Imperial family would meet with a secure and dignified future. But under the circumstances direct help is impossible, and any step of mine or my government would only worsen the fate of the imperial family . . .

Emperor William II, letter to the king of Denmark (also a relative of Tsar Nicholas), March 17, 1918.

Is a great new step in human government coming from the sad travail of Russia? Unless Western Allies comprehend significance of Bolshevism, they'll not only never lick Germany, but will have internal trouble themselves. This war is ending, but there may be a worse one ahead.

H.V. O'Brien, diary entry, May 5, 1918, Wine, Women and War *(1926).*

While we dream over dreadfulness of such things as *Lusitania,* busy Boche goes about his propaganda. Trotsky once ran a newspaper in N.Y. The bitterest Bolsheviks learned their class hatred in sweat shops of the East Side. They know—or think they know—

the U.S. Derision for our expressed purpose in fighting for Democracy and oppressed people.

H.V. O'Brien, diary entry, May 9, 1918, Wine, Women and War.

One has to make oneself as inconspicuous as possible. More than ever I shall go out in an old hat and a very dark overcoat whose fur collar I have folded inside. I am freezing all the more around my ears. I had given my worn boots to my servant maid, but under these circumstances I have taken them back. Because I am not interested to be molested by these brutal fellows of the Red Guards who . . . may not be shy about undressing me in public, if they consider my dress too luxurious.

Paulette Pax, French actress, Journal d'une comédienne *(1919).*

In the streets one sees refugees of the aristocracy in strange outfits. Mostly they are dressed only in pants and a shirt, their head is covered by their hairs. Fortunately it is oppressively hot now. On the other hand, soldiers who only yesterday were running around in rags, suddenly appear in elegant suits, white flannel trousers, wearing officers' dolmans, hussar jackets and good shoes.

Louise Patin, summer of 1918, in Journal d'une française.

Externally, the Tsar was always quiet. Every day he went for a walk in the garden with his children. His son could not walk, he had a bad leg. The wife of the Tsar never went to the garden but only to the outdoor stairs next to the fence around the house . . . The Tsar seemed to be in good health. He had no white hair, but his wife had; she also had lost a lot of weight. The children behaved as usual and joked with the guards. It was prohibited to talk to them.

Witness Medvedev, describing the Tsar at Ekaterinburg, June 1918, in Nicolas Sokoloff, Legal Inquiry into the Assassination *(1929).*

The Red Army units were unsufficient and we had to anticipate the occupation of the city of Ekaterinburg within three days. Under the circumstances the local Soviet decided to shoot the Romanovs without waiting for a verdict. The shooting and disposal of the bodies was entrusted to the commandant of the house and some reliable Communist workers . . . in order not to give to the counter-revolution the possibility to exploit the ignorance of the masses by providing them with "relics" of the Ex-Tsar.

P.M. Bikow, Les derniers jours des Romanov *(1931).*

The Tsar was carrying his son. Behind them came Medvedev and the Letts, the ten men who lived below and whom Jurovskij had brought from the Ceka. Two of them carried rifles. After the prisoners had entered the room (No. 2), they were made to stand as follows: The Tsar in the middle, at his right the Tsarevich sitting on a chair, and further to the right Botkin. Behind them stood the Tsarina, her daughters and all the others. Derjabin saw through the window that Jurovskij [the commandant] said something and moved his hand. Klescev assured he had heard him say to the Tsar—and I well remember it—"Nicholas Aleksandrovic, your people have tried to save you, but they did not succeed. It is our duty to shoot you!" At this moment, some shots rang. They were all pistol shots. After the first shots one could hear the groaning and the crying of female voices. The victims fell, one after the other. First the Tsar, after him the Tsarevich. Demidova [the lady-in-waiting] tried to escape and to protect herself with a pillow. I do not know if she was wounded by the bullets or not.

Nicolas Sokoloff, reports on the assassination of the Imperial Russian family, July 16, 1918 in Ekaterinburg, Legal Inquiry into the Assassination.

Well, nobody would have stood guard in this cursed assignment had he known that these beasts who acted like bandits, planned to rob their prisoners, to murder and burn them. The horde that had the power perpetrated this deed in a state of intoxication, and then they were the first to be afraid.

The worker Zlokcov, member of the execution squad, as reported in Nicolas Sokoloff, Legal Inquiry into the Assassination.

This execution of the imperial family was necessary, not only to frighten the enemy, to daze and deprive him of any hope, but also to wake up our own people and to show them that there was no way back, and that what was in store for them was victory or total destruction. Among the intellectuals of the party there were, it is true, some misgivings and some shaking of heads. But the mass of the workers and soldiers had no doubts for a minute; they would not have understood or approved of any other decision. Lenin felt that.

Leon Trotsky, Lénine.

We have come across some unheard of sabotage among the functionaries. Therefore, we had to be merciless and to extinguish all those who were convicted of belonging to the organisation of the White Guards. It was necessary to demobilise completely demoralized military units . . . The red terror was nothing but the expression of the unbreakable will of the poor peasants and the proletariat to nip in the bud the slightest attempt of an uprising against us.

F.E. Dzerzhinsky, head of the Cheka (secret police), in Izvestija *("News"), official government newspaper in Moscow, February 18, 1919.*

15. The West: Germany's Last Great Offensive and Failure: March to November 1918

THE HISTORICAL CONTEXT

By the end of 1917, the Allies finally established a somewhat closer coordination between their various commands. A Supreme War Council was established, consisting of the leading Allied statesmen and their military advisers. But dickering between the French and British commands as to their respective fronts, the use of their reserves, etc., continued. It was clear to Haig and Pétain that a major blow could be expected in the west by the increased German armies, and that as long as the American contribution was limited to a few divisions, they would not be able to launch a major offensive themselves. In fact, there was talk about 1919 being the year of decision.

LUDENDORFF'S MARCH OFFENSIVE

What Ludendorff planned was one gigantic attack and breakthrough in the spring of 1918, before the pinch of the blockade and the arrival of a large American contingent would turn the table in favor of the Allies. The attack was expected, but not where Ludendorff concentrated it—on the southern part of the British sector—and not with the intensity with which the blow was delivered.

The British armies along the Somme consisted of 26 divisions and fewer than 1,000 pieces of heavy artillery. They stood against 71 German divisions with 2,500 heavy-caliber guns. British general Julian Byng's Third Army and Hubert Gough's Fifth Army faced three German armies, including Otto von Below's Seventeenth, which had just returned from Caporetto. All troops had been carefully trained for the new assault tactics so successfully employed by General Oskar von Huitier, which ran contrary to the trench warfare tactics used during the last years: the bypassing of strong points, massive infiltration and short but heavy artillery barrages. The attack began on March 21, after a bombardment by 6,000 guns and a heavy gas attack. Heavy fog helped the Germans, and their armies drove deep into the British lines on a 40-mile sector. British reserves were inadequate, since Lloyd George, distrusting Haig's belief in bloody offensives, had retained large forces in England. Péronne, Bapaume, Chauny and Noyon were taken, and the German armies advanced 14 miles in four days, more than any attack had achieved since 1914.

Sudden heavy explosions took place in Paris which were first blamed on air bombardments, until it was learned that the Germans were employing special long-range guns to shell the city. There were still misunderstandings within the Allied command: the French suspected that the main concern of the British was the securing of the Channel ports for eventual escape, while the British thought that Pétain was more interested in safeguarding his capital than in helping the Allied front. In this crisis, Ferdinand Foch was named first coordinator of the French-British forces, and shortly thereafter he was made commander in chief of all Allied armies in France. Actually, the national commanders—Haig, King Albert and the commander in chief of the American Expeditionary Force, John Joseph Pershing retained some of their control nevertheless, and in many cases Foch had to get results by persuasion where he could not command; but at least a unified military leadership had been established.

Amiens was threatened, but the stubborn resistance of the British frustrated the German attack. After two weeks of heavy fighting, the

British soldiers at St. Quentin, 1918. Photo courtesy of the National Archives.

breakthrough had been patched up and Amiens was still in Allied possession. Still, the British had lost 160,000 men—including 90,000 prisoners—and the French, 70,000, while the Germans had captured a great amount of war materiel and had retaken a good part of the Noyon salient which they had given up the year before. Their second main assault started on the northern front, south of Ypres, just a few days later on a 12-mile stretch. Most of the opposing British divisions had not recovered from the Somme fighting, and after a few days, Haig had thrown in his last reserves. A Portuguese division ordered into one gap gave way very quickly.

Although the German troops were strafed by hundreds of British planes, they captured most of the Messines Ridge and took Armentières. In three weeks of bitter struggle, the fighting extended into the lowlands along the coast. With the help of seven French divisions, the attackers were repulsed in the end but not before Haig had issued his "Backs to the Wall" order, prohibiting any further retreat. The British divisions were exhausted, and the Allies had suffered more than 350,000 casualties in the first six weeks of the great offensive. But the Germans had lost almost as many and could not take full advantage of the strategic situation for lack of reserves. Before the next blow fell, reinforcements were rushed to France from Italy, Macedonia, Palestine and across the Channel.

GERMANY'S MAY AND JUNE OFFENSIVES

Ludendorff struck again in an offensive known as the Third Battle of the Aisne, which started at the end of May. Forty-two divisions attacked between Soissons and Rheims, and the French were driven back 13 miles on the first day of attack. The Chemin des Dames, which the French had won in such hard fighting a year earlier, was retaken and Soissons was occupied. Within a few days, German troops were again at the Marne. A huge salient, at some points more than 30 miles deep, had been punched into the French lines, and the Germans were at Château-Thierry, only 56 miles from Paris.

It seems that Ludendorff had not expected such a spectacular success. The initial purpose in this attack had been to draw French units from the Flanders front where he intended to launch his main offensive. Now he decided to push on in the south towards Compiègne. His first assault was met by the French; the American second and third divisions joined the fighting at Château-Thierry and repulsed German units attempting to cross the Marne. The Americans were inexperienced but good fighters, and they learned quickly; their very appearance lifted the morale of the battle-weary French troops.

But the situation of the Allied armies was close to desperate. German troops were as close to Paris as they had been in 1914, and the

John J. ("Black Jack") Pershing, commander of the American Expeditionary Force.

Germans had a clear numerical superiority: By June 1, there were more than 200 German divisions on the western front, against 162 Allied, and about 1,640,000 infantrymen against 1,450,000 Allied. Clemenceau, Lloyd George and Italian Premier Vittorio Orlando sent most urgent appeals to Washington, asking for one hundred American divisions, almost four million men! In the meantime, the French and British wished to fill their decimated units with American troops, while General John J. "Black Jack" Pershing insisted on having American troops fighting as a separate army under his own command.

The fourth German offensive, which attempted to expand the newly won Marne base and link it up with the great Amiens salient in the north, started on June 9. General von Huitier's Eighteenth Army, again employing his infiltration tactics, gained about six miles but did not reach his objectives. The main and last great offensive was started on July 15 and became known as the Second Battle of the Marne. In this ultimate German effort, Ludendorff threw 52 divisions into the battle east and west of Rheims. In the eastern section, the Germans got nowhere, stopped by the French under General Henri Gouraud. In the west, however, the Germans crossed the Marne and set up bridgeheads four miles deep. This was the high tide of the great offensive, which had taken as much ground as the first huge drive in 1914. But it was less dangerous as the exhausted German troops had overextended themselves. Foch replied with incessant artillery fire and bombings, which all but interrupted German supply routes across the Marne.

While Clemenceau was furious about the German advance, Foch never lost control; by July 18, the offensive was called off and all German units again retreated north across the Marne. The slogan of the day, *Ils ne passeront pas* ("They shall not pass"), had been enforced.

U.S. PARTICIPATION. ALLIED COUNTERATTACKS

Only three American divisions had participated in the great battle, but by mid-July, 29 U.S. divisions were in France or on their way across the Atlantic. The convoy system transported 250,000 to 300,000 men each month. By the end of August, 35 divisions were in France; by the end of September, 39; by the end of October, 42. In late June, German rifle strength in the west fell below that of the Allies, and the trend continued. In their great western offensives, the Germans had inflicted almost a million casualties on the Allies, including 225,000 prisoners. But they had not reached their main objectives, and now it was Foch's turn. His counterattack began promptly on July 18. It was aimed at the salients the Germans had pushed into the Allied lines. The French Tenth Army under General Charles Mangin attacked the Aisne-Marne salient, with eight American and some British divisions participating. In almost three weeks of heavy fighting, the salient was reduced, Soissons was retaken and Ludendorff's plans for an attack on the British were frustrated.

The next salient was the bulge at Amiens and Noyon. After well-concealed and careful preparation, the British Fourth Army under General Henry Rawlinson, supported by French units, attacked the apex of the big salient on August 8, employing 450 tanks and almost 400 airplanes. A Canadian corps led the 12-mile advance in which the bulge was flattened out and the threat to Amiens eliminated. About 30,000 prisoners were taken, and the Allies had inflicted higher casualties than they had suffered. The attack had been an unqualified Allied success, but the German forces had not been decisively defeated. Yet Ludendorff had good reason to call August 8 the "black day of the German Army." For the first time, it had shown weaknesses. Discipline was faltering and units moving in from the eastern front showed signs of Communist indoctrination, undermining the morale of the western troops. At a conference at German General Headquarters, the opinion prevailed that the German government should try to end the war at a favorable moment. But this moment did not materialize. The next Allied attack came on August 20, with both the British and the French attacking German flanks at Arras and in the Soissons area: The French reached the Oise, the British made major gains around Arras, and the Australians took Peronne. Ludendorff withdrew his troops by about 10 miles on a 50-mile front, but the Allied attacks did not stop. The retreats were executed in good order, supplies were evacuated,

Two-man U.S. tank, made by the Ford Motor Co. Photo courtesy of the National Archives, Washington, D.C.

bridges were destroyed and an area of scorched earth was left behind. At the same time, the fortifications along the Hindenburg line were strengthened, and that is where the advancing Allies met the main German defense system on September 25.

Meanwhile, U.S. troops had operated for the first time as a separate army. They had launched an offensive against the St. Mihiel salient, south of Verdun, still an important strong-point for the Germans, as it protected an area of iron mines, two important railroad lines and the fortress of Metz. But the Germans no longer had the manpower to defend the area, and Pershing's 14 divisions—assembled from all over France—supported by French and British tanks, overwhelmed the German defenders, mostly very young or very old men. About 1,400 planes, the largest air force ever assembled, joined in the attack under the command of Colonel William (Billy) Mitchell, though most of them were flown by French and British pilots. The offensive could not fail, particularly since the Germans had already begun to evacuate the area, but they lost more than 16,000 Allied prisoners and 440 guns.

The tremendous successes of August and September encouraged Foch to revise his plans and deliver the final blow immediately instead of waiting for the next year. His new slogan was *Tout le monde à la bataille!* ("The whole world into the battle!").

THE ALL-OUT ALLIED OFFENSIVE

The strategy for the final attack was a huge pincer movement consisting of an American-French thrust through the Argonne—in a northern direction—and a British-French thrust eastward toward Cambrai and Lille. These offensives would bring under Allied control vital railway junctions on which the German armies had depended. For this gigantic battle, 29 American divisions were available for combat—each almost twice the size of a French or British division—plus 60 British, 102 French and 12 Belgian divisions. They were opposed by 193 German and four Austrian divisions, but many of these were below their normal strength. Only a few American divisions fought under French or British command; all others served in the First American Army and the newly created Second American Army under Generals Hunter Liggett and Robert Bullard, holding a front of about 90 miles. The great drives began on September 26, but the advance was slower than expected. The American First Army got into heavy fighting in the Argonne forest and the hills of Montfaucon, and by October 3 had fought their way only through half the forest. Simultaneously, the British attacked with 40 divisions in Picardy and the Belgians along the coast one day later. By October 5, the British had penetrated the Hindenburg line with the German armies retreating slowly, delaying all advances with machine guns and other rear-guard actions. By stubborn resistance, they managed to give little at the two flanks, yielding more at the center, thus shortening their line of defense. Some of the hardest fighting was still to come, but Ludendorff knew on September 28 that he was beaten and told Hindenburg that an immediate armistice was necessary. Apparently his nerves failed him at the moment when all Allied armies attacked simultaneously in the west and news came that his Bulgaria ally had withdrawn from the war and had asked for an armistice. The civil government in Berlin fell, and the new chancellor, Prince Max von Baden, approached President Wilson on October 4, asking for an armistice. But the fighting did not yet stop.

The British continued to advance throughout October, taking Ostend, Zeebrugge, Lille and Bruges by the middle of the month. The American advance through the Argonne was much slower and extremely costly. Pershing relieved some of the green divisions by sending more experienced units from the St. Mihiel sector and replacing a number of generals who had not performed to his satisfaction. The attack in the Argonne region cost more than 100,000 American casualties, but by the end of the month, Pershing had reached open country, and the Hindenburg line was broken on a wide front. From now on, rapid progress was made, and on November 11, the day of the armistice, the American Forty-Second (Rainbow) Division, under General

Brigadier General Douglas MacArthur in St. Benoit Chateau, France. Photo courtesy of the National Archives, Washington, D.C.

Douglas MacArthur, stood in front of Sedan, the Belgians had taken Ghent and were advancing to the Scheldt River, the British were at Maubeuge, and the Canadians were at Mons. While some sporadic fighting continued, most of it died on this day. Soldiers crawled out of their trenches and celebrated—victorious or defeated—the end of the four years' horror. Only one small part of the German army remained undefeated: In northern Rhodesia, General Paul von Lettow-Vorbeck's small contingent, which had eluded the British for four years, learned of the armistice on November 23. He then surrendered.

COLLAPSE OF GERMANY AND ITS ALLIES

There were many reasons for the collapse of the seemingly invincible German army, all converging in the final months of the war: the shortage of food and materials caused by four years of British and British-American blockade; the huge losses in man power and war materiel encountered fighting in France, Russia, Italy, the Balkans and the Near East; and the antiquated structure of German society, built on an unbridgeable gap between the ruling classes and the masses, who had to make all the sacrifices. In addition, at the very end, the effect of the Bolshevik peace propaganda undermined the morale of some army units and had a deadly effect on the navy personnel, which had been kept idle at the ports ever since the battle of Jutland in 1916. On Octo-

Group of German soldiers. The man in the bottom row far left is Adolf Hitler. Photo courtesy of the National Archives, Washington, D.C.

ber 29, mutinies of the sailors stationed in Wilhelmshaven and Kiel began, and by November 3, Kiel was in their hands. All last-minute efforts to democratize the German government in order to prevent a wholesale revolution came too late. Ludendorff resigned on October 27. When the armistice with Germany was signed, the German army still stood on foreign soil, save for some Alsacian villages the French had held throughout the war. After the armistice was signed, German troops were withdrawn, not only from France and Belgium, but also from Romania, Austria, Turkey and, finally, Russia. Allied troops also withdrew. Everybody was anxious to go home, and the withdrawal procedures worked much too slowly for some units. There were some mutinies in the American army camps in France. Some British and Canadian camps also mutinied, and in London a body of troops demonstrated against the secretary of war. The last German troops crossed the frontier of France on November 18 and the Belgian frontier on November 26. Strasbourg was occupied by the French on November 25, and British-American occupation of Germany began on December 1.

Germany's allies had collapsed more readily. Bulgaria had been the first to go. In December 1917, French general Marie-Louis Guillaumat had taken over the command of the Allied forces in the Balkans and reorganized the forces at Salonika. He prepared a great attack of 29 divisions, which began in September 1918 at Monastir-Doiran. Allied forces—Italians on the left, Serbians in the center, Greeks, French and British on the right—began an offensive all the way from Albania to the Struma River under the overall command of French marshal Franchet d'Esperey. The Bulgarians were badly equipped, and their German allies had no troops to spare. The Serbs in the center advanced almost 40 miles in a week and threatened to split the Bulgarian front wide open. The Bulgarians, who had tried for peace talks since June, now appealed for an armistice, which was concluded on September 30. The Allied armies then entered Romania, and the Serbs continued into their own country, taking Belgrade on November 1.

In Turkey, an armistice had been concluded on October 30, after British and French forces had taken Damascus, Beirut, Homs and Aleppo. and after the new sultan, Mohammed VI, had dismissed his Young Turk ministers and appealed to President Wilson.

Finally, the Habsburg Monarchy concluded an armistice with the Allies on November 3. All through the preceding summer, the empire had gone through a process of disintegration. Austrian troops were still fighting in Italy, France and Russia, but within these contingents Polish, Czech and Yugoslav legions were formed that went over to the Allies. National councils for the racial minorities in the empire were set up in Paris, London and in the provinces. These activities were welcomed by the Allies and by American secretary of state Robert Lansing, in accordance with the Wilsonian principle of self-determination for the peoples. In spite of all this, the Austrian army launched an offensive in Italy in June, crossing the Piave River; but it was unable to maintain its position and withdrew after losing about 100,000 men. After this, the army's morale deteriorated rapidly, and on September 15, the Vienna government appealed to Wilson to arrange for a peace conference. The plea was rejected by the U.S. president. Emperor Charles's attempts to reorganize the non-Hungarian part of the monarchy as a federal state in which the various nationalities were to enjoy complete self-government came too late. On October 21, the Czechoslovaks declared their independence. A few days later, the Italians finally attacked on a front from the Adriatic to the Trentino. The key position on the Monte Grappa was defended by the Austrians for a week, but their lines on the lower Piave collapsed, and the Italians advanced to Vittorio Veneto, taking about 300,000 unresisting prisoners. The rest of the Habsburg forces retired from the battlefront and went home, while in the first days of November the Italians occupied Trieste and Fiume. At Zagreb on October 29, an independent Yugoslavia was proclaimed. The Austro-Hugarian Empire offered no further resistance.

CHRONICLE OF EVENTS

1917:

November 27: A Supreme War Council is established by the Allies, including General Ferdinand Foch, Henry Wilson, General Tasker H. Bliss and General Luigi Cadorna.

1918:

March 21: Beginning of the great German offensive on the west.

March 26: At a conference at Doullens, General Ferdinand Foch is appointed to coordinate Allied operations on the western front.

Ferdinand Foch, commander of the Allied armies, in 1918. Photo courtesy of the New York Public Library.

April 9–29: Battle of the Lys, south of Ypres. Germans storm Messines ridge and take Armentières.

April 14: General Foch is named commander in chief of the Allied armies in France.

April 21: Manfred von Richthofen, German air fighter ace, is shot down.

May 27: Ludendorff's third offensive begins.

May 29: Germans take Soissons.

May 30: Germans reach again the Marne River, only 37 miles from Paris.

June 4: American forces at Château-Thierry break the German advance.

June 9–14: Battle of the Matz. Ludendorff attempts to join his salients at Noyon and Soissons, but is stopped.

July: Allied air aces James Thomas McCudden, William Avery (Billy) Bishop and Edward Mannock are shot down.

July 15–August 7: Second Battle of the Marne. German troops cross the river, but thereafter make little progress.

July 18: Foch orders a counterattack in which nine American divisions take part.

August 2: French units retake Soissons.

August 8–11: Battle of Amiens. The British attack with 450 tanks. August 8 is Ludendorff's "black day for the German Army."

August 21–September 3: Second battles of the Somme and Arras. British continue their advance.

August 27: British take Roye.

August 28: British take Bapaume and Noyon.

August 31: British take Péronne.

September 12–13: American forces attack the St. Mihiel salient on both sides and occupy it, taking 15,000 prisoners.

September 26–October 15: Battles of the Argonne and of Ypres.

October 1–2: British take St. Quentin, Lens and Armentières.

October 15: American forces have broken through the Argonne region.

October 18: In their sweep in the northern sector, British troops have taken Ostend, Zeebrugge, Roubaix, Lille and Douai.

October 19: British take Bruges.
October 27: The German government accepts Ludendorff's resignation.
November 1: British take Valenciennes.

November 10: American units have reached Sedan.
November 11: Hostilities cease on the western front.

Eyewitness Testimony

Now in "extreme danger zone." Ship zig-zags continually. Blue lights. All noise muffled. Orders to sleep in clothes. These U-boats a damned nuisance!

H.V. O'Brien, American officer, on crossing the Atlantic, January 13, 1918, in his diary, published as Wine, Women and War *(1926).*

Country liveliest in France . . . and le vin de Saumur not hard to take. Get a great hate for the Boche. To think what he's done to this pleasant land and gentle people. The faces so sad—but so unfailingly cheerful. And so much black (mourning). Makes the throat ache, to go down the street.

H.V. O'Brien, diary, January 22, 1918, near Saumur, France. Wine, Women and War.

Newspapers full of peace talk—none whatsoever among the military . . . Exceedingly strict discipline. Every detail of life regulated. Like German prisoners I saw today. Stolidly docile—animal-like. Hard to believe they ever think. Therefore—good soldiers. No brutes—automata, rather. Pitiful, a little nauseating.

H.V. O'Brien, diary, January 25, 1918. Wine, Women and War.

About one awakened by wail of sirens. Guns going hell-bent by time I got to window, and colored lights of defense planes high in sky. Flash of bursting shrapnel plainly visible. Bomb explosions distant at first, but one presently fell one block away. Terrific racket. No special alarm among people. Streets and roofs crowded with gapers. Funny to see wearers of the Medaille Militaire . . . scuttle for shelter like rabbits when the "alerte" (warning signal) starts. Their contention that they're reasonable beings sounds reasonable . . . Sleepy long before it was over . . .

H.V. O'Brien, diary, January 30, 1918, in Paris. Wine, Women and War.

Reports of strikes in Austria, and hopes of early peace. Funny how notions change. Back we drooled about "democracy" and "glory." Like Burgundy wine, that stuff doesn't stand a sea voyage. Most of the people whom the papers squeak about being "eager for the front" about as eager for the small pox.

H.V. O'Brien, diary, February 2, 1918. Wine, Women and War.

Much-touted German drive may never come off. Probably just feint, designed to scare Allies into negotiating peace. If the bluff's called, he may lay down his cards. . . . Maybe end before summer. But no such notion officially. Extent of our preparations staggering. Tremendous lot of matériel delivered already. Heinie will never be able to stand against us.

H.V. O'Brien, diary, February 7, 1918. Wine, Women and War.

The war will be won all right. But *we* won't win it. We'll merely help finish it sooner. Humility still our cue . . . Blunders, of course. But my guess no worse than what the Allies went through at beginning—or Germans, either.

H.V. O'Brien, diary, February 15, 1918. Wine, Women and War.

Not same thrill at Bonaparte's tomb I got ten years ago. Seem to feel differently about military men now—especially generals. Makes me realize how much gilt has chipped off war's pictureframe. M— quoted Grant: "never was a good war or a bad peace." That would be treason at home. Nice thing about being here is you can be treasonable in safety.

H.V. O'Brien, diary, February 17, 1918, Paris. Wine, Women and War.

French student officers took a couple of days. We have more ingenuity, more open minds and greater initiative. They find us dumb at mathematics. We find them impractical, wasting time terribly on nonessentials. Humor and exasperation on both sides. Anyway, we're learning a lot—and so are they. Fair exchange.

H.V. O'Brien, diary, February 17, 1919. Wine, Women and War.

One of these days Jerry Hun is going to learn something to his disadvantage. Yanks hate war. Crab incessantly. Anxious to go home, so all for hurry-up in Kultur-extermination. French joyful over prospects and Germans massing their dirtiest players—the "butchers"—for us. When it reaches the rough-and-tumble, there'll be some startled Jerries. We're good imitators. Fritz will see some stuff that'll make him think he's been to the stockyards.

H.V. O'Brien, diary, March 2, 1918. Wine, Women and War.

Dinner with French officers . . . One of them . . . his home, up North, completely sacked by Germans.

Machine-gun crew, June 1918. Photo courtesy of the National Archives, Washington, D.C.
37 мм Gun

"I suppose they carted off everything?" I said. "No", he answered, with a little smile. "They took very little—the French had already been there." There's a good "atrocity" story.

H.V. O'Brien, diary, March 2, 1918. Wine, Women and War.

Job of censoring enlisted men's letters . . . Three classes: (1) To best girl. Magnifying hardship. Full of vainglory and heroics. (2) To boy friend. Nonchalant, sophisticated, bold comments on wine and women . . . Contemptuous of war and danger. Hard guy. (3) To mother. Usually brief. Laborious explanations and apologies for not writing oftener. Mostly truthful . . . Hardships glossed over and "we won't go up for months yet."

H.V. O'Brien, diary, March 8, 1918. Wine, Women and War.

No mail. When I'm old and feeble, sitting by fire telling lies to grandchildren, the postman will bring me the letters sent to me in France in 1918 . . . The war, alone, holds German Empire together. The extraneous menace removed, the whole fabric, if it doesn't disintegrate, ought to take on a cast far from military and imperialistic. Cling to faith in common people. In the end, they'll settle their fate—and ours. Regardless of the length of the war, or its outcome, Kaiserism is done for. Feel sure of that.

H.V. O'Brien, diary, March 10, 1918. Wine, Women and War.

Visit from [Newton D. Baker, Secretary of War]. Poked fingers in breech blocks and made usual helpless remarks of layman. Looked about as uncomfortable as he probably was. Gen. Pershing with him. Had the honor of saluting him. Seemed more interested in state of my buttons than soul. Generals get that way.

H.V. O'Brien, diary, March 13, 1918. Wine, Women and War.

Got a copy of *New Republic*, Pacifist leanings. Most of army has, too. War spirit in inverse ration to proximity of war. Quickest way to end it, put all journalists and politicians under arms. Leave peace arrangements to soldiers, under rank of Lieut. Make talkers fight and fighters talk.

H.V. O'Brien, diary, March 16, 1918. Wine, Women and War.

And all the squawk about "slackers" . . . No special virtue in being here. Most of us here because we are afraid to stay home—afraid of our women. It's the women who have made all the wars in history. But the draft-evador—he's not playing fair. Defaulted on the social contract, and ought to be made to pay up. Funny, he and "Conscientious Objector" unknown in France.

H.V. O'Brien, diary, March 1918. Wine, Women and War.

In quick, decisive succession blow after blow was struck until Château-Thierry had been overrun and

Paris seemed within grasp. The wedge, aimed to divide the north English front from the south French front, had almost penetrated and completed the separation of the two armies. For the Allies those were alarming, depressing days, full of fear lest Germany should after all achieve victory. In America anxiety was keen as one began to fear that we had arrived too late. In Germany an "I told you so" attitude prevailed among the officers. Never was one's temper as an American so tried as then when one had to listen to their tales of triumph, told with cynical, cold arrogance. The German people, more prejudiced, were none the less enthusiastic, grateful, but still anxious of ultimate success. Somehow they were not so sure that the glowing reports of the press concerning the victories achieved really spelled victory.

Conrad Hoffmann, In the Prison Camps of Germany (1918).

Even if checked in this push, Boche may dig in and trust to diplomacy and defeatist propaganda to get better terms. The German people must be fed up with promises. When Allies attack, ought to go through like stone through tissue paper hoop. Germans haven't failed yet, by a long shot, but in ticklish position. Caught between reinforced wings of French and British.

H.V. O'Brien, diary, March 27, 1918. Wine, Women and War.

What a dreadful sight is the cathedral of St. Quentin with its trembling crest raised above ruins piled mountain high, inside it the heavens looking down through the roof, which has been crushed to the very floor. A few poor stumps are all that is left of the buttresses and pillars of the cross-vault. The remains of marvellous rose-windows, splinters of stained-glass windows iridescent with colour, still stick here and there . . . The remnants of the ceiling painted absurdly as a starlit sky continue to blink stupidly down upon us in a few places, while next to it the real sky stretches blue and austere above the ruins of beautifully curved arches.

Otto Braun, letter to his father, on the way to the French front, April 4, 1918.

This terrain should stay the way it is . . . Every ruler, every leading statesman, every president of a nation should be shown this sight, instead of swearing an oath to hold up the constitution. There would be no more wars, from now till eternity.

Rudolf G. Binding, German writer, referring to a battlefield after the Siegfried offensive, April 4, 1918, in his war memoirs, Dies war das Mass (n.d.).

Too much "war to bitter end—Destroy Germany" talk. . . . That keeps war going . . . Our bitter-enders play directly into Junker hands. German people just about ready to quit. Great danger is our safe and sound jingoes in high place won't give the chance. Wilson is the boy. Incomparably, *the* statesman of the time. Vacillating, at times, but far-seeing. Germany can certainly thank God for him.

H.V. O'Brien, diary, April 7, 1918. Wine, Women and War.

With our backs to the wall, and believing in the justice of our cause, each one must fight to the end. The safety of our homes and the freedom of mankind depend alike upon the conduct of each one of us at the critical moment.

Field Marshal Sir Douglas Haig, Proclamation, April 12, 1918.

To poor, war and peace, all one. Merely suffer more dramatically, more suddenly, under guns than under crushing weight of "peaceful" industrialism. The dispossessed, the broken bodies, the numbed minds, in peace as in war—and fewer friendly hands to help.

H.V. O'Brien, diary, April 12, 1918. Wine, Women and War.

Busy Bertha still booming. Its chief objection—suddenness. Bang! Glass in windows goes out in fine spray, and cobblestones try to crawl over one another. Doesn't do much damage, though. Supposed to wreck Parisian morale. Doesn't. *Parigot* refuses even to get mad about it. The chief wrath seems to be against newspapers for calling it "Bertha" when there are so many nice French girls of that name.

H.V. O'Brien, diary, Paris, April 18, 1918. Wine, Women and War.

The completely devastated district around here—the old Somme line—the shelled villages, often entirely shot to pieces, have something about them that depresses one terribly . . . But do not think that I am complaining. When one sees here the horrors of war's devastation, one can only be thankful that this time our country was spared the unfettered fury,and can only want to go on fighting till the danger is over.

Otto Braun, letter to Julie V. from the French front, April 21, 1918.

We have got a big cellar, which is now being eagerly fortified. The 20th . . . got two direct hits in their column while marching yesterday. Today the dead still lay in the street, swimming in their blood. I wanted to go forward . . . but the Major forbade it, to my great annoyance; I do not feel at rest till I know the whole position.

Otto Braun, diary (last entry), at Marcelcave, France, April 27, 1918.

. . . made me think of British Tommy, with 32 wounds in him who wrote home: "Top hole and feeling fine." Also, by contrast, with letter from enlisted man at Souge, who described rain of machine gun bullets on his dugout as making noise like a kid running a stick along a picket fence. Five hundred miles from the nearest machine gun!

H.V. O'Brien, diary, April 17, 1918. Wine, Women and War.

We have reached the darkest hours of the War, and though the clouds have not yet lifted, though the rate of the German advance has already begun to slow down . . . The ordeal of Paris has been renewed by shelling from the German long-distance gun, the last and most sensational of German surprise-packets. These are indeed dark days, yet already lit by hopeful omens—the closer union of the Allies, the appointment of the greatest French military genius, General Foch, as Generalissimo of the Allied Forces, and his calm assurance that we have as yet lost "nothing vital."

Punch, London, April 1918.

Saw bunch German prisoners. Ferocity, bestiality, dreadful purposiveness with which we endow ensemble so completely lacking in individual. Man for man, as attractive as any one knows. Device of partisan journalists to photograph Hun just emerging from a week in line—preferably a repulsive one. Then say this is enemy "type." Lies. These prisoners notable in physique and intelligent in appearance.

H.V. O'Brien, diary, May 3, 1918. Wine, Women and War.

Humor of France its salvation. If Chamber becomes unruly, the President puts on his hat, as signal for *cloture*. In recent crisis . . . president reached for hat. Horrors! Not to be found. Fortunately, one of members had his. President clapped it on. Proved three or four sizes too large. Chamber gave one look and dissolved in laughter. Crisis averted!

H.V. O'Brien, diary, May 17, 1918. Wine, Women and War.

However great a man's faith in the strength of homeland forces, it was difficult to keep up hope during these days of the continued advance of the German armies in spite of the maximum efforts put forth by the Allied armies. It will not be easy to forget the anxiety of those days for all in America. How much greater must have been the concern of the prisoners of war interned in the enemy country.

Then the miracle occurred: A halt in the advance, in which our own American doughboys played no small part.

Conrad Hoffman, In the Prison Camps of Germany.

Pitiable spectacle of some of our best clergy trying to write foot-note to words of Christ about forgiveness of enemies. Church cutting sorry figure in this business. Incredible puerility of "Jesus never knowing Germans." Don't seem to grasp utter sterility of hate . . . Damned be he who tries to carry venom that has rotted entrails of this generation into as-yet sweet lives of the next!

H.V. O'Brien, diary, May 18, 1918. Wine, Women and War.

L'Humanité Socialist sheet—most interesting. May be cracked in its economics but at least trying to see beyond next week—which is more than any of our God-damned governments do. Representative of Manchester *Guardian* chased out of France—probably for suggesting we spend a few minutes thinking about what we're fighting for . . . Only country today which is unit, is Germany—through fear and repression only. In all the others, lion and lamb march together against common national foe. But remove foe, and the two will fly apart . . .

H.V. O'Brien, diary, May, 21, 1918. Wine, Women and War.

Just read, in *Lit. Digest*, eulogy of Liebknecht—"heroism tried and found true." On next page, de-

English women in a munitions factory, 1918. Photo courtesy of the National Archives, Washington, D.C.

nunciation of pacifists and defeatists in our midst. What's crime in an American is glorious in a German. Why the hell can't we fight a decent war without drooling hypocrisy all the time?

H.V. O'Brien, diary, May 22, 1918. Wine, Women and War.

. . . Col. S — [American] sprang this one: "Why is Germany like Holland?" Ans.: "Because it is a low-lying country damned on all sides". Insisted that I translate it to M. le Général. Explained that it was a non-translatable calembourg [pun] and that he would materially aid the Entente . . . by laughing when I did. He did . . .

H.V. O'Brien, diary, May 25, 1918. Wine, Women and War.

The ordeal of our men on the Western Front is terrible, but they have at least one grand and heart-ening stand-by in the knowledge that they have plenty of guns and no lack of shells behind them . . . Our mercurial Premier lays himself open to a good deal of legitimate criticism, but for this immense relief, unstinted thanks are due to his energy and the devoted labors of the munition workers, women as well as men.

Punch, London, June 1918.

Do folk who gabble about "imposing our will" etc. want to maintain garrisons of a couple of million in Germany for the rest of time? Do they think the capture of Berlin would change the German heart . . . And the "teaching a lesson" nonsense. Was Wilhelm deterred by the fate of Napoleon? Will future Kriegsherren be frightened by his? Nix.

H.V. O'Brien, diary, June 4, 1918. Wine, Women and War.

Curious that most anathemized man to-day is quiet dreamer Nietzsche. They say words accomplish nothing—but nothing's ever done save as conse-quence of words. . . . How thin and tawdry that word Democracy has been worn. Yet it remains the Word. *Must.*

H.V. O'Brien, diary, June 13, 1918. Wine, Women and War.

Unpleasant twist of French character. Have no regard and little knowledge of anyone but selves. Frankly contemptuous of British army. Despise Bel-gians no less than Portuguese. Hate Germans, but not very violently, recognizing in him soldier as good as themselves. For us, amiable tolerance, though think we've been taking hell of a time to make good on promises. Think we're smart kids in some ways, but never amount to much in military way.

H.V. O'Brien, diary, June 16, 1918. Wine, Women and War.

Efforts were made to maintain even greater secrecy than ever before about the contemplated plans. At all railroad stations, in most of the trains, in fact everywhere, signs were displayed cautioning the soldiers to be careful in their conversation and urging the men working in the factories to avoid telling secrets of manufacture, because of the danger of espionage. One such sign issued by the railway officials which was widely circulated and displayed read as follows:

"Attention, soldiers! to guard against enemy spies and their conspirators who have been discovered to frequent in large numbers our railway stations and trains, the War Ministry forbids all military individuals, our wounded men especially, making any reference whatsoever regarding troop positions, movements, new formations, and other military information of any character, especially to strange men and women. Soldiers, be careful of your conversation in the presence of others. Do not allow yourself to be drawn out into conversation. A careless word may cost the lives of many of your comrades. Report to the railway authorities any suspicious strangers who seek your company or attempt to listen to your conversations. The German soldier must not only be able to fight for his Fatherland, but must also remain silent for his Fatherland."

Conrad Hoffmann, In the Prison Camps of Germany.

Lots of talk . . . about free love. In Europe, *fait accompli.* Maybe youth and beauty that won't fall, but damned few. Axiomatic that any woman, whatever her position, ready for business until she proves contrary. Sex-morality badly jarred in France. Worse in England, they say. What must it be in Germany! . . . The Yank, healthy, amiable, moneyed and with the lure of novelty, can have anything he wants.

H.V. O'Brien, diary, June 19, 1918. Wine, Women and War.

Anglo-Saxon ideas of love n'existe pas in France. Frenchman talks more and knows less about it than anybody in the world. Women either mistresses or wives . . . Knows nothing of chivalry. We're differ-

ent, not superior. Toss-up. We treat wives better, he treats mistresses better.

H.V. O'Brien, diary, June 22, 1918. Wine, Women and War.

Attila, to Little Willie: "Speaking as one barbarian to another, I don't recommend the neighborhood. I found it a bit unhealthy myself."

Cartoon in Punch, *London, July 1918, alluding to Attila's defeat at Chalons, France, in 451* A.D.

Occasional instances of bad behavior of Americans. In general, simply marvelous. Drunken soldier a rarity. M.P's very much on the job. In T—'s battery a soldier accused by French family of having stolen 200 fr. Before wheels of military justice begin to turn, battery took up collection. Right or wrong, we weren't going to give anybody excuse to say Yank soldiers were thieves. French so moved at that, refused to accept money. Thief so moved at refusal, collection etc., he confessed, and told where money was.

H.V. O'Brien, diary, July 10, 1918. Wine, Women and War.

Wounded American infantryman at Varennes, France, September 1918. Photo courtesy of the National Archives, Washington, D.C.

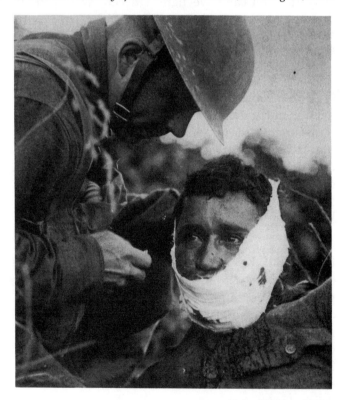

The French woman—marvelous! Not a family the hand of war hasn't scarred. But got to know them long and intimately before you know *how* scarred. No talk of life's hardness, not many words wasted on enemy. Don't talk of "carrying on"; just do it.

H.V. O'Brien, diary, July 15, 1918. Wine, Women and War.

During the last year of the war, when the food supplies which the Germans could give to the prisoners were entirely inadequate for their needs, and when tuberculosis and influenza were widespread, the number of graves in many cemeteries was greatly augmented. This was particularly true of the camps where Russians, Roumanians, and Serbians were interned. To see row on row of earth mounds, each with its cross, and to be conscious of the fact that each grave held some mother's son, brought home to one as perhaps nothing else could have done the awfulness of war.

Conrad Hoffman, In the Prison Camps of Germany.

Antipathy in French army, as in ours, between professional and amateur. Each, though making exceptions, despises other as class. In French army, this antagonism is intensified, because remaining regulars are well on in years. To natural hostility is added that between youth and age.

H.V. O'Brien, diary, July 19, 1918. Wine, Women and War.

G.H.Q. [American General Headquarters] a shock. Expected to see Gen. Pershing like Napoleon at Friedland, on white charger, spy glass under arm, surrounded by gold laced officers in swords and high boots. Found instead group huge stone barracks, around court, with million typewriters all clicking at once. Reminded me of Sears Roebuck. More field clerks and stenogs than soldiers . . .

H.V. O'Brien, diary, July 30, 1918. Wine, Women and War.

In the north of us, we had a division brought over from the eastern front after two years of no fighting. Our men had this experience . . . with other units of this kind and called them the "Bolshevik-divisions." We soon discovered that our expectation of increasing our army in the west by a great number of divisions after making peace with Lenin and Trotzki would be met numerically but in reality it would mean the disintegration of our western front.

Heinrich Bruening, captain at the western front in August 1918 (later chancellor of Germany), Memoirs *(1970).*

16. The Collapse of the Central Powers: Revolution, Armistice and Peace Treaties: October 1918–1920

THE HISTORICAL CONTEXT

GERMANY ASKS FOR PEACE

As early as September 29, 1918, Ludendorff had insisted that he would have to get an immediate armistice. He feared an Allied break-through—which never took place—and hoped that an armistice would allow the German army to withdraw to its border and take up a strong defensive position. When his government pointed out that the Allies would force much harsher terms on a Germany run by the military, Ludendorff arranged for a "revolution from above." The liberal Prince Max of Baden was appointed chancellor, and press restriction was relaxed. The prince would have preferred negotiations first, since he foresaw that an immediate request for armistice would break the fighting spirit of the German people once and for all; but Ludendorff insisted and—for the last time—had his way.

The German request, however, was not addressed to the Allied supreme commander Foch but to President Wilson, whose Fourteen Point platform was now accepted by Germany. By this move, the prince tried to put himself on the same idealistic level as Wilson, who, it seems, still saw himself more as the neutral peace mediator than as the head of a belligerent nation. Ignoring objections from France and Britain and from hot-heads in his own country, he advised Germany

287

Prince Max (Maximilian) von Baden, last chancellor of Imperial Germany. Photo courtesy of the German Information Center, New York City.

that he would promote an armistice if Germany would first evacuate all occupied territories. On October 12, when the German chancellor accepted this condition, a German submarine sank the *Leinster*, a British boat shuttling between England and Ireland, with the loss of 450 lives. Now Wilson demanded immediate cessation of the submarine warfare and further proof that Germany had been democratized according to the will of the people. He added that the armistice should be concluded by the military commanders rather than civilian authorities.

The great debate started within Germany. Ludendorff had apparently recovered his nerves; he and the High Command proposed to go on fighting. But for the first time, the generals were overruled by the civilian government, which now included liberal and Socialist ministers, a sign that Germany had really begun to become democratic, and the submarine warfare was called off. Wilson asked the generals to draft an armistice, using his Fourteen Points as a basis for the coming peace. This, in a way, was an imposition. The United States had done much less fighting than Britain, France, Belgium or Italy, and the Allies had never accepted his Fourteen Points. On the other hand, the Allies had never agreed on their war aims among themselves. The French wanted the Rhineland; the British, the German colonies; yet they had never openly claimed these territories. As to the armistice, Haig would have been satisfied with the German withdrawal from all occupied territory, while Pershing, unlike his political chief Wilson, did not want armistice at all (instead, he pleaded to give his army further chances to win victories). Foch wanted the Rhineland and struck a bargain with the British admirals, who wanted the ships of the German navy and sided with Foch against Haig's moderation. All were afraid of the spreading of Bolshevism and, therefore, in order to hasten an armistice, accepted the Fourteen Points, though Lloyd George rejected the "freedom of the seas" clause, pointing out that the United States had not abided by these principles either when enforcing the blockade during the last year and a half. Yet, by leaving the main questions open for the peace conference, the Allies were ready for the armistice. But just then, Wilson's strong position suddenly weakened. The Republicans won the November elections, and their program did not embrace an idealistic peace, but simply the defeat of Germany and thereafter a quick retreat from European affairs. Germany's position was also weakened by the collapse of its allies, which left its rear wide open. The German admirals were still defiant. They resented the ending of the submarine war and planned a last desperate attack on the British fleet, perhaps in the hope of wrecking the armistice talks. But when the crews began to mutiny, the chancellor knew he had to conclude an armistice right away, not just to end the war but to prevent a revolution.

THE KAISER ABDICATES

It was too late. When Mathias Erzberger (the head of the German Armistice Commission) and his colleagues met with Foch and Admiral Wemyss (the spokesman for the Navy) in a railway carriage at Rethondes in the forest of Compiègne on November 8, a revolution was in full swing in Munich, and the Bavarian king abdicated. On the following day, the pressure had become so great that the cabinet urged the kaiser to abdicate in order to preserve the monarchy. At the headquarters in Spa William hesitated, but Prince Max felt that he could no longer wait and announced the Kaiser's abdication. The same day, Socialist leader Philipp Scheidemann proclaimed the German Republic. One day later, the Kaiser listened to Hindenburg and General Wilhelm Groener, Ludendorff's successor, who advised him that the soldiers would perhaps keep on fighting for Germany but not for him. He declared he could not leave his family—but then decided to go after all. After some delay, he was allowed to cross the Dutch frontier. Two days later he signed his formal abdication as German emperor and king of Prussia.

Mathias Erzberger, who led the German delegation that signed the armistice. Photo courtesy of the German Information Center, New York City.

ARMISTICE

The armistice terms read by Foch to Erzberger called not only for the evacuation of all occupied territories but also for renunciation of the treaties of Brest-Litovsk and Bucharest (with Romania) and the surrender of 5,000 locomotives, 150,000 freight cars and 160 submarines and other warships. The German delegation had no choice and signed. The armistice was concluded for a period of 30 days and was renewed each month until peace had been signed. A relaxation of the blockade was not granted by Foch, whose only concession was to leave the Germans some machine guns—to fight Bolshevism.

All hostilities ceased on November 11, 1918 and wild celebrations burst out in the Allied capitals. In London, crowds poured into the streets, where they cheered, danced and lit bonfires. The celebrations became more and more riotous and after two days had to be stopped by the police. In Paris the joy was more subdued. The country had suffered too much. In Moscow, there was a note of somber triumph and the expectation that now the revolution would spread all over Europe. The same was feared by many in the Western countries as well, but a general mood of optimism and the expectation of a lasting peace prevailed.

The English prime minister, David Lloyd George, favored some kind of conciliation with Germany; but he had an election to win and during the campaign felt compelled to join in with the radicals whose election slogan was "Hang the Kaiser!" This deterioration of the high principles pronounced by Wilson was perhaps inevitable. One cannot preach to a people that it fights against a vicious and culturally inferior enemy, and then, after he is beaten, settle with the defeated aggressor on more or less equal terms and go back to a status quo. This was the problem Wilson had to face when he joined the international peace conference that assembled in Paris on January 18, 1919, thereby becoming the first American president to leave the States during his term of office.

THE VERSAILLES PEACE CONFERENCE AND THE LEAGUE OF NATIONS

The plenary sessions of the conference were of little importance, as the decisions were to be made by the Supreme Council, the Big Ten who represented the five major powers: Wilson and Secretary of State Robert Lansing for the United States, Lloyd George and Foreign Secretary Arthur James Balfour for England, Clemenceau and Foreign Minister Stéphen-Jean-Marie Pichon for France, Premier Vittorio Emanuele Orlando and Foreign Minister Sidney Barone Sonnino for Italy, and Premier Marquis Kimmochi Saionji and Baron Shinken Makino for Japan. Germany was not invited to participate, and Russia did not participate either, since Clemenceau refused to invite delegates of revolutionary and counterrevolutionary parties who were engaged in unresolved conflicts at the time. Since public opinion in France and England was overwhelmingly anti-Bolshevik, an agreement would probably have been impossible to reach anyway.

The leading statesmen were expected to create peace built on the ideas expressed on Wilson's Fourteen Points: democratic governments, self-determination of peoples, cessation of secret diplomacy, and an international organization to maintain justice and peace among the nations. At first Wilson had his way, as on January 25, a resolution for the creation of a League of Nations was unanimously adopted. A committee to draft a constitution was appointed, and several other committees dealing with the question of territorial adjustments and reparations followed. It turned out that Allies' ideas of maintaining peace in the league differed widely. The British scheme was to rely on moral force, the French on armed might, and the Japanese wanted to include the principle of racial equality. The Japanese had to be bought off by Wilson, who promised them former German possessions in China. When these questions were settled, Wilson lost interest in the other details under discussion. He felt that any mistakes would be rectified by the league once it got under way. U.S. domestic problems called him back to Washington to deal with Congress in the middle of February, and Lloyd George had to return to London several times to deal with complaints in the House of Commons. Clemenceau, remaining in Paris, was also inactivated for a time, as he was seriously wounded by an assassin.

After Wilson's return, the Big Ten were replaced by the Big Four—Wilson, Lloyd George, Clemenceau and Orlando—to expedite the business at hand, the settlement with Germany. Actually, it turned out to be a council of the big three, as Orlando played a minor role in the discussions. All three statesmen were overworked and constantly interrupted by domestic or other immediate questions. No meeting of the three ever concentrated on a single topic, and all debates were slowed down by the work of the translator, since only Clemenceau understood both French and English. Both he and Lloyd George had accepted Wilson's high principles only half-heartedly, but they also disagreed violently with one another. England had secured promise of one of its main objectives, possession of the German fleet, which—as no neutral port was willing to receive it—was by now interned at Scapa Flow. But Lloyd George also wanted the German colonies—although they were of questionable value—and he met the resistance not only of the French but also of some British Dominions. South Africa wanted German South West Africa; Australia wanted New Guinea. These problems were finally solved by the creation of so-called mandates of the League of Nations, which then distributed all of these territories among the Allies, mainly between the British and French. Even greater clashes occurred when Clemenceau insisted on separating the left bank of the Rhine from Germany, on the annexation of the Saar Basin, and on the question of reparations to be paid by Germany. Lloyd George felt that the impoverished, exhausted Germany could not pay the huge sums Clemenceau demanded; but he

The Big Four at Versailles: Lloyd George, Orlando, Clemenceau and Wilson. Photo courtesy of the National Archives, Washington, D.C.

had committed himself to reparations during this recent election campaign.

The first agreement was the Covenant of the League of Nations, which had been worked out by a committee consisting of Wilson, his adviser Edward Mandell House, British Viscount Edgar Algernon Cecil, South African minister Jan Christiaan Smuts, the French delegate Léon Bourgeois and Greek premier Eleutherios Venizelos. The covenant was incorporated into the treaty with Germany, although Germany was not to be a member until it had demonstrated its peaceful and democratic character. The league was to consist of the signatory states and new members to be admitted by a two-thirds vote. Members were to protect each other from aggression, would submit disputes to arbitration and would abstain from war. Previous treaties incompatible with these provisions were pronounced cancelled, and all new treaties were to be registered with the league, which would devote itself to disarmament, labor and health problems and similar international causes. At Geneva, Switzerland, a permanent secretariat was established, presided by Sir Eric James Drummond, Earl of Perth. In the General Assembly, all members had one vote, while the executive powers rested with a Council consisting of delegates of the five great powers and four others chosen by the assembly.

As its fate was discussed in Paris, Germany was never given a chance to bring up its own arguments. Of course, it had set a bad example by the brutal treatment of beaten Russia at Brest-Litovsk, but at least Russian delegates had been admitted to the conference table. As time went by, the Allies started to demobilize but kept their most effective weapon, the blockade against Germany. This seemed inhuman, since the fighting was long over. British troops occupying the Rhineland protested the blockade and began sharing their food with hungry woman and children. Yet both Paris and London insisted that a peace treaty had to be signed and German disarmament carried out before the blockade could be lifted. Neither Clemenceau nor Lloyd George admitted that there could be any "good" Germans. They pointed out that the German Socialists now heading the government had supported the war until its very end, and the few radical leftists who had opposed it were suspected as Bolshevist sympathizers and considered traitors in their own country. Even Wilson saw no point in listening to the Germans. He engaged in long and bitter wrangles with Clemenceau and Lloyd George over reparations and annexations, objected to Polish claims and Italian claims in Dalmatia, but in the end compromised, and the treaty was submitted to the German delegation on May 7. Count Ulrich von Brockdorff-Rantzau, the German foreign secretary, immediately protested that the terms were not compatible with those under which Germany had laid down its arms and that many demands were impossible to fulfill. But only a few slight modifications were allowed by the Allies.

GERMAN DEBATES OVER THE PEACE CONDITIONS

When the Allied terms became known in Germany, a violent debate arose. After the Kaiser's abdication—and that of all other heads of German states—the Majority Socialists, led by Friedrich Ebert and Philipp Scheidemann, had taken over the government. They were involved immediately in a struggle with the extreme left, the so-called Spartacus group led by Karl Liebknecht and Rosa Luxemburg, who tried to establish a Communist regime built on a system of soviets as Lenin had introduced in Russia. Late in November, the representatives of the new state governments decided that a National Constituent Assembly should be elected. In spite of the violent opposition of the Spartacists, who revolted in Berlin, Munich and other cities, the elections were held in January and showed an overwhelming majority for the moderate parties—Majority Socialists, Catholics and Liberals. Ebert was chosen as president, Scheidemann was appointed chancellor of the new republic.

Work on the new constitution was interrupted when the question of the Allied peace terms had to be decided. All parties were split wide open, as many delegates felt that accepting the proposed peace would mean the slow death of the nation, while others considered the treaty as the lesser evil, compared to Allied occupation, civil war, anarchy and possibly Bolshevism. Scheidemann, who had committed himself against the treaty, resigned and so did Brockdorff-Rantzau. But the assembly voted finally for unconditional acceptance, and on June 28, 1919 the new German foreign secretary, Hermann Mueller, a moderate socialist, and Hans Bell, minister for colonies, signed the treaty in the same Hall of Mirrors in Versailles in which, in 1871, after the German victory over France, the German Empire had been founded.

In the treaty, Germany ceded Alsace-Lorraine to France, some small border regions to Belgium, the larger part of the provinces of Posen and West Prussia to Poland, and the Memel district—at the northern end of East Prussia—to the Allies. The Saar area was put under international administration for 15 years; northern and central Schleswig and Upper Silesia were to decide their allegiance by plebiscite. The city of Danzig (Gdansk) became a free state within the Polish customs union, and all German colonies were ceded to the Allies and organized as mandates under the supervision of the League of Nations.

Germany's future army was limited to 100,000 men; no large guns and only a limited number of small ones were permitted; and the navy was limited to six warships and some smaller boats, without submarines or military aircraft. Allied troops were to occupy the Rhineland for 15 years or longer, and a 30-mile zone on the right bank of the Rhine was demilitarized. The fortifications of Heligoland were to be dismantled, the Kiel Canal between the Baltic and the North Sea was opened to the military and merchant ships of all nations, and all major German rivers were internationalized. All merchant ships of more than 1,600 tons, half of the smaller ones and one-quarter of Germany's fishing fleet were to be handed over to the Allies. Large quantities of coal were to be supplied to France, Belgium and Italy for 10 years. In Article 231 of the treaty, Germany accepted the sole responsibility for starting the war. The kaiser and other prominent persons were to be tried as war criminals, and Germany would pay for all civilian damage caused by the war, the final amount to be determined later. Control commissions were to enforce all conditions. The province of East Prussia was separated from the bulk of Germany by the so-called Polish Corridor, a strip 20 to 70 miles wide that gave the new Polish state an access to the sea. Germany was to pay for the upkeep of the armies of occupation. Austria, now a small, poor country with a purely German population, was forbidden to join up with Germany. This was a clear violation of Wilson's principle of self-determination of the people; but Clemenceau argued successfully that victory would become a mockery if Germany emerged from the war with more inhabitants than when it had entered the war.

Although these conditions were extremely harsh, Germany ratified the treaty and so did France, England, Italy and Japan in the course of 1919. The United States never signed the treaty.

PEACE TREATIES WITH GERMANY'S ALLIES

Peace negotiations with Germany's allies were conducted simultaneously in and around Paris. Charles, emperor of Austria-Hungary, abdicated on November 12, and during the next days, an Austrian and a Hungarian republic had been declared. King Peter of Serbia became the monarch of the new kingdom of the Serbs, Croats and Slovenes. In Montenegro, King Nicholas was deposed, and the parliament voted for union with the new Yugoslav kingdom. The old Habsburg empire no longer existed. German Austria, with a population of less than eight million people (two million of whom lived in Vienna), was to become the most unfortunate result of the peace conference. The country was shut off by high tariffs from its neighbors and politically torn between the Catholic-conservative countryside and the Socialist-oriented metropolis. Its assembly voted in March 1919 to become part of the German Reich but was forbidden to do so by the peace treaty of St. Germain signed in September of the same year, which registered the dissolution of the old Dual Monarchy. As the remaining representative of the old regime, Austria was penalized as the beaten enemy. It recognized the independence of Yugoslavia, Czechoslovakia, Hungary and Poland and ceded Eastern Galicia, South Tyrol, Trieste, the Trentino and Istria to its neighbors. The Austrian army was reduced to 30,000 men, and Austria was to pay reparations for 30 years. The name of the state was changed from German Austria to the Republic of Austria.

The settlement with Hungary was complicated by two events, the Bolshevik coup of Bela Kun and the Romanian invasion. The country of about eight million inhabitants was still organized on a semifeudal basis and was predominantly agricultural. The Hungarian parliament had proclaimed independence from Austria in October 1918, and Count Michael Karolyi, a liberal republican, was made prime minister, then president of the newly proclaimed republic. He resigned in protest when the Allies assigned Transylvania to Romania in March 1919 and was succeeded by a Socialist-Communist government, in which the Socialists were soon pushed out by foreign minister Bela Kun, who then established a Communist dictatorship. He declared war on Czechoslovakia and attempted to reconquer Slovakia. Now Romania interfered, fearing an invasion of Transylvania. A counterrevolution started in the country as the Romanians advanced. Kun had to flee to Vienna and a few days later, on August 4, Romanian troops occupied Budapest. Now the monarchists gained the upper hand, and when, under Allied pressure, the Romanians finally evacuated the country, Admiral Nicholas Horthy, the military commander, was made head of the state. He declared Hungary a monarchy with the throne vacant, and in June 1920 signed the peace treaty of Trianon, in which the old Hungary was deprived of about two-thirds of its former territory and inhabitants. Slovakia was ceded to Czechoslovakia, western Hungary to Austria, Croatia-Slavonia to Yugoslavia, and the Banat was split between Romania and Yugoslavia. Romania also received Transylvania. Hungary also had to pay reparations and was allowed an army of only 35,000 men.

Bulgaria signed the peace treaty of Neuilly in November 1919. The country was deprived of a seaboard on the Aegean Sea and had to pay reparations in the amount of $445 million. It also had to surrender its war materials and had its army limited to 20,000 men.

Finally, the settlement with Turkey developed into a prolonged problem. During the war, the Allies had promised Constantinople to the Russians, but the collapse of the tsarist regime and the publication of the secret treaties by Lenin changed the whole situation, since Wilson was opposed to the partition of the Turkish Empire as the Allies had envisioned it. The government of the sultan was practically helpless, and Greek troops, supported by the Allies, landed at Smyrna in May 1919. Meanwhile, a strong nationalist movement under Mustapha Kemal violently opposed all Allied partition plans. Nevertheless, a treaty was finally concluded at Sèvres in August 1920, in which the sultan renounced all claims to non-Turkish territories. Syria was to become a mandate of France, Mesopotamia and Palestine were given to the British; Smyrna, Thrace and some Aegean Islands went to Greece; and the Dodecanese and Rhodes went to Italy. Armenia was declared independent, the Dardanelles Straits were internationalized. Nothing was left of all the promises that had been made to the Arabs during the war. Furthermore, nothing was left. But this treaty was not recognized by Turkish nationalists, who steadily grew in strength under the vigorous leadership of Mustapha Kemal. Within three years, he managed to defeat the Greeks in spite of British help, to abolish the sultanate, and to conclude a new treaty at Lausanne which radically revised the Treaty of Sèvres and secured Constantinople for the Turks.

CHRONICLE OF EVENTS

1918:

September 29: Ludendorff demands an armistice and peace negotiations.

September 30: German chancellor Georg Graf von Hertling and his cabinet resign.

October 4: Prince Max von Baden, a Liberal, is appointed chancellor and foreign minister.

Both the German and Austrian governments appeal to President Wilson to arrange for an armistice and accept the Fourteen Points mentioned in his speech of January 8.

October 12: The German government accepts Wilson's condition that all occupied territories be evacuated.

The *Leinster*, shuttling between Ireland and England, is sunk by a German submarine. 450 lives are lost.

October 27: General Wilhelm Groener, quartermaster general, succeeds Ludendorff.

End of October: Wilson asks the generals to draft an armistice on the basis of his Fourteen Points.

November 3: A mutiny breaks out in the German fleet stationed at Kiel and spreads to other ports.

November 7: A revolution breaks out in Munich, and the Bavarian king abdicates.

November 8: A German commission headed by Mathias Erzberger is received by Foch in his railroad car near Compiègne, in Ile-de-France.

November 9: Prince Max von Baden announces the abdication of the German emperor.

Socialist leader Philipp Scheidemann proclaims the German Republic.

November 11: The armistice is signed and all fighting in the west stops.

November 18: The last German troops leave French territory.

November 26: The last German troops leave Belgian territory.

December 1: British and American troops begin the occupation of German territories.

Philipp Scheidemann, who proclaimed the German Republic on November 9, 1918. Photo courtesy of the German Information Center, New York City.

1919:

January 18: The Peace Conference opens formally at Paris.

January 25: The creation of a League of Nations is unanimously approved at the conference.

February: The conference is interrupted as President Wilson is forced to return to the United States and Lloyd George to London.

March 22: In Hungary, the republican government led by Count Michael Karolyi is overthrown by a Bolshevik coup headed by Bela Kun.

March 25: In Paris, negotiations are resumed, and the Council of Ten (Big Ten) is replaced by a Council of Four (Big Four).

April 7: Because of disagreements among the Allies, Wilson prepares to return home, but then decides to stay.

April 23–May 6: The Italian delegation leaves the conference.

April 28: The Covenant of the League of Nations is presented in Paris.

April 29: The German delegation, headed by Count Ulrich von Brockdorff-Rantzau, arrives at the conference.

May 7: The peace treaty is submitted to the German delegation, which protests vigorously. Only slight modifications are made.

May 15: Greek troops occupy Smyrna, and Italian troops land in Anatolia.

June 28: The Peace Treaty is signed in the Hall of Mirrors at Versailles.

July 7: The German government ratifies the treaty.

August 1: In Hungary,the Bolshevik government is overthrown.

August 4: Romanian troops invade Hungary and occupy Budapest.

September 10: Austria signs the Peace Treaty of St. Germain which dissolves the Habsburg Empire and recognizes the independence of Poland, Hungary, Czechoslovakia and Yugoslavia.

October 13: France ratifies the Treaty of Versailles.

October 15: England ratifies the Treaty of Versailles.

Italy ratifies the Treaty of Versailles.

October 30: Japan ratifies the Treaty of Versailles.

November 27: Bulgaria signs the peace treaty of Neuilly.

December 10: Romanian forces withdraw from Hungary.

1920:

February: The monarchists regain control in Hungary. Admiral Nicholas Horthy is appointed regent.

April 18: At the conference of San Remo, the Allies agree on peace conditions for Turkey.

August 20: The sultan's government signs the Treaty of Sèvres and renounces all claims to non-Turkish territory.

EYEWITNESS TESTIMONY

. . . This government will fall anyway, will go to pieces in the terrific upheaval of events . . . No matter how this war will end, the Government will surely die of it. If the war lasts long, it will die early; if it is over soon, it may survive a little longer.

Otto Braun, letter to his parents from Lithuania, August 21, 1915.

Any leaning the soldier may have towards socialism is, after all, mainly negative. He is furious with the whole rotten bourgeois society, furious with the stay-at-homes, in fact, furious with everything at home. For the present I see no sign of any constructive political ideas . . . When the armies return, the self-assurance of the people will have grown tremendously. There will be at the back of them a great amount of knowledge and a consciousness of power.

Otto Braun, letter to his parents from the Russian front, September 12, 1915.

No doubt during the winter months of 1917 and 1918 the representatives of the Russian Bolshevik Government, who had come to Berlin under the leadership of Joffe, carried on extensive propaganda and agitation among the more radical elements of the Left wing, with the result that the demand was made for an immediate and complete revision of the political basis of representation.

Conrad Hoffman, In the Prison Camps of Germany (1918).

Der Tag! Nothing happened all day. Kidded by everybody. Then K — bounced in, with evening paper and Von Kühlmann's address to Reichstag. Admits frankly Germany's inability to reach a military decision. So far as I know, first official recognition of fact! Dumbfounded! Begin to believe I *am* a prophet!

H.V. O'Brien, June 26, in his diary, Wine, Women and War (1926).

So Washington thinks we can finish this God damned war by 1920. Nice of them to set date . . . At least now we talk about ending it ourselves. Everybody here says next summer. Still think Boche can't stick it through winter. Significant, no news coming out of Austria. When tough old hide of

German Empire finally punctured, we'll find nothing in it but rotting bones.

H.V. O'Brien, diary, July 6, 1918, Wine, Women and War.

Germans having some difficulty disposing of us. Their communiqué announced taking of Cantigny by "the enemy." Did not mention Americans. Prisoners asked what they think of the Yanks, say they aren't Yanks, but Canadians dressed up in a new British trick!

H.V. O'Brien, diary, July 6, 1918, Wine, Women and War.

The Hun having rude and rather comic awakening as to Yanks. Finding them fighters more savage than his own ideal. Has tried "Kamarad" stuff several times—hasn't proved profitable. American, aroused by what he considers unfair play, a murderous fighter. Refuses to hate Hun. Considers him merely a peculiarly objectionable pig – to be quickly stung.

H.V. O'Brien, diary, July 31, 1918, Wine, Women and War.

War just as pictured. Mud. Wrecked buildings. Loot accumulated in dugouts, but not carried off. Dead horses at roadside. First sign of Front, unutterable smell thereof. Troops, guns, dispatch riders bursting shells, balloons, planes—everything just as movies show it. Most impressive thing—the cleaning up. Dead quickly buried. Small army goes through fields salvaging equipment. Hard to find souvenirs three days after battle.

H.V. O'Brien, diary, at the front near Château-Thierry, August 6, 1918, Wine, Women and War.

Rumor that present quiet on Italian presages separate peace. Constant remarks of German prisoners, being taken back after Marne battle, and seeing enormous masses of Americans: "We have been fooled." Significant of what must soon reach their civilians. Americans no longer a promise—delivering. Have heartened French tremendously . . . Big Bertha's shells continue to drop. No effect. One fell near Embassy other day, killing two people. Less excitement than a street car accident at home.

H.V. O'Brien, diary, Paris, August 7, 1918, Wine, Women and War.

In Germany, as the tide began to turn, universal disillusionment resulted. Then came the revelations

of Lichnowsky, former German Ambassador to England, which gave the people evidence that Germany was the chief culprit in the initiation of the Great War. The Government tried to undo the harm occasioned by these revelations, but in vain. The failure of the submarine warfare was also apparent, for month by month the amount of tonnage destroyed had decreased by extradorinary and unexpected degrees, while on the other hand, the amount of tonnage being constructed in Allied dockyards was rapidly overcoming the losses of the previous months due to the submarines; and added to all these discouraging signs of the times were the increasingly serious food conditions. The health of the civilians in the large cities was being undermined most dangerously. The community kitchens which had been organized a year or so before were now feeding 100,000 to 250,000 people in the city of Berlin alone. The death rate due to malnutrition and the resultant intestinal diseases was overwhelming and disastrous.
Conrad Hoffman, In the Prison Camps.

Lunch with Julius Rosenwald (American merchant and philanthropist). Crude, unpolished, naïve, but genuine and likable and worthy of respect. Very friendly and democratic, stopping soldiers on street to . . . get their names, so that he could write home about them. Not subtle, but refreshingly direct and honest.
H.V. O'Brien, diary, August 25, 1918, Wine, Women and War.

The unutterable stupid Germans! Not yet to have learned, what all her spies know, that the will to victory on our side is now practically universal . . . What was once hyperbole—"peace in Berlin"—is now a conviction. The Yanks thoroughly aroused, thinking they have Jerry on the run. And with a savage but understandable desire to shell German towns—which, as sure as next summer comes, they'll do.
H.V. O'Brien, diary, August 26, 1918, Wine, Women and War.

July was a glorious month for the Allies, and August is even better. It began with the recovery of Soissons; a week later it was the turn of the British . . . The 8th of August was a bad day for Germany, for it showed that the counter-offensive was not to be confined to one section; that henceforth no respite would be allowed from hammer-blows. The German

High Command endeavours to tranquilize the German people by *communiqués* . . .
Punch, London, August 1918.

Party of Congressmen to Front . . . Chief interest of party—souvenirs. Half the time spent collecting iron . . . Lord, what questions! . . . Tried to answer honestly, at first—which meant "I don't know" 99% of time. But was human. By end of the day had Munchhausen looking like a piker . . . it's their God-damned frivolity that infuriates. Treat the war as a circus, put on for their especial benefit. Most of them here as nothing but curiosity seekers, getting material for re-election campaigns . . .
H.V. O'Brien, diary, August 26, 1918, Wine, Women and War.

Never have such crazy rumors gone around in Germany as during the last weeks, since we are in the defense in the west. Men who are closest to our hearts are constantly declared dead . . . One should not and cannot excuse this moral weakness as war psychosis . . . When conducting a war, one has to reckon with vicissitudes. A hundred victories against one defeat? Who would not want to be on our position?
Captain Felix Neumann, in the German weekly Reklams Universum, *September 7, 1918.*

Comfort in official report on information gathered from 12,000 prisoners. "Morale lowering rapidly. Only hope—'holding' " . . . Food difficulties acute, even in army . . . Criticism of indecision and vacillation of High Command. Also growing friction between German states. In prison camps, actual fighting between Bavarians, Prussians etc.
H.V. O'Brien, diary, September 9, 1918, Wine, Women and War.

Saw G.H.Q. report on conditions in Italy. French tried to teach them something about war, but Italians too busy to listen. High praise for enlisted man, but nix on officer. Cocky as hell—think they've got Caesar's blood in them, etc. Bad case of swelled head . . . Every time Italians get too cocky, Allies threaten to shut off coal. Military power of future evidently going to reside where coal and iron do.
H.V. O'Brien, diary, September 9, 1918, Wine, Women and War.

The more I learn of European politics and what lies behind the countless veils, the more I am struck

by fact that of all nations in war, U.S. is by far the most thoroughly homogeneous and united. All others torn constantly with internal dissension. We alone present perfect front. We the one guaranty of Germany's through defeat.
H.V. O'Brien, diary, September 27, 1918,
Wine, Women and War.

Belgians' nationalistic problem hard to solve, and has led them into foolish and unhappy paths. But can't forget it was her heroic decision to stand against the might of the Hun for a few bloody weeks that saved the Western world. The U.S. may give the *coup de grace*, but Belgium made it possible.
H.V. O'Brien, diary, September 27, 1918,
Wine, Women and War.

. . . Those two points of view [German and English] basis of whole war. Cavell [Edith C., English nurse shot by the Germans] incident another illustration. Undoubtedly everything Germans said she was. But British would have turned her loose, with some grand remark about British lion never touching lady, etc,—loud cheers from the gallery. Poor Germans too damned logical. Committed capital military crime. Even admitted it. Had to be shot.
H.V. O'Brien, diary, September 29, 1918,
Wine, Women and War.

Strikingly anti-British feeling among Yanks. Much more hostile than toward Germans. Common remark: "When we get through with Jerry, we'll clean up them God damned limeys!"
H.V. O'Brien, diary, September 30, 1918,
Wine, Women and War.

The German, true to his character of the world's worst loser and winner, leaves behind him all manners of booby-traps, some puerile, many diabolical which give our sappers plenty of work, cause a good many casualties, and only confirm the resolve of the victors.
Punch, *London, October 1918.*

Visited C—, Commissaire Spéciale . . . Characteristic treatment of spy. Latter came in tears, said he'd been spying for some time, but French people of neighborhood been so kind to him, could not bear to keep it up. C— told him not to be troubled. Had known all along he was spying. Was, in fact, rather grateful than otherwise, since he'd been rather dumb

spy, and furnished excellent channels for news of things that weren't so. Counter-espionage developed along those lines. Difficult and costly to catch spy, try him etc. Much more satisfactory to isolate him, and either feed false information . . . or intercept dope he sends. Like talking into telephone with wires cut. Keeps spy busy and no harm done.
H.V. O'Brien, diary, October 3, 1918, Wine,
Women and War.

Germans, and *a* German—so different. Fishing through poor torn pockets of shabby German body, drooped over wreck of machine gun, to find well-thumbed photograph of woman and little boy and little girl—so like one's own . . . impossible to hate what had been that body.
H.V. O'Brien, diary, October 6, 1918, Wine,
Women and War.

We are all for peace. We, the few, have been warning and imploring, but no Government of ours would bring itself to look facts in the face. Now they have let themselves be stampeded without due reflection and with the time not yet ripe. When the army is in retreat, that is no time to begin negotiations; you must first steady the front line . . . Our country is unviolated, its resources are not exhausted, its people is unwearied. We have gone back, but we have not been beaten . . . The people must be prepared to rise in the defence of the nation . . .
Walter Rathenau, October 7, 1918, to Prince
Max von Baden, quoted in the latter's Memoirs.

Curious that rank counts so much more among Yanks, than with any of Allies. Newer at game, look more closely at insignia. Promotion very slow in French army. Chap may have functions of general, with one stripe on sleeve. In consequence, pay small attention to tunic. We pay a lot . . .
H.V. O'Brien, diary, October 13, 1918, Wine,
Women and War.

English criticism of American delay in entering war, as tactless as unjustified. Failure to grasp enormity of Wilson's task in bringing territorial agglomeration, of doubtful homogeneity, into struggle spiritually and geographically so remote.
H.V. O'Brien, diary, October 14, 1918, Wine,
Women and War.

Danger of an approaching invasion of the Fatherland by the Allies seemed imminent and created a state of chaos not only in the German army, but especially among the German people at home. The hopelessness of the German cause gradually became apparent, and very soon there was an insistent demand for peace. It was argued, "Why sacrifice more lives in this war which has already cost so many, for a cause which is now hopelessly lost?" The Social Democrats and Independent Socialists took up this as yet unvoiced desire of the German people and became the opposition party in the Government.

Conrad Hoffmann, In the Prison Camps of Germany.

Sent home saw-tooth bayonet picked up near Cambrai. Supposed evidence of German ferocity. Really used for woodcutting, only one issued to squad . . . Ironic that French "Joséphine" doesn't get share of attention as atrocity producer. Makes neat hole that closes up, with sepsis inevitable. French not keen for bayonet-work. Silly to fight close-in, when more damage possible with gun at half a mile. Disapprove of even odds in war. Not a *game.*

H.V. O'Brien, diary, October 15, 1918, Wine, Women, and War.

Captain Rickenbacker furnished, by his example, an ideal squadron leader . . . It is absolutely essential that squadron commanders be experienced and daring pilots . . . Captain Rickenbacker obtained results himself and his pilots could not help but emulate him and do likewise.

Report to General Billy Mitchell, October 1918, in Quentin Reynolds, They Fought for the Sky *(1957).*

Drunken soldiers. Profuse apologies on discovering American officer. Salutes and handshaking. One reason why Germans have no chance against us. Couldn't picture German officer shaking hands with drunken privates and giving advice on how to elude M.P.s.

H.V. O'Brien, diary, October 16, 1918, Wine, Women and War.

The morale of the troops has suffered considerably and their power of resistance is declining steadily. The men are surrendering in droves during enemy attacks, and thousands of marauders are loitering around the rear areas. We have no more dug-in positions and can not build them any longer . . . I want to emphasize that already at this moment our position is an extremely dangerous one, and according to circumstances, may turn into a catastrophe overnight. Ludendorff does not realize the seriousness of the situation.

Bavarian Crown Prince Rupprecht, letter to the German chancellor, October 18, 1918.

Vast amount of nonsense about Germany. Silly idea of demanding huge indemnities, and in the same breath refusing to allow access to raw material, i.e. ask tree to give fruit, but shut off sun and air . . . Policy of forgive and forget not merely laudable on moral grounds. Only way out.

H.V. O'Brien, diary, October 18, 1918, Wine, Women and War.

On October 23rd, *Vorwaerts,* the organ of the Social Democrats, commented on this session as follows:

"Without song or music, without honor and without warm applause, but more as one condemned and with the hisses of the masses, someone was buried yesterday in Parliament. The bankrupt Junker regime, the system of Prussian feudalism was forevermore abolished. The Reichstag through the mouth of its first speaker gave final condemnation to the system which has brought Germany into the abyss. Upon the gravestone of this regime the following epitaph will be placed: 'It lived as it died, in dishonor.'

In Conrad Hoffmann, In the Prison camps of Germany.

In bed all A.M. having pants repaired. News that Ludendorff's got the hook. Dreadful suspicion of another "trick." So often underestimated Hun that now going other way. Devil himself couldn't be as full of wicked cleverness as Boche supposed to be. About time to wonder if he isn't really in bad way. Kaiser next for skids, with more or less of revolution to follow, and probably of German Republic in full working order before it dawns on us war actually *finie.*

H.V. O'Brien, diary, October 27, 1918, Wine, Women and War.

There seemed to be no hope of achievement on the battlefield, in spite of the continued newspaper reports that the retreat on the west front was purely for strategic purposes and that a final stand would

be made by the time the Rhine was reached. Whether or not the recognition of this fact was the cause for the proposed sea battle is not known. It is true, however, that in the first days of November the ship crews at Kiel received orders to stack up with coal, which meant getting ready for sea and in all probability a last effort to attack the British sea fleet and render to it an overwhelming and crushing blow.
Conrad Hoffmann, In the Prison Camps of Germany.

To average European, Wilson has Messiah quality: not too much to say, he's *revered.* T.R. [Theodore Roosevelt] simply n'existe plus. Never hear him mentioned . . . Wilson's appeal less to intellectual than to the emotional and religious. No conception at home of aura surrounding him in mind of common man here . . . first message of hope and good will among men heard these many years. Tommy and *poilu* hungry for such word-sick of politician's empty jargon. If Germany doesn't know it yet, she will presently, that W.W.'s her best friend.
H.V. O'Brien, diary, November 2, 1918, Wine, Women and War.

. . . King Albert of Belgium who defied Germany at the outset, shared the dangers of his soldiers in retreat and disaster . . . His decision to resist Germany was perhaps the most heroic act of the war, and he has emerged from his tremendous ordeal with world-wide prestige and unabated distaste for the limelight. The liberation and resurrection of Belgium and Serbia have been two of the most splendid outcomes of the World War . . .
Punch, *London, November 1918.*

In the record of acknowledgment France stands first since her sacrifices and losses have been heaviest, and she gave us in Foch the chief organizer of victory, in Clemenceau the most inspiring example of intrepid statesmanship.
Punch, *London, November 1918.*

It must be the first duty of all in both city and rural communities not to hinder the production of food supplies or their transportation to the cities. On the contrary, all must help to facilitate the same. Food scarcity means plundering and robbery, bringing suffering to all. The poorest will suffer the most. The industrial laborers will be hit hardest. He who in any way hinders the transportation of food supplies or

Friedrich Ebert, first president of the Weimar Republic. Photo courtesy of the German Information Center, New York City.

other necessary supplies, or who in any way withholds and prevents their proper distribution sins most severely against the entire people.
Friedrich Ebert, Proclamation of November 9, 1918, in Conrad Hoffmann, In the Prison Camps of Germany.

Berlin, November 9th. To the German citizens: The new Chancellor Ebert issues the following proclamation for the German citizens:

"Fellow-Citizens: The recent Chancellor, Prince Max of Baden, in agreement with all state secretaries, has entrusted me with the responsibility of the Chancellor's position. I am about to organize the new Government in cooperation with the various parties, and will report to the public very shortly the result of this organization. The new Government will be a people's government."
In Conrad Hoffmann, In the Prison Camps of Germany.

I witnessed many a scene where a general or other officer was rudely attacked by private soldiers, his saber torn from him, the epaulets ripped off from his shoulders, and he then ordered to move on. Every soldier was ordered to remove the red, white, and black cockade and all decorations.

It was reported that in several of the cafés, notably Victoria, Kranzler, and Bauer, officers had entrenched themselves prepared to resist to the limit. Similar resistant groups of officers were reported to have entrenched themselves in several of the university buildings, in the palace and stables of the Crown Prince, and in the royal stables (Marstall). Parties were sent out immediately to storm these citadels with the result that extensive shooting took place. A few deaths resulted. Such was the beginning of the German Revolution on that memorable November 9, 1918.

Conrad Hoffmann, In the Prison Camps of
Germany.

On November 9 Germany, lacking any firm hand, bereft of all will, robbed of her princes, collapsed like a house of cards. All we had lived for, all that we had bled four years to maintain, was gone. We no longer had a native land of which we might be proud. Order in state and society vanished. All authority disappeared. Chaos, Bolshevism, terror, un-German in name and nature, made their entry into the German Fatherland.

General Erich Ludendorff, in A.A. Hoehling,
The Great War at Sea *(1965).*

Dominant note in all stories—irritating pettiness of Hun. Belgians hate him more for what he is, than for things he did. Might forgive him for murdering wife, burning home and taking sons into slavery. But when put in jail for two weeks and fined because employee reputed to have talked back to officer, become implacable . . . Many things he did would be laughable if not so tragic. Basis of harshness, his never-absent fear.

H.V. O'Brien, diary, in Belgium, November 9,
1918. Wine, Women and War.

We are not shedding any tears after him, he has not left us any to shed.

Th. Th. Heine in Simplicissimus, *Munich satirical journal, November 1918, after abdication*
of William II.

The end has come with a swiftness that has outdone the hopes of the most sanguine optimists. In the first eleven days of November we have seen history in the making on a larger scale and with larger possibilities than at any time since the age of Napoleon, perhaps since the world began.

Punch, *London November 1918.*

Some time later I visited the camp at Rastatt again. This was after the German revolution had occurred resulting in the overthrow of the military power and the establishment of the Soldiers' and Workmen's Councils. On arriving in Rastatt I thought an American invasion had struck town, for doughboys in large numbers were strolling up and down the principal streets. On questioning a number of them, I was told that the Soldiers' Council which had usurped power at the prison camp had hailed the American boys as brothers, declaring that they, too, were now free and had thrown open the gates of the camp, giving our men the freedom of the town. Needless to say, dangers were involved in such promiscuous mingling of our American prisoners with the German population without any discipline or regulations. The situation was aggravated by the fact that an epidemic of influenza was raging in the city, from which our boys in the prison camps had so far kept free.

Conrad Hoffmann, In the Prison Camps of
Germany.

Only the curious student of history knows that a clamor of revenge and inhumanity all but drowned the clear, wise, humane voice of Lincoln at the close of the Civil War. A hundred years from now the young American citizen will study the policy and read the utterances of President Wilson, and his heart will glow with the feeling that in her third time of trial America again gave proof not only of material greatness but of moral grandeur. He will not know that an obscene clamor arose in these great days, demanding that the helpless civil population of a vanquished state be left to perish in famine and anarchy.

The New Republic, *November 23, 1918, as in*
Allan Nevins, American Press Opinion
(1969).

I had the feeling . . .that I had been the victim of an enormous nonsense . . . I was going to forget the nightmare, burn my uniform as soon as I would be finally discharged, throw away my badges and tokens into Lake Ontario, and efface every trace of my shame and humiliation.

Pierre Van Passen, about the end of the war, in
Days of Our Years *(1934).*

The plain truth is that if I were to obey my native animal instincts—and there was little hope for anything else while I was in the trenches—I should enlist

again in any future war, or take part in any sort of fighting, merely to experience again that voluptuous thrill of the human brute who realizes his power to take away life from other human beings who try to do the same to him. What was first accepted as a moral duty became a habit . . . had become a need.
Henry De Man, Belgian socialist and soldier,
Scribner's Magazine (1919).

The Left wing took advantage of the universal dissatisfaction and the growing complaint among the masses of the people in the large cities and industrial centers. These had suffered most. A large percentage of their men folks had been killed in battle or were prisoners. Prices continued to soar, while food and clothing supplies were rapidly diminishing. All these factors had a marked effect in undermining the morale of the civilian population.
Conrad Hoffmann, In the Prison Camps of Germany.

If during the next two years the spread of Leninism is to be checked and the road cleared for an orderly social advance, based on the popular education and an enlightened public opinion, the western democracies must depend on Wilsonism to do the job. But it must be a thoroughgoing Wilsonism which can distinguish true from false democracy and is not afraid to trust the people to do many unprecedented things. The chief trouble with Mr. Wilson during the war was that he was not sufficiently Wilsonian.
The New Republic, *November 30, 1918, as quoted in Allan Nevins,* American Press Opinion.

Time to abolish censorship. Necessary in war. Not now. On contrary, nothing more needed now than free thought and free speech. The opinion even of that shrewd old tyrant, Clemenceau. Droll to see Americans getting more Prussian than Prussians ever were.
H.V. O'Brien, diary, December 11, 1918,
Wine, Women and War.

He (Wilson) insisted that the guaranties should be general rather than specific and should strike at the root of the international competition for power. The world was to be made safe not merely for France, Great Britain and America as against Germany, but for democracies of all countries . . . He proposed

the League of Nations as the instrument of this general guaranty of future security . . .
The New Republic, *December 14, 1918, as quoted in Allan Nevins,* American Press Opinion.

At Danzig 20,000 to 30,000 Russian prisoners, maddened by hunger and the desire to get home which had been so long frustrated, stormed and took possession of four of the ships in the harbor which had been secured by the British military commission for the transportation of British prisoners. The situation with reference to the Russians was further aggravated by the fact that Russia refused to permit these prisoners access to Russia.
Conrad Hoffmann, In the Prison Camps of Germany.

In other camps the conditions were most chaotic. All prisoners from working commandos, when they heard the news of possible early repatriation, flocked immediately to their parent camps, fearing that they would be forgotten if they remained on the working detachments. The Russians, believing that they, too, were to be repatriated, swarmed to the camps and by their overwhelming numbers threatened to crowd out the other nationalities. The camps, needless to say, did not have food supplies for this sudden influx of thousands of men, and shelter in all was entirely inadequate.
Conrad Hoffmann, In the Prison Camps of Germany.

L'Union Sacrée, etc.—all shot. Used to think if nations could only meet each other personally, most cause for strife would vanish. Here we are—and national differences only intensified. Can't separate individual from country . . . As it stands, French dislike English, English dislike Americans, and all join in detesting Belges. A cockeyed world!
H.V. O'Brien, diary, December 15, 1918,
Wine, Women and War.

At present there is no church here worthy of the name. The fall of the Kaiser and the system of Prussian militarism of which he was the exponent automatically necessitated the fall of the German Church, which was part and parcel of the system the Kaiser created. For the Church of the Universal God which endures and will arise newborn out of the present chaos, it is good that the old is dead. It may be of interest to know that during the War the pastors of the old German Church invariably received from their superiors the Bible text on which they were to preach the following Sunday, and which, especially in the case of nationalistic themes, was accompanied by a suggested outline for handling it. It is thus evident how efficiently the Church served the State as a mouthpiece.

Conrad Hoffmann, In the Prison Camps of Germany.

[The children's] interrogations at strangeness of life, these days, answered with "daddy's killing Germans." So easy to dispose of tiring subjects. Whatever daddy does is right: therefore Germans forever wrong and bad. Perplexing world of tomorrow not going to solve difficulties by such easy distribution of rightness and wrongness.

H.V. O'Brien, diary, December 22 1918, Wine, Women and War.

Freedom of the press and freedom of public meetings have given the forces of evil free reign, which they are utilizing to the fullest capacity. Last night I went down Friedrich Street, the café and cabaret center, and came away shuddering. It was a filthy lane through a slough of immorality. The War's four years of concentration on the material interests of the body, with little if any strengthening spiritual influence, have resulted in a frightful moral degeneration.

Conrad Hoffmann, In Prison Camps of Germany.

The monarchists are assuming the 'I told you so' attitude. One frequently hears the Berlin citizen on street cars and street corners grumbling about the chaotic conditions that prevail. Then one hears one of the monarchists reply with words something to this effect: 'That is what you get in a democracy. It is what you wanted.' The result is that unconsciously in the hearts of many there is a longing for the old-time law and order, the security, prosperity, and the like which it must be conceded the old form of government gave the people. This dissatisfaction is being capitalized by the nationalistic press.

Conrad Hoffmann, In the Prison Camps of Germany.

Today was a momentous one. The various political parties had scheduled mass demonstrations, the So-

cial Democrats as a protest against the use of force by the Spartacist and sailor group, and the latter as a condemnation of the murderous action of the Social Democratic Party, at present the party in power. The objective of the demonstrations was lost in the extravagant efforts put forth by both parties to secure the greater number of people to parade with them. The Spartacist group had the advantage so far as drawing cards were concerned, for they had scheduled as a feature of their demonstration the burial of the victims of the battle last Tuesday.

Conrad Hoffmann, In the Prison Camps of Germany.

Dismissed from parade . . . thousands of men marched into the city, tearing down street signs in the French language on the way. Streetcars were commandeered; local citizens found driving in their sleighs were stopped, pushed out and forced to surrender their conveyances to the veterans. The walking sticks, donated by the patriotic citizens of Quebec, were used to batter in their own shop windows.

Pierre Van Passen, on the discharge of soldiers in Montreal, early 1919, in Days of Our Years.

Clemenceau was by far the most formidable member of the Council of Four, and he had taken the measure of his colleagues. He alone had an idea, and had considered it in all its consequences. His age, his character, his wit and his appearance joined to give him objectivity and a defined outline in an environment of confusion. One could not despise Clemenceau or dislike him, but only take a different view as to the nature of civilized man, or indulge, at least, a different hope.

J.M. Keynes, British economist in "The Economic Consequences of the Peace Treaty," on the Conference of Versailles, in Guy Chapman (ed.), Vain Glory (1937).

. . . [Wilson] was not only insensitive to his surroundings in the external sense, he was not sensitive to his environment at all. What chance could such a man have against Mr. Lloyd George's unerring, almost medium-like, sensibility to everyone immediately round him? To see the British Prime Minister watching the company, with six or seven senses not available to ordinary men, judging character, motive and sub-conscious impulse, perceiving what each was thinking and even what each was going to say next, and compounding with telepathic instinct the argument of appeal best suited to the vanity, weakness, or self-interest of his immediate auditor, was to realize that the poor President was being played blind man's buff in that party. Never could a man have stepped into the parlour a more perfect and predestined victim to the finished accomplishments of the Prime Minister.

J.M. Keynes, British economist, in "The Economic Consequences of the Peace Treaty," on the Conference of Versailles. Quoted in Guy Chapman (ed.), Vain Glory.

One must also remember the serious food and industrial conditions which prevailed. The thousands upon thousands of returning troops were crowding into the cities. Unable to find work, they very soon joined the vast ranks of the unemployed and furnished most fertile ground for agitation such as that conducted by the Spartacists. During the months of January and February, 1919, it was estimated that in Berlin alone there were over 350,000 unemployed, made up largely of returned troops.

Conrad Hoffmann, In the Prison Camps of Germany.

It has, of course, been everything but a peace conference. So far as the world is concerned, it is a palpable fraud upon the world. A small executive committee, first of ten men, then of five, then of four, has been parcelling out the globe in sessions so secret that their closest associates, the members of their own delegations, have not known what is going on. The very existence of this committee is the result

Victory parade of U.S. troops in front of the New York Public Library. Photo courtesy of the National Archives, Washington, D.C.

of an arrogant, unauthorized assumption of power, for never and nowhere did the conference endow Messrs. Wilson, Orlando, Clemenceau and Lloyd George with the authority to transact all business and come to all decisions. The Germans need not complain if they are arbitrarily summoned to Versailles and told to take the treaty and sign it without discussion. They are only in the same category with all the various Allied delegates . . . except four . . . A democratic peace, frankly, it can never be; a lasting peace it can be only if heaven shows an unexampled favor . . . Who hears today in Paris of the "freedom of the seas?" Who . . . recalls the fine phrase about "no punitive indemnities or annexations"? Actually, we seem to have progressed but little since Napoleon. If there are today four Napoleons setting up new governments and redrawing the map, at least the great emperor spared the world the hypocrisy of clothing his acts in language to charm. And while the Big Four have wrangled, argued, reargued, and fought, Europe has come to the very edge of the abyss. It is civilization itself that is now trembling in the balance.

The Nation, *April 26, 1919, as in Allan Nevins*, American Press Opinion.

And now we read in the news that Lloyd George is hoping to come to this country as to attend the first formal meeting of the League of Nations at Washington in October. The impudent Welshman! Doesn't he know that the most august assembly on earth has not yet made up its mind whether it will allow the League to come into being at all?

New York Evening Post, *May 28, 1919, in Allan Nevins*, American Press Opinion.

It was the more unappropriate, to use no stronger term, for the President to present such stuff to the Senate because of two major reasons. One was the secrecy with which the Treaty had been made . . . the other reason was that there had been raised very specific points of objections to the Treaty . . . The President . . . knew what these points were. He knew that they were what the Senate was most interested in. And he dodged them, every one . . . What it [the Senate] wanted, what it was entitled to, was an explicit and practical report upon the President's extraordinary mission and it did not get it . . . It wanted facts: it got "words, words, words."

Harvey's Weekly, *July 19, 1919, after Wilson's return from Paris, in Allan Nevins*, American Press Opinion.

If Article Ten of the League Covenant means what Mr. Wilson says it means, then it means nothing . . . If Article Ten be interpreted to mean anything that meaning necessarily is that we engage to send our armed forces wherever and whenever a supergovernment of Foreigners sitting in Switzerland orders us to send them . . . One interpretation is an insult to our self-respect as an nation. The other reduced the whole of Article Ten to a vacuum. The way to treat Article Ten is to strike it out.

Harvey's Weekly, *August 9, 1919, in Allan Nevins*, American Press Opinion.

17. Summary and Outlook

WAR LOSSES, WAR DEBTS AND REBUILDING

The grim statistics of the war:

France (Population in 1914: about 40 million)
1,385,000 dead; 3,044,000 wounded; 446,000 prisoners.

Great Britain: (Population in 1914: about 37 million)
947,000 dead; 2,122,000 wounded; 192,000 prisoners.

Russia: (Population in 1914: about 145 million)
1,700,000 dead; 4,950,000 wounded; 2,500,000 prisoners.

Italy: (Population in 1914: about 35 million)
460,000 dead; 947,000 wounded; 530,000 prisoners.

United States: (Population in 1914: about 85 million)
115,000 dead; 206,000 wounded; 4,500 prisoners.

Germany: (Population in 1914: about 68 million)
1,808,000 dead; 4,247,000 wounded; 618,000 prisoners.

Austria-Hungary: (Population in 1914: about 52 million)
1,200,000 dead; 3,260,000 wounded; 2,200,000 prisoners.

Turkey: (Population in 1914: about 40 million)
325,000 dead; 400,000 wounded.

(Some statistics on prisoners of war are in chapter 11.)

This adds up to almost eight million dead, 20 million wounded and more than six million prisoners. In addition, an influenza epidemic of unheard of proportions, no doubt caused by the war, swept over the whole world in 1918–19, leaving another 20 million dead.

The total direct cost of the war worldwide has been estimated at $180,500,000,000; the direct cost at $151,612,500,000.

Obviously, a continent that had lived through five years of desperate fighting and had suffered such ghastly losses in human lives, as well as encountering such tremendous material losses, could not be the same when this period of waste and destruction had come to an end. The financial stability of prewar years was never again attained by the European countries. All European Allies were deeply indebted to the United States, which had lent a total of $10,350,000,000 to foreign powers for war material purchases. It took more than 10 years for the 17 nations involved to come to refunding agreements, Britain being the first to settle for a payment over 62 years at 3.3% interest in 1923. The defeated nations were totally unable to meet their internal war debts. In Germany, a devastating inflation ruined the middle class in particular and even after the currency was stabilized in 1923—and all government war debts cancelled out—the huge payments of reparations imposed on the nation in accordance with the Versailles Treaty prevented any genuine recovery.

Still, the overall economical picture in Europe after the first few turbulent years was good. The war had called into existence new industrial resources; new technologies were developed in the early 1920s. Within a few years, most of the destruction caused by the war had been put right, leaving little evidence of the destroyed areas in France, Italy, Poland and Serbia. Most countries reached or surpassed their prewar production by 1925; even Russia, devastated by the war and years of inner conflict, did so in 1927. All in all, the years 1922–29 were prosperous. By 1929, over-production led to the next big economic crisis and the depression.

POSTWAR POLITICS

The political consequences of the war were far more permanent. Europe was no longer the center of the world. The United States, which had suffered the least losses, emerged as the strongest nation, while Russia, having lost the Polish and Baltic territories and having transferred its capital from Petrograd to Moscow, had moved away from Europe. The remaining victorious powers—France, Britain and Italy—almost as exhausted as the losers, pursued entirely different political aims after the peace treaties had been concluded. France wanted, above all, security from future German aggression and therefore aimed to detach the left bank of the Rhine from Germany. Britain opposed this, claiming it was contrary to Wilson's principle of self-determination of the peoples and also because Britain wanted to prevent France from becoming too powerful on the continent. Italy had not contributed much to the Allied victory and got the worst of the Paris conference deals. Italian claims on the town of Fiume (Rijeka) had been rejected by Wilson; Italian representatives had thereupon left the conference table, and Italy considered itself to be among the losers of the war.

Germany's chief aim, of course, would be the revision of the Versailles Treaty. The situation on the eastern front had not been solved by the peace treaties at all, except that Germany's treaty of Brest-Litovsk had been annulled. The deep distrust between the Soviets and the Western powers continued, and Russia remained an outcast. Its existence was not officially acknowledged by the other powers until 1924 and not by the United States until 1933. Even after Russia returned as a great power, it was not accepted as an equal by the capitalist nations, and the world was from now on divided into a Communist and a non-Communist half, possibly the direct consequence of the Paris treaties.

While Woodrow Wilson had not been able to incorporate all of his ideas of democracy and self-determination into the Paris treaties, some of them prevailed, at least temporarily. The new frontiers drawn were not perfect from the national point of view, and in some cases were outright unjust—usually at the expense of a defeated power. But fewer people were under alien national sovereignty after 1919 than ever before in Europe, and the borders hastily drawn in 1919 and 1920 did survive into the 1980s, except for the eastern border between Germany and Poland. The democratic ideal proclaimed by Wilson also seemed to have prevailed in Paris. In 1914, there had been 17 monarchies and only three republics in Europe. In 1919, there were 13 monarchies and 13 republics, and of the former, many were democratic.

But the democratic idea was soon confronted with other foes, dictatorships and fascism. These new forms of government developed in countries that had little or no previous experience in democratic procedures and were disappointed by the outcome of the war. Italy was the first nation to go this way in 1922; Bulgaria, Spain, Turkey, Albania, Poland, Portugal, Lithuania and finally Germany followed.

WILSON'S FAILURE

Perhaps this development, which led directly into World War II, would not have taken place if the nation that had inspired the ideas of reconciliation, democracy and peace had continued to participate in European politics. But public opinion in the United States had refused to support Woodrow Wilson's initiatives and the peace treaties he brought back from Paris. The U.S. Congress refused to join the League of Nations and even killed an Anglo-American guarantee for France against future German aggression, which Lloyd George had proposed to silence the French clamor for additional security. Wilson, who had won the Nobel Prize for peace, in 1919, had been greeted as the great savior in Europe, but he found upon his return that Congress was unwilling to accept any further involvements in European politics. Wilson then set out to seek popular support for his policies by making a speaking tour through the United States, but he suffered a breakdown in September 1919, and shortly thereafter he had a stroke, from which he never recovered fully. He died a bitterly disillusioned man, three years after his term had expired. A period of strict isolationism followed in the United States after its first adventure into world politics. Yet Wilson's main legacy, the League of Nations, provided a fairly effective instrument for maintaining peace among the nations for the next 12–15 years, and set the pattern for its successor, the United Nations.

COLONIALISM

One of the most significant phenomena of the prewar world situation—colonialism—began to decline after the war. At first, appearances seemed to point in the opposite direction. The war brought the British and French empires to the peak of their expansion. But respect for the white man diminished among the natives of Africa and Asia when they observed their rulers fighting each other. Contributions from the colonies had greatly strengthened the British and French war efforts; 200,000 men from British overseas possessions had died in the war. Consequently, expectations of increased measures of self-government were raised among the more advanced colonial populations, and the spirit of nationalism enacted in Europe had its effect among colonial peoples all over the world. Gradually, the great colonial powers had to give in to the ever-increasing pressures emanating from their colonies, and the great colonial empires of Britain, France, Belgium, and the Netherlands disintegrated more and more. Although German diplomacy in the 1920s made some feeble attempts to regain some of the former colonies, the Allies had actually done a favor to Germany by depriving it of colonial problems in the future and improving Germany's status among the less-developed colonies and dependencies, which contended that control by the imperialist nations was retarding their economic development.

WAR CRIMINALS

One condition of the Treaty of Versailles was never enforced: the demand that the former German emperor and other offenders be tried as war criminals. In accordance with Section VII of the Versailles Treaty, the Allies, on January 20, 1920, produced a list with 895 names of men to be extradited. German resistance was fierce since the list included not just the former emperor but popular heroes such as Hindenburg. The government submitted a counter-proposal according to which these men were to be tried by the German Supreme Court, rather than by the Allies. The English finally agreed to this and persuaded the

French to play along. The Reichsgericht never even indicted any of the accused, and the Dutch government had made clear that it would never extradite William II, whom it had received as a guest. The whole matter was then quietly dropped. It was the first time a German "No" had had its desired effect and probably encouraged the German government to openly resist the French occupation of the Ruhr district in 1923—with disastrous consequences.

Ten years after the signing of the peace treaties, it looked as if Europe were entering a period of prosperity, reconciliation and peace. The German Republic seemed stable, it had joined the League of Nations, and while the problem of reparations remained unsolved, at least some relief had been provided by the newly adopted Young Plan, which regulated reparation payments in a way more acceptable to Germany. The radical nationalists on both sides of the Rhine were subdued. But in October of the same year, the stock market crash on Wall Street ushered in an international depression and a rise of radicalism that, 10 years later, ended in an international catastrophe even greater than the First World War.

EYEWITNESS TESTIMONY

Dear remembered dead; friendless dead, for whom no one weeps, and therefore doubly glorious, there is in you a force, and a power, and a leaven that we must not lose. You have the right to exact of us, the wounded, above all, the following up of your task. You died to save the French spirit. You died that we may hold our heads high, in order that we be not like the men of the defeat whom we see with their sad vanquished faces . . . Thanks to you we can be ourselves . . . You died that all people might be free; that all men should be better; that there should be more love and less suffering on the earth. And your voices say to us: "Righteousness and justice are the supreme wisdom. Be good without weakness and without illusion. Abhor violence, and regard force as a means, but not as an end. Love one another for the love of us."

André Fribourg, concluding sentences of his war memoirs; The Flaming Crucible (1918).

Appendix A
List of Documents

1. Treaty of Alliance between Austria-Hungary and Germany, October 7, 1879

2. League of the Three Emperors, Berlin, June 18, 1881

3. The Austro-Serbian Alliance, June 16–28, 1881

4. The "Reinsurance Treaty" between Germany and Russia, Berlin, June 18, 1887

5. Letter of the German Secretary for Foreign Affairs, Count Herbert Bismarck, to the German Ambassador of London, Count Hatzfeldt, November 8, 1887

6. Prince Otto von Bismarck's Suggestion of an Anglo-German Alliance, January 11, 1889

7. The Franco-Russian Alliance, 1891–1894

8. William II, Telegram to President Kruger, January 3, 1896

9. William II, Revelation of English Proposal in Letter to the Tsar, May 30, 1898

10. The Fashoda Crisis, September–October 1898

11. Joseph Chamberlain, Colonial Secretary, Speech of November 30, 1899

12. Chancellor von Bülow, Advice to William II to Delay Negotiations for a British Alliance, January 21, 1901

13. Marques of Salisbury, British Prime Minister, Proposal to Include England in the Triple Alliance, May 29, 1901

14. The Anglo-French Entente, April 8, 1904

15. The Bjoerkoe Treaty, July 1905

16. Nicholas II, Letter to William II, November 1905

17. William II, Letter to Nicholas II, 1905

18. German Chancellor von Bethmann-Hollweg, Extracts of Speech of November 9, 1911

19. David Lloyd George, "Mansion House Speech," July 21, 1911

20. Colonel Edward M. House, Extract from Diary on His Meeting with William II, 1914

21. Extracts from Statutes of the "Union or Death" organization

22. Chancellor von Bethmann-Hollweg, Letter to the German Ambassador at Vienna, July 6, 1914

23. Colonel House, Letter to William II, July 8, 1914

24. Count Pourtalès, German Ambassador at St. Petersburg, Telegram to the German Foreign Office, July 25, 1914

25. Special Journal of the Russian Council of Ministers, Advice to Serbia, July 11 (24), 1914

26. British Foreign Secretary, Sir Edward Grey, Telegram to Sir F. Bertie, July 26, 1914

27. The Serbian Reply to the Austrian Ultimatum, July 25, 1914

28. Chancellor von Bethmann-Hollweg, Note to William II, July 26, 1914

29. Sir Edward Grey, Telegram to the British Ambassador at Berlin, July 27, 1914

30. Chancellor von Bethmann-Hollweg, Telegram to the German Ambassador at Vienna, July 27, 1914

31. Telegram of the British Ambassador at Berlin to Sir Edward Grey, July 27, 1914

32. Sir Edward Grey to Sir F. Bertie, July 31, 1914

33. Telegram of the Austrian Ambassador in Rome to Austrian Foreign Minister, July 30, 1914

34. Telegram of the German Ambassador at Rome to the German Foreign Office, July 31, 1914

35. Telegram of the Austrian Minister to Romania to the Austrian Foreign Secretary, August 1, 1914

36. The Secret Treaty of London, April 26, 1915

37. Declaration of France, Great Britain, Italy and Russia, April 26, 1915

38. Emperor Francis Joseph of Austria-Hungary, Proclamation of May 23, 1915

39. The Zimmermann Note to the German Minister to Mexico, January 19, 1917

40. Note of the Russian Foreign Minister to the French Ambassador at Petrograd, February 14, 1917

41. Telegram of the German Ambassador at Washington to the German Foreign Office, January 26, 1917

42. Austria's Peace Offer, March 5, 1917

43. Secret Treaty on the Partitioning of Asiatic Turkey, March 6, 1917

44. Emperor Charles of Austria-Hungary, Letter of March 24, 1917

45. Joint Resolution of the U.S. Congress to Create a State of War, April 6, 1917

46. Senator George William Norris, Extracts of Speech on the Joint Resolution, April 4, 1917

47. Some German Reactions to the U.S. Declaration of War, April 9, 1917

48. Resolution of the German Reichstag on Peace Terms, July 19, 1917

49. Pope Benedict XV, Peace Proposal, August 1, 1917

50. Joint Socialist Statement at the Stockholm Conference, July 1917

51. Lord Balfour, British Foreign Secretary, Statement on Palestine, November 8, 1917

52. President Woodrow Wilson's Fourteen Points, January 8, 1918

53. Anglo-French Statement of Aims in Mesopotamia and Syria, November 7, 1918

54. Example of Northcliffe Propaganda, 1918

55. The Peace Treaty of Brest-Litovsk between the Central Powers and Russia, March 3, 1918

56. The Peace Treaty of Versailles, June 28, 1919 (Excerpts)

1. Treaty of Alliance between Austria-Hungary and Germany

October 7, 1879

Article I. Should, contrary to their hope, and against the loyal desire of the two High Contracting Parties, one of the two Empires be attacked by Russia, the High Contracting Parties are bound to come to the assistance one of the other with the whole war strength of their Empires, and accordingly only to conclude peace together and upon mutual agreement.

Article II. Should one of the High Contracting Parties be attacked by another Power, the other High Contracting Party binds itself hereby, not only not to support the aggressor against its high Ally, but to observe at least a benevolent neutral attitude towards its fellow Contracting Party.

Should, however, the attacking party in such a case be supported by Russia, either by an active coöperation or by military measures which constitute a menace to the Party attacked, then the obligation stipulated in Article I of this Treaty, for reciprocal assistance with the whole fighting force, becomes equally operative, and the conduct of the war by the two High Contracting Parties shall in this case also be in common until the conclusion of a common peace.

Article III. The duration of this Treaty shall be provisionally fixed at five years from the day of ratification. One year before the expiration of this period the two High Contracting Parties shall consult together concerning the question whether the conditions serving as the basis of the Treaty still prevail, and reach an agreement in regard to the further continuance or possible modification of certain details. If in the course of the first month of the last year of the Treaty no invitation has been received from either side to open these negotiations, the Treaty shall be considered as renewed for a further period of three years.

Article IV. This Treaty shall, in conformity with its peaceful character, and to avoid any misinterpretation, be kept secret by the two High Contracting Parties, and only communicated to a third Power upon a joint understanding between the two Parties, and according to the terms of a special Agreement.

The two High Contracting Parties venture to hope, after the sentiments expressed by the Emperor Alexander at the meeting at Alexandrovo, that the armaments of Russia will not in reality prove to be menacing to them, and have on that account no reason for making a communication at present; should, however, this hope, contrary to their expectations, prove to be erroneous, the two High Contracting Parties would consider it their loyal obligation to let the Emperor Alexander know, at least confidentially, that they must consider an attack on either of them as directed against both.

Article V. This Treaty shall derive its validity from the approbation of the two Exalted Sovereigns and shall be ratified within fourteen days after this approbation has been granted by Their Most Exalted Majesties.

In witness whereof the Plenipotentiaries have signed this Treaty with their own hands and affixed their arms.

Done at Vienna, October 7, 1879

ANDRÁSSY   H. VII v. REUSS

L.S.   L.S.

2. League of the Three Emperors, Berlin, June 18, 1881

Article I. In case one of the High Contracting Parties should find itself at war with a fourth Great Power, the two others shall maintain towards it a benevolent neutrality and shall devote their efforts to the localization of the conflict.

This stipulation shall apply likewise to a war between one of the three Powers and Turkey, but only in the case where a previous agreement shall have been reached between the three Courts as to the results of this war.

In the special case where one of them shall obtain a more positive support from one of its two Allies, the obligatory value of the present Article shall remain in all its force for the third.

Article II. Russia, in agreement with Germany, declares her firm resolution to respect the interests arising from the new position assured to Austria-Hungary by the Treaty of Berlin.

The three Courts, desirous of avoiding all discord between them, engage to take account of their respective interests in the Balkan Peninsula. They further promise one another that any new modifications in the territorial status quo of Turkey in Europe can be accomplished only in virtue of a common agreement between them.

In order to facilitate the agreement contemplated by the present Article, an agreement of which it is impossible to foresee all the conditions, the three Courts from the present moment record in the Protocol annexed to this Treaty the points on which an understanding has already been established in principle.

Article III. The three Courts recognize the European and mutually obligatory character of the principle of the closing of the Straits of the Bosporus and of the Dardanelles, founded on international law, confirmed by treaties, and summed up in the declaration of the second Plenipotentiary of Russia at the session of July 12 of the Congress of Berlin.

They will take care in common that Turkey shall make no exception to this rule in favor of the interests of any Government whatsoever, by lending to warlike operations of a belligerent Power the portion of its Empire constituted by the Straits.

In case of infringement, or to prevent it if such infringement should be in prospect, the three Courts will inform Turkey that they would regard her, in that event, as putting herself in a state of war towards the injured Party, and as having deprived herself thenceforth of the benefits of the security assured to her territorial status quo by the Treaty of Berlin.

Article IV. The present Treaty shall be in force during a period of three years, dating from the day of the exchange of ratifications.

Article V. The High Contracting Parties mutually promise secrecy as to the contents and the existence of the present Treaty, as well as of the Protocol annexed thereto.

Article VI. The secret Conventions concluded between Austria-Hungary and Russia and between Germany and Russia in 1873 are replaced by the present Treaty. . . .

SZÉCHÉNYI
V. BISMARCK
SABOURDROFF

SEPARATE PROTOCOL ON THE SAME DATE TO THE
CONVENTION OF BERLIN. JUNE 18,1881

1. *Bosnia and Herzegovina.* Austria-Hungary reserves the right to annex these provinces at whatever moment she shall deem opportune.

2. *Sanjak of Novibazar.* The Declaration exchanged between the Austro-Hungarian Plenipotentiaries and the Russian Plenipotentiaries at the Congress of Berlin under the date of July 13/1, 1878, remains in force.

3. *Eastern Rumelia.* The three Powers agree in regarding the eventuality of an occupation either of Eastern Rumelia or of the Balkans as full of perils for the general peace. In case this should occur, they will employ their efforts to dissuade the Porte from such an enterprise, it being well understood that Bulgaria and Eastern Rumelia on their part are to abstain from provoking the Porte by attacks emanating from their territories against the other provinces of the Ottoman Empire.

4. *Bulgaria.* The three Powers will not oppose the eventual reunion of Bulgaria and Eastern Rumelia within the territorial limits assigned to them by the Treaty of Berlin, if this question should come up by the force of circumstances. They agree to dissuade the Bulgarians from all aggressions against the neighboring provinces, particularly Macedonia; and to inform them that in such a case they will be acting at their own risk and peril.

5. In order to avoid collisions of interests in the local questions which may arise, the three Courts will furnish their representatives and agents in the Orient with a general instruction, directing them to endeavor to smooth out their divergences by friendly explanations between themselves in each special case; and, in the cases where they do not succeed in doing so, to refer the matters to their Governments.

6. The present Protocol forms an integral part of the secret Treaty signed on this day at Berlin, and shall have the same force and validity. . . .

3. The Austro-Serbian Alliance, June 16/28, 1881 [Excerpt]

Article I. There shall be stable peace and friendship between Austria-Hungary and Serbia. The two Governments engage to follow mutually a friendly policy.

Article II. Serbia will not tolerate political, religious, or other intrigues, which, taking her territory as a point of departure, might be directed against the Austro-Hungarian Monarchy, including therein Bosnia, Herzegovina, and the Sanjak of Novibazar.

Austria-Hungary assumes the same obligation with regard to Serbia and her dynasty, the maintenance and strengthening of which she will support with all her influence.

Article III. If the Prince of Serbia should deem it necessary, in the interest of His dynasty and of His country, to take in behalf of Himself and His descendants the title of King, Austria-Hungary will recognize this title as soon as its proclamation shall have been made in legal form, and will use her influence to secure recognition for it on the part of the other Powers.

Article IV. Austria-Hungary will use her influence with the other European Cabinets to second the interest of Serbia.

Without a previous understanding with Austria-Hungary, Serbia will neither negotiate nor conclude any political treaty with another Government, and will not admit to her territory a foreign armed force, regular or irregular, even as volunteers.

Article V. If Austria-Hungary should be threatened with war or find herself at war with one or more other Powers, Serbia will observe a friendly neutrality towards the Austro-Hungarian Monarchy, including therein Bosnia, Herzegovina and the Sanjak of Novibazar, and will accord to it all possible facilities, in conformity with their close friendship and spirit of this Treaty.

Austria-Hungary assumes the same obligation towards Serbia, in case the latter should be threatened with war or find herself at war.

4. The "Reinsurance Treaty," 1887

Treaty between Germany and Russia. Berlin, June 18, 1887

The Imperial Courts of Germany and of Russia, animated by an equal desire to strengthen the general peace by an understanding destined to assure the defensive position of their respective States, have resolved to confirm the agreement established between them by a special arrangement, in view of the expiration on June 15/27, 1887, of the validity of the secret Treaty and Protocol, signed in 1881 and renewed in 1884 by the three Courts of Germany, Russia, and Austria-Hungary.

To this end the two Courts have named as Plenipotentiaries:

His Majesty the Emperor of Germany, King of Prussia, the Sieur Herbert Count Bismarck-Schoenhausen, His Secretary of State in the Department of Foreign Affairs;

His Majesty the Emperor of All the Russias, the Sieur Paul Count Schouvaloff, His Ambassador Extraordinary and Plenipotentiary to His Majesty the Emperor of Germany, King of Prussia, who, being furnished with full powers, which have been found

in good and due form, have agreed upon the following Articles:

Article I. In case one of the High Contracting Parties should find itself at war with a third great Power, the other would maintain a benevolent neutrality towards it, and would devote its efforts to the localization of the conflict. This provision would not apply to a war against Austria or France in case this war should result from an attack directed against one of these two latter Powers by one of the High Contracting Parties.

Article II. Germany recognizes the rights historically acquired by Russia in the Balkan Peninsula, and particularly the legitimacy of her preponderant and decisive influence in Bulgaria and in Eastern Rumelia. The two Courts engage to admit no modification of the territorial status quo of the said peninsula without a previous agreement between them, and to oppose, as occasion arises, every attempt to disturb this status quo or to modify it without their consent.

Article III. The two Courts recognize the European and mutually obligatory character of the principle of the closing of the Straits of the Bosphorus and of the Dardanelles, founded on international law, confirmed by treaties, and summed up in the declaration of the second Plenipotentiary of Russia at the session of July 12 of the Congress of Berlin (Protocol 19).

They will take care in common that Turkey shall make no exception to this rule in favor of the interests of any Government whatsoever, by lending to warlike operations of a belligerent power the portion of its Empire constituted by the Straits. In case of infringement, or to prevent it if such infringement should be in prospect, the two Courts will inform Turkey that they would regard her, in that event, as putting herself in a state of war towards the injured Party, and as depriving herself thenceforth of the benefits of the security assured to her territorial status quo by the Treaty of Berlin.

Article IV. The present Treaty shall remain in force for the space of three years, dating from the day of the exchange of ratifications.

Article V. The High Contracting Parties mutually promise secrecy as to the contents and the existence of the present Treaty and of the Protocol annexed thereto.

Article VI. The present Treaty shall be ratified and ratifications shall be exchanged at Berlin within a period of a fortnight, or sooner if may be.

In witness whereof the respective Plenipotentiaries have signed the present Treaty and have affixed thereto the seal of their arms.

Done at Berlin, the eighteenth day of the month of June, one thousand eight hundred and eighty-seven.

(L. S.)   COUNT BISMARCK
(L. S.)   COUNT PAUL SCHOUVALOFF

ADDITIONAL PROTOCOL. BERLIN, JUNE 18, 1887

In order to complete the stipulations of Articles II and III of the secret Treaty concluded on this same date, the two Courts have come to an agreement upon the following points:

1. Germany, as in the past, will lend her assistance to Russia in order to reëstablish a regular and legal government in Bulgaria. She promises in no case to give her consent to the restoration of the Prince of Battenberg.

2. In case His Majesty the Emperor of Russia should find himself under the necessity of assuming the task of defending the entrance of the Black Sea in order to safeguard the interests of Russia, Germany engages to accord her benevolent neutrality and her moral and diplomatic support to the measures which His Majesty may deem it necessary to take to guard the key of His Empire.

3. The present Protocol forms an integral part of the secret Treaty signed on this day at Berlin, and shall have the same force and validity.

In witness whereof the respective Plenipotentiaries have signed it and have affixed thereto the seal of their arms.

Done at Berlin, the eighteenth day of the month of June, one thousand eight hundred and eighty-seven.

COUNT BISMARCK
COUNT PAUL SCHOUVALOFF

5. Secretary for Foreign Affairs, Count Herbert Bismarck, to the Ambassador at London, Count Hatzfeldt

Secret   Berlin, November 8, 1887

While in Berlin you were told of the secret negotiations for an understanding between England, Austria, and Italy on the basis of the maintenance of peace and the status quo in the East, and also of our attitude concerning them. For your added personal information and with an urgent request for strict secrecy in handling it, I send you a copy of the "8 Points" which are a result of the ambassadorial conferences in Constantinople. . . .

With reference to our conversation and to the instructions given you at Friedrichsruh, I request again that you use your influence to try to bring Lord Salisbury to conclude an agreement in some form with Austria and Italy on the above basis.

If, as you expected, you find that Lord Salisbury proposes certain alterations in the drafting, his Austrian and Italian colleagues will without doubt agree. The Constantinople Points are described by the ambassadors themselves as merely "bases d'un accord" and are in any case not drawn up in the form of an agreement. Obviously they still require final editing.

It is of the greatest significance not only that an entente be arrived at between Austria and Italy, but that England should join it in some binding form. The entente between the two former powers will begin to have effectiveness and permanency only when England joins it. Germany could form without England a lasting alliance with Italy, but to hold Austria and Italy firmly together English cement is necessary.

In addition, the Sultan will put more trust in the group of three than in a mere entente between Austria and Italy which England remains out of. English prestige is greater in Turkey and more influential than that of the remaining powers, and the Sultan pays more attention to the movements of the British fleet than to the numerical strength of the armies of the rest. . . .

ANNEX: EIGHT-POINT BASIS OF ACCORD À TROIS
(England, Austria, and Italy)

Secret

1. Maintenance of peace by the exclusion of all policy of aggression.

2. Maintenance of the status quo in the East founded on the treaties by the exclusion of all policy of compensations.

3. Maintenance of local autonomies established by the same treaties.

4. Independence of Turkey, trustee of important European interests (independence of the Caliphate, freedom of the Straits, etc.) of all preponderating foreign influence.

5. As a consequence, the Porte may neither cede

nor delegate its suzerain rights over Bulgaria to any other power, not intervene to establish there a foreign administration, nor tolerate any acts of coercion, undertaken for this last purpose, under a form, be it military occupation, be it by the dispatch of volunteers, which would constitute not only an infraction of the legal status quo but would be injurious to the interests of the three Powers.

6. The desire of these Powers to associate Turkey with them for the common defense of these principles.

7. In case of resistance on the part of the Porte to the illegal enterprises above indicated, the three Powers will immediately advise with each other on the support to be given it.

8. In case, however, the Porte should be in connivance with an illegal enterprise of the kind indicated, or even in case she should not oppose such with serious resistance, the three Powers shall unite in the provisional occupation by their land or sea forces of certain points of Turkish territory, with the aim of reëstablishing such political and military equilibrium as is necessary to safeguard the principles and interests above mentioned.

[Bismarck's note: "It is not to our interest to fight for the program and equally so not to oppose it. We can fight only for *Germany's interests,* and they are not concerned here."]

6. Bismarck's Suggestion of an Anglo-German Alliance, 1889

Prince Bismarck to Count Hatzfeldt

Berlin, January 11, 1889

During your recent visit to Friedrichsruh I requested you to make use of the next opportunity for a private conversation with Lord Salisbury to express my conviction that peace, which England and Germany equally desire, or even the respite required by them in order to arm suitably for the magnitude of the dangers of the next wars, could not be more certainly obtained than through the conclusion of a treaty between England and Germany in which both Powers bind themselves for a limited period to combined resistance against a French attack upon either of them. Such a secret treaty, if it should be possible, would give to both Powers considerable security against the result of such a war, while an impediment to war might possibly come from its mere publication.

England and Germany are not threatened with an attack by any Power other than France. Only through Russian-Austrian difficulties could Germany be brought into a war with Russia, and as there would be no acceptable reward for Germany as a result of such a war, we must do our utmost to keep Austria from being involved in war.

The only threatening element for the two friendly Powers, England and Germany, is their sole common neighbor, France. England possesses divergent interests with North America and Russia, as well as with France. But a war with one of those Powers, even with both at once, can only be threatening for England if France is allied with England's enemies. And the behavior of America would be more prudent toward England than it was on the Canadian and Sackville questions, if America were made to realize that a break with England would leave her without material or moral aid from France. The most practical means to prevent America from counting on France in a quarrel with England is the certainty that France would not be able to make an attack upon England without at the same time having to face a German army of more than a million men. America will not be inclined to emphasize by war the chauvinistic tendencies of her future government and of her former unfriendliness towards England unless she is assured of eventual French support. British foreign policy would enjoy freedom of movement in all directions only is she were fully protected from the French war danger by adequate alliances. Even then, if such alliances are only concluded for the short period required by England for the restoration of her fighting power on the sea, it would seem to me that the absolute certainty of peace for one or more years thus created might be of great service to all peace-loving Powers. It is not a question of being stronger in case of war, but of the prevention of war. Neither France nor Russia will break the peace if they are officially told that they will certainly find England against them if they do so. They will break it only if they may hope that they might be able to attack the peace-loving nations of Europe in succession. When once it is clearly understood that England would be protected against a French attack by a German alliance and Germany against a French attack by an English alliance, I hold that European peace would be assured for the duration of such a publicly announced alliance.

It is a question whether the conviction that European peace can be considered as assured for a given time may not be bought too dearly at the price of taking an open and parliamentary position in favor of a defensive alliance in the interests of the maintenance of peace.

My idea is that, if His Majesty consents, an alliance should be concluded between the English and the German Governments through which both should bind themselves to support each other in case the French should attack either of them in the next 1, 2, or 3 years, and that this treaty, which would be binding on Germany even without the consent of the Reichstag, should be submitted to the English Parliament for approval and publicly communicated to the Germany Reichstag.

I think that the effect of such an open and manly step in this direction would be an easing and a calming of feeling not only in England and Germany, but all over Europe, and would secure for the English cabinet the reputation of being the Protector of World Peace. . . .

7. The Franco-Russian Alliance, 1891–1894

Definition of the Russo-French Understanding

M. de Mohrenheim, Ambassador of Russia at Paris, to M. Ribot, Minister of Foreign Affairs of France, communicating the instructions of M. de Giers, Russian Minister of Foreign Affairs

Paris, August 15/27, 1891

During my recent sojourn in St. Petersburg, whither I was ordered by my August Sovereign, it pleased the Emperor to provide me with special instructions, set forth in the letter, subjoined in copy, which His Excellency, M. de Giers, Minister of Foreign Affairs, addressed to me, and which His Majesty has deigned to direct me to communicate to the Government of the Republic.

In execution of this Supreme order, I am making it my pressing duty to bring this document to the knowledge of Your Excellency, in the firm hope that its contents, previously concerted and formulated by common agreement between our two Cabinets, will meet with the full approbation of the French Government; and that you will be kind enough, Mr. Minister, in conformity with the wish expressed by M. de Giers, to honor me with a reply testifying to the perfect agreement fortunately established from this time on between our two Governments.

The ulterior developments, of which the two points thus agreed upon not only are susceptible, but which will form their necessary complement, may be made the subject of confidential and intimate conferences at the moment judged opportune by either Cabinet, when they believe they can proceed to it at a good time.

Holding myself for this purpose at the entire disposition of Your Excellency, I am happy to be able to take advantage of such an occasion to ask you to be kind enough to accept the renewed homage of my highest consideration and of my most unalterable devotion.

Mohrenheim

Letter of M. de Giers, Minister of Foreign Affairs of Russia, to M. De Mohrenheim, Ambassador of Russia at Paris

Petersburg, August 9/12, 1891

The situation created in Europe by the open renewal of the Triple Alliance and the more or less probable adhesion of Great Britain to the political aims which that alliance pursues, has, during the recent sojourn here of M. de Laboulaye, prompted an exchange of ideas between the former Ambassador of France and myself, tending to define the attitude which, as things now stand and in the presence of certain eventualities, might best suit our respective Governments, which having kept out of any league, are none the less sincerely desirous of surrounding the maintenance of peace with the most efficacious guaranties.

It is thus that we have been led to formulate the two points below:

1. In order to define and consecrate the cordial understanding which unites them, and desirous of contributing in common agreement to the maintenance of the peace which forms the object of their sincerest aspirations, the two Governments declare that they will take counsel together upon every question of a nature to jeopardize the general peace;

2. In case that peace should be actually in danger, and especially if one of the two parties should be threatened with an aggression, the two parties undertake to reach an understanding on the measures whose immediate and simultaneous adoption would be imposed upon the two Governments by the realization of this eventuality.

Having submitted to the Emperor the fact of this exchange of ideas as well as the text of the conclusions resulting therefrom, I have the honor to inform you today that His Majesty has deigned to approve completely these principles of agreement, and would view with favor their adoption by the two Governments.

In informing you of these Sovereign dispositions, I beg that you be kind enough to bring them to the knowledge of the French Government and to communicate to me the decisions which it may take on its side.

GIERS

M. Ribot, French Minister of Foreign Affairs, to M. de Mohrenheim, Russian Ambassador at Paris, in reply to the preceding

Paris, August 27, 1891

You have been kind enough, by order of your Government, to communicate to me the text of the letter of the Minister of Foreign Affairs of the Empire, wherein are set forth the special instructions with which the Emperor Alexander decided to provide you in pursuance of the last exchange of ideas to which the general situation of Europe had given rise between M. de Giers and the Ambassador of the French Republic at St. Petersburg.

Your Excellency was instructed to express at the same time the hope that the contents of this document, previously concerted and formulated in common agreement between the two Cabinets, would meet with the full assent of the French Government.

I hasten to thank Your Excellency for this communication.

The Government of the Republic can only take the same view as does the Imperial Government of the situation created in Europe by the conditions under which the renewal of the Triple Alliance has come to pass, and believes with it that the moment has arrived to define the attitude which, as things now stand and in the presence of certain eventualities, might seem best to the two Governments, equally desirous of assuring the guaranties for the maintenance of peace which result from the European balance of power.

I am, therefore, happy to inform Your Excellency that the Government of the Republic gives its entire adhesion to the two points which form the subject of the communication of M. de Giers and which are formulated as follows: [See points 1 and 2 in preceding letter.]

I furthermore hold myself at your disposal for the examination of all questions which, under present political conditions, make more particular demand upon the attention of the two Governments.

Conversely, the Imperial Government will doubtless appreciate, as do we, the importance of confiding to special delegates, who should be designated as soon as possible, the practical study of measures designed to meet the eventualities foreseen by the second point of the agreement.

In begging you to bring the reply of the French Government to the knowledge of the Government of His Majesty, I wish to emphasize how much I cherish the opportunity to participate in the consecration of an understanding which has been the constant object of our common efforts.

RIBOT

DRAFT OF MILITARY CONVENTION

France and Russia, being animated by an equal desire to preserve peace, and having no other object than to meet the necessities of a defensive war, provoked by an attack of the forces of the Triple Alliance against the one or the other of them, have agreed upon the following provisions:

1. If France is attacked by Germany, or by Italy supported by Germany, Russia shall employ all her available forces to attack Germany.

If Russia is attacked by Germany, or by Austria supported by Germany, France shall employ all her available forces to fight Germany.

2. In case the forces of the Triple Alliance, or of one of the Powers composing it, should mobilize, France and Russia, at the first news of the event and without the necessity of any previous concert, shall mobilize immediately and simultaneously the whole of their forces and shall move them as close as possible to their frontiers.

3. The available forces to be employed against Germany shall be, on the part of France, 1,300,000 men, on the part of Russia, 700,000 or 800,000 men.

These forces shall engage to the full, with all speed, in order that Germany may have to fight at the same time on the East and on the West.

4. The General Staffs of the Armies of the two countries shall coöperate with each other at all times in the preparation and facilitation of the execution of the measures above foreseen.

They shall communicate to each other, while there is still peace, all information relative to the armies of the Triple Alliance which is or shall be within their knowledge.

Ways and means of corresponding in times of war shall be studied and arranged in advance.

5. France and Russia shall not conclude peace separately.

6. The present Convention shall have the same duration as the Triple Alliance.

7. All the clauses above enumerated shall be kept rigorously secret.

Signature of the Minister:
Signature of the Minister:
General Aide-de-Camp,
    Chief of the General Staff,
    Signed: Obrucheff

General of Division,
    Councillor of State,
Sub-Chief of the General
    Staff of the Army,
    Signed: boisdeffre

General de Boisdeffre's interview with the Tsar regarding the Military Convention. "Mobilization is a declaration of war"

Saint Petersburg, August 18, 1892

This morning, Tuesday, I received from the Minister of War a letter dated August 5/17, in which . . . he made known to me that the Emperor had approved in principle the project as a whole. [The draft of the Military Convention.] . . . The Emperor had evidently held that the basis of the entente would have to be precisely and officially fixed before his audience.

We have now, awaiting the exchange of ratifications with ministerial signatures, an official basis for a definite convention, a basis that can be considered as absolutely sure and decisive when one knows the reserve and the prudence of the Russian Government and the firmness of the Emperor in his engagements.

At eleven o'clock, I was received by the Emperor. His Majesty declared to me immediately that he had read, re-read, and studied the project of the convention, that he gave it his full approbation, taking it as a whole, and that he thanked the French Government for accepting some changes of wording that he had requested.

His Majesty added that the convention contained, to his mind, some political articles which he desired to have examined by the Minister of Foreign Affairs; that there might be, as a result, some minor changes of wording to be made. Finally, His Majesty repeated that the project gave him entire satisfaction and that everything seemed to him to be adjusted to the best interests of the two countries.

I did not believe it necessary to take up again the defence of the first text, since the new text had received the approval of the Government. I only said to the Emperor that the French Government had wished to testify once more through this concession to its confidence in him. The Emperor did not fail to tell me of his strong desire that we guard the secret absolutely. . . .

The Emperor spoke of his desire for peace. I remarked to him that we were no less pacific than His Majesty. "I know it," he responded. "You have given proof of it for twenty-two years." I believe, moreover, that at this moment, peace is not threatened. The German Emperor has enough internal troubles, and England has as many. Moreover, with our convention, I estimate that our situation will be favorable. I surely desire to have at least two more years of peace, for it is necessary for us to complete our armament, our railways, and to recover from want and from the cholera. In fine, it is necessary to hope that peace will be maintained for a long time yet, and let us wish for it.

The Emperor then spoke of mobilization under Article 2. I ventured to remark that mobilization was the declaration of war; that to mobilize was to oblige one's neighbor to do so also; that the mobilization entailed the execution of strategic transportation and of concentration. Without that, to allow the mobilization of a million men on one's frontier without doing the same simultaneously was to deny to one's self all possibility of stirring later. It would be like the situation an individual would be in if he had a pistol in his pocket and would allow his neighbor to point a gun at his forehead without drawing his own. "That is the way I understand it," the Emperor responded. . . .

8. Emperor William to President Kruger, January 3, 1896

I express my sincere congratulations that, supported by your people, without appealing for the help of friendly Powers, you have succeeded by your own energetic action against armed bands which invaded your country as disturbers of the peace, and have thus been enabled to restore peace and safeguard the independence of the country against attacks from the outside.

Wilhelm I.R.

9. Kaiser's Revelation of English Proposal in a Letter to the Tsar, May 3, 1898

Dearest Nicky   Berlin 30/v 98

With a suddenness wholly unexpected to me am I placed before a grave decision which is of vital importance to my country, and which is so far reaching that I cannot foresee the ultimate consequences. The traditions in which I was reared by my beloved Grandfather of blessed memory as regards our two houses and countries, have as you will own always been kept up by me as a holy bequest from him, and my loyalty to you and your family is, I flatter myself, above suspicion. I therefore come to you as my friend and "confidant" to lay the affairs before you as one who expects a frank and loyal answer to a frank and loyal question.

In the beginning of April the attacks on my country and person, till then showered on us by the British Press and people, suddenly fell off, and there was, as you will have perceived, a momentary lull. This rather astonished us at home and we were at loss for an explanation. In a private inquiry I found out that H. M. the Queen herself through a friend of hers had sent word to the British Papers, that she wished this unnoble and false game to cease. This in the Land of the "Free Press"! Such an unwonted step naturally led us to the conclusion that something was in the air.

10. The Fashoda Crisis

Mr. Rodd to the Marquess of Salisbury

Cairo, D. September 25, 1898

I have received the following telegram this morning from Sir Herbert Kitchener:—

"I have just returned here from Fashoda where I found Captain Marchand, accompanied by eight officers and 120 men, located in the old Government buildings, over which they had hoisted the French flag; I sent a letter announcing my approach the day before my arrival at Fashoda. A small rowboat carrying the French flag brought me a reply from Captain Marchand on the following morning, the 19th September, stating that he had reached Fashoda on the 10th July, his Government having given him instruction to occupy the Bahr-el-Ghazal as far as the confluence of the Bahr-el-Jebel, as well as the Shilluk country on the left bank of the White Nile as far as Fashoda. He stated that he had concluded a Treaty with the Chief of the Shilluk tribe, whereby the latter placed his country under the protection of France, and that he had sent this Treaty to his Government for ratification by way of Abyssinia, as well as by the Bahr-el-Ghazal. Captain Marchand described the fight which he had had with the Dervishes on the 25th August, and said that, in anticipation of a second and more severe attack, he had sent his steamer south for reinforcements, but our arrival had averted this danger.

"When we arrived at Fashoda, Captain Marchand and M. Germain came on board, and I at once stated that the presence of a French force at Fashoda and in the Valley of the Nile was regarded as a direct infringement of the rights of the Egyptian Government and of that of Great Britain, and I protested in the strongest terms against their occupation of Fashoda and their hoisting the French flag in the dominions of His Highness the Khedive. In reply, Captain Marchand stated that he had precise orders to occupy the country and to hoist the French flag over the Government buildings at Fashoda, and that it was impossible for him to retire without receiving orders from his Government to that effect, but he did not expect that these orders would be delayed. On my pressing him to say whether, seeing that I had a preponderating force, he was prepared to resist the hoisting of the Egyptian flag at Fashoda, he hesitated and replied that resistance was impossible. I then caused the flag to be hoisted on a ruined bastion of the old Egyptian fortifications about 500 yards south of the French flag, and on the only road which leads to the interior from the French position, which is surrounded by impassable marshes on all sides. Before leaving for the south, I handed to Captain Marchand a formal protest in writing, on behalf of the British and Egyptian Governments, against any occupation by France of any part of the Nile Valley, such occupation being an infringement of the rights of these Governments which I could not recognise.

"I appointed Major Jackson to be Commandant of the Fashoda district, where I left a garrison consisting of one Soudanese battalion, four guns, and a gunboat, after which I proceeded to the Sobat, where, on the 20th September, a post was established and the flag hoisted. We neither saw nor heard anything of the Abyssinians on the Sobat River, but we were told that their nearest post was situated some 350 miles further up. The Bahr-el-Jebel is completely blocked by the 'sudd,' and in consequence I ordered a gun-boat to patrol up the Bahr-el-Ghazal towards Meshra-er-Rek. On my way north, as I passed Fashoda, I sent a letter to Captain Marchand, stating that all transport of war material on the Nile was absolutely prohibited, as the country was under military law. The Shilluk Chief, with a large following, has come into Major Jackson's camp; the whole tribe are delighted to return to their allegiance to us, and the Chief absolutely denies having made any Treaty with the French.

"The position in which Captain Marchand finds himself at Fashoda is as impossible as it is absurd. He is cut off from the interior, and his water transport is quite inadequate; he is, moreover, short of ammunition and supplies, which must take months to reach him; he has no following in the country, and nothing could have saved him and his expedition from being annihilated by the Dervishes had we been a fortnight later in crushing the Khalifa.

"The futility of all their efforts is fully realised by Captain Marchand himself, and he seems quite as anxious to return as we are to facilitate his departure. In his present position he is powerless, but I hope that Her Majesty's Government will take the necessary steps for his removal as soon as possible, as the presence of a French force and flag on the Nile is manifestly extremely undesirable.

"Captain Marchand only lost four natives on the journey, and his expedition is all well.

"I am sending a complete despatch by Lord Edward Cecil, who is leaving with it for Cairo at once."

Mr. Rodd to the Marquess of Salisbury
Cairo, September 25, 1898

Further from Sirdar:

"If the French Government will at once give telegraphic instructions for the explorer M. Marchand and his expedition to leave Fashoda and come down Nile, I can now send special steamer with such orders to fetch them.

"I am quite sure that no one would be more pleased than M. Marchand and his officers to secure release from their unpleasant position."

He suggests taking over their boats and launch at a valuation.

The Marquess of Salisbury to Mr. Rodd

Foreign Office, October 1, 1898

The following is secret:—

I request that you will inform the Sirdar that it has become clear that the French Government will not instruct M. Marchand to leave Fashoda. They expect that Her Majesty's Government will purchase his departure by large concessions of territory. This Her Majesty's Government will not do.

Under these circumstances, the question remains how M. Marchand is to be dealt with if he persists in remaining at Fashoda.

The Sirdar has already stated that he will not allow any reinforcements or munitions of war to pass upon the Nile. Nothing further remains to be done in this respect. The Sirdar has, no doubt, taken care that there is a sufficient force to secure that his declaration is carried into effect.

M. Marchand's position should be made as untenable as possible. If he is in want of food supplies, it will be very necessary to use circumspection in helping him to obtain them. Until he expresses his intention of going down the river, no such supplies should be furnished to him except in case of extreme necessity.

11. Chamberlain's Leicester Speech of November 30, 1899

. . .But there is something more which I think any far-seeing statesman must have long desired, and that is that we should not remain permanently isolated on the continent of Europe; and I think that the moment that aspiration was formed it must have appeared evident to everybody that the natural alliance is between ourselves and the great German Empire. [Loud cheers.] We have had our differences with Germany; we have had our quarrels and contentions; we have had our misunderstandings. I do not conceal that the people of this country have been irritated and justly irritated by circumstances which we are only too glad to forget, but at the root of things there has always been a force which has necessarily brought us together. What does unite nations? Interest and sentiment. What interest have we which is contrary to the interest of Germany? We have had, as I said, differences, but they have all been about matters so petty as regards the particular merits of the case that they have not really formed occasion for anything like serious controversy. These differences have, under Lord Salisbury's wise administration of foreign affairs [Cheers], been one by one gradually removed, until at the present time I cannot conceive any point which can arise in the immediate future which would bring ourselves and the Germans into antagonism of interests. [Cheers.] On the contrary, I can foresee many things in the future which must be a cause of anxiety to the statesmen of Europe, but in which our interests are clearly the same as the interests of Germany, and in which that understanding of which I have spoken in the case of America might, if extended to Germany, do more perhaps than any combination of arms in order to preserve the peace of the world. [Cheer.] . . .

It is with the German people [that we desire to have an understanding]; and I may point out to you that at bottom the character, the main character, of the Teutonic race differs very slightly indeed from the character of the Anglo-Saxon [Cheers], and the same sentiments which bring us into close sympathy with the United States of America may also be evoked to bring us into closer sympathy and alliance with the Empire of Germany. What do we find? We find our system of justice, we find our literature, we find the very base and foundation on which our language is established the same in the two countries, and if the union between England and America is a powerful factor in the cause of peace, a new Triple Alliance between the Teutonic race and the two great branches of the Anglo-Saxon race will be a still more potent influence in the future of the world. [Cheers.] . . .

12. Bülow's Advice to Delay Negotiations for a British Alliance

The Imperial Chancellor, Count von Bülow, to Emperor William II, temporarily at Osborne

Berlin, January 21, 1901

Your Majesty is quite right in feeling that the English must come to us. In Africa they have lost much hair, America shows herself to be uncertain. Japan unreliable, France full of hate, Russia perfidious, public opinion in all countries antagonistic. In 1897 at the Diamond Jubilee English self-confidence reached its height, the English peacock spread out his proud tail and was pleased with its splendid isolation. In 1898 the first efforts toward *rapprochement* appeared in the letter of Her Majesty, the Empress Frederick. In December 1899 the English wishes took form in the Chamberlain addresses and now the English are gradually becoming aware that they will not be able to maintain their world dominion with

their own strength against so many adversaries. It is now a matter of neither discouraging the English nor of letting oneself be prematurely pinned down by them. The embarrassment of the English will be enhanced in the next few months and thereby the price which we will be able to demand will increase. We must not show the English too great readiness—for that would increase the English demands and curtail our prospects of advantages—but we must at the same time keep the English convinced that we desire the perpetuation of a powerful England, that we believe in the solidarity of German and English cultural, political and economic interests, and that we would eventually be ready with the proper conduct on the English side to come to some sort of an agreement with them.

In this connection, according to my humble opinion, a dilatory behavior is demanded on our part, partly because very little solid gain can be made until Lord Salisbury has retired. It is true that he is no longer our avowed enemy, but still he is distrustful, indecisive, and slow in pulling the trigger. With reference to the general world situation and also to our own vital interests, Your Majesty would make a master stroke if Your Majesty were to succeed in letting Englishmen in authority hope for future firm relations with us without Your Majesty's now being prematurely pinned down. The understanding which the English threaten to make with the Dual Alliance is only a bugbear for our intimidation, with which the English have been maneuvering for years. The sacrifices which such an agreement would impose upon England are so enormous that the English government, even at the time of greatest irritation between us and England, did not decide in its favor. This agreement, which through the sacrifices required would weaken England, would strengthen and encourage the Dual Alliance for further opposition to England; it could only delay for a short time England's decisive battle for existence and would therefore be not only useless but directly harmful for her. Your Majesty will certainly know how to make the English conscious of this in a friendly but evident manner.

It seems to me very important, too, to avoid everything that might give the British the idea that the political relations between us and Russia and the personal relations between Your Majesty and the Tsar are strained or indeed irremediably bad. If the English believed that, they would no longer make us serious concessions in the hope and expectation that by the force of things Germany would be forced into conflict with Russia and France, and England would thereby be relieved of the necessity of risking her own skin.

God grant that Your Majesty may not have any too painful impressions in Osborne!

BÜLOW

13. Memorandum by Marquess of Salisbury, May 29, 1901

Proposal for including England within the Triple Alliance

This is a [German] proposal for including England within the bounds of the Triple Alliance. I understand its practical effect to be:

1. If England were attacked by two Powers—say France and Russia—Germany, Austria, and Italy could come to her assistance.

2. Conversely, if either Austria, Germany, or Italy were attacked by France and Russia, or, if Italy were attacked by France and Spain, England must come to the rescue.

Even assuming that the Powers concerned were all despotic, and could promise anything they pleased, with a full confidence that they would be able to perform the promise, I think it is open to much question whether the bargain would be for our advantage. The liability of having to defend the German and Austrian frontiers against Russia is heavier than that of *having to defend the British Isles against France.* Even, therefore, in its most naked aspect the bargain would be a bad one for this country. Count Hatzfeldt speaks of our *"isolation"* as constituting a serious danger for us. *Have we ever felt that danger practically?* If we had succumbed in the revolutionary war, our fall would not have been due to our isolation. We had many allies, but they would not have saved us if the French Emperor had been able to command the Channel. Except during his reign we have never even been in danger; and, therefore, it is impossible for us to judge whether the "isolation" under which we are supposed to suffer, does or does not contain in it any elements of peril. It would hardly be wise to incur novel and most onerous obligations, in order to guard against *a danger in whose existence we have no historical reason for believing.*

But though the proposed arrangement, even from this point of view, does not seem to me admissible, these are not by any means the weightiest objections that can be urged against it. The fatal circumstance is that *neither we nor the Germans are competent to make the suggested promises.* The British Government cannot undertake to declare war, for any purpose, unless it is a purpose of which the electors of this country would approve. If the Government promised to declare war for an object which did not commend itself to public opinion, the promise would be repudiated, and the Government would be turned out. I do not see how, in common honesty, we could invite other nations to rely upon our aids in a struggle, which must be formidable and probably supreme, when we have no means whatever of knowing what may be the humour of our people in circumstances which cannot be foreseen. We might, to some extent, divest ourselves of the full responsibility of such a step, *by laying our Agreement with the Triple Alliance before Parliament* as soon as it is concluded. But there are very grave objections to such a course, and I do not understand it to be recommended by the German Ambassador.

The impropriety of attempting to determine by a *secret contract* the future conduct of a Representative Assembly upon an issue of peace or war would apply to German policy as much as to English, only that the German Parliament would probably pay more deference to the opinion of their Executive than would be done by the English Parliament. But a *promise of defensive alliance with England would excite bitter murmurs in every rank of German society*—if we may trust the indications of German sentiment, which we have had an opportunity of witnessing during the last two years.

It would not be safe to stake any important national interest upon the fidelity with which, in case of national exigency, either country could be trusted to fulfil the obligations of the Alliance, if the Agreement had been concluded without the assent of its Parliament.

Several times during the last sixteen years Count Hatzfeldt has tried to elicit from me, in conversation, some opinion as to the probable conduct of England, if Germany or Italy were involved in war with France. I have always replied that no English minister could venture on such a forecast. The course of the English Government in such a crisis must depend on the view taken by public opinion in this country, and public opinion would be largely, if not exclusively, governed by the nature of the *casus belli.*

14. The Anglo-French Entente, April 8, 1904

Article 1. His Britannic Majesty's Government declare that they have no intention of altering the political status of Egypt.

The Government of the French Republic, for their part, declare that they will not obstruct the action of Great Britain in that country by asking that a limit of time be fixed for the British occupation or in any other manner, and that they give their assent to the draft Khedivial Decree annexed to the present arrangement, containing the guarantees considered necessary for the protection of the interests of the Egyptian bondholders, on the condition that, after its promulgation, it cannot be modified in any way without the consent of the Powers signatory of the Convention of London of 1885.

It is agreed that the post of Director-General of Antiquities in Egypt shall continue, as in the past, to be entrusted to a French *savant*.

The French schools in Egypt shall continue to enjoy the same liberty as in the past.

Article 2. The Government of the French Republic declare that they have no intention of altering the political status of Morocco.

His Britannic Majesty's Government, for their part, recognise that it appertains to France, more particularly as a Power whose dominions are conterminous for a great distance with those of Morocco, to preserve order in that country, and to provide assistance for the purpose of all administrative, economic, financial, and military reforms which it may require.

They declare that they will not obstruct the action taken by France for this purpose, provided that such action shall leave intact the rights which Great Britain, in virtue of treaties, conventions, and usage, enjoys in Morocco, including the right of coasting trade between the ports of Morocco, enjoyed by British vessels since 1901.

Article 3. His Britannic Majesty's Government, for their part, will respect the rights which France, in virtue of treaties, conventions, and usage, enjoys in Egypt, including the right of coasting trade between Egyptian ports accorded to French vessels.

Article 4. The two Governments, being equally attached to the principle of commercial liberty both in Egypt and Morocco, declare that they will not, in those countries, countenance any inequality either in the imposition of customs duties or other taxes, or of railway transport charges.

The trade of both nations with Morocco and with Egypt shall enjoy the same treatment in transit through the French and British possessions in Africa. An agreement between the two Governments shall settle the conditions of such transit and shall determine the points of entry.

This mutual engagement shall be binding for a period of thirty years. Unless this stipulation is expressly denounced at least one year in advance, the period shall be extended for five years at a time.

Nevertheless, the Government of the French Republic reserve to themselves in Morocco, and His Britannic Majesty's Government reserve to themselves in Egypt, the right to see that the concessions for roads, railways, ports, etc., are only granted on such conditions as will maintain intact the authority of the State over these great undertakings of public interest.

Article 5. His Britannic Majesty's Government declare that they will use their influence in order that the French officials now in the Egyptian service may not be placed under conditions less advantageous than those applying to the British officials in the service.

The Government of the French Republic, for their part, would make no objection to the application of analogous conditions to British officials now in the Moorish service.

Article 6. In order to ensure the free passage of the Suez Canal, His Britannic Majesty's Government declare that they adhere to the treaty of the 29th October, 1888, and that they agree to their being put in force. The free passage of the Canal being thus guaranteed, the execution of the last sentence of paragraph 1 as well as of paragraph 2 of article 8 of that treaty will remain in abeyance.

Article 7. In order to secure the free passage of the Straits of Gibraltar, the two Governments agree not to permit the erection of any fortifications or strategic works on that portion of the coast of Morocco comprised between, but not including, Melilla and the heights which command the right bank of the River Sebou.

This condition does not, however, apply to the places at present in the occupation of Spain on the Moorish coast of the Mediterranean.

Article 8. The two Governments, inspired by their feeling of sincere friendship for Spain, take into special consideration the interests which that country derives from her geographical position and from her territorial possessions on the Moorish coast of the Mediterranean. In regard to these interests the French Government will come to an understanding with the Spanish Government.

The agreement which may be come to on the subject between France and Spain shall be communicated to His Britannic Majesty's Government.

Article 9. The two Governments agree to afford to one another their diplomatic support, in order to obtain the execution of the clauses of the present Declaration regarding Egypt and Morocco.

In witness whereof his Excellency the Ambassador of the French Republic at the Court of His Majesty the King of the United Kingdom of Great Britain and Ireland and of the British Dominions beyond the Seas, Emperor of India, and His Majesty's Principal Secretary of State for Foreign Affairs, duly authorised for that purpose, have signed the present Declaration and have affixed thereto their seals.

Done at London, in duplicate, the 8th day of April, 1904.

(L.S.) LANSDOWNE
(L.S.) PAUL CAMBON

SECRET ARTICLES

Article 1. In the event of either Government finding themselves constrained, by the force of circumstances, to modify their policy in respect to Egypt or Morocco, the engagements which they have undertaken towards each other by articles, 4, 6, and 7 of the Declaration of to-day's date would remain intact.

Article 2. His Britannic Majesty's Government have no present intention of proposing to the Powers any changes in the system of the Capitulations, or in the judicial organisation of Egypt.

In the event of their considering it desirable to introduce in Egypt reforms tending to assimilate the Egyptian legislative system to that in force in other civilised Countries, the Government of the French Republic will not refuse to entertain any such proposals, on the understanding that His Britannic Majesty's Government will agree to entertain the suggestions that the Government of the French Republic may have to make to them with a view of introducing similar reforms in Morocco.

Article 3. The two Governments agree that a certain extent of Moorish territory adjacent to Melilla, Ceuta, and other *présides* should, whenever the Sultan ceases to exercise authority over it, come within the sphere of influence of Spain, and that the administration of the coast from Melilla as far as, but not including, the heights on the right bank of the Sebou shall be entrusted to Spain.

Nevertheless, Spain would previously have to give her formal assent to the provisions of articles 4 and 7 of the Declaration of to-day's date, and undertake to carry them out.

She would also have to undertake not to alienate the whole, or a part, of the territories placed under her authority or in her sphere of influence.

Article 4. If Spain, when invited to assent to the provisions of the preceding article, should think proper to decline, the arrangement between France and Great Britain, as embodied in the Declaration of to-day's date, would be none the less at once applicable.

Article 5. Should the consent of the other Powers to the draft Decree mentioned in article 1 of the Declaration of to-day's date not be obtained, the Government of the French Republic will not oppose the repayment at par of the Guaranteed, Privileged, and Unified Debts after 15th July, 1910.

Done at London, in duplicate, the 8th day of April, 1904.

(L.S.) LANSDOWNE
(L.S.) PAUL CAMBON

15. Final Text of the Bjoerkoe Treaty, July 1905

Björkoe 24/VII 1905 11/VII
Their Majesties the Emperors of all the Russias and of Germany, in order to assure the maintenance of peace in Europe have agreed upon the following articles of a Treaty of defensive alliance:

Article I. In case one of the two Empires is attacked by an European Power, its ally will aid it in Europe with all its land and sea forces.

Article II. The High Contracting Parties engage not to conclude separate peace with any common adversary.

Article III. The present treaty will be in force from the moment of the conclusion of peace between Russia and Japan, and may be denounced only by giving a year's previous notice.

Article IV. After this treaty has become effective, the Emperor of all the Russias will take the necessary steps to make its terms known to France and invite her to subscribe to it as an ally.

WILLIAM I. R.   NICOLAS
VON TSCHIRSCHKY and   A. BIRILEFF
BÖGENDORFF

16. Emperor Nicholas II of Russia to Emperor William II

[In his own handwriting in English]

Nov. 10/23, 1905

Six weeks have passed since I wrote to You last and many events have happened in this short space of time.

But first of all I must come back to the question of our Björkoe treaty. You remember that when it was signed, the war with Japan was continuing and it seemed that there would be ample time to prepare France to participate. Events of the last weeks have shown that there is not much chance of winning her over to our treaty "à trois" at least for the present.

Russia has no reasons to abandon her old ally suddenly nor to violate her.

Our influence must be cautious and perservering to become fruitful and certainly must take some time.

But a very serious difficulty would arise if France refused to join in our understanding. In that case Germany and Russia would remain alone and if the *secret* of Björkoe were to transpire, I am positively sure, a strong coalition will form itself against us two.

17. Emperor William II to Emperor Nicholas II of Russia 1905

[Undated draft in English]

Dearest Nicky,

I thank you for your letter and two telegrams, and also for ordering the coaling question to be regulated. We cannot to-day foresee, whether the declaration given by your Government will prove sufficient for every kind of complication, which may arise out of the present train of affairs. It is, however, not my intention, to press any sort of solution, which might appear undesirable to you. True and loyal friends we shall remain under all circumstances.

We cannot take France into our confidence, before we two have come to a definite arrangement. I look upon Loubet and Delcassé as statesmen of experience. But naturally I cannot place them on the same footing with you in a question of confidence. If therefore you think it imperative eventually to acquaint the French with our negotiations, before we have

arrived at a settlement, then it is better for all parties, to continue in our present condition of mutual independence, and spontaneously to promote each others ends as far as the situation will permit. I trust that the hope of our being useful to each other may be realized not only during war, but also during the peace-negotiations, for our interests in the far East are identical in more than one respect.

18. Extracts from the Speech Delivered by Bethmann-Hollweg in the Reichstag, November 9, 1911

For the consideration of the agreements laid before you it will first of all be of value to inform you as to the latest phase of the Morocco question, and as to the important points of the agreements concluded. The Algeciras Act was intended to maintain the independence of Morocco with a view to the economic development of the country for the benefit of the trade of all the Powers parties to it. It was soon evident that one of the essential conditions was lacking, namely, a Sultan who was actual ruler of the country, and was in a position to carry out the reforms contemplated. Even Sultan Mulai Hafid could not do so in spite of his personal qualities. He became more and more dependent upon foreign influence, and came into constantly increasing conflict with the tribes of his own country in consequence. This led to ever-growing influence on the part of France, for, of the four Powers which since the seventies possessed treaty rights to maintain military missions at the Sultan's Court, only the French Mission had succeeded in establishing its position. In the same way France had for long supplied Morocco with money. The position of the Sultan, surrounded by hostile tribes and shut up in Fez, became eventually so precarious that France informed the Powers that grave apprehensions must be felt for the lives and property of her officers at the Sultan's Court and of the European colony.

France accordingly declared that she proposed to send troops to Fez, and to conduct the Europeans back to the coast. We had received no such threatening reports from Fez and, therefore, declared that our colony did not require foreign assistance. Since, however, we could naturally assume no responsibility for the lives of the French citizens who were apparently threatened, we raised no objection to the advance to Fez to bring back the threatened French citizens to the coast. We added the explicit reservation, however, which we also announced publicly, that we retained our liberty of action, should the French expedition go beyond its alleged object, even should such action be merely the result of circumstances arising out of the expedition. This occurred, as was to be expected. France exerted practically unlimited sway over the relieved Sultan in virtue of her influence, which had gradually become absolute. The independence of the Sultan assumed by the Algeciras Act thus ceased to exist. It has, indeed, been urged that the Sultan himself summoned the French to his assistance, but a ruler who summons foreign troops to his assistance and who relies solely upon the support of foreign bayonets, is no longer the independent ruler on whose existence the Algeciras Act was based. We let this be known and suggested to France an understanding, leaving, of course, the initiative to her. We indicated the general outlines only of our programme to the effect that we should be ready to take into account the altered position of France resulting from the changed conditions, but that in return we must demand more precise guarantees for the equality assured to us in the domain of commerce and industry, especially in regard to public works, besides compensations for the rights assumed by France without previous understanding with us and going beyond the letter and spirit of the Algeciras Act. At first we received no positive proposals from Paris, whilst the French military power continued to spread in Morocco, and the fiction began gradually to become established, not only in France but also with the other Powers, that France was acting in pursuance of a European mandate. When, therefore, German interests appeared to be threatened in consequence of the events in Morocco, we sent a war-ship to Agadir. The dispatch of this ship was primarily intended for the protection of the lives and property of our subjects.

19. Lloyd George's "Mansion House Speech," July 21, 1911

. . . But I am also bound to say this—that I believe it is essential in the highest interests, not merely of this country but of the world, that Britain should at all hazards maintain her place and her prestige amongst the Great Powers of the world. [Cheers.] Her potent influence has many a time been in the past, and may yet be in the future, invaluable to the cause of human liberty. It has more than once in the past redeemed Continental nations, who are sometimes too apt to forget that service, from overwhelming disaster and even from international extinction. I would make great sacrifices to preserve peace. I conceive that nothing would justify a disturbance of international good will except questions of the gravest national moment. But if a situation were to be forced upon us in which peace could only be preserved by the surrender of the great and beneficent position Britain has won by centuries of heroism and achievement, by allowing Britain to be treated where her interests were vitally affected as if she were of no account in the Cabinet of nations, then I say emphatically that peace at that price would be a humiliation intolerable for a great country like ours to endure. [Cheers.] National honour is no party question. [Cheers.] The security of our great international trade is no party question; the peace of the world is much more likely to be secured if all nations realize fairly what the conditions of peace must be. And it is because I have the conviction that nations are beginning to understand each other better, to appreciate each other's points of view more thoroughly, to be more ready to discuss calmly and dispassionately their differences, that I feel assured that nothing will happen between now and next year which will render it difficult for the Chancellor of the Exchequer in this place to respond to the toast proposed by you, my Lord Mayor, of the continued prosperity of the public purse.

20. The House Mission, 1914

Extract from House's Diary

"Afterwards we adjourned to one of the larger drawing-rooms, where I was presented to the Empress. We talked of Corfu, the beauty of Germany in the spring, and other generalities. When this formality was over, the Kaiser's Aide-de-Camp came to say that His Majesty was ready to receive me on the terrace. . . .

"I found that he had all the versatility of Roosevelt with something more of charm, something less of force. He has what to me is a disagreeable habit of bringing his face very close to one when he talks most earnestly. His English is clear and well chosen and, though he talks vehemently, yet he is too much the gentleman to monopolize conversation. It was give-and-take all the way through. He knew what he wanted to say, so did I; and since we both talk rapidly, the half-hour was quite sufficient.

"Gerard and Zimmermann stood in conversation some ten or fifteen feet away, quite out of hearing. At first I thought I would never get His Majesty past his hobbies, but finally I drew him to the subject I had come to discuss. . . . I found him much less prejudiced and much less belligerent than von Tirpitz. He declared he wanted peace because it seemed to Germany's interest. Germany had been poor, she was now growing rich, and a few more years of peace would make her so. 'She was menaced on every side. The bayonets of Europe were directed at her,' and much more of this he gave me. Of England, he spoke kindly and admiringly. England, America, and Germany were kindred peoples and should draw closer together. Of other nations he had but little opinion. . . .

"He spoke of the impossibility of Great Britain being able to make a permanent and satisfactory alliance with either Russia or France. I told him that the English were very much concerned over his ever-growing navy, which taken together with his enormous army constituted a menace; and there might come a time when they would have to decide whether they ran more danger from him and his people making a successful invasion than they did from Russia, and the possibility of losing their Asiatic colonies. I thought when that point was reached, the decision would be against Germany.

"I spoke of the community of interests between England, Germany, and the United States, and thought if they stood together the peace of the world could be maintained. He assented to this quite readily. However, in my opinion, there could be no understanding between England and Germany so long as he continued to increase his navy. He replied that he must have a large navy in order to protect Germany's commerce in an adequate way, and one commensurate with her growing power and importance. He also said it was necessary to have a navy large enough to be able to defend themselves against the combined efforts of Russia and France.

"I asked when he would reach the end of his naval programme. He said this was well known, since they had formulated a policy for building and, when that was completed, there would be an end; that Great Britain had nothing to fear from Germany, and that he personally was a friend of England and was doing

her incalculable service in holding the balance of power against Russia.

"I told him that the President and I thought perhaps an American might be able to better compose the difficulties here and bring about an understanding with a view to peace than any European, because of their distrust and dislike for one another. He agreed to this suggestion. I had undertaken the work and that was my reason for coming to Germany, as I wanted to see him first. After leaving Germany it was my purpose to go directly to England, where I should take the matter up with that Government as I had done with him.

"I explained that I expected to feel my way cautiously and see what could be accomplished, and, if he wished it, I would keep him informed. He asked me to do this and said letters would reach him through our friend Zimmermann here in the Foreign Office." . . .

21. Extracts from the Statutes of "Union or Death"

Article 1. This organisation has been created with the object of realising the national ideal: The union of all the Serbs. All Serbs without distinction of sex, religion, place of birth and all who are sincerely devoted to this cause, may become members.

Article 2. This organisation prefers terrorist action to intellectual propaganda and for this reason must be kept absolutely secret from persons who do not belong to it.

Article 3. This organisation bears the name "Union or Death."

Article 4. To accomplish its task, the organisation:

1. Brings influence to bear on Government circles, on the various social classes and on the whole social life of the Kingdom of Serbia, regarded as Piémont.
2. Organises revolutionary action in all territories inhabited by Serbs.
3. Outside the frontiers of Serbia uses every means available to fight the adversaries of this idea.
4. Maintains amicable relations with all states, peoples, organisations and individuals who entertain feelings of friendship towards Serbia and the Serbian element.

5. Lends help and support in every way possible to all peoples and all organisations struggling for their national liberation and for their union.

Article 5. A Central Committee having its headquarters at Belgrade is at the head of this organisation and exercises executive authority. . . .

Article 25. Members of the organisation are not known to each other personally. It is only the members of the Central Committee who are known to one another.

Article 26. In the organisation itself the members are known by numbers. Only the Central Committee at Belgrade is to know their names. . . .

Article 31. Anyone who once enters the organisation may never withdraw from it. . . .

Article 33. When the Central Committee at Belgrade has pronounced penalty of death [on one of the members] the only matter of importance is that the execution take place without fail. . . .

22. The Imperial Chancellor, Bethmann-Hollweg, to the German Ambassador at Vienna, Tschirschky

Berlin, July 6, 1914

Confidential. For Your Excellency's
   personal information and guidance

The Austro-Hungarian Ambassador yesterday delivered to the Emperor a confidential personal letter from the Emperor Franz Joseph, which depicts the present situation from the Austro-Hungarian point of view, and describes the measures which Vienna has in view [cf. doc. No. 56 (a)]. A copy is now being forwarded to Your Excellency.

I replied to Count Szögyeny today on behalf of His Majesty that His Majesty sends his thanks to the Emperor Franz Joseph for his letter and would soon answer it personally. In the meantime His Majesty desires to say that he is not blind to the danger which threatens Austria-Hungary and thus the Triple Alliance as a result of the Russian and Serbian Panslavic agitation. Even though His Majesty is known to feel no unqualified confidence in Bulgaria and her ruler, and naturally inclines more toward our old ally Roumania and her Hohenzollern prince, yet he quite understands that the Emperor Franz Joseph, in view

of the attitude of Roumania and of the danger of a new Balkan alliance aimed directly at the Danube Monarchy, is anxious to bring about an understanding between Bulgaria and the Triple Alliance. His Majesty will, therefore, direct his minister at Sofia to lend the Austro-Hungarian representative such support as he may desire in any action taken to this end. His Majesty will, furthermore, make an effort at Bucharest, according to the wishes of the Emperor Franz Joseph, to influence King Carol to the fulfilment of the duties of his alliance, to the renunciation of Serbia, and to the suppression of the Roumanian agitations directed against Austria-Hungary.

Finally, as far as concerns Serbia, His Majesty, of course, cannot interfere in the dispute now going on between Austria-Hungary and that country, as it is a matter not within his competence. The Emperor Franz Joseph may, however, rest assured that His Majesty will faithfully stand by Austria-Hungary, as is required by the obligations of his alliance and of his ancient friendship.

BETHMANN-HOLLWEG

23. House's Letter to the Kaiser

Colonel Edward M. House to Emperor William

London, July 8, 1914

Sir!

Your Imperial Majesty will doubtless recall our conversation at Potsdam, and that with the President's consent and approval I came to Europe for the purpose of ascertaining whether or not it was possible to bring about a better understanding between the Great Powers, to the end that there might be a continuation of peace, and later a beneficent economic readjustment, which a lessening of armaments would ensure. Because of the commanding position Your Majesty occupies, and because of your well-known desire to maintain peace, I came, as Your Majesty knows, directly to Berlin. I can never forget the gracious acceptance of the general purposes of my mission, the masterly exposition of the worldwide political conditions as they exist today, and the prophetic forecast as to the future which Your Majesty then made. I received every reasonable assurance of Your Majesty's cordial approval of the President's purpose, and I left Germany happy in the belief that Your Majesty's great influence would be thrown in behalf of peace and the broadening of the world's commerce. In France I tried to reach the thoughts of her people in regard to Germany and to find what hopes she nursed. My conclusion upon leaving was that her statesmen have given over all thought of revenge, or of recovery of the two provinces. Her people in general still have hopes in both directions, but her better-informed rulers would be quite content if France would be sure of her autonomy as it now exists. It was then, Sir, that I came to England and with high hopes, in which I have not been disappointed. I first approached Sir Edward Grey, and I found him sympathetic to the last degree. After a two hours' conference, we parted with an understanding that we should meet again within a few days. This I inferred to mean that he wished to consult with the Prime Minister and his colleagues. At our next conference, which again lasted for two hours, he had to meet me, the Lord Chancellor [Lord Haldane], Lord Crewe, and Sir William Tyrrell. Since then I have met the Prime Minister and practically every important member of the British Government, and I am convinced that they desire such an understanding as will lay the foundation for permanent peace and security. England must necessarily move cautiously lest she offend the sensibilities of France and Russia; but, with the changing sentiment in France, there should be a gradual improvement of relations between Germany and that country which England will now be glad to foster. While much has been accomplished, yet there is something still to be desired in order that there may be a better medium created for an easy and frank exchange of thoughts and purposes. No one knows better than Your Majesty of the unusual foment that is now going on throughout the world, and no one is in so fortunate a position to bring about a sane and reasonable understanding among the statesmen of the Western peoples, to the end that our civilization may continue uninterrupted. While this communication is, as Your Majesty knows, quite unofficial, yet it is written in sympathy with the well-known views of the President, and, I am given to understand, with the hope from His Britannic Majesty's Government that it may bring a response from Your Majesty which may permit another step forward.

Permit me, Sir, to conclude by quoting a sentence from a letter which has come to me from the President: "Your letter from Paris, written just after coming from Berlin, gives me a thrill of deep pleasure. You have, I hope and believe, begun a great thing and I rejoice with all my heart."

I have the honour to be, Sir, with the greatest respect, Your Majesty's very obedient Servant,

EDWARD M. HOUSE

24. German View That Russia Was the Key to the European Situation (Kaiser's Comments Shown)

The German Ambassador at St. Petersburg to the Foreign Office

Telegram 149   St. Petersburg, July 25, 1914

Have just had long interview with Sazonoff at which subject of dispatch 592 figured exhaustively. Minister, who was *very much excited* and gave vent to boundless reproaches against Austria-Hungary, stated in the most determined manner that it would be impossible for Russia to admit that the Austro-Serb quarrel could be settled between the two parties concerned. The obligations which Serbia had assumed after the Bosian crisis and to which the Austrian note refers, were assumed toward Europe, consequently the affair was a European affair, and it was for *Europe* to investigate as to whether Serbia had lived up to these obligations. He therefore proposes that the documents in relation to the inquiry be laid before the Cabinets of the six Powers. Austria could not be both accuser and judge in her own case. Sazonoff announced that he could in no way consider as proven the facts alleged by Austria in her note, that the inquiry, on the other hand, inspired him with the greatest (suspicion). He continued by saying that, in case the facts asserted should be proved to be true, Serbia could give Austria satisfaction in the purely legal questions, but not, on the other hand, in the matter of the demands of a political nature. I called attention to the fact that it was impossible to separate the legal from

Good.

Rot!

That's a question of the point of view!

Cannot be separated.

the political side of the matter, as the assassination was inseparably connected with the Greater-Serbia propaganda.

I promised to lay his ideas before my Government, but did not believe that we would suggest to our ally to submit the results of an inquiry conducted by her *once more to a European tribunal.* Austria would object to this suggestion just as any Great Power would have to refuse to submit itself to a court of arbitration in a case in which its vital interests were at stake.

My references to the monarchical principle made little impression on the minister. Russia *knew* what she *owed to the monarchical principle,* with which, however, this case had nothing to do. I requested Sazonoff very seriously, avoiding everything that might have the appearance of a threat, not to let himself be led astray by his hatred of Austria and *"not to defend a bad cause."* Russia could not possibly constitute herself the advocate of *regicides.*

In the course of the conversation Sazonoff exclaimed: "If Austria-Hungary devours Serbia, we will go to war with her." From this it may perhaps be concluded that Russia will only take up arms in the event of Austria's attempting to acquire territory at the expense of Serbia. The expressed desire to Europeanize the question also seems to point to the fact that immediate intervention on the part of Russia is not to be anticipated.

POURTALÈS

25. Russian Advice to Serbia

Special Journal of the Council of Ministers
11 [24] July, 1914

Subsequent to the declaration made by the Minister of Foreign Affairs regarding the most recent measures taken by the Austro-Hungarian Government against Serbia.

The Minister of Foreign Affairs informed the Council of Ministers that, according to information received by him and according to the announcement made by the Austro-Hungarian Ambassador to the Imperial Court, the Austro-Hungarian Government had turned upon the Serbian Government with demands which appeared, in fact, to be quite unacceptable to the Serbian Government as a sovereign State, and which were drawn up in the form of an ultimatum calling for a reply within a definite time, expiring tomorrow, July 12, at 6 o'clock in the evening.

Therefore, foreseeing that Serbia would turn to us for advice, and perhaps also for aid, there arose a need to prepare an answer which might be given to Serbia.

Having considered the declaration made by Marshal Sazonov in its relation to the information reported by the Ministers of War, Marine and Finance concerning the political and military situation, the Council of Ministers decreed:

1—To approve the proposal of the Minister of Foreign Affairs to get in touch with the Cabinets of the Great Powers in order to induce the Austro-Hungarian Government to grant a postponement in the matter of the answer to the ultimatum demands presented by the Austro-Hungarian Government, so that it might be possible for the Governments of the Great Powers to become acquainted with and to investigate the documents on the Sarajevo crime which are in the hands of the Austro-Hungarian Government, and which, according to the declaration of the Austro-Hungarian Ambassador, it is willing to communicate to the Russian Government.

2—To approve the proposal of the Minister of Foreign Affairs to advise the Serbian Government, in case the situation of Serbia should be such that she could not with her own strength protect herself against the possible armed invasion by Austro-Hungary, not to offer armed resistance to the invasion of Serbian territory, if such an invasion should occur, but to announce that Serbia yields to force and that she entrusts her fate to the judgment of the Great Powers.

3—To authorize the Ministers of War and of Marine, in accordance with the duties of their offices, to beg your Imperial Majesty to consent, according to the progress of events, to order the mobilization of the four military districts of Kiev, Odessa, Moscow and Kazan, and the Baltic and Black Sea fleets.

(Note by the Acting Secretary of the Council:

"In the original the word 'Baltic' has been added by his Imperial Majesty's own hand, and the word 'fleet' corrected to read 'fleets' ")

4—To authorize the War Minister to proceed immediately to gather stores of war material.

5—To authorize the Minister of Finance to take measures instantly to diminish the funds of the Ministry of Finance which may be at present in Germany or Austria.

The Council of Ministers considers it its loyal duty to inform your Imperial Majesty of these decisions which it has made.

26. Sir Edward Grey to Sir F. Bertie (British Ambassador to Paris)

Foreign Office, July 26, 1914

Tel. (No. 232)

Ask Minister for Foreign Affairs if he would be disposed to instruct Ambassador here to join with representatives of Italy, Germany, France, and myself in a conference to be held here at once in order to endeavour to find an issue to prevent complications. With this view representatives at Vienna, St. Petersburg and Belgrade should be authorised in informing Governments to which they are accredited of above suggestion to request that pending results of conference all active military operations shall be suspended.

(Repeated to Vienna, St. Petersburg, and Nish.)
(Sent also to Berlin, and Rome.)

27. The Serbian Reply to the Austrian Ultimatum, July 25, 1914

This declaration will be brought to the knowledge of the Royal Army in an order of the day, in the name of His Majesty the King, by his Royal Highness the Crown Prince Alexander, and will be published in the next official army bulletin.

The Royal Government further undertake:—

1. To introduce at the first regular convocation of the Skuptchina a provision into the press law providing for the most severe punishment of incitement to hatred or contempt of the Austro-Hungarian Monarchy, and for taking action against any publication the general tendency of which is directed against the territorial integrity of Austria-Hungary. The Government engage at the approaching revision of the Constitution to cause an amendment to be introduced into article 22 of the Constitution of such a nature that such publication may be confiscated, a proceeding at present impossible under the categorical terms of article 22 of the Constitution.

2. The Government possess no proof, nor does the note of the Imperial and Royal Government furnish them with any, that the "Narodna Odbrana" and other similar societies have committed up to the present any criminal act of this nature through the proceedings of any of their members. Nevertheless, the Royal Government will accept the demand of the Imperial and Royal Government, and will dissolve the "Narodna Odbrana" Society and every other society which may be directing its efforts against Austria-Hungary.

3. The Royal Servian Government undertake to remove without delay from their public educational establishments in Servia all that serves or could serve to foment propaganda against Austria-Hungary, whenever the Imperial and Royal Government furnish them with facts and proofs of this propaganda.

4. The Royal Government also agree to remove from military service all such persons as the judicial enquiry may have proved to be guilty of acts directed against the integrity of the territory of the Austro-Hungarian Monarchy, and they expect the Imperial and Royal Government to communicate to them at a later date the names and the acts of these officers and officials for the purposes of the proceedings which are to be taken against them.

5. The Royal Government must confess that they do not clearly grasp the meaning or the scope of the demand made by the Imperial and Royal Government that Servia shall undertake to accept the collaboration of the organs of the Imperial and Royal Government upon their territory, but they declare that they will admit such collaboration as agrees with the principle of international law, with criminal procedure, and with good neighbourly relations.

6. It goes without saying that the Royal Government consider it their duty to open an enquiry against all such persons as are, or eventually may be, implicated in the plot of the 15th June, and who happen to be within the territory of the kingdom. As regards the participation in this enquiry of Austro-Hungarian agents or authorities appointed for this purpose by the Imperial and Royal Government, the Royal Government cannot accept such an arrangement, as it would be a violation of the Constitution and of the law of criminal procedure; nevertheless, in concrete

cases communications as to the results of the investigation in question might be given to the Austro-Hungarian agents.

7. The Royal Government proceeded, on the very evening of the delivery of the note, to arrest Commandant Voislav Tankossitch. As regards Milan Ziganovitch, who is a subject of the Austro-Hungarian Monarchy and who up to the 15th June was employed (on probation) by the directorate of railways, it has not yet been possible to arrest him.

The Austro-Hungarian Government are requested to be so good as to supply as soon as possible, in the customary form, the presumptive evidence of guilt, as well as the eventual proofs of guilt which have been collected up to the present, at the enquiry at Serajevo for the purposes of the later enquiry.

8. The Servian Government will reinforce and extend the measures which have been taken for preventing the illicit traffic of arms and explosives across the frontier. It goes without saying that they will immediately order an enquiry and will severely punish the frontier officials on the Schabatz-Loznitza line who have failed in their duty and allowed authors of the crime of Serajevo to pass.

28. German Chancellor's Attempt to Hold Back the Kaiser and Allow Mediation to Have Its Effect (Latter's Comments Are Shown)

The Imperial Chancellor to the Emperor

There is a Russian fleet! In the Baltic there are now five Russian torpedo boat flotillas engaged in practice cruises, which as a whole or in part can be at the Belts within sixteen hours and close

Berlin, July 26, 1914

As Your Majesty has just been informed by the Admiralty Staff, the naval attaché at London reports that the *English* fleet is discharging its reservists, and giving crews leave according to schedule. In agreement with this fact, I venture most humbly to suggest to Your Majesty to order the High Seas Fleet to remain in Nor-

them. Port Arthur should be a lesson! My fleet has orders to sail for Kiel, and to Kiel it is going to sail! W.

way for the present, as this would materially lighten the burden of England's proposed mediation action at Petersburg, which is *evidently beginning to get shaky*.
BETHMANN-HOLLWEG

Where does he get that idea? *Not* from the material submitted to me.

29. Grey's Request That Germany Urge Moderation at Vienna

Sir Edward Grey to Sir E. Goschen

Tel. (No. 208)   Foreign Office, July 27, 1914

German Ambassador has informed me that German Government accept in principle mediation between Austria and Russia by the four Powers, reserving, of course, their right as an ally to help Austria if attacked. He has also been instructed to request me to use influence in St. Petersburg to localise the war and to keep up the peace of Europe.

I have replied that the Servian reply went further than could have been expected to meet the Austrian demands. German Minister for Foreign Affairs has himself said that there were some things in the Austrian note that Servia could hardly be expected to accept. I assumed that Servian reply could not have gone as far as it did unless Russia had exercised conciliatory influence at Belgrade, and it was really at Vienna that moderating influence was now required. If Austria put the Servian reply aside as being worth nothing and marched into Servia, it meant that she was determined to crush Servia at all costs, being reckless of the consequences that might be involved. Servian reply should at least be treated as a basis for discussion and pause. I said German Government should urge this at Vienna.

I recalled what German Government had said as to the gravity of the situation if the war could not be localised, and observed that if Germany assisted Austria against Russia it would be because, without any reference to the merits of the dispute, Germany could no afford to see Austria crushed. Just so other issues might be raised that would supersede the dispute between Austria and Servia, and would bring other Powers in, and war would be the biggest ever known; but as long as Germany would work to keep the peace I would keep closely in touch. I repeated that after the Servian reply it was at Vienna that some moderation must be urged.

30. German Advice to Austria in Pursuance of Grey's Request

The Imperial Chancellor to the German Ambassador at Vienna

Telegram 169   Berlin, July 27, 1914

Prince Lichnowsky has just telegraphed:

"Sir E. Grey had me call on him just now and requested me to inform Your Excellency as follows:

"The Serbian Chargé d'Affaires had just transmitted to him the text of the Serbian reply to the Austrian note. It appeared from the reply that Serbia had agreed to the Austrian demands to an extent such as he would never have believed possible; except in one point, the participation of Austrian officials in the judicial investigation, Serbia had actually agreed to everything that had been demanded of her. It was plain that this compliance of Serbia's *was to be attributed to the pressure exerted from Petersburg.*

"Should Austria fail to be satisfied with this reply, in other words, should this reply not be accepted at Vienna as a foundation for peaceful negotiations, or should Austria even proceed to the occupation of Belgrade, which lay quite defenseless before her, it would then be absolutely evident that Austria was only seeking an excuse for crushing Serbia. And thus, that Russia and Russian influence in the Balkans were to be struck at through Serbia. It was plain that Russia could not regard such action with equanimity, and would have to accept it as a direct challenge. The result would be the most frightful war that Europe had ever seen, and no one could tell to what such a war might lead.

"We had repeatedly, and even yesterday, stated the Minister, turned to him with the request that he *make a plea for moderation at Petersburg. He had always gladly complied with this request* and during the last crisis had subjected himself to reproaches from Russia to the effect that he was placing himself too much on our side and too little on theirs. Now he was turning to us with the request that we should make use of our influence at Vienna either to get them to accept the reply from Belgrade as satisfactory or as the basis for conferences. He was convinced that it lay in our hands to bring the matter to a settlement by means of the proper representations, and he would regard it as a good augury for the future *if we two should once again succeed in assuring the peace of Europe by means of our mutual influence on our allies.*

"I found the Minister irritated for the first time.

He spoke with great seriousness and seemed absolutely to expect that we should successfully make use of our influence to settle the matter. He is also going to make a statement in the House of Commons today in which he is to express his point of view. In any event, I am convinced that in case it should come to war after all, we should no longer be able to count on British sympathy or British support, as every evidence of ill-will would be seen in Austria's procedure."

Since we have already refused one English proposal for a conference, it is impossible for us to waive *a limine* this English suggestion also. By refusing every proposition for mediation, we should be held responsible for the conflagration by the whole world, and be set forth as the original instigators of the war. That would also make our position impossible in our own country, where we must appear as having been forced into the war. Our situation is all the more difficult, inasmuch as Serbia has apparently yielded to a very great degree. Therefore we cannot refuse the mediator's rôle, and must submit the English proposal to the consideration of the Vienna Cabinet, especially as London and Paris continue to make their influence felt in Petersburg. I request Count Berchtold's opinion on the English suggestion, as likewise his views on M. Sazonoff's desire to negotiate directly with Vienna.

31. German Refusal of Grey's Proposal of a Conference

Sir E. Goschen to Sir Edward Grey

Tel. (No. 96)   Berlin, July 27, 1914

Your telegram No. 232 of 26th of July to Paris

Secretary of State for Foreign Affairs says that conference you suggest would practically amount to a court of arbitration and could not, in his opinion, be called together except at the request of Austria and Russia. He could not therefore, desirous though he was to cooperate for the maintenance of peace, fall in with your suggestion. I said I was sure that your idea had nothing to do with arbitration, but meant that representatives of the four nations not directly interested should discuss and suggest means for avoiding a dangerous situation. He maintained, however, that such a conference as you proposed was not practicable. He added that news he had just received from St. Petersburg showed that there was an intention on the part of M. Sazonof to exchange views with Count Berchtold. He thought that this method of procedure might lead to a satisfactory result, and that it would be best, before doing anything else, to await outcome of the exchange of views between the Austrian and Russian Governments.

In the course of a short conversation Secretary of State for Foreign Affairs said that as yet Austria was only partially mobilising, but that if Russia mobilised against Germany latter would have to follow suit. I asked him what he meant by "mobilising against Germany." He said that if Russia only mobilised in south Germany would not mobilise, but if she mobilised in north Germany would have to do so too, and Russian system of mobilisation was so complicated that it might be difficult exactly to locate her mobilisation. Germany would therefore have to be very careful not to be taken by surprise. . . .

32. Grey to Bertie

(No. 513)   Foreign Office, July 31, 1914
Sir,

M. Cambon referred today to a telegram that had been shown to Sir Arthur Nicolson this morning from the French Ambassador in Berlin saying that it was the uncertainty with regard to whether we would intervene which was the encouraging element in Berlin, and that, if we would only declare definitely on the side of Russia and France, it would decide the German attitude in favour of peace.

I said that it was quite wrong to suppose that we had left Germany under the impression that we would not intervene. I had refused overtures to promise that we should remain neutral. I had not only definitely declined to say that we would remain neutral; I had even gone so far this morning as to say to the German Ambassador that, if France and Germany became involved in war, we should be drawn into it. That, of course, was not the same thing as taking an engagement to France, and I told M. Cambon of it only to show that we had not left Germany under the impression that we would stand aside.

M. Cambon then asked me for my reply to what he had said yesterday.

I said that we had come to the conclusion, in the Cabinet today, that we could not give any pledge at the present time. The commercial and financial situation was exceedingly serious; there was danger of a complete collapse that would involve us and everyone else in ruin; and it was possible that our standing aside might be the only means of preventing a complete collapse of European credit, in which we should

be involved. This might be a paramount consideration in deciding our attitude.

I went on to say to M. Cambon that though we should have to put our policy before Parliament, we could not pledge Parliament in advance. Up to the present moment, we did not feel, and public opinion did not feel, that any treaties or obligations of this country were involved. Further developments might alter this situation and cause the Government and Parliament to take the view that intervention was justified. The preservation of the neutrality of Belgium might be, I would not say a decisive, but an important factor, in determining our attitude. Whether we proposed to Parliament to intervene or not to intervene in a war, Parliament would wish to know how we stood with regard to the neutrality of Belgium, and it might be that I should ask both France and Germany whether each was prepared to undertake an engagement that she would not be the first to violate the neutrality of Belgium.

M. Cambon expressed great disappointment at my reply. He repeated his question of whether we would help France if Germany made an attack on her.

I said that I could only adhere to the answer that, as far as things had gone at present, we could not take any engagement. *The latest news was that Russia had ordered a complete mobilisation of her fleet and army. This, it seemed to me, would precipitate a crisis, and would make it appear that German mobilisation was being forced by Russia.*

M. Cambon urged that Germany had from the beginning rejected proposals that might have made for peace. It could not be to England's interest that France should be crushed by Germany. We should then be in a very diminished position with regard to Germany. In 1870, we had made a great mistake in allowing an enormous increase of German strength; and we should not be repeating the mistake. He asked me whether I could not submit his question to the Cabinet again.

I said that the Cabinet would certainly be summoned as soon as there was some new development, but at the present moment the only answer I could give was that we could not undertake any definite engagement.

I am, &c.
E. GREY

33. Italian Reasons for Neutrality

[Von Mérey was Austrian Ambassador in Rome. The Italian Minister of Foreign Affairs in 1914 was San Giuliano.]

(a) *Von Mérey to Count Berchtold*

Telegram   Rome, July 30, 1914

Minister of Foreign Affairs spontaneously brought up today the question of Italy's attitude in the event of a European war.

As the character of the Triple Alliance is purely defensive; as our measures against Servia may precipitate a European conflagration, and finally as we had not previously consulted this government, Italy would not be bound to join us in the war. This, however, does not preclude the alternative that Italy might, in such an event, have to decide for herself whether her interests would best be served by taking sides with us in military operations or by remaining neutral. Personally he feels more inclined to favor the first solution, which appears to him as the more likely one, provided that Italy's interests in the Balkan Peninsula are safeguarded and that we do not seek changes likely to give us a predominance detrimental to Italy's interests in the Balkans.

34. The German Ambassador at Rome to the German Foreign Office

Telegram 161   Rome, July 31, 1914

The local Government has discussed, at the Ministerial Council held today, the question of Italy's attitude in the war. Marquis San Giuliano told me that the Italian Government had considered the question thoroughly, and had again come to the conclusion that Austria's procedure against Serbia must be regarded as an act of aggression, and that consequently a *casus foederis*, according to the terms of the Triple Alliance treaty, did not exist. Therefore Italy would have to declare herself neutral. Upon my violently opposing this point of view, the Minister went on to state that since Italy had not been informed in advance of Austria's procedure against Serbia, she could with less reason be expected to take part in the war, as Italian interests were being directly injured by the Austrian proceeding. All that he could say to me now was that the local Government reserved the right to determine whether it might be possible for Italy to intervene later in behalf of the allies, if, at the time of doing so, Italian interests should be satisfactorily protected. The Minister, who was in a state of great excitement, said in explanation that the entire Ministerial Council, with the exception of himself, had shown a distinct dislike for Austria. It had been all the more difficult for him to contest this feeling, because Austria, as I myself knew, was continuing so persistently with a recognized injury to Italian interests, as to violate Article 7 of the Triple Alliance treaty, and because she was declining to give a guaranty for the independence and integrity of Serbia. He regretted that the Imperial Government had not done more to intervene in this connection to persuade Austria to a timely compliance. I have the impression that it is not yet necessary to give up all hope for the future here, if the Italians should be met halfway with regard to the demands mentioned above, or in other words, if compensation should be offered them. Nevertheless, it cannot be denied that the attitude England has assumed has decidedly diminished the prospects of an active Italian participation in our favor.

35. Roumanian Decision for Neutrality

[Count Czernin was Austrian Minister to Roumania.]

Czernin to Berchtold, Aug. 1, 1914

Bucharest

The Prime Minister has just notified me the result of the Cabinet Council. After a warm appeal from the King to bring the treaty into force, the Cabinet Council, with one exception, declared that no party could undertake the responsibility of such action.

The Cabinet Council has resolved that *as Roumania was neither notified nor consulted concerning the Austro-Hungarian action in Belgrade no casus foederis exists*. The Cabinet Council further resolved that military preparations for the safety of the frontier be undertaken, which would be an advantage for the Austro-Hungarian Monarchy, as several hundred miles of its frontiers would thereby be covered.

The Prime Minister added that he had already given orders to strengthen all military posts, after which by degrees general mobilization would follow.

The government intends only to publish a short *communiqué* relating to the military measures taken for the safety of the country.

36. Secret Treaty of London, April 26, 1915

Article 1. A military convention shall be immediately concluded between the General Staffs of France, Great Britain, Italy and Russia. This convention shall settle the minimum number of military forces to be employed by Russia against Austria-Hungary in order to prevent that Power from concentrating all its strength against Italy, in the event of Russia deciding to direct her principal effort against Germany.

This military convention shall settle question of armistices, which necessarily comes within the scope of the Commanders-in-chief of the Armies.

Article 2. On her part, Italy untertakes to use her entire resources for the purpose of waging war jointly with France, Great Britain and Russia against all their enemies.

Article 3. The French and British fleets shall render active and permanent assistance to Italy until such time as the Austro-Hungarian fleet shall have been destroyed or until peace shall have been concluded.

A naval convention shall be immediately concluded to this effect between France, Great Britain and Italy.

Article 4. Under the Treaty of Peace, Italy shall obtain the Trentino, Cisalpine Tyrol with its geographical and natural frontier (the Brenner frontier), as well as Trieste, the counties of Gorizia and Gradisca, all Istria as far as the Quarnero and including Volosca and the Istrian islands of Cherso and Lussin, as well as the small islands of Plavnik, Unie, Canidole, Palazzuoli, San Pietro di Nembi, Asinello, Gruica, and the neighbouring islets. . . . [Note tracing this frontier in detail]

Article 5. Italy shall also be given the province of Dalmatia within its present administrative boundaries, including to the north [here follow details of boundary].

To be neutralized:—

(1) The entire coast from Cape Planka on the north to the southern base of the peninsula of Sabbioncello in the south, so as to include the whole of that peninsula; (2) the portion of the coast which begins in the north at a point situated 10 kilometres south of the headland of Ragusa Vecchia extending southward as far as the River Voïussa, in such a way as to include the gulf and ports of Cattaro, Antivari, Dulcigno, St. Jean de Medua and Durazzo, without prejudice to the rights of Montenegro consequent on the declarations exchanged between the Powers in April and May 1909. As these rights only apply to the present Montenegrin territory, they cannot be extended to any territory or ports which may be assigned to Montenegro. Consequently neutralisation shall not apply to any part of the coast now belonging to Montenegro. There shall be maintained all restrictions concerning the port of Antivari which were accepted by Montenegro in 1909; (3) finally, all the islands not given to Italy.

NOTE: The following Adriatic territory shall be assigned by the four Allied Powers to Croatia, Serbia and Montenegro:—

In the Upper Adriatic, the whole coast from the bay of Volosca on the borders of Istria as far as the northern frontier of Dalmatia, including the coast which is at present Hungarian and all the coast of Croatia, with the port of Fiume and the small ports of Novi and Carlopago, as well as the islands of Veglia, Pervichio, Gregorio, Goli and Arbe. And, in the Lower Adriatic, (in the region interesting Serbia and Montenegro) the whole coast from Cape Planka as far as the River Drin, with the important harbours of Spalato, Ragusa, Cattaro, Antivari, Dulcigno and St. Jean de Medua and the islands of Greater and Lesser Zirona, Bua, Solta, Brazza, Jaclian and Calamotta. The port of Durazzo to be assigned to the independent Moslem State of Albania.

Article 6. Italy shall receive full sovereignty over Valona, the island of Saseno and surrounding territory of sufficient extent to assure defence of these points (from the Voïussa to the north and east, approximately to the northern boundary of the district of Chimara on the south).

Article 7. Should Italy obtain the Trentino and Istria in accordance with the provisions of Article 4, together with Dalmatia and the Adriatic islands within the limits specified in Article 5, and the Bay of Valona (Article 6), and if the central portion of Albania is reserved for the establishment of a small autonomous neutralised State, Italy shall not oppose the division of Northern and Southern Albania between Montenegro, Serbia and Greece, should France, Great Britain and Russia so desire. The coast from the southern boundary of the Italian territory of Valona (see Article 6) up to Cape Stylos shall be neutralised.

Italy shall be charged with the representation of the State of Albania in its relations with foreign Powers.

Italy agrees, moreover, to leave sufficient territory in any event to the east of Albania to ensure the existence of a frontier line between Greece and Serbia to the west of Lake Ochrida.

Article 8. Italy shall receive entire sovereignty over the Dodecanese Islands which she is at present occupying.

Article 9. Generally speaking, France, Great Britain and Russia recognise that Italy is interested in the maintenance of the balance of power in the Mediterranean and that, in the event of the total or partial partition of Turkey in Asia, she ought to obtain a just share of the Mediterranean region adjacent to the province of Adalia, where Italy has already acquired rights and interests which formed the subject of an Italo-British convention. The zone which shall eventually be allotted to Italy shall be delimited, at the proper time, due account being taken of the existing interests of France and Great Britain.

The interests of Italy shall also be taken into consideration in the event of the territorial integrity of the Turkish Empire being maintained and of alterations being made in the zones of interest of the Powers.

If France, Great Britain and Russia occupy any territories in Turkey in Asia during the course of the war, the Mediterranean region bordering on the Province of Adalia within the limits indicated above shall be reserved to Italy, who shall be entitled to occupy it.

Article 10. All rights and privileges in Libya at present belonging to the Sultan by virtue of the Treaty of Lausanne are transferred to Italy.

Article 11. Italy shall receive a share of any eventual war indemnity corresponding to her efforts and her sacrifices.

Article 12. Italy declares that she associates herself in the declaration made by France, Great Britain and Russia to the effect that Arabia and the Moslem Holy Places in Arabia shall be left under the authority of an independent Moslem Power.

Article 13. In the event of France and Great Britain increasing their colonial territories in Africa at the expense of Germany, those two Powers agree in principle that Italy may claim some equitable compensation, particularly as regards the settlement in her favour of the questions relative to the frontiers of the Italian colonies of Eritrea, Somaliland and Libya and the neighbouring colonies belonging to France and Great Britain.

Article 14. Great Britain undertakes to facilitate the immediate conclusion, under equitable conditions, of a loan of at least £50,000,000, to be issued on the London market.

Article 15. France, Great Britain and Russia shall support such opposition as Italy may make to any proposal in the direction of introducing a representative of the Holy See in any peace negotiations or negotiations for the settlement of questions raised by the present war.

Article 16. The present arrangement shall be held secret. The adherence of Italy to the Declaration of the 5th September, 1914, shall alone be made public, immediately upon declaration of war by or against Italy.

.   .   .   .

After having taken act of the foregoing memorandum the representatives of France, Great Britain and Russia, duly authorised to that effect, have concluded the following agreement with the representative of Italy, also duly authorised by his Government:—

France, Great Britain and Russia give their full assent to the memorandum presented by the Italian Government.

With reference to Articles 1, 2, and 3 of the memorandum which provide for military and naval coöperation between the four Powers, Italy declares that she will take the field at the earliest possible date and within a period not exceeding one month from the signature of these presents.

In faith where of the undersigned have signed the present agreements and have affixed thereto their seals.

Done at London, in quadruplicate, the 26th day of April, 1915.

(L. S.) E. GREY
(L. S.) IMPERIALI
(L. S.) BENCKENDORFF
(L. S.) PAUL CAMBON

37. Declaration by Which France, Great Britain, Italy and Russia Undertake Not to Conclude a Separate Peace during the Course of the Present European War

The Italian Government, having decided to participate in the present war with the French, British and Russian Governments, and to accede to the Declaration made at London, the 5th September, 1914, by the three above-named Governments,

The undersigned, being duly authorised by their respective Governments, make the following declaration:—

The French, British, Italian and Russian Governments mutually undertake not to conclude a separate peace during the course of the present war.

The four Governments agree that, whenever there maybe occasion to discuss the the terms of peace, none of the Allied Powers shall lay down any conditions of peace without previous agreement with each of the other Allies.

.   .   .   .

DECLARATION

The Declaration of the 26th April, 1915, whereby France, Great Britain, Italy and Russia undertake not to conclude a separate peace during the present European war, shall remain secret.

After the declaration of war by or against Italy, the four Powers shall sign a new declaration in identical terms, which shall thereupon be made public.

38. Proclamation of Francis Joseph, Emperor of Austria, on May 23, 1915

To my peoples! The King of Italy has declared war on me. A breach of faith as history has never known has been committed by the Kingdom of Italy against her two Allies. After an alliance of more than 30 years during which she could extend her territorial possessions and achieve an unimagined prosperity, Italy has forsaken us in the hour of danger and went over into the camp of our enemies with flying colors.

39. The Zimmermann Note to the German Minister to Mexico, January 19, 1917

Berlin, January 19, 1917

On the first of February we intend to begin submarine warfare unrestricted. In spite of this, it is our intention to endeavor to keep neutral the United States of America.

If this attempt is not successful, we propose an alliance on the following basis with Mexico: That we shall make war together and together make peace. We shall give general financial support, and it is understood that Mexico is to reconquer the lost territory in New Mexico, Texas, and Arizona. The details are left to you for settlement.

[Mexico to bring in Japan]

You are instructed to inform the President of Mexico of the above in the greatest confidence as soon as it is certain that there will be an outbreak of war with the United States and suggest that the President of Mexico, on his own initiative, should communicate with Japan suggesting adherence at once to this plan; at the same time, offer to mediate between Germany and Japan.

Please call to the attention of the President of Mexico that the employment of ruthless submarine warfare now promises to compel England to make peace in a few months.

ZIMMERMANN

40. Franco-Russian Plan for the German Frontiers Note of the Russian Foreign Minister (Pokrovsky) to the French Ambassador at Petrograd, February 14, 1917

In your Note of today's date your Excellency was good enough to inform the Imperial Government that the Government of the Republic was contemplating the inclusion in the terms of peace to be offered to Germany the following demands and guarantees of a territorial nature:

1. Alsace-Lorraine to be restored to France.

2. The frontiers are to be extended at least up to the limits of the former principality of Lorraine, and are to be drawn up at the discretion of the French Government so as to provide for the strategical needs and for the inclusion in French territory of the entire iron district of Lorraine and of the entire coal district of the Saar Valley.

3. The rest of the territories situated on the left bank of the Rhine which now form part of the German Empire are to be entirely separated from Germany and freed from all political and economic dependence upon her.

4. The territories of the left bank of the Rhine outside French territory are to be constituted an autonomous and neutral State, and are to be occupied by French troops until such time as the enemy States have completely satisfied all the conditions and guarantees indicated in the Treaty of Peace.

Your Excellency stated that the Government of the Republic would be happy to be able to rely upon the support of the Imperial Government for the carrying out of its plans. By order of His Imperial Majesty my most august master, I have the honour, in the name of the Russian Government, to inform your Excellency by the present Note that the Government of the Republic may rely upon the support of the Imperial Government for the carrying out of its plans as set out above.

41. Ambassador Count Bernstorff to the Foreign Office

Washington, January 26, 1917

Telegram No. 238

. . . The commencement of the U-boat war without preliminary negotiations with regard to the above proposals would, in my opinion, put us absolutely in the wrong and make the avoidance of a break impossible on account of personal affront to Wilson.

BERNSTORFF

42. Austria's Peace Offer

Memorandum by Prince Sixte de Bourbon-Parma, read by him to the President of the French Republic at Paris, March 5, 1917

On December 5 and 14 my mother [Duchess of Parma, mother of Empress Zita of Austria] wrote to say that she was particularly anxious to see me. She also sent a letter to the Queen of the Belgians which arrived on December 20, begging her and the King to insist that my brother and I should go to our mother. And, before this letter reached her, the Queen

had received a subsequent telegram, sent through the Consulate of Luxembourg, at Berne, in which the Grand Duchess Adelaide of Luxembourg asked her, on my mother's behalf, whether she had received the letter. While all this was happening, we left our Regiment to spend Christmas Eve (December 24, 1916) with the King and Queen. We had the idea of this journey in our minds, and discussed its difficulties with Their Majesties. In the end they gave their consent and we decided to go.

We left the front on January 23 and reached Paris the same evening. We there procured the necessary papers and started again on the evening of the 28th; about noon next day we arrived at the prearranged meeting-place in Switzerland. My mother had been there for two days, travelling strictly incognita with my sister Maria-Antonia. She explained to us how much the Emperor wished to see us and to discuss with us directly the possibilities of peace. All arrangements had been made for conveying us with the strictest secrecy to Vienna. The Colonel in charge of the police on the frontier had received instructions from the Emperor to take us by motor to his presence. Absolute secrecy had been observed; but, if we felt that the scheme was impracticable, the Emperor was ready to send a confidential envoy to us in Switzerland, who would communicate his views to us. We considered that the latter course alone was possible, and that only after we had sent word to Paris. Meanwhile, to avert suspicion, we should proceed on the journey into Italy, which we had planned three months earlier, to look after our estates there. The Italian Government knew of this intention.

My mother insisted, in the Emperor's name, that time was of vital importance. She handed us a letter from the Empress, endorsed with a few lines by the Emperor, in which she implored us both most urgently to assist her in realising the ideal of peace which the Emperor had formulated on his accession. In answer to this, I told my mother of the conditions which I, personally, thought fundamental and prerequisite, on the Entente side, to peace: namely, the restoration to France of the Alsace-Lorraine of 1814, without any colonial or other compensation; the restoration of Belgium, with the Congo; the similar restoration of Serbia, and her eventual extension so as to include Albania; and, lastly, the cession of Constantinople to the Russians. If Austria could manage to conclude a secret armistice with Russia upon these points, that would be a good base for the Peace we all desired.

We left Switzerland on February 1, reached le Pianore next day, and returned to Paris on the morning of Saturday February 10. On the evening of the 12th, at the express wish, as we were told, of the French Government, we both set out again for Switzerland, where at 1.30 on the 13th the Emperor's Envoy was presented to us, bringing with him a letter in which the Empress accredited him to us as the Emperor's representative.

He told us that the Emperor was keenly interested by the first impressions which he had gathered from my mother. He was most anxious for Peace and was prepared to consider it upon the following terms:

1. A secret armistice with Russia in which the question of Constantinople would not be made an issue.

2. Alsace-Lorraine and

3. Belgium to be restored.

4. The formation of a Southern-Slav Monarchy, embracing Bosnia-Herzegovina, Serbia, Albania, and Montenegro. He urgently begged that I would spare no pains to secure Peace upon this footing.

I answered that the situation was enormously complicated by our growing difficulties with America; while I felt that there was no hope of succeeding through diplomatic channels, so long as both Italy and Germany were directly interested in the failure of such a scheme. Austria need show no consideration for Germany, whose interests were quite different from her own, and who might very well abandon her at any moment. It would be preferable to protect the Monarchy by direct action, and only to inform Germany after the event. This direct action would be stimulated by an Imperial Rescript in which Austria, while keeping up an appearance of friendship and alliance with Germany, would offer Peace to her enemies on the terms cited above, except with regard to Serbia, which must be restored *in statu quo* and given a reasonable avenue to the sea by the addition of Albania.

Should the Emperor feel unable to act thus openly, and prefer to attempt to make peace by diplomatic methods, I requested the Envoy to let me have, at the earliest possible moment, the proposals from which the preliminary steps of diplomacy might start. I emphatically insisted that these points would be clearly defined in the document.

The Envoy made a careful note of my requirements, and returned to Vienna. No one else but the Emperor, the Empress and my mother knew of our interview. Count Czernin, the Foreign Minister of the Monarchy, was told no more than that the Emperor had found a means of negotiating with the Entente. On February 21 the Envoy rejoined me. In the interval the Emperor had, by a strongly worded rescript of the 12th, superseded the Archduke Frederick; while on the 13th the Emperor William had come to Vienna; but the Austrian Emperor, in spite of the toasts and other compliments exchanged between them, had declined to sever relations with America, so that the German Emperor went home again without much satisfaction.

The Envoy brought me: (1) a document written in French and signed by himself, but founded on a minute in German, either written or dictated by Count Czernin; (2) a secret and personal message written in German by the Emperor; (3) a letter from my sister Maria-Antonia, written at her dictation to accredit the Envoy; (4) two letters from the Empress; and (5) a long letter from my mother containing many personal details which she had elicited from the Emperor. The Empress, in her two letters, implored me, not only from herself and the Emperor, but also from Count Czernin, to come to Vienna secretly and discuss matters with them there. In Count Czernin's words, "Half an hour's conversation is worth a dozen journeys." In addition to this, I was told again, from the Emperor, how anxious he was to make Peace, not only as an urgent and immediate obligation laid upon him by military conditions, but as his solemn duty, before God, towards the peoples of his Empire and all the belligerents. He repeated his expressions of sympathy for his "dear France," his admiration for the valour of her troops and for the spirit of self-sacrifice and devotion which seemed to prevail throughout the country. I was reminded that I must act with absolute secrecy, into which no one except Count Czernin had been admitted by Their Majesties.

43. Secret Treaty Partitioning Asiatic Turkey

Memorandum dated March 6, 1917

As a result of negotiations which took place in London and Petrograd in the Spring of 1916, the Allied British, French and Russian Governments came to an agreement as regards the future delimitation of their respective zones of influence and territorial acquisitions in Asiatic Turkey, as well as the formation in Arabia of an independent Arab State, or a federation of Arab States. The general principles of the agreement are as follows:

1. Russia obtains the provinces of Erzerum, Trebizond, Van, and Bitlis, as well as territory in the

southern part of Kurdistan, along the line Mush-Sert-Ibn-Omar-Amadjie-Persian frontier. The limit of Russian acquisitions on the Black Sea coast will be fixed later on at a point lying west of Trebizond.

2. France obtains the coastal strip of Syria, the vilayet of Adana, and a territory bounded on the south by a line Aintab-Mardin to the future Russian frontier, and on the north by a line Ala-Dagh-Zara-Egin-Kharput.

3. Great Britain obtains the southern part of Mesopotamia with Bagdad, and stipulates for herself in Syria the ports of Haifa and Akka.

4. By agreement between France and England, the zone between the French and the British territories forms a confederation of Arab States, or one independent Arab State, the zones of influence in which are determined at the same time.

5. Alexandretta is proclaimed a free port.

With a view to securing the religious interests of the Entente Powers, Palestine, with the Holy places, is separated from Turkish territory and subjected to a special régime to be determined by agreement between Russia, France and England.

As a general rule the contracting Powers undertake mutually to recognise the concessions and privileges existing in the territories now acquired by them which have existed before the war.

They agree to assume such portions of the Ottoman Debt such as correspond to their respective acquisitions.

44. The Text of the Emperor's Letter of March 24, Published by Clemenceau on April 12, 1918. The Emperor's Autographed Letter

Laxenburg, March 24, 1917

My dear Sixte—The third anniversary of a war which has plunged the world in mourning is now drawing near. All the peoples of my Empire are united more firmly than ever in the determination to preserve the integrity of the Monarchy, even at the cost of the greatest sacrifices. By virtue of their unity, of the generous collaboration of all the races of my Empire, we have been able to hold out, for nearly three years, against the most fierce attacks. No one can deny the success of my troops in the field, especially in the Balkan Theatre.

France, too, has shown the greatest strength in resisting invasion, and a magnificent vitality. We must all admire without reservation the traditional valour of her gallant army and the willing spirit of sacrifice shown by the whole French people. And I am particularly pleased to note that, although for the time we are in opposite camps, my Empire is not divided from France by any real differences of outlook or of aspiration; while I am justified in hoping that my own keen sympathy for France, supported by the affection which she inspires throughout the Monarchy, will prevent the recurrence at any future time of a state of war for which I myself must disclaim all responsibility. Therefore, and in order that I may express in words what I so strongly feel, I request that you will secretly and unofficially convey to M. Poincaré, the President of the French Republic, my assurance that I will use all my personal influence and every other means in my power to exact from my Allies a settlement of her just claims in Alsace-Lorraine.

As for Belgium, she must be restored in her entirety as a Sovereign State, with the whole of her African possessions, and without prejudice to the compensations she may receive for the losses she has already suffered. Serbia, too, shall be restored as a Sovereign State, and, as a mark of our goodwill towards her, we are prepared to allow her a just and natural approach to the Adriatic, as well as economic concessions on a liberal scale. In return, Austria-Hungary will insist, as a primordial and absolute condition, that the Kingdom of Serbia abandon for the future all relations and suppress all groups or societies whose political object is the disintegration of the Monarchy, and especially the Society called "Narodna Obrana"; and that she take every means in her power loyally to prevent all forms of political agitation, whether within her borders or without, that may tend towards this object, giving her assurance under a guarantee from the Entente Powers.

Recent events in Russia make it desirable that I should withhold my views with regard to her until such time as a reign of law and order is established there.

Now that I have shown you what I feel, I request that you in your turn, after consultation with France and England, will inform me of their views, so that we may prepare a common ground of mutual understanding on which official negotiations may be based, to the ultimate satisfaction of all parties.

Trusting that we may soon be able to put an end to the sufferings of all the millions of men and all their families, who are now oppressed by sorrow and anxiety, I beg you to be assured of my most warm and brotherly affection.

CHARLES

45. Speech of Senator Norris on the Joint Resolution, April 4, 1917 (extracts)

Mr. President, while I am most emphatically and sincerely opposed to taking any step that will force our country into the useless and senseless war now being waged in Europe, yet if this resolution passes I shall not permit my feeling of opposition to its passage to interfere in any way with my duty either as a Senator or as a citizen in bringing success and victory to American arms. I am bitterly opposed to my country entering the war, but if, notwithstanding my opposition, we do enter it, all of my energy and all of my power will be behind our flag in carrying it on to victory.

The resolution now before the Senate is a declaration of war. Before taking this momentous step, and while standing on the brink of this terrible vortex, we ought to pause and calmly and judiciously consider the terrible consequences of the step we are about to take. We ought to consider likewise the route we have recently traveled and I have outlined the beginning of the controversy. I have given in substance the orders of both of these great Governments that constituted the beginning of our controversy with each. There have been other orders made by both Governments subsequent to the ones I have given that interfered with our rights as a neutral Nation, but these two that I have outlined constitute the origin of practically the entire difficulty, and subsequent orders have only been modifications and reproductions of those I have already mentioned. It is unnecessary to cite authority to show that both of these orders declaring military zones were illegal and contrary to international law. It is sufficient to say that our Government has officially declared both of them to be illegal and has officially protested against both of them.

The only difference is that in the case of Germany we have persisted in our protest, while in the case of England we have submitted. What was our duty as a Government and what were our rights when we were confronted with these extraordinary orders declaring these military zones? First, we could have defied both of them and could have gone to war against both of these nations for this violation of international law and interference with our neutral rights. Second, we had the technical right to defy one and to acquiesce in the other. Third, we could, while denouncing them both as illegal, have acquiesced in them both and thus remained neutral with both sides, although not agreeing with either as to the righteousness of their respective orders. We could have said to American shipowners that, while these orders are both contrary to international law and are both unjust, we do not believe that the provocation is sufficient to cause us to go to war for the defense of our rights as a neutral nation and, therefore, American ships and American citizens will not go into these zones at their own peril and risk. Fourth, we might have declared an embargo against the shipping from American ports of any merchandise to either one of these Governments that persisted in maintaining its military zone. We might have refused to permit the sailing of any ship from any American port to either of these military zones. In my judgment, if we had pursued this course, the zones would have been of short duration. England would have been compelled to take her mines out of the North Sea in order to get any supplies from our country. When her mines were taken out of the North Sea then the German ports upon the North Sea would have been accessible to American shipping and Germany would have been compelled to cease her submarine warfare in order to get any supplies from our Nation into German North Sea ports.

There are a great many American citizens who feel that we owe it as a duty to humanity to take part in this war. Many instances of cruelty and inhumanity can be found on both sides. Men are often biased in their judgment on account of their sympathy and their interests. To my mind, what we ought to have maintained from the beginning was the strictest neutrality. If we had done this I do not believe we would have been on the verge of war at the present time. We had a right as a nation, if we desired, to cease at any time to be neutral. We had a technical right to respect the English war zone and to disregard the German war zone, but we could not do that and be neutral. I have no quarrel to find with the man who does not desire our country to remain neutral. While many such people are moved by selfish motives and hopes of gain, I have no doubt but that in a great many instances, through what I believe to be a misunderstanding of the real condition, there are many honest, patriotic citizens who think we ought to engage in this war and who are behind the President in his demand that we should declare war against Germany. I think such people err in judgment and to a great extent have been misled as to the real history and the true facts by the almost unanimous demand of the great combination of wealth that has a direct financial interest in our participation in the war. We have loaned many hundreds of millions of dollars to the allies in this controversy. While such action was legal and countenanced by international law, there is no doubt in my mind but the enormous amount of money loaned to the allies in this country has been instrumental in bringing about a public sentiment in favor of our country taking a course that would make every bond worth a hundred cents on the dollar and making the payment of every debt certain and sure. Through this instrumentality and also through the instrumentality of others who have not only made millions out of the war in the manufacture of munitions, etc., and who would expect to make millions more if our country can be drawn into the catastrophe, a large number of the great newspapers and news agencies of the country have been controlled and enlisted in the greatest propaganda that the world has ever known, to manufacture sentiment in favor of war. It is now demanded that the American citizens shall be used as insurance policies to guarantee the safe delivery of munitions of war to belligerent nations. The enormous profits of munition manufacturers, stockbrokers, and bond dealers must be still further increased by our entrance into the war. This has brought us to the present moment, when Congress urged by the President and backed by the artificial sentiment, is about to declare war and engulf our country in the greatest holocaust that the world has ever known. . . .

To whom does war bring prosperity? Not to the soldier who for the munificent compensation of $16 per month shoulders his musket and goes into the trench, there to shed his blood and to die if necessary; not to the broken-hearted widow who waits for the return of the mangled body of her husband; not to the mother who weeps at the death of her brave boy; not to the little children who shiver with cold; not to the babe who suffers from hunger; nor to the millions of mothers and daughters who carry broken hearts to their graves. War brings no prosperity to the great mass of common and patriotic citizens. It increases the cost of living of those who toil and those who already must strain every effort to keep soul and body together. War brings prosperity to the stock gambler on Wall Street—to those who are already in possession of more wealth than can be realized or enjoyed. . . .

Their object in having war and in preparing for war is to make money. Human suffering and the sacrifice of human life are necessary, but Wall Street considers only the dollars and the cents. The men who do the fighting, the people who make the sacrifices, are the ones who will not be counted in the measure of this great prosperity. . . . The stock brokers would not, of course, go to war, because the very object they have in bringing on the war is profit, and therefore they must remain in their Wall Street offices in order to share in that great prosperity which they say war will bring. The volunteer officer, even the drafting officer, will not find them. They will be concealed in their palatial offices on Wall Street, sitting behind mahogany desks, covered up with clipped coupons—coupons soiled with the sweat of honest toil, coupons stained with mothers' tears, coupons dyed in the lifeblood of their fellow men.

We are taking a step today that is fraught with untold danger. We are going into war upon the command of gold. We are going to run the risk of sacrificing millions of our countrymen's lives in order that other countrymen may coin their lifeblood into money. And even if we do not cross the Atlantic and go into the trenches, we are going to pile up a debt that the toiling masses that shall come many generations after us will have to pay. Unborn millions will bend their backs in toil in order to pay for the terrible step we are now about to take. We are about to do the bidding of wealth's terrible mandate. By our act we will make millions of our countrymen suffer, and the consequences of it may well be that millions of our brethren must shed their life-blood, millions of broken-hearted women must weep, millions of children must suffer with the cold, and millions of babes must die from hunger, and all because we want to preserve the commercial right of American citizens to deliver munitions of war to belligerent nations. . . .

46. Joint Resolution to Create a State of War (April 6, 1917)

Resolved by the Senate and House of Representatives of the United States of America in Congress assembled, That the state of war between the United States and the Imperial German Government which has thus been thrust upon the United States is hereby formally declared; and that the President be, and he is hereby, authorized and directed to employ the entire naval and military forces of the United States and the resources of the Government to carry on war against the Imperial German Government; and to bring the conflict to a successful determination all of the resources of the country are hereby pledged by the Congress of the United States.

47. Some German Reactions to the Declaration of War by the United States

The *Frankfurter Zeitung* (Apr. 9):—

Germany to-day is fighting the same war that Athens once fought against the Persians, that the Swiss fought against the Habsburgers, and that the Dutch fought against Spain—a struggle of a minority whose liberty and life are threatened by a brutal, overwhelming majority. The participation of ever new nations in the war proves the truth of the old idea of the gods striking people with blindness. Motives of human reason are not adequate to explain the entry of America into the war. It is not reason, humaneness, and justice that have driven our enemies into this war, but the lack of them and nationalist passion, the striving for power, the wish to repress and oppress Germany, and inability to comprehend our perfect right to live and act as a great nation. . . .

. . . In America, where hardly anything is known of war except the sanguinary profits made from supplying war materials, Wilson and Congress are throwing fresh firebrands on to the funeral pile that had died down to the smouldering heap. In Europe all nations are weary of the war. Peace is over-ripe; it depends on our enemies when it comes. Unless we are greatly mistaken the notes blown from the horns of the war men of the Entente no longer resound as they did three months ago; but even should the entry of America reinflame their war zeal we shall yet succeed in achieving our aim.

The *Leipziger Neuste Nachrichten* (extreme Jingo National-Liberal) (Apr. 9):—

The United States can now be called upon to advance to the impoverished Entente nations the money that will be demanded as an indemnity by the Central Powers. It suggests that Canada should be held by the United States as a mortgage until the money thus advanced is repaid. The declaration of war, which was preceded by a "Parliamentary comedy," means merely that millions of American money will be flung across the ocean in the vain hope of recovering the American millions already lost. The commanders of German submarines will take care that the Americans are taught the frightful seriousness of the war, of which "they have as yet no idea."

The *Fremden-Blatt* (Apr. 9):—
The Americans will not be more fortunate than were the Italians and Rumanians. The worst is now over, and the sun will soon shine again.

The *Neue Freie Presse* (Apr. 9):—
America is falling upon Germany without any sufficient reason as an excuse for the rupture of diplomatic relations.

The *Reichspost* (Jingo Clerical) (Apr. 9):—
The United States is entering the war with the sole object of ensuring the gains resulting from her unneutral attitude pursued hitherto, and generally augmenting the profit made out of the European War. . . . President Wilson never was a philanthropist; the public statements he has made hitherto were deliberately hypocritical and part of a plan conceived long ago.

48. Reichstag Resolution on Peace Terms, July 19, 1917

"The Reichstag declares: As on August 4, 1914, so now on the threshold of the fourth year of war, that it approves the words in the Address from the Throne: 'We are not actuated by lust for conquest.' For the defense of its freedom and independence, for the inviolability of its territory, Germany has taken arms.

"The Reichstag strives for a peace of understanding and lasting reconciliation of the nations. [Cheers from the Center, the Progressive Peoples' Party and the Social Democrats.] With such a peace, forcible acquisitions of territory and political, economic, or financial coercion are irreconcilable. [Renewed cheers from the Center, the Progressive Peoples' Party and the Social Democrats.] The Reichstag also rejects all plans for the economic isolation and antagonizing of the nations after the War. ['Very true' from the Center, the Progressive Peoples' Party and the Social Democrats.] The Freedom of the seas must be secured. [Approval in the Center, the Progressive Peoples' Party and the Social Democrats.] Only economic peace can prepare the ground for friendly relations among the nations. [Renewed approval from the Center, the Progressive Peoples' Party and the Social Democrats.] The Reichstag will energetically promote the creation of international judicial organizations. [Cheers from the Center, the Progressive Peoples' Party and the Social Democrats.]

"As long, however, as the enemy governments will not enter upon such a peace, as long as they threaten Germany and her allies with conquest and coercion, the German People will stand together as a man [lively approval from the Center, the Progressive Peoples' Party and the Social Democrats], unflinchingly persevere, and fight until their own and their allies' right to life and development are secured. [Cheers from the Center, the Progressive Peoples' Party, and the Social Democrats.] The German People are invincible in their unity. [Lively approval.] The Reichstag knows itself to be in harmony with the men who are defending the Fatherland in heroic struggle. The imperishable gratitude of the entire people is assured them. [Lively agreement from the Center, the Progressive Peoples' Party and the Social Democrats.]"

49. Peace Proposal of Pope Benedict XV, August 1, 1917

To the Heads of the Belligerent Peoples:

From the beginning of our pontificate, in the midst of the horrors of the terrible war which has been let loose upon Europe, there were three objects above all which we set before ourselves: to maintain a perfect impartiality in regard to all belligerents as is fitting for him who is the common father, and who loves all his children with a like affection; to strive always to do to all the greatest amount of good possible, and that without distinction of persons, and without difference of nationality or religion, even as is enjoined upon us by the universal law of charity as well as by the supreme spiritual charge entrusted to us by Christ; finally, as is demanded also by our mission of peace, to omit nothing, in so far as may be in our power, which might contribute to hasten the end of this calamity by endeavouring to induce the peoples of the world and their leaders to adopt more moderate resolutions, and to enter into the calm consideration of peace—of a peace "just and durable."

Whoever has followed our work during these last three painful years must surely recognise that, while remaining always faithful to our determination of absolute impartiality and to our humanitarian activities, we have nonetheless continued to exhort the belligerent nations and Governments to resume their brotherhood, although all that we have done to attain this noble object has not become public knowledge.

Towards the end of the first year of the war we addressed the most lively exhortations to the belligerent nations, and we at the same time indicated the road that they should follow, in order to arrive at a stable peace such as would be honourable for all.

Unfortunately our appeal was not regarded; the war has continued pitilessly and with all its horrors for another two years; it has, in truth, increased in cruelty, and spread over the earth, over the sea, and even into the air, and desolation and death have been showered upon defenceless cities, peaceful villages, and innocent populations. No one can now imagine to what extent this universal suffering will be increased and intensified if further months or, worse still, if further years are to be added to the blood-stained period that has elapsed. Is the civilised world then to become no more than a field of death? And is Europe, so glorious and flourishing in the past, to plunge into the abyss, as if driven by some universal madness, and to contrive her own suicide?

In this agonising situation, in the presence of this grave menace, we, who have no private political object, who give ear to the suggestions and interests of no special one of the belligerent parties, but who are inspired solely by the feeling of our supreme duty as common father of the faithful by the prayers of our children who beg for our intervention and for our words of peace, by the voice even of humanity and reason, we again raise a cry of peace and we renew an urgent appeal to those who hold in their hands the destinies of nations.

50. The Stockholm Conference, July 1917

Joint Socialist Statement on the Refusal of Passports to Stockholm

The Stockholm conference, called at the instance of the Russian Council of Workmen's and Soldiers' Delegates to discuss and formulate the basis of a democratic and durable peace between the masses of the peoples, has been postponed because the governments of Italy, France, England and the United States have refused passports to delegates. For this action the American government is largely responsible.

At the entente conference in Paris, it was the Italian government, through Baron Sonnino, which headed the opposition to the Stockholm conference. France also voted no, though the favorable attitude of Petrograd was known. The Russian representative did not vote. England declared herself in favor of allowing Socialists and labor delegates to go to Stockholm.

There remained only the American government, which practically cast the deciding vote. The American government voted no.

We do not understand President Wilson's course of action. When, in the Senate in December, 1916, he addressed the peoples of the world, the Socialists and labor organizations of Europe supported him with all their strength.

In all Wilson's public utterances it has been made perfectly plain that the main obstacle to American peace with Germany is the German political autocracy, and that America's object in the war is to secure the democratization of the German government.

The Stockholm conference is the best and, perhaps, the only opportunity for the representatives of the entente peoples to make clear to the German masses the conditions upon which peace is possible. And yet President Wilson refuses to allow the delegates of American Socialist and Labor groups to come to Stockholm.

The peoples of the world are sick of war, whatever policy their governments see fit publicly to adopt.

In the invitation to the Stockholm conference and its acceptance by democratic political and economic elements in all the belligerent countries is to be seen the first action of the international masses, growing conscious of their power, awakening to the colossal error of unending war and determination that government shall be of, by and for the Social Democracy.

51. Statement of British Policy in Palestine by Foreign Secretary Balfour, November 8, 1917

His Majesty's Government view with favor the establishment in Palestine of a national home for the Jewish people, and will use their best endeavors to facilitate the achievement of this object, it being clearly understood that nothing shall be done which may prejudice the civil and religious rights of existing non-Jewish communities in Palestine, or the rights and political status enjoyed by Jews in any other country.

I should be grateful if you would bring this declaration to the knowledge of the Zionist Federation.

52. President Wilson's Fourteen Points, January 8, 1918

It will be our wish and purpose that the processes of peace, when they are begun, shall be absolutely open and that they shall involve and permit henceforth no secret understandings of any kind. The day of conquest and aggrandizement is gone by; so is also the day of secret covenants entered into in the interest of particular governments and likely at some unlooked-for moment to upset the peace of the world. It is this happy fact, now clear to the view of every public man whose thoughts do not still linger in an age that is dead and gone, which makes it possible for every nation whose purposes are consistent with justice and the peace of the world to avow nor or at any other time the objects it has in view.

We entered this war because violations of right had occurred which touched us to the quick and made the life of our own people impossible unless they were corrected and the world secure once for all against their recurrence. What we demand in this war, therefore, is nothing peculiar to ourselves. It is that the world be made fit and safe to live in; and particularly that it be made safe for every peace-loving nation which, like our own, wishes to live its own life, determine its own institutions, be assured of justice and fair dealing by the other peoples of the world as against force and selfish aggression. All the peoples of the world are in effect partners in this interest, and for our own part we see very clearly that unless justice be done to others it will not be done to us. The programme of the world's peace, therefore, is our programme; and that programme, the only possible programme, as we see it, is this:

I. Open covenants of peace, openly arrived at, after which there shall be no private international understandings of any kind but diplomacy shall proceed always frankly and in the public view.

II. Absolute freedom of navigation upon the seas, outside territorial waters, alike in peace and in war, except as the seas may be closed in whole or in part by international action for the enforcement of international covenants.

III. The removal, so far as possible, of all economic

barriers and the establishment of an equality of trade conditions among all the nations consenting to the peace and associating themselves for its maintenance.

IV. Adequate guarantees given and taken that national armaments will be reduced to the lowest point consistent with domestic safety.

V. A free, open-minded, and absolutely impartial adjustment of all colonial claims, based upon a strict observance of the principle that in determining all such questions of sovereignty the interests of the populations concerned must have equal weight with the equitable claims of the government whose title is to be determined.

VI. The evacuation of all Russian territory and such a settlement of all questions affecting Russia as will secure the best and freest coöperation of the other nations of the world in obtaining for her an unhampered and unembarrassed opportunity for the independent determination of her own political development and national policy and assure her of a sincere welcome into the society of free nations under institutions of her own choosing; and, more than a welcome, assistance also of every kind that she may need and may herself desire. The treatment accorded Russia by her sister nations in the months to come will be the acid test of their good will, of their comprehension of her needs as distinguished from their own interests, and of their intelligent and unselfish sympathy.

VII. Belgium, the whole world will agree, must be evacuated and restored, without any attempt to limit the sovereignty which she enjoys in common with all other free nations. No other single act will serve as this will serve to restore confidence among the nations in the laws which they have themselves set and determined for the government of their relations with one another. Without this healing act the whole structure and validity of international law is forever impaired.

VIII. All French territory should be freed and the invaded portions restored, and the wrong done to France by Prussia in 1871 in the matter of Alsace-Lorraine, which has unsettled the peace of the world for nearly fifty years, should be righted, in order that peace may once more be made secure in the interest of all.

IX. A readjustment of the frontiers of Italy should be effected along clearly recognizable lines of nationality.

X. The peoples of Austria-Hungary, whose place among the nations we wish to see safeguarded and assured, should be accorded the freest opportunity to autonomous development.

XI. Rumania, Serbia, and Montenegro should be evacuated; occupied territories restored; Serbia accorded free and secure access to the sea; and the relations of the several Balkan states to one another determined by friendly counsel along historically established lines of allegiance and nationality; and international guarantees of the political and economic independence and territorial integrity of the several Balkan states should be entered into.

XII. The Turkish portion of the present Ottoman Empire should be assured a secure sovereignty, but the other nationalities which are now under Turkish rule should be assured an undoubted security of life and an absolutely unmolested opportunity of autonomous development, and the Dardanelles should be permanently opened as a free passage to the ships and commerce of all nations under international guarantees.

XIII. An independent Polish state should be erected which should include the territories inhabited by indisputably Polish populations, which should be assured a free and secure access to the sea, and whose political and economic independence and territorial integrity should be guaranteed by international covenant.

XIV. A general association of nations must be formed under specific covenants for the purpose of affording mutual guarantees of political independence and territorial integrity to great and small states alike.

In regard to these essential rectifications of wrong and assertions of right we feel ourselves to be intimate partners of all the governments and peoples associated together against the Imperialists. We cannot be separated in interest or divided in purpose. We stand together until the end.

For such arrangements and covenants we are willing to fight and to continue to fight until they are achieved; but only because we wish the right to prevail and desire a just and stable peace such as can be secured only by removing the chief provocations to war, which this programme does remove. We have no jealousy of German greatness, and there is nothing in this programme that impairs it. We grudge her no achievement or distinction of learning or of pacific enterprise such as have made her record very bright and very enviable. We do not wish to injure her or to block in any way her legitimate influence or power. We do not wish to fight her either with arms or with hostile arrangements of trade if she is willing to associate herself with us and the other peace-loving nations of the world in covenants of justice and law and fair dealing. We wish her only to accept a place of equality among the peoples of the world,—the new world in which we now live,—instead of a place of mastery.

53. Anglo-French Statement of Aims in Mesopotamia and Syria, November 7, 1918

The aim of France and Great Britain in carrying on in the Near East the war let loose by Germany's ambitions is the complete and final liberation of the peoples so long oppressed by the Turks and the establishment of governments and administrations deriving their authority from the initiative and the free choice of the native populations.

In view of following out this intention, France and Great Britain are agreed to encourage and help the establishment of native governments and administrations in Syria and Mesopotamia actually liberated by the allies, and in the territories they are now striving to liberate, and to recognize them as soon as effectively established.

Far from seeking to force upon the populations of these countries any particular institution, France and Great Britain have no other concern than to ensure by their support and their active assistance the normal working of the governments and institutions which the populations shall have freely adopted, so as to secure just impartiality for all, and also to facilitate the economic development of the country in arousing and encouraging local initiative by the diffusion of instruction, and to put an end to discords which have too long been taken advantage of by Turkish rule.

Such is the rôle that the two Allied Governments claim for themselves in the liberated territories.

54. Examples of Northcliffe Propaganda Dropped Into German Trenches, 1918

What Are You Fighting for, Michel?

BY BALLOON

They tell you that you are fighting to secure victory for your Fatherland. But have you ever thought about what you are fighting for?

You are fighting for the glory of, and for the enrichment of the Krupps. You are fighting to save the Kaiser, the Junkers and the War Lords who caused the war from the anger of the people.

The Junkers are sitting at home with their bejewelled wives and mistresses. Their bank accounts are constantly growing, accounts to which you and your comrades pay with your lives. For your wives and brides there are no growing bank accounts. They are at home working and starving, sacrifices like yourselves to the greed of the ruling class to whose pipes you have to dance.

What a dance! The dance of death. But yesterday you marched over the corpses of your comrades against the English cannon. Tomorrow another German soldier will march over your corpse.

You have been promised victory and peace. You poor fool! Your comrades were also promised these things more than three years ago. Peace indeed they have found—deep in the grave. But victory did not come.

Your Kaiser has adorned the glorious Hindenburg with the Iron Cross with golden beams. What has the Kaiser awarded to you? Ruin, suffering, poverty, hunger for your wives and children, misery, disease, and tomorrow the grave.

It is for the Fatherland, you say, that you go out as a brave patriot to death for the Fatherland.

But of what does your Fatherland consist? Is it the Kaiser with his fine speeches? Is it the Crown Prince with his jolly companions, who sacrificed 600,000 men at Verdun? Is it Hindenburg, who sits with Ludendorf, both covered with medals many kilometers behind you and who plans how he can furnish the English with still more cannon fodder. Is it Frau Bertha Krupp for whom through year after year of war you pile up millions upon millions of marks?

Is it the Prussian Junkers who cry out over your dead bodies for annexations?

No, the Fatherland is not any of these. You are the Fatherland, Michel! You and your sisters and your wives and your parents and your children. You, the common people are the Fatherland. And yet it is you and your comrades who are driven like slaves into the hell of English cannon-fire, driven by the command of the feelingless slave-drivers.

When your comrades at home were striking, they were shot at with machine guns. If you, after the war, strike a blow for your rights, the machine guns will be turned upon you, for you are fighting only to increase the power of your lords.

Do you perhaps believe your rulers who love war as you hate it? Of course not. They love war for it brings them advancement, honor, power, profit. The longer the war lasts, the longer they will postpone the revolution.

They promise you that you can compel the English to beg for peace. Do you really believe that? You have advanced a few kilometers but for every Englishman whom you have shot down, six Germans have fallen. And all America is still to come.

Your commanders report to you wonderful stories of English losses. But did they tell you that Germany in the first five days of battle lost 315,000 men?

Arrayed against Germany in battle today stands the entire world because it knows that German rulers caused the war to serve their own greedy ambition. The entire power of the Western World stands behind England and France and America. An army of ten million men is being prepared. Soon it will go forth to battle. Have you thought of that, Michel?

55. The Peace Treaty of Brest-Litovsk, March 3, 1918

Article I. Germany, Austria-Hungary, Bulgaria, and Turkey, for the one part, and Russia, for the other part, declare that the state of war between them has ceased. They are resolved to live henceforth in peace and amity with one another.

Article II. The contracting parties will refrain from any agitation or propaganda against the Government or the public and military institutions of the other party. In so far as this obligation devolves upon Russia, it holds good also for the territories occupied by the Powers of the Quadruple Alliance.

Article III. The territories lying to the west of the line agreed upon by the contracting parties which formerly belonged to Russia, will no longer be subject to Russian sovereignty; the line agreed upon is traced on the map submitted as an essential part of this treaty of peace. The exact fixation of the line will be established by a Russo-German commission.

No obligations whatever toward Russia shall devolve upon the territories referred to, arising from the fact that they formerly belonged to Russia.

Russia refrains from all interference in the internal relations of these territories. Germany and Austria-Hungary purpose to determine the future status of these territories in agreement with their population.

Article IV. As soon as a general peace is concluded and Russian demobilization is carried out completely, Germany will evacuate the territory lying to the east of the line designated in paragraph 1 of Article III, in so far as Article VI does not determine otherwise.

Russia will do all within her power to insure the immediate evacuation of the provinces of eastern Anatolia and their lawful return to Turkey.

The districts of Erdehan, Kars, and Batum will likewise and without delay be cleared of the Russian troops. Russia will not interfere in the reorganization of the national and international relations of these districts, but leave it to the population of these districts, to carry out this reorganization in agreement with the neighboring States, especially with Turkey.

Article V. Russia will, without delay, carry out the full demobilization of her army inclusive of those units recently organized by the present Government.

Furthermore, Russia will either bring her warships into Russian ports and there detain them until the day of the conclusion of a general peace, or disarm them forthwith. Warships of the States which continue in the state of war with the Powers of the Quadruple Alliance, in so far as they are within Russian sovereignty, will be treated as Russian warships.

The barred zone in the Arctic Ocean continues as such until the conclusion of a general peace. In the Baltic sea, and, as far as Russian power extends within the Black sea, removal of the mines will be proceeded with at once. Merchant navigation within these maritime regions is free and will be resumed at once. Mixed commissions will be organized to formulate the more detailed regulations, especially to inform merchant ships with regard to restricted lanes. The navigation lanes are always to be kept free from floating mines.

Article VI. Russia obligates herself to conclude peace at once with the Ukrainian People's Republic and to recognize the treaty of peace between that State and the Powers of the Quadruple Alliance. The Ukrainian territory will, without delay, be cleared of Russian troops and the Russian Red Guard. Russia is to put an end to all agitation or propaganda against the Government or the public institutions of the Ukrainian People's Republic.

Esthonia and Livonia will likewise, without delay, be cleared of Russian troops and the Russian Red Guard. The eastern boundary of Esthonia runs, in general, along the river Narwa. The eastern boundary of Livonia crosses, in general, lakes Peipus and Pskow, to the southwestern corner of the latter, then across Lake Luban in the direction of Livenhof on the Dvina. Esthonia and Livonia will be occupied by a German police force until security is insured by proper national institutions and until public order has been established. Russia will liberate at once all arrested or deported inhabitants of Esthonia and Livonia, and insures the safe return of all deported Esthonians and Livonians.

Finland and the Aaland Islands will immediately be cleared of Russian troops and the Russian Red Guard, and the Finnish ports of the Russian fleet and of the Russian naval forces. So long as the ice prevents the transfer of warships into Russian ports, only limited forces will remain on board the warships. Russia is to put an end to all agitation or propaganda against the Government or the public institutions of Finland.

The fortresses built on the Aaland Islands are to be removed as soon as possible. As regards the permanent non-fortification of these islands as well as their further treatment in respect to military technical navigation matters, a special agreement is to be concluded between Germany, Finland, Russia, and Sweden; there exists an understanding to the effect that, upon Germany's desire, still other countries bordering upon the Baltic Sea would be consulted in this matter.

Article VII. In view of the fact that Persia and Afghanistan are free and independent States, the contracting parties obligate themselves to respect the political and economic independence and the territorial integrity of these states.

Article VIII. The prisoners of war of both parties will be released to return to their homeland. The settlement of the questions connected therewith will be effected through the special treaties provided for in Article XII.

Article IX. The contracting parties mutually renounce compensation for their war expenses, i.e., of the public expenditures for the conduct of the war, as well as compensation for war losses, i.e., such losses as were caused [by] them and their nationals within the war zones by military measures, inclusive of all requisitions effected in enemy country.

Article X. Diplomatic and consular relations between the contracting parties will be resumed immediately upon the ratification of the treaty of peace. As regards the reciprocal admission of consuls, separate agreements are reserved.

Article XI. As regards the economic relations between the Powers of the Quadruple Alliance and Russia the regulations contained in Appendices II-V are determinative. . . .

Article XII. The reëstablishment of public and private legal relations, the exchange of war prisoners and interned citizens, the question of amnesty as well as the question anent the treatment of merchant ships which have come into the power of the opponent, will be regulated in separate treaties with Russia which form an essential part of the general treaty of peace, and, as far as possible, go into force simultaneously with the latter.

Article XIII. In the interpretation of this treaty, the German and Russian texts are authoritative for the relations between Germany and Russia; the German, the Hungarian, and Russian texts for the relations between Austria-Hungary and Russia; the Bulgarian and Russian texts for the relations between Bulgaria and Russia; and the Turkish and Russian texts for the relations between Turkey and Russia.

Article XIV. The present treaty of peace will be ratified. The documents of ratification shall, as soon as possible, be exchanged in Berlin. The Russian Government obligates itself, upon the desire of one of the Powers of the Quadruple Alliance, to execute the exchange of the documents of ratification within a period of two weeks. Unless otherwise provided for in its articles, in its annexes, or in the additional treaties, the treaty of peace enters into force at the moment of its ratification.

In testimony whereof the Plenipotentiaries have signed this treaty with their own hand.

Executed in quintuplicate at Brest-Litovsk, 3 March, 1918.

56. The Peace Treaty of Versailles, Signed on June 28, 1919 (Excerpts)

PART I

THE COVENANT OF THE LEAGUE OF NATIONS

THE HIGH CONTRACTING PARTIES,

In order to promote international co-operation and to achieve international peace and security

by the acceptance of obligations not to resort to war,

by the prescription of open, just and honourable relations between nations,

by the firm establishment of the understandings of international law as the actual rule of conduct among Governments,

and by the maintenance of justice and a scrupulous respect for all treaty obligations in the dealings of organised peoples with one another,

Agree to this Covenant of the League of Nations.

Article 1. 1. The original Members of the League of Nations shall be those of the Signatories which are named in the Annex to this Covenant and also such of those other States named in the Annex as shall accede without reservation to this Covenant. Such accession shall be effected by a Declaration deposited with the Secretariat within two months of the coming into force of the Covenant. Notice thereof shall be sent to all other Members of the League.

2. Any fully self-governing State, Dominion or Colony not named in the Annex may become a Member of the League if its admission is agreed to by two-thirds of the Assembly, provided that it shall give effective guarantees of its sincere intention to observe its international obligations, and shall accept such regulations as may be prescribed by the League in regard to its military, naval and air forces and armaments.

3. Any Member of the League may, after two years' notice of its intention so to do, withdraw from the League, provided that all its international obligations and all its obligations under this Covenant shall have been fulfilled at the time of its withdrawal.

Article 2. The action of the League under this Covenant shall be effected through the instrumentality of an Assembly and of a Council, with a permanent Secretariat.

Article 3. 1. The Assembly shall consist of Representatives of the Members of the League.

2. The Assembly shall meet at stated intervals and from time to time as occasion may require at the Seat of the League or at such other place as may be decided upon.

3. The Assembly may deal at its meetings with any matter within the sphere of action of the League or affecting the peace of the world.

4. At meetings of the Assembly, each Member of the League shall have one vote, and may have not more than three Representatives.

Article 4. 1. The Council shall consist of Representatives of the Principal Allied and Associated Powers, together with Representatives of four other Members of the League. These four Members of the League shall be selected by the Assembly from time to time in its discretion. Until the appointment of the Representatives of the four Members of the League first selected by the Assembly, Representatives of Belgium, Brazil, Spain and Greece shall be members of the Council.

2. With the approval of the majority of the Assembly, the Council may name additional Members of the League whose Representatives shall always be Members of the Council; the Council with like approval may increase the number of Members of the League to be selected by the Assembly for representation on the Council.

2bis. The Assembly shall fix by a two-thirds majority the rules dealing with the election of the non-permanent Members of the Council, and particularly such regulations as relate to their term of office, and the conditions of re-eligibility.

3. The Council shall meet from time to time as occasion may require, and at least once a year, at the Seat of the League, or at such other place as may be decided upon.

4. The Council may deal at its meetings with any matter within the sphere of action of the League or affecting the peace of the world.

5. Any Member of the League not represented on the Council shall be invited to send a Representative to sit as a member at any meeting of the Council during the consideration of matters specially affecting the interests of that Member of the League.

6. At meetings of the Council, each Member of the League represented on the Council shall have one vote, and may have not more than one Representative.

Article 5. 1. Except where otherwise expressly provided in this Covenant or by the terms of the present Treaty, decisions at any meeting of the Assembly or of the Council shall require the agreement of all the Members of the League represented at the meeting.

2. All matters of procedure at meetings of the Assembly or of the Council, including the appointment of Committees to investigate particular matters shall be regulated by the Assembly or by the Council and may be decided by a majority of the Members of the League represented at the meeting.

3. The first meetings of the Assembly and the first meeting of the Council shall be summoned by the President of the United States of America.

Article 6. 1. The permanent Secretariat shall be established at the Seat of the League. The Secretariat shall comprise a Secretary-General and such secretaries and staff as may be required.

2. The first Secretary-General shall be the person named in the Annex; thereafter the Secretary-General shall be appointed by the Council with the approval of the majority of the Assembly.

3. The secretaries and staff of the Secretariat shall be appointed by the Secretary-General with the approval of the Council.

4. The Secretary-General shall act in that capacity at all meetings of the Assembly and of the Council.

5. The expenses of the League shall be borne by the Members of the League in the proportion decided by the Assembly.

Article 7. 1. The Seat of the League is established at Geneva.

2. The Council may at any time decide that the Seat of the League shall be established elsewhere.

3. All positions under or in connection with the League, including the Secretariat, shall be open equally to men and women.

4. Representatives of the Members of the League and officials of the League when engaged on the business of the League shall enjoy diplomatic privileges and immunities.

5. The buildings and other property occupied by the League or its officials or by Representatives attending its meetings shall be inviolable.

Article 8. 1. The Members of the League recognise that the maintenance of peace requires the reduction of national armaments to the lowest point consistent with national safety and the enforcement by common action of international obligations.

2. The Council, taking account of the geographical situation and circumstances of each State, shall formulate plans for such reduction for the consideration and action of the several Governments.

3. Such plans shall be subject to reconsideration and revision at least every ten years.

4. After these plans shall have been adopted by the several Governments, the limits of armaments therein fixed shall not be exceeded without the concurrence of the Council.

5. The Members of the League agree that the manufacture by private enterprise of munitions and implements of war is open to grave objections. The Council shall advise how the evil effects attendant upon such manufacture can be prevented, due regard being had to the necessities of those Members of the League which are not able to manufacture the munitions and implements of war necessary for their safety.

6. The Members of the League undertake to interchange full and frank information as to the scale of their armaments, their military, naval and air programmes and the conditions of such of their industries as are adaptable to warlike purposes.

Article 9. A permanent Commission shall be constituted to advise the Council on the execution of the provisions of Articles 1 and 8 and on military, naval and air questions generally.

Article 10. The Members of the League undertake to respect and preserve as against external aggression the territorial integrity and existing political independence of all Members of the League. In case of any such aggression aggression or in case of any threat or danger of such the Council shall advise upon the means by which this obligation shall be fulfilled.

Article 11. 1. Any war or threat of war, whether immediately affecting any of the Members of the League or not, is hereby declared a matter of concern to the whole League, and the League shall take any action that may be deemed wise and effectual to safeguard the peace of nations. In case any such emergency should arise the Secretary-General shall on the request of any Member of the League forthwith summon a meeting of the Council.

2. It is also declared to be the friendly right of each Member of the League to bring to the attention of the Assembly or of the Council any circumstance whatever affecting international relations which threatens to disturb international peace or the good understanding between nations upon which peace depends.

Article 12. 1. The Members of the League agree that if there should arise between them any dispute likely to lead to a rupture they will submit the matter either to arbitration *or judicial settlement* or to enquiry by the Council, and they agree in no case to resort to war until three months after the award by the arbitrators *or the judicial decision* or the report by the Council.

2. In any case under this Article the award of the

arbitrators *or the judicial decision* shall be made within a reasonable time, and the report of the Council shall be made within six months after the submission of the dispute.

Article 13. 1. The Members of the League agree that whenever any dispute shall arise between them which they recognise to be suitable for submission to arbitration *or judicial settlement,* and which cannot be satisfactorily settled by diplomacy, they will submit the whole subject-matter to arbitration *or judicial settlement.*

2. Disputes as to the interpretation of a treaty, as to any question of international law, as to the existence of any fact which, if established would constitute a breach of any international obligation, or as to the extent and nature of the reparation to be made for any such breach, are declared to be among those which are generally suitable for submission to arbitration *or judicial settlement.*

3. For the consideration of any such dispute, the court to which the case is referred shall be the Permanent Court of International Justice, established in accordance with Article 14, or any tribunal agreed on by the parties to the dispute or stipulated in any convention existing between them.

4. The Members of the League agree that they will carry out in full good faith any award *or decision* that may be rendered, and that they will not resort to war against a Member of the League which complies therewith. In the event of any failure to carry out such an award *or decision,* the Council shall propose what steps should be taken to give effect thereto.

Article 14. The Council shall formulate and submit to the Members of the League for adoption plans for the establishment of a Permanent Court of International Justice. The Court shall be competent to hear and determine any dispute of an international character which the parties thereto submit to it. The Court may also give an advisory opinion upon any dispute or question referred to it by the Council or by the Assembly.

Article 15. 1. If there should arise between Members of the League any dispute likely to lead to a rupture, which is not submitted to arbitration *or judicial settlement* in accordance with Article 13, the Members of the League agree that they will submit the matter to the Council. Any party to the dispute may effect such submission by giving notice of the existence of the dispute to the Secretary-General, who will make all necessary arrangements for a full investigation and consideration thereof.

2. For this purpose the parties to the dispute will communicate to the Secretary-General, as promptly as possible, statements of their case with all the relevant facts and papers, and the Council may forthwith direct the publication thereof.

3. The Council shall endeavour to effect a settlement of the dispute, and if such efforts are successful, a statement shall be made public giving such facts and explanations regarding the dispute and the terms of settlement thereof as the Council may deem appropriate.

4. If the dispute is not thus settled, the Council either unanimously or by a majority vote shall make and publish a report containing a statement of the facts of the dispute and the recommendations which are deemed just and proper in regard thereto.

5. Any Member of the League represented on the Council may make public a statement of the facts of the dispute and of its conclusions regarding the same.

6. If a report by the Council is unanimously agreed to by the members thereof other than the Representatives of one more of the parties to the dispute, the Members of the League agree that they will not go to war with any party to the dispute which complies with the recommendations of the report.

7. If the Council fails to reach a report which is unanimously agreed to by the members thereof, other than the Representatives of one or more of the parties to the dispute, the Members of the League reserve to themselves the right to take such action as they shall consider necessary for the maintenance of right and justice.

8. If the dispute between the parties is claimed by one of them, and is found by the Council, to arise out of a matter which by international law is solely within the domestic jurisdiction of that party, the Council shall so report, and shall make no recommendation as to its settlement.

9. The Council may in any case under this Article refer the dispute to the Assembly. The dispute shall be so referred at the request of either party to the dispute provided that such request be made within fourteen days after the submission of the dispute to the Council.

10. In any case referred to the Assembly, all the provisions of this Article and of Article 12 relating to the action and powers of the Council shall apply to the action and powers of the Assembly, provided that a report made by the Assembly, if concurred in by the Representatives of those Members of the League represented on the Council and of a majority of the other Members of the League, exclusive in each case of the Representatives of the parties to the dispute, shall have the same force as a report by the Council concurred in by all the members thereof other than

the Representative of one or more of the parties to the dispute.

Article 16. 1. Should any Member of the League resort to war in disregard of its covenants under Articles 12, 13 or 15, it shall *ipso facto* be deemed to have committed an act of war against all other Members of the League, which hereby undertake immediately to subject it to the severance of all trade or financial relations, the prohibition of all intercourse between their nationals and the nationals of the covenant-breaking State, and the prevention of all financial, commercial or personal intercourse between the nationals of the convenant-breaking State and the nationals of any other State, whether a Member of the League or not.

2. It shall be the duty of the Council in such a case to recommend to the several Governments concerned what effective military, naval or air force the Members of the League shall severally contribute to the armed forces to be used to protect the covenants of the League.

3. The Members of the League agree, further that they will mutually support one another in the financial and economic measures which are taken under this Article, in order to minimise the loss and inconvenience resulting from the above measures, and that they will mutually support one another in resisting any special measures aimed at one of their number by the covenant-breaking State, and that they will take the necessary steps to afford passage through their territory to the forces of any of the Members of the League which are cooperating to protect the covenants of the League.

4. Any Member of the League which has violated any covenant of the League may be declared to be no longer a Member of the League by a vote of the Council concurred in by the Representatives of all the other Members of the League represented thereon.

Article 17. 1. In the event of a dispute between a Member of the League and a State which is not a Member of the League, or between States not Members of the League, the State or States not Members of the League shall be invited to accept the obligations of membership in the League for the purposes of such dispute, upon such conditions as the Council may deem just. If such invitation is accepted, the provisions of Articles 12 to 16 inclusive shall be applied with such modifications as may be deemed necessary by the Council.

2. Upon such invitation being given the Council shall immediately institute an inquiry into the circumstances of the dispute and recommend such ac-

tion as may seem best and most effectual in the circumstances.

3. If a State so invited shall refuse to accept the obligations of membership in the League for the purposes of such dispute, and shall resort to war against a Member of the League, the provisions of Article 16 shall be applicable as against the State taking such action.

4. If both parties to the dispute when so invited refuse to accept the obligations of membership in the League for the purposes of such dispute, the Council may take such measures and make such recommendations as will prevent hostilities and will result in the settlement of the dispute.

Article 18. Every treaty or international engagement entered into hereafter by any Member of the League shall be forthwith registered with the Secretariat and shall as soon as possible be published by it. No such treaty or international engagement shall be binding until so registered.

Article 19. The Assembly may from time to time advise the reconsideration by Members of the League of treaties which have become inapplicable and the consideration of international conditions whose continuance might endanger the peace of the world.

Article 20. 1. The Members of the League severally agree that this Covenant is accepted as abrogating all obligations or understandings *inter se* which are inconsistent with the terms thereof, and solemnly undertake that they will not hereafter enter into any engagements inconsistent with the terms thereof.

2. In case any Member of the League shall, before becoming a Member of the League, have undertaken any obligations inconsistent with the terms of this Covenant, it shall be the duty of such Member to take immediate steps to procure its release from such obligations.

Article 21. Nothing in this covenant shall be deemed to affect the validity of international engagements, such as treaties of arbitration or regional understandings like the Monroe doctrine, for securing the maintenance of peace.

Article 22. 1. To those colonies and territories which as a consequence of the late war have ceased to be under the sovereignty of the States which formerly governed them and which are inhabited by peoples not yet able to stand by themselves under the strenuous conditions of the modern world, there should be applied the principle that the well-being and development of such peoples form a sacred trust of civilisation and that securities for the performance of this trust should be embodied in this Covenant.

2. The best method of giving practical effect to this

principle is that the tutelage of such peoples should be entrusted to advanced nations who by reason of their resources, their experience or their geographical position can best undertake this responsibility, and who are willing to accept it, and that this tutelage should be exercised by them as Mandatories on behalf of the League.

3. The character of the mandate must differ according to the stage of the development of the people, the geographical situation of the territory, its economic conditions and other similar circumstances.

4. Certain communities formerly belonging to the Turkish Empire have reached a stage of development where their existence as independent nations can be provisionally recognised subject to the rendering of administrative advice and assistance by a Mandatory until such time as they are able to stand alone. The wishes of these communities must be a principal consideration in the selection of the Mandatory.

5. Other peoples, especially those of Central Africa, are at such a stage that the Mandatory must be responsible for the administration of the territory under conditions which will guarantee freedom of conscience and religion, subject only to the maintenance of public order and morals, the prohibition of abuses such as the slave trade, the arms traffic and the liquor traffic, and the prevention of the establishment of fortifications or military and naval bases and of military training of the natives for other than police purposes and the defence of territory, and will also secure equal opportunities for the trade and commerce of other Members of the League.

6. There are territories, such as South-West Africa and certain of the South Pacific Islands, which, owing to the sparseness of their population, or their small size, or their remoteness from the centres of civilisation, or their geographical contiguity to the territory of the Mandatory, and other circumstances, can be best administered under the laws of the Mandatory as integral portions of its territory, subject to the safeguards above mentioned in the interest of the indigenous population.

7. In every case of mandate, the Mandatory shall render to the Council an annual report in reference to the territory committed to its charge.

8. The degree of authority, control or administration to be exercised by the Mandatory shall, if not previously agreed upon by the Members of the League, be explicitly defined in each case by the Council.

9. A permanent Commission shall be constituted to receive and examine the annual reports of the Mandatories and to advise the Council on all matters relating to the observance of the mandates.

Article 23. Subject to and in accordance with the provisions of international conventions existing or hereafter to be agreed upon, the Members of the League:

(a) will endeavour to secure and maintain fair and humane conditions of labour for men, women, and children, both in their own countries and in all countries to which commercial and industrial relations extend, and for that purpose will establish and maintain the necessary international organisations;

(b) undertake to secure just treatment of the native inhabitants of territories under their control;

(c) will entrust the League with the general supervision over the execution of agreements with regard to the traffic in women and children, and the traffic in opium and other dangerous drugs;

(d) will entrust the League with the general supervision of the trade in arms and ammunitions with the countries in which the control of this traffic is necessary in the common interest;

(e) will make provision to secure and maintain freedom of communications and of transit and equitable treatment for the commerce of all Members of the League. In this connection, the special necessities of the regions devastated during the war of 1914–1918 shall be borne in mind;

(f) will endeavour to take steps in matters of international concern for the prevention and control of disease.

Article 24. 1. There shall be placed under the direction of the League all international bureaux already established by general treaties if the parties to such treaties consent. All such international bureaux and all commissions for the regulation of matters of international interest hereafter constituted shall be placed under the direction of the League.

2. In all matters of international interest which are regulated by general conventions but which are not placed under the control of international bureaux or commissions, the Secretariat of the League shall, subject to the consent of the Council and if desired by the parties, collect and distribute all relevant information and shall render any other assistance which may be necessary or desirable.

3. The Council may include as part of the expenses of the Secretariat the expenses of any bureau or commission which is placed under the direction of the League.

Article 25. The Members of the League agree to

encourage and promote the establishment and co-operation of duly authorised voluntary national Red Cross organisations having as purposes the improvement of health, the prevention of disease and the mitigation of suffering throughout the world.

Article 26. 1. Amendments of this Covenant will take effect when ratified by the Members of the League whose Representatives compose the Council and by a majority of the Members of the League whose Representatives compose the Assembly.

2. No such amendments shall bind any Member of the League which signifies its dissent therefrom but in that case it shall cease to be a Member of the League.

PART VII

PENALTIES

Article 227. The Allied and Associated Powers publicly arraign William II of Hohenzollern, formerly German Emperor, for a supreme offence against international morality and the sanctity of treaties.

A special tribunal will be constituted to try the accused, thereby assuring him the guarantees essential to the right of defence. It will be composed of five judges, one appointed by each of the following Powers: namely, the United States of America, Great Britain, France, Italy and Japan.

In its decision the tribunal will be guided by the highest motives of international policy, with a view to vindicating the solemn obligations of international undertakings and the validity of international morality. It will be its duty to fix the punishment which it considers should be imposed.

The Allied and Associated Powers will address a request to the Government of the Netherlands for the surrender to them of the ex-Emperor in order that he may be put on trial.

. . . . . .

PART VIII

REPARATION

SECTION I: GENERAL PROVISIONS

Article 231. The Allied and Associated Governments affirm and Germany accepts the responsibility of Germany and her allies for causing all the loss and damage to which the Allied and Associated Governments and their nationals have been subjected as a consequence of the war imposed upon them by the aggression of Germany and her allies.

Article 232. The Allied and Associated Governments recognize that the resources of Germany are not adequate, after taking into account permanent diminutions of such resources which will result from other provisions of the present Treaty, to make complete reparation for all such loss and damage.

The Allied and Associated Governments, however, require, and Germany undertakes, that she will make compensation for all damage done to the civilian population of the Allied and Associated Powers and to their property during the period of the belligerency of each as an Allied or Associated Power against Germany by such aggression by land, by sea and from the air, and in general all damage as defined in Annex I hereto.

In accordance with Germany's pledges, already given, as to complete restoration for Belgium, Germany undertakes, in addition to the compensation for damage elsewhere in this Part provided for, as a consequence of the violation of the Treaty of 1839, to make reimbursement of all sums which Belgium has borrowed from the Allied and Associated Governments up to November 11, 1918, together with interest at the rate of five per cent. (5%) per annum on such sums. This amount shall be determined by the Reparation Commission, and the German Government undertakes thereupon forthwith to make a special issue of bearer bonds to an equivalent amount payable in marks gold, on May 1, 1926, or, at the option of the German Government, on May 1 in any year up to 1926. Subject to the foregoing, the form of such bonds shall be determined by the Reparation Commission. Such bonds shall be handed over to the Reparation Commission, which has authority to take and acknowledge receipt thereof on behalf of Belgium.

. . . . . .

SECTION II: SPECIAL PROVISIONS

Article 245. Within six months after the coming into force of the present Treaty the German Government must restore to the French Government the trophies, archives, historical souvenirs or works of art carried away from France by the German authorities in the course of the war of 1870–1871 and during this last war, in accordance with a list which will be communicated to it by the French Government; particularly the French flags taken in the course of the war of 1870–1871 and all the political papers taken by the German authorities on October 10, 1870, at the château of Cerçay, near Brunoy (Seine-et-Oise) belonging at the time to Mr. Rouher, formerly Minister of State.

PART XIV

GUARANTEES

SECTION I: WESTERN EUROPE

Article 428. As a guarantee for the execution of the present Treaty by Germany, the German territory situated to the west of the Rhine, together with the bridgeheads, will be occupied by Allied and Associated troops for a period of fifteen years from the coming into force of the present Treaty.

Article 429. If the conditions of the present Treaty are faithfully carried out by Germany, the occupation referred to in Article 428 will be successively restricted as follows:

(1) At the expiration of five years there will be evacuated: the bridgehead of Cologne and the territories north of a line running along the Ruhr, then along the railway Jülich, Düren, Euskirchen, Rheinbach, thence along the road Rheinbach to Sinzig, and reaching the Rhine at the confluence with the Ahr; the roads, railways and places mentioned above being excluded from the area evacuated.

(2) At the expiration of ten years there will be evacuated: the bridgehead of Coblenz and the territories north of a line to be drawn from the intersection between the frontiers of Belgium, Germany and Holland, running about 4 kilometres south of Aix-la-Chapelle, then to and following the crest of Forst Gemünd, then east of the railway of the Urft Valley, then along Blankenheim, Valdorf, Dreis, Ulmen to and following the Moselle from Bremm to Nehren, then passing by Kappel and Simmern, then following the ridge of the heights between Simmern and the Rhine and reaching this river at Bacharach; all the places, valleys, roads and railways mentioned above being excluded from the area evacuated.

(3) At the expiration of fifteen years there will be evacuated: the bridgehead of Mainz, the bridgehead of Kehl and the remainder of the German territory under occupation.

If at that date the guarantees against unprovoked aggression by Germany are not considered sufficient by the Allied and Associated Governments, the evacuation of the occupying troops may be delayed to the extent regarded as necessary for the purpose of obtaining the required guarantees.

Article 430. In case either during the occupation or after the expiration of the fifteen years referred to above the Reparation Commission finds that Germany refuses to observe the whole or part of her obligations under the present Treaty with regard to reparation, the whole or part of the areas specified in Article 429 will be reoccupied immediately by the Allied and Associated forces.

Article 431. If before the expiration of the period of fifteen years Germany complies with all the undertakings resulting from the present Treaty, the occupying forces will be withdrawn immediately.

Article 432. All matters relating to the occupation and not provided for by the present Treaty shall be regulated by subsequent agreements, which Germany hereby undertakes to observe.

Appendix B
Biographies of Major Personalities

Albert I (1875–1934): king of the Belgians (1909–34), married to a Bavarian princess. He offered heroic resistance to the German invasion in 1914, and greatly helped the Allied cause. He spent the entire war at the head of his army and led the offensive in 1918 that recovered the Belgian coast. He died in a rock-climbing accident.

Alexander (1893–1920): king of the Hellenes (1917–20), succeeded to the Greek throne after his father Constantine was forced to abdicate. Supported the Allied cause. Died of a monkey-bite. Shortly thereafter, his father was restored to the throne.

Alexandra Feodorovna (1872–1918): wife of Tsar Nicholas II, the last Russian tsarina. She was a Hessian princess and a granddaughter of Queen Victoria. She was dominated by Rasputin, who apparently succeeded in checking the hemophilia of her son, the successor to the throne. With her husband absent at the front, she assumed control in St. Petersburg and replaced liberal ministers with those favored by Rasputin. She was unpopular and suspected to be pro-German. She was shot by the Bolsheviks, together with her husband and children.

Allenby, Viscount Edmund Henry Hynman (1861–1936): British field marshal, fought in the colonies and the Boer War. Commanded first the cavalry, then the Third British Army in France during the war. In June 1917, he was appointed commander of the Egyptian Expeditionary Force and invaded Palestine in the last great cavalry campaign. He captured Jerusalem and after the battle of Megiddo in September 1918 ended Turkish resistance.

Asquith, Herbert Henry, 1st earl of Oxford and Asquith (1852–1928): British statesman. A Liberal Im-

perialist, he became prime minister in 1908. Promoted social welfare legislation, and was instrumental in stripping the House of Lords of its veto power. Formed a coalition government with the Conservatives in 1915. Resigned at the end of 1916 as a result of an intrigue of Lloyd George and the Conservatives.

Balfour, Arthur James, 1st earl of (1841–1930): British statesman, Conservative leader in the House of Commons, opponent to the Irish Home Rule movement. Became first lord of the Admiralty in 1915, and foreign secretary under Lloyd George in 1916. In the "Balfour Declaration" of 1917, he pledged British support to the Zionist hope for a Jewish national home in Palestine. Attended the Versailles Peace Conference.

Ball, Albert (1896–1917): British pilot in the Royal Flying Corps, credited with shooting down 43 enemy planes. Killed in action.

Beatty, David, 1st Earl (1871–1936): British admiral, served in Egypt, the Sudan, and in China. Commanded successful naval actions at Heligoland Bight (1914) and Dogger Bank (1915), and played an important role in the battle of Jutland (1916). Became then commander of the fleet, and in 1919 first sea lord of the navy.

Below, Fritz von (1853–1918): German general, fought at the Masurian Lakes 1914, at St. Quentin 1915–16, at Cambrai and at the Somme 1918.

Below, Otto von (1857–1944): German general, brother of Fritz von Below. Fought at Tannenberg and the Masurian Lakes 1914, in Italy 1917, and commanded the new German First Army 1918.

Benedict XV (1854–1922): original name Giacomo della Chiesa, pope (1914–22), kept strictest neutrality during the war and was respected by all belligerents. Founder of the Vatican service for prisoners of war, and very charitable toward war victims. He was also the originator of several peace proposals, the most important of which was in August 1917.

Berchtold, Count Leopold von (1863–1942): Austrian foreign minister (1912–15), worked for an independent Albania during the Balkan wars to block Serbian expansion to the Adriatic. His reckless policy after the assassination of the Austrian successor to the throne contributed much to the outbreak of the war. He probably exaggerated a border incident to secure Emperor Francis Joseph's approval of the declaration of war on Serbia.

Bernstorff, Count Johann Heinrich (1862–1939): German ambassador to the United States (1908–17), tried to conciliate feelings in the United States toward Germany and consistently warned the German government against the introduction of unrestricted submarine warfare. Later became a member of the German Reichstag and a delegate to the League of Nations disarmament conference. When Hitler came to power, he went into exile.

Bethmann-Hollweg, Theobald von (1856–1921): German chancellor (1909–17), pursued a moderate policy and worked for a greater autonomy of Alsace-Lorraine, and for the preservation of peace. When war broke out, he did his best to justify Germany's violation of the neutrality of Belgium, calling the treaty guaranteeing the neutrality a "scrap of paper." Stood against unrestricted submarine warfare and tried to bring the war to an end in 1916, thereby getting into conflict with Ludendorff and Hindenburg, who forced his resignation.

Bishop, William Avery ("Billy") (1894–1956): Canadian military aviator, credited with downing 72 enemy aircraft. Member of the Canadian Expeditionary Force in France.

Boelcke, Oswald (1891–1916): German military aviator, one of the first prominent German fighter pilots, credited with downing 40 enemy planes. Killed in action.

Bratianu, Ion (1864–1927): Romanian politician, succeeded his father as leader of the Liberals and served as prime minister, 1909–11 and 1914–18. Early in 1918, he resigned because of the humiliating peace terms offered by the victorious General Powers, but he returned to power in December 1918 and repre-sented his country at the Paris Peace Conference. He resigned again in protest against the Treaty of Trianon.

Briand, Aristide (1862–1932): French statesman. Started out as a socialist, but was ejected from his party for joining a bourgeois cabinet in 1906. Was prime minister 10 times, for the first time in 1909. Headed two wartime cabinets in 1915–17, and made the decision to hold Verdun at any price. Overthrown by Poincaré in 1917 for trying to negotiate a peace with Germany. After the war, he criticized the Treaty of Versailles and worked for reconciliation with Germany. In 1925, he became the chief architect of the Locarno Pact and he shared the Nobel Peace Prize with Gustav Stresemann in 1926. One of the prominent figures in the League of Nations. He also advocated a plan for a United States of Europe.

Brockdorff-Rantzau, Count Ulrich von (1869–1928): German diplomat, ambassador in Denmark 1912–18, then, from December 1918 on, foreign secretary. Though a member of an old noble family, he believed in democracy. When his endeavors for a just and honorable peace treaty failed, he resigned, together with chancellor Philipp Scheidemann and his cabinet, in June 1919. Between 1922 and 1928 he was German ambassador in Moscow, where he was highly respected.

Brooke, Rupert (1887–1915): English poet. He joined the Royal Naval division at the outbreak of the war and served at Antwerp. He was then in the Dardanelles expedition and died of blood poisoning at the island of Skiros.

Brusilov, Aleksei A. (1853–1926): the most successful Russian general of the war. After winning victories in Galicia he organized the great Russian offensive against Austria in 1916, which was successful at first but was finally stopped and cost his country approximately one million lives. Under Kerensky he was briefly commander in chief but could not stop the German advances. Served also in the Soviet Army's staff in the 1920 war against Poland.

Bryan, William Jennings (1860–1925): American political leader, ran unsuccessfully three times as Democratic candidate for the presidency, then, in 1912, supported Woodrow Wilson, who made him secretary of state. In this position, he pursued an antiwar and strictly neutral course when war broke out in Europe. In June 1915 he refused Wilson's second *Lusitania* note and resigned. He maintained thereafter an influential position in the Democratic party, and played an important role in the Scopes Trial of 1925.

Bülow, Bernhard Heinrich Martin (1849–1929): German foreign secretary in 1897 and chancellor from 1900 to 1908. His aggressive policy increased German isolation. He antagonized France in the Moroccan crisis of 1905 and Russia by supporting Austria-Hungary's annexation of Bosnia and Herzegovina in 1908. After the *Daily Telegraph* incident of October 1908 he lost his emperor's confidence and resigned. In 1914–15 he served as ambassador to Italy.

Byng, Viscount Julian Hedworth George (1862–1935): British general, served in India and South Africa and held several commands during the Great War. In April 1917 he commanded Canadian units including Vimy Ridge in northern France. After the war, he was made governor general of Canada (1921–26).

Cadorna, Luigi (1850–1928): Italian field marshal, served as chief of staff under the nominal leadership of King Victor Emanuel III. His operations against the Austrians in the Isonzo area were indecisive. After the crushing defeat at Caporetto he was replaced and he fell in disgrace after the war. He then supported Mussolini, who rehabilitated him.

Casement, Sir Roger David (1864–1916): Irish revolutionary. After the war broke out, he went to the United States, then to Germany, trying to secure aid for an Irish uprising. He returned to Ireland in April 1916 because he considered the promised German help to be insufficient. Tried in vain to delay the outbreak of the Easter Rebellion. After its failure he was arrested, tried for treason and hanged.

Cavell, Edith (1865–1915): English nurse and head of the nursing staff of the Berkendael Medical Institute in Brussels. In 1915 she was arrested by the German occupation forces and admitted harboring and helping Allied prisoners, some 130 of whom she had assisted to cross the Dutch border. In spite of efforts of the U.S. minister to Belgium, she was shot by the Germans.

Cecil of Chelwood, Viscount Edgar Algernon Robert (1864–1958): conservative British statesman, held several cabinet posts and advocated internationalism. In 1919 he worked with President Wilson in drafting the League of Nations Covenant. Was awarded the Nobel Peace Prize in 1937.

Charles (Karl) of Habsburg (1887–1922): last emperor of Austria and king of Hungary (1916–18). Grandnephew of Emperor Francis Joseph and, after the assassination of his uncle Francis Ferdinand at Sarajevo, heir to the Austrian throne. Commander during the first years of the war. After his accession he attempted to come to an understanding with the Allies through his brother-in-law, Prince Sixtus of Bourbon-Parma. The negotiations failed because he could not satisfy Italian demands. The Allies published his correspondence in April 1918 and caused severe friction between Germany and Austria, also diminished his popularity. In October 1918 he proclaimed an Austrian federative state, but he could not save the Austro-Hungarian monarchy. He abdicated as emperor on November 11, 1918 and two days later as king of Hungary. Went to exile in Switzerland and tried, after the monarchists had won in Hungary, to regain the Hungarian throne. After the second attempt, the Hungarian regent Nicholas Horthy had him arrested. He was then exiled to Madeira. He was married to Zita of Bourbon-Parma, who never renounced her aim to see her son Otto crowned king of Hungary.

Churchill, Sir Winston Leonard Spencer (1874–1965): British soldier and statesman. Served as an officer in India and in the Sudan under Kitchener, then as journalist covering the South African War, where he was captured by the Boers but managed to escape. Was elected to Parliament as a Conservative in 1900, but then switched to the Liberal party and held several cabinet posts. Became first lord of the admiralty in 1911, but had to resign after the failure of the Dardanelles Expedition, which he had vigorously advocated. Served then in the front lines in France as a major with a battalion of the Grenadier Guards but was made minister of munitions by Lloyd George in 1917, then secretary for war and for air in 1918. Continued to play a leading role in British politics between the two world wars and led the British nation through World War II. Was prime minister 1940–45 and 1951–55.

Clemenceau, Georges (1841–1929): French statesman, started his political career as a socialist, opposed Jules Ferry and General Boulanger. In 1893, his career almost came to an end as he was involved in the Panama Canal scandal, and accused of being in the pay of the British. Defender of Alfred Dreyfus in 1902. Prime minister 1906–09 and again from 1917 to 1920. During his first tenure, he used harsh measures against strikers and broke with the socialists. In the first years of the war he attacked his government for defeatism. In his second tenure, he formed a coalition cabinet, served also as minister of war and did everything possible to revive patriotism and morale in France. At Versailles he was the chief opponent to Woodrow Wilson and succeeded in wrecking most of Wilson's plans. Yet he considered the Versailles Treaty as insufficient for French security. After his defeat in the presidential election of 1920 he retired.

Conrad von Hoetzendorf, Count Franz (1852–1925): Austrian field marshal, headed the armies of the empire during the war. He opposed Emperor Charles' peace plans and was dismissed in 1917. Then commanded the Austro-Hungarian armies at the Italian front, 1917–18. After the failure of the June 1918 offensive he was replaced. During the crisis of July 1914 he had been a chief promoter of an aggressive Austrian policy against Serbia.

Constantine I (1868–1923): king of the Hellenes, succeeded to the throne in 1913. He was married to the sister of the German emperor and opposed the pro-Allied policy of his prime minister Venizelos. Under Allied pressure, he was forced to abdicate in 1917 and was succeeded by his second son, Alexander. After Alexander's death in 1920 he was recalled, but was again deposed in 1922 after the Turkish victory over the Greeks had caused a military rebellion.

Czernin, Count Ottokar (1872–1932): adviser to Archduke Francis Ferdinand, then foreign minister of Austria-Hungary (1916–18). He aided Emperor Charles' efforts for a negotiated peace, but opposed the sacrifice of Austrian designs in Italy and the Balkans. One of the chief negotiators at Brest-Litovsk. When Charles' peace feelers behind the back of his German allies were disclosed by Clemenceau, Czernin was dismissed.

D'Annunzio, Gabriele (1863–1938): Italian poet, novelist and dramatist. At the outbreak of the war, he returned from France to Italy where his oratory helped to persuade Italians to join the Allies. He became a daring aviator and, in 1919, led an expedition against Fiume, where he established a regime which was opposed by the Italian government as well as the rest of Europe. It lasted until January 1921. He was courted by Mussolini, and the black shirts of his troops against Fiume became the official fascist uniform.

Delcassé, Théophile (1852–1923): French diplomat, foreign minister from 1898 to 1905. Helped to settle the Fashoda incident and started the Franco-British rapprochement which led to the Entente Cordiale of 1904, after colonial differences between the two countries had been settled. He also worked for closer ties with Russia and concluded a secret non-aggression agreement with Italy. He also urged a firm stand

against Germany in the Morocco crisis of 1905, but lacking support in his country caused him to resign. Served again as naval minister (1911–13) and foreign minister (1914–15).

Denikin, Alexander Ivanovich (1872–1947): Russian general and counterrevolutionary. In November 1917 he joined General Kornilov and succeeded him as commander of the antirevolutionary forces in the south. He managed to control a great section of southern Russia, but did not succeed in taking Moscow in 1919. Thereafter, his forces were driven back by the Bolsheviks and his troops became demoralized. He resigned in 1920 and moved to France.

De Robeck, John (1862–1928): British admiral, attempted on March 18, 1915 to force the Dardanelles Narrows with 18 warships. Four of his ships were sunk, due to insufficient mine sweeping before the attack, and De Robeck gave up the attempt, possibly prematurely.

Drummond, James Eric, earl of Perth (1876–1951): British diplomat and promoter of the idea of the League of Nations. He became its first secretary and served from 1919–1933. Thereafter ambassador to Rome.

Ebert, Friedrich (1871–1925): German Socialist leader and first president of the Weimar Republic. Started as a saddler, then as union leader and journalist. Member of the Reichstag in 1912 and in 1913 head of the Social Democratic party as successor to August Bebel. He supported the war effort but opposed any policy of annexations, as well as all strikes in wartime instigated by the radical left. In November 1918 he wanted to preserve the monarchy. Became chancellor when Max von Baden resigned. In February 1919 he was elected president of the new German Republic by the National Assembly in Weimar.

Enver Pasha (1881–1922): Turkish political leader and general, played a prominent part in the Young Turk Revolution of 1908 in which the old liberal constitution of 1876 was reinstituted. Obtained dictatorial powers by a coup d'état in 1913, after having fought in the Turkish-Italian war of 1911–12 and both Balkan wars. Because of Turkish territorial losses in the Balkan wars, he worked toward bringing his country into the great war on the German side. When the armistice was signed, he fled to Berlin. Killed during an anti-Soviet expedition in Uzbekistan.

Erzberger, Mathias (1876–1921): German politician and public official. Since 1903 leader of the left wing of the Catholic Center party in the Reichstag. At first an annexionist, but in 1917 leader of the move for a Reichstag peace resolution. Member of Prince Max von Baden's cabinet in October 1918 and head of the German delegation that signed the armistice. Then member of Scheidemann's cabinet, and when Scheidemann resigned rather than sign the proposed peace treaty, Erzberger pressed for acceptance and became vice chancellor and finance minister under Scheidemann's successor, Bauer. Later was ruthlessly attacked by the radical right and assassinated by fanatics in 1921.

Faisal (ibn Hussein) (1885–1933): son of Hussein, sherif of Mecca, served with the Turkish army in Syria until 1916, then escaped to Arabia and joined with T.E. Lawrence in a revolt against the Turkish regime. His hopes to rule as king over all Arabs liberated from Turkish rule after the war were disappointed. Though a Syrian nationalist congress proclaimed him king in 1920, France forced him to abdicate.

Falkenhayn, Erich von (1861–1922): Prussian minister of war and chief of the German Supreme Command after Moltke's attack on the Marne had failed in 1914. He believed in concentrating all available German forces on the French front, in contrast to Hindenburg and Ludendorff. Attempted the great breakthrough at Verdun in 1916 that had to be abandoned after huge losses had been incurred by both sides, and because of the British attack at the Somme. He was replaced by Hindenburg and Ludendorff in August 1916 and later fought successfully in the Balkans.

Ferdinand (1865–1927): king of Romania, son of a Prussian prince and married to a granddaughter of Queen Victoria and Tsar Alexander II. In 1916, he took his country into the war on the Allied side, but failed to provide any substantial help to the Triple Entente. He annexed Bessarabia from Russia in 1918, but could not prevent the occupation of his country by the Central Powers. Through the peace treaties of St. Germain and Trianon his country was given Siebenbuergen, Bessarabia, the Bukovina and the Dobrudja. He also intervened in Hungary to break the Communist regime of Bela Kun.

Foch, Ferdinand (1851–1929): marshal of France. As professor of the Ecole de Guerre and then as its director, he formulated French military policies in case of war with Germany. In 1914 he, with Joffre and Gallieni, was responsible for stopping the German advance to the Marne. He then took part in the battles of Ypres in 1915 and of the Somme in 1916,

and in 1917 was appointed chief of the French general staff. In April 1918, when the great German offensive threatened Paris again, he was given the unified command of the French, British and American armies, and in this capacity led the great Allied counterattack that resulted in the collapse of the German western front. At the end of the war, he was often in conflict with Clemenceau. Although his demand that the German-French border run along the Rhine was not considered at Versailles, he continued to serve latter governments as military consultant.

Francis Ferdinand (1863–1914): archduke of Austria, grandnephew of Emperor Francis Joseph and heir apparent after Crown Prince Rudolf had committed suicide. His right to succession was, however, questioned at times because of his frail health. The emperor was never reconciled to Francis Ferdinand's marriage to Sophie Chotek, who was of minor nobility so that the marriage was declared morganatic, thus barring her children from succession. Francis Ferdinand was arrogant, brusque and unfriendly and quite unpopular, but he saw the weaknesses of the empire much more clearly than did the emperor. His efforts to transform the Dual Monarchy into a Triple Monarchy including a Slavic kingdom under Croatian leadership won him the enmity of the Pan-Serbians and the Pan-Germans, as well as the hostility of the Hungarian nobility. He worked to reform the Austrian army, but had little influence in Vienna, and opposed Conrad von Hoetzendorf's military designs. His and his wife's assassination at Sarajevo by Gavrilo Princip was the occasion which led to the outbreak of war.

Francis Joseph I of Habsburg (1830–1916): emperor of Austria (1848–1916) and king of Hungary (1867–1916), subdued Hungary in 1849 after the 1848 revolution, but lost all influence in Italy in the following years and all control over Germany after his defeat in 1866. In 1867 he established the Dual Monarchy with Hungary and in 1879 an alliance with Germany, later joined by Italy. His personal life was full of tragedies: His brother Maximilian was shot in Mexico (1867), his wife Elizabeth was assassinated (1889), his son Rudolph committed suicide and his heir apparent was assassinated at Sarajevo. His personal misfortunes and the length of his regime made him a popular figure and it was his personality which held the various diverging people of his waning, obsolete empire together during the first years of the war. He died before the Dual Monarchy actually fell apart.

François, Hermann von (1856–1933): German general under Prittwitz in East Prussia, attacked the

Russian First Army at Gumbinnen against his superior's orders and after initial successes was thrown back. Subsequently he played an important part in the battle of Tannenberg under Hindenburg and Ludendorff's command.

French, John Denton Pinkstone, Earl of Ypres (1852–1925): British field marshal. Served in the British army in the Sudan, in South Africa and commanded the British Expeditionary Force in Belgium and France from the beginning of the war to December 1915. He failed to coordinate the movements of his forces with those of the French and was more concerned about the safety of his troops than about aiding his allies. Nevertheless, his troops suffered heavy losses at Ypres and Loos. After his relief he reorganized the British home defenses.

Gallieni, Joseph-Simon (1849–1916): French colonial administrator and general. Served in the Sudan and Tonkin and organized the French administration in Madagascar. In 1914, he was called in from retirement and, as military governor of Paris, became the decisive figure in the battle of the Marne, although most of the credit for the French victory went to Joffre. In 1915, he was made minister of war by Briand, but he resigned after his proposals for reorganization of command were refused by the cabinet. He died shortly thereafter but many of his proposed reforms were carried out after his death.

George V (1865–1936): king of Great Britain and Ireland (1910–36), second son of Edward VII, became heir to the throne when his elder brother Clarence died in 1892. As king, he acted as moderator in the debates over the Irish Home Rule. In 1917, he abandoned his German titles and changed the name of his house from Saxe-Coburg-Gotha to Windsor. Aside from this, he had little influence on the British conduct of the war.

Giolitti, Giovanni (1842–1928): Italian statesman, five times prime minister, the last three times 1906–09, 1911–14 and 1920–21. He was a progressive liberal, carried out social and agrarian reforms and introduced universal male suffrage in 1912. Supported the Italian conquest of Libya, but opposed his country's participation in the Great War. His insistence on strict neutrality was vigorously opposed by D'Annunzio and Mussolini. The end of the "Era Giolitti" came with the rise of fascism and Mussolini.

Grey, Edward, viscount of Fallodon (1862–1933): British statesman. Entered Parliament as a Liberal in 1885, and was foreign secretary from 1905 to 16. He supported France in the Morocco crisis and authorized secret military conversations with France. Again supported France during the Agadir crisis in 1911 and arranged a conference of the Great Powers during the Balkan wars. During the July crisis of 1914 he tried to find a compromise and to maintain peace. Concluded a secret treaty with Italy in 1915 which brought Italy into the war on the Allied side. Maintained good relations with the United States throughout his tenure and served as ambassador in Washington (1919–20).

Groener, Wilhelm (1867–1939): German general and politician. Organized the railroad system for the great offensives of 1914 and served as administrator of munitions production and troop reinforcements. Opposed the radical war aims of the extreme right and thereby antagonized Ludendorff, whose successor he became on October 26, 1918. Appealed in vain to the emperor to personally appear at the front. After the German revolution he cooperated with Ebert in establishing a democratic regime in the country. Advised to accept the Versailles Treaty and resigned shortly thereafter, but played again an important role in the last years of the Weimar Republic.

Guillaumat, Marie-Louis Adolphe (1863–1940): French general, commanded the Second French army defending Verdun. The commander in chief of Allied armies in the east, 1918. Finally commanded the Fifth French Army in October 1918, forcing the passage of the Aisne River.

Guynemer, Georges-Marie (1894–1917): French military aviator. He was credited with destroying 54 enemy planes. Killed in action.

Haig, Earl Douglas (1861–1928): British field marshal. Served in the Sudan and in the South African Corps, and at the outbreak of the Great War commanded the first British Army Corps in France. As successor to French, he became the commander in chief of the British Expeditionary Force in December 1915. He commanded the great Somme offensive in the summer of 1916 which gained little and resulted in very high casualties. Prime Minister David Lloyd George opposed most of Haig's ideas and put some British under French command. Consequently, Haig had to conduct the Ypres campaign under Nivelle's orders in the fall of 1917, and Haig's whole Flanders campaign resulted in huge losses and little territorial gain. But in 1918, Haig foresaw the forthcoming collapse of the German armies and insisted on wholesale offensives when Foch still believed the war would last into 1919.

Hamilton, Sir Ian Standish Monteith (1853–1947): British general, fought with distinction in the South African War and was military attaché with the Japanese in their war against Russia (1904–05). He commanded the British Expeditionary Force during the Gallipoli campaign, which ended in failure and his replacement. Later engaged in pacifist activities.

Hausen, Max Klemens von (1846–1922): German general, commanded the Third Army at the Belgian frontier. He kept in close contact with the army on his right flank, the Second Army under von Below, advanced close to the Marne River and then retreated together with the whole German right wing to the Aisne River.

Hertling, Count Georg von (1843–1919): German philosopher and politician. Professor of philosophy, then right-wing leader of the Center Party in the Reichstag. In 1912 he became Bavarian prime minister. After Bethmann-Hollweg resigned, the German emperor asked Hertling to become his successor, but he declined because of old age. But on November 1, 1917, when Michaelis resigned, he did accept and was appointed German chancellor and Prussian prime minister. He could not overcome resistance of the Prussian conservatives against more democratic election reforms and was powerless against the Supreme Military Command under Hindenburg and Ludendorff. He resigned September 30, 1918.

Hindenburg, Paul von Beneckendorff und von (1847–1934): German field marshal, fought in the Prussian-Austrian war of 1866 and the Franco-Prussian war of 1870–71. Retired as general in 1911, but called back as commander in East Prussia after the initial Russian successes in this area. Ludendorff was his chief of staff throughout the war, and he was mainly responsible for the victories Hindenburg received credit for. After the victory of Tannenberg against superior Russian forces and the further defeat of the Second Russian Army at the Masurian Lakes, he became a legend and commanded immense prestige. As commander of the German army in the east he constantly asked for reinforcements from the western theater, but was resisted by Moltke and Falkenhayn. But in 1916 he was made successor to Falkenhayn and as commander of all the German armies, he and Ludendorff became virtual dictators in Germany who took over control of the civilian government. His greatest military successes occurred in 1917 after Russia and Romania had been decisively beaten. His and Ludendorff's great Spring Offensive broke through the Allied lines, and brought German units once more close to Paris, but ultimately failed. When, after the

Allied counterattack, Ludendorff resigned, Hindenburg remained in office and led back the German troops. He also swore allegiance to the new republican government. Hindenburg was to be tried as a war criminal, but the German Supreme Court never even indicted him. In 1925, after Ebert's death, he was called out of retirement again and persuaded to run for president. He was elected in 1925 and again in 1932, and in January 1933 appointed Adolf Hitler chancellor.

Hipper, Franz von (1863–1932): German admiral. On May 31, 1916, his squadron met a British squadron under Admiral Beatty 60 miles west of the coast of Jutland. When both Hipper and Beatty were joined by the bulk of the British and German navies, the only major naval engagement of the war ensued in which the outnumbered German forces inflicted the greater damage. He remained commander of the German naval reconnaissance, and from August to November 1918 was commander of the German High Seas Fleet.

Hoffman, Max (1869–1927), German general. He prepared the battle of Tannenberg before Hindenburg's and Ludendorff's arrival and is considered to be one of the great strategists of the war. In 1916 he was made chief of staff of the eastern armies. He then was Germany's main representative at Brest-Litovsk. In his diaries and later writings he criticized the German High Command.

Horthy, Nicholas de Nagybanya (1868–1957): Hungarian admiral and regent. Commanded the Austro-Hungarian fleet during the war. As vice admiral, he turned over the Austrian fleet to the South Slavian Committee on October 31, 1918. After the overthrow of Bela Kun's Communist regime in Budapest, Horthy was made regent and head of state. Two attempts of former Emperor Charles to regain the throne of Hungary were checked by Horthy, one by persuasion, one by armed force (March and October 1921), and also by the resistance of the Little Entente controlled by postwar France.

House, Edward Mandell (1858–1938): American politician and adviser to President Wilson. He was sent to Europe in 1914 in an attempt to prevent the outbreak of the war, and in 1915 to propose a peace conference. After the United States entered the war, he was its representative at the conference for coordinating Allied activities, and became a member of the U.S. peace commission. He also worked on the draft of the Versailles Treaty and the League of Nations Covenant. He disagreed with Wilson on the conduct of the Paris negotiations by suggesting to accept Senator Lodge's conditions to secure the acceptance of the Treaty in the U.S. Senate.

Jaurès, Jean (1859–1914): French Socialist historian and political leader. He helped unify the French Socialist party in 1905 and in 1914 proposed arbitration instead of military action, declaring that the capitalist nations, including France, were responsible for the conflict. He was assassinated by a right-wing fanatic at the end of July 1914.

Jellicoe, Earl John Rushworth (1859–1935): British admiral. After a long naval career he served as commander in chief of the Grand Fleet, which he commanded during the indecisive battle of Jutland in 1916, the conduct of which earned him much criticism and some praise. Thereafter appointed first sea lord, he opposed the use of convoys to counteract the great German submarine threat, and was dismissed by Lloyd George. After the war, he served as governor of New Zealand (1920–24).

Joffre, Joseph-Jacques-Césaire (1852–1931): marshal of France. Served first in the colonies and was appointed commander in chief in 1911. At the outbreak of the war he launched an abortive offensive in Alsace-Lorraine and underestimated the power of the German offensive through Belgium. Yet he managed a fairly orderly retreat and, with the help of Gallieni and others, was able to counterattack when a gap developed between the advancing First and Second German armies. He then organized the trench warfare and gained great prestige by his unshakable calmness and sound common sense. He was less successful at the Salonika front, was replaced by Nivelle and finally served as chairman of the Allied War Council.

Karolyi, Count Michael (1875–1955): Hungarian politician, of ancient noble descent. In 1918, he organized a national council for Hungary and was made prime minister after the Austro-Hungarian Monarchy was dissolved. As a liberal, he tried to keep a balance between the extreme right and left faction in his country. In January 1919 he was elected provisional president, but he had to surrender to the Communists under Bela Kun in March of that year.

Kemal Atatürk (1881–1938): Turkish soldier and statesman, founder of modern Turkey. As a young officer he joined the Young Turks, who fought for a constitutional government of the Ottoman Empire. He participated in the Young Turk revolution as chief of staff to Enver Pasha and fought in Libya and the second Balkan War. In World War I, he fought successfully at the Dardanelles, in Armenia and in Palestine. After the Turkish collapse, he organized the Turkish National Party and built up an army. He was outlawed by the sultan in Constantinople, who was under Allied control, and set up his own government at Ankara. After the sultan signed the treaty of Sèvres, Atatürk moved against the Greek Anatolia and, in November 1922, abolished the sultanate. In the treaty of Lausanne, which undid the treaty of Sèvres, nationalist Turkey under Atatürk triumphed, and he was elected president of the newly founded Turkish Republic.

Kerensky, Alexander Feodorovich (1881–1970): Russian revolutionary. He was elected to the Duma in 1912 as delegate of the moderate Labor Party and joined the Social Revolutionary Party after the 1917 February revolution. He served as minister of justice and minister of war under Prince Lvov, whom he succeeded as premier in July 1917. He insisted on continuing the war and failed to deal with urgent economic problems, such as land distribution. This enabled the Bolsheviks to overthrow his government in October 1917. He fled to Paris and continued his propaganda against the Soviet regime. In 1940 he fled to the United States.

Kitchener, Horatio Herbert, earl of Kitchener (1850–1916): British field marshal and statesman. Served in the colonies and participated in the unsuccessful attempt of General Gordon at Khartoum in 1885. As governor general of Eastern Sudan he repulsed the last Mahdist invasion of Egypt and reconquered the Sudan 1896–98. He frustrated the French in their attempt to claim part of the Sudan in the Fashoda incident and then served as chief of staff in the South African War. There he had to fight Boer guerrilla warfare, but he finally secured their submission in 1902. Then he served as commander in chief of the Indian forces, was made field marshal and served in Egypt as consul general from 1911 to 1914. At the outbreak of the war, he was called to London as secretary of state for war. Unlike most of his countrymen, he was convinced the war would last for several years and called for a vast expansion of the army. The response of the British public who idolized him was overwhelming, but soon after he was criticized by newspaper king Lord Northcliffe and others for munition shortages and the failure at the Dardanelles. His offer to resign was refused because he was still immensely popular. Upon the request of the tsar, Kitchener embarked on a mission to Russia in June 1916 in order to encourage Russia to continue resistance. His ship hit a German mine and sank off the Orkney Islands, and Kitchener was drowned. His main achievement was the fast creation of a large British land army.

Kluck, Alexander von (1846–1934): German general. He commanded the right wing of the German advance through Belgium at the beginning of the war. He advanced rapidly, but could not follow the original plan of swinging around west of Paris. After his troops had crossed the Marne, he was forced to turn west and a gap developed between his forces and the Second Army under Karl von Bülow which was exploited by Allied counterattacks. His and the other German armies then retreated behind the Aisne River.

Kolchak, Alexander Vasilyevich (1874–1920): Russian admiral, leader of anti-Bolshevik forces in Western Siberia, 1918–20. He had fought in the Russo-Japanese war and commanded the Black Sea fleet during the war. In October 1918, an antirevolutionary government was set up at Omsk, and Kolchak, as minister of war, carried out a coup d'état and established a dictatorship over Siberia. He was recognized by the Allies, but his great offensive of 1919, aimed at joining up with the British and Russian counter-revolutionaries at the White Sea, collapsed. He retreated to Irkutsk, lost most of his troops and was betrayed to the Bolsheviks, who had him shot.

Kornilov, Lavr Georgyevich (1870–1918): Russian general and anti-Bolshevik. Fought in the Russo-Japanese war. In the Great War, he was captured by the Austrians in 1915, but he escaped in the following year. Kerensky made him commander in chief, and his army was joined by conservatives who tried to reconstruct the provisional government. When Kornilov sent troops to Petrograd (Leningrad), Kerensky dismissed him fearing that Kornilov was planning a military dictatorship. Since Kornilov refused to obey, Kerensky had him arrested. After the October revolution, Kornilov escaped and joined antirevolutionary forces in southern Russia. His troops were greatly weakened when the Cossacks defected, and Kornilov had to retreat to the Kuban region. When he was attacking Ekaterinodar (Kranodar), he was killed and was succeeded by Denikin.

Kun, Bela (1886–1939 ?): Hungarian Communist. He was taken prisoner of war in Russia, became a Bolshevist and was sent to Hungary as a propagandist. His chance came when the liberal Count Michael Karolyi had to resign in March 1919 and the Communists and Social Democrats formed a coalition government. Kun then carried out a coup d'état; he assumed dictatorial powers and nationalized banks, large estates and businesses and private property above a certain minimum. He suppressed all opposition, raised an army and invaded Slovakia. When the Allies forced Kun to withdraw from Slovakia, a counterrevolution broke out. After some initial successes, Kun was defeated when a Romanian army intervened. He fled to Vienna, and his Red Terror was followed by a wave of White Terror. Kun then went to Soviet Russia. He disappeared during the great Stalinist purges in the 1930s.

Lanrezac, Charles (1852–1925): French general, appointed by Joffre to command the Fifth French Army. He fought at Charleroi and participated in the battle of the Marne. He had a low opinion of Joffre and French and repeatedly clashed with them. He refused to counterattack at the Marne, then fought at St. Quentin. After too much disagreement with Joffre's headquarters, he was relieved, but his objection to the folly of Plan 17 made the recovery at the Marne possible.

Lansing, Robert (1864–1928): U.S. secretary of state (1915–20). Served as counsel for the United States in several international disputes. When William Jennings Bryan resigned as secretary of state because of Wilson's aggressive policy toward Germany, Lansing was appointed his successor. He was in favor of U.S. participation in the war. He was nominal head of the U.S. commission to the Paris Peace Conference but did not think the Covenant of the League of Nations was essential to the peace treaty, and thereby lost Wilson's confidence. He resigned, at Wilson's request, in February 1920.

Lawrence, Thomas Edward (1888–1935): British soldier and adventurer, known as Lawrence of Arabia. He spent his prewar years in the Middle East, learning colloquial Arabic and engaged in archaeological surveys. When war broke out, he was attached to the British intelligence section in Egypt. In 1916, he contacted the Arab forces under Faisal ibn Hussein and organized the Arab revolt against the Turkish regime. He managed to tie down large Turkish contingents with only a few thousand Arab troops. He sympathized with the Arabs and fought hard at the Paris Conference to achieve independence for them. Since this could not be achieved, he felt he had betrayed his friends and fellow fighters. After the war, he joined the Royal Air Force and then the tank corps under assumed names. His accounts of his war adventures became extremely popular.

Leman, Gerard Mathieu (1851–1920): Belgian soldier and administrator, was governor of Liège at the time of the German attack in August 1914. He offered all possible resistance to the German onslaught and held Fort Loncin until the last possible moment. When the fort was smashed by the big German guns. He was taken prisoner while unconscious.

Lenin, Vladimir Ilyich (1870–1924): (Born Vladimir Ilyich Ulyanov.) Russian revolutionary and statesman. Became a revolutionary when his brother, who had participated in the assassination of Tsar Alexander II, was executed in 1887. As revolutionary he was exiled to Siberia, where he stayed from 1887 to 1900, and he then continued his activities abroad. When, at a meeting in London, the Russian Socialist Party, Lenin headed the more radical Bolsheviks. He returned to Russia when the revolution of 1905 broke out but left again in 1907 and spent the first years of World War I in Switzerland, convinced that the war would bring about a general uprising of the proletariat. In February 1917 the German government arranged for Lenin and several of his companions to cross through Germany from Switzerland to Sweden in a sealed rail car and proceeded from there to Russia. However, after an unsuccessful uprising in July 1917, he was compelled to flee to Finland. He returned to Russia in October when the Bolsheviks had gained sufficient strength to overthrow Kerensky's provisional government. Lenin now became chairman of the Council of the People's Commissars, and virtual dictator. With the help of Trotsky, Rykow, Stalin and others, he established a dictatorship of the Communist party, oppressing all opposition and accepting the humiliating peace treaty of Brest-Litovsk. Civil war raged through the country all through 1920. He launched the New Economic Policy in 1921 which permitted some private enterprise. He suffered a stroke in 1922 and died in January 1924, and in the contest for his succession, Stalin emerged victorious over Trotsky.

Lettow-Vorbeck, Paul von (1870–1964): German general, commander of the colonial forces in German East Africa, conducted a brilliant defense against greatly superior British forces, though completely cut off from his home country. He surrendered only after an armistice had been signed in Europe.

Lichnowsky, Prince Karl Max von (1860–1928): German diplomat, ambassador to London 1912–14. Admirer of the British, he tried very hard to prevent the outbreak of hostilities between Germany and England, but misunderstood a last minute message by foreign secretary Grey. In a privately circulated pamphlet, written in 1916, he criticized German diplomacy and the attitude of the German government during the July crisis 1914. The pamphlet was published without his permission, whereupon he was expelled from the Prussian Upper House.

Liebknecht, Karl (1871–1919): radical German socialist leader who refused to support his government during the war. In 1915, he and Rosa Luxemburg founded a revolutionary group later called the Spartacus Party. He was repeatedly imprisoned for anti-war activities. He opposed the moderate Socialist government that took over after the German monarchy collapsed and in January 1919 led an uprising against the provisional Republican government which failed. He was arrested and was killed by right-wing fanatics while being taken to prison.

Liman von Sanders, Otto (1855–1929): German general. In 1913, his appointment to reorganize the Turkish army led to a diplomatic crisis between Russia and Germany. After the British attacked in the Dardanelles, he took over the command of the Turkish defenses, and in 1918 he was given supreme command in Palestine where he was defeated by the British under General Allenby and the Arabs organized by T.E. Lawrence.

Lloyd George, David (1863–1945): British statesman of Welsh origin. Started out as an anti-imperialist liberal, and opposed the South African War. Member of a liberal cabinet in 1905, and in 1908 chancellor of the exchequer under Asquith. He and Asquith forced the passage of the Parliament Act of 1911 by which the House of Lords lost its veto power. During the same year, he warned Germany in his Mansion House Speech not to interfere with Britain's international interests. In 1915 he became minister of munitions, and in the following year minister or war. In December 1916 he formed his own government, ousting Asquith, and created a small war cabinet. Often at odds with Britain's military leaders, in particular Haig, he nevertheless pursued a very bold and aggressive policy and was instrumental in unifying the Allied command under Marshal Foch. He also was the spirit behind the introduction of the convoy system that saved Britain from the German submarine menace. At Versailles, he tried to moderate Clemenceau, but at the same time fought Wilson's idealistic plans. A substantial part of the final agreement was his work. He and his liberal cabinet fell in 1922 and were replaced by a conservative leadership under Bonar Law.

Ludendorff, Erich (1865–1937): German general and chief of staff to Field Harshal Hindenburg. He was a disciple of Schlieffen. His first success was during the German onslaught against Liège in August 1914. He was then assigned to the East Prussian front, where he and Hindenburg won a brilliant victory over superior Russian forces at Tannenberg, then at the Masurian Lakes. When Hindenburg became supreme military commander in 1916, Ludendorff also intervened in matters of civilian government. In 1917, he forced Chancellor Bethmann-Hollweg to resign. He was the driving spirit behind the great German offensive at the western front in Spring 1918 that was stopped by French, British and American forces at the last moment. On September 29, he suddenly demanded an armistic, and he was dismissed by the kaiser by the end of October. He fled to Sweden, returned in 1919 and participated in radical rightist uprisings, including that of Adolf Hitler in 1923, with whom he split in 1925.

Luxemburg, Rosa (1871–1919): German revolutionary, of Polish-Jewish descent, one of the founders of the Polish Socialist party, became a German citizen through marriage and became a leader in the German Socialist party, but also participated in the Russian revolution of 1905. During the war, she founded what became known as the Spartacus Party with Karl Liebknecht. She spent much of the war years in protective custody and was released when the revolution of 1918 broke out. She edited the Communist paper *Rote Fahne* and was active in the Communist uprising in January 1919. When it failed, she and Liebknecht were arrested, and both were slain by right-wing radicals on their way to prison.

Lvov, Prince Georgi Yevgenyevich (1861–1925): Russian politician. Member of the Constitutional Democratic party in the Duma and head of the Provisional government after the tsar's abdication in February 1917. He was averse to any kind of violence and unfit to control the turbulent situation. During his tenure, the Socialists gained power by organizing the workers and peasants councils. His foreign minister and war minister were forced to resign in May 1917, and after an uprising in Petrograd was suppressed in July he resigned in favor of a moderate Socialist government headed by Kerensky. Lvov then emigrated to Paris.

MacArthur, Douglas (1880–1964): American general, served in the Philippines and in Japan, then as aide to President Theodore Roosevelt. Attached to the Army General Staff from 1913 to 1917. Fought in France as chief of staff of the 42nd (Rainbow) Division, and, as brigadier general, commanded the 84th Infantry Brigade. After the war he was appointed superintendent at West Point. His main career took place in the Far East during World War II.

Mackensen, August von (1849–1945): German field marshal. Victor in the battle of the Masurian Lakes, 1914–15, and chief of various operations in Serbia, Galicia and Romania. Throughout the war, he was one of the most successful and popular German generals.

Mahan, Alfred Thayer (1840–1914): American naval officer and historian, wrote major works on the importance of sea power and naval strategy. Both Theodore Roosevelt and William II were much influenced by his writings, in which he showed that naval power was the key to success in modern warfare.

Mata Hari (1876–1917): (Pseudonym of Margaretha Geertruida Zelle.) Dutch dancer and spy for the German secret service from 1907 to 1917. She betrayed many military secrets confided to her by high Allied officers with whom she was on intimate terms. The French arrested, convicted and executed her in 1917.

Maunoury, Michel-Joseph (1847–1923): French general who played a major part in the operations on the western front in August 1914. Commander of the Army of Lorraine, then of the newly formed Sixth Army. His troops were driven back by Kluck's First Army and nearly defeated, but then contributed to the final French victory at the Marne.

Max (Maximilian) von Baden (1867–1929): the last chancellor of Imperial Germany. He was a liberal and when the German defeat had become inevitable, he was appointed chancellor. During his brief tenure, from October 3 to November 11, he tried to bring about political reforms, in particular a parliamentary form of government. He insisted on Ludendorff's dismissal, formed a coalition government with the center party, the Progressives and the Socialists, and began the armistice negotiations. He tried to save the monarchy by announcing William's abdication on November 9, before the emperor had made up his mind. Several hours later he resigned and surrendered the government to Friedrich Ebert.

Michaelis, Georg (1857–1936): German chancellor from July to October 1917, was dominated by Ludendorff and avoided endorsement of the Reichstag peace resolution. He also refused to promise Germany's withdrawal from Belgium.

Milyukov, Pavel Nikolayevich (1859–1943): Russian political leader. Founder of the Constitutional Democratic Party and member of the Duma. He became foreign minister in the provisional government of

Prince Lvov. Unpopular because of his insistence to carry out Russia's military obligations toward her allies, he was forced to resign in May 1917. Opposed to the Bolsheviks, he settled in Paris.

Mitchell, William (Billy) (1879–1936): American pilot and army officer. Commanded the American Expeditionary Air Force. Advocate of air power and an independent air force.

Moltke, Count Helmuth Johannes Ludwig von (1848–1916): also known as Moltke the Younger, nephew of the famous Prussian field marshal Helmuth von Moltke and a favorite of William II. He succeeded Schlieffen as chief of the general staff in 1906, and changed his predecessor's plan by assigning more troops to the eastern front, fearing a Russian invasion, and to the Alsacian front fearing a French attack there. He refused the kaiser's last-minute request to reverse the mobilization plans. During the great attack through Belgium, he probably stayed too far behind the lines and was constantly plagued by self-doubts. He never visited the front lines and may have lost Germany's chance to win the war during the first month by his indecisiveness and lack of control. He ordered general withdrawal to the Aisne River when gaps between the First and Second armies threatened to endanger the whole German position. He was succeeded as chief of staff by Falkenhayn on September 14, 1914.

Murray, Sir Archibald (1860–1945): British general, chief of staff under French in the British Expeditionary Force. He and his chief gave only limited support to the French in their efforts to stem the German tide in August 1914.

Nicholas I (1841–1921): king of Montenegro (1910–18), sided with Serbia in 1914, but tried to conclude a separate peace with the Central Powers when his army was defeated. His country was occupied by Austrian troops and he went into exile. He resisted a proposed union of his country with Serbia and was therefore deposed by a national assembly in 1918.

Nicholas II Romanov (1868–1918): the last tsar of Russia (1894–1917), married to Princess Alix (Alexandra) of Hesse. He maintained the autocratic regime of his predecessors and suppressed all opposition. He initiated the Hague Peace Conferences but pursued an aggressive policy in the Far East. After Russia's humiliating defeat in its war against Japan and the subsequent revolution of 1905, he promised a representative government and basic civil liberties, but he soon curtailed the new parliament, the Duma, and dismissed his liberal minister Count Sergei Witte.

In the critical days of July 1914, his order to mobilize made the war almost inevitable. In 1915, he took over the command of the army from Grand Duke Nicholas, leaving his wife in control at the capital. Her German sympathies, the influence of her favorite Rasputin, military setbacks and the deteriorating food situation undermined his authority and he was forced to abdicate in March 1917. He and his family were first held at the Tsarskoe Selo palace, then near Tobolsk. When counterrevolutionary forces were threatening Ekaterinburg, the local Bolsheviks had the tsar and his whole family shot on July 16, 1918, possibly with Lenin's approval.

Nicholas (Nikolai Nikolayevich) (1856–1929): Russian grand duke, and first cousin to Tsar Alexander III. He served as an army officer in the Russo-Turkish war of 1877–78. During the 1905 revolution he refused the Tsar Nicholas' request to become a military dictator. At the outbreak of the war, he was made commander in chief of the Russian armies, and he may have saved France by his prompt invasion of East Prussia, forcing the German High Command to divert troops to the east. He was opposed by the tsarina and Rasputin, who induced the tsar to dismiss him in 1915. He then served as commander in the Caucasus region and won successes against the Turks. After the revolution of February 1917 he was deprived of his command. He then lived in France.

Nivelle, Robert-Georges (1856–1924): French general. He was chief assistant to Pétain at Verdun and then succeeded Joffre as commander in chief of the French armies. His long prepared Aisne offensive was frustrated before it began by Ludendorff's strategic withdrawal, and when launched, resulted in huge losses and little territorial gains. He was then dismissed and given a command in North Africa.

Norris, George William (1861–1944): American legislator. Served as U.S. Senator from 1912 to 1942. A liberal Republican, he opposed U.S participation in the war and denounced the Peace Treaty of Versailles. Later supported President Franklin Delano Roosevelt's domestic and foreign policies.

Northcliffe, Alfred Charles William Harmsworth, Viscount Northcliffe (1865–1922): British journalist and newspaper publisher, founder of the *Daily Mail* and the *Daily Mirror*. He also revived the London *Times*. He was a virulent critic of Asquith and was instrumental in the downfall of his government. Supporter of Lloyd George.

Orlando, Vittorio Emanuele (1860–1952): Italian statesman. He held several cabinet posts between

1903 and 1917 and became prime minister in 1917. As one of the Big Four at Versailles, he insisted on receiving all the Dalmatian territories promised to Italy in the secret treaty of London 1915 for its entry into the war. Wilson disagreed with him, and since he could not secure any help from Lloyd George or Clemenceau, he left the conference in April 1919, but returned in May. Since no solution satisfactory to Italy could be agreed upon, Orlando resigned on June 19, 1919 and was succeeded by Francesco Nitti.

Painlevé, Paul (1863–1933): French mathematician and politician. When professor of mathematics at the Sorbonne, he became interested in politics through the Dreyfus Affair. He held several cabinet posts during the war and was made prime minister for a short time in 1917, but after two months he was replaced by Clemenceau, who was more successful in lifting the sunken morale of the French people.

Paléologue, Maurice (1859–1944): French diplomat, ambassador to Russia in 1914. He urged the Russian government and the tsar to attack Germany immediately to relieve German pressure on France.

Papen, Franz von (1879–1969): German politician. As military attaché at the German embassy in Washington, he became involved in espionage activities. The U.S. government then requested his recall. Subsequently he served as diplomat in Turkey, and after the war he entered politics as a member of the Catholic Center party. In 1932 he was appointed chancellor by President Hindenburg.

Péguy, Charles (1873–1914): French poet and writer, supporter of Dreyfus and one of the foremost modern Catholic writers. Killed at the battle of the Marne.

Pershing, John Joseph (1860–1948): Commander in chief of the American Expeditionary Force during the war. Fought against the American Indians (Geronimo) and in the Spanish-American War, also taught at West Point. Later fought in the Philippines and was American military attaché in the Russo-Japanese war. Fought unsuccessfully against Pancho Villa in Mexico (1916–17). When America entered the war, he transformed his hastily trained troops into efficient combat units. He refused to have his soldiers used as replacements in French or British units, but insisted on their operating as a separate force. In the last months of the war his troops contributed largely to the final defeat of the German armies in France. Even after the Allied command was unified under Foch, Pershing, known as "Black Jack" among his troops, managed to have his own way.

Pétain, Henri-Philippe (1856–1951): French general. He was mainly responsible for stopping the German onslaught on Verdun in 1916, and became a military hero. In 1917 he was appointed French commander in chief, and in 1918 was made marshal. After the war, he fought for France in Morocco, and much later, during World War II, concluded the armistice with Germany and became head of the Vichy government which collaborated with the Hitler regime.

Peter I (1844–1921): king of Serbia (1903–18), led his country through the Balkan wars and the Great War, with the help of his prime minister Nicola Pasic. However, because of ill health, he retired from active rule in 1914 in favor of his son Alexander. He participated in the Serbian retreat through Albania to Corfu. In 1918, he was chosen to rule what was to become known as Yugoslavia, while Alexander remained regent.

Poincaré, Raymond (1860–1934): French statesman, president of France (1913–20). Held various cabinet posts between 1893 and 1906 and became premier and foreign minister in 1912. As president, he worked to strengthen France militarily. During the great crisis of 1917, he called Clemenceau to form a new cabinet although he disliked him intensely. He was a staunch nationalist and conservative, considered the Versailles to be too lenient and continued to ask for additional guarantees for France's security.

Princip, Gavrilo (1895–1918): Serbian nationalist and agitator. As a student, he joined the secret society Union or Death, known as the "Black Hand." He assassinated Archduke Francis Ferdinand and his wife at Sarajevo on June 28, 1914, thus precipitating the outbreak of the war. He was imprisoned and died there of tuberculosis.

Prittwitz und Gaffron, Friedrich Wilhelm von (1848–1917), commander of the Eighth German Army in East Prussia when the Russian armies invaded in August 1914. He suffered a setback at Gumbinnen and proposed to Moltke withdrawal of the entire army behind the Vistula, leaving East Prussia to the Russians. Moltke was shocked and immediately replaced him with Hindenburg and Ludendorff, who saved the situation for Germany.

Radek, Karl (1885–1939?): Communist leader and journalist. His original name was Sobelsohn. Participated in the 1905 revolution in Warsaw, and wrote for various Eastern European newspapers. During the war, he lived in Switzerland, expecting the war to turn into an international revolution. After the October revolution, he joined the Communist party and attended the Brest-Litovsk peace negotiations. In 1918, Lenin sent him to Germany to help organize the German Communist movement. He was imprisoned for a time, then returned to Russia and became a leading official of the Comintern, the Third Communist International founded in Moscow in 1919. Since no Communist takeover took place in Germany, he lost his post and was expelled from the party in 1927, but he recanted and was readmitted in 1930. He disappeared during the great Stalinist purges.

Rasputin, Grigori Yefimovich (1872–1916): notorious figure at the St. Petersburg court and favorite of the Tsarina. He was a semiliterate peasant and self-appointed "holy man" who apparently exerted some personal magnetism and practiced a doctrine of religious fervor and sexual indulgence. He apparently checked the bleeding of the Tsarevich Alexei, who suffered from hemophilia, and thereby achieved a strong hold over his mother and the tsar. From 1911 on his followers began to fill high positions. He had no clear political program, but managed to dominate the court, particularly when the tsar took over command at the front. His scandals and disgraceful behavior completely undermined the tsarist regime, and he was even suspected of working on a separate peace with Germany, through the tsarina. In December 1916, a group of nationalist patriots led by Prince Felix Yussupov and Grand Duke Dmitri, the tsar's cousin, managed to assassinate him by riddling him with bullets after poison had failed to affect him. His body was thrown in the Neva River.

Rathenau, Walther (1867–1922): German industrialist and statesman, son of the well known founder of the A.E.G., Emil Rathenau. As a writer, he was highly critical of the capitalist system and of feudalistic government still ruling Germany. He directed the distribution of raw materials during the war and succeeded his father as president of the A.E.G. in 1915. He spoke vigorously against the introduction of unrestricted submarine warfare. After the war, he became minister of reconstruction and later foreign minister. In June 1922 he was assassinated by two right-wing radicals.

Rennenkampf, Pavel K. (1854–1918): commander of the First Russian Army invading East Prussia. He pushed back the German Eighth Army at Gumbinnen and proceeded in the direction of Koenigsberg, failing to established a link with the Second Russian Army under Samsonov in the south. Consequently, Hindenburg and Ludendorff were able to concentrate on Samsonov, whose army was annihilated at Tan-nenberg. Rennenkampf's army was then attacked and defeated by the Germans under Mackensen in the Masurian Lakes region.

Richthofen, Manfred Baron von (1892–1918): German aviator who was credited with shooting down 80 aircraft. Richthofen, known as the "Red Baron," was shot down in action on April 21, 1918. Hermann Göring belonged to his squadron.

Rickenbacker, Edward Vernon (Eddie) (1890–1973): American aviator who volunteered for the air service and was credited with downing 26 enemy planes. After the war, he became an executive in several airline companies.

Roosevelt, Franklin Delano (1882–1945): American statesman. He was elected to the New York state senate in 1910, fought the influence of Tammany Hall and became an ardent supporter of Woodrow Wilson. He served as assistant secretary of the Navy from 1913 to 1920, then ran unsuccessfully as vice presidential candidate with James M. Cox against Harding and Coolidge. Elected president in 1932, he served four terms.

Rupprecht von Wittelsbach (1869–1955): crown prince of Bavaria, was made general of the infantry in 1912 and commanded the Sixth German Army during the war, with considerable success. First optimistic about German chances of victory, he changed his mind around 1916 and in a letter in the summer of 1917 asked Chancellor Hertling to initiate peace negotiations to avoid a catastrophy for Germany. After the war, he never gave up the thought of restoring the Bavarian monarchy.

Salandra, Antonio (1853–1931): Italian prime minister (1914–16). Held various cabinet posts between 1891 and 1910 and succeeded Giolitti as premier in 1914. Although an expansionist, he continued Giolitti's policy of neutrality, but then he began to prepare for war and to secure territory from the Entente as a reward for entering the war on the Allied side. After promises were made in the secret treaty of London in 1915, he denounced the Triple Alliance and, under the slogan of *sacro egoismo* ("sacred egotism") declared war on Austria. When the Italian armies retreated in the Trentino in 1916, he resigned, but he served as delegate for Italy at the Paris Peace Conference and at the League of Nations.

Samsonov, Alexander (1859–1914): Russian general and commander of the Second Russian Army invading East Prussia at the beginning of the war. When the German army, under Hindenburg and Ludendorff, attacked him, he was thoroughly beaten at Tannenberg and his army was destroyed. He received no help from the First Russian Army in the north, possibly because he was on bad terms with its commander, Rennenkampf. After the defeat he committed suicide.

Sarrail, Maurice (1856–1929): French general, fought first in Lorraine, then at Salonika, where he bolstered Venizelos' efforts to bring in Greece on the Allied side. There he was replaced by General Guillaumat in December 1917. After the war, he served as High Commissioner in Syria.

Sazonov, Sergei Dimitriyevich (1861–1927): Russian foreign minister (1910–16). His policy vaccillated between efforts to preserve the peace and to further the Russian interests in the Balkans. He did not aim for war in July 1914, but he was unable to check the military who insisted on immediate mobilization. He may also have hoped to counteract the revolutionary movement in his country by drawing Russia into a war. In 1916 Tsar Nicholas asked him to resign.

Scheer, Reinhard (1863–1928): German admiral. In 1913, Tirpitz made him admiral in the High Seas Fleet, command of which he took over in 1916. He advocated active intervention of the High Seas Fleet, and in spite of its numerical inferiority he led it in the battle of Jutland where he, on May 31, 1916, achieved a tactical success over the British navy. He was in favor of unrestricted submarine warfare. Shortly before the end of the war he planned to lead the navy into one last, desperate battle, and this plan caused the riots in Kiel and Wilhelmshaven that started the German revolution.

Scheidemann, Philipp (1865–1939): German Social Democrat and chancellor. Member of the Reichstag from 1898 and member of Prince Max von Baden's short-lived cabinet. On November 9 he proclaimed the German republic, without the knowledge and the approval of his friend and colleague, Chancellor Ebert. He succeeded Ebert as chancellor of the provisional government, but resigned four months later in protest against the Versailles Treaty he had called unacceptable.

Schlieffen, Alfred Count von (1833–1913): chief of the German General Staff from 1898 and originator of the famous plan that provided an overwhelming attack against France in any future war. His proposed strategy was only partly followed by his successor Moltke when the war broke out.

Smuts, Jan Christiaan (1870–1950): South African soldier and statesman. In the South African War, he commanded Boer guerrilla forces, but from 1904 on he worked for cooperation between Boers and British. After the creation of the Union of South Africa, he served as its minister of defense and finance. When the great war broke out, he suppressed a Boer uprising and served as a general in German East Africa. In 1917–18, he became a member of the imperial war cabinet in London and signed the Versailles Treaty, although protesting that its terms would prevent any harmonious coexistence between the nations, which he believed should be served by the League of Nations. From 1919 to 1924 he was prime minister of the Republic of South Africa. He stood by the British Empire in the Second World War.

Souchon, Wilhelm (1864–   ): German admiral, commanded the German warships *Goeben* and *Breslau* that were in the Mediterranean when war broke out. He was ordered to proceed to Constantinople and, although British were searching for him, managed to avoid them. His arrival in Constantinople played a considerable part in causing the swaying Turkish government to join the Central Powers.

Spee, Maximilian Count von (1861–1914): German admiral. When war broke out, he commanded a squadron in the Far East. In November he met and destroyed a British naval unit under Admiral Cradock off the Chilean coast. He delayed his immediate departure home and thereby was caught by a superior squadron under British admiral Sir Frederick Sturdee. All but one of his ships were sunk, and Spee and his two sons perished.

Stresemann, Gustav (1878–1929): German statesman. Member of the Reichstag from 1907 as deputy of the National Liberal Party that represented the interests of big business. During the war he supported the monarchy and a policy of annexations, but after the defeat he founded the moderately conservative German People's Party, which advocated a conciliatory policy toward the former enemies and a gradual relaxation of the Versailles Treaty. He pursued this policy as chancellor (19232) and foreign minister.

Stuermer, Boris Vladimirovich (1848–1917): Russian politician. The tsar appointed him prime minister in 1916 and he also replaced Sazonov as foreign minister shortly thereafter. In the Duma, he was violently attacked for his connections with Rasputin and the pro-German elements in the court. He was forced to resign in November 1916 and was arrested during the February revolution of 1917. He died in prison.

Sturdee, Sir Frederick Charles Doveton (1859–1925):

British admiral. In the battle of the Falklands (December 1914) he decisively defeated a German squadron under Spee. He also commanded a squadron in the battle of Jutland, and was made admiral of the fleet in 1921.

Stürgkh, Count Karl von (1859–1916): Austrian prime minister (1911–16). He was opposed to all reforms and during the war governed without the unruly Austrian parliament, against the opposition of liberals and leftists. He was assassinated by a young socialist, Friedrich Adler.

Sukhomlinov, Valdimir (1848–1926): Russian minister of war at the outbreak of the war. Indolent, pleasure-loving and utterly corrupt, he befriended Rasputin, hated Grand Duke Nicholas and opposed all military innovations and reforms. In 1917, after the fall of the monarchy, he was arrested and sentenced to hard labor for life. But a few months later the Bolsheviks freed him and he moved to Berlin. He dedicated his memoirs to the former German emperor.

Tirpitz, Alfred von (1849–1930): German admiral, the founder and spiritual father of the German navy. He helped develop the recently invented torpedo and held the post as minister for naval affairs longer than any minister since Bismarck (1897–1916). Under him the German navy was built up to be the second most powerful in the world. When war broke out, he urged the use of the German High Seas Fleet aggressively, but he was resisted by the chief of the admiral staff, Hugo von Pohl. He then urged rapid construction of submarines and resigned when Chancellor von Bethmann-Hollweg and others opposed his demand of unrestricted submarine warfare. After the war he joined the radical right. He continued to have considerable influence on Hindenburg, even after the latter was elected president of the Weimar Republic.

Tisza, Count Stephen (1861–1918): Hungarian statesman. He served as prime minister from 1903 to 1905 and 1913 to 1917. His regime was based on the support of the large estate owners. He suppressed the Serbian and Romanian minorities in Hungary, and opposed Berchtold's aggressive foreign policy. He finally agreed to the declaration of war under the condition that no Serbian territory would be annexed. His influence receded after Emperor Francis Joseph's death, and his ministry fell when the leftist opposition blamed the hardships of the third year of war on him. He then served as military commander on the Italian front. In October 1918 he was assassinated by soldiers who thought him responsible for the outbreak of the war.

Trotsky, Leon (Lev Davidovich Bronstein) (1879–1940): Russian Communist revolutionary, son of a prosperous farmer in the Ukraine. He became a Marxist in 1896 and was arrested many times. Exiled to Siberia in 1900, he escaped in 1902 and met Lenin in London, but after the Social Democratic Party split he became a spokesman for the Mensheviks, then followed his own independent course. When again in prison in 1905, he developed his theory of permanent revolution. Again sent to Siberia, he escaped to Vienna, then Switzerland and Paris, where he was expelled in 1917, then went to New York. During all these years, he was active as a journalist. He returned to Russia after the fall of the tsar, but was imprisoned by Kerensky in July of 1917. Released in September, he became the chief organizer of the October revolution. He served as chief Russian negotiator at Brest-Litovsk, then became commissar of war in 1918 and organized the Red Army. During the civil war he clashed with Stalin, and when the latter took over after Lenin's death, Trotsky was expelled from the party and exiled in 1928. He was killed in Mexico City, probably by an agent of Stalin, in 1940.

Udet, Ernst (1896–1941): German fighter pilot during the war, later aircraft designer and administrator in Hitler's Air Ministry. He committed suicide after clashes with Goering and Hitler.

Venizelos, Eleutherios (1864–1936): Greek statesman. Fought for and finally achieved the union of his native Crete with Greece. During his first term as prime minister, 1910–15, he led Greece through the Balkan wars and greatly increased Greek territory. Favored the Allied cause in the Great War, until King Constantine forced him to resign. He was prime minister again in August 1915, and when the king made him resign again, he established a provisional government at Thessaloniki (Salonica). When the king abdicated in 1917, Venizelos became prime minister for the third time. He attended the Paris Peace Conference, but in 1920 his cabinet fell and King Constantine was restored. However, Venizelos continued as Greece's leading politician after the king abdicated in 1922.

Viviani, René (1863–1925): French statesman. Started as a socialist and helped Jean Jaurès unite the French Socialist Party. Minister for labor from 1906 to 1910 under Clemenceau and Briand. He became prime minister in June 1914. When war started, he appealed for a "sacred union" of all parties. Resigned in 1915, but served as minister of justice until 1917.

Weddigen, Otto (1882–1915): German submarine commander. On September 22, 1914, his submarine *U-9* sank three British cruisers off the Dutch coast. As commander of the submarine *U-29,* he sank several British merchant ships, but in March 1915 his boat was rammed by a British dreadnought and sank with all men aboard.

William (Wilhelm) II Hohenzollern, also known as Kaiser Wilhelm (1859–1941): German emperor and king of Prussia, grandson of Queen Victoria of England. In contrast to his liberal-minded parents, he believed in the divine nature of his rule and loved military display. Shortly after he ascended the throne (1888), he dismissed Chancellor Otto von Bismarck, who had controlled German politics since 1871. He did not permit the Reinsurance Treaty with Russia to be renewed in 1890 and, while he admired England and strove to be on friendly terms with its rulers, at the same time he alienated them by building a strong navy that the British considered a menace to them. Although on intimate terms with Tsar Nicholas, he alienated the Russians by supporting the Balkan policies of his ally, Austro-Hungary. He combined eloquence and impetuosity and on several occasions spoke out and acted unadvisedly, thereby shocking British as well as German public opinion. In July 1914, he was convinced that England would not take up arms against Germany. As the war progressed, his power declined, and by 1917 not he, but Hindenburg and Ludendorff were the rulers of Germany. When President Wilson made his abdication a prerequisite of peace negotiations, and navel mutinies as well as civil uprisings started in several German cities, he hesitated until his chancellor, Prince Max of Baden, announced his abdication. William then fled to Holland and formally abdicated two weeks later. While the Allies demanded his trial for instigating the war, the Dutch refused to extradite him. He alienated many of his loyal followers in Germany when he entered a second marriage in 1922.

William (Wilhelm) Hohenzollern (1882–1951): crown prince of Germany, oldest son of William II. In 1914 he commanded an army on the western front and nominally headed the Army Group Deutscher Kronprinz which attacked Verdun in 1916. He was influenced by Pan-German ideas, but distanced himself from the Pan-Germans, advocating a negotiated peace. In internal politics, he remained an arch-conservative and contributed to the fall of Chancellor Bethmann-Hollweg. He went into exile in Holland on November 13, 1918, although Ebert had not objected to his remaining in Germany. He supported the Hitler movement for a while apparently hoping that with the fall of the Weimar Republic the Hohenzollern throne would be restored.

Wilson, Sir Henry Hughes (1864–1922): British field marshal. He was a friend of French general Foch and worked for years on plans for French-British cooperation in case of war. In 1914 he was made assistant chief of staff of the British Expeditionary Force, and he later acted as liaison officer between the French and British armies. He went on a military mission to Russia in 1917 and was a member of the Allied Supreme War Council. In 1918 he was appointed chief of the British Imperial General Staff.

Wilson, Woodrow (1856–1924): the 28th president of the United States (1913–21). Taught history and political economy and was elected president of Princeton University in 1902. In 1910, he was elected governor of New Jersey as a Democrat. In 1912 he was nominated as Democratic candidate for president and won since the Republican party was split. As president, he initiated many progressive reforms. When war broke out, Wilson pursued at first a policy of strict neutrality, but public opinion began to mount against Germany and Wilson followed this trend, replacing his strictly neutral foreign secretary William Jennings Bryan with Robert Lansing, who leaned toward intervention on the Allied side. The sinking of the *Lusitania* deteriorated the German position in the United States, and after the American *Sussex* was sunk, Wilson sent an ultimatum, after which Germany changed its submarine warfare policy. In 1916, Wilson was reelected under the slogan "He kept us out of war," defeating Charles Evans Hughes by a very close margin. Wilson now attempted to mediate between the warring parties, but without success, and when Germany renewed unrestricted submarine warfare, war became inevitable. After war was declared, his speeches united the country behind him and permitted him to pursue his war aims energetically. But he still tried to search for a basis of a negotiated peace, particularly in his proposal of Fourteen Points, which, however, was ignored by Germany until it was defeated in October 1918. Wilson was looked upon in Europe as the savior of the future and he played the central figure at the Paris Peace Conference. Yet he could not cope with the policies pursued by the European leaders who had little use for his idealistic approach. Little of his proposal was realized in the Versailles Treaty, except for the Covenant of the League of Nations, and Wilson left Europe a bitterly disappointed man. Back in the United States he found that Congress was not inclined to accept the Paris treaties. Rather than compromise, Wilson tried to secure popular support by making a speaking tour through the United States, but he suffered a breakdown in September 1919 and shortly thereafter a stroke from which he never recovered fully.

Zeppelin, Count Ferdinand (1838–1917): German airship builder. Served in the Prussian army in 1866 and 1870–71, and was an observer on the Union side in the American Civil War. Retired from the Prussian army in 1891. Invented the first rigid airship and built one with a speed of about 30 miles per hour in 1906. In his Zeppelin Foundation, established in Friedrichshafen on Lake Constance in 1908, were built the motor-driven airships that raided London during the Great War.

Zimmermann, Arthur (1864–1940): German foreign minister from November 20, 1916 to August 5, 1916. On January 16, 1917 he sent a note to the German ambassador in Washington suggesting that in case of war with the United States, Mexico should declare war on the United States and, as a reward, would then have restored the lost territories of Arizona, Texas and New Mexico. The note was intercepted by the British and sent to President Wilson, who published it on March 1, 1917. The note turned public opinion in the United States against Germany. Zimmermann was replaced by Richard von Kuehlmann.

Zinoviev, Grigori Evseyevich (1883–1936): Russian Communist leader. His original name was Radomylsky. He went into exile in 1908 and became one of Lenin's closest collaborators, and returned to Russia with him after the February 1917 revolution. He opposed Lenin's plan of a coup d'état in October 1917 as premature, but after the takeover he served as head of the Comintern. After Lenin's death he aligned himself with Trotsky and was expelled from the party in 1927. In 1936, during the Stalinist purges, he was sentenced to death and executed.

Zita (1892–1989): daughter of Duke Robert of Parma and last empress of Austria and wife of Emperor Charles. She had great influence over Charles and is blamed for his attempts to negotiate peace with the Allies behind Germany's back, and his attempts to the throne in 1921. After Charles' death in 1922, she lived in Belgium, the United States, Canada and finally Switzerland.

Appendix C
Maps

Western Front: 1914–18

Eastern Front: 1914–18

Southern Fronts: Italian Front 1915–18

Turkish Fronts: Sinai, Western Desert and Palestine 1914–18

African Operations: East Africa 1914–18

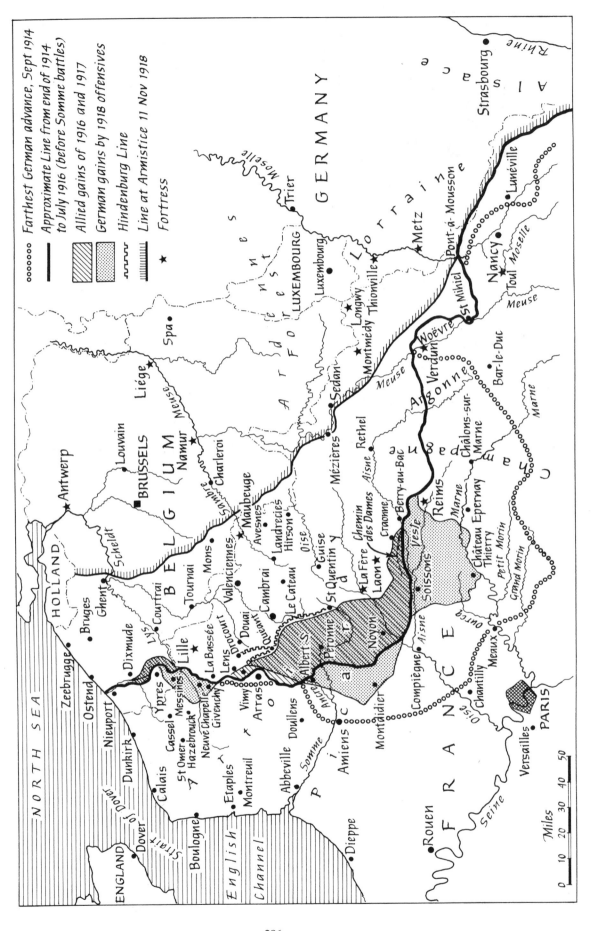

Western Front: 1914-18

Legend:

- ○○○○○○○ Farthest German advance, Sept 1914
- —— Approximate Line from end of 1914 to July 1916 (before Somme battles)
- ▨ Allied gains of 1916 and 1917
- ▨ German gains by 1918 offensives
- ⌇⌇⌇ Hindenburg Line
- ⁗⁗⁗ Line at Armistice 11 Nov 1918
- ★ Fortress

NORTH SEA

ENGLAND

Dover · Strait of Dover

English Channel

Dieppe · Rouen · Seine

Boulogne · Étaples · Montreuil · Abbeville · Doullens · Amiens · Somme

Calais · St Omer · Cassel · Hazebrouck · Neuve Chapelle · Givenchy · Arras · Vimy · Ancre · Albert

Dunkirk · Nieuport · Ostend · Zeebrugge · Bruges · Ghent · Ypres · Messines · La Bassée · Lens · Drocourt · Douai

Dixmude · Lille · Courtrai · Lys · Tournai · Valenciennes · Quéant · Cambrai · Le Cateau · Péronne

BELGIUM · Antwerp · Louvain · BRUSSELS · Namur · Charleroi · Sambre · Mons · Avesnes · Landrecies · Hirson · Guise · St Quentin · Noyon · Oise

HOLLAND · Scheldt · Liège · Meuse · Spa

Maubeuge

FRANCE

Montdidier · Compiègne · Chantilly · Meaux · Aisne · Oise

PARIS · Versailles

Soissons · Château Thierry · Petit Morin · Grand Morin · Ourcq

Laon · La Fère · Chemin des Dames · Craonne · Berry-au-Bac · Vesle · Reims · Épernay · Châlons-sur-Marne · Marne

Mézières · Rethel · Aisne · Sedan · Argonne · Verdun · Woëvre · St Mihiel · Bar-le-Duc · Meuse

GERMANY

Trier · Moselle

LUXEMBOURG · Luxembourg · Longwy · Montmédy · Thionville · Metz · Pont-à-Mousson

Lorraine · Nancy · Toul · Moselle · Lunéville · Meurthe

Alsace · Strasbourg · Rhine

Ardennes Forest

Miles
0 10 20 30 40 50

Eastern Front: 1914-18

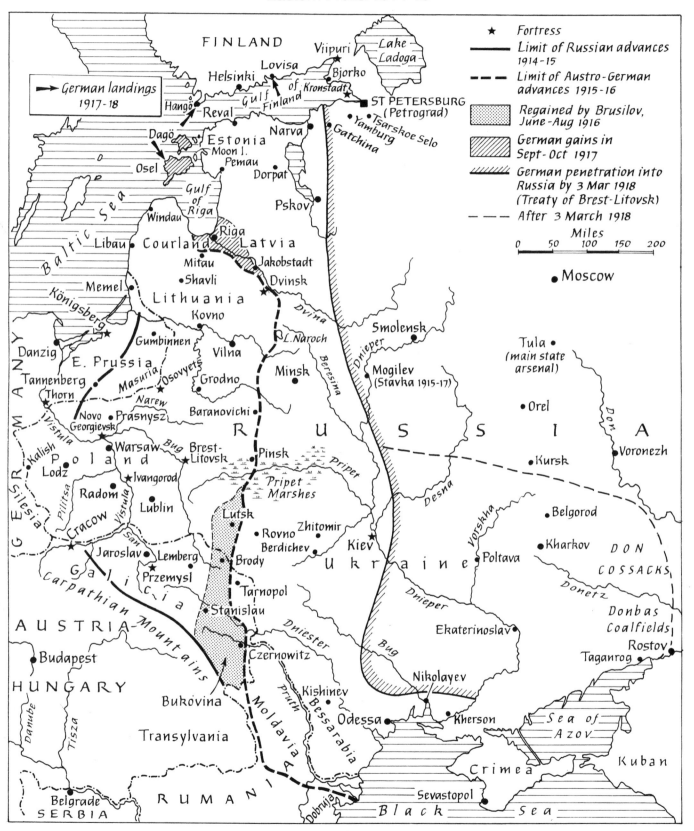

★	Fortress
▬▬▬	Limit of Russian advances 1914-15
▬ ▬ ▬	Limit of Austro-German advances 1915-16
(stippled)	Regained by Brusilov, June-Aug 1916
(hatched)	German gains in Sept-Oct 1917
(lined)	German penetration into Russia by 3 Mar 1918 (Treaty of Brest-Litovsk)
– – –	After 3 March 1918

Miles
0   50   100   150   200

German landings 1917-18

Southern Fronts: Italian Front 1915-18

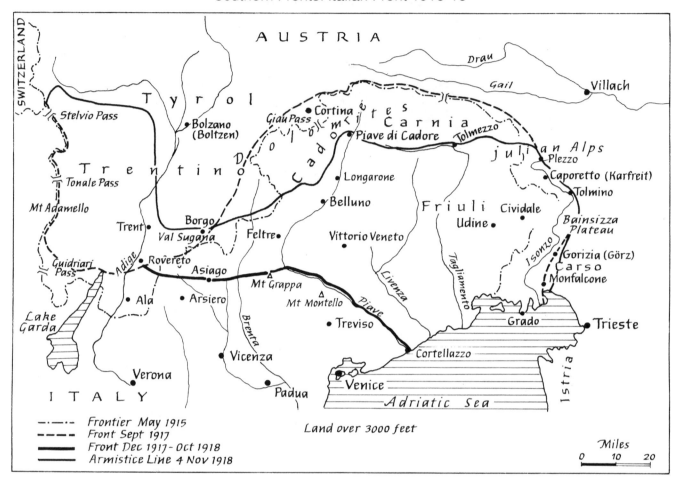

Frontier May 1915
Front Sept 1917
Front Dec 1917 – Oct 1918
Armistice Line 4 Nov 1918

Land over 3000 feet

Miles
0   10   20

Turkish Fronts: Sinai, Western Desert and Palestine 1914-18

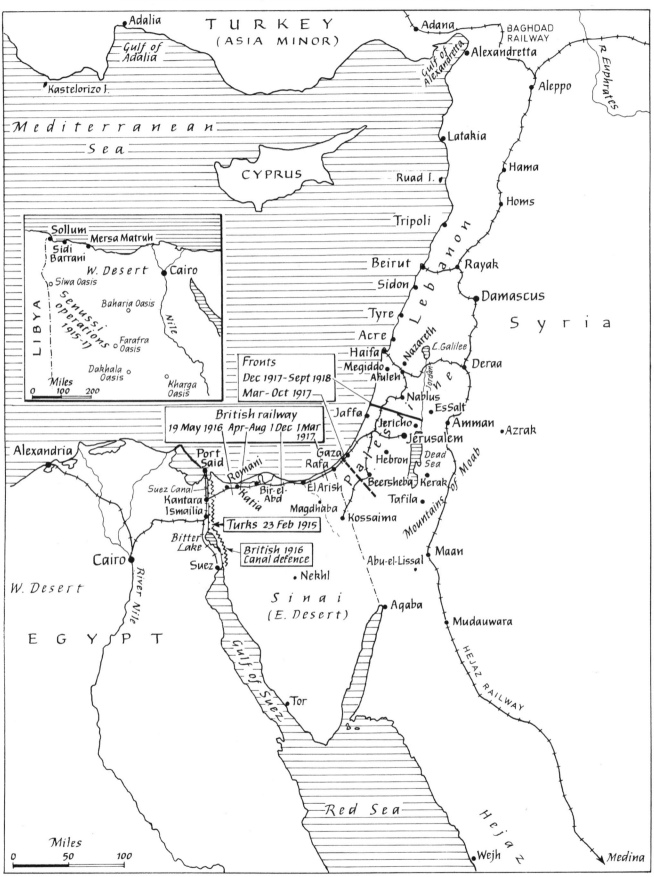

African Operations: East Africa 1914-18

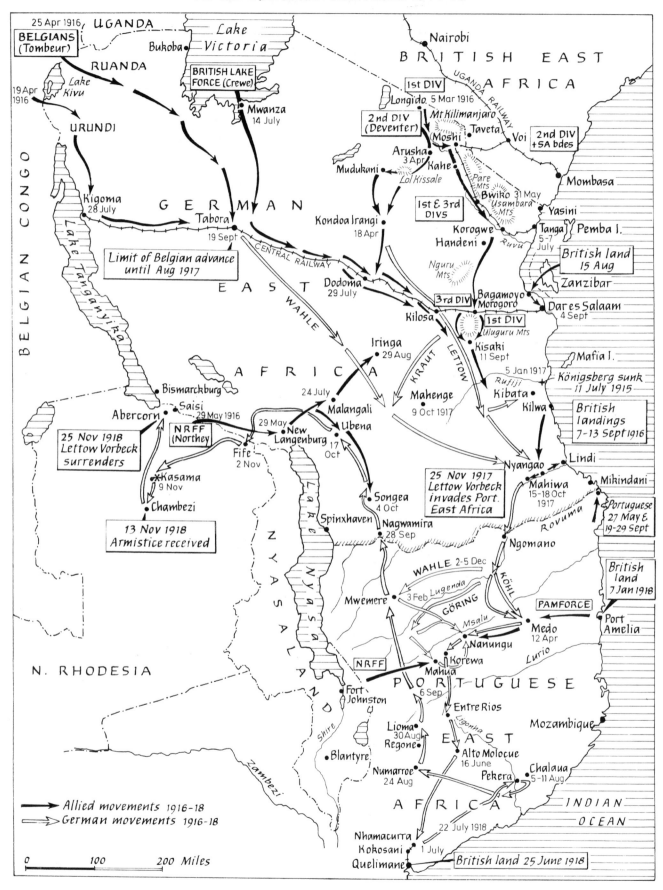

Bibliography

Alexinsky, Grégoire. *Memoirs*. Paris, n.d.

Ashmead-Bartlett, Ellis. *Diary*. London, 1915–16.

Baldwin, Hanson W., *World War One*. New York, 1962.

Barbusse, Henri. *I Saw It Myself*. New York, 1928.

Barnett, Corelli, *The Sword Bearers*. Bloomington and London, 1963.

Bell, Herbert Douglas, *A Soldier's Diary*. London, 1929.

Bennett, G., *Naval Battles of the First World War*. New York, 1968.

Bikow, P.M. *Les derniers jours des Romanov*. Paris, 1931.

Binding, Rudolf, *War Poems and Diaries*. Potsdam, 1940.

———, *Memoirs*. 1928.

Bismarck, Otto von. *Gedanken und Erinnerungen*. 3 vols. Stuttgart, 1898–1921.

Braun, Otto, *The Diary*, ed. J. Vogelstein. New York, 1924.

Chambrun, Charles de, *Letters*. Paris, 1941.

Chapman, Guy (ed.), *Vain Glory*. London, 1937.

Churchill, Winston, *The Unknown War*. New York, 1931.

Conrad von Hoetzendorf, Franz, *Memoirs*. 1921–25.

Courant, Richard, *Memoirs*. 1915.

Daheim (German journal), 1915.

Die Aktion (German journal), 1914.

Engel, Eduard, *Ein Tagebuch*. Braunschweig, 1915.

Edmunds, Charles, *Subaltern's War*. London, 1929.

Eddalin, Alexander, *La Révolution Russe*. Paris, 1920.

Falls, Cyril, *The Great War*. New York, 1959.

Ferro, Marc, *The Great War 1914–1918* (trans. by N. Stone). London, 1973.

Frankfurter Zeitung (German newspaper), 1918.

Freud, Sigmund, *Sein Leben in Bildern*. Frankfurt, 1976.

Fribourg, André, *The Flaming Crucible*. New York, 1918.

Gilliard, Pierre, *The Tragic Destiny of Nicholas*. Paris, 1921.

Graves, Robert, *Good-bye to All That*. New York, 1929.

Guilbeaux, Henri, *Authentic Portrait of Lenin*. Paris, 1924.

Hamilton, Ian, *Gallipoli Diary*. 1920.

Hedin, Sven Anders, *Ein Volk in Waffen* (A Nation in Arms). Leipzig, 1915.

Hoehling, A.A., *The Great War at Sea*. New York, 1965.

Hoffmann, Conrad, *In the Prison Camps of Germany*. New York, 1920.

Hoffmann, Max, *Der Krieg*. München, 1923.

Hofmiller, J., *Diary*. Munich, 1918.

Imbrie, Robert Whitney, *Behind the Wheel*. New York, 1918.

Izvestija (Russian newspaper), 1919.

Joffre, Joseph-Jacques-Césaire, *Narrative of the Battle of the Marne*. New York, 1927.

Journal de Genève, 1915.

Journal de Petrograd, 1917.

Juenger, Ernst, *Fire and Blood*. Hamburg, 1935.

————, *Sturm*. Olten, 1963.

Kerensky, Alexander Feodorovich, *La Révolution Russe*. Paris, 1917.

————, *Memoires*. Paris, 1927.

————, *The Truth about the Massacre of the Romanovs*. Paris, 1936.

Kipling, Rudyard, "For all we have and are" (poem). 1914.

Kohn, Richard, "Memoirs" (unpublished).

Kreisler, Fritz, *Four Weeks in the Trenches*. Boston, 1915.

Kuehlmann, Richard von, *Memoirs*. Heidelberg, 1948.

Lapradelle, A.G. de, *War Letters from France*. Boston, 1915.

Lawrence, T.E., *Revolt in the Desert*. New York, 1926.

Le carnet (Notebook), Paris, 1916.

Lee, A.G., *No Parachute*. New York, 1968.

Leed, Eric J., *No Man's Land*. Cambridge, 1979.

Le Matin (Paris newspaper), 1914.

Le Monde Slave. Paris, 1926.

Le Temps (Paris newspaper), 1917.

Letters of Fallen Englishmen. London, 1930.

Liebknecht, Karl, *Briefe aus dem Felde* (Letters from the Field). Berlin, 1920.

Livesey, Anthony, *Great Battles of World War I*. New York, 1989.

Lloyd George, David, *War Memoirs*. London, 1933–36.

London *Daily Telegraph*, 1914.

Ludwig, Emil, *Wilhelm der Zweite*. Berlin, 1920.

Markovich, Marylie, *La Révolution Russe*. Paris, 1918.

Max von Baden, Prince, *Memoirs*. Stuttgart, 1927.

McCormick, R.R., *With the Russian Army*. New York, 1915.

Mackenzie, Compton, *My Life and Times* (Memoirs). 1963–71.

Michaels, Robert, *Briefe eines Hauptmanns* (Letters of a Captain). Berlin, 1916.

Moltke, Helmut Graf von, *Memoirs, Letters, Documents*. Stuttgart, 1922.

Mommsen, W., *Max Weber*. Tuebingen, 1959.

Moorehead, Alan, *Gallipoli*. New York, 1956.

Naudeau, Ludovic, *Les Dessous de Chaos Russe*. Paris, 1921.

Neue Zuercher Zeitung (Swiss newspaper), 1917.

Nevins, Alan, *American Press Opinion*. Port Washington, N.Y., 1969.

Nicholas II of Russia, *Diary*. Paris, 1925.

Noulens, Joseph, *Mémoires*. Paris, 1933.

O'Brien, H.V., *Wine, Women and War*. New York, 1926.

Oskine, J., *Le Carnet*. Paris, 1931.

Paléologue, Maurice, *Alexandra Feodorovna*. Paris, 1932.

Palmer, Frederick, *My Year of the Great War*. New York, 1915.

———, *My Second Year of the War*. New York, 1917.

Paley, Princesse, *Souvenirs de Russie*. Paris, 1923.

Patin, Louise, "Journal d'une française," 1917–19 (unpublished).

Pax, Paulette, *Journal d'une comédienne*. Paris, 1919.

Poincaré, Raymond, *Mémoires*. Paris, 1930.

Pross, Harry, *Die Zerstoerung der deutschen Politik*. Frankfurt, 1959.

Punch, *Mr. Punch's History of the Great War*. New York, 1919.

Radbruch, Gustav, *Der innere Weg*. Stuttgart, 1951.

Rathenau, Walther, *Briefe (Letters)*. Dresden, 1926.

Reynolds, Quentin, *They Fought for the Sky*. New York, 1957.

Richter, Werner, *Bismarck*. Frankfurt, 1962.

Sadoul, Jacques, *Notes on the Bolshevik Revolution*. Paris, 1919.

Schauwecker, Franz, *The Fiery Way*. London, 1921.

Schurz, Carl. *Lebenserinnerungen*. Berlin, 1907.

Scribner's Magazine 66, 1919.

Seeger, Alan, *Letters and Diary*, New York, 1917.

Sellman, R.R., *The First World War*. New York, 1962.

Simonovice, Aron, *Raspoutine*. Paris, 1930.

Simplisissimus (German periodical), Munich 1898, 1918.

Sokoloff, Nicolas, *Enquête judiciaire sur l'assassinat*. Paris, 1929.

Stalin, Josef, *My Life*. Paris, 1956.

Stinton, Jones. *Russia in Revolution*. London, 1917.

Stumpf, Richard, *Kriegs-Tagebuch (War Diary)*. Berlin, 1927.

Sulzberger, Arthur, *The Fall of the Eagles*. New York, 1977.

Sweetser, Arthur, *Roadside Glimpses of the Great War*. New York, 1916.

Taylor, A.J.P., *The Struggle for Mastery in Europe*. Oxford, 1954.

————, *Illustrated History of the First World War*. New York, 1964.

Taylor, Edmond, *The Fall of the Dynasties*. New York, 1963.

The Times (London newspaper), 1915.

Tirpitz, Alfred von, *Erinnerungen*. Leipzig, 1919.

Trotsky, Leon, *Ma Vie*. Paris, 1930.

———, *Lénine*. Paris, 1925.

———, *Histoire de la Révolution*. Paris, 1934.

The Two Battles of the Marne (Joffre, Ludendorff, Foch, Crown Prince Wilhelm). New York, 1927.

Tuchman, Barbara W., *The Guns of August*. New York, 1962.

Tucholsky, Kurt, *Selected Letters*. Hamburg, 1962.

Der Tuermer (German monthly), 1917.

Van Passen, Pierre, *Days of Our Years*. New York, 1934.

Vorwaerts (German Socialist newspaper), Berlin, 1914.

Vossische Zeitung (German newspaper), Berlin, 1915.

Vysotski, V., *Alexandr Kerenski*. Moscow, 1917.

War Letters of Fallen Students. Munich, 1929. ed by P. Witkop.

Welchert, H.H., *Weltgewitter*. Hamburg, n.d.

Wiese, Leopold von. *Der Liberalismus*. 1917.

Winter, J.M., *The Experience of World War One*. Oxford, 1990.

Witte, Count Serge de. *Mémoirs*. Paris, 1921.

Zenzinov, Vladimir, *Mémoirs*. Paris, 1919.

Zweig, Stefan, Letters, in *"Die Insel."* Stuttgart, 1965.

INDEX